# Lecture Notes in Computer Science 6702

Commenced Publication in 1973
Founding and Former Series Editors:
Gerhard Goos, Juris Hartmanis, and Jan van Leeuwen

W0246092

## Editorial Board

David Hutchison
*Lancaster University, UK*

Takeo Kanade
*Carnegie Mellon University, Pittsburgh, PA, USA*

Josef Kittler
*University of Surrey, Guildford, UK*

Jon M. Kleinberg
*Cornell University, Ithaca, NY, USA*

Alfred Kobsa
*University of California, Irvine, CA, USA*

Friedemann Mattern
*ETH Zurich, Switzerland*

John C. Mitchell
*Stanford University, CA, USA*

Moni Naor
*Weizmann Institute of Science, Rehovot, Israel*

Oscar Nierstrasz
*University of Bern, Switzerland*

C. Pandu Rangan
*Indian Institute of Technology, Madras, India*

Bernhard Steffen
*TU Dortmund University, Germany*

Madhu Sudan
*Microsoft Research, Cambridge, MA, USA*

Demetri Terzopoulos
*University of California, Los Angeles, CA, USA*

Doug Tygar
*University of California, Berkeley, CA, USA*

Gerhard Weikum
*Max Planck Institute for Informatics, Saarbruecken, Germany*

Oege de Moor  Georg Gottlob  Tim Furche
Andrew Sellers (Eds.)

# Datalog Reloaded

First International Workshop, Datalog 2010
Oxford, UK, March 16-19, 2010
Revised Selected Papers

 Springer

Volume Editors

Oege de Moor
Oxford University, Department of Computer Science, Wolfson Building
Parks Road, Oxford OX1 3QD, UK
E-mail: oege@cs.ox.ac.uk

Georg Gottlob
Oxford University, Department of Computer Science, Wolfson Building
Parks Road, Oxford OX1 3QD, UK
E-mail: georg.gottlob@cs.ox.ac.uk

Tim Furche
Oxford University, Department of Computer Science, Wolfson Building
Parks Road, Oxford OX1 3QD, UK
E-mail: tim@furche.net

Andrew Sellers
Oxford University, Department of Computer Science, Wolfson Building
Parks Road, Oxford OX1 3QD, UK
E-mail: andrew.sellers@cs.ox.ac.uk

ISSN 0302-9743                        e-ISSN 1611-3349
ISBN 978-3-642-24205-2                e-ISBN 978-3-642-24206-9
DOI 10.1007/978-3-642-24206-9
Springer Heidelberg Dordrecht London New York

Library of Congress Control Number: 2011937827

CR Subject Classification (1998): H.2.4, H.4, I.2.4, C.2, H.3, H.5, D.1.6

LNCS Sublibrary: SL 3 – Information Systems and Application, incl. Internet/Web
and HCI

*Typesetting:* Camera-ready by author, data conversion by Scientific Publishing Services, Chennai, India

Printed on acid-free paper

Springer is part of Springer Science+Business Media (www.springer.com)

# Preface

This volume contains the proceedings of Datalog 2.0, a workshop celebrating the reemergence of datalog in academia and industry. Datalog 2.0 was held in 2010 during March 16–19 in Magdalen College, Oxford. We are proud to have contributions from many of the top researchers in deductive databases for this publication.

These proceedings consist of selected papers from the workshop, additionally refereed for this volume. They showcase the state of the art in theory and systems for datalog, divided into three sections: properties, applications, and extensions of datalog. Many exciting developments in datalog have occurred since the first datalog workshop in 1977 organized by Herve Gallaire and Jack Minker. By Datalog 2.0, datalog has surpassed its beginnings as an area of strictly academic interest and matured into a powerful tool for industrial use and scientific research. One need look no further than the papers in this volume for proof of this assertion. At the event itself, the Enterprise CIO of BestBuy, Neville Roberts, gave a talk on "Challenges of Enterprise IT," making the case for datalog-based systems.

We would like to thank all the members of the Program Committee and the external reviewers for their excellent reviews. Further, we would like to express our appreciation to Magdalen College, Oxford, and the Oxford University Computing Laboratory for their gracious support of the workshop. In particular, we would like to thank Wendy Adams and Julie Sheppard for their hard work in organizing the workshop. We would also like to thank Springer for facilitating the publication of these proceedings as an LNCS volume. Finally, neither the workshop nor this volume would have been possible without the support from LogicBlox Inc., Semmle Ltd., and the DIADEM project (funded from the European Research Council under the European Community's Seventh Framework Programme (FP7/2007–2013) / ERC grant agreement no. 246858).

April 2011

Oege de Moor
Georg Gottlob
Tim Furche
Andrew Sellers

# Organization

## Program Committee

| | |
|---|---|
| François Bry | University of Munich, Germany |
| Thomas Eiter | Vienna University of Technology, Austria |
| Ömer Farukhan Güneş | Oxford University, UK |
| Tim Furche | Oxford University, UK |
| Georg Gottlob | Oxford University, UK |
| Giovanni Grasso | University of Calabria, Italy |
| Giovambattista Ianni | University of Calabria, Italy |
| Jakub Kotowski | University of Munich, Germany |
| Clemens Ley | Oxford University, UK |
| Jan Maluszynski | Linköping University, Sweden |
| Marco Manna | University of Calabria, Italy |
| Giorgio Orsi | Politecnico di Milano, Italy |
| Simona Perri | University of Calabria, Italy |
| Reinhard Pichler | Vienna University of Technology, Austria |
| Andreas Pieris | Oxford University, UK |
| Christian Schallhart | Oxford University, UK |
| Andrew Sellers | Oxford University, UK |
| Mantas Simkus | Vienna University of Technology, Austria |
| Letizia Tanca | Politecnico di Milano, Italy |
| Giorgio Terracina | University of Calabria, Italy |
| Antonius Weinzierl | Vienna University of Technology, Austria |

## Sponsors

# Table of Contents

# Section 3: New Languages Extending Datalog

# Datalog-Based Program Analysis
# with BES and RWL*

María Alpuente, Marco Antonio Feliú,
Christophe Joubert, and Alicia Villanueva

Universidad Politécnica de Valencia, DSIC / ELP
Camino de Vera s/n, 46022 Valencia, Spain
{alpuente,mfeliu,joubert,villanue}@dsic.upv.es

**Abstract.** This paper describes two techniques for Datalog query evaluation and their application to object-oriented program analysis. The first technique transforms Datalog programs into an implicit Boolean Equation System (BES) that can then be solved by using linear-time complexity algorithms that are available in existing, general purpose verification toolboxes such as CADP. In order to improve scalability and to enable analyses involving advanced meta-programming features, we develop a second methodology that transforms Datalog programs into rewriting logic (RWL) theories. This method takes advantage of the preeminent features and facilities that are available within the high-performance system Maude, which provides a very efficient implementation of RWL. We provide evidence of the practicality of both approaches by reporting on some experiments with a number of real-world Datalog-based analyses.

## 1 Introduction

Datalog [31] is a simple relational query language that allows complex interprocedural program analyses involving dynamically created objects to be described in an intuitive way. The main advantage of formulating data-flow analyses in Datalog is that analyses that traditionally take hundreds of lines of code can be expressed in a few lines [34]. In real-world problems, the Datalog clauses that encode a particular analysis must generally be solved under the huge set of Datalog facts that are automatically extracted from the analyzed program.

We propose two different Datalog query answering techniques that are specially-tailored to object-oriented program analysis. Our techniques essentially consist of transforming the original Datalog program into a suitable set of rules which are then executed under an optimized top-down strategy that caches and reuses "rewrites" in the target language. We use two different formalisms for transforming any given set of definite Datalog clauses into an efficient implementation, namely Boolean Equation Systems (BES) [5] and Rewriting Logic

---

* This work has been partially supported by the EU (FEDER), the Spanish MEC/MICINN under grants TIN 2007-68093-C02 and TIN 2010-21062-C02-02, and the Generalitat Valenciana under grant Emergentes GV/2009/024. M. A. Feliú was partially supported by the Spanish MEC FPU grant AP2008-00608.

O. de Moor et al. (Eds.): Datalog 2010, LNCS 6702, pp. 1–20, 2011.
© Springer-Verlag Berlin Heidelberg 2011

(RWL) [25], a very general *logical* and *semantical framework* that is efficiently implemented in the high-level executable specification language Maude [9]. This paper provides a comprehensive overview of both techniques, which are fully automatable. For a detailed description of the methods, see [3,4].

In the BES-based program analysis methodology, the Datalog clauses that encode a particular analysis, together with a set of Datalog facts that are automatically extracted from program source code, are dynamically transformed into a BES whose local resolution corresponds to the demand-driven evaluation of the program analysis. This approach allows us to reuse existing general purpose analysis and verification toolboxes such as CADP, which provides local BES resolution with linear-time complexity. Similarly to the *Query/Subquery* technique [32], computation proceeds with a set of tuples at a time. This can be a great advantage for large datasets since it makes disk access more efficient.

Our motivation for developing our second, RWL-based query answering technique for Datalog was to provide purely declarative yet efficient program analyses that overcome the difficulty of handling meta-programming features such as reflection in traditional analysis frameworks [21]. Tracking reflective method invocations requires not just tracking object references through variables but actually tracking method values and method name strings. The interaction of static analysis with meta-programming frameworks is non-trivial, and analysis tools risk losing correctness and completeness, particularly when reflective calls are improperly interpreted during the computation. By transforming Datalog programs into Maude programs, we take advantage of the flexibility and versatility of Maude in order to achieve meta-programming capabilities, and we make significant progress towards scalability without losing the declarative nature of specifying complex program analyses in Datalog. The current version of Maude can do more than 3 million rewritings per second on standard PCs, so it can be used as an implementation language [29]. Also, as a means to scale up towards handling real programs, we wanted to determine to what extent Maude is able to process a sizable number of constraints that arise in real-life problems, like the static analysis of Java programs. After exploring the impact of different implementation choices (equations *vs* rules, unraveling *vs* conditional term rewriting systems, explicit *vs* implicit consistency check, etc.) in our working scenario (i.e., sets of hundreds of facts and a few clauses that encode the analysis), we elaborate on an equation-based transformation that leads to efficient transformed Maude-programs.

## Datalog-Based Program Analysis

The Datalog approach to static program analysis [34] can be summarized as follows. Each program element, namely variables, types, and code locations are grouped in their respective *domains*. Thus, each argument of a predicate symbol is typed by a domain of values. Each program statement is decomposed into *basic program operations* such as load, store, and assignment operations. Each kind of basic operation is described by a relation in a Datalog program. By considering only finite program domains, and applying standard loop-checking techniques, Datalog program execution is ensured to terminate.

```
public A foo { ... p = new Object(); /* o1 */     vP0(p,o1).
                   q = new Object(); /* o2 */     vP0(q,o2).
                   p.f = q;                        store(p,f,q).
                   r = p.f; ... }                  load(p,f,r).


   vP(V1,H1)      :- vP0(V1,H1).
   vP(V1,H1)      :- assign(V1,V2), vP(V2,H1).
   hP(H1,F,H2)    :- store(V1,F,V2), vP(V1,H1), vP(V2,H2).
   vP(V1,H1)      :- load(V2,F,V1), vP(V2,H2), hP(H2,F,H1).
```

**Fig. 1.** Datalog specification of a context-insensitive points-to analysis

In order to describe the general transformations from Datalog programs into BES (resp. Maude programs), let us introduce our running example: a context-insensitive points-to analysis borrowed from [34].

*Example 1.* The upper left side of Fig. 1 shows a simple Java program where o1 and o2 are heap allocations (extracted by a Java compiler from corresponding bytecode). The Datalog pointer analysis approach consists in first extracting Datalog facts (relations at the upper right side of the figure) from the program. For instance, the relation vP0 represents the direct points-to information of a program, i.e., vP0(v,h) holds if there exists a direct assignment of heap object reference h to program variable v. Other Datalog relations such as store, load and assign relations are inferred similarly from the code. Using these extracted facts, the analysis deduces further pointer-related information, like points-to relations from local variables and method parameters to heap objects (vP(V1,H1) in Fig. 1) as well as points-to relations between heap objects through field identifiers (hP(H1,F,H2) in Fig. 1).

A Datalog query consists of a goal over the relations defined in the Datalog program, e.g., :- vP(X,Y). This goal aims at computing the complete set of program variables in the domain of X that may point to any heap object Y during program execution. In the example above, the query computes the following answers: {X/p,Y/o1}, {X/q,Y/o2}, and {X/r,Y/o2}.

In the related literature, the solution for a Datalog query is classically constructed following a bottom-up approach; therefore, the information in the query is not exploited until the model has been built [18]. In contrast, the typical top-down, logic programming interpreter would produce the output by reasoning backwards from the query. Between these two extremes, there is a whole spectrum of evaluation strategies [6,7,32]. In this work, we essentially consider the top-down approach for developing our techniques since it is closer to BES local resolution as well as to Maude's evaluation principle, which is based on (non-deterministic) rewriting.

*Related Work.* The description of data-flow analyses as a database query was pioneered by Ullman [31] and Reps [28], who applied Datalog's bottom-up magic-set implementation to automatically derive a *local* implementation.

Recently, BEss with typed parameters [23], called PBES, have been successfully used to encode several hard verification problems such as the first-order value-based modal $\mu$-calculus model-checking problem [24], and the equivalence checking of various bisimulations [8] on (possibly infinite) labeled transition systems. However, PBESs were not used to compute complex interprocedural program analyses involving dynamically created objects until our work in [3]. The work that is most closely related to the BEs-based analysis approach of ours is [19], where Dependency Graphs (DGs) are used to represent satisfaction problems, including propositional Horn Clauses satisfaction and BEs resolution. A linear time algorithm for propositional Horn Clause satisfiability is described in terms of the least solution of a DG equation system. This corresponds to an alternation-free BEs, which can only deal with propositional logic problems. The extension of Liu and Smolka's work [19] to Datalog query evaluation is not straightforward. This is testified by the encoding of data-based temporal logics in equation systems with parameters in [24], where each boolean variable may depend on multiple data terms. DGs are not sufficiently expressive to represent such data dependencies on each vertex. Hence, it is necessary to work at a higher level, on the PBES representation.

The idea of using a tabled implementation of Prolog for the purpose of program analysis is a recurring theme in the logic programming community [15]. Oege de Moor *et al.* [15] have developed fast Datalog evaluators that are implemented via optimizing compilation to SQL which performs a specialized version of the well-known 'magic sets' transformation. The system, named *CodeQuest* is specifically suited for source code querying. *CodeQuest* consists of two parts: an implementation of Datalog on top of a relational database management system (RDBMS), and an Eclipse (`www.eclipse.org`) plugin for querying Java code via the Datalog implementation. Datalog queries are compiled in SQL and evaluated by the database system. The database is updated incrementally as the source code changes. Typical queries in *CodeQuest* refer to the enforcement of general rules such as the correct usage of APIs and coding style rules (*e.g.*, declarations and naming conventions), or framework-specific rules (*e.g.*, identify which classes have a method with a given name). Other queries aim to program understanding (*e.g.*, analyse which methods implement a given abstract method or are never called transitively from the *main* method). The use of a database system as the backend, together with its powerful RDBMS optimizations, makes the evaluation mechanism of *CodeQuest* very scalable. A commercial version has been implemented on top of this work by Semmle [11]. It offers a complete code analysis environment, that stores Java projects as relational databases, and provides an object-oriented query language, called .QL, to allow SQL-like queries on the databases. .QL is first translated into a pure Datalog intermediate representation, that is then optimised and translated to SQL. Finally, the SQL program can be executed on a number of databases such as Microsoft SQL Server,

PostgreSQL and H2. Apart from the completely different evaluation mechanisms and implementation technology, the main differences of our tools, DATALOG_SOLVE and DATALAUDE, with respect to *CodeQuest* is in their focus. While *CodeQuest* focuses on source code queries during the development process, we are more interested in performing dataflow analysis (particularly points-to analysis), that require deeper semantic analysis.

A very efficient Datalog program analysis technique based on binary decision diagrams (BDDs) is available in the BDDBDDB system [34], which scales to large programs and is competitive w.r.t. the traditional (imperative) approach. The computation is achieved by a fixpoint computation starting from the everywhere false predicate (or some initial approximation based on Datalog facts). Datalog rules are then applied in a bottom-up manner until saturation is reached so that all the solutions that satisfy each relation of a Datalog program are exhaustively computed. These sets of solutions are then used to answer complex formulas. In contrast, our approach focuses on demand-driven techniques to solve the considered query with no *a priori* computation of the derivable atoms. In the context of program analysis, note that all program updates, like pointer updates, might potentially be inter-related, leading to an exhaustive computation of all results. Therefore, improvements to top-down evaluation are particularly important for program analysis applications. Recently, Zheng and Rugina [35] showed that demand-driven CFL-reachability with worklist algorithm compares favorably with an exhaustive solution. Our technique to solve Datalog programs based on local BES resolution goes in the same direction and provides a novel approach to demand-driven program analyses almost for free.

As for the RWL-based approach, it essentially consists of a suitable transformation from Datalog into Maude. Since the operational principles of logic programming (*resolution*) and functional programming (*term rewriting*) share some similarities [16], many proposals exist for transforming logic programs into term rewriting systems [22,27,30]. These transformations aim at reusing the term rewriting infrastructure to run the (transformed) logic program while preserving the intended observable behavior (*e.g.*, termination, success set, computed answers, etc.) Traditionally, translations of logic programs into functional programs are based on imposing an input/output relation (mode) on the parameters of the original program [27]. However, one distinguished feature of Datalog programs that burdens the transformation is that predicate arguments are not *moded*, meaning that they can be used both as input or output parameters. One recent transformation that does not impose modes on parameters was presented in [30]. The authors defined a transformation from definite logic programs into (infinitary) term rewriting for the termination analysis of logic programs. Contrary to our approach, the transformation of [30] is not concerned with preserving the computed answers, but only the termination behavior. Moreover, [30] does not tackle the problem of efficiently encoding logic (Datalog) programs containing a huge amount of facts in a rewriting-based infrastructure such as Maude.

*Plan of the Paper.* The rest of the paper is organized as follows: Section 2 describes the application of Datalog and BES to program analysis and reports on experimental results for a context-insensitive pointer analysis of realistic Java programs. Section 3 describes the RWL-based analysis technique and the analysis infrastructure that we deployed to effectively deal with reflection. Finally, Section 4 concludes and discusses some lines for future work.

## 2   The BES-Based Datalog Evaluation Approach

This section summarizes how Datalog queries can be solved by means of Boolean Equation System [5] (BES) resolution. The key idea of our approach is to translate the Datalog specification representing a specific analysis into an implicit BES, whose resolution corresponds to the execution of the analysis [3]. We implemented this technique in the Datalog solver DATALOG_SOLVE that is based on the well-established verification toolbox CADP, which provides a generic library for local BES resolution.

A Boolean Equation System is a set of equations defining boolean variables that can be resolved with linear-time complexity. Parameterised Boolean Equation System [23] (PBES) are defined as BES with typed parameters. Since PBES are a more compact representation than BESs for a system, we first present an elegant and natural intermediate representation of a Datalog program as a PBES. In [3], we established a precise correspondence between Datalog query evaluation and PBES resolution, which is formalized as a linear-time transformation from Datalog to PBES, and vice-versa. As in [34], we assume that Datalog programs have stratified negation (no recursion through negation) and totally-ordered finite domains.

### 2.1   From Datalog to BES

In the following, we illustrate how a PBES can be obtained from a Datalog program in an automatic way. In Fig. 2 we introduce a simplified version of the analysis given in Fig. 1 that contains four facts and the first two clauses that define the predicate vP:

Given the query :- vP(V,o2)., our transformation constructs the PBES shown below, which defines the boolean variable $x_0$ and three parameterised boolean variables ($x_{vP0}$, $x_{assign}$ and $x_{vP}$), one for each Datalog relation in the analysis. Parameters of these boolean variables are defined on a specific domain and may be either variables or constants. The domains in the example are the heap domain ($D_h = \{o1, o2\}$) and the source program variable domain ($D_v = \{p, q, r, w\}$).

```
vP0(p,o1).
vP0(q,o2).
assign(r,q).
assign(w,r).
vP(V,H)  :- vP0(V,H).
vP(V,H)  :- assign(V,V2), vP(V2,H).
```

**Fig. 2.** Datalog partial context-insensitive points-to analysis

PBES are evaluated by a least fixpoint computation ($\mu$) that sets the boolean variable $x_0$ to *true* if there exists a value for $V$ that makes the parameterised boolean variable $x_{vP}(V, o2)$ true. Logical connectives are interpreted as usual.

$$x_0 \stackrel{\mu}{=} \exists V \in D_v . x_{vP}(V, o2)$$
$$x_{vP0}(p, o1) \stackrel{\mu}{=} \text{true}$$
$$x_{vP0}(q, o2) \stackrel{\mu}{=} \text{true}$$
$$x_{assign}(r, q) \stackrel{\mu}{=} \text{true}$$
$$x_{assign}(w, r) \stackrel{\mu}{=} \text{true}$$
$$x_{vP}(V : D_v, H : D_h) \stackrel{\mu}{=} x_{vP0}(V, H) \vee \exists V2 \in D_v.(x_{assign}(V, V2) \wedge x_{vP}(V2, H))$$

Intuitively, the Datalog query is transformed into the *relevant* boolean variable $x_0$, i.e., the boolean variable that will guide the PBES resolution. Each Datalog fact is transformed into an *instantiated* parameterised boolean variable (no variables appear in the parameters), whereas each predicate symbol defined by Datalog clauses (different from facts) is transformed into a parameterised boolean variable (in the example $x_{vP}(V : D_v, H : D_h)$). This parameterised boolean variable is defined by the disjunction of the corresponding Datalog clauses' bodies, in terms of boolean variables and variable quantifications. Variables that do not appear in the parameters of the boolean variable are existentially quantified on the specific domain (in the example $\exists V \in D_v$ and $\exists V2 \in D_v$).

**From PBES to BES.** Among the different known techniques for solving a PBES (see [10] and the references therein), we consider the resolution method based on transforming the PBES into an alternation-free parameterless boolean equation system (BES) that can be solved by linear time and memory algorithms when data domains are finite [23].

The first step towards the resolution of the analysis is to write the PBES in a simpler format, where, by using new auxiliary boolean variables, each formula at the right-hand side of a boolean equation contains at most one operator. Hence, boolean formulae are restricted to pure disjunctive or conjunctive formulae.

Thereafter, by applying the instantiation algorithm of Mateescu [23], we obtain a parameterless BES where all possible values of each typed data term are enumerated over their corresponding finite data domains. Actually, we do not explicitly construct the parameterless BES. Instead, an implicit representation of the instantiated BES is defined. The interested reader will find the implicit representation in [3]. This implicit representation is then used by the CADP toolbox to generate the explicit parameterless BES on-the-fly. Intuitively, the construction of the BES can be seen as the resolution of the analysis.

However, the idea of naïvely instantiating all the boolean variable parameters in the parameterised BES results in an inefficient implementation since a huge number of possible instantiations are enumerated at each computation step. In order to avoid this, we derive and subsequently optimize a version that instantiates only the parameters necessary to resume the computation. Similarly to *Query/Subquery* [32], we consider the binding of variables occurring in different atoms when transforming a clause: boolean equations only instantiate parameters to the values of variable arguments that appear more than once in the body of the corresponding Datalog clause; otherwise, arguments are kept unbound. In this way, instantiation takes place only when values are needed. Moreover, if the corresponding predicate symbol is extensively defined by a set of facts, the only possible values of its variable arguments in the instantiation are those in the defining facts.

To illustrate the idea behind this optimized version of the generated BES, in Fig. 3 we show (a part of) the BES that results from our running example. Boolean variables, whose name starts with $x$ (shown in bold in the figure) are those that correspond to the goal and subgoals of the original program. Boolean variables starting with $r$ or $g$ are auxiliary boolean variables that are defined during unfolding and instantiation of (sub)goals. The first fragment of the BES (four equations) shows the definition process for the initial query, represented by the boolean variable $x_0$. The query is unfolded and partially instantiated. In our example, there is only one query (:- vP(V,o2).) with one single subgoal. Since no variables are shared, $V$ is kept unchanged. Then, the partially instantiated (sub)query is solved by means of its associated boolean variable $(x_{vP(V,o2)})$. Finally, $x_{vP(V,o2)}$ is defined as the disjunction of the boolean variables that correspond to querying the *facts* $(x^f)$ and querying the *clauses* $(x^c)$.

A query to the clauses of a predicate is defined as the disjunction of the boolean variables that represent the body of the Datalog clauses. In the case of the query $vP(V,H)$ defined by two clauses, the corresponding boolean variable $x^c_{vP(V,H)}$ is defined in terms of two boolean variables $r_{vP0(V,H)}$ and

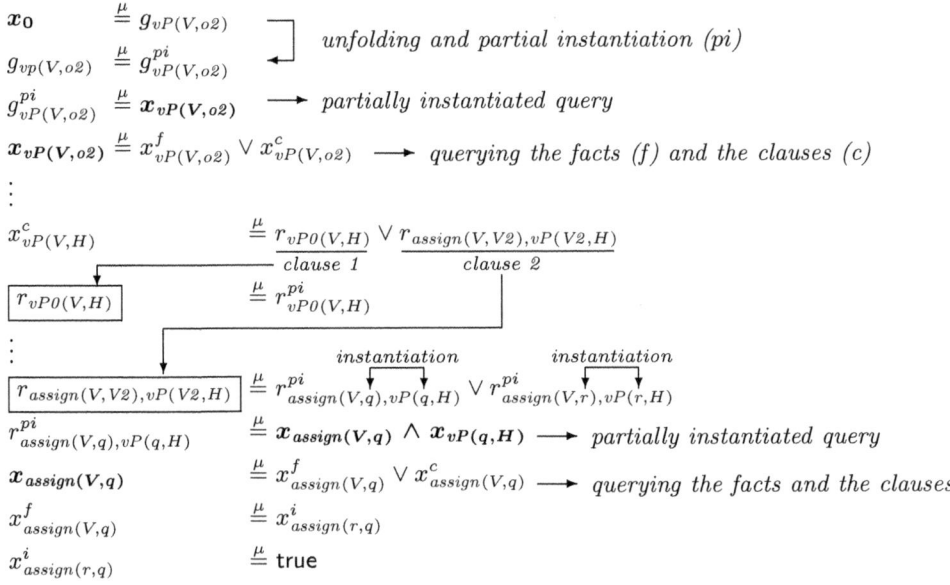

**Fig. 3.** An excerpt of the generated BES

$r_{assign(V,V2),vP(V2,H)}$. The $r$ boolean variable is defined as the disjunction of the different possible instantiations of the query on the shared variables. These *partial instantiations* are represented by $r^{pi}$ boolean variables. For instance, we can observed that $r_{assign(V,V2),vP(V2,H)}$ can be instantiated with the two possible values for $V2$, the only shared variable. The $r^{pi}$ boolean variables are defined as the conjunction of the (partially instantiated) subqueries, which are represented by $x$ boolean variables. As before, boolean variables $x$ are defined as the disjunction of the boolean variables that correspond to querying the *facts* ($x^f$) and querying the *clauses* ($x^c$), as shown in the equation for $x_{assign(V,q)}$. Finally, facts are instantiated to final values and are represented as boolean variables $x^i$, set to true.

As stated above, when the $r^{pi}$ boolean variables are generated, only variables that are shared by two or more subgoals in the body of the Datalog program are instantiated, and only values that appear in the corresponding parameters of the program facts are used. In other words, we do not generate spurious boolean variables, such as $r^{pi}_{assign(V,w),vP(w,H)}$, which can never be true.

**Solution extraction.** By considering the optimized parameterless BES defined above, the query satisfiability problem is reduced to the local resolution of boolean variable $x_0$. The value (true or false) computed for $x_0$ indicates whether or not there exists at least one satisfiable goal. In order to compute all the different solutions of a Datalog query, it is sensible to use a breadth-first search strategy (BFS) for the resolution of the BES. Such a strategy forces the resolution of all boolean variables in the BFS queue that are potential solutions to the query. Query solutions are extracted from all the boolean variables that are reachable from boolean variable $x_0$ following a path of true-valued boolean variables.

## 2.2   The Prototype Datalog_Solve

We implemented the Datalog transformation to BES in a fully automated Datalog solver tool, called DATALOG_SOLVE[1], which was developed within the CADP verification toolbox [14]. Of course, other source languages and problems can be specified in Datalog and solved by our tool as well.

DATALOG_SOLVE takes as input the Datalog facts that are automatically extracted by the JOEQ compiler [33] and a Datalog query that consists of the initial goal and the specification for the analysis.

The DATALOG_SOLVE architecture (120 lines of Lex, 380 lines of Bison and 3 500 lines of C code) consists of two components, as illustrated in Fig. 4. The front-end of DATALOG_SOLVE constructs the (implicit) optimized BES representation from the considered Datalog analysis. The back-end of our tool carries out the interpretation of the BES that is generated and solved on-the-fly by means of the generic CÆSAR_SOLVE library of CADP.

---

[1] http://www.dsic.upv.es/users/elp/datalog_solve/

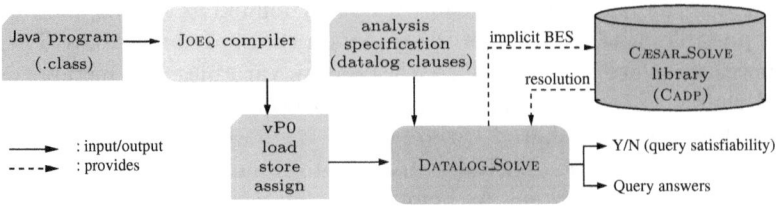

**Fig. 4.** Java program analysis using the DATALOG_SOLVE tool

This architecture clearly separates the implementation of **Datalog**-based static analyses from the resolution engine, which can be extended and optimized independently.

### 2.3   Experimental Results

In order to test the scalability and applicability of the transformation, the DATALOG_SOLVE tool was applied to a number of Java programs by computing the context-insensitive pointer analysis described in Fig. 1. We have compared our prototype against BDDBDDB on four of the most popular 100% Java standalone applications hosted on Sourceforge used as benchmarks for the BDDBDDB tool [34]. All experiments were conducted on a Intel Core 2 duo E4500 2.2 GHz (only one core used), with 2048 KB cache, 4 GB of RAM, and running Linux Ubuntu 10.04. BDDBDDB is executed with the best variable ordering that we have found for the points-to analysis example, namely: V V H H F. Execution times (in seconds) are presented in Table 1: "Time" column refers to the analysis computed by our prototype; "BDDBDDB" column shows the execution time of the BDDBDDB solver; and "Opt.Time" column shows some preliminary results of an ongoing optimization of our prototype, that makes use of an auxiliary data structure (tries) to improve efficiency. This "optimized" approach is still under development [12,13] and is not fully automated; however, the results are very promising. The results show that our approach works on large amounts of facts as can be encountered in the analysis of real programs. Even with the best encountered boolean variable ordering, the BDD-based approach appears to be penalized by the poor regularity of the points-to analysis domains and poor redundancy of the analysis relations with respect to our approach based on an explicit encoding.

**Table 1.** Description of the Java projects used as benchmarks

| Name | Classes | Methods | Vars | Allocs | Time | BDDBDDB | Opt.Time |
|------|---------|---------|------|--------|------|---------|----------|
| freetts (1.2.1) | 215 | 723 | 8K | 3K | 10 | 3.8 | 0.02 |
| nfcchat (1.1.0) | 283 | 993 | 11K | 3K | 8 | 3.86 | 0.01 |
| jetty (6.1.10) | 309 | 1160 | 12K | 3K | 73 | 6.41 | 0.04 |
| joone (2.0.0) | 375 | 1531 | 17K | 4K | 4 | 3.45 | 0.01 |

# 3   The RWL-Based Datalog Evaluation Approach

With the aim to achieve higher expressiveness for static-analysis specification, we translate Datalog into a powerful and highly extensible framework, namely, rewriting logic. Due to the high level of expressiveness of RWL, many ways for translating Datalog into RWL can be considered. Because efficiency does matter in the context of Datalog-based program analysis, our proposed transformation is the result of an iterative process that is aimed at optimizing the running time of the transformed program. The basic idea of the translation is to automatically compile Datalog clauses into deterministic equations. Queries and answers are consistently represented as terms so that the query is evaluated by reducing its term representation into a *constraint set* that represents the answers.

## 3.1   From Datalog to Maude

*Membership equational logic* [26] is the subset of RWL that we use for representing the translated Datalog programs. A *membership equational theory* consists of a signature and a set of equations and membership axioms. Its operational semantics is based on *term rewriting* modulo algebraic axioms, where equations are considered as left-to-right rewriting rules, while membership axioms are assertions of membership to a given sort.

The translated programs have been expressed in Maude [9], which provides many powerful features, like ACI-matching[2], efficient set-representation, meta-programming capabilities (*e.g.*, reflection), and memoization. In this subsection, we first summarize the key ideas of the transformation and its Maude representation, and then we describe how we deal with points-to analyses involving reflection in our framework. The complete transformation is given in [4], and the proof of its correctness and completeness can be found in [2].

**Answer representation.** Datalog answers are expressed as equational *constraints* that relate the variables of the queries to values. Values are represented as *ground terms* of sort Constant that are constructed by means of Maude *Quoted Identifiers* (Qids). Since logical variables cannot be represented with rewriting rule variables because of their dual input-output nature, we give a representation for them as ground terms of sort Variable by means of the overloaded vrbl constructor. A Term is either a Constant or a Variable. These elements are represented in Maude as follows:

```
sorts Variable Constant Term .
subsort Variable Constant < Term .
subsort Qid < Constant .
op vrbl : Term -> Variable [ctor] .
```

In our formulation, answers are recorded within the term that represents the ongoing partial computation of the Maude program. Thus, we represent a (partial)

---

[2] Matching modulo Associativity, Commutativity, and Identity.

answer for the original Datalog query as a set of equational constraints (called answer constraints) that represent the substitution of (logical) variables by (logical) constants that are incrementally computed during the program execution. We define the sort Constraint as the composition of answer equations. Elements of sort Constraint represent single answers for a Datalog query as follows:

```
sort Constraint .

op _=_ : Term Constant -> Constraint .
op T : -> Constraint .
op F : -> Constraint .
op _,_ : Constraint Constraint -> Constraint [assoc comm id: T] .

eq F, C:Constraint = F .                    --- Zero element
```

Constraints are constructed[3] by the conjunction (_,_) of solved equations of the form T:Term = C:Constant, the *false* constraint F, or the *true* constraint T. Note that the conjunction operator _,_ obeys the laws[4] of associativity and commutativity. T is defined as the identity of (_,_), and F is used as the zero element.

Unification of expressions is performed by combining the corresponding answer constraints and checking the satisfiability of the compound. Simplification equations are introduced in order to simplify trivial constraints by reducing them to T, or to detect inconsistencies (unification failure) so that the whole conjunction can be drastically replaced by F, as shown in the following code excerpt:

```
var Cst Cst1 Cst2 : Constant . var V : Variable .
eq (V = Cst)  , (V = Cst)  = (V = Cst) , T . --- Idempotence
eq (V = Cst1) , (V = Cst2) = F [owise] .      --- Unsatisfiability
```

In our setting, a failing computation occurs when a query is reduced to F. If a query is reduced to T, then the original (ground) query is proven to be satisfiable. On the contrary, if the query is reduced to a set of solved equations, then the computed answer is given by a substitution $\{x_1/t_1, \ldots, x_n/t_n\}$ that is expressed by the computed normal form $x_1 = t_1$ , $\ldots$ , $x_n = t_n$.

Since equations in Maude are run deterministically, all the non-determinism of the original Datalog program has to be embedded into the term under reduction. This means that we need to carry all the possible (partial) answers at a given execution point. To this end, we introduce the notion of *set of answer constraints*, and we define a new sort called ConstraintSet as follows:

```
sorts ConstraintSet .
subsort Constraint < ConstraintSet .
op _;_ : ConstraintSet ConstraintSet -> ConstraintSet  [assoc comm id: F] .
```

---

[3] The actual transformation defines a more complex hierarchy of sorts in order to obtain simpler equations and improve performance.

[4] Associativity, commutativity, and identity are easily expressed by using ACI attributes in Maude, thus simplifying the equational specification and also achieving a more efficient implementation.

The set of constraints is constructed as the (possibly empty) disjunction _;_ of accumulated constraints. The disjunction operator _;_ obeys the laws of associativity and commutativity and is also given the identity element **F**.

Transformed predicates are naturally expressed as functions (with the same arity) whose codomain is the `ConstraintSet` sort. They will be reduced to the set of constraints that represent the satisfiable instantiations of the original query. The transformed predicates of our running example are represented in Maude as follows:

```
op vP vP0 assign : Term Term -> ConstraintSet .
```

In order to incrementally add new constraints throughout the program execution, we define the composition operator x for constraint sets as follows:

```
op _x_ : ConstraintSet ConstraintSet -> ConstraintSet [assoc] .
```

The composition operator x allows us to combine (partial) solutions of the subgoals in a clause body.

**A glimpse of the transformation.** Let us describe the transformation by evaluating queries in our running example. For instance, by executing the Datalog query :- vP0(p,Y) on the program in Fig. 2, we obtain the solution {Y/o1}. Here, vP0 is a predicate defined only by facts, so the answers to the query represent the variable instantiations as given by the existing facts. Thus, we would expect the query's RWL representation vP0('p, vrbl('Y)) to be reduced to the `ConstraintSet` (with just one constraint) vrbl('Y) = 'o1. This is accomplished by representing facts according to the following equation pattern:

```
var T0 T1 : Term .
eq vP0(T0,T1) = (T0 = 'p , T1 = 'o1) ; (T0 = 'q , T1 = 'o2) .
eq assign(T0,T1) = (T0 = 'r , T1 = 'q) ; (T0 = 'w , T1 = 'r) .
```

The right-hand side of the RWL equation that is used to represent the facts that define a given predicate (in the example vP0 and assign) consists of the set of constraints that express the satisfiable instantiations of the original predicate. As can be observed, arguments are propagated to the constraints, thus allowing the already mentioned equational simplification process on the constraints. For this particular case, the reduction proceeds as follows:

```
vP0('p,vrbl('Y))
   → ('p = 'p , vrbl('Y) = 'o1) ; ('p = 'q , vrbl('Y) = 'o2)
   →* (T , vrbl('Y) = 'o1) ; (F , vrbl('Y) = 'o2)
   →* vrbl('Y) = 'o1 ; F
   → vrbl('Y) = 'o1
```

Another example of Datalog query is :- vP(V,o2), whose execution for the leading example delivers the solutions {{V/q},{V/r},{V/w}}. Thus, we expect vP(vrbl('V),'o2) to be reduced to the set of constraints (vrbl('V) = 'q) ; (vrbl('V) = 'r) ; (vrbl('V) = 'w). In this case, vP is a predicate defined by clauses, so the answers to the query are the disjunction of the answers provided by all the clauses defining it. This is represented in RWL by introducing auxiliary functions to separately compute the answers for each clause, and the equation to join them is as follows:

```
op vP-clause-1 vP-clause-2 : Term Term -> ConstraintSet .
var X Y : Term .
eq vP(X,Y) = vP-clause-1(X , Y) ; vP-clause-2(X , Y) .
```

In order to compute the answers delivered by a clause, we search for the satisfiable instantiations of its body's subgoals. In our translation, we explore the possible instantiations from the leftmost subgoal to the rightmost one. In order to impose this left-to-right exploration, we create a different (auxiliary) unraveling function for each subgoal. Each of these auxiliary functions computes the partial answer depending on the corresponding and previous subgoals and propagates it to the subsequent unraveling function[5]. Additionally, existential variables that occur only in the body of original Datalog clauses, e.g., Z, are introduced by using a ground representation that is parameterised with the corresponding call pattern in order to generate fresh variables (in the example below vrblZ(X,Y)).

As shown in the following code excerpt, in our example, the first Datalog clause can be transformed without using unraveling functions. For the second Datalog clause (with two subgoals) only one unraveling function is needed in order to force the early reduction of the first subgoal.

```
op vrblZ : Term Term -> Variable .
op unrav : ConstraintSet TermList -> ConstraintSet .

eq vP-clause-1(X,Y) = vP0(X,Y) .
eq vP-clause-2(X,Y) = unrav( assign(X, vrblZ(X,Y)) , X Y ) .
```

The unrav function has two arguments: a ConstraintSet, which is the first (reduced) subgoal (the original subgoal assign(X,Z) in this case); and the X Y call pattern. This function is defined as follows:

```
var Cnt : Constant . var TS : TermList .
var C : Constraint . var CS : ConstraintSet .

eq unrav( ( (vrblZ(X,Y) = Cnt , C) ; CS ) , X Y ) =
    ( vP(Cnt,Y) x (vrblZ(X,Y) = Cnt , C) ) ; unrav( CS , X Y ) .
eq unrav( F , TS ) = F .
```

The unraveling function (in the example unrav) takes a set of partial answers as its first argument. It requires the partial answers to be in solved equation form by pattern matching, thus ensuring the left-to-right execution of the goals. The second argument is the call pattern of the translated clause and serves to reference the introduced existential variables. The propagated call pattern is represented as a TermList, that is, a juxtaposition (__ operator) of Terms. The two unrav equations (recursively) combine each (partial) answer obtained from

---

[5] Conditional equations could also be used to impose left-to-right evaluation, but in practice they suffer from poor performance as our experiments revealed.

the first subgoal with every (partial) answer computed from the (instantiated) subsequent subgoal (vP(Cnt,Y) in the example).

Consider again the Datalog query :- vP(V,o2). We undertake all possible query reduction by using the equations above. Given the size of the execution trace, we will use the following abbreviations: V stands for vrbl('V), vPci for vP-clause-i, and Z-T0-T1 for vrblZ(T0,T1).

```
vP(V,'o2 )
   → vPc1(V,'o2) ; vPc2(V,'o2)
   →* vP0(V,'o2) ; unrav( assign(V,Z-V-o2) , V 'o2 )
   →* ((V = 'p , 'o2 = 'o1) ; (V = 'q , 'o2 = 'o2))
      ; unrav( ((V = 'r , Z-V-o2 = 'q) ; (V = 'w , Z-V-o2 = 'r)) , V 'o2 )
   →* (F ; (V = 'q , T)) ; (vP('q,'o2) x (V = 'r , Z-V-o2 = 'q))
      ; unrav( (V = 'w , Z-V-o2 = 'r) , V 'o2 )
   →* (V = 'q) ; ((vPc1('q,'o2) ; vPc2('q,'o2)) x (V = 'r , Z-V-o2 = 'q))
      ; (vP('r,'o2) x (V = 'w , Z-V-o2 = 'r)) ; unrav( F , V 'o2 )
   . . .

   →* (V = 'q) ; (V = 'r) ; (V = 'w)
```

**Reflection.** Reflection in Java is a powerful technique that is used when a program needs to examine or modify the runtime behavior of applications running on the Java virtual machine. For example, by using reflection, it is possible to write to object fields and invoke methods that are not known at compile time.

The main difficulty of reflective analysis is that we do not have all the basic information for the points-to analysis at the beginning of the computation. This is because Java methods that handle reflection may generate new basic points-to information. A sound approach for handling Java reflection in Datalog analyses is proposed in [21]. We transform Datalog clauses that specify the reflection analysis into Maude conditional rules in a natural way. Then, the Maude reflection capability is used during the analysis to automatically generate the rules that represent the deduced points-to information and adds them to the program. This is in contrast to [21], which resorts to an external artifact with ad-hoc notation and operational principle.

We have implemented a small prototype which essentially consists of a module at the Maude meta-level that implements a generic infrastructure to deal with reflection. Fig. 5 shows the structure of a typical reflection analysis as it is run in our tool. The static analysis is specified in two object-level modules, a *basic module* and a *reflective module*. These modules can be written in either Maude or Datalog since Datalog analyses are automatically compiled into Maude code. The *basic program analysis* module contains the rules for the classical analysis (which neglects reflection), whereas the *reflective program analysis* module contains the part of the analysis that deals with the reflective components of the Java program. At the meta-level, the *solver* module consists of a generic fixpoint algorithm that feeds the reflective module with the points-to information inferred by the basic analysis. Then, rules that encode the new inferred information are built by the

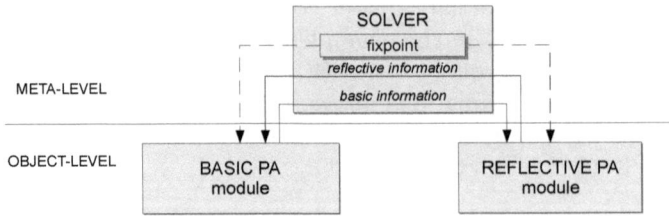

**Fig. 5.** The structure of the reflective analysis

reflective analysis and added to the basic module in order to infer new information, until a fixpoint is reached. A detailed description can be found in [2].

### 3.2   The Prototype Datalaude

We implemented the Datalog to RWL transformation in DATALAUDE[6] (700 lines of Haskell code and 50 lines of Maude code). The prototype transforms the set of Datalog rules and facts into a Maude membership equational theory. Then, the generated theory is used to reduce each query into its answer constraint set representation in Maude.

**Experimental results.** We report on the performance of DATALAUDE by comparing it to a previous *rule-based* Datalog-to-RWL transformation that consisted of a one-to-one mapping from Datalog rules into Maude conditional rules. We briefly present the results obtained by using the rule-based approach and the enhanced *equational-based* DATALAUDE approach with and without the optimization of using the memoization capability of Maude.

Table 2 shows the resolution times of the three selected versions for different sets of initial Datalog facts (`assign/2` and `vP0/2`), which were extracted by the JOEQ compiler [33] from a Java program (with 374 lines of code) that implements a tree visitor algorithm. All experiments were conducted on a Intel Core 2 duo E4500 2.2 GHz (only one core used), with 2048 KB cache, 4 GB of RAM, and running Linux Ubuntu 10.04. The evaluated query is `?- vP(Var,Heap)`. Note that the results obtained are progressively better, which emphasizes the fact that by favoring determinism and unconditional equations the computation time can be greatly reduced. On the largest set of initial facts (last line of the table), when memoization is used, 1 293 984 rewritings are realized in 0.87 seconds to compute all solutions of the analysis. *Memoization* is a table-based mechanism that stores the canonical form (equational simplification) of subterms having operators, at the top, tagged with the `memo` attribute. Whenever such subterm is encountered during the computation, its canonical form is searched in the table and used instead. Since subcomputations involving the `vP` operator will be repeated many times in the points-to analysis, the overall computation is substantially sped up when the operator `vP` is given the `memo` attribute.

---

[6] http://www.dsic.upv.es/users/elp/datalaude

**Table 2.** Number of initial facts (`assign/2` and vP0/2) and computed answers (vP/2), and resolution time (in seconds) for the three implementations

| assign/2 | vP0/2 | vP/2 | rule-based | equational | equational+memo |
|---|---|---|---|---|---|
| 100 | 100 | 144 | 1.32 | 0.24 | 0.01 |
| 150 | 150 | 222 | 4.86 | 0.76 | 0.01 |
| 200 | 200 | 297 | 12.47 | 1.76 | 0.02 |
| 403 | 399 | 602 | 117.94 | 15.42 | 0.10 |
| 807 | 1669 | 2042 | 1540.55 | 277.09 | 0.87 |

These results confirm that the current DATALAUDE implementation is the one that best fits our program analysis purposes. More details of this experiment and a comparison with other implementations can be found in [4].

# 4  Conclusion and Future Work

This article overviews two novel complementary approaches for solving Datalog queries. Both approaches are fully automatable and applicable to a large class of Datalog programs. In this article, we illustrated them on a popular application domain, namely Datalog-based pointer analysis.

- We used boolean equation systems (BES) to efficiently compute fixpoints in Datalog evaluations. BES resolutions achieve the robustness of bottom-up evaluation, satisfactorily coping with redundant infinite computations. Our transformation also achieves the effectiveness of demand-driven techniques by propagating values and constraints that are part of the query's subgoals in order to speed up the computation.
- We defined, formalized, and proved the correctness of another novel transformation from Datalog programs into Maude programs. By taking advantage of the cogent RWL reflection capabilities, we also demonstrated the adequacy of Maude to support declarative, accurate, and sound complex pointer analyses that include meta-programming features such as reflection in Java programs.

Two new Datalog solvers, called DATALOG_SOLVE and DATALAUDE, respectively, were designed, implemented, and successfully used for the evaluation of the Datalog-based program analysis over several realistic Java programs. The BES-approach is really fast and can analysis in few milliseconds a context-insensitive points-to analysis on a real Java project. Such an approach would perfectly fit in *Integrated Development Environments* (IDEs) to provide rapid feedback to a developer during the development of its code. However, this evaluation technique is not so appropriate to define, compose and experiment new analyses as it would be with a purely declarative approach based on rewriting logic. RWL offers a sound framework to design complex program analyses in just a few lines.

As ongoing work, we recently endowed DATALOG_SOLVE with new, optimized strategies for local BES resolution, where Datalog rules are first decomposed in order to allow goal-directed bottom-up evaluation with complexity guarantees [20].

As future work, we plan to explore such sophisticated Datalog optimizations in a purely declarative framework like Maude. Inversely, we could also benefit from the regular structure of our BES encoding by distributing the BES resolution over a network of workstations with balanced partitioning while still preserving locality, similarly to [17]. A promising alternative approach to explore would distribute the workload directly at the Datalog level by using Map-Reduce-based algorithms such as [1].

**Acknowledgements.** We are grateful to Fernando Tarín and Adam Kepa for their valuable contributions to the experiments shown in this paper.

# References

1. Afrati, F.N., Ullman, J.D.: Optimizing joins in a map-reduce environment. In: Manolescu, I., Spaccapietra, S., Teubner, J., Kitsuregawa, M., Léger, A., Naumann, F., Ailamaki, A., Özcan, F. (eds.) EDBT. ACM International Conference Proceeding Series, vol. 426, pp. 99–110. ACM, New York (2010)
2. Alpuente, M., Feliú, M., Joubert, C., Villanueva, A.: Defining Datalog in Rewriting Logic. Technical Report DSIC-II/07/09, DSIC, Universidad Politécnica de Valencia (2009)
3. Alpuente, M., Feliú, M., Joubert, C., Villanueva, A.: Using Datalog and Boolean Equation Systems for Program Analysis. In: Cofer, D., Fantechi, A. (eds.) FMICS 2008. LNCS, vol. 5596, pp. 215–231. Springer, Heidelberg (2009)
4. Alpuente, M., Feliú, M.A., Joubert, C., Villanueva, A.: Defining datalog in rewriting logic. In: De Schreye, D. (ed.) LOPSTR 2009. LNCS, vol. 6037, pp. 188–204. Springer, Heidelberg (2010)
5. Andersen, H.R.: Model checking and boolean graphs. Theoretical Computer Science 126(1), 3–30 (1994)
6. Bancilhon, F., Maier, D., Sagiv, Y., Ullman, J.D.: Magic Sets and Other Strange Ways to Implement Logic Programs. In: Proc. 5th ACM SIGACT-SIGMOD Symp. on Principles of Database Systems, PODS 1986, pp. 1–15. ACM Press, New York (1986)
7. Ceri, S., Gottlob, G., Tanca, L.: Logic Programming and Databases. Springer, Heidelberg (1990)
8. Chen, T., Ploeger, B., van de Pol, J., Willemse, T.A.C.: Equivalence Checking for Infinite Systems Using Parameterized Boolean Equation Systems. In: Caires, L., Vasconcelos, V.T. (eds.) CONCUR 2007. LNCS, vol. 4703, pp. 120–135. Springer, Heidelberg (2007)
9. Clavel, M., Durán, F., Ejer, S., Lincoln, P., Martí-Oliet, N., Meseguer, J., Talcott, C.: All About Maude - A High-Performance Logical Framework. LNCS, vol. 4350. Springer, Heidelberg (2007)
10. Dam, A., Ploeger, B., Willemse, T.: Instantiation for Parameterised Boolean Equation Systems. In: Fitzgerald, J.S., Haxthausen, A.E., Yenigun, H. (eds.) ICTAC 2008. LNCS, vol. 5160, pp. 440–454. Springer, Heidelberg (2008)
11. de Moor, O., Sereni, D., Verbaere, M., Hajiyev, E., Avgustinov, P., Ekman, T., Ongkingco, N., Tibble, J.: QL: Object-oriented queries made easy. In: Lämmel, R., Visser, J., Saraiva, J. (eds.) GTTSE 2008. LNCS, vol. 5235, pp. 78–133. Springer, Heidelberg (2008)

12. Feliú, M., Joubert, C., Tarín, F.: Efficient BES-based Bottom-Up Evaluation of Datalog Programs. In: Gulías, V., Silva, J., Villanueva, A. (eds.) Proc. X Jornadas sobre Programación y Lenguajes (PROLE 2010), Garceta, pp. 165–176 (2010)
13. Feliú, M., Joubert, C., Tarín, F.: Evaluation strategies for datalog-based points-to analysis. In: Bendisposto, J., Leuschel, M., Roggenbach, M. (eds.) Proc. 10th Workshop on Automated Verification of Critical Systems (AVoCS 2010), pp. 88–103. Technical Report of Düsseldorf University (2010)
14. Garavel, H., Mateescu, R., Lang, F., Serwe, W.: CADP 2006: A Toolbox for the Construction and Analysis of Distributed Processes. In: Damm, W., Hermanns, H. (eds.) CAV 2007. LNCS, vol. 4590, pp. 158–163. Springer, Heidelberg (2007)
15. Hajiyev, E., Verbaere, M., de Moor, O.: CodeQuest: Scalable Source Code Queries with Datalog. In: Hu, Q. (ed.) ECOOP 2006. LNCS, vol. 4067, pp. 2–27. Springer, Heidelberg (2006)
16. Hanus, M.: The Integration of Functions into Logic Programming: From Theory to Practice. Journal on Logic Programming 19 & 20, 583–628 (1994)
17. Joubert, C., Mateescu, R.: Distributed On-the-Fly Model Checking and Test Case Generation. In: Valmari, A. (ed.) SPIN 2006. LNCS, vol. 3925, pp. 126–145. Springer, Heidelberg (2006)
18. Leeuwen, J. (ed.): Formal Models and Semantics, vol. B. Elsevier, The MIT Press (1990)
19. Liu, X., Smolka, S.A.: Simple Linear-Time Algorithms for Minimal Fixed Points. In: Larsen, K.G., Skyum, S., Winskel, G. (eds.) ICALP 1998. LNCS, vol. 1443, pp. 53–66. Springer, Heidelberg (1998)
20. Liu, Y.A., Stoller, S.D.: From datalog rules to efficient programs with time and space guarantees. ACM Trans. Program. Lang. Syst. 31(6) (2009)
21. Livshits, B., Whaley, J., Lam, M.: Reflection Analysis for Java. In: Yi, K. (ed.) APLAS 2005. LNCS, vol. 3780, pp. 139–160. Springer, Heidelberg (2005)
22. Marchiori, M.: Logic Programs as Term Rewriting Systems. In: Rodríguez-Artalejo, M., Levi, G. (eds.) ALP 1994. LNCS, vol. 850, pp. 223–241. Springer, Heidelberg (1994)
23. Mateescu, R.: Local Model-Checking of an Alternation-Free Value-Based Modal Mu-Calculus. In: Proc. 2nd Int'l Workshop on Verication, Model Checking and Abstract Interpretation, VMCAI 1998 (1998)
24. Mateescu, R., Thivolle, D.: A Model Checking Language for Concurrent Value-Passing Systems. In: Cuellar, J., Sere, K. (eds.) FM 2008. LNCS, vol. 5014, pp. 148–164. Springer, Heidelberg (2008)
25. Meseguer, J.: Conditional Rewriting Logic as a Unified Model of Concurrency. Theoretical Computer Science 96(1), 73–155 (1992)
26. Meseguer, J.: Membership algebra as a logical framework for equational specification. In: Parisi-Presicce, F. (ed.) WADT 1997. LNCS, vol. 1376, pp. 18–61. Springer, Heidelberg (1998)
27. Reddy, U.: Transformation of Logic Programs into Functional Programs. In: Proc. Symposium on Logic Programming (SLP 1984), pp. 187–197. IEEE Computer Society Press, Los Alamitos (1984)
28. Reps, T.W.: Solving Demand Versions of Interprocedural Analysis Problems. In: Adsul, B. (ed.) CC 1994. LNCS, vol. 786, pp. 389–403. Springer, Heidelberg (1994)
29. Rosu, G., Havelund, K.: Rewriting-Based Techniques for Runtime Verification. Autom. Softw. Eng. 12(2), 151–197 (2005)
30. Schneider-Kamp, P., Giesl, J., Serebrenik, A., Thiemann, R.: Automated Termination Analysis for Logic Programs by Term Rewriting. In: Puebla, G. (ed.) LOPSTR 2006. LNCS, vol. 4407, pp. 177–193. Springer, Heidelberg (2007)

31. Ullman, J.D.: Principles of Database and Knowledge-Base Systems, Volume I and II, The New Technologies. Computer Science Press, Rockville (1989)
32. Vieille, L.: Recursive Axioms in Deductive Databases: The Query/Subquery Approach. In: Proc. 1st Int'l Conf. on Expert Database Systems, EDS 1986, pp. 253–267 (1986)
33. Whaley, J.: Joeq: a Virtual Machine and Compiler Infrastructure. In: Proc. Workshop on Interpreters, Virtual Machines and Emulators, IVME 2003, pp. 58–66. ACM Press, New York (2003)
34. Whaley, J., Avots, D., Carbin, M., Lam, M.S.: Using Datalog with Binary Decision Diagrams for Program Analysis. In: Yi, K. (ed.) APLAS 2005. LNCS, vol. 3780, pp. 97–118. Springer, Heidelberg (2005)
35. Zheng, X., Rugina, R.: Demand-driven alias analysis for C. In: Proc. 35th ACM SIGPLAN-SIGACT Symp. on Principles of Programming Languages, POPL 2008, pp. 197–208. ACM Press, New York (2008)

# Datalog for Security, Privacy and Trust

Piero A. Bonatti

Università di Napoli "Federico II", Italy

**Abstract.** Logic-based policy languages are appreciated because of their clean semantics and expressiveness. Datalog has been used for a long time as a foundation of many security models and policy languages. Recently, Description Logics (DLs for short) have been adopted as policy languages, too. In this paper we carry out a comparison of Datalog and Description Logics as policy languages, based both on expressiveness analysis and on an assessment of the current maturity of the two fields, expressly related to the representation and reasoning tasks involved in policy authoring, enforcement, and management. We shall argue that Datalog-based approaches are currently more powerful and mature than those based on pure DLs, although the ongoing research on the latter might change the picture in a near future. The potential of hybrid approaches will be briefly discussed.

## 1 Introduction

Logic-based languages have been regarded as appealing policy languages for a long time, since the seminal work by Woo and Lam [91]. The computer security community appreciates the independent, clean, and unambiguous semantics of logic languages (that constitutes an ideal implementation-independent specification for policy languages) and the expressiveness of logic-based specifications, that is becoming more and more important in modern open application contexts characterized by unprecedented needs for flexibility [75,73,53]. The first approaches in the literature are essentially rule-based [91] and founded on Datalog and extensions thereof [56,62,45,12,22]. Recently, the advent of the semantic web fostered the adoption of Description Logics (DLs) as policy languages [85,44,92,61]. This is a natural choice, given that policies frequently express decisions based on the information and metadata they are meant to protect; when such policy inputs are organized and/or formulated by means of DLs, a policy language based on the same formalism has obvious potential advantages in terms of uniformity and integration.

Such a wide landscape of alternative policy languages calls for criteria and tools for comparing and assessing different approaches. This paper carries out a comparison of Datalog and Description Logics as policy languages, based both on expressiveness analysis and on an assessment of the current maturity of the two fields, expressly related to the representation and reasoning tasks involved in policy authoring, enforcement, and management. We shall argue that Datalog-based approaches are currently more powerful and mature than those based on pure DLs, although the ongoing research on the latter might change the picture in a near future. The potential advantages and disadvantages of hybrid approaches will be briefly mentioned.

O. de Moor et al. (Eds.): Datalog 2010, LNCS 6702, pp. 21–36, 2011.

The paper is organized as follows. In Section 2 we recall the main policy languages based on Datalog and DLs. In Section 3 the expressiveness of these languages is analyzed using descriptive complexity—a technique developed in the area of database theory—and the tree-model property of Description Logics. Section 4 outlines the main reasoning tasks related to policy enforcement and management, and for each task compares the maturity level of the methods and technologies based on Datalog and DLs. Although hybrid approaches that combine rules and DLs are not yet popular in the area of policy languages, they have an interesting potential. Hybrid approaches are briefly discussed in Section 5. The paper is concluded by a final discussion. Throughout the paper we will point to interesting directions for future work.

We assume the reader to be familiar with Logic Programming, Description Logics, and Logic-based policies. For background on these topics we refer to [3,7,25].

# 2   Logic-Based Policy Languages

## 2.1   Datalog-Based Approaches

Nonmonotonic semantics is fundamental for policy languages, that need to encode default policies such as open and closed policies (where authorizations are granted or denied—respectively—unless stated otherwise), authorization inheritance with exceptions (which is helpful to formulate policies incrementally, by iterative refinements, and supports exception handling, such as user blacklisting for crisis management), and prioritized conflict resolution. The initial approach by Woo and Lam [91], based on general default logic, has been later refined into a framework called *Flexible Authorization Framework* (FAF) [56], based on stratified Datalog with negation. Stratification has three important roles. First, it reduces data complexity from NP to P. Second, it removes the potential ambiguities arising in the general case, where a policy may have multiple stable models. Third, the layers induced by stratification may be regarded as the steps of a methodology for constructing policies in a principled way, starting with explicit authorizations, then adding derived authorizations (e.g. by inheritance along hierarchies of subjects, objects, and roles), and finally filling in policy gaps with default authorizations and resolving conflicts. In FAF, the policy evaluation context (defining entities such as users, resources, and roles, the corresponding hierarchies, as well as histories and other pieces of information relevant to policy evaluation) is defined by means of ground facts. Policy rules define and propagate authorizations. A distinguished predicate *do(Subject, Object, Operation)* expresses authorizations: the subject is allowed to perform the specified operation on the object iff *do(Subject, Object, Operation)* belongs to the unique stable model of $P \cup C$, where $P$ is the set of policy rules and $C$ the evaluation context.

Rei [58] integrates RDF documents and logic programming rules. In Rei default policies and conflict resolution must be managed with meta-rules. Rei is not Datalog; function symbols are extensively used.

A conspicuous amount of recent work has been devoted to *trust negotiation* (TN) [90], where peers progressively exchange digital credentials to reach a level of mutual agreement sufficient to complete a transaction. Logic-based policies tell which credentials must be disclosed to access a web resource, as well as which credentials should be received by a peer before a local credential—possibly encoding sensitive information—can be disclosed. This process, based on requests and counter-requests, gives rise to *credential negotiations*. Credentials are represented in the policies by means of distinguished predicates; when a peer receives a credential, the policy engine verifies it and—in case of success—asserts the corresponding ground fact in the current context (called *negotiation state* in the TN jargon). Roughly speaking, the credential selection process consists in searching a portfolio of credentials $D$ for a set of credentials $D' \subseteq D$ that together with the policy $P$ implies the desired authorization formula.

The RT family [62] has an ad-hoc rule language for manipulating credentials that encode roles and permissions. RT's semantics, however, is specified by a translation into Datalog.

Cassandra [12] is a TN framework based on Datalog with constraints. In Cassandra, atoms are labelled with a location where the atom holds, and with an issuer that digitally signs the atom (thereby certifying that inference).

PeerTrust [45] is a Datalog dialect with atom annotations expressing locations and signatures analogous to Cassandra's. Locations are used for distributed policy evaluation: subgoals are sent over the Internet and a proof tree supporting an authorization typically consists of rules and facts gathered across the network.

Protune [22,13] is a TN framework based on Datalog with stratified negation. It supports an object oriented syntax for manipulating semi-structured objects such as X509 digital credentials. The object-oriented extension is only syntactic sugar; the internal form is standard Datalog with negation.

Clear requirements have been formulated for the policy languages of TN frameworks [80]. One of them states that policies should be monotonic w.r.t. credentials, because it is technically impossible to check whether a peer does *not* have a specific credential. Negation, however, can be applied to any predicate that does not depend on credentials. Detailed comparisons of these and other policy languages can be found in [16,36,13].

As for applications, SecPAL [10], a decentralized authorization language developed at Microsoft Research, has been applied to the management of electronic health records. For further details, see the project's web site at http://research.microsoft.com/en-us/projects/securitypolicy/.

Moreover, the standard policy framework XACML [61] is considered a rule-based language, with nonmonotonic features such as rule priorities and majority decisions. XACML's syntax can be regarded as a factorized representation of Datalog rule sets, supporting bounded forms of recursion. XACML can be translated into Datalog with a mapping similar to the translation from the policy composition algebra into Datalog illustrated in [17].

## 2.2  DL-Based Approaches

The use of Description Logics as policy languages is more recent. One of the major projects is KAoS [85], that focusses on several distributed access control scenarios, ranging from computational grids to military applications [57].[1] Description logics have been used to provide an alternative logical account of the standard policy

---

[1] Demonstration videos are available on http://www.ihmc.us/coopsmovs/

language XACML [61]. Moreover, in [44] and [92], respectively, DLs have been applied to encode role-based access control (RBAC) and a variant thereof.

There are two main approaches to policy encoding in the literature. In the first approach (which is adopted by KAoS and [61]), policy evaluation contexts are *reified*, that is, represented as individuals. A context *c* typically has several attributes (called *roles* in DL jargon), some of which encode the current access request, e.g., by means of roles *subject, object, operation*. A policy *P* is encoded by a TBox defining concepts such as *Permit-P* and *Deny-P*, for example, that define for each possible policy output the class of contexts that yield that output according to *P*. With this approach, authorization checking can be carried out by encoding the context *c* with an ABox (a set of ground assertions) and then checking whether the resulting knowledge base (TBox+ABox) entails the assertion *Permit-P(c)*.

The second approach (adopted by [92]) associates each privilege to a role (i.e. a binary predicate, in the sense of DLs) and encodes authorization triples by means of role assertions. For example, given an ABox that describes the properties of a subject *s* and a resource *r*, *s* is authorized to perform *op* on *r* iff the resulting knowledge base entails the assertion *op(s, r)*.

## 3   Expressiveness Analysis

In order to analyze the expressiveness of policy languages formally, it is convenient to adopt an abstract, language-independent notion of policy. Most policies are *mappings* from contexts (comprising sets of users and roles along with their properties, resources and their metadata, current time and location, etc.) to decisions (such as access control decisions). In their simplest form, contexts are finite structures (say, encoded within relational databases and XML documents) and decisions may range over *permit, deny*, and *error*, like in XACML, or be encoded as a set of valid authorizations (i.e., an access control matrix), which yields the following mapping type:

$$Policy : Contexts \rightarrow Subjects \times Objects \times Privileges .$$

More general classes of policies will be discussed later. Under the above "simple" abstract perspective, policies are nothing but mappings over finite relational structures, that is, *queries*, as understood in database theory.

Database theory provides us with an excellent notion of expressiveness for query languages: *descriptive complexity* [54,55]. The same idea can be profitably applied to policy languages: the *expressiveness* of a policy language is the class of policy mappings that can be expressed with the language. Such classes frequently correspond to complexity classes.

In this setting, policies (queries) are expressed as logical theories, and contexts (instances) are sets of ground facts. Policy outputs (query answers) are encoded as authorization formulas like *do(Subject, Object, Operation)*, *Permit-P(c)*, or *op(s, r)* (see the previous section). Given a policy *P*, and a context *C*, the policy returns the decision encoded by a formula *A* iff $P \cup C \models_x A$, where $\models_x$ is a suitable consequence relation (stable model reasoning in the case of stratified Datalog, or classical inference in the case of DLs).

### 3.1 Expressiveness of Datalog Policy Languages

It is well-known that Datalog can express exactly the queries in P, provided that input instances are equipped with a total ordering of their domain, consisting of two unary predicates *first* and *last*, satisfied by the first and last elements, respectively, and a binary predicate *succ* associating each domain element with its successor [72,33]. Datalog with negation can autonomously produce such total ordering using non-stratified negation [33]. Stratified Datalog is not able to encode such ordering, as witnessed by the fact that it cannot encode some queries in P [60]. This is relevant to our paper because the main approaches to Datalog policies adopt stratified negation [25] (see also Sec. 2.1). In this setting, it is possible to capture all the policies in P by analogy with the case of (monotonic) Datalog queries, that is, assuming that contexts are equipped with a binary relation *succ* that totally orders the individuals occurring in the context (represented as a set of ground facts). The unary predicates *first* and *last* can be defined with stratified negation by extending any given policy as follows:

- Introduce a fresh predicate *dom*, and for each $n$-ary predicate $p$ occurring in the context and all nonnegative indexes $i \leq n$, add a rule

$$dom(X_i) \leftarrow p(X_1, \ldots, X_i, \ldots, X_n).$$

- Add the rules

$$first(X) \leftarrow dom(X), \neg succ(Y, X).$$
$$last(X) \leftarrow dom(X), \neg succ(X, Y).$$

Now the results reported in [33] can be easily adapted to prove that:

**Proposition 1.** *Stratified Datalog with negation can express exactly all the polynomial-time computable policies over the class of contexts that embody a total order succ over their domain.*

Note that the assumption on *succ* is really mild—essentially equivalent to having a built-in term comparison predicate like @< of standard Prolog.

### 3.2 Expressiveness of Description Logics

To the best of our knowledge, the *descriptive* complexity of description logics has not been studied so far. However, it is not difficult to see that the expressiveness of DLs has "holes"; in particular there exist simple policies in P that cannot be expressed by means of DLs. The reason of such weakness lies in the *tree model property* of DLs without nominals—such as $\mathcal{ALC}$, $\mathcal{ALCQI}$, and $\mathcal{SHIQ}$—and in its counterpart for nominals, the *quasi-forest model property* [79]. The tree model property states that if a theory $\mathcal{T}$ has a model $\mathcal{I}$, then $\mathcal{T}$ has also a tree-shaped model $\mathcal{J}$; in other words, $\mathcal{T}$ is not able to distinguish cyclic contexts from acyclic contexts. Since cycle detection can be performed in polynomial time, it turns out that there are polynomial-time computable policies that cannot be expressed with $\mathcal{ALC}$, $\mathcal{ALCQI}$, $\mathcal{SHIQ}$, or any other description logic enjoying the tree model property. To make this general argument more concrete, let us consider a few policies that typically arise in modern application scenarios and involve the recognition of cyclic patterns in the given context.

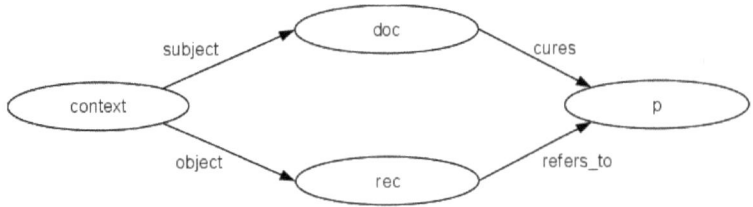

**Fig. 1.** The cyclic pattern of the medical record access policy

**Accessing medical records.** In normal conditions, access to a medical record $r$ referring to a patient $p$ should be allowed only to the doctors $d$ that are explicitly in charge of curing $p$. Suppose that the context's schema consists of two binary relations: $refers\_to(r, p)$ and $cures(d, p)$. A first obstacle to be overcome is that DLs can only express unary or binary relations, while the above policy is essentially based on a ternary relation between records, patients, and doctors. The classical solution to this problem is *reification*: $n$-tuples can be represented as individuals with $n$ attributes (cf. the logic $\mathcal{DLR}$ [27] for a general approach). In our example, one could represent the context as an individual $c$ with two attributes: *subject* (the doctor requesting the access) and *object* (the medical record requested). The policy should check whether the following facts hold:

$$subject(c, doc), \ object(c, rec), \ refers\_to(rec, p), \ cures(doc, p).$$

This pattern is cyclic (cf. Fig. 1), therefore no policy $P$ written in $\mathcal{ALC}$ or any other DL with the tree model property can uniformly check it: if the above context is a model of $P$ then $P$ has also tree-shaped models where the composed roles *subject* ∘ *cures* and *object* ∘ *refer_to* do not commute. Note that this medical record example is a classical motivation for *role templates*, an extension of the RBAC model that attracted quite some interest in the computer security community [47,64,32,8]. The above discussion shows the limitations of DLs in modelling role templates.

**Picture sharing.** Consider a social network where users can share their pictures with their friends and forbid access from non-friends. Technically, this example is similar to the medical record example: the policy should allow access only in the presence of cyclic patterns like:

$$subject(c, s), \ object(c, p), \ owner(p, o), \ friend(s, o),$$

where $c$ represent the context, $s$ is the user trying to get the picture, $p$ is the picture, and $o$ is the picture's owner. This pattern is cyclic, as in the previous example, and hence it cannot be encoded with standard DLs.

**Payment with identification.** This is a popular example in the world of trust negotiation. Access is granted if the subject pays for the resource by exhibiting a credit card and an ID with the same name on top [22]. This example is analogous to the previous two examples, as it involves the recognition of cyclic patterns like:

$$credit\_card(c, cc), \ ID(c, id), \ owner(cc, s), \ owner(id, s),$$

where $c$ represent the context, $s$ is the user, $cc$ and $id$ are the two digital credentials.

The same limitations apply to DLs with nominals (i.e., singleton concepts, denoted by $\{a\}$, that re-introduce in DLs the expressiveness of individual constants). Such DLs can express some cyclic patterns by using nominals themselves. For example, given a specific individual $s$, one can force different role chains to converge to $s$ by defining contexts like

$$\exists \, credit\_card.\exists \, owner.\{s\} \sqcap \exists \, ID.\exists \, owner.\{s\} \, .$$

However, this formulation depends on the specific constant $s$ and cannot be generalized to arbitrary individuals. The quasi-forest model property states that every consistent theory has a model such that if all the binary relations involving a nominal are removed, then the model becomes a forest. In other words, nominals allow to express cyclic patterns only if such patterns involve explicitly the nominals themselves.

The KAoS team run into a similar expressiveness problem, trying to model policy rules within DLs [68] and tackled it by extending $\mathcal{ALC}$ with *role-value maps* [7, Chap. 5], that can force roles chains to converge to a same individual, as required by the above examples. An example of the syntax of the role-value maps like those adopted by KAoS is:

$$credit\_card.owner = ID.owner \, .$$

Unfortunately, extending $\mathcal{ALC}$ or even much weaker languages like $\mathcal{FL}^-$ with role-value maps over role chains makes reasoning undecidable [7, Chap. 5]. This problem has not been discussed in [68] nor any other KAoS paper that we know of.

An interesting direction for extending the expressiveness of DL-based policy languages consists in extending the theory on *concrete feature agreements*. In many cases, the attributes of credentials are functional and their value belongs to a primitive data type such as strings or numbers. Such attributes are called *concrete features*. It has been proved that in some cases concrete features may be forced to commute with a construct called *feature agreement* without affecting decidability, see for example [65]. Currently, the limitation of these results is that they do not apply to the combinations of concrete features and normal roles that naturally arise in the above examples. For example, while roles like *owner* in the picture sharing scenario are naturally functional, other roles like *friend* are not. Mixed chains of normal roles and concrete features can be compared only under some restrictions: one of the two chains must be of the form $R.f$ where $R$ is a normal role and $f$ a concrete feature, while the second chain must consist of a single concrete feature $f'$ [65]. This is not sufficient to model our examples, but we conjecture that these restrictions can be relaxed to some extent without affecting decidability. This is an interesting motivation for further foundational work on DLs.

## 4   Reasoning: Foundations and Technology

There are several reasoning tasks relevant to policies. The obvious one is *entailment*, which is at the core of authorization checking: given a context $C$ (represented as a set of ground facts) a policy $P$ and an authorization $A$, decide whether $A$ is granted in $C$ by checking whether $P \cup C \models_n A$, where $\models_n$ is a suitable consequence relation. As we pointed out in Sec. 2.1, $\models_n$ in general cannot be simply the standard entailment relation of classical logic; it should rather be a nonmonotonic relation capable of encoding default policies and authorization inheritance.

The second policy reasoning task is *abduction*: given a server policy $P$, a context $C$, and a portfolio of digital credentials $D$ (modelled as a set of ground atoms), find a set of credentials that grant a desired authorization $A$. In symbols, find a set $D' \subseteq D$ such that $P \cup C \cup D' \models_n A$. This is the reasoning task underlying credential selection at each step of a trust negotiation process; the set $D'$ is a candidate for disclosure.[2] Abduction has been applied to credential selection in several works, including [24,13,11].

Another form of policy processing relevant to trust negotiation is *filtering*. In PSPL [24] and Protune [13], peers disclose their policies and part of their local context to let the other peers select a set of credentials to be disclosed. Policies and contexts must be filtered before disclosure for efficiency and confidentiality reasons. This process is essentially based on partial evaluation techniques, that remove irrelevant details and hide sensitive facts and formulas.

The fourth major reasoning task is *policy comparison*, namely, given two policies $P_1$ and $P_2$ check whether for all contexts $C$ and all authorizations $A$, $P_1 \cup C \models_n A$ implies $P_2 \cup C \models_n A$. If this condition holds, then we say that $P_1$ is *contained* in $P_2$. This task needs to be solved to check whether a server policy $P_1$ complies with a user's privacy preferences, encoded as a policy $P_2$. For example, a similar task is one of the main intended uses of P3P policies [87].

Further reasoning tasks are related to *explanations* and *automated documentation*, that is, automated explanation facilities for explaining a policy or a policy-based decision in nontechnical terms, accessible to end users. There is no single, widely adopted explanation technique; the existing approaches manipulate policies by representing proofs, premises, and conclusions in various ways [84,9,63,67,30,52].

### 4.1   Maturity

Entailment techniques are highly mature in both areas. Logic programming has very efficient and stable engines based on tabling, such as XSB [78] (widely used in logic-based security). The stable model semantics has very well-engineered and scalable implementations such as SMODELS [70] and DLV [39]. The Answer Set Programming community has continuosly promoted the improvement of these and other engines over the years, by means of systematic benchmarking initiatives. Classical DL reasoning is equally well-developed; it exploits advanced tableaux optimization techniques [7, Cap. 9] and specialized implementations for restricted languages of practical interest such as $\mathcal{EL}$ [5,6]. However, nonmonotonic reasoning is still far from being supported in DLs. In general, the complexity of nonmonotonic DL reasoning is very high [35,20] and so far the attempts at reducing complexity through language restrictions have not

---

[2] In [59], abduction is erroneously considered an unsound procedure because the philosophical notion of abduction is confused with the specific technical notion adopted in logic programming and AI. Obviously, if $\models_n$ is classical entailment then, by the implication theorem, abduction is equivalent to proving that $\bigwedge D' \to A$ is a classical consequence of $P \cup C$. When $\models_n$ is nonmonotonic, the restriction that policies must be monotonic w.r.t. credentials (cf. Sec. 2.1) allows to prove an implication theorem for the stable semantics, and abduction is equivalent to proving that $\bigwedge D' \to A$ holds in the unique stable model of $P \cup C$.

pushed complexity below the second level of the polynomial hierarchy [19]. The major DL reasoning engines do not support nonmonotonic reasoning. Said so, we have to remark that there is an intense ongoing research activity on nonmonotonic DL reasoning that may soon change the picture [19,46,49,29].

The situation is similar for abduction. Most works on abduction have been carried out in the logic programming area, starting with the seminal work by Eshghi [43]. Many systems have been deployed, such as CIFF [66], SCIFF [2], ProLogICA [76], some ASP-based implementation [37], etc. In the DL area, the study of abduction has a much shorter history. It has been introduced in [71], and one year later a tableaux algorithm has been provided [31]. More general forms of abduction have been introduced in [42]. Currently, the main DL engines give no direct support to abduction. In TN, credential selection should minimize the sensitivity of disclosed credentials. In general, this is not possible, unless policies are entirely public. The report [14] studies the complexity of the weighted abduction problem corresponding to minimizing the sensitivity of disclosed credentials. This problem is FNP//log-complete for any *fixed* Datalog policy (the equivalent of data complexity), that is, a solution can be nondeterministically computed in polynomial time given an oracle for an optimization problem in NP. The complexity of the same problem for DL policies is currently unknown.

Trust negotiation is usually not tackled with DLs, probably in relation to the aforementioned lack of support to abduction (and hence to credential selection). Accordingly, policy filtering is not addressed, either. Datalog approaches could benefit of very well-understood partial evaluation techniques that have been developed many years ago, for program optimization. An articulated discussion of such techniques can be found, for example, in the excellent book by Sterling and Shapiro [83].

Policy comparison is essentially a query containment problem ($P_1$ and $P_2$ correspond to queries, $C$ to database instances, and $A$ to answers) [21]. In DLs, policy comparison can be a very natural task; within the encoding approach based on *Permit-P* and *Deny-P*, policy comparison boils down to checking subsumptions like $Permit\text{-}P_1 \sqsubseteq Permit\text{-}P_2$. It is not clear how to compare policies in the second encoding approach, based on role assertions (cf. Sec. 2.2). Policy comparison is definitely difficult for Datalog policies, because of recursion. It is well-known that Datalog query containment is in general undecidable [81]. Several decidable cases have been identified by restricting recursion [28,15] but complexity may be high. Recently, a specialized approach focussed on the most common forms of recursion used in security and trust negotiation (e.g., certificate chains and authorization inheritance) has been published in [21]. The experimental results, based on a prototype implementation, are encouraging. In general, this restricted version of the problem is NP-complete; if rule length is bounded by a constant, then policy comparison is quadratic in the cardinality of the two policies.

Explanation facilities have first been designed for rule-based expert systems, that are closer to Datalog than DLs. Research on explanation facilities has eventually produced recommendations for building so-called *second generation explanation facilities* [89], that emphasize usability in several ways, for example by means of navigational aids, heuristics for removing irrelevant details, and heuristics for replacing internal identifiers (that are meaningless to the user) with key attributes. Most approaches to Datalog and DL policy explanation and documentation, on the contrary, are limited to printing out comments and dumping proof trees on the user [82,59]. To the best of our knowledge, the only exception is ProtuneX [23,13], the second-generation explanation facility of Protune. It is innovative also with respect to previous second-generation facilities, as the peculiarities of policy frameworks are exploited to give an automated solution to problems (such as removing details and identifying key attributes) that in other settings are solved manually by knowledge engineers. Another innovative feature is the hypertext structure of the explanations that permits to navigate smoothly across different proof attemtps, including both successful and failed proofs. The ability of explaining failures is one of the characteristic features of ProtuneX.

## 5   Hybrid Approaches

Recently, a significant amount of effort has been devoted to integrating rule-based and DL-based approaches to the Semantic Web. The interested reader is referred to the survey in [38]. From a policy language point of view, such hybrid approaches are potentially interesting because they support the DL-based knowledge representation languages at the core of the semantic web, and at the same time they overcome the lack of expressiveness of DLs illustrated in the previous sections. However, integrating the two families of logics is a challenging problem, as witnessed by the large number of approaches to hybrid frameworks. A major problem is that the naive approach—consisting in extending DLs with Datalog rules under classical first-order semantics—makes reasoning undecidable. Further difficulties arise from the need of integrating a classical open-world formalisms such as DLs with logic programming languages that are nonmonotonic and adopt a closed-world semantics. Solutions range from "loosely coupled" formalisms such as [40,88] (where the rule-based and DL parts of the knowledge base are treated like separate components that interact by querying each other) to fully integrated approaches (where the vocabulary and semantics are homogeneous) [69,34,50].

So far, the application and the appropriateness of the above integrated approaches to the design of policy languages has not been studied. Expressiveness is not the only issue, as hybrid formalisms usually have high computational complexity. Since access control comes into play for each and every transaction, complexity issues may eventually prevent certain languages to be effectively adopted.

Some hybrid approaches, such as the OWL2RL profile, simply consist in identifying a common fragment of Horn rules and DLs. Of course such formalisms inherit the expressiveness limitations of DLs by definition and hence do not address the expressiveness needs of policy languages.

Given the analogies between policies and queries, another potentially relevant area is DL querying (see for example the recent works [74,48,41,4]). Not surprisingly, recursive Datalog query evaluation is undecidable when combined with DLs, therefore the works in this area usually focus on *conjunctive queries* that are not recursive. This restriction, however, prevents several simple queries in P from being computed, e.g., transitive closures. From a policy perspective, this means that credential chains and authorization inheritance along hierarchies of subjects and objects cannot be expressed (just to name a few).

# 6 Conclusions

As of today, the policy frameworks based on Datalog are significantly more mature than those based on DLs, both from a foundational perspective and from a technological perspective. Expressiveness results show that Datalog is well-suited to expressing all the policy mappings of practical interest. On the contrary, DL-based policies currently suffer from serious expressiveness limitations, and lack the flexibility for tackling several important access control scenarios that naturally arise in modern applications. This problem can only be overcome with more foundational work, e.g. aimed at generalizing the decidability results for concrete feature agreement.

As far as reasoning is concerned, on the Datalog side the need is felt for more general, efficient techniques for policy comparison. DL-based policies, instead, need more work on crucial reasoning tasks like abduction, nonmonotonic reasoning, and user-friendly explanations. In particular, stable and efficient implementations need to be deployed.

Hybrid solutions are appealing because they integrate the expressiveness of Datalog languages with widely adopted formats for knowledge representation on the semantic web. However, hybrid approaches inherit several drawbacks from pure approaches. For example, policy containment has not been studied in this area, and in general is undecidable, because hybrid formalisms generalize recursive Datalog. Furthermore, technological maturity is probably not yet sufficient. Since access control places an overhead on every transaction, a lightweight implementation of hybrid frameworks—and perhaps a clever use of knowledge compilation—are of paramount importance in this context.

A major unsolved problem is usability. Recent studies [77] show that users write poor policies, even if the policy language is very simple and intuitive. Explanations and documentation only partially address this issue. Logic-based policy languages potentially enable the development of new intelligent policy authoring tools aimed at improving the quality of user policies and supporting their management; this is an appealing area for further work.

Last but not least, it should be mentioned that modern application scenarios increasingly need more and more general notions of policies, that hardly fit the query-like view adopted by standard policy frameworks (and by this paper as well). A first novel issue arises from the incomplete and generally unreliable nature of semantic web knowledge: a correct and complete representation of the current state of the world, that is, the context, is generally not available (not even its restriction to the aspects relevant to policy decisions). If we change the domain of policy mappings by replacing complete contexts with an incomplete representation thereof, then the classical theoretical expressiveness results are affected. For example, if contexts are represented by means of positive clauses, then nonmonotonic query languages—that have the same expressiveness over complete contexts—exhibit different capabilities in the generalized framework [18]. In such a framework, it is generally difficult to capture all the mappings in P.

Another aspect that may conflict with the query-like view arises from *usage control* policies, that may specify actions, obligations, and time constraints over them. In the simplest cases, actions must be executed (and obligations fulfilled) immediately, and the query-like approach can be adapted simply by modifying policy range, e.g.:

$$Policy : Contexts \rightarrow Subjects \times Objects \times Privileges \times Obligations.$$

However, some policy languages can express very complex dynamic behaviors by means of dynamic logics [51]. In this case it is not clear how to generalize the abstract, language independent notion of policy mapping.

# References

1. Agrawal, D., Al-Shaer, E., Kagal, L., Lobo, J. (eds.): 9th IEEE International Workshop on Policies for Distributed Systems and Networks (POLICY 2008), June 2-4. IEEE Computer Society, Palisades (2008)
2. Alberti, M., Chesani, F., Gavanelli, M., Lamma, E., Mello, P., Torroni, P.: Verifiable agent interaction in abductive logic programming: The SCIFF framework. ACM Trans. Comput. Log. 9(4) (2008)
3. Apt, K.R.: Logic programming. In: Handbook of Theoretical Computer Science. Formal Models and Semantics (B), vol. B, pp. 493–574 (1990)
4. Armando, A., Baumgartner, P., Dowek, G. (eds.): IJCAR 2008. LNCS (LNAI), vol. 5195. Springer, Heidelberg (2008)
5. Baader, F., Brandt, S., Lutz, C.: Pushing the EL envelope. In: Proc. of the Nineteenth International Joint Conference on Artificial Intelligence, IJCAI 2005, pp. 364–369. Professional Book Center (2005)
6. Baader, F., Lutz, C., Suntisrivaraporn, B.: CEL - a polynomial-time reasoner for life science ontologies. In: Furbach, U., Shankar, N. (eds.) IJCAR 2006. LNCS (LNAI), vol. 4130, pp. 287–291. Springer, Heidelberg (2006)
7. Baader, F., McGuiness, D.L., Nardi, D., Patel-Schneider, P.: The Description Logic Handbook: Theory, implementation and applications. Cambridge University Press, Cambridge (2003)
8. Bacon, J., Moody, K., Yao, W.: A model of OASIS role-based access control and its support for active security. ACM Trans. Inf. Syst. Secur. 5(4), 492–540 (2002)
9. Barzilay, R., McCullough, D., Rambow, O., DeChristofaro, J., Korelsky, T., Lavoie, B.: A new approach to expert system explanations. In: 9thInternational Workshop on Natural Language Generation, pp. 78–87 (1998)
10. Becker, M.Y., Fournet, C., Gordon, A.D.: SecPAL: Design and semantics of a decentralized authorization language. Journal of Computer Security 18(4), 619–665 (2010)
11. Becker, M.Y., Nanz, S.: The role of abduction in declarative authorization policies. In: Hudak, P., Warren, D.S. (eds.) PADL 2008. LNCS, vol. 4902, pp. 84–99. Springer, Heidelberg (2008)
12. Becker, M.Y., Sewell, P.: Cassandra: Distributed access control policies with tunable expressiveness. In: POLICY 2004, pp. 159–168. IEEE Computer Society, Los Alamitos (2004)
13. Bonatti, P., Coi, J.D., Olmedilla, D., Sauro, L.: A rule-based trust negotiation system. IEEE Transactions on Knowledge and Data Engineering 99(PrePrints) (2010)
14. Bonatti, P., Eiter, T., Faella, M.: Automated negotiation mechanisms. Technical Report I2-D6, REWERSE (April 2006), http://rewerse.net/deliverables/m24/i2-d6.pdf
15. Bonatti, P.A.: On the decidability of containment of recursive datalog queries - preliminary report. In: Deutsch, A. (ed.) PODS, pp. 297–306. ACM, New York (2004)
16. Bonatti, P.A., Coi, J.L.D., Olmedilla, D., Sauro, L.: Rule-based policy representations and reasoning. In: Bry, F., Małuszyński, J. (eds.) Semantic Techniques for the Web. LNCS, vol. 5500, pp. 201–232. Springer, Heidelberg (2009)
17. Bonatti, P.A., di Vimercati, S.D.C., Samarati, P.: An algebra for composing access control policies. ACM Trans. Inf. Syst. Secur. 5(1), 1–35 (2002)

18. Bonatti, P.A., Eiter, T.: Querying disjunctive databases through nonmonotonic logics. Theor. Comput. Sci. 160(1&2), 321–363 (1996)
19. Bonatti, P.A., Faella, M., Sauro, L.: Defeasible inclusions in low-complexity DLs: Preliminary notes. In: Boutilier (ed.) [26], pp. 696–701
20. Bonatti, P.A., Lutz, C., Wolter, F.: Description logics with circumscription. In: Proc. of the Tenth International Conference on Principles of Knowledge Representation and Reasoning, KR 2006, pp. 400–410. AAAI Press, Menlo Park (2006)
21. Bonatti, P.A., Mogavero, F.: Comparing rule-based policies. In: Agrawal, et al. (eds.) [1], pp. 11–18
22. Bonatti, P.A., Olmedilla, D.: Driving and monitoring provisional trust negotiation with metapolicies. In: 6th IEEE International Workshop on Policies for Distributed Systems and Networks (POLICY 2005), pp. 14–23. IEEE Computer Society, Los Alamitos (2005)
23. Bonatti, P.A., Olmedilla, D., Peer, J.: Advanced policy explanations on the web. In: 17th European Conference on Artificial Intelligence (ECAI 2006), pp. 200–204. IOS Press, Riva del Garda (2006)
24. Bonatti, P.A., Samarati, P.: A uniform framework for regulating service access and information release on the web. Journal of Computer Security 10(3), 241–272 (2002)
25. Bonatti, P.A., Samarati, P.: Logics for authorization and security. In: Chomicki, J., van der Meyden, R., Saake, G. (eds.) Logics for Emerging Applications of Databases, pp. 277–323. Springer, Heidelberg (2003)
26. Boutilier, C. (ed.): Proceedings of the 21st International Joint Conference on Artificial Intelligence, IJCAI 2009, Pasadena, California, USA, July 11-17 (2009)
27. Calvanese, D., Giacomo, G.D., Lenzerini, M.: On the decidability of query containment under constraints. In: PODS, pp. 149–158. ACM Press, New York (1998)
28. Calvanese, D., Giacomo, G.D., Vardi, M.Y.: Decidable containment of recursive queries. Theor. Comput. Sci. 336(1), 33–56 (2005)
29. Casini, G., Straccia, U.: Rational closure for defeasible description logics. In: Janhunen, T., Niemelä, I. (eds.) JELIA 2010. LNCS, vol. 6341, pp. 77–90. Springer, Heidelberg (2010)
30. Chalupsky, H., Russ, T.A.: Whynot: debugging failed queries in large knowledge bases. In: 14th National Conference on Artificial Intelligence, pp. 870–877 (2002)
31. Colucci, S., Noia, T.D., Sciascio, E.D., Donini, F.M., Mongiello, M.: A uniform tableaux-based method for concept abduction and contraction in description logics. In: de Mántaras, R.L., Saitta, L. (eds.) ECAI, pp. 975–976. IOS Press, Amsterdam (2004)
32. Covington, M.J., Long, W., Srinivasan, S., Dev, A.K., Ahamad, M., Abowd, G.D.: Securing context-aware applications using environment roles. In: SACMAT 2001: Proceedings of the Sixth ACM Symposium on Access Control Models and Technologies, pp. 10–20. ACM, New York (2001)
33. Dantsin, E., Eiter, T., Gottlob, G., Voronkov, A.: Complexity and expressive power of logic programming. ACM Comput. Surv. 33(3), 374–425 (2001)
34. de Bruijn, J., Eiter, T., Polleres, A., Tompits, H.: Embedding non-ground logic programs into autoepistemic logic for knowledge-base combination. In: Veloso (ed.) [86], pp. 304–309
35. Donini, F.M., Nardi, D., Rosati, R.: Description logics of minimal knowledge and negation as failure. ACM Trans. Comput. Log. 3(2), 177–225 (2002)
36. Duma, C., Herzog, A., Shahmehri, N.: Privacy in the semantic web: What policy languages have to offer. In: POLICY 2007, pp. 109–118. IEEE Computer Society, Los Alamitos (2007)
37. Eiter, T., Faber, W., Leone, N., Pfeifer, G.: The diagnosis frontend of the DLV system. AI Commun. 12(1-2), 99–111 (1999)
38. Eiter, T., Ianni, G., Krennwallner, T., Polleres, A.: Rules and ontologies for the semantic web. In: Baroglio, C., Bonatti, P.A., Małuszyński, J., Marchiori, M., Polleres, A., Schaffert, S. (eds.) Reasoning Web. LNCS, vol. 5224, pp. 1–53. Springer, Heidelberg (2008)

39. Eiter, T., Leone, N., Mateis, C., Pfeifer, G., Scarcello, F.: A deductive system for non-monotonic reasoning. In: Fuhrbach, U., Dix, J., Nerode, A. (eds.) LPNMR 1997. LNCS, vol. 1265, pp. 364–375. Springer, Heidelberg (1997)
40. Eiter, T., Lukasiewicz, T., Schindlauer, R., Tompits, H.: Combining answer set programming with description logics for the semantic web. In: Dubois, D., Welty, C.A., Williams, M.-A. (eds.) KR, pp. 141–151. AAAI Press, Menlo Park (2004)
41. Eiter, T., Lutz, C., Ortiz, M., Simkus, M.: Query answering in description logics with transitive roles. In: Boutilier (ed.) [26], pp. 759–764
42. Elsenbroich, C., Kutz, O., Sattler, U.: A case for abductive reasoning over ontologies. In: Grau, B.C., Hitzler, P., Shankey, C., Wallace, E. (eds.) OWLED. CEUR Workshop Proceedings, vol. 216. CEUR-WS.org (2006)
43. Eshghi, K.: Abductive planning with event calculus. In: ICLP/SLP, pp. 562–579 (1988)
44. Finin, T.W., Joshi, A., Kagal, L., Niu, J., Sandhu, R.S., Winsborough, W.H., Thuraisingham, B.M.: ROWLBAC: representing role based access control in OWL. In: Ray, I., Li, N. (eds.) SACMAT, pp. 73–82. ACM, New York (2008)
45. Gavriloaie, R., Nejdl, W., Olmedilla, D., Seamons, K.E., Winslett, M.: No registration needed: How to use declarative policies and negotiation to access sensitive resources on the semantic web. In: Bussler, C.J., Davies, J., Fensel, D., Studer, R. (eds.) ESWS 2004. LNCS, vol. 3053, pp. 342–356. Springer, Heidelberg (2004)
46. Giordano, L., Gliozzi, V., Olivetti, N., Pozzato, G.: Reasoning about typicality in preferential description logics. In: Hölldobler, S., Lutz, C., Wansing, H. (eds.) JELIA 2008. LNCS (LNAI), vol. 5293, pp. 192–205. Springer, Heidelberg (2008)
47. Giuri, L., Iglio, P.: Role templates for content-based access control. In: RBAC 1997: Proceedings of the Second ACM Workshop on Role-based Access Control, pp. 153–159. ACM, New York (1997)
48. Glimm, B., Lutz, C., Horrocks, I., Sattler, U.: Conjunctive query answering for the description logic shiq. J. Artif. Intell. Res. (JAIR) 31, 157–204 (2008)
49. Grimm, S., Hitzler, P.: A preferential tableaux calculus for circumscriptive ALCO. In: Polleres, A., Swift, T. (eds.) RR 2009. LNCS, vol. 5837, pp. 40–54. Springer, Heidelberg (2009)
50. Heymans, S., Nieuwenborgh, D.V., Vermeir, D.: Open answer set programming for the semantic web. J. Applied Logic 5(1), 144–169 (2007)
51. Hilty, M., Pretschner, A., Basin, D.A., Schaefer, C., Walter, T.: A policy language for distributed usage control. In: Biskup, J., López, J. (eds.) ESORICS 2007. LNCS, vol. 4734, pp. 531–546. Springer, Heidelberg (2007)
52. Huang, X.: Reconstructing proofs at the assertion level. In: Bundy, A. (ed.) CADE 1994. LNCS, vol. 814, pp. 738–752. Springer, Heidelberg (1994)
53. Iannella, R., Guth, S. (eds.): Proceedings of the First International Workshop on the Open Digital Rights Language (ODRL), Vienna, Austria, April 22-23 (2004)
54. Immerman, N.: Relational queries computable in polynomial time. Information and Control 68(1-3), 86–104 (1986)
55. Immerman, N.: Descriptive and computational complexity. In: Csirik, J., Demetrovics, J., Gécseg, F. (eds.) FCT 1989. LNCS, vol. 380, pp. 244–245. Springer, Heidelberg (1989)
56. Jajodia, S., Samarati, P., Sapino, M.L., Subrahmanian, V.S.: Flexible support for multiple access control policies. ACM Trans. Database Syst. 26(2), 214–260 (2001)
57. Johnson, M., Intlekofer, K., Jung, H., Bradshaw, J.M., Allen, J., Suri, N., Carvalho, M.: Coordinated operations in mixed teams of humans and robots. In: First IEEE Conference on Distributed Human-Machine Systems, DHMS 2008 (2008) (in press)
58. Kagal, L., Finin, T.W., Joshi, A.: A policy language for a pervasive computing environment. In: 4th IEEE International Workshop on Policies for Distributed Systems and Networks (POLICY), p. 63. IEEE Computer Society, Lake Como (2003)

59. Kagal, L., Hanson, C., Weitzner, D.J.: Using dependency tracking to provide explanations for policy management. In: Agrawal, et al. (eds.) [1], pp. 54–61

60. Kolaitis, P.G.: The expressive power of stratified programs. Inf. Comput. 90(1), 50–66 (1991)

61. Kolovski, V., Hendler, J.A., Parsia, B.: Analyzing web access control policies. In: Williamson, C.L., Zurko, M.E., Patel-Schneider, P.F., Shenoy, P.J. (eds.) WWW, pp. 677–686. ACM, New York (2007)

62. Li, N., Mitchell, J.C., Winsborough, W.H.: Design of a role-based trust-management framework. In: IEEE Symposium on Security and Privacy, pp. 114–130 (2002)

63. Lowe, H., Cumming, A., Smyth, M.: Lessons from experience: Making theorem provers more co-operative. In: 2nd Workshop on User Interfaces for Theorem Provers (July 1996)

64. Lupu, E., Sloman, M.: Reconciling role based management and role based access control. In: ACM Workshop on Role-Based Access Control, pp. 135–141 (1997)

65. Lutz, C.: Adding numbers to the $\mathcal{SHIQ}$ description logic—First results. In: Proceedings of the Eighth International Conference on Principles of Knowledge Representation and Reasoning (KR 2002), pp. 191–202. Morgan Kaufmann, San Francisco (2002)

66. Mancarella, P., Terreni, G., Sadri, F., Toni, F., Endriss, U.: The CIFF proof procedure for abductive logic programming with constraints: Theory, implementation and experiments. TPLP 9(6), 691–750 (2009)

67. McGuinness, D.L., da Silva, P.P.: Explaining answers from the semantic web: The Inference Web approach. Journal of Web Semantics 1(4), 397–413 (2004)

68. Moreau, L., Bradshaw, J.M., Breedy, M.R., Bunch, L., Hayes, P.J., Johnson, M., Kulkarni, S., Lott, J., Suri, N., Uszok, A.: Behavioural specification of grid services with the KAoS policy language. In: CCGRID, pp. 816–823. IEEE Computer Society, Los Alamitos (2005)

69. Motik, B., Rosati, R.: A faithful integration of description logics with logic programming. In: Veloso (ed.) [86], pp. 477–482

70. Niemelä, I., Simons, P.: Smodels — an implementation of the stable model and well-founded semantics for normal lp. In: Fuhrbach, U., Dix, J., Nerode, A. (eds.) LPNMR 1997. LNCS, vol. 1265, pp. 421–430. Springer, Heidelberg (1997)

71. Noia, T.D., Sciascio, E.D., Donini, F.M., Mongiello, M.: Abductive matchmaking using description logics. In: Gottlob, G., Walsh, T. (eds.) IJCAI, pp. 337–342. Morgan Kaufmann, San Francisco (2003)

72. Papadimitriou, C.H.: A note the expressive power of Prolog. Bulletin of the EATCS 26, 21–22 (1985)

73. Park, J., Sandhu, R.S.: The $UCON_{ABC}$ usage control model. ACM Trans. Inf. Syst. Secur. 7(1), 128–174 (2004)

74. Pérez-Urbina, H., Motik, B., Horrocks, I.: Tractable query answering and rewriting under description logic constraints. J. Applied Logic 8(2), 186–209 (2010)

75. Pretschner, A., Hilty, M., Basin, D.: Distributed usage control. Commun. ACM 49(9), 39–44 (2006)

76. Ray, O., Kakas, A.: ProLogICA: a practical system for abductive logic programming. In: Proceedings of the 11th International Workshop on Non-monotonic Reasoning, pp. 304–312 (2006)

77. Sadeh, N.M., Hong, J.I., Cranor, L.F., Fette, I., Kelley, P.G., Prabaker, M.K., Rao, J.: Understanding and capturing people's privacy policies in a mobile social networking application. Personal and Ubiquitous Computing 13(6), 401–412 (2009)

78. Sagonas, K., Swift, T., Warren, D.: XSB as an efficient deductive database engine. In: Proceedings of the 1994 ACM SIGMOD International Conference on Management of Data, pp. 442–453. ACM Press, Minneapolis (1994)

79. Sattler, U., Vardi, M.Y.: The hybrid $\mu$-calculus. In: Goré, R.P., Leitsch, A., Nipkow, T. (eds.) IJCAR 2001. LNCS (LNAI), vol. 2083, pp. 76–91. Springer, Heidelberg (2001)

80. Seamons, K.E., Winslett, M., Yu, T., Smith, B., Child, E., Jacobson, J., Mills, H., Yu, L.: Requirements for policy languages for trust negotiation. In: 3rd International Workshop on Policies for Distributed Systems and Networks (POLICY), pp. 68–79. IEEE Computer Society, Monterey (2002)
81. Shmueli, O.: Equivalence of DATALOG queries is undecidable. J. Log. Program 15(3), 231–241 (1993)
82. Shvaiko, P., Giunchiglia, F., da Silva, P.P., McGuinness, D.L.: Web explanations for semantic heterogeneity discovery. In: Gómez-Pérez, A., Euzenat, J. (eds.) ESWC 2005. LNCS, vol. 3532, pp. 303–317. Springer, Heidelberg (2005)
83. Sterling, L., Shapiro, E.Y.: The Art of Prolog - Advanced Programming Techniques, 2nd edn. MIT Press, Cambridge (1994)
84. Tanner, M.C., Keuneke, A.M.: Explanations in knowledge systems: The roles of the task structure and domain functional models. IEEE Expert: Intelligent Systems and Their Applications 6(3), 50–57 (1991)
85. Uszok, A., Bradshaw, J.M., Jeffers, R., Suri, N., Hayes, P.J., Breedy, M.R., Bunch, L., Johnson, M., Kulkarni, S., Lott, J.: KAoS policy and domain services: Towards a description-logic approach to policy representation, deconfliction, and enforcement. In: 4th IEEE International Workshop on Policies for Distributed Systems and Networks (POLICY), pp. 93–96. IEEE Computer Society, Lake Como (2003)
86. Veloso, M.M. (ed.): Proceedings of the 20th International Joint Conference on Artificial Intelligence, IJCAI 2007, Hyderabad, India, January 6-12 (2007)
87. W3C. Platform for Privacy Preferences (P3P) Specification, `http://www.w3.org/TR/WD-P3P/Overview.html`
88. Wang, K., Billington, D., Blee, J., Antoniou, G.: Combining description logic and defeasible logic for the semantic web. In: Antoniou, G., Boley, H. (eds.) RuleML 2004. LNCS, vol. 3323, pp. 170–181. Springer, Heidelberg (2004)
89. Wick, M.R.: Second generation expert system explanation. In: David, J.-M., Krivine, J.-P., Simmons, R. (eds.) Second Generation Expert Systems, pp. 614–640. Springer, Heidelberg (1993)
90. Winsborough, W., Seamons, K., Jones, V.: Automated trust negotiation. In: Proceedings of DARPA Information Survivability Conference and Exposition, DISCEX 2000, pp. 88–102. IEEE Computer Society, Los Alamitos (2000)
91. Woo, T.Y.C., Lam, S.S.: Authorizations in distributed systems: A new approach. Journal of Computer Security 2(2-3), 107–136 (1993)
92. Zhang, R., Artale, A., Giunchiglia, F., Crispo, B.: Using description logics in relation based access control. In: Grau, B.C., Horrocks, I., Motik, B., Sattler, U. (eds.) Description Logics. CEUR Workshop Proceedings, vol. 477. CEUR-WS.org (2009)

# Answer Set Modules for Logical Agents

Stefania Costantini

Università degli Studi di L'Aquila,
Dipartimento di Informatica,
Via Vetoio, Loc. Coppito, I-67010 L'Aquila, Italy
Stefania.Costantini@univaq.it

**Abstract.** Various approaches exist to the application of Answer Set Programming (ASP) in the agent realm. Nonetheless, a controversial point is how to combine answer set modules with the other modules an agent is composed of, considering that an agent can be seen as a set of "capabilities" that in suitable combination produce the overall agent behavior as an emergent behavior. In this paper, we outline a possible fruitful integration of ASP into many agent architectures, by introducing two kinds of modules: one that allows for complex reaction, the other one that allows for reasoning about necessity and possibility.

## 1  Introduction

Logic programming under the answer set semantics (Answer Set Programming, for short ASP) is nowadays a well-established programming paradigm, with applications in many areas, including problem solving, configuration, information integration, security analysis, agent systems, semantic web, and planning (see among many [1,2,3,4,5] and the references therein).

The application of ASP in agents has been advocated since long, with ASP mainly taking the form of Action Description Languages. These kind of ASP-based languages were first introduced in [6] and [7] and have been since then extended and refined in many subsequent papers by several authors. Action Description Languages are formal models used to describe dynamic domains, by focusing on the representation of effects of actions. In particular, an action specification represents the direct effects of each action on the state of the world, while the semantics of the language takes care of all the other aspects concerning the evolution of the world (e.g., the ramification problem).

The first approaches have been extended in many ways, recently also in order to cope with, interpret, and recover from, exogenous events and unexpected observations, on the line of [8]. In this direction we mention [7], [9], and the recent work presented in [10]. In this work, an architecture (called AAA) is described where both the description of the domain's behavior and the reasoning components are written in Answer Set Programming, selected because of its ability to represent various forms of knowledge including defaults, causal relations, statements referring to incompleteness of knowledge, etc. An AAA agent executes a main cycle according to the *Observe-Think-Act* model proposed in the seminal paper [11]. Unexpected observations are coped with by hypothesizing the undetected occurrence of exogenous actions. In [12], this notion of an agent is extended to enable communication between agents through the introduction of special named sets of fluents known as "requests".

O. de Moor et al. (Eds.): Datalog 2010, LNCS 6702, pp. 37–58, 2011.

In other directions, we mention a different line of work, focusing upon modeling agent decisions in an extended ASP by means of game theory [13]. In [14,15] and other papers by the same group, ASP is exploited to model dynamic updates of an agent's knowledge base. We are also aware of ongoing work about modeling properties of multi-agent systems in ASP, e.g., [16].

Despite this corpus of work is technically and conceptually very well-developed, the view of an agent based upon having an ASP program as its "core" does not appear to be fully convincing. One reason is that the basic feature of ASP, which is that a program may have several answer sets that correspond to alternative coherent views of the world, is in our opinion not fully suitable for the agent main cycle, while it can be very useful for many of the agent reasoning activities. Another reason is that the architecture outlined above appears to be too rigid with respect to the other approaches to defining agent architectures in computational logic, among which one has to mention at least MetateM, 3APL, AgentSpeak, Impact, KGP and DALI [17,18,19,20,21,22,23,24,25] (for a recent survey the reader may refer to [26]). All these architectures, and their operational models, are in practice or at least in principle more dynamic and flexible. If we consider for instance the KGP [24,25] architecture, we find many modules ("capabilities") and many knowledge bases, integrated by *control theories* that can be interchanged according to the agent's present context and tasks. In KGP, capabilities are supposed to be based upon abductive logic programming [27] but the architecture might in principle accommodate modules defined in different ways.

We believe that an "ideal" agent architecture should exploit the potential of integrating several modules/components representing different behaviors/forms of reasoning, with these modules possibly based upon different formalisms. The "overall agent" should emerge from dynamic, non-deterministic combination of these behaviors that should occur also in consequence of the evolution of the agent's environment. Therefore, in our view an important present and future direction of ASP is that of being able to encapsulate ASP programs into modules suitable to be integrated into an overall agent program, the latter expressed in whatever languages/formalisms. There is a growing corpus of literature about modules in ASP (see Section 3). However, the existing approaches mainly refer to traditional programming techniques and to software engineering methodologies. To the best of our knowledge, except for the approach of [28] in the context of action theories, there is no existing approach to modules which is tailored for the agent realm.

Building upon our long-termed experience in logical agents, involving the definition and implementation of the DALI agent-oriented logic language [22,23,29,30], in this paper we propose two kinds of ASP modules to be possibly integrated into a variety of agent architectures. A first perspective is that of "Reactive ASP modules", aimed at defining complex reaction strategies to cope with external events and establish what could be done. An ASP module will determine the different possibilities, among which the agent will choose according either to preferences or to an overall planning strategy. A second particularly relevant perspective is that of "Modal ASP modules", that exploit the multi-model nature of answer set semantics to allow for reasoning about possibility and necessity in agents, at a comparatively low complexity. The proposed approach allows for interesting forms of reasoning suitable for real applications. From the implementation point of view, we implemented and we have been experimenting ASP modules within the DALI multi-agent system [31].

The paper is structured as follows. In Section 2 we briefly introduce answer set programming to the non-expert reader. In Sections 3 and 4 we review the existing research about modules in ASP and we quickly discuss logical agents. In Sections 5 and 6 we introduce Reactive and Modal ASP modules respectively, of which we propose a possible operative usage and some examples of application. Finally, we conclude in Section 7.

## 2    Answer Set Programming in a Nutshell, and Some Terminology

"Answer set programming" (ASP) is the well-established logic programming paradigm adopting logic programs with default negation under the *answer set semantics*, shortly summarized below. For the applications of ASP, the reader can refer for instance to [1,2,3,4,5]. Several well-developed answer set solvers [32] that compute the answer sets of a given program can be freely downloaded by potential users [32].

In the rest of the paper, whenever it is clear from the context, by "a (logic) program $\Pi$" we mean a datalog program $\Pi$ (for datalog the reader may refer for instance to [33]), and we will implicitly refer to the "ground" version of $\Pi$. The ground version of $\Pi$ is obtained by replacing in all possible ways the variables occurring in $\Pi$ with the constants occurring in $\Pi$ itself, and is thus composed of *ground atoms*, i.e., atoms which contain no variables. The Herbrand base $\mathbf{B}_\Pi$ of a ground ASP program $\Pi$ is composed of all ground atoms that can be constructed out of the set of predicate symbols and the set of constant symbols occurring in $\Pi$. We indicate with $\mathcal{B}_\Pi$ the restriction of $\mathbf{B}_\Pi$ to the atoms actually occurring in the ground version of $\Pi$. This assumption is due to the fact that ASP solvers produce the grounding of the given program as a first step. In fact, they are presently able to find the answer sets of ground programs only (though work is under way to overcome at least partially this limitation, cf.,e.g., [34,35]).

Let $\mathcal{V}$ be a set of variables. To the purposes of this paper, we will call *abstract atom* (referring to program $\Pi$) any non-ground atom built out of a ground atom $A \in \mathcal{B}_\Pi$ by substituting some of the constants occurring in it by variables in $\mathcal{V}$. We will call $\mathcal{B}_\Pi^a$ the set of all the abstract atoms obtained from $\mathcal{B}_\Pi$. Vice versa, a *proper* instantiation (w.r.t. program $\Pi$) of an abstract atom $B \in \mathcal{B}_\Pi^a$ is an instantiation (ground instance) $A$ of $B$ such that $A \in \mathcal{B}_\Pi$. If $S$ is a set of abstract atoms, we let $Ground(S)$ be the set of its proper instantiations. Instantiations and proper instantiations of a conjunction of abstract atoms have the obvious definition.

A normal program (or, for short, just "program") $\Pi$ is a collection of *rules* of the form

$$H \leftarrow L_1, \ldots, L_m, \, not \; L_{m+1}, \ldots, not \; L_{m+n}.$$

where $H$ is an atom, $m \geqslant 0$ and $n \geqslant 0$, and each $L_i$ is an atom. An atom $L_i$ and its negative counterpart $not \; L_i$ are called *literals*. In the examples, $\leftarrow$ will often be indicated with $:-$, which is the symbol adopted in practical programming systems. In the version of $\Pi$ defined by a programmer, all atoms will be in general abstract atoms. In the ground version of $\Pi$ they become ground atoms, as each original rule is substituted by all its ground instantiations. Various extensions to the basic paradigm exist, that we do not consider here as they are not essential in the present context. The left-hand side and the right-hand side of the clause are called *head* and *body*, respectively. A rule with empty body is called a *fact*. A rule with empty head is a *constraint*, where a constraint of the form

$$\leftarrow L_1, ..., L_n.$$

states that literals $L_1, \ldots, L_n$ cannot be simultaneously true in any answer set.

The answer sets semantics [36,37] is a view of logic programs as sets of inference rules (more precisely, default inference rules). Alternatively, one can see a program as a set of constraints on the solution of a problem, where each answer set represents a solution compatible with the constraints expressed by the program. Consider the simple program $\{q \leftarrow not\, p.\ p \leftarrow not\, q.\}$. For instance, the first rule is read as "assuming that $p$ is false, we can *conclude* that $q$ is true." This program has two answer sets. In the first one, $q$ is true while $p$ is false; in the second one, $p$ is true while $q$ is false. The programming paradigm based upon logic programs under the answer set semantics is called "Answer Set Programming" (ASP), and programs are called "answer set programs" (ASP programs).

A subset $M$ of $\mathcal{B}_\Pi$ is an answer set of $\Pi$ if $M$ coincides with the least model of the reduct $P^M$ of $P$ with respect to $M$. This reduct is obtained by deleting from $\Pi$ all rules containing a condition $not\, a$, for some $a$ in $M$, and by deleting all negative conditions from the other rules. Answer sets are minimal supported models, and form an anti-chain. Referring to the original terminology of [36], answer sets are sometimes called *stable models*. Unlike other semantics, a program may have several answer sets, or may have no answer set, because conclusions are included in an answer set only if they can be justified. The following program has no answer set:
$\{a \leftarrow not\, b.\ b \leftarrow not\, c.\ c \leftarrow not\, a.\}$

The reason is that in every minimal model of this program there is a true atom that depends (in the program) on the negation of another true atom, which is strictly forbidden in this semantics, where every answer set can be considered as a self-consistent and self-supporting set of consequences of a given program. Whenever a program has no answer sets, we will say that the program is *inconsistent*. Correspondingly, checking for consistency (or stability) means checking for the existence of answer sets.

By some abuse of notation, given program $\Pi$ and a set of facts and rules $I$, by $\Pi \cup I$ we indicate the new program obtained by adding the atoms and rules occurring in $I$ to $\Pi$. Also, if a consistent program $\Pi$ has a number $k$ of answer sets, we will assume an arbitrary enumeration $M_1, \ldots, M_k$ of these answer sets, and we will refer to $M_h$ ($h \leq k$) as the $h - th$ answer set. Given answer set program $\Pi$ which is inconsistent, we call a set of atoms $R \subseteq \mathcal{B}_\Pi$ a *trigger* for $\Pi$ whenever $\Pi \cup R$ is consistent.

As it is well known (cf., e.g., [38]), an ASP program is inconsistent whenever there is some *odd cycle*, like for instance the above one
$\{a \leftarrow not\, b.\ b \leftarrow not\, c.\ c \leftarrow not\, a.\}$

For obtaining a potentially consistent program from one including such a cycle, the cycle should *constrained* by adding, in the terminology of [38], some *handle* for the cycle. A handle for the above cycle can consist of, e.g., rule $\{a \leftarrow d.\}$. Or, it can consist of an additional literal, e.g., $not\, r$, added to any of the rules of the cycle, say for instance the second one. If at least one handle of an odd cycle is *active*, then the program fragment including the odd cycle and the handles is consistent. The former handle is active if $d$ occurs somewhere in the overall program. Thus, the head $a$ of the rule becomes true. The latter handle is active if $r$ occurs somewhere in the overall program. Thus, $not\, r$ is false and then the head $b$ of the rule where this literal occurs becomes true. In both cases, the circularity is broken, i.e., if there are active handles the cycle becomes (again in the terminology of [38]) *actually constrained*. For the overall program to be consistent, every odd cycle must be actually constrained. This requires that, if there are several odd cycles, they admit handles which are *compatible*, i.e., that do not expect opposite truth values for the same atom.

An inconsistent program $\Pi$ necessarily involves some "problematic" odd cycle which is not actually constrained. Therefore, a trigger $R$ for $\Pi$ includes a set of atoms that make all the odd cycles in $\Pi$ actually constrained. I.e., a trigger includes atoms that make at least one handle for each problematic odd cycle active, where these handles are compatible among themselves and with those already present in $\Pi$.

In the following sections, triggers will be exploited as a "control" device to manage modules consisting of an ASP program. Such a module will be supposed to provide some kind of answer to an agent which "invokes" it by providing suitable input. We will assume the ASP program defining a module to be inconsistent on purpose, and to be designed so that a trigger must include the significant input the module needs in order to provide meaningful answers. Then, providing a trigger will be the way for an agent to invoke a module and get answers.

As mentioned before, ASP has the peculiarity that an ASP program may have none, one or several answer sets. These answer sets can be interpreted in various possible ways. If the program formalizes a search problem, e.g., a colorability problem or a path finding problem for graphs, then the answer sets represents the possible solutions to the problem, namely, in the examples, the possible colorings or the existing paths for given graph. In knowledge representation, an ASP program may represent a formal definition of the known features of a situation/world of interest. In this case, the answer sets represent the possible consistent states of this world, that can be several whenever the formalization involves some kind of uncertainty. Also, and ASP program can be seen as the formalization of the knowledge and beliefs of a rational agent about a situation/world, and the answer sets represent the possible belief states of such an agent, that can be several if either uncertainty or alternative possible choices are involved in the description. Such an agent can exploit an ASP module for several purposes, such as answering questions, building plans, explaining observations, making choices, etc. Some potential uses of ASP modules in agents will be proposed and discussed in the rest of the paper.

## 3  Related Work on ASP Modules

There are several approaches to modularization of ASP programs with software engineering purposes, i.e., to govern the complexity of programs and their development process. For a review of the state of the art in this field the reader may refer for instance to [39] and to the references therein.

In the approach of [40,39], in conformance with programming-in-the-large principles, a suitable input-output interface for ASP modules is defined, in order to compute the combination of compatible answer sets of joinable modules. By providing a notion of equivalence for modules, the approach tackles the issue of the replacement of a module with another one without altering the semantics of the program when seen as an overall entity.

This proposal is related to that of [41], then evolved into [42], as each one can be rephrased in terms of the other. However, in the latter proposal the point of view is different, as modules are seen as "procedures" that can invoke each other, even recursively, by providing input parameters. An overall program is composed of several modules where a "main" module without input can be identified. Providing the semantics of a program requires to identify, via a *call graph*, the relevant modules, i.e., those that are actually invoked. Complexity ranges from exponential to double exponential, due to the complex module interaction that the approach admits.

In [43], modules import answer sets from other modules in order to compute the overall solution, where no cycles are admitted among modules. [44] provides modules specification with information hiding, where modules exchange information with a global state.

Some approaches exist [45,46] that, in order to encourage code reusability, define modules in terms of macros or "templates" that factorize predefined definitions, again with no cycle allowed among these entities.

In [47], a technique is proposed that allows an answer set program to access the brave or cautious consequences of another answer set program. The technique is based upon joining the two programs into a single one and then performing a suitable rewriting with the addition of weak constraints.

In the following sections we will propose *Reactive ASP Modules*, where complex forms of reaction can be specified in an agent program, in contrast to the simple "condition-action rules" that are often adopted. Namely, an ASP module will describe how an agent might behave upon the occurrence of certain events, also depending upon particular circumstances and/or the agent's past experiences (e.g., when and why lend or not lend a certain resource upon request). When provided with information about the present context, the answer sets of such a module will encode the possible courses of action that the agent might undertake. We will also propose *Modal ASP Modules*, where an agent will be enabled to reason about possibility and necessity. I.e., such a module will describe what an agent knows or believes about some situation, and the agent will be enable to inspect its answer sets so as to "bring to consciousness" its own mental states and understand what is possible in that situation (because it occurs in some answer set) and/or what is mandatory (because it occurs in every answer set). In previous example, lending some resource to a certain requester might be possible given some conditions, or even mandatory if for instance the agent has previously contracted an obligation. This will imply encoding in an ASP module a fragment of the domain of interest of the agent and examining the answer sets of the module. In the present proposal, ASP modules do not interact with each other. For future extensions in the direction of interacting modules, the techniques presented in [47] might be of use for a principled implementation.

The first idea of exploiting possibility and necessity in ASP is due to Michael Gelfond and presented in [48]. In this proposal, possibility and necessity operators can occur in ASP programs, thus called "epistemic logic programs", in the body of rules. Therefore, concluding or not the head of these rules will depend upon the contents of a program's own answer sets. A suitable extension of the answer set semantics is introduced to cope with the enhanced expressivity. The work presented in [49,50] investigates computational complexity of this approach by redefining its semantics as *world view semantics*. On the one hand it is concluded that the consistency check problem under this semantics is PSPACE-complete. On the other hand however, non-trivial classes of programs where the complexity is $\Sigma_2^P$-complete or even NP-complete are identified. In [16], the authors adopt a different perspective and employ meta-programming techniques to model in an ASP program multi-agent systems involving agents with knowledge about other agent's knowledge.

Related to the present work is ASP-PROLOG [51], that proposes an integration between prolog and ASP where prolog programs are enabled to invoke ASP modules and examine the answers sets. These modules can be customized by adding and removing rules prior to invocation. The similarity with the approach presented in this paper lays in the fact the the prolog program invoking ASP modules can be seen as analogous to a logical agent program exploiting ASP modules, though the kind of application and the envisaged use of modules is different. ASP-PROLOG is procedural in nature and extends the standard prolog notation. It might be a good implementation tool for many kinds of ASP modules, included those presented here.

In Section 6.1 we will show how to exploit possibility and necessity to perform interesting forms of meta-reasoning. An approach to meta-reasoning within ASP programs is that of [52], which proposes "template" rules with variables in place of predicates (to be suitable instantiated to actual predicate symbols occurring in the program), in the style of Reflective Prolog [53,54]. The work presented in [55] interprets ASP programs as agents and allows for various forms of reasoning by introducing deontic operators (such as for instance *Obligation*) in such programs.

# 4   Logical Agents in Short

Recently, the computing landscape has changed from a focus on standalone computer systems to a situation characterized by distributed, open and dynamic heterogeneous systems that must interact, and must operate effectively within rapidly changing circumstances and with increasing quantities of available information. In this context, agents constitute a suitable design metaphor, that provides designers and developers with a way of structuring an application around autonomous, communicative and flexible elements [56].

Agents should be *intelligent* so as to face changing situations by modifying their behavior, or their goals, or the way to achieve their goals. This requires agents to be able to perform, interleave and combine various forms of commonsense reasoning, possibly based upon different kinds of representation. Several agent-oriented languages and architecture exist and in particular several computational logic-based agent architectures and models. A common feature is the aim at building agents that are able to adapt or change their behavior when they encounter a new or different situation.

A logical agent is based upon an "agent program" which consists of a knowledge base and of a set of rules aimed at providing the entity with the needed capabilities.

Rules may include object-level rules and meta-(meta-...)rules that determine the agent behavior. The knowledge base may itself include rules, which either define knowledge (and meta-knowledge) in an abstract way or constitute part of the agent knowledge. The knowledge base constitutes in fact the agent "memory" while rules define the agent behavior. An underlying inference engine, or more generally a control mechanism, puts an agent at work. Agents in general evolve in time as a result of both their interaction with the environment and their own self-modifications. Despite the differences, all logical agent-oriented architectures and languages, or "agent models", exhibit at least the following basic features (for a general discussion about logical agent models the reader may see, e.g., [57] and [58], and for a general logical semantics for evolving agents [29]):

- A logical "core", that for instance in both KGP and DALI is a resolution-based logic program (prolog-like for DALI and abductive for KGP).
- Reactivity, i.e., the capability of managing external stimuli.
- Proactivity, i.e., the capability of managing internal "initiatives".
- The capability of performing actions.
- The capability of recording what has happened and has been done in the past.
- The capability of managing communication with other agents.
- A basic cycle that interleaves the application of formerly specified capabilities. E.g., in DALI the basic cycle is integrated within the logical core into an extended resolution, while in KGP the basic cycle has a meta-level definition and thus can be varied.

Taking for instance KGP and DALI, which are two well-known and fully implemented agent models based upon logic programming, we can identify the following more specific features.

KGP agents are equipped with the following components.

(1) A set of beliefs, equipped with a set of *reasoning capabilities*, for reasoning with the information available in the agent state. These capabilities include Planning, Temporal Reasoning, Reactivity, Goal Decision, and Temporal Constraint Satisfiability. Beliefs include a records of the information sensed from the environment, as well as a history of executed actions.

(2) A set of *goals* and *plans* to which the agent is committed.

(3) A sensing capability, allowing agents to observe their environment and actions (including utterances) by other agents.

(3) An actuating capability, allowing agents to affect their environment (including by performing utterances).

(4) Control information, including a set of *transition rules*, changing the agent's state and a set of *selection functions* to select inputs to transitions.

(5) A control component, for deciding which enabled transition should be next [59].

The DALI agent model includes:

(i) A set of beliefs, including reactive rules, support for proactivity and reasoning, planning, constraint satisfiability. Beliefs also include *past events* that record what has happened in the past: events perceived and reacted to, proactive initiatives, goals reached, etc. Past events can be organized into histories on which properties can be verified by means of constraints.

(ii) A sensing capability, allowing agents to observe their environment and actions by other agents.

(iii) A set of constraints for verifying that the agent's course of actions respects some properties and does not present anomalies.

(iv) A learning component for recording past events and building histories; a belief revision component for removing old information based on conditions and for either incorporating or dropping knowledge acquired from other agents.

(v) Control information that may influence proactive behavior and the recording of past events.

Both KGP and DALI are by their very natural modular architectures, as agents are composed of various modules. ASP modules may be exploited in these architectures to implement various capabilities, for instance planning. In subsequent sections, we will propose however some kinds of ASP modules that may actually under some respects empower these agent models.

## 5   Reactive ASP Modules

Since [60], it is universally recognized that *reactivity* is an essential feature in logical agents, in the sense of an agent being able to respond in a timely and appropriate way to the reception of stimuli coming from an external environment which is in general subject to change and that can generate events in an unforeseeable sequence. Reactions are often expressed in condition-action rules, say e.g. of the form

$IF \langle Conditions \rangle \ DO \ \langle Actions \rangle$

which are also present in ASP-based action languages, where however they are not meant to be triggered by the conditions, but are rather processed contextually to the rest of the program. The problem was tackled in [28] where *reactive control modules* composed of condition-action rules were introduced and the problem of their correctness w.r.t. the overall program (action theory) was discussed.

Here, we intend to introduce modules that allow for "complex" reactivity, where some kind of reasoning has to be performed in order to devise suitable reactions. These modules are intended to "sleep" in the background and enter into play when activated by the occurrence of external events. In order to choose among the different actions that is possible to perform, corresponding to different answer sets of a reactive module, we build upon previous work [61], where we introduced priorities among (conditional) actions in logic agent-oriented languages.

In the rest of this section, we propose a formulation, a possible operational behavior and some examples of use of reactive ASP modules. Technically, we will specify reactive ASP modules by exploiting a distinguished, ASP feature, i.e., the constraints. We also make the reactive behavior parametric w.r.t. context conditions that may be different in different module invocations.

The basic idea is that of constructing a reactive ASP module around an inconsistent ASP program, where inconsistency is due to one or more constraints of the form

$:- not \ A_1, \ldots, not \ A_n$

where the $A_i$'s are atoms, which represent the events that must happen in order to *activate* the module. In fact, if no event has happened, all the $A_i$'s are false which implies that the constraint is violated (as all the *not* $A_i$'s are true) and therefore the module is inconsistent. A module will stay "asleep" until one or more events happen: events which have occurred will be asserted as facts, thus acting as triggers that make the module consistent. The module will now have answer sets which encompass the possible reactions to these events. The proposed formulation of reactive ASP modules is aimed at their introduction in the basic cycle of the agent architecture at hand. In this basic cycle, there will be at some stage a check of reactive modules that, whenever active, will generate possible reactions one of which will be chosen and put into play either nondeterministically or based on preferences.

A reactive ASP module will have an input/output interface. The input interface specifies the events that may trigger the module. The output interface specifies the actions that the module answer sets (if any) can possibly encompass. However, at the *invocation* the module will return not only the actions, but also the conditions (if any) for their being actually performed. For instance, if the module performs some form of default reasoning [62], the output may include the normality/abnormality assumptions.

We introduce below the definition that specifies an ASP reactive module after giving some guidelines about the logic program which constitutes its "core".

**Definition 1.** *A completed logic program $\Pi$ is obtained from an inconsistent logic program $\Pi_{given}$ containing at least one constraint of the form* $:-not\ A_1, \ldots, not\ A_n$ *by adding, for each atom $A$ that in $\Pi_{given}$ does not occur in a constraint and does not occur as the head of a rule, the even cycle (composed of two rules):* $A :-not\ noA$, $noA :-not\ A$ *where $noA$ is a fresh atom.*

$A$ will be called an *assumption* (w.r.t. program $\Pi$) and the set of all the assumptions will be called $\mathcal{A}_\Pi$. The purpose of assumptions will be illustrated below in relation to an example.

**Definition 2.** *A reactive ASP module $\mathcal{M}$ is a triple $\langle In, \Pi, Out \rangle$ where $\Pi$ is a completed logic program and $In, Out \subseteq \mathcal{B}_\Pi^a$ are sets of abstract atoms, called the* abstract inputs *and* abstract outputs *respectively, where $\mathcal{A}_\Pi \subseteq Ground(Out)$.*

A reactive ASP module can be invoked by providing an input including the proper instantiations of (some of) the atoms in $In$ (i.e., it is not mandatory to provide *all* the specified inputs). Symmetrically, it may be the case that only part of the outputs is returned. However, the input may also include facts and rules that represent additional contextual knowledge useful for the evaluation of the reaction. These facts and rules are here required to be ground.

Given *actual input $I$*, an invocation implies to determine the answer sets of $\Pi \cup I$ and to extract proper instantiations for the outputs. If $\Pi \cup I$ is consistent, there may be different results corresponding to the different answer sets. Otherwise, no result will be returned. We may notice that the assumptions which belong to each answer set are returned in the output by definition, unless they have been provided as input. In fact, no input atom is returned as output.

**Definition 3.** *An* invocation result *of a reactive ASP module* $\mathcal{M} = \langle In, \Pi, Out \rangle$ *is a triple* $\langle I, \Pi, O \rangle$, *where: I, called the* actual input, *is a set of ground facts and rules[1], including proper instantiations of (some of the) atoms in In; $O \subseteq \mathcal{B}_\Pi$, called the* actual output, *includes proper instantiations of (some of the) atoms in Out, where either $\Pi \cup I$ is inconsistent and $O = \emptyset$ or $O \subseteq (M \setminus I)$ where M is an answer set of $\Pi \cup I$ and O is composed of all the proper instantiations of atoms in Out which occur in M, except those given in the input.*

It is easy to see that, given input $I$, there are as many invocation results as the answer sets of $\Pi \cup I$ (among which the actual course of action must be somehow selected by the agent), and that $O \neq \emptyset$ only if $I$ includes a trigger $R$ for $\Pi$.

Operationally, invocation of ASP modules can explicitly occur in an agent program, where the precise way to invoke a module will depend upon the agent language at hand. In DALI for instance, the simple reactive rules of the language can be used to directly resort to a reactive module whenever the relevant events occur together (where DALI provides a way of specifying what does it mean to happen together for a given set of events, e.g., in the same day, same second, etc.). Other methods for invocation are also possible: e.g., the inputs related to an invocation can be written on a blackboard which is examined from time to time by an underlying control component which performs the invocation, and puts the results on the blackboard.

The ASP modules so defined are suitable for specifying the reaction to external stimuli, where, in an invocation, the inputs include the external stimuli and the outputs include a set of actions to be executed in response to the stimuli according to the assumptions. In our view in fact, reactive ASP modules should be used to describe knowledge and beliefs concerning how an agent would cope with some events in a given situation. The answer sets of a reactive module are meant to represent the possible courses of action that the agent might undertake whenever these events actually occur, given the present context. They will in general contain plans that the agent might execute to cope with the events together with the assumptions these plans are based upon. In simple cases, like in the examples below, a plan may plainly consist of few actions whose order does not matter. The module "core" is a completed program so that whatever is not known and is not provided as input can possibly be assumed. An agent invokes an ASP module by providing an actual input including a trigger for the module and all the relevant information which is available. Among the resulting answer sets, the agent will have to choose according to some criteria and put the selected course of action into operation.

Below we propose an example of an ASP module. For the sake of clarity, here and in the rest of the paper we adopt the DALI syntax, and thus we assume to indicate predicates denoting actions with suffix 'A' and those denoting external stimuli with suffix 'E'. The external stimulus to be coped with is *bell_ringsE*. Program $\Pi$ is the following. It is a completed program, where *good_weather* is an assumption, i.e., if not provided as input, the agent may assume that the weather is good or not. The agent will open the door if the bell rings whenever the situation does not look dangerous (i.e.,

---

[1] Facts and rules composed of ground atoms. Notice, here and in what follows, that they are not required to be composed only of atoms in $\mathbf{B}_\Pi$, i.e., fresh predicate and constant symbols are allowed to occur.

we are not at night with strangers around). It opens the window whenever the weather
good, or, precisely, whenever either it is known to be good (because this information
has been received in input) or it has been assumed to be good. Notice that the former
action is generated by means of a very simple form of *proactivity*, i.e., on the agent's
own initiative. In fact, it is not a reaction to an external event and it is not necessarily
a consequence of what is known (the weather being good can arbitrarily be assumed if
not known). Proactivity is commonly assumed to be a main feature of agents.

```
:- not bell_ringsE.
openA(door) :- bell_ringsE.
:- openA(door), at_night, strangers_around.
openA(window):- good_weather.
good_weather :- not nogood_weather.
nogood_weather :- not good_weather.
```

The trigger that makes $\Pi$ consistent is the external event *bell_ringsE* and the resulting program $\Pi \cup bell\_ringsE$ has a number of answer sets which depends upon whether
both *at_night* and *strangers_around* are given, and whether *good_weather* is either
given or assumed. If we do not either have as input or assume *good_weather* we can
possibly conclude *openA(door)* but not *openA(window)*, which has *good_weather*
as a condition. If we have both *at_night* and *strangers_around*, we cannot conclude *openA(door)* but, if we assume *good_weather*, then we can possibly conclude
*openA(window)*.

A reactive ASP module associated to $\Pi$ can be for instance:
$\langle\{bell\_ringsE, at\_night, strangers\_around\}, \Pi, \{openA(X)\}\rangle$

Among the possible invocation results, each one corresponding to an answer set of
$\Pi \cup I$, we have the following :
$\langle\{bell\_ringsE\}, \Pi, \{openA(door)\}\rangle$
$\langle\{bell\_ringsE, good\_weather\}, \Pi, \{openA(door), openA(window)\}\rangle$
$\langle\{bell\_ringsE\}, \Pi, \{good\_weather, openA(door), openA(window)\}\rangle$
$\langle\{bell\_ringsE, at\_night, strangers\_around\}, \Pi, \emptyset\rangle$
$\langle\{bell\_ringsE, at\_night\}, \Pi, \{good\_weather, openA(window)\}\rangle$

As another example, program $\Pi$ below states that the agent may or may not lend money
to somebody, however: (s)he never lends money to unreliable persons; (s)he normally
lends money to friends, unless this friend is an unreliable person. Notice that lending/not
lending money is chosen arbitrarily, unless conditions occur (stated in the constraints)
to force an agent to make a certain choice. Going back to the definition of completed
program (Definition 1), it may be noticed that every item of information occurring in
the program can be assumed if not provided in input, except the conditions occurring
in the constraints. For instance, in the module below the agent will force itself to lend
the money if the request comes from a friend, but the requester being a friend must be
explicitly specified in input (of course, if at the invocation the agent believes that this is
the case).

```
:- not requestE.
lend_moneyA :- not no_land, requestE.
no_land :- not lend_moneyA.
:- lend_moneyA, unreliable_person.
:- not lend_moneyA, requestE, friend.
```

A reactive ASP module associated to $\Pi$ can be for instance:

$\langle \{ requestE, friend, unreliable\_person \}, \Pi, \{ lend\_moneyA \} \rangle$

We may have for instance the following invocation results, where notice that, if the requester is stated to be unreliable, the output is empty (thus no action is prescribed) as the module is inconsistent.

$\langle \{ requestE, friend \}, \Pi, \{ lend\_moneyA \} \rangle$
$\langle \{ requestE, friend, unreliable\_person \}, \Pi, \emptyset \rangle$
$\langle \{ requestE \}, \Pi, \emptyset \} \rangle$ and $\langle \{ requestE \}, \Pi, \{ lend\_moneyA \} \rangle$

With input *requestE*, one of the two possible outcomes must be chosen as the actual course of action.

## 6  Reasoning on Possibility and Necessity: Modal ASP Modules

In this section, we propose another kind of ASP module, defined so as to allow forms of reasoning to be expressed on possibility and necessity analogous to those of modal logic. As it is well-known, in classical modal logic (see [63]) a proposition is said to be possible if and only if it is not necessarily false (regardless of whether it is actually true or actually false), and to be *necessary* if and only if it is not possibly false. The meaning of these terms refers to the existence of multiple "possible worlds": something "necessary" is true in all possible worlds, something "possible" is true in at least one possible world. These "possible world semantics" are formalized with Kripke semantics. Either the notion of possibility or that of necessity may be taken to be basic, where the other one is defined in terms of it. Possibility and necessity are related to *credulous* and *skeptical* (or *brave* and *cautious*) reasoning in non-monotonic reasoning, where in the credulous (brave) approach a proposition is believed if it is possible, while in the skeptical (cautious) approach it is believed only if it is necessary.

In our setting, the "possible worlds" that we consider refer to an ASP program $\Pi$ and are its answer sets. Therefore, given $A \in \mathcal{B}_\Pi$, we will say that $A$ is possible if it belongs to some answer set, and that $A$ is necessary if it belongs to the intersection of all the answer sets.

A comment is in order about why we do not choose to refer to the well-founded model (wfm) [64]. In fact, as it is well-known every answer set $M$ of a given program $\Pi$ is a superset of the wfm of the program. This means that, given $WFM = \langle T; F \rangle$ where atoms in $T$ are considered to be true, atoms in $F$ are considered to be false and all the other atoms are considered to be undefined (i.e., the WFM is a three-valued semantics) we have $T \subseteq M$. However, $T$ is in general smaller than the intersection of all the answer sets, as it includes only the consequences derivable from the acyclic part of the program. Therefore, $T$ does not include consequences deriving from assumptions, even when these assumptions lead to the same conclusion in all the answer sets[2].

## 6.1  Definition, Use and Applications of Modal ASP Modules

We introduce below an operator of possibility, that we indicate with $P$ (instead of the traditional $\diamond$, or $M$), and an operator of necessity, that we indicate with $N$ (instead of the classical $\square$, or $L$). We change the terminology as we re-define the operators w.r.t. the answer sets of a program considered as a theory. In this specific setting, properties of the operators can be proved rather than defined axiomatically. These operators define *Modal ASP Expressions* that can be either *possibility expressions* or *necessity expressions*.

**Definition 4.** *Given answer set program $\Pi$ with answer sets enumerated as $M_1, \ldots, M_k$, and an atom $A$, the* possibility *expression $P(w_i, A)$ is deemed to hold (w.r.t. $\Pi$) whenever $A \in M_{w_i}$, $w_i \in \{1, \ldots, k\}$. The possibility operator $P(A)$ is deemed to hold whenever $\exists M \in \{M_1, \ldots, M_k\}$ such that $A \in M$.*

**Definition 5.** *Given answer set program $\Pi$ with answer sets $M_1, \ldots, M_k$, and an atom $A$, the* necessity *expression $N(A)$ is deemed to hold (w.r.t. $\Pi$) whenever $A \in (M_1 \cap \ldots \cap M_k)$.*

We are now able to define the negation of possibility and necessity operators.

**Definition 6.** *Given answer set program $\Pi$ with answer sets enumerated as $M_1, \ldots, M_k$, and an atom $A$: the* possibility *expression $\neg P(w_i, A)$ is deemed to hold (w.r.t. $\Pi$) whenever $A \notin M_{w_i}$, $w_i \in \{1, \ldots, k\}$; the expression $\neg P(A)$ is deemed to hold whenever $\neg \exists M \in \{M_1, \ldots, M_k\}$ such that $A \in M$; the* necessity *expression $\neg N(A)$ is deemed to hold (w.r.t. $\Pi$) whenever $A \notin (M_1 \cap \ldots M_k)$.*

It is easy to see that, given answer set program $\Pi$:

**Proposition 1.** $N(A)$ implies $P(A)$ and implies that $\exists w_i$ such that $P(w_i, A)$.

**Proposition 2.** $\neg P(A)$ implies $\neg N(A)$.

The extension of the above operators to conjunctions is straightforward, where a conjunction is deemed to be possible in a certain answer set $w_i$ (resp. possible in general) whenever all conjuncts belong to $w_i$ (resp. to the same answer set) and a conjunction is deemed to be necessary whenever all conjuncts belong to the intersection of the answer sets.

We now extend the definition of modal ASP expressions to include a context for their evaluation

**Definition 7.** *Let $E(Args)$ be either a possibility or a necessity expression. The corresponding contextual expression has the form $E(Args) : Context$ where $Context$ is a set of ground facts and rules. $E(Args) : Context$ is deemed to hold whenever $E(Args)$ holds w.r.t. $\Pi \cup Context$.*

---

[2] For the interested reader, in previous work [38] we have discussed the role of cycles and of connections between cycles for the consistency of the program.

The abstract counterparts of modal ASP expressions are expressions of the form $P(I, X)$, $P(X)$ and $N(X)$ (resp. $P(I, X) : C$, $P(X) : C$ and $N(X) : C$ for their contextual version) where: $I$ is a variable ranging over natural numbers; $X$ can be either an abstract atom or a conjunction of abstract atoms or also a metavariable intended to denote either an abstract atom or a conjunction of abstract atoms; $C$ can be either a set of abstract atoms or a metavariable intended to denote a set of abstract atoms.

Possibility and necessity expressions are evaluated w.r.t. an underlying *modal ASP module* of the following form.

**Definition 8.** *A modal ASP module $\mathcal{M}$ is a tuple*
$\langle Module\_name, AbstrQuery, AbstrContext, \Pi, AbstrPos, AbstrNec \rangle$ *where:*

- *Module_name is the name of the module;*
- *$\Pi$ is a logic program;*
- *AbstrQuery is either an abstract atom or a conjunction of abstract atoms (that can be intended as a set), i.e., $AbstrQuery \subseteq \mathcal{B}_\Pi^a$ and $AbstrQuery \neq \emptyset$;*
- *AbstrContext is a metavariable denoting a set of ground facts and rules;*
- *AbstrPos is a metavariable denoting a set of abstract possibility expressions of the form $P(I, AbstrQuery)$;*
- *Nec is a metavariable denoting either a necessity expressions of the form $N(AbstrQuery)$ or the empty set.*

A modal ASP module is invoked whenever a modal ASP expression has to be evaluated, by providing a proper instantiation of the abstract query and of the context by means of the arguments of the modal ASP expression at hand.

**Definition 9.** *An invocation result of a modal ASP module $\mathcal{M}$ is a tuple*
$\langle Module\_name, Query, Context, \Pi, Pos, Nec \rangle$ *where:*

- *$Query \subseteq \mathcal{B}_\Pi$, $Query \neq \emptyset$, is composed of proper instantiations of (some of) the abstract atoms in AbstrQuery;*
- *Context is a set of ground facts and rules;*
- *Pos is the set of the expressions $P(w_i, Query)$ that hold w.r.t. $\Pi \cup Context$, or the expression $\neg P(Query)$ if no possibility has been found to hold;*
- *Nec is either $N(Query)$ or $\neg N(Query)$ depending upon which of the two holds w.r.t. $\Pi \cup Context$.*

Notice that, from the practical point of view, once the module has been invoked on some input, its invocation result can be stored for subsequent use.

For the case where there are several modal ASP modules, the straightforward extension of the above-defined modal ASP expressions can be $E(T, Args)$ (resp. $E(T, Args) : Context$ for the contextual form) where the given expression is meant to be evaluated w.r.t. module (theory) $T$ (precisely, w.r.t. program $\Pi$ included in $T$).

The Kripke structure that we propose is simple, but yet it allows significant forms of reasoning to be performed. For instance, one is able to define meta-axioms, like, e.g., the following, which states that a proposition is plausible w.r.t. theory $T$ if, say, it is possible in at least two different worlds:

$$plausible(T, Q) :- P(T, I, Q), P(T, J, Q), I \neq J.$$

We can also formulate the contextual counterpart of the above:

$$plausible(T, Q, C) :- P(T, I, Q) : C, P(T, J, Q) : C, I \neq J.$$

As we were mentioning before, to evaluate an instance of the meta-axioms above one has to invoke module $T$ on query $Q$ just once.

Among the relevant realms of possible application of modal ASP expressions are in our view normative reasoning and negotiation. Consider for instance the famous example proposed in the seminal work about meta-interpreters [65]:

$$guilty(X) :- demo(Facts, guilty(X))$$

meaning that one can be considered to be guilty only if (s)he is provably guilty within theory $Facts$ representing both the laws/regulations and the evidence. We can generalize this kind of reasoning by allowing $Facts$ to be an answer set program, i.e., by allowing non-monotonic reasoning and multiple possible solutions. In our setting, we might rephrase this example as follows:

$$guilty(X) :- N(Facts, guilty(X))$$

We might also allow evidence that one proposes to her/his excuse, e.g.,

$$innocent(X) :- \neg P(Facts, guilty(X)) : Evidence$$

Here, we have used a contextual expression where we say that one has to be considered innocent if it is impossible that (s)he is not, assuming to accept the $Evidence$ (s)he proposes as excuse.

## 6.2   Extension to Multi-agent Setting

It can be interesting to extend our setting so as to allow an agent to reason not only about what is possible or necessary for herself/himself, but also about what is possible or necessary for other agents.

In this discussion, we assume that there are several agents, which are able to communicate with each other. We will however abstract from the details of the communication mechanism, assuming the existence of two primitives: $tell(Ag, Prop)$, to signify that the agent in which it occurs communicates proposition $Prop$ to agent $Ag$; $told(Ag, Prop)$, to signify that the agent in which it occurs receives proposition $Prop$ from agent $Ag$.

As a first simple example, let us assume for instance that agent Mary includes a modal ASP module where she decides whether to spend the evening going out (e.g, to cinema) or not. Let us also assume that there exists another agent, say John, who would like to invite Mary to cinema. In our approach, John can reason about Mary's possibilities, e.g., by means of a condition-action rule that might look like the following:

$told(mary, P(go\_to\_cinema))\ OR$
$told(mary, P(go\_to\_cinema) : lend\_money)$
$\qquad\qquad DO\ tell(mary, lend\_money\_if\_needed, invite\_to\_cinema)$

stating that if John is told by Mary that she would possibly go to cinema, either at her own expenses or upon the condition she can borrow some money, he offers to lend the money and invites her to go.

The next example refers to negotiation between agents. In the example, a benevolent agent accepts the justification of a partner agent for a contract violation if the partner is known to be reliable and offers a justification which is plausible w.r.t. a theory describing the negotiation domain, given a context (that presumably includes common knowledge about what has been going on). We refer to the above definition of *plausible*.

$$excused(Ag, Viol, Context\_facts) :-$$
$$N(Reputation\_theory, reliable(Ag)), told(Ag, Justification),$$
$$plausible(Domain\_theory, Justification, Context\_facts)$$

### 6.3 Complexity

As it is well-known, deciding the existence of an answer set has been proved NP-complete and the same for deciding whether an atom is a member of some answer set, while the problem whether a given atom is in the intersection of all stable models is co-NP-complete (see [66] and [67])[3].

It is useful to remark that complexity of epistemic logic programs [48] recalled in Section 3 is not related to the complexity of the approach presented here. In fact, in epistemic logic programs necessity and possibility operators may occur *within* a theory, while here we reason about an inner theory which is a plain ASP program.

We state here the complexity of reasoning about possibility and necessity with the above-mentioned operators, that is in accordance with the above results. In fact, we may notice that there is no real difference between computing the answer sets and enumerating them. Therefore, deciding whether an atom is a member of the $i$-th answer set has the same complexity of deciding whether an atom is a member of some answer set. We can then easily state the following.

**Proposition 3.** *Given atom A, the problem of deciding whether $P(w_i, A)$ holds w.r.t. program $\Pi$ is NP-complete.*

**Proposition 4.** *Given atom A, the problem of deciding whether $N(A)$ holds w.r.t. program $\Pi$ is co-NP-complete.*

Notice however that the above complexity results refers to the ground version of the logic program included in an ASP module: in fact, this is always the case when one adopts ASP. Therefore, either one bases a module upon ground programs as we have assumed up to now, or it is necessary to be careful about possible exponential blowup of program size (e.g., by stating constraints on the program structure or by avoiding to introduce too many new constants in the input). In the present setting, the input and the context of modal ASP expressions are provided by the overall agent (logic) program, and we have seen in the examples that several modal expressions may occur in the same rule. However, we assume (cf. Definition 9) that every modal ASP expression can be

---

[3] These results hold for normal ASP programs as defined in Section 2. If one considers additional constructs such as for instance disjunction, the complexity increases.

evaluated whenever all its arguments are ground. Then, no interaction is possible due to conjunctions of modal atoms. Relaxing at least to some extent this limitation, i.e., allowing modal ASP expressions to return results rather than simply evaluate to true or false will be a subject of future work.

Notice also that the increase of complexity that one can find, e.g., in the approach of [42] due to the interaction between modules that invoke each other even recursively cannot be found here. This because in the present setting modules cannot be nested and do not interact: in fact, an agent uses the possibility and necessity operator without nesting in its main agent program. Thus, there is no possible interaction among different invocations of such operators. The topic of allowing the use of possibility and necessity operators within modal ASP modules, where a module is allowed to refer to another one (presumably in an acyclic fashion) and the topic of nesting of possibility and necessity will be interesting subjects of future work, but have not been tackled here.

Whenever a logical agent uses only possibility in the body of its rules, the resulting system fits into the framework of [68]. In fact, rules with the possibility operator in the body can easily be seen in their terminology as "bridge rules". The agent program under, e.g., the semantics defined in [29] and the invoked modules under the answer set semantics form, again in their terminology, a set of logics. Finally, the belief state composed of the semantics of the agent program and the answer sets of the invoked modules and selected by the possibility operator constitutes what they call an "equilibrium". However, the complexity is lower that the more general case that they consider, because bridge rules can be used in the agent program only.

## 7  Concluding Remarks

We have proposed a framework for integrating ASP modules into virtually any agent architecture so as to allow for complex reactivity, and for hypothetical reasoning based upon possibility and necessity. From the implementation point of view, the integration of such modules into logic-based architectures is straightforward. In fact, we have implemented the approach within the DALI interpreter. The implementation is described in detail in [69], and uses the DLV answer set solver [70].

Our approach is different from previous ones under several respects. To the best of our knowledge in fact, except for the approach of [28] in the context of action theories, there is no existing approach which is comparable with the proposed one. On the first place, ASP modules are adopted for empowering reasoning capabilities of logical intelligent agents. Then, they are exploited to introduce forms of complex reactivity. Finally, we allow an agent to reason about what is possible given the corpus of agent's knowledge. The forms of hypothetical reasoning which are allowed are interesting, and may be used to design real applications at a comparatively low complexity.

## References

1. Baral, C.: Knowledge representation, reasoning and declarative problem solving. Cambridge University Press, Cambridge (2003)
2. Anger, C., Schaub, T., Truszczyński, M.: ASPARAGUS – the Dagstuhl Initiative. ALP Newsletter 17(3) (2004), http://asparagus.cs.uni-potsdam.de

3. Leone, N.: Logic programming and nonmonotonic reasoning: From theory to systems and applications. In: Baral, C., Brewka, G., Schlipf, J. (eds.) LPNMR 2007. LNCS (LNAI), vol. 4483, p. 1. Springer, Heidelberg (2007)
4. Truszczyński, M.: Logic programming for knowledge representation. In: Dahl, V., Niemelä, I. (eds.) ICLP 2007. LNCS, vol. 4670, pp. 76–88. Springer, Heidelberg (2007)
5. Gelfond, M.: Answer sets. In: Handbook of Knowledge Representation, ch. 7. Elsevier, Amsterdam (2007)
6. Gelfond, M., Lifschitz, V.: Action languages. ETAI, Electronic Transactions on Artificial Intelligence (6) (1998)
7. Baral, C., Gelfond, M.: Reasoning agents in dynamic domains. In: Minker, J. (ed.) Workshop on Logic-Based Artificial Intelligence, pp. 257–279. Kluwer Academic Publishers, Dordrecht (2001)
8. Baral, C., McIlraith, S., Son, T.C.: Formulating diagnostic problem solving using an action language with narratives and sensing. In: Proc. of the Int. Conference on the Principles of Knowledge Representation and Reasoning (KRR 2000), pp. 311–322 (2000)
9. Balduccini, M.: Answer Set Based Design of Highly Autonomous, Rational Agents. PhD thesis (2005)
10. Balduccini, M., Gelfond, M.: The AAA architecture: An overview. In: AAAI Spring Symposium 2008 on Architectures for Intelligent Theory-Based Agents, AITA 2008 (2008)
11. Kowalski, R.A., Sadri, F.: From logic programming towards multi-agent systems. Annals of Mathematics and Artificial Intelligence 25(3-4), 391–419 (1999)
12. Gelfond, G., Watson, R.: Modeling cooperative multi-agent systems. In: Costantini, S., Watson, R. (eds.) Proc. of ASP 2007, 4th International Workshop on Answer Set Programming at ICLP 2007 (2007)
13. De Vos, M., Vermeir, D.: Extending answer sets for logic programming agents. Annals of Mathematics and Artifical Intelligence, Special Issue on Computational Logic in Multi-Agent Systems 42(1-3), 103–139 (2004)
14. Alferes, J.J., Brogi, A., Leite, J.A., Pereira, L.M.: Evolving logic programs. In: Flesca, S., Greco, S., Leone, N., Ianni, G. (eds.) JELIA 2002. LNCS (LNAI), vol. 2424, pp. 50–61. Springer, Heidelberg (2002)
15. Alferes, J.J., Dell'Acqua, P., Pereira, L.M.: A compilation of updates plus preferences. In: Flesca, S., Greco, S., Leone, N., Ianni, G. (eds.) JELIA 2002. LNCS (LNAI), vol. 2424, pp. 62–74. Springer, Heidelberg (2002)
16. Baral, C., Gelfond, G., Son, T.C., Pontelli, E.: Using answer set programming to model multi-agent scenarios involving agents' knowledge about other's knowledge. In: Proc. of the 9th Int. Conference on Autonomous Agents and Multiagent Systems (AAMAS 2010), Copyright 2010 by the International Foundation for Autonomous Agents and Multiagent Systems, IFAAMAS (2010)
17. Rao, A.S., Georgeff, M.: Modeling rational agents within a bdi-architecture. In: Proc. of the Second Intl. Conf. on Principles of Knowledge Representation and Reasoning (KR 1991), pp. 473–484. Morgan Kaufmann, San Francisco (1991)
18. Rao, A.S.: Agentspeak(l): BDI agents speak out in a logical computable language. In: Perram, J., Van de Velde, W. (eds.) MAAMAW 1996. LNCS, vol. 1038. Springer, Heidelberg (1996)
19. Hindriks, K.V., de Boer, F., van der Hoek, W., Meyer, J.C.: Agent programming in 3APL. Autonomous Agents and Multi-Agent Systems 2(4) (1999)
20. Fisher, M.: Metatem: The story so far. In: Bordini, R.H., Dastani, M.M., Dix, J., El Fallah Seghrouchni, A. (eds.) PROMAS 2005. LNCS (LNAI), vol. 3862, pp. 3–22. Springer, Heidelberg (2006)
21. Subrahmanian, V.S., Bonatti, P., Dix, J., Eiter, T., Kraus, S., Ozcan, F., Ross, R.: Heterogeneous Agent Systems. MIT Press/AAAI Press, Cambridge, MA, USA (2000)

22. Costantini, S., Tocchio, A.: A logic programming language for multi-agent systems. In: Flesca, S., Greco, S., Leone, N., Ianni, G. (eds.) JELIA 2002. LNCS (LNAI), vol. 2424, p. 1. Springer, Heidelberg (2002)
23. Costantini, S., Tocchio, A.: The DALI logic programming agent-oriented language. In: Alferes, J.J., Leite, J. (eds.) JELIA 2004. LNCS (LNAI), vol. 3229, pp. 685–688. Springer, Heidelberg (2004)
24. Kakas, A.C., Mancarella, P., Sadri, F., Stathis, K., Toni, F.: The KGP model of agency. In: Proc. ECAI 2004 (2004)
25. Bracciali, A., Demetriou, N., Endriss, U., Kakas, A., Lu, W., Mancarella, P., Sadri, F., Stathis, K., Terreni, G., Toni, F.: The KGP model of agency: Computational model and prototype implementation. In: Priami, C., Quaglia, P. (eds.) GC 2004. LNCS (LNAI), vol. 3267, pp. 340–367. Springer, Heidelberg (2005)
26. Fisher, M., Bordini, R.H., Hirsch, B., Torroni, P.: Computational logics and agents: a road map of current technologies and future trends. Computational Intelligence Journal 23(1), 61–91 (2007)
27. Kakas, A.C., Kowalski, R.A., Toni, F.: The role of abduction in logic programming. In: Gabbay, D., Hogger, C., Robinson, A. (eds.) Handbook of Logic in Artificial Intelligence and Logic Programming, vol. 5, pp. 235–324. Oxford University Press, Oxford (1998)
28. Baral, C., Son, T.: Relating theories of actions and reactive control. ETAI (Electronic Transactions of AI) 2(3-4), 211–271 (1998)
29. Costantini, S., Tocchio, A.: About declarative semantics of logic-based agent languages. In: Baldoni, M., Endriss, U., Omicini, A., Torroni, P. (eds.) DALT 2005. LNCS (LNAI), vol. 3904, pp. 106–123. Springer, Heidelberg (2006)
30. Costantini, S., Tocchio, A.: DALI: An architecture for intelligent logical agents. In: Proc. of the Int. Workshop on Architectures for Intelligent Theory-Based Agents (AITA 2008). AAAI Spring Symposium Series. AAAI Press, Stanford (2008)
31. Costantini, S., D'Alessandro, S., Lanti, D., Tocchio, A.: Dali web site, download of the interpreter (2010); With the contribution of many undergraduate and graduate students of Computer Science, L'Aquila
32. implementations, A.: Web references for some ASP solvers, ASSAT: http://assat.cs.ust.hk; Ccalc: http://www.cs.utexas.edu/users/tag/ccalc; Clasp: http://www.cs.uni-potsdam.de/clasp; Cmodels: http://www.cs.utexas.edu/users/tag/cmodels; DeReS and aspps: http://www.cs.uky.edu/ai/; DLV: http://www.dbai.tuwien.ac.at/proj/dlv; Smodels: http://www.tcs.hut.fi/Software/smodels
33. Ceri, S., Gottlob, G., Tanca, L.: What you always wanted to know about datalog (and never dared to ask). IEEE Transactions on Knowledge and Data Engineering 1(1), 146–166 (1989)
34. Dal Palù, A., Dovier, A., Pontelli, E., Rossi, G.: Answer set programming with constraints using lazy grounding. In: Hill, P.M., Warren, D.S. (eds.) ICLP 2009. LNCS, vol. 5649, pp. 115–129. Springer, Heidelberg (2009)
35. Lefèvre, C., Nicolas, P.: A first order forward chaining approach for answer set computing. In: Erdem, E., Lin, F., Schaub, T. (eds.) LPNMR 2009. LNCS, vol. 5753, pp. 196–208. Springer, Heidelberg (2009)
36. Gelfond, M., Lifschitz, V.: The stable model semantics for logic programming. In: Kowalski, R., Bowen, K. (eds.) Proc. of the 5th Intl. Conference and Symposium on Logic Programming, pp. 1070–1080. The MIT Press, Cambridge (1988)
37. Gelfond, M., Lifschitz, V.: Classical negation in logic programs and disjunctive databases. New Generation Computing 9, 365–385 (1991)

38. Costantini, S.: On the existence of stable models of non-stratified logic programs. J. on Theory and Practice of Logic Programming 6(1-2) (2006)

39. Oikarinen, E.: Modularity in Answer Set Programs. Doctoral dissertation, TKK Dissertations in Information and Computer Science TKK-ICS-D7, Helsinki University of Technology, Faculty of Information and Natural Sciences, Department of Information and Computer Science, Espoo, Finland (2008) ISBN 978-951-22-9581-4

40. Janhunen, T., Oikarinen, E., Tompits, H., Woltran, S.: Modularity aspects of disjunctive stable models. In: Baral, C., Brewka, G., Schlipf, J. (eds.) LPNMR 2007. LNCS (LNAI), vol. 4483, pp. 175–187. Springer, Heidelberg (2007)

41. Veith, H., Eiter, T., Eiter, T., Gottlob, G.: Modular logic programming and generalized quantifiers. In: Fuhrbach, U., Dix, J., Nerode, A. (eds.) LPNMR 1997. LNCS, vol. 1265, pp. 290–309. Springer, Heidelberg (1997)

42. Dao-Tran, M., Eiter, T., Fink, M., Krennwallner, T.: Modular nonmonotonic logic programming revisited. In: Hill, P.M., Warren, D.S. (eds.) ICLP 2009. LNCS, vol. 5649, pp. 145–159. Springer, Heidelberg (2009)

43. Tari, L., Baral, C., Anwar, S.: A language for modular answer set programming: Application to acc tournament scheduling. In: Proc. of the Int. Workshop on Answer Set Programming, ASP 2005. CEUR Workshop Proceedings, vol. 142, pp. 277–292 (2005)

44. Balduccini, M.: Modules and signature declarations for a-prolog: Progress report. In: Proc. of the Software Engineering for Answer Set Programming Workshop, SEA 2007 (2007)

45. Baral, C., Dzifcak, J., Takahashi, H.: Macros, macro calls and use of ensembles in modular answer set programming. In: Etalle, S., Truszczyński, M. (eds.) ICLP 2006. LNCS, vol. 4079, pp. 376–390. Springer, Heidelberg (2006)

46. Calimeri, F., Ianni, G.: Template programs for disjunctive logic programming: An operational semantics. AI Communications 19

47. Faber, W., Woltran, S.: Manifold answer-set programs for meta-reasoning. In: Erdem, E., Lin, F., Schaub, T. (eds.) LPNMR 2009. LNCS, vol. 5753, pp. 115–128. Springer, Heidelberg (2009)

48. Gelfond, M.: Logic programming and reasoning with incomplete information. Annals of Mathematics and Artificial Intelligence 12 (1994)

49. Zhang, Y.: Computational properties of epistemic logic programs. In: Principles of Knowledge Representation and Reasoning: Proc. of the 10th Int. Conference (KR 2006), pp. 308–317. AAAI Press, Menlo Park (2006)

50. Zhang, Y.: Epistemic reasoning in logic programs. In: Proc. of the 20th International Joint Conference on Artificial Intelligence, IJCAI 2007, pp. 647–652 (2007)

51. El-Khatib, O., Pontelli, E., Son, T.C.: Asp-prolog: a system for reasoning about answer set programs in prolog. In: Proc. of the 10th International Workshop on Non-Monotonic Reasoning, NMR 2004, pp. 155–163 (2004)

52. Eiter, T., Ianni, G., Schindlauer, R., Tompits, H.: A uniform integration of higher-order reasoning and external evaluations in answer-set programming. In: Proc. of the 19th International Joint Conference on Artificial Intelligence, IJCAI 2005, pp. 90–96 (2005)

53. Costantini, S., Lanzarone, G.A.: A metalogic programming language, pp. 218–233. The MIT Press, Cambridge (1989)

54. Barklund, J., Dell'Acqua, P., Costantini, S., Lanzarone, G.A.: Reflection principles in computational logic. J. of Logic and Computation 10(6), 743–786 (2000)

55. Eiter, T., Subrahmanian, V., Pick, G.: Heterogeneous active agents, i: Semantics. Artificial Intelligence 108(1-2), 179–255 (1999)

56. Luck, M., McBurney, P., Preist, C.: A manifesto for agent technology: Towards next generation computing. Autonomous Agents and Multi-Agent Sytems 9, 203–252 (2004)

57. Fisher, M., Bordini, R.H., Hirsch, B., Torroni, P.: Computational logics and agents: a road map of current technologies and future trends. Computational Intelligence Journal 23(1), 61–91 (2007)
58. Costantini, S., Tocchio, A., Toni, F., Tsintza, P.: A multi-layered general agent model. In: Basili, R., Pazienza, M.T. (eds.) AI*IA 2007. LNCS (LNAI), vol. 4733, pp. 121–132. Springer, Heidelberg (2007)
59. Kakas, A.C., Mancarella, P., Sadri, F., Stathis, K., Toni, F.: Declarative agent control. In: Leite, J., Torroni, P. (eds.) CLIMA 2004. LNCS (LNAI), vol. 3487, pp. 96–110. Springer, Heidelberg (2005)
60. Kowalski, R., Sadri, F.: Towards a unified agent architecture that combines rationality with reactivity. In: Pedreschi, D., Zaniolo, C. (eds.) LID 1996. LNCS, vol. 1154, pp. 135–149. Springer, Heidelberg (1996)
61. Costantini, S., Dell'Acqua, P., Tocchio, A.: Expressing preferences declaratively in logic-based agent languages. In: McCarthy, J. (ed.) Proc. of Commonsense 2007, the 8th International Symposium on Logical Formalizations of Commonsense Reasoning. AAAI Spring Symposium Series, AAAI Press (2007) a Special Event in Honor, Stanford University (March 2007)
62. Gabbay, D.M., Smets, P.: Handbook of Defeasible Reasoning and Uncertainty Management Systems. Kluwer Academic Publishers, Dordrecht (2000); edited collection
63. Blackburn, P., van Benthem, J., Wolter, F.: Handbook of Modal Logic. Elsevier, Amsterdam (2006); collection of contributions
64. Van Gelder, A., Ross, K.A., Schlipf, J.: The well-founded semantics for general logic programs. Journal of the ACM (3) (1990)
65. Bowen, K.A., Kowalski, R.A.: Amalgamating language and metalanguage in logic programming. In: Clark, K.L., Tärnlund, S.Å. (eds.) Logic Programming, pp. 153–172. Academic Press, London (1982)
66. Marek, V.W., Truszczyński, M.: Autoepistemic logic. Journal of the ACM 38(3), 587–618 (1991)
67. Marek, V.W., Truszczyński, M.: Computing intersection of autoepistemic expansions. In: Proceedings of the First International Workshop on Logic Programming and Non Monotonic Reasoning, pp. 35–70. The MIT Press, Cambridge (1991)
68. Brewka, G., Eiter, T.: Equilibria in heterogeneous nonmonotonic multi-context systems. In: Proc. of the 22nd Conference on Artificial Intelligence, AAAI 2007, pp. 385–390 (2007)
69. Nisar, M.A.: Integration of answer set programming modules with logical agents. Master's thesis, University of the Punjab, Lahore, Pakistan (2010); Supervisor Prof. Stefania Costantini, University of L'Aquila, Italy
70. Eiter, T., Faber, W., Leone, N., Pfeifer, G.: Declarative problem-solving using the DLV system, pp. 79–103. Kluwer Academic Publishers, USA (2000)

# First-Order Encodings for
# Modular Nonmonotonic Datalog Programs*

Minh Dao-Tran, Thomas Eiter, Michael Fink, and Thomas Krennwallner

Institut für Informationssysteme, Technische Universität Wien
Favoritenstraße 9–11, 1040 Vienna, Austria
{dao,eiter,fink,tkren}@kr.tuwien.ac.at

**Abstract.** Recently Modular Nonmonotonic Logic Programs (MLP) have been
introduced which incorporate a call-by-value mechanism and allow for unrestricted calls between modules, including mutual and self recursion, as an approach to provide module constructs akin to those in conventional programming
in Nonmonotonic Logic Programming under Answer Set Semantics. This paper considers MLPs in a Datalog setting and provides characterizations of their
answers sets in terms of classical (Herbrand) models of a first-order formula,
extending a line of research for ordinary logic programs. To this end, we lift
the well-known loop formulas method to MLPs, and we also consider the recent
ordered completion approach that avoids explicit construction of loop formulas
using auxiliary predicates. Independent of computational perspectives, the novel
characterizations widen our understanding of MLPs and they may prove useful
for semantic investigations.

## 1 Introduction

Since the early days of Datalog, modularity aspects have been recognized as an important issue, and already the seminal notion of stratification [1] builds on an evaluation of
subprograms in an ordered way. This has been later largely elaborated to notions like
modular stratification [20] and XY-stratification incorporated in the $\mathcal{LDL}$++ system [2],
and has been generalized to a syntactic notions of modularity for disjunctive Datalog
programs [7,9] that, in the context of non-monotonic logic programming, has been independently found as Splitting Sets [18]. More recently, research on modularity where
in contrast subprograms may mutually depend on each other has been intensified, with
DLP-functions [15] being the most prominent example to provide a Gaifman-Shapiro-
style module architecture [13].

However the above concepts do not cater a module concept as familiar in conventional imperative and object-oriented languages, where procedures come with parameters that are passed on during the evaluation. To provide support for this, [8] developed
modular logic programs, based on an extension of logic programs with genuine generalized quantifiers, where modules can receive input that is passed on in a call-by-value
mode, in addition to the usual call-by-reference access to atoms in other modules. Limitations of this seminal approach have been recently overcome with an generalized and

---

* This research has been supported by the Austrian Science Fund (FWF) project P20841 and the
Vienna Science and Technology Fund (WWTF) project ICT-08 20.

O. de Moor et al. (Eds.): Datalog 2010, LNCS 6702, pp. 59–77, 2011.

semantically refined notion of Modular Nonmonotonic Logic Programs (MLPs) in [6] under the answer set semantics [14].

Roughly, an MLP is a system $\mathbf{P} = (m_1, \ldots, m_n)$, of modules, where each module $m_i = (P_i[\mathbf{q_i}], R_i)$ has a module name $P_i$ with an associated list $\mathbf{q_i}$ of formal input atoms, and an associated set of rules $R_i$ (the "implementation"). A module $m_i$ can access another module $m_j$ using *module atoms* (in the body of a rule in $R_i$) of the form $P_j[\mathbf{p}].o$. Intuitively, the module atom evaluates to true if, on input of the atoms in $\mathbf{p}$ to the module $P_j$, the atom $o$ will be true in $P_j$. Such programs allow unrestricted cyclic calls between modules; they can be seen as a generalization of DLP-functions from propositional to Datalog programs that allow for positive cyclic calls between modules (including recursion), and provide a call-by-value mechanism.

For example, the following MLP $\mathbf{P} = (m_1, m_2, m_3)$ recursively checks whether the number of facts over predicate $q$ in the main module $m_1$, which has no input ($\mathbf{q_1}$ is empty) and implementation $R_1 = \{q(a).\ q(b).\ ok \leftarrow P_2[q].even.\}$, is even. Intuitively, $m_1$ calls $m_2$ with a rule for the check, and assigns the result to $ok$. The module $m_2$ is mutual recursive with module $m_3$. They have the formal inputs $\mathbf{q_2} = q_2$ and $\mathbf{q_3} = q_3$, respectively, and the implementations

$$
R_2 = \left\{
\begin{array}{l}
q_2'(X) \leftarrow q_2(X), q_2(Y), \\
\qquad\quad \text{not } q_2'(Y), X \neq Y. \\
skip_2 \leftarrow q_2(X), \text{not } q_2'(X). \\
even \leftarrow \text{not } skip_2. \\
even \leftarrow skip_2, P_3[q_2'].odd.
\end{array}
\right\}
,\quad
R_3 = \left\{
\begin{array}{l}
q_3'(X) \leftarrow q_3(X), q_3(Y), \\
\qquad\quad \text{not } q_3'(Y), X \neq Y. \\
skip_3 \leftarrow q_3(X), \text{not } q_3'(X). \\
odd \leftarrow skip_3, P_2[q_3'].even.
\end{array}
\right\}
.
$$

A call to $m_2$ 'returns' *even*, if either the input $q_2$ to $m_2$ is empty (as then $skip_2$ is false), or the call of $m_3$ with $q_2'$ resulting from $q_2$ by randomly removing one element (then $skip_2$ is true) returns *odd*. Module $m_3$ returns *odd* for input $q_3$, if a call to $m_2$ with $q_3'$ analogously constructed from $q_3$ returns *even*. In any answer set of $\mathbf{P}$, $ok$ is true.

In this paper, we further the work on MLPs and turn to characterizing of answer sets in terms of classical models, in line with recent research in Answer Set Programming. To this end, we first explore the notion of *loop formulas* to MLPs. Lin and Zhao [19] first used loop formulas to characterize the answer sets of normal, i.e., disjunction-free, propositional logic programs by the models of a propositional formula built of the Clark completion [5] and of additional formulas for each positive loop in the dependency graph of the program. They built on this result developing the ASP solver ASSAT, which uses a SAT solver for answer sets computation [19]. The loop formula characterization has subsequently been extended to disjunctive logic programs [16], and to general propositional theories under a generalized notion of answer set [12]. In the latter work, the notion of a loop has been adapted to include trivial loops (singletons) in order to recast Clark's completion as loop formulas. Besides their impact on ASP solver development, loop formulas are a viable means for the study of semantic properties of ASP programs, as they allow to resort to classical logic for characterization. For instance, in the realm of modular logic programming, loop formulas have recently been fruitfully extended to DLP-functions [15], simplifying some major proofs.

The expedient properties of MLPs, however, render a generalization of loop formulas more involved. Due to the module input mechanism, it is necessary to keep track of different module instantiations. Furthermore, because of unlimited recursion in addition to loops that occur inside a module, loops across module boundaries, i.e., when modules refer to each other by module atoms, have to be captured properly. To cope with this requirements,

- we adapt Clark's completion for module atoms w.r.t. different module instantiations;
- we provide a refined version of the positive dependency graph for an MLP, the *modular dependency graph*, and *cyclic instantiation signature*: the combination then relates module instantiations with the atoms of a module;
- based on it, we define *modular loops* and their external support formulas; and
- eventually, we define *modular loop formulas*, and show that the conjunction of all modular loop formulas for an MLP characterizes the answer sets of **P** in its (Herbrand) models.

Furthermore, the definition of the MLP semantics in terms of the FLP-reduct [11] and the underlying principal idea of loop formulas requires us to restrict module atoms under negation to be monotonic. This is often not a limitation, since negated module atoms may be easily replaced by unnegated ones using a simple rewriting technique (e.g., for stratified program parts). Intuitively, the restriction seems to be the trade off for the benign property that under the FLP-reduct, answer sets of a MLP – even with nonmonotonic module atoms – are always minimal models of the program. The latter would not be the case if they were defined under the traditional GL-reduct [14], for which loop formulas have been developed.

Second, we explore the recent approach of [3] to modify the Clark completion in order to characterize answer set semantics of non-monotonic logic programs with finite Herbrand universes but without using loop formulas explicitly. The idea is to introduce predicates of the form $T_{qp}(\mathbf{y}, \mathbf{x})$ which intuitively holds when $q(\mathbf{y})$ is used to derive $p(\mathbf{x})$, and to respect a derivation order; the completion is allowed to take effect only if no positive loop is present, which is ensured by adding $T_{qp}(\mathbf{y}, \mathbf{x}) \wedge \neg T_{pq}(\mathbf{x}, \mathbf{y})$ in the completion of rules with head $p(\mathbf{x})$ and $q(\mathbf{y})$ in the positive body; for this to work, it must be ensured that $T_{qp}$ respects transitive derivations, i.e., the composition of $T_{qr}$ and $T_{rp}$ must be contained in $T_{qp}$. The resulting translation is called *ordered completion*.

An advantage of this approach is that, at the cost of fresh (existential) predicates, constructing the (possible exponentially) many loop formulas can be avoided, while answer sets may be extracted from the (Herbrand) models of a first-order sentence, which may be fed into a suitable theorem prover. This similarly applies to MLPs, where unrestricted call-by-value however leads to an unavoidable blowup, which may be avoided by resorting to higher-order logic. Independent of computational perspectives, the novel characterizations widen our understanding of MLPs and they may prove, similarly as those in [15], useful for semantic investigations.

## 2   Preliminaries

We first recall syntax and semantics of modular nonmonotonic logic programs [6].

**Syntax.** Let $\mathcal{V}$ be a vocabulary $\mathcal{C}$, $\mathcal{P}$, $\mathcal{X}$, and $\mathcal{M}$ of mutually disjoint sets whose elements are called of *constants, predicate, variable,* and *module names*, respectively, where each $p \in \mathcal{P}$ has a fixed associated arity $n \geq 0$, and each module name in $\mathcal{M}$ has a fixed associated list $\mathbf{q} = q_1, \ldots, q_k$ $(k \geq 0)$ of predicate names $q_i \in \mathcal{P}$ (the formal input parameters). Unless stated otherwise, elements from $\mathcal{X}$ (resp., $\mathcal{C} \cup \mathcal{P}$) are denoted with first letter in upper case (resp., lower case).

Elements from $\mathcal{C} \cup \mathcal{X}$ are called *terms*. An ordinary atom (simply atom) has the form $p(t_1, \ldots, t_n)$, where $p \in \mathcal{P}$ and $t_1, \ldots, t_n$ are terms; $n \geq 0$ is its *arity*. A *module atom* has the form $P[p_1, \ldots, p_k].o(t_1, \ldots, t_n)$, where $P \in \mathcal{M}$ is a module name with associated $\mathbf{q}$, $p_1, \ldots, p_k$ is a list of predicate names $p_i \in \mathcal{P}$, called *module input list*, such that $p_i$ has the arity of $q_i$ in $\mathbf{q}$, and $o \in \mathcal{P}$ is a predicate name with arity $n$ such that for the list of terms $t_1, \ldots, t_n$, $o(t_1, \ldots, t_n)$ is an ordinary atom. Intuitively, a module atom provides a way for deciding the truth value of a ground atom $o(\mathbf{c})$ in a program $P$ depending on the truth of a set of input atoms.

A *normal rule* $r$ (or rule for short) is of the form

$$\alpha \leftarrow \beta_1, \ldots, \beta_m, \text{not } \beta_{m+1}, \ldots, \text{not } \beta_n \quad (m, n \geq 0), \tag{1}$$

where $\alpha$ is an atom and each $\beta_j$ is an ordinary or a module atom. We define $H(r) = \{\alpha\}$ and $B(r) = B^+(r) \cup B^-(r)$, where $B^+(r) = \{\beta_1, \ldots, \beta_m\}$ and $B^-(r) = \{\beta_{m+1}, \ldots, \beta_n\}$. For $\star \in \{+, -\}$ we let $B_m^\star(r)$ and $B_o^\star(r)$ be the set of module and ordinary atoms that appear in $B^\star(r)$, respectively. If $B(r) = \emptyset$ and $H(r) \neq \emptyset$, then $r$ is a *fact*; $r$ is *ordinary*, if it does not contain module atoms.

We now formally define the syntax of modules and normal MLPs. A *module* is a pair $m = (P[\mathbf{q}], R)$, where $P \in \mathcal{M}$ with associated input $\mathbf{q}$, and $R$ is a finite set of normal rules. It is either a *main module* (then $|\mathbf{q}| = 0$) or a *library module*, and is *ordinary* iff all rules in $R$ are ordinary. We omit empty $[]$ from (main) modules if unambiguous.

A *normal modular logic program (MLP)* is a tuple $\mathbf{P} = (m_1, \ldots, m_n), n \geq 1$, where all $m_i$ are modules and at least one is a main module, where $\mathcal{M} = \{P_1, \ldots, P_n\}$.

*Example 1.* Let $m_1 = (P_1[], R_1)$ with $R_1 = \{p \leftarrow P_2[p].r\}$ and $m_2 = (P_2[q], R_2)$ with $R_2 = \{r \leftarrow q\}$. Then $\mathbf{P} = (m_1, m_2)$ is a normal MLP with the main module $m_1$.

*Example 2.* Let $m_1 = (P_1[], R_1)$ with $R_1 = \{p_1 \leftarrow P_2.p_2\}$ and $m_2 = (P_2[], R_2)$ with $R_2 = \{p_2 \leftarrow P_1.p_1\}$. Putting both modules together, we get the MLP $\mathbf{P} = (m_1, m_2)$ with the main modules $m_1, m_2$.

W.l.o.g, in the rest of this paper, we assume that for all $i \neq j$, the atoms in $m_i$ and $m_j$ are distinct; thus, $\mathcal{P} = \bigcup_{i=1}^{n} \mathcal{P}_i$ where all $\mathcal{P}_i$ are disjoint.

**Semantics.** The semantics of MLPs is defined in terms of Herbrand interpretations and grounding as customary in traditional logic programming and ASP. The *Herbrand base* w.r.t. vocabulary $\mathcal{V}$, $HB_\mathcal{V}$, is the set of all ground ordinary and module atoms that can be built using $\mathcal{C}$, $\mathcal{P}$ and $\mathcal{M}$; if $\mathcal{V}$ is implicit from an MLP $\mathbf{P}$, it is the *Herbrand base of* $\mathbf{P}$ and denoted by $HB_\mathbf{P}$. The grounding of a rule $r$ is the set $gr(r)$ of all ground instances of $r$ w.r.t. $\mathcal{C}$; the grounding of rule set $R$ is $gr(R) = \bigcup_{r \in R} gr(r)$, and the one of a module $m$, $gr(m)$, is defined by replacing the rules in $R(m)$ by $gr(R(m))$; the grounding of an MLP $\mathbf{P}$ is $gr(\mathbf{P})$, which is formed by grounding each module $m_i$ of $\mathbf{P}$. The semantics of an arbitrary MLP $\mathbf{P}$ is given in terms of $gr(\mathbf{P})$.

Let $S \subseteq HB_\mathbf{P}$ be any set of atoms. For any list of predicates $\mathbf{p} = p_1, \ldots, p_k$ and $\mathbf{q} = q_1, \ldots, q_k$, we use the notation $S|_\mathbf{p} = \{p_i(\mathbf{c}) \in S \mid 1 \leq i \leq k\}$ and $S|_\mathbf{p}^\mathbf{q} = \{q_i(\mathbf{c}) \mid p_i(\mathbf{c}) \in S, 1 \leq i \leq k\}$.

For a module name $P \in \mathcal{M}$ with associated formal input $\mathbf{q}$ and $S \subseteq HB_\mathbf{P}|_\mathbf{q}$, we say that $P[S]$ is a *value call with input* $S$; we denote by $VC(\mathbf{P})$ the set of all such $P[S]$ for $\mathbf{P}$. Intuitively, $VC(\mathbf{P})$ names all instances of modules in $\mathbf{P}$, which we thus also use as an index set. A *rule base* is an (indexed) tuple $\mathbf{R} = (R_{P[S]} \mid P[S] \in VC(\mathbf{P}))$ of sets $R_{P[S]}$ of rules. For a module $m_i = (P_i[\mathbf{q_i}], R_i)$ from $\mathbf{P}$, its *instantiation with* $S \subseteq HB_\mathbf{P}|_{\mathbf{q_i}}$, is $I_\mathbf{P}(P_i[S]) = R_i \cup S$. For an MLP $\mathbf{P}$, its *instantiation* is the rule base $I(\mathbf{P}) = (I_\mathbf{P}(P_i[S]) \mid P_i[S] \in VC(\mathbf{P}))$.

We next define (Herbrand) interpretations and models of MLPs.

**Definition 1 (model).** *An interpretation* $\mathbf{M}$ *of an MLP* $\mathbf{P}$ *is an (indexed) tuple* $(M_{P_i[S]} \mid P_i[S] \in VC(\mathbf{P}))$, *where all* $M_{P_i[S]} \subseteq HB_\mathbf{P}$ *contain only ordinary atoms. To ease notation, we also write* $M_i/S$ *for* $M_{P_i[S]}$. *We say that* $\mathbf{M}$ *is a* model *of*

- *an atom* $\alpha$ *at* $P_i[S]$, *denoted* $\mathbf{M}, P_i[S] \models \alpha$, *iff (i)* $\alpha \in M_i/S$ *when* $\alpha$ *is ordinary, and (ii)* $o(\mathbf{c}) \in M_k/((M_i/S)|_\mathbf{p}^\mathbf{q_k})$, *when* $\alpha = P_k[\mathbf{p}].o(\mathbf{c})$ *is a module atom;*
- *a rule* $r$ *at* $P_i[S]$ *(*$\mathbf{M}, P_i[S] \models r$*), iff* $\mathbf{M}, P_i[S] \models H(r)$ *or* $\mathbf{M}, P_i[S] \not\models B(r)$, *where (i)* $\mathbf{M}, P_i[S] \models H(r)$, *iff* $\mathbf{M}, P_i[S] \models \alpha$ *for* $H(r) = \{\alpha\}$, *and (ii)* $\mathbf{M}, P_i[S] \models B(r)$, *iff* $\mathbf{M}, P_i[S] \models \alpha$ *for all* $\alpha \in B^+(r)$ *and* $\mathbf{M}, P_i[S] \not\models \alpha$ *for all* $\alpha \in B^-(r)$;
- *a set of rules* $R$ *at* $P_i[S]$ *(*$\mathbf{M}, P_i[S] \models R$*) iff* $\mathbf{M}, P_i[S] \models r$ *for all* $r \in R$;
- *a rule base* $\mathbf{R}$ *(*$\mathbf{M} \models \mathbf{R}$*) iff* $\mathbf{M}, P_i[S] \models R_{P_i[S]}$ *for all* $P_i[S] \in VC(\mathbf{P})$.

*Finally,* $\mathbf{M}$ *is a* model *of* $\mathbf{P}$, *denoted* $\mathbf{M} \models \mathbf{P}$, *iff* $\mathbf{M} \models I(\mathbf{P})$ *in case* $\mathbf{P}$ *is ground resp.* $\mathbf{M} \models gr(\mathbf{P})$, *if* $\mathbf{P}$ *is nonground. An MLP* $\mathbf{P}$ *is* satisfiable, *iff it has a model.*

For any interpretations $\mathbf{M}$ and $\mathbf{M}'$ of $\mathbf{P}$, we define $\mathbf{M} \leq \mathbf{M}'$, iff $M_i/S \subseteq M_i'/S$ for every $P_i[S] \in VC(\mathbf{P})$, and $\mathbf{M} < \mathbf{M}'$, iff $\mathbf{M} \neq \mathbf{M}'$ and $\mathbf{M} \leq \mathbf{M}'$. A model $\mathbf{M}$ of $\mathbf{P}$ (resp., a rule base $\mathbf{R}$) is *minimal*, if $\mathbf{P}$ (resp., $\mathbf{R}$) has no model $\mathbf{M}'$ such that $\mathbf{M}' < \mathbf{M}$.

We next recall answer sets for MLPs. To focus on relevant modules, we use a *call graph*, which intuitively captures the relationship between module instances and potential module calls. The nodes correspond to module instances and edges to presumptive calls from one instance to others; edge labels distinguish different syntactical calls. Given an interpretation $\mathbf{M}$, one can determine the actual calls, starting from the main modules, following the edges whose labels match with the atoms in $\mathbf{M}$. This leads then to the *relevant call graph* with respect to $\mathbf{M}$.

**Definition 2 (call graph).** *The* call graph *of an MLP* $\mathbf{P}$ *is a labeled digraph* $CG_\mathbf{P} = (V, E, l)$ *with vertex set* $V = VC(\mathbf{P})$ *and an edge* $e$ *from* $P_i[S]$ *to* $P_k[T]$ *in* $E$ *iff* $P_k[\mathbf{p}].o(\mathbf{t})$ *occurs in* $R_i$, *and* $e$ *has the input list* $\mathbf{p}$ *in its label, i.e.,* $\mathbf{p} \in l(e)$. *Given an interpretation* $\mathbf{M}$ *of* $\mathbf{P}$, *the* relevant call graph $CG_\mathbf{P}(\mathbf{M}) = (V', E')$ *of* $\mathbf{P}$ *w.r.t.* $\mathbf{M}$ *is the smallest subgraph of* $CG_\mathbf{P}$ *such that* $E'$ *contains all edges from* $P_i[S]$ *to* $P_k[T]$ *of* $CG_\mathbf{P}$ *where* $(M_i/S)|_{l(e)}^{\mathbf{q_k}} = T$ *and* $V'$ *contains all* $P_i[S]$ *that are main module instantiations or induced by* $E'$; *any such* $P_i[S]$ *is called* relevant *w.r.t.* $\mathbf{M}$.

For instance, the call graphs of the MLPs in Example 1 and 2 are shown in Fig. 1a and 1b, respectively.

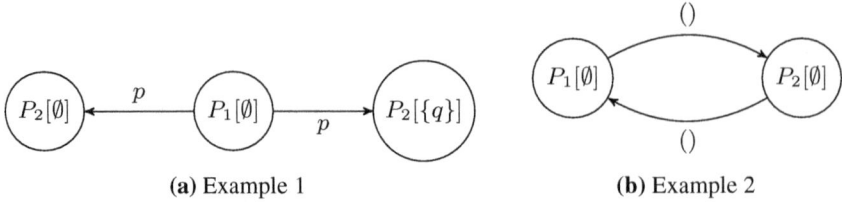

(a) Example 1                                    (b) Example 2

**Fig. 1.** Call graphs

For answer sets of an MLP **P**, we use a reduct of the instantiated program as customary in ASP; for reasons discussed in [6], we use the FLP reduct [11] rather than the traditional Gelfond-Lifschitz reduct [14]. As **P** might have inconsistent module instantiations, which compromises the existence of an answer set of **P**, we contextualize reducts and answer sets. Let $V(G)$ and $E(G)$ denote the vertex and edge set of a graph $G$, respectively.

**Definition 3 (context-based reduct).** *A* context *for an interpretation* **M** *of an MLP* **P** *is any set* $C \subseteq VC(\mathbf{P})$ *such that* $V(CG_{\mathbf{P}}(\mathbf{M})) \subseteq C$. *The* reduct of **P** *at* $P[S]$ *w.r.t.* **M** *and* $C$, *denoted* $f\mathbf{P}(P[S])^{\mathbf{M},C}$, *is the rule set* $I_{gr(\mathbf{P})}(P[S])$ *from which, if* $P[S] \in C$, *all rules* $r$ *such that* $\mathbf{M}, P[S] \not\models B(r)$ *are removed. The* reduct of **P** *w.r.t.* **M** *and* $C$ *is* $f\mathbf{P}^{\mathbf{M},C} = (f\mathbf{P}(P[S])^{\mathbf{M},C} \mid P[S] \in VC(\mathbf{P}))$.

That is, outside $C$ the module instantiations of **P** remain untouched, while inside $C$ the FLP-reduct [11] is applied.

**Definition 4 (answer set).** *Let* **M** *be an interpretation of a ground MLP* **P**. *Then* **M** *is an* answer set *of* **P** *w.r.t. a context* $C$ *for* **M**, *iff* **M** *is a minimal model of* $f\mathbf{P}^{\mathbf{M},C}$.

In particular, if $\mathbf{P} = (m_1)$ consists of a single module $m_1$ with no calls to itself, the answer sets of **P** coincide with the answer sets of $R_1$.

Note that $C$ is a parameter that allows to select a degree of overall-stability for answer sets of **P**. The minimal context $C = V(CG_{\mathbf{P}}(\mathbf{M}))$ is the relevant call graph of **P**. For the rest of this paper, we assume that $C = VC(\mathbf{P})$, i.e., all module instances have answer sets (see Section 7 for further discussion).

*Example 3.* The program in Example 1 has the single answer set $(M_1/\emptyset := \emptyset, M_2/\emptyset := \emptyset, M_2/\{q\} := \{r, q\})$ while the program in Example 2 has the single answer set $(M_1/\emptyset := \emptyset, M_2/\emptyset := \emptyset)$.

A module atom $\beta = P_k[\mathbf{p}].o(\mathbf{c})$ that appears in a rule in $m_i = (P_i[\mathbf{q}_i], R_i)$ in an MLP **P** is *monotonic*, if for all interpretations **M**, **N** of **P** such that $\mathbf{M} \leq \mathbf{N}$ and $\mathbf{M} \neq \mathbf{N}$, and all $P_i[S] \in VC(\mathbf{P})$, we have that $\mathbf{M}, P_i[S] \models \beta$ implies $\mathbf{N}, P_i[S] \models \beta$.

In the sequel, we will characterize the answer sets of MLPs via loop formulas and program completion where all module atoms under negation are monotonic. Such characterizations consist of two parts: (1) the completion, which singles out classical models, which is studied in Section 3; (2) the loop formulas, which take care of minimality (foundedness) aspects; this will be considered in Section 4. Alternatively, the completion can be made ordered, which we do in Section 5.

## 3   Program Completion for MLPs

We start with adapting the classical Clark completion [5] with module atoms. The intuition behind this adaption is to replace every module atom $\beta = P_k[\mathbf{p}].o(\mathbf{c})$ in $m_i$ by a formula $\mu(m_i, \beta, S)$ which selects, based on the value of the input atoms $\mathbf{p}$ in the value call $P_i[S]$, the "right" instance $P_k[T]$ of $P_k$ and retrieves the value of $o(\mathbf{c})$ in it.

Given a set $S \subseteq HB_\mathbf{P}$ of ordinary atoms, we assume that $S$ is enumerated, i.e., $S = \{a_1, \ldots, a_n\}$ where $n = |S|$. We identify subsets $B$ of $S$ with their characteristic function $\chi^B \colon S \to \{0, 1\}$ such that $\chi^B(a) = 1$ iff $a \in B$.

For any ordinary atom $a \in HB_\mathbf{P}$ and any set of ordinary atoms $A$, let $a^A$ denote a fresh atom, and for any set $B \subseteq HB_\mathbf{P}$ of ordinary atoms, let $B^A = \{a^A \mid a \in B\}$. Next, we define support rules. Intuitively, support rules are used to define the completion of an atom. The *support rules* of a set of rules $R$ w.r.t. an ordinary atom $\alpha \in HB_\mathbf{P}$ is

$$SR(\alpha, R) = \{r \in R \mid H(r) = \{\alpha\}\} \ .$$

Let $\neg.A = \{\neg a \mid a \in A\}$ and, as usual, $\bigvee F = \bigvee_{f \in F} f$ and $\bigwedge F = \bigwedge_{f \in F} f$ (note that $\bigvee \emptyset = \bot$ and $\bigwedge \emptyset = \top$).

Then, for every module atom $\beta = P_k[\mathbf{p}].o(\mathbf{c}) \in HB_\mathbf{P}$ from some module $m_i = (P_i[\mathbf{q_i}], R_i)$ (where $P_k$ has formal input $\mathbf{q_k} = q_{k,1}, \ldots, q_{k,n_k}$) and $S \subseteq HB_\mathbf{P}|_{\mathbf{q_i}}$, let

$$\beta_{m_i, S, T} = \bigwedge_{\chi^T(q_{k,j}(\mathbf{c}))=1} p_j^S(\mathbf{c}) \wedge \bigwedge_{\chi^T(q_{k,j}(\mathbf{c}))=0} \neg p_j^S(\mathbf{c})$$

and

$$\mu(m_i, \beta, S) = \bigvee_{T \subseteq HB_\mathbf{P}|_{\mathbf{q_k}}} \left( \beta_{m_i, S, T} \wedge o^T(\mathbf{c}) \right) \ ,$$

$$\bar{\mu}(m_i, \beta, S) = \bigvee_{T \subseteq HB_\mathbf{P}|_{\mathbf{q_k}}} \left( \beta_{m_i, S, T} \wedge \neg o^T(\mathbf{c}) \right) \ .$$

We can now define the modular completion, which relates instantiations of the rules in modules to propositional formulas.

**Definition 5 (Modular Completion).** *Let $r$ be a rule from module $m_i = (P_i[\mathbf{q_i}], R_i)$, and let $S \subseteq HB_\mathbf{P}|_{\mathbf{q_i}}$. Then*

$$\gamma(m_i, r, S) = \bigwedge B_o^+(r)^S \wedge \bigwedge_{\beta \in B_m^+(r)} \mu(m_i, \beta, S) \wedge \tag{2}$$

$$\bigwedge \neg.B_o^-(r)^S \wedge \bigwedge_{\beta \in B_m^-(r)} \bar{\mu}(m_i, \beta, S) \supset H(r)^S \ ,$$

*and*

$$\sigma(m_i, r, S) = \bigwedge B_o^+(r)^S \wedge \bigwedge_{\beta \in B_m^+(r)} \mu(m_i, \beta, S) \wedge \tag{3}$$

$$\bigwedge \neg.B_o^-(r)^S \wedge \bigwedge_{\beta \in B_m^-(r)} \bar{\mu}(m_i, \beta, S) \ ,$$

*For a set of rules $R$, we let $\sigma(m_i, R, S) = \bigvee_{r \in R} \sigma(m_i, r, S)$ and $\gamma(m_i, R, S) = \bigwedge_{r \in R} \gamma(m_i, r, S)$.*

*For any value call $P_i[S]$ of module $m_i = (P_i[\mathbf{q_i}], R_i)$, $\mathbf{q_i} = q_{i,1}, \ldots, q_{i,n_i}$, in $\mathbf{P}$, let*

$$\gamma(\mathbf{P}, P_i[S]) = \gamma(m_i, R_i, S) \wedge \bigwedge_{\chi^S(q_{i,j}(\mathbf{c}))=1} q_{i,j}^S(\mathbf{c}) , \tag{4}$$

$$\sigma(\mathbf{P}, P_i[S]) = \bigwedge_{r \in R_i, a \in H(r)} a^S \supset \sigma(m_i, SR(a, R_i), S) \tag{5}$$

*and*

$$\gamma(\mathbf{P}) = \bigwedge_{P_i[S] \in VC(\mathbf{P})} \gamma(\mathbf{P}, P_i[S]) ,$$

$$\sigma(\mathbf{P}) = \bigwedge_{P_i[S] \in VC(\mathbf{P})} \sigma(\mathbf{P}, P_i[S]) .$$

*Example 4.* Continuing with $\mathbf{P}$ of Example 1, we get the following formulas (here, $S_1 = \emptyset$, $S_2^0 = \emptyset$ and $S_2^1 = \{q\}$):

- $\gamma(\mathbf{P}, P_1[\emptyset]) = (\neg p^{S_1} \wedge r^{S_2^0}) \vee (p^{S_1} \wedge r^{S_2^1}) \supset p^{S_1}$,
- $\gamma(\mathbf{P}, P_2[\emptyset]) = q^{S_2^0} \supset r^{S_2^0}$,
- $\gamma(\mathbf{P}, P_2[\{q\}]) = \left(q^{S_2^1} \supset r^{S_2^1}\right) \wedge q^{S_2^1}$,
- $\sigma(\mathbf{P}, P_1[\emptyset]) = p^{S_1} \supset (\neg p^{S_1} \wedge r^{S_2^0}) \vee (p^{S_1} \wedge r^{S_2^1})$,
- $\sigma(\mathbf{P}, P_2[\emptyset]) = r^{S_2^0} \supset q^{S_2^0}$,
- $\sigma(\mathbf{P}, P_2[\{q\}]) = r^{S_2^1} \supset q^{S_2^1}$.

The conjunction of the first three formulas yields $\gamma(\mathbf{P})$, and the last three give us $\sigma(\mathbf{P})$.

*Example 5.* For the MLP $\mathbf{P}$ in Example 2, we get the following formulas ($S = \emptyset$):

- $\gamma(\mathbf{P}) = p_2^S \supset p_1^S \wedge p_1^S \supset p_2^S$
- $\sigma(\mathbf{P}) = p_1^S \supset p_2^S \wedge p_2^S \supset p_1^S$

The formula $\gamma(\mathbf{P})$ now captures the (classical) models of $\mathbf{P}$.

**Lemma 1.** *The models of $\gamma(\mathbf{P})$ correspond 1-1 to the models of $\mathbf{P}$. That is, (i) if $M \models \gamma(\mathbf{P})$, then $\mathbf{M} \models \mathbf{P}$, where $M_i/S = \{p(\mathbf{c}) \in HB_\mathbf{P} \mid p^S(\mathbf{c}) \in M \wedge p \in \mathcal{P}_i\}$, for all $P_i[S]$, and (ii) if $\mathbf{M} \models \mathbf{P}$, then $M \models \gamma(\mathbf{P})$, where $M = \bigcup_{P_i[S]} (M_i/S)^S$.*

*Proof (sketch).* (i) Suppose $M \models \gamma(\mathbf{P})$, and let $\mathbf{M}$ as described. We need to show that $\mathbf{M}, P_i[S] \models r$ for each $r \in I_\mathbf{P}(P_i[S]) = R_i \cup S$ and $P_i[S] \in VC(\mathbf{P})$. If $r$ is a fact $q_j(\mathbf{c})$ for a formal input parameter $q_j$ of $P_i[\mathbf{q}]$, then $q_j(\mathbf{c}) \in S$ and, by formula (4), $M \models q_j^S(\mathbf{c})$; hence, $q_j(\mathbf{c}) \in M_i/S$, and thus $\mathbf{M}, P_i[S] \models r$. Otherwise, $r \in R_i$. As $M \models \gamma(m_i, R_i, S)$, we have that $M$ satisfies the formula (2). By construction, for each ordinary atom $\beta$ in $r$, we have $M \models \beta^S$ iff $\mathbf{M}, P_i[S] \models \beta$; furthermore, $M \models \mu(m_i, \beta, S)$ for $P_k[\mathbf{p}].o(\mathbf{c})$ iff $M \models o^T(\mathbf{c})$, where $T \subseteq HB_\mathbf{P}|_{\mathbf{q_k}}$ is the unique set $T$ such that $M \models \bigwedge_j (p_j^S(\mathbf{c}) \equiv q_{i,j}^T(\mathbf{c}))$. That is, $M \models \mu(m_i, \beta, S)$ iff $\mathbf{M}, P_i[S] \models \beta$. Hence, it follows that $\mathbf{M}, P_i[S] \models r$.

(ii) Suppose $\mathbf{M} \models \mathbf{P}$, and let $M = \bigcup_{P_i[S]} (M_i/S)^S$. To show that $M \models \gamma(\mathbf{P})$, we must show that $M \models \gamma(\mathbf{P}, P_i[S])$ for all $P_i[S]$. As $S \subseteq I_{\mathbf{P}}(P_i[S])$ and $\mathbf{M}, P_i[S] \models I_{\mathbf{P}}(P_i[S])$, all conjuncts $q_j^S$ (representing the formal input) in $\gamma(\mathbf{P}, P_i[S])$ are satisfied by $M$; thus it remains to show $M \models \gamma(m_i, R_i, S)$, i.e., $M \models \gamma(m_i, r, S)$ for each $r \in R_i$. For each ordinary atom $\beta$ in $r$, we have by construction of $M$ that $M \models \beta^S$ iff $\mathbf{M}, P_i[S] \models \beta$; furthermore, for each module atom $\beta = P_k[\mathbf{p}].o(\mathbf{c})$ in $r$, we have that $M \models \mu(m_i, \beta, S)$ iff $M \models o^T(\mathbf{c})$, i.e., $o(\mathbf{c}) \in M_k/T$, where $T \subseteq HB_{\mathbf{P}}|_{\mathbf{q_k}}$ contains $q_{k,j}(\mathbf{c})$ iff $M \models p_j^S(\mathbf{c})$, i.e., $p_j(\mathbf{c}) \in M_i/S$. Thus, $M \models \mu(m_i, \beta, S)$ iff $o(\mathbf{c}) \in M_k/(M_i/S)|_{\mathbf{P}}^{\mathbf{q_k}}$; in other words, iff $\mathbf{M}, P_i[S] \models o(\mathbf{c})$. As $\mathbf{M}, P_i[S] \models r$, it follows that $M \models \gamma(m_i, r, S)$.

Call a model $\mathbf{M}$ of $\mathbf{P}$ *supported*, if for every atom $\alpha \in M_i/S$, $P_i[S] \in VC(\mathbf{P})$, there is some rule $r \in SR(\alpha, I_{\mathbf{P}}(P_i[S]))$ such that $\mathbf{M}, P_i[S] \models B(r)$. Then, based on Lemma 1 the following can be shown.

**Lemma 2.** *The models of $\gamma(\mathbf{P}) \wedge \sigma(\mathbf{P})$ correspond 1-1 to the supported models of $\mathbf{P}$.*

In particular, if $\mathbf{P}$ is acyclic (no atom depends recursively on itself), then it has a single supported model, which gives rise to an answer set of $\mathbf{P}$.

*Example 6.* Continuing with Example 4, we get for $\gamma(\mathbf{P})$ the classical models $M_1 = \{r^{S_2^1}, q^{S_2^1}\}$, $M_2 = \{p^{S_1}, r^{S_2^0}, r^{S_2^1}, q^{S_2^1}\}$, $M_3 = \{p^{S_1}, r^{S_2^1}, q^{S_2^1}\}$, and $M_4 = \{p^{S_1}, r^{S_2^0}, r^{S_2^1}, q^{S_2^0}, q^{S_2^1}\}$. They correspond to the classical models $\mathbf{M}_1 = (M_1/\emptyset := \emptyset, M_2/\emptyset := \emptyset, M_2/\{q\} := \{r, q\})$, $\mathbf{M}_2 = (M_1/\emptyset := \{p\}, M_2/\emptyset := \{r\}, M_2/\{q\} := \{r, q\})$, $\mathbf{M}_3 = (M_1/\emptyset := \{p\}, M_2/\emptyset := \emptyset, M_2/\{q\} := \{r, q\})$, and $\mathbf{M}_4 = (M_1/\emptyset := \{p\}, M_2/\emptyset := \{r, q\}, M_2/\{q\} := \{r, q\})$ of $\mathbf{P}$. The formula $\gamma(\mathbf{P}) \wedge \sigma(\mathbf{P})$ has only the classical models $M_1, M_3$, and $M_4$, which will give us the supported models $\mathbf{M}_1$, $\mathbf{M}_2$, and $\mathbf{M}_4$ of $\mathbf{P}$.

*Example 7.* In Example 5, the models of $\gamma(\mathbf{P})$ are $M_1 = \emptyset$ and $M_2 = \{p_1^S, p_2^S\}$, which are also the models of $\gamma(\mathbf{P}) \wedge \sigma(\mathbf{P})$. Both of them correspond to the classical as well as supported models of $\mathbf{P}$, namely $\mathbf{M}_1 = (M_1/\emptyset := \emptyset, M_2/\emptyset := \emptyset)$ and $\mathbf{M}_2 = (M_1/\emptyset := \{p_1\}, M_2/\emptyset := \{p_2\})$.

## 4 Loop Formulas for MLPs

In this section, we develop *modular loop formulas* that instantiate each program module with possible input to create the classical theory of the program, and then add loop formulas similar as in [16]. However, we have to respect loops not only inside a module, but also across modules due to module atoms. The latter will be captured by a *modular dependency graph*, which records positive dependencies that relates module instantiations with the atoms in a module. The instantiation of the modules makes it necessary to create fresh propositional atoms very similar to grounding of logic programs; complexity results in [6] suggest that there is no way to circumvent this: with arbitrary input, already propositional Horn MLPs are EXP-complete and normal propositional MLPs are NEXP-complete (considering brave inference of a ground atom, i.e., membership in some answer set). In the non-ground case, Horn MLPs are 2EXP-complete, while

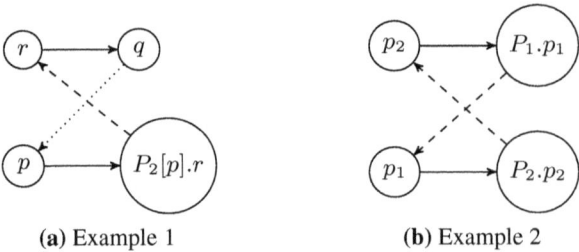

(a) Example 1                    (b) Example 2

**Fig. 2.** Module dependency graphs

normal non-ground MLPs are 2NEXP-complete. In the rest of this section, we assume that all negated module atoms in a MLP are monotonic and that $\mathbf{P}$ is ground.

We define now the modular dependency graph to keep track of dependencies between modules and rules. It is a ground dependency graph with two additional types of edges.

**Definition 6 (Modular Dependency Graph).** *Let* $\mathbf{P} = (m_1, \ldots, m_n)$ *be an MLP. The dependency graph of* $\mathbf{P}$ *is the digraph* $MG_{\mathbf{P}} = (V, E)$ *with vertex set* $V = HB_{\mathbf{P}}$ *and edge set* $E$ *containing the following edges:*

- $p(\mathbf{c_1}) \rightarrow q(\mathbf{c_2})$, *for each* $r \in R_i$ *with* $H(r) = \{p(\mathbf{c_1})\}$ *and* $q(\mathbf{c_2}) \in B^+(r)$.
- $a \rightarrow b$, *if one of* (i)–(ii) *holds, where* $\alpha$ *is of the form* $P_j[\mathbf{p}].o(\mathbf{c})$ *in* $R_i$ *and* $P_j$ *has the associated input list* $\mathbf{q_j}$:
   *(i)* $a = \alpha$ *and* $b = o(\mathbf{c}) \in HB_{\mathbf{P}}$;
   *(ii)* $a = q_\ell(\mathbf{c}) \in HB_{\mathbf{P}}|_{\mathbf{q_j}}$ *and* $b = p_\ell(\mathbf{c}) \in HB_{\mathbf{P}}|_{\mathbf{p}}$ *for* $1 \leq \ell \leq |\mathbf{q_j}|$.

Intuitively, the module graph is "uninstantiated", i.e., all module atoms are purely syntactic. This also means that loops that show up in the module graph must be "instantiated" in the formulas.

*Example 8.* The module dependency graphs of the programs in Examples 1 and 2 are shown in Fig. 2a and 2b, resp. In both figures, the two upper nodes are from $m_2$, while the nodes below stem from $m_1$. Note that the dashed edges stem from condition (i) in Definition 6, while dotted edges are from condition (ii). Straight edges are standard head-body dependencies.

We define now modular loops based on the modular dependency graph.

**Definition 7 (Modular Loops).** *A set of atoms* $\mathcal{L} \subseteq V(MG_{\mathbf{P}})$ *is called a* modular loop *for* $\mathbf{P}$ *iff the subgraph of* $MG_{\mathbf{P}}$ *induced by* $\mathcal{L}$ *is strongly connected.*

Note that $\mathcal{L}$ may contain module atoms, and single-atom loops are allowed.

Modular loop formulas have then the same shape as standard loop formulas [19,16], with the important distinction that external support formulas may take the input $S$ from the value call $P_i[S]$. For that, we define first the *external support rules* of rule set $R$ w.r.t. a set $\mathcal{L} \subseteq HB_{\mathbf{P}}$ as

$$ER(\mathcal{L}, R) = \{r \in R \mid H(r) \cap \mathcal{L} \neq \emptyset, B^+(r) \cap \mathcal{L} = \emptyset\} \ .$$

Note that $\mathcal{L}$ may contain module atoms.

Modular loops may go through the atoms of multiple modules, but do not take care of "instantiated loops" that stem from the input. Given a modular loop, the instantiated loop may be exponentially longer in the propositional case, whereas it could have double-exponential length in the non-ground case. To keep record of these loops, we next define cyclic instantiation signatures that are used to instantiate modular loops.

**Definition 8 (Cyclic instantiation signature).** *Let $\mathcal{L}$ be a modular loop for* $\mathbf{P} = (m_1, \ldots, m_n)$. *A cyclic instantiation signature for $\mathcal{L}$ is a tuple $\mathcal{S} = (\mathcal{S}_1, \ldots, \mathcal{S}_n)$ such that for all $i \in \{1, \ldots, n\}$, (i) $\mathcal{S}_i \subseteq 2^{HB_{\mathbf{P}}|q_i}$ with $\mathcal{S}_i \neq \emptyset$ and all $S \in \mathcal{S}_i$ have $S \cap \mathcal{L} = \emptyset$, if $\mathcal{L}$ has some ground atoms with predicates from $\mathcal{P}_i$, and (ii) $\mathcal{S}_i = \emptyset$ otherwise.*

Intuitively, we use a modular loop as template to create loops that go over instantiations.

*Example 9.* The MLP $\mathbf{P}$ in Example 1 has the loop $\mathcal{L} = \{p, P_2[p].r, r, q\}$ for which we get one cyclic instantiation signature $\mathcal{S}_1 = (\{\emptyset\}, \{\emptyset\})$; $(\{\emptyset\}, \{\{q\}\})$ and $(\{\emptyset\}, \{\emptyset, \{q\}\})$ are not cyclic instantiation signatures as they share atoms with $\mathcal{L}$, thus always get support from input $S$. Intuitively, this captures those module instantiations that cycle over module input, but have no support from the formal input, viz., $P_1[\emptyset] \leftrightarrow P_2[\emptyset]$.

*Example 10.* In Example 2, we have a loop $\mathcal{L} = \{p_1, P_2.p_2, p_2, P_1.p_1\}$. We get one cyclic instantiation signatures: $\mathcal{S}_1 = (\{\emptyset\}, \{\emptyset\})$. Here, $\mathcal{S}_1$ builds a cycle over module instantiations from the mutual calls in $m_1$ and $m_2$.

**Definition 9 (Modular Loop Formulas).** *Let $\mathcal{S} = (\mathcal{S}_1, \ldots, \mathcal{S}_n)$ be an instantiation signature for the modular loop $\mathcal{L}$ in MLP $\mathbf{P}$. The* loop formula *for $\mathcal{L}$ w.r.t. $\mathcal{S}$ in $\mathbf{P}$ is*

$$\lambda(\mathcal{S}, \mathcal{L}, \mathbf{P}) \;=\; \bigvee_{i=1}^{n} \bigvee_{T \in \mathcal{S}_i} \left( \bigvee (\mathcal{L}|_{\mathcal{P}_i})^T \right) \;\supset\; \bigvee_{i=1}^{n} \bigvee_{S \in \mathcal{S}_i} \sigma(m_i, ER(\mathcal{L}, R_i), S) \ .$$

*Given $\mathbf{P}$, the* loop formula *for a modular loop $\mathcal{L}$ in $\mathbf{P}$ is the conjunction $\lambda(\mathcal{L}, \mathbf{P}) = \bigwedge_{\mathcal{S}} \lambda(\mathcal{S}, \mathcal{L}, \mathbf{P})$ for all cyclic instantiation signatures $\mathcal{S}$ of $\mathcal{L}$, and the* loop formula *for $\mathbf{P}$ is the conjunction $\lambda(\mathbf{P}) = \bigwedge_{\mathcal{L}} \lambda(\mathcal{L}, \mathbf{P})$ for all modular loops $\mathcal{L}$ in $\mathbf{P}$.*

Intuitively, the formal input in a value call $P_i[S]$ always adds external support for the input atoms in $S$ as we add $S$ to the instantiation $I_{\mathbf{P}}(P_i[S])$. Since we obtain all supported models with $\gamma(\mathbf{P}) \wedge \sigma(\mathbf{P})$, thus also have $S$ there, we can restrict to those instantiation signatures $\mathcal{S}$ for a modular loop $\mathcal{L}$ that have no support from formal input. Putting things together, let us define

$$\Lambda(\mathbf{P}) = \gamma(\mathbf{P}) \wedge \sigma(\mathbf{P}) \wedge \lambda(\mathbf{P}) \ .$$

*Example 11.* Continuing with Example 4, we get the following modular loop formulas based on the loop $\mathcal{L}$ and instantiation signature $\mathcal{S}_1$ for $\mathcal{L}$ shown in Example 9 (here, $S_1 = \emptyset$, $S_2^0 = \emptyset$): $\lambda(\mathcal{S}_1, \mathcal{L}, \mathbf{P}) = (p^{S_1} \vee r^{S_2^0} \vee q^{S_2^0}) \supset \bot$. This formula and $\gamma(\mathbf{P}) \wedge \sigma(\mathbf{P})$ yields $\Lambda(\mathbf{P})$, whose model is $M_1 = \{r^{S_2^1}, q^{S_2^1}\}$, which coincides with the answer set $\mathbf{M}_1 = (\emptyset, \emptyset, \{r, q\})$ of $\mathbf{P}$.

*Example 12.* Based on Example 5 and 10 we get the following modular loop formulas using the loop $\mathcal{L}$ and instantiation signature $\mathcal{S}_1$ ($S = \emptyset$): $\lambda(\mathcal{S}_1, \mathcal{L}, \mathbf{P}) = p_1^S \vee p_2^S \supset \bot \vee \bot$. The classical model of the conjunction of $\gamma(\mathbf{P}) \wedge \sigma(\mathbf{P})$ and above formula ($= \Lambda(\mathbf{P})$) is thus $M_1 = \emptyset$, which coincides with the answer set $\mathbf{M}_1 = (\emptyset, \emptyset)$ of $\mathbf{P}$.

We have the following result.

**Theorem 1.** *Given an MLP $\mathbf{P}$ in which all negated module atoms are monotonic, the answer sets of $\mathbf{P}$ and the classical models of $\Lambda(\mathbf{P})$ correspond, such that (i) if $M \models \Lambda(P)$, then there is some answer set $\mathbf{M}$ of $\mathbf{P}$ such that $M_i/S = \{p(\mathbf{c}) \in HB_{\mathbf{P}} \mid p^S(\mathbf{c}) \in M \wedge p \in \mathcal{P}_i\}$ for all $P_i[S] \in VC(\mathbf{P})$, and (ii) if $\mathbf{M}$ is an answer set of $\mathbf{P}$, then $M \models \Lambda(\mathbf{P})$, where $M = \bigcup_{P_i[S]}(M_i/S)^S$.*

## 5   Ordered Completion for MLPs

In this section, we follow the idea in [3] to provide an ordered completion for non-ground MLPs. We consider MLPs in the Datalog setting, i.e., an MLP $\mathbf{P}$ can be viewed as a *modular nonmonotonic Datalog program* which has an infinite set of constants $\mathcal{C}$ and is independent from the domains (this is ensured by forcing safety conditions to rules in $\mathbf{P}$). Grounding of $\mathbf{P}$ is done with respect to a *finite relational structure* $\mathfrak{M}$ (extended to MLPs), having a finite universe $U_{\mathfrak{M}}$ accessible by constants; it is the active domain we are restricted to. We also need to adapt the notion of answer set for this setting. Like above, we assume that all negated module atoms in a MLP are monotonic. Moreover, we assume that MLPs do not contain facts, i.e., rules of form (1) have non-empty body.[1]

**Finite Structures for MLPs.** Given an MLP $\mathbf{P}$, we call a predicate in $\mathbf{P}$ *intensional* if it occurs in the head of a rule in $\mathbf{P}$ or in the formal input parameters $\mathbf{q_i}$ of a module $m_i = (P_i[\mathbf{q_i}], R_i)$, and *extensional* otherwise. Intuitively, intensional predicates are defined by the rules in $\mathbf{P}$ and the input given to a module instantiation, whereas extensional predicates stem from the extension given by a relational structure. The *signature* of an MLP $\mathbf{P}$ contains all intensional predicates, extensional predicates, and constants occurring in $\mathbf{P}$. The set of intensional (resp., extensional) predicates in a module $m$ is denoted by $Int(m)$ (resp., $Ext(m)$).

A *finite (Herbrand) relational structure for* $\mathbf{P}$ (H-structure) can be defined as a pair $\mathfrak{M} = (U_{\mathfrak{M}}, \cdot^{\mathfrak{M}})$, where the finite universe $U_{\mathfrak{M}}$ consists of constants in $\mathbf{P}$ and $\cdot^{\mathfrak{M}}$ is a mapping associating (i) each constant in $\mathbf{P}$ with itself, i.e., $c^{\mathfrak{M}} = c$, (ii) each extensional predicate $q$ in $\mathbf{P}$ with a relation $q^{\mathfrak{M}}$ over $\mathfrak{M}$, where $q^{\mathfrak{M}}$ has the same arity as $q$, (iii) each intensional predicate $p$ in a module $m_i = (P_i[\mathbf{q_i}], R_i)$, together with each input $S$ from the value calls $P_i[S] \in VC(\mathbf{P})$, with a relation $p^{\mathfrak{M},S}$ whose arity is the same as $p$. The grounding process is gradually defined as follows. The grounding of a rule $r$ under $\mathfrak{M}$ is the set $gr(r, \mathfrak{M})$ of all ground instances of $r$ by replacing all variables in the rules by some domain objects in $\mathfrak{M}$. The grounding of a rule set $R$ w.r.t. $\mathfrak{M}$ is $gr(R, \mathfrak{M}) = \bigcup_{r \in R} gr(r, \mathfrak{M}) \cup \{q(\mathbf{c}) \mid q \in Ext(R) \wedge \mathbf{c} \in q^{\mathfrak{M}}\}$; intuitively,

---

[1] This is w.l.o.g., since we can remove facts from an MLP and map them to extensional relations in a finite relational structure.

it means that rules are grounded wrt. $\mathfrak{M}$ and facts are taken from the finite structure as a database. The grounding of a module $m$ wrt. $\mathfrak{M}$, denoted by $gr(m, \mathfrak{M})$, is defined by replacing the rules in $R(m)$ by $gr(R(m), \mathfrak{M})$. Finally, the grounding of $\mathbf{P}$ wrt. $\mathfrak{M}$ is $gr(\mathbf{P}, \mathfrak{M})$, which is formed by grounding each module $m_i$ of $\mathbf{P}$ wrt. $\mathfrak{M}$.

We say that $\mathfrak{M}$ is an answer set of $\mathbf{P}$ iff the interpretation $\mathbf{M} = (M_i/S \mid P_i[S] \in VC(\mathbf{P}))$, where

$$M_i/S = \{q(\mathbf{c}) \mid q \in Ext(m_i) \wedge \mathbf{c} \in q^{\mathfrak{M}}\} \cup \{p(\mathbf{c}) \mid p \in Int(m_i) \wedge \mathbf{c} \in p^{\mathfrak{M},S}\} \ ,$$

is an answer set of $gr(\mathbf{P}, \mathfrak{M})$ according to Definition 4.

**Ordered Completion.** Given an MLP $\mathbf{P}$, our goal now is to give a translation of $\mathbf{P}$ to a first-order formula such that the models of the latter correspond to the answer sets of the former.

Suppose that we are in a value call $P_i[S]$ of the module $m_i = (P_i[\mathbf{q}_i], R_i)$ and consider a module atom $\beta = P_j[\mathbf{p}].o(\mathbf{y})$ from a module $m_j = (P_j[\mathbf{q}_j], R_j)$. Formula $\beta_{m_i,S,T}$, as defined in Section 3, can then match the interpretation of $\mathbf{p}$ to an input $T$ of $\beta$.

Once this is done, we can "guess" the right $T$ by ranging over all possible subsets of the restricted Herbrand base $HB_{\mathbf{P}}|_{\mathbf{q}_j}$ of the called module $m_j$ with formal input parameters $\mathbf{q}_j$. For each guess, we translate the module atom $\beta$ to its output predicate labeled with the corresponding input $T$. Depending on whether $\beta$ appears in the positive (resp. negative) part of the body of a rule, one uses the translation $\mu'$ (resp., $\overline{\mu}'$):

$$\mu'(m_i, \beta, S) = \bigvee_{T \subseteq HB_{\mathbf{P}}|_{\mathbf{q}_j}} \beta_{m_i,S,T} \wedge o^T(\mathbf{y})$$

$$\overline{\mu}'(m_i, \beta, S) = \bigvee_{T \subseteq HB_{\mathbf{P}}|_{\mathbf{q}_j}} \beta_{m_i,S,T} \wedge \neg o^T(\mathbf{y}) \ .$$

Compared to $\mu$ and $\overline{\mu}$, the primed version here deals with non-ground output of $\beta$.

Now we can build the left direction of the completion, which intuitively says that if there is some ground body which holds, then the respective head is concluded. We assume that rules are standardized apart, i.e., a predicate $a$ appearing in the head of a rule always has the form $a(\mathbf{x})$. Suppose that free variables in the body of a rule $r$ are $y_1, \ldots, y_n$, the left hand side of the completion $\gamma'(m_i, a(\mathbf{x}), S)$ is a lifted version of $\gamma(m_i, r, S)$ to the non-ground case which merges all supporting rules for $a(\mathbf{x})$. We define

$$\gamma'(m_i, a(\mathbf{x}), S) =$$

$$\forall \mathbf{x} \left[ \bigvee_{r \in SR(a(\mathbf{x}), R_i)} \exists y_1, \ldots, y_n \left( \bigwedge_{p_l(\mathbf{y}_l) \in B_o^+(r)} p_l^S(\mathbf{y}_l) \wedge \bigwedge_{p_l(\mathbf{y}_l) \in B_o^-(r)} \neg p_l^S(\mathbf{y}_l) \wedge \right. \right.$$

$$\left. \left. \bigwedge_{\beta \in B_m^+(r)} \mu'(m_i, \beta, S) \wedge \bigwedge_{\beta \in B_m^-(r)} \overline{\mu}'(m_i, \beta, S) \right) \supset a^S(\mathbf{x}) \right] \ .$$

*Example 13.* Take $\mathbf{P}$ from Example 1 and the labels $S_1$, $S_2^0$, and $S_2^1$ from Example 11.
We have $\gamma'(m_1, p, \emptyset) = (\neg p^{S_1} \wedge r^{S_2^0}) \vee (p^{S_1} \wedge r^{S_2^1}) \supset p^{S_1}$.

We next turn to build the right hand side of the completion, with a modification concerning the order between predicates. Similar to [3], we use a predicate $D$ to keep track of the derivation/dependency ordering between labeled predicates. Basically, $D$ is labeled with subscripts describing the two related predicates (the former is used in deriving the latter, in a transitive way), and superscripts referring to the respective inputs. For example, $D_{oa}^{TS}(\mathbf{y}, \mathbf{x})$ means that $o(\mathbf{y})$ in a value call $P_j[T]$ is used to derive $a(\mathbf{x})$ in $P_i[S]$; hence, $D_{oa}^{TS}(\mathbf{y}, \mathbf{x}) \wedge \neg D_{ao}^{ST}(\mathbf{x}, \mathbf{y})$ means that there is no loop between the two. Using this, the ordinary predicates in a rule $r$ can be ordered as follows:

$$\delta(m_i, r, S) = \bigwedge_{a(\mathbf{x}) \in H(r)} \bigwedge_{b \in Int(m_i)} \bigwedge_{b(\mathbf{z}) \in B_o^+(r)} D_{ba}^{SS}(\mathbf{z}, \mathbf{x}) \wedge \neg D_{ab}^{SS}(\mathbf{x}, \mathbf{z}) \ .$$

Concerning module atoms, we upgrade the translation for module atoms $\mu'$ to $\mu^\star$ with atom $a(\mathbf{x})$ as an additional argument. This new translation not only takes care of matching labels but also prevents loops between the output atom of $\beta$ and $a(\mathbf{x})$, as well as loops between input predicates and formal arguments of the respective module call. In the following formula, $p_k$ and $q_{j,k}$ come correspondingly from the input predicate list $\mathbf{p}$ of $\beta$ and the formal arguments $\mathbf{q}_j$ of module $m_j$:

$$\mu^\star(m_i, \beta, S, a(\mathbf{x})) = \bigvee_{T \subseteq HB_{\mathbf{P}}|_{\mathbf{q}_j}} \beta_{m_i, S, T} \wedge o^T(\mathbf{y}) \wedge D_{oa}^{TS}(\mathbf{y}, \mathbf{x}) \wedge \neg D_{ao}^{ST}(\mathbf{x}, \mathbf{y}) \wedge$$

$$\forall \mathbf{z} \left( \bigwedge D_{p_k q_{j,k}}^{ST}(\mathbf{z}, \mathbf{z}) \wedge \neg D_{q_{j,k} p_k}^{TS}(\mathbf{z}, \mathbf{z}) \right) \ .$$

The right hand side of the completion applies to every intensional predicate. Intuitively, this formula makes sure that whenever a head is true, then there must be some rule with the body satisfied, plus there is no loop involving the head and any atom in the body (both ordinary and module atoms), or between the input predicates and the corresponding formal input parameters of the called module; this is encoded in $\delta$ and $\mu^\star$, respectively:

$$\rho(m_i, a(\mathbf{x}), S) =$$

$$\forall \mathbf{x} \left[ a^S(\mathbf{x}) \supset \bigvee_{r \in SR(a(\mathbf{x}), R_i)} \exists \mathbf{y}_1, \dots, \mathbf{y}_n \left( \bigwedge_{p_l(\mathbf{y}_l) \in B_o^+(r)} p_l^S(\mathbf{y}_l) \wedge \bigwedge_{p_l(\mathbf{y}_l) \in B_o^-(r)} \neg p_l^S(\mathbf{y}_l) \wedge \right. \right.$$

$$\left. \left. \delta(m_i, r, S) \wedge \bigwedge_{\beta \in B_m^+(r)} \mu^\star(m_i, \beta, S, a(\mathbf{x})) \wedge \bigwedge_{\beta \in B_m^-(r)} \overline{\mu'}(m_i, \beta, S) \right) \right] \ .$$

*Example 14.* Continuing with Example 13, we get

$$\rho(m_1, p, \emptyset) = p^{S_1} \supset (\neg p^{S_1} \wedge r^{S_2^0} \wedge D_{rp}^{S_2^0 S_1} \wedge \neg D_{pr}^{S_1 S_2^0} \wedge D_{pq}^{S_1 S_2^0} \wedge \neg D_{qp}^{S_2^0 S_1})$$

$$\vee (p^{S_1} \wedge r^{S_2^1} \wedge D_{rp}^{S_2^1 S_1} \wedge \neg D_{pr}^{S_1 S_2^1} \wedge D_{pq}^{S_1 S_2^1} \wedge \neg D_{qp}^{S_2^1 S_1}).$$

Then, the ordered completion for an intensional predicate $a$ is simply the conjunction of $\gamma'$ and $\rho$:

$$\psi(m_i, a(\mathbf{x}), S) = \gamma'(m_i, a(\mathbf{x}), S) \wedge \rho(m_i, a(\mathbf{x}), S).$$

The ordered completion for a value call $P_i[S]$ is the collection of ordered completions of all intensional predicates and the realization of the input via predicates in $\mathbf{q}_i$, all labeled with $S$:

$$\psi(\mathbf{P}, P_i[S]) = \bigwedge_{a \in Int(m_i)} \psi(m_i, a(\mathbf{x}), S) \wedge \bigwedge_{\chi^S(q_{i,j}(\mathbf{c}))=1} q_{i,j}^S(\mathbf{c}) \ .$$

The only thing left is to capture the closure condition of the dependencies $D_{qp}^{ST}$, not only inside but also across module instances. In the formula below, we consider triples of value calls $P_i[S]$, $P_j[T]$, and $P_k[U]$ (not necessarily distinct) coming from the call graph $VC(\mathbf{P})$. Then,

$$\tau(P_i[S], P_j[T], P_k[U]) =$$
$$\bigwedge_{p \in Int(m_i)} \bigwedge_{q \in Int(m_j)} \bigwedge_{r \in Int(m_k)} \forall \mathbf{xyz}(D_{pq}^{ST}(\mathbf{x}, \mathbf{y}) \wedge D_{qr}^{TU}(\mathbf{y}, \mathbf{z}) \supset D_{pr}^{SU}(\mathbf{x}, \mathbf{z})).$$

Finally, the ordered completion of the whole MLP $\mathbf{P}$ is given by collecting the completions for all value calls in the call graph $VC(\mathbf{P})$ and the closure axiom of the dependency ordering between labeled predicates,

$$\tau(\mathbf{P}) = \bigwedge_{P_i[S], P_j[T], P_k[U] \in VC(\mathbf{P})} \tau(P_i[S], P_j[T], P_k[U]) \ ,$$

i.e.,

$$\Omega(\mathbf{P}) = \tau(\mathbf{P}) \wedge \bigwedge_{P_i[S] \in VC(\mathbf{P})} \psi(\mathbf{P}, P_i[S]) \ ,$$

*Example 15.* The formulas in Examples 13 and 14 give us the encoding $\psi(\mathbf{P}, P_1[]) = \gamma'(m_1, p, \emptyset) \wedge \rho(m_1, p, \emptyset)$ for module $m_1$ of the MLP $\mathbf{P}$ in Example 1. For $m_2$, we have:

- $\psi(\mathbf{P}, P_2[\emptyset]) = (q^{S_2^0} \supset r^{S_2^0}) \wedge (r^{S_2^0} \supset q^{S_2^0} \wedge D_{qr}^{S_2^0 S_2^0} \wedge \neg D_{rq}^{S_2^0 S_2^0})$,

- $\psi(\mathbf{P}, P_2[\{q\}]) = q^{S_2^1} \wedge (q^{S_2^1} \supset r^{S_2^1}) \wedge (r^{S_2^1} \supset q^{S_2^1} \wedge D_{qr}^{S_2^1 S_2^1} \wedge \neg D_{rq}^{S_2^1 S_2^1})$,

- $\tau(\mathbf{P}) = \bigwedge D_{p_1 p_2}^{T_1 T_2} \wedge D_{p_2 p_3}^{T_2 T_3} \supset D_{p_1 p_3}^{T_1 T_3}$, where $p_i \in \{p, q, r\}$; $T_i = S_1$ if $p_i = p$ and $T_i \in \{S_2^0, S_2^1\}$ otherwise.

The ordered completion $\Omega(\mathbf{P}) = \tau(\mathbf{P}) \wedge \psi(\mathbf{P}, P_1[]) \wedge \psi(\mathbf{P}, P_2[\emptyset]) \wedge \psi(\mathbf{P}, P_2[\{q\}])$ has a single model whose projection to labeled atoms is $\{r^{S_2^1}, q^{S_2^1}\}$. This model corresponds to the answer set mentioned in Example 1.

The following theorem shows the correctness of our translation. For this, given an MLP $\mathbf{P}$ and an H-structure $\mathfrak{M}$, we define the *derivation ordering* of $\mathbf{P}$ wrt. $\mathfrak{M}$ as the set $D^{\mathfrak{M}}(\mathbf{P})$ of all facts $D_{qp}^{TS}(\mathbf{c}_2, \mathbf{c}_1)$ such that (i) there exists a path from $p(\mathbf{c}_1)$ to $q(\mathbf{c}_2)$ in the modular dependency graph $MG_{\mathbf{P}}$, (ii) $\mathbf{c}_1 \in p^{\mathfrak{M},S}$ as $p$ is an intensional predicate, and (iii) $\mathbf{c}_2 \in q^{\mathfrak{M},T}$ if $q$ is an intensional predicate or $\mathbf{c}_2 \in q^{\mathfrak{M}}$ if $q$ is an extensional predicate, where $T \in VC(\mathbf{P})$.

**Theorem 2.** *Let $\mathbf{P} = (m_1, \ldots, m_n)$ be an MLP in which all negated module atoms are monotonic. Then, (i) if an H-structure $\mathfrak{M}$ for $\mathbf{P}$ is an answer set of $gr(\mathbf{P}, \mathfrak{M})$, then $M \cup D(\mathbf{P})$ is a model of $\Omega(\mathbf{P})$, where*

$$M = \bigcup_{P_i[S] \in VC(\mathbf{P})} \{q^S(\mathbf{c}) \mid q \in Ext(m_i) \wedge \mathbf{c} \in q^{\mathfrak{M}}\} \cup \{p^S(\mathbf{c}) \mid p \in Int(m_i) \wedge \mathbf{c} \in p^{\mathfrak{M},S}\};$$

*(ii) if $M$ is a finite model of $\Omega(\mathbf{P})$, then the H-structure $\mathfrak{M}$ for $\mathbf{P}$ where (a) for each extensional predicate $q$, $q^{\mathfrak{M}} = \{\mathbf{c} \mid P_i[S] \in VC(\mathbf{P}) \wedge q^S(\mathbf{c}) \in M\}$, and (b) for each intensional predicate $p$ in module $m_i$ with input $S$, $p^{\mathfrak{M},S} = \{\mathbf{c} \mid P_i[S] \in VC(\mathbf{P}) \wedge p^S(\mathbf{c}) \in M\}$, is an answer set of $gr(\mathbf{P}, \mathfrak{M})$.*

## 6   Discussion

The translations $\Lambda(\mathbf{P})$ and $\Omega(\mathbf{P})$ from above allow us to express the existence of answer sets of an MLP $\mathbf{P}$ as a satisfiability problem in propositional respectively predicate logic that is decidable; however, for arbitrary call-by-value, the resulting formulas are huge in general, given that there are double exponential many value calls $P_i[S]$ for an input $\mathbf{q}$ in general. Furthermore, loops can be very long; in the general case, they can have double exponential length. However, the intrinsic complexity of MLPs already mentioned in Section 4 suggests that even in the propositional case (where the number of different inputs $S$ is at most exponential) we can not expect a polynomially computable transformation of brave inference $\mathbf{P} \models a$ into a propositional SAT instance, as the problem is EXP-complete for propositional Horn MLPs and NEXP-complete for propositional normal MLPs.

The ordered completion formula $\Omega(\mathbf{P})$, which can be seen as a $\Sigma_1^1$ formula over a finite structure and is thus evaluable in nondeterministic exponential time. Here, in the propositional case the input values $S$ and $T$ may be encoded using (polynomially many) predicate arguments (e.g., $o^T(\mathbf{y})$ becomes $o(\mathbf{x}, \mathbf{y})$ where $\mathbf{x} = x_1, \ldots, x_k$ encodes $T$) and disjunction/conjunction over $S$ and $T$ expressed by (first-order) quantification. In this way, it is possible to obtain a $\Sigma_1^1$ formula of polynomial size over a finite structure, such that this modified transformation is worst-case optimal with respect to the complexity of propositional normal MLPs. Similar encoding techniques can be applied for non-ground MLPs if the predicate arities of formal input predicates are bounded by a constant.

In the general non-ground case, such polynomial encoding techniques are not evident; already in the Horn case deciding $\mathbf{P} \models a$ is 2EXP-complete, and for normal MLPs brave inference is 2NEXP-complete. One may resort to predicate variables for encoding $S$ and $T$, and naturally arrive at a formula in higher-order logic (e.g., $o^T(\mathbf{y})$

becomes $o(\mathbf{T}, \mathbf{y})$ where $\mathbf{T} = T_1, \ldots, T_k$ is a list of predicate variables for the formal input predicates $\mathbf{q} = q_1, \ldots, q_k$). It remains to be seen, however, whether the structure of the resulting (polynomial-size) formula would readily permit worst-case optimal evaluation with respect to the complexity of MLPs.

Noticeably, however, we do not get a blowup if no call-by-value is made, i.e., if all inputs lists are empty (which means all $S$ and $T$ have the single value $\emptyset$). This setting is still useful for structured programming, and amounts in the propositional case to the DLP-functions of [15] (but in contrast permits unlimited recursion through modules, in particular positive recursion). Our results thus also provide ordered completion formulas for DLP-functions over normal programs.

## 7 Conclusion

In this paper, we have studied encodings of answer sets of Modular Nonmonotonic Logic Programs (MLPs) into first-order formulas, in the line of recent work in Answer Set Programming.

As for future work, refinement of the results and exploitation of the results for answer sets computation using SAT and QBF solvers, as well as theorem provers remains to be investigated; here, fragments of MLPs that allow for reasonable encodings might be considered, and the suitability of higher-order theorem provers evaluated.

For this paper, we have considered as context $C$ the set $VC(\mathbf{P})$ of all value calls, which thus can be omitted. Intuitively, a given context $C$ may be incorporated by ensuring that loop formulas are built only for relevant instantiation signatures $(\mathcal{S}_1, \ldots, \mathcal{S}_n)$; for modular loops, which are those that contain some value call $\mathcal{S}_i$ inside $C$; furthermore, either none or all value calls $\mathcal{S}_i$ must be in $C$. Relative to an interpretation $\mathbf{M}$, the minimal context $C = V(CG_{\mathbf{P}}(\mathbf{M}))$ may be defined using suitable predicates respective propositions. The technical elaboration of these ideas is beyond this paper.

Another assumption that we have made was that module atoms under negation are monotonic, in order to readily apply loop formula techniques despite the semantics of MLPs based on the FLP-reduct. It would be interesting to look into the full case of MLPs with arbitrary module atoms. Recently, unfounded sets for logic programs with arbitrary aggregates have been defined in [10]. Given that for ordinary logic programs unfounded sets are a semantic counterpart of loop formulas, this may inspire a similar notion of unfounded set for MLPs and help developing a syntactic counterpart in terms of loop formulas. The papers [17,21], which inspect the FLP-semantics on a more principled level, may also be useful in this respect. Different from answer semantics under the GL-reduct, not only positive atoms need to be considered for derivability, but also negated non-montonic module atoms.

A further issue are encodings for disjunctive MLPs, i.e., MLPs where the head of a rule may be a disjunction $\alpha_1 \vee \cdots \vee \alpha_k$ of atoms. Loop formulas for ordinary disjunctive logic programs have been developed in [16], and for general propositional theories under Answer Set Semantics in [12]. There is no principal obstacle to extend the loop formula encoding of this paper to disjunctive MLPs, and doing this is routine. In contrast, ordered completion formulas for disjunctive MLPs and already ordinary LPs needs further work; they may require a blowup given that ordinary disjunctive Datalog programs have $\text{NEXP}^{\text{NP}}$ complexity.

Finally, relationships to other semantics of logic programming is an interesting issue. Chen et al. [4] showed that loops with at most one external support rule in the program have a close connection to (disjunctive) well-founded semantics. Studying MLPs under similar restrictions could provide similar results, yet well-founded semantics for MLPs remains to be formalized.

# References

1. Apt, K., Blair, H., Walker, A.: Towards a Theory of Declarative Knowledge. In: Foundations of Deductive Databases and Logic Programming, pp. 89–148. Morgan Kaufmann, San Francisco (1988)
2. Arni, F., Ong, K., Tsur, S., Wang, H., Zaniolo, C.: The deductive database system $\mathcal{LDL}$++. Theor. Pract. Log. Prog. 3(1), 61–94 (2003)
3. Asuncion, V., Lin, F., Zhang, Y., Zhou, Y.: Ordered completion for first-order logic programs on finite structures. In: AAAI 2010, pp. 249–254. AAAI Press, Menlo Park (2010)
4. Chen, X., Ji, J., Lin, F.: Computing loops with at most one external support rule for disjunctive logic programs. In: Hill, P.M., Warren, D.S. (eds.) ICLP 2009. LNCS, vol. 5649, pp. 130–144. Springer, Heidelberg (2009)
5. Clark, K.L.: Negation as failure. In: Logic and Data Bases, pp. 293–322 (1978)
6. Dao-Tran, M., Eiter, T., Fink, M., Krennwallner, T.: Modular Nonmonotonic Logic Programming Revisited. In: Hill, P.M., Warren, D.S. (eds.) ICLP 2009. LNCS, vol. 5649, pp. 145–159. Springer, Heidelberg (2009)
7. Eiter, T., Gottlob, G., Mannila, H.: Disjunctive Datalog. ACM T. Database Syst. 22(3), 364–417 (1997)
8. Eiter, T., Gottlob, G., Veith, H.: Modular Logic Programming and Generalized Quantifiers. In: Fuhrbach, U., Dix, J., Nerode, A. (eds.) LPNMR 1997. LNCS, vol. 1265, pp. 290–309. Springer, Heidelberg (1997)
9. Eiter, T., Leone, N., Saccà, D.: On the Partial Semantics for Disjunctive Deductive Databases. Ann. Math. Artif. Intell. 19(1/2), 59–96 (1997)
10. Faber, W.: Unfounded sets for disjunctive logic programs with arbitrary aggregates. In: Baral, C., Greco, G., Leone, N., Terracina, G. (eds.) LPNMR 2005. LNCS (LNAI), vol. 3662, pp. 40–52. Springer, Heidelberg (2005)
11. Faber, W., Leone, N., Pfeifer, G.: Semantics and complexity of recursive aggregates in answer set programming. Artif. Intell. 175(1), 278–298 (2011)
12. Ferraris, P., Lee, J., Lifschitz, V.: A generalization of the Lin-Zhao theorem. Ann. Math. Artif. Intell. 47(1-2), 79–101 (2006)
13. Gaifman, H., Shapiro, E.: Fully abstract compositional semantics for logic programs. In: POPL 1989, pp. 134–142. ACM, New York (1989)
14. Gelfond, M., Lifschitz, V.: Classical negation in logic programs and disjunctive databases. New Generat. Comput. 9(3-4), 365–385 (1991)
15. Janhunen, T., Oikarinen, E., Tompits, H., Woltran, S.: Modularity Aspects of Disjunctive Stable Models. J. Artif. Intell. Res. 35, 813–857 (2009)
16. Lee, J., Lifschitz, V.: Loop formulas for disjunctive logic programs. In: Palamidessi, C. (ed.) ICLP 2003. LNCS, vol. 2916, pp. 451–465. Springer, Heidelberg (2003)
17. Lee, J., Meng, Y.: On reductive semantics of aggregates in answer set programming. In: Erdem, E., Lin, F., Schaub, T. (eds.) LPNMR 2009. LNCS, vol. 5753, pp. 182–195. Springer, Heidelberg (2009)
18. Lifschitz, V., Turner, H.: Splitting a Logic Program. In: ICLP 1994, pp. 23–38. MIT-Press, Cambridge (1994)

19. Lin, F., Zhao, Y.: ASSAT: computing answer sets of a logic program by SAT solvers. Artif. Intell. 157(1-2), 115–137 (2004)
20. Ross, K.: Modular Stratification and Magic Sets for Datalog Programs with Negation. J. ACM 41(6), 1216–1267 (1994)
21. Truszczyński, M.: Reducts of propositional theories, satisfiability relations, and generalizations of semantics of logic programs. Artif. Intell. 174(16-17), 1285–1306 (2010)

# Datalog Programs and Their Stable Models

Vladimir Lifschitz

Department of Computer Science
University of Texas at Austin, USA

**Abstract.** This paper is about the functionality of software systems used in answer set programming (ASP). ASP languages are viewed here, in the spirit of Datalog, as mechanisms for characterizing intensional (output) predicates in terms of extensional (input) predicates. Our approach to the semantics of ASP programs is based on the concept of a stable model defined in terms of a modification of parallel circumscription.

## 1 Introduction

This paper is about the functionality of software systems used in answer set programming (ASP) [11,14,1,7]. ASP languages are viewed here, in the spirit of Datalog, as mechanisms for characterizing intensional (output) predicates in terms of extensional (input) predicates.

**Example 1.** The ASP program

```
q(X,Y) :- p(X,Y).
q(X,Z) :- q(X,Y), q(Y,Z).
```

can be viewed as a definition of the output predicate $q$ in terms of the input predicate $p$; it tells us that $q$ is the transitive closure of $p$. To illustrate this assertion, consider what happens when we extend the program above by a set of ground atoms defining $p$, such as

```
p(a,b). p(b,c).
```

Given the file consisting of these three lines, an ASP system such as CLINGO[1] or DLV[2] returns the transitive closure of $p$:[3]

```
{q(a,b), q(a,c), q(b,c)}.
```

**Example 2.** Take the disjunctive ASP program consisting of one rule

```
q(X) ; r(X) :- p(X).
```

---

[1] http://potassco.sourceforge.net
[2] http://www.dlvsystem.com
[3] To be precise, the set of atoms generated by these systems includes also the atoms defining $p$.

O. de Moor et al. (Eds.): Datalog 2010, LNCS 6702, pp. 78–87, 2011.
© Springer-Verlag Berlin Heidelberg 2011

It can be thought of as a description of all possible ways to partition an input $p$ into disjoint[4] (and possibly empty) subsets $q$, $r$. Consider, for instance, what happens when we combine this rule with a set of ground atoms defining $p$, such as

```
p(a). p(b). p(c).
```

Given this file, DLV returns the list of 8 partitions:

```
{r(a), r(b), r(c)},
{q(a), r(b), r(c)},
{r(a), q(b), r(c)},
{q(a), q(b), r(c)},
{r(a), r(b), q(c)},
{q(a), r(b), q(c)},
{r(a), q(b), q(c)},
{q(a), q(b), q(c)}.
```

**Example 3.** The choice rule

```
{q(X)} :- p(X).
```

describes all possible ways to choose a subset $q$ of a given set $p$. Given this one-rule program and the same input as in Example 2, CLINGO generates all subsets of $\{a, b, c\}$:

```
{ },
{q(a)},
{q(b)},
{q(b), q(a)},
{q(c)},
{q(c), q(a)},
{q(c), q(b)},
{q(c), q(b), q(a)}.
```

We describe here a declarative semantics for a class of ASP programs that includes many examples of this kind. Our approach is based on the concept of a stable model [5] generalized as proposed in [3]. We will see, for instance, that the stable models of the program from Example 1 are arbitrary interpretations (in the sense of first-order logic) of the language with binary predicate constants $p$, $q$ in which $q$ is the transitive closure of $p$. The stable models of the program from Example 3 are arbitrary interpretations of the language with unary predicate constants $p$, $q$ in which $q$ is a subset of $p$.

---

[4] Disjunction in the head of an ASP rule often behaves as exclusive disjunction, but there are exceptions. See Remark 1 in Section 4.

## 2    A Few More Examples

We will now extend the program from Example 2 by adding a "constraint"—a rule with the empty head. The effect of adding a constraint to an ASP program is to weed out the solutions satisfying the body of the constraint.

**Example 4.** The program

```
q(X) ; r(X) :- p(X).
:- q(a).
```

describes the partitions of the input $p$ into subsets $q$, $r$ such that $a$ is not in $q$. Given this program and the same input as in Example 2, DLV returns

```
{r(a), r(b), r(c)},
{r(a), q(b), r(c)},
{r(a), r(b), q(c)},
{r(a), q(b), q(c)}.
```

**Example 5.** If $p$ is the set of vertices of a directed graph, and $q$ is the set of its edges, then the program

```
r(X) :- q(X,Y).
s(X) :- p(X), not r(X).
```

describes the set $s$ of terminal vertices. It uses the auxiliary symbol $r$, representing the complement of $s$. The combination `not r(X)` in the body of the second rule employs "negation as failure" to express that the rules of the program do not allow us to establish `r(X)`. (In Section 5 we will see how the stable model semantics makes this idea precise.) Given this program and the input

```
p(a). p(b). q(a,b).
```

both CLINGO and DLV return

```
{r(a), s(b)}.
```

**Example 6.** For $p$ and $q$ as in the previous example, the program below defines the sets of vertices of out-degrees 0, 1, and 2:

```
r0(X) :- p(X), #count{Y:q(X,Y)}=0.
r1(X) :- p(X), #count{Y:q(X,Y)}=1.
r2(X) :- p(X), #count{Y:q(X,Y)}=2.
```

In particular, $r_0$ has the same meaning as $s$ from Example 5. The "aggregate" symbol `#count` used in these rules represents the cardinality of a set. Given this program and the input

```
p(a). p(b). p(c). q(a,b). q(a,c).
```

DLV returns

```
{r0(b), r0(c), r2(a)}.
```

| | Logic programming notation | First-order formula |
|---|---|---|
| 1 | q(X,Y) :- p(X,Y). | $\forall xy(p(x,y) \to q(x,y))$ |
| 2 | q(X,Z) :- q(X,Y), q(Y,Z). | $\forall xyz(q(x,y) \land q(y,z) \to q(x,z))$ |
| 3 | q(X) ; r(X) :- p(X). | $\forall x(p(x) \to q(x) \lor r(x))$ |
| 4 | {q(X)} :- p(X). | $\forall x(p(x) \to q(x) \lor \neg q(x))$ |
| 5 | :- q(a). | $q(a) \to \bot$ |
| 6 | r(X) :- q(X,Y). | $\forall xy(q(x,y) \to r(x))$ |
| 7 | s(X) :- p(X), not r(X). | $\forall x(p(x) \land \neg r(x) \to s(x))$ |
| 8 | r0(X) :- p(X), #count{Y:q(X,Y)}=0. | $\forall x(p(x) \land \neg(\exists y)q(x,y) \to r_0(x))$ |
| 9 | r1(X) :- p(X), #count{Y:q(X,Y)}=1. | $\forall x(p(x) \land (\exists y)q(x,y) \land \neg(\exists_2 y)q(x,y) \to r_1(x))$ |
| 10 | r2(X) :- p(X), #count{Y:q(X,Y)}=2. | $\forall x(p(x) \land (\exists_2 y)q(x,y) \land \neg(\exists_3 y)q(x,y) \to r_2(x))$ |

**Fig. 1.** Rules as formulas

## 3   Rules and Programs

In first-order formulas, we take the symbols $\neg, \land, \lor, \to, \forall, \exists$ to be primitives, along with the 0-place connectives $\top$ (truth) and $\bot$ (falsity).

A first-order sentence is a *rule* if it has the form

$$\widetilde{\forall}(B \to H) \tag{1}$$

and has no occurrences of $\to$ other than the one explicitly shown.[5] Formula $B$ is the *body* of rule (1), and $H$ is its *head*. The expressions that were called rules in Examples 1–6 can be viewed as rules in the sense of this definition written in "logic programming notation," as shown in Figure 1.

In the last two lines, we use the abbreviation $\exists_n x F(x)$ for

$$\exists x_1 \cdots x_n \left( \bigwedge_{1 \le i \le n} F(x_i) \land \bigwedge_{1 \le i < j \le n} x_i \ne x_j \right).$$

Note that $\neg r(x)$ in line 7 of the table corresponds to `not r(X)` in logic programming notation. When we write a rule as a formula, the negation symbol $\neg$ corresponds to negation as failure, and not to "classical" (or "strong") negation in the sense of [6]. (To represent rules containing strong negation as first-order formulas, we would have to eliminate strong negation from them in favor of additional predicate constants.)

In this paper, a *(Datalog) program* is a pair $(F, \mathbf{p})$, where $F$ is a conjunction of rules, and $\mathbf{p}$ is a tuple of distinct predicate constants.[6] The members of $\mathbf{p}$ are called the *intensional predicates* of the program. The other predicate constants occurring in $F$ are its *extensional predicates*. In many cases, including Examples 1–6, $\mathbf{p}$ is the list of all predicate constants occurring in the heads of the rules of $F$.

---

[5] $\widetilde{\forall}F$ stands for the universal closure of $F$.

[6] In this paper, equality is not considered a predicate constant, so that it is not allowed to be a member of $\mathbf{p}$.

We will define the semantics of Datalog programs by specifying which models of $F$ are considered "stable models" of $(F, \mathbf{p})$. The definition of a stable model is based on a syntactic transformation that turns any Datalog program $(F, \mathbf{p})$ into a second-order sentence, denoted by $\mathrm{SM}_{\mathbf{p}}[F]$. We will define the *stable models* of $(F, \mathbf{p})$ as the models of $\mathrm{SM}_{\mathbf{p}}[F]$ in the sense of second-order logic.[7]

## 4   Positive Programs

Consider first the simpler case of rules and programs that do not contain intensional predicates in the scope of negation. We will call them *positive*. In Figure 1, the only rules that are not positive are those in lines 4 and 7. In the special case of positive programs, $\mathrm{SM}_{\mathbf{p}}$ is the well-known parallel circumscription operator [12], [2, Section 6.4.2].

The definition of parallel circumscription uses the following notation. If $p$ and $q$ are predicate constants of the same arity then $p \leq q$ stands for the formula $\forall \mathbf{x}(p(\mathbf{x}) \to q(\mathbf{x}))$, where $\mathbf{x}$ is a tuple of distinct object variables. If $\mathbf{p}$ and $\mathbf{q}$ are tuples $p_1, \ldots, p_n$ and $q_1, \ldots, q_n$ of predicate constants then $\mathbf{p} \leq \mathbf{q}$ stands for the conjunction

$$(p_1 \leq q_1) \wedge \cdots \wedge (p_n \leq q_n).$$

Furthermore, $\mathbf{p} < \mathbf{q}$ stands for $(\mathbf{p} \leq \mathbf{q}) \wedge \neg(\mathbf{q} \leq \mathbf{p})$. This formula expresses that each $p_i$ is a subset of the corresponding $q_i$, and at least one of these subsets is proper. In second-order logic, we apply the same notation to tuples of predicate variables.

For any positive Datalog program $(F, \mathbf{p})$, we define $\mathrm{SM}_{\mathbf{p}}[F]$ as the sentence

$$F \wedge \neg \exists \mathbf{u}((\mathbf{u} < \mathbf{p}) \wedge F(\mathbf{u})), \tag{2}$$

where $\mathbf{u}$ is a list of distinct predicate variables of the same length as $\mathbf{p}$, and $F(\mathbf{u})$ is the formula obtained from $F$ by substituting the variables $\mathbf{u}$ for the constants $\mathbf{p}$.

The second conjunctive term of (2) expresses the minimality of the extents of the predicates $\mathbf{p}$ (with respect to set inclusion) subject to constraint $F$. Thus the stable models of a positive program $(F, \mathbf{p})$ are the models of $F$ in which $\mathbf{p}$ cannot be made smaller without making $F$ false.

**Example 1, continued.** Let $F$ be the conjunction of the first-order formulas in lines 1 and 2 of Figure 1. These formulas express that $q$ is a superset of $p$, and that $q$ is a transitive relation. The formula $\mathrm{SM}_q[F]$ says in addition that $q$ cannot be made smaller without violating property $F$. Consequently the stable models of the program from Example 1 can be characterized as the interpretations in which $q$ is the transitive closure of $p$.

**Example 2, continued.** Let $F$ be the first-order formula in line 3 of Figure 1. It expresses that the union of $q$ and $r$ covers $p$. The formula $\mathrm{SM}_{qr}[F]$ says

---

[7] The semantics of second-order formulas is described, for instance, in [8, Section 1.2.3].

in addition that this property will be lost if we change the interpretation by replacing $q$ and $r$ with their subsets. It is clear that this condition is equivalent to the first-order formula

$$\forall x(p(x) \leftrightarrow q(x) \lor r(x)) \land \neg \exists x(q(x) \land r(x)).$$

The stable models of the program from Example 2 represent arbitrary partitions of $p$ into disjoint subsets $q$, $r$.

**Remark 1.** Consider the result of addings the facts

p(a). q(a). r(a).

to the program from Example 2. The corresponding first-order formula is

$$\forall x(p(x) \rightarrow q(x) \lor r(x)) \land (\top \rightarrow p(a)) \land (\top \rightarrow q(a)) \land (\top \rightarrow r(a)),$$

and the result of applying $\mathrm{SM}_{qr}$ to this formula is equivalent to

$$\forall x(p(x) \leftrightarrow q(x) \lor r(x)) \land \forall x(q(x) \land r(x) \leftrightarrow x = a).$$

In the presence of the additional facts shown above, minimizing $q$ and $r$ does not make these sets disjoint, and it does not make the disjunction exclusive.

**Example 4, continued.** Let $F$ be the conjunction of the first-order formulas in lines 3 and 5 of Figure 1. These formulas express that the union of $q$ and $r$ covers $p$, and that $a$ does not belong to $q$. The formula $\mathrm{SM}_{qr}[F]$ says in addition that the extents of $q$ and $r$ cannot be made smaller without violating property $F$. This condition is equivalent to

$$\forall x(p(x) \rightarrow q(x) \lor r(x)) \land \neg q(a) \land \neg \exists x(q(x) \land r(x)).$$

The stable models of the program from Example 4 represent arbitrary partitions of $p$ into disjoint subsets $q$, $r$ such that $a$ is not in $q$.

**Example 6, continued.** Let $F$ be the conjunction of the first-order formulas in lines 8–10 of Figure 1. These formulas express that $r_0$ contains all terminal vertices, that $r_1$ contains all vertices of out-degree 1, and that $r_2$ contains all vertices of out-degree 2. The result of applying the operator $\mathrm{SM}_{r_0 r_1 r_2}$ to this formula expresses that the sets $r_i$ are minimal subject to these conditions. In the stable models of the program from Example 6, $r_0$ is the set of terminal vertices, $r_1$ is the set of vertices of out-degree 1, and $r_2$ is the set of vertices of out-degree 2.

# 5   General Definition of a Stable Model

Sentence (2) can be formed even if the Datalog program $(F, \mathbf{p})$ is not positive. But for a nonpositive program the models of that sentence usually match neither the intended meaning of the program nor the behavior of ASP solvers.

This discrepancy can be resolved by modifying (2) as follows. Let $p_1, \ldots, p_n$ be the members of the list $\mathbf{p}$, and let $u_1, \ldots, u_n$ be the corresponding members of $\mathbf{u}$. By $F^\diamond(\mathbf{u})$ we denote the formula obtained from $F$ by replacing each part $p_i(\mathbf{t})$ that does not belong to the scope of any negation with $u_i(\mathbf{t})$; here $\mathbf{t}$ is an arbitrary tuple of terms. For any Datalog program $(F, \mathbf{p})$, $\mathrm{SM}_{\mathbf{p}}[F]$ stands for the sentence

$$F \wedge \neg\exists\mathbf{u}((\mathbf{u} < \mathbf{p}) \wedge F^\diamond(\mathbf{u})). \tag{3}$$

It is clear that if $(F, \mathbf{p})$ is positive then $F^\diamond(\mathbf{u})$ is identical to the result $F(\mathbf{u})$ of substituting $\mathbf{u}$ for $\mathbf{p}$ in $F$. Consequently the new definition of $\mathrm{SM}_{\mathbf{p}}$ is a generalization of the definition from Section 4.

**Example 3, continued.** Let $F$ be the first-order formula in line 4 of Figure 1. Then $\mathrm{SM}_q[F]$ is

$$\forall x(p(x) \to q(x) \vee \neg q(x)) \wedge \neg\exists u((u < q) \wedge \forall x(p(x) \to u(x) \vee \neg q(x))). \tag{4}$$

Note the disjunction $u(x) \vee \neg q(x)$ at the end of the formula; the occurrence of $q$ in the second disjunctive term is not replaced with $u$ because it is in the scope of a negation. The first conjuctive term of (4) is logically valid, so that it can be dropped. The second term says that the intersection of $p$ and $q$ is not contained in any proper subset of $q$. This is equivalent to saying that this intersection is itself not a proper subset of $q$, that is, to the formula $q \leq p$. In the stable models of the program from Example 3, $q$ is an arbitrary subset of $p$.

**Example 5, continued.** Let $F$ be the conjunction of the first-order formulas in lines 6 and 7 of Figure 1. Then $\mathrm{SM}_{rs}[F]$ is

$$\forall xy(q(x, y) \to r(x)) \wedge \forall x(p(x) \wedge \neg r(x) \to s(x))$$
$$\wedge \neg\exists uv(((u, v) < (r, s)) \wedge \forall xy(q(x, y) \to u(x)) \wedge \forall x(p(x) \wedge \neg r(x) \to v(x))). \tag{5}$$

Note that $r(x)$ in the second line did not become $u(x)$: it is in the scope of a negation. Since the subformula $\forall xy(q(x, y) \to u(x))$ does not contain $v$, and the subformula $\forall x(p(x) \wedge \neg r(x) \to v(x))$ does not contain $u$, (5) can be rewritten as

$$\forall xy(q(x, y) \to r(x)) \wedge \forall x(p(x) \wedge \neg r(x) \to s(x))$$
$$\wedge \neg\exists u((u < r) \wedge \forall xy(q(x, y) \to u(x)))$$
$$\wedge \neg\exists v((v < s) \wedge \forall x(p(x) \wedge \neg r(x) \to v(x))).$$

This formula expresses, first, that each nonterminal vertex belongs to $r$, and that $r$ is the smallest set with this property; second, that $s$ contains the complement of $r$, and that $s$ is the smallest set with this property. In the stable models of the program from Example 5, $r$ is the set of nonterminal vertices, and $s$ is its complement—the set of terminal vertices.

**Remark 2.** The definition of a stable model above looks very different from the definition proposed in [5], which involves grounding, constructing the reduct, and checking a fixpoint condition. But it is actually a generalization of the 1988 definition (limited to finite programs); see [3, Corollary 1]. The 1988 definition corresponds to the special case when

- the head of each rule is an atom,
- the body of each rule is a conjunction of literals,
- all predicate constants are intensional,
- we are interested in Herbrand interpretations only.

**Remark 3.** The definition above differs from the definition of a stable model from [3] in two ways. It is limited to "Datalog programs"—conjuctions of rules; the definition from [3] is applicable to arbitrary first-order sentences. On the other hand, it uses the transformation $F \mapsto F^{\diamond}(\mathbf{u})$ instead of the more complex transformation $F \mapsto F^{*}(\mathbf{u})$ from that paper. (This complexity is the price that one has to pay for the additional generality—for allowing arbitrary first-order sentences as arguments of $\mathrm{SM_p}$.) In application to Datalog programs, the two definitions are equivalent.

## 6  Equivalent Transformations of Datalog Programs

Recall that the definition of $\mathrm{SM_p}[F]$ for positive $F$ given in Section 4 uses the notation $F(\mathbf{u})$ for the formula obtained from $F$ by substituting the predicate variables $\mathbf{u}$ for the predicate constants $\mathbf{p}$. It is clear that if formulas $F_1$ and $F_2$ are equivalent to each other then the formulas $F_1(\mathbf{u})$ and $F_2(\mathbf{u})$ are equivalent to each other as well. It follows that for any positive and equivalent $F_1$, $F_2$, the formula $\mathrm{SM_p}[F_1]$ is equivalent to $\mathrm{SM_p}[F_2]$. More generally, if $F_1$ and $F_2$ are equivalent to each other and positive then $\mathrm{SM_p}[F_1 \wedge G]$ is equivalent to $\mathrm{SM_p}[F_2 \wedge G]$ for any conjunction $G$ of rules. In other words, replacing a group of positive rules within a Datalog program with an equivalent group of positive rules does not affect the class of stable models of the program.

But without the assumption that the rules involved in the replacement are positive this assertion would be incorrect. For instance, replacing the fact

p(a).

where p is an intensional predicate with the constraint

:- not p(a).

can change the stable models of the program, even though these rules, written as first-order formulas

$$\top \rightarrow p(a), \quad \neg p(a) \rightarrow \bot, \tag{6}$$

are equivalent to each other. The reason is that the transformation $F \mapsto F^{\diamond}(\mathbf{u})$, applied to two equivalent formulas, may produce non-equivalent formulas. For instance, in application to formulas (6) this transformation gives the non-equivalent formulas

$$\top \rightarrow u(a), \quad \neg p(a) \rightarrow \bot.$$

The results of [15,9,10,3] show, on the other hand, that replacing a group of rules within a Datalog program with another group of rules does not affect the class of stable models whenever the two sets of rules are *intuitionistically*

equivalent.[8] (Formulas (6) are equivalent to each other classically, but not intuitionistically.)

We can say even more: Datalog programs $(F_1, \mathbf{p})$ and $(F_2, \mathbf{p})$ have the same
stable models if $F_1 \leftrightarrow F_2$ is intuitionistically entailed by the sentences

$$\widetilde{\forall}(F \vee \neg F) \tag{7}$$

for formulas $F$ that do not contain members of the list $\mathbf{p}$.[9]

Compare, for instance, the rule

```
q(X) ; r(X) :- p(X).
```

from Example 2 and the rule

```
q(X) :- p(X), not r(X).
```

The corresponding formulas

$$\forall x(p(x) \rightarrow q(x) \vee r(x)), \ \forall x(p(x) \wedge \neg r(x) \rightarrow q(x)) \tag{8}$$

are not intuitionistically equivalent to each other; it is not surprising then that replacing one rule by the other within a Datalog program usually changes the class
of stable models. But the rules above are interchangeable if $r$ is an extensional
predicate, because the equivalence between formulas (8) is intuitionistically entailed by

$$\forall x(r(x) \vee \neg r(x)).$$

# 7    Discussion

The definition of a stable model based on a modification of the circumscription
operator provides a declarative semantics for several constructs used in answer
set programming, including choice and negation as failure.

Two classes of constructs are conspicuously absent, however, from the examples studied in this paper. One is built-in functions and predicates, such as
operations on integers. The other includes aggregates other than #count, such
as #sum (the sum of a set of integers). It appears that such "difficult" aggregates
can be handled by extending the operator SM to expressions more general than
first-order formulas [4].

**Acknowledgements.** Thanks to Paolo Ferraris, Joohyung Lee, Yuliya Lierler,
Fangkai Yang, and the anonymous referee for useful comments. This work was
partially supported by the National Science Foundation under grant IIS-0712113.

---

[8] See [13] for an introduction to intuitionistic logic.

[9] This assertion will remain true if we allow $F$ in (7) to have occurrences of intensional
predicates as long as each of them is in the scope of a negation or in the antecedent
of an implication.

# References

1. Baral, C.: Knowledge Representation, Reasoning and Declarative Problem Solving. Cambridge University Press, Cambridge (2003)
2. Brewka, G., Niemelä, I., Truszczyński, M.: Nonmonotonic reasoning. In: van Harmelen, F., Lifschitz, V., Porter, B. (eds.) Handbook of Knowledge Representation. Elsevier, Amsterdam (2008)
3. Ferraris, P., Lee, J., Lifschitz, V.: Stable models and circumscription. Artificial Intelligence 175, 236–263 (2011)
4. Ferraris, P., Lifschitz, V.: The stable model semantics for first-order formulas with aggregates[10]. In: Proceedings of International Workshop on Nonmonotonic Reasoning, NMR (2010)
5. Gelfond, M., Lifschitz, V.: The stable model semantics for logic programming. In: Kowalski, R., Bowen, K. (eds.) Proceedings of International Logic Programming Conference and Symposium, pp. 1070–1080. MIT Press, Cambridge (1988)
6. Gelfond, M., Lifschitz, V.: Classical negation in logic programs and disjunctive databases. New Generation Computing 9, 365–385 (1991)
7. Lifschitz, V.: What is answer set programming? In: Proceedings of the AAAI Conference on Artificial Intelligence, pp. 1594–1597. MIT Press, Cambridge (2008)
8. Lifschitz, V., Morgenstern, L., Plaisted, D.: Knowledge representation and classical logic. In: van Harmelen, F., Lifschitz, V., Porter, B. (eds.) Handbook of Knowledge Representation, pp. 3–88. Elsevier, Amsterdam (2008)
9. Lifschitz, V., Pearce, D., Valverde, A.: Strongly equivalent logic programs. ACM Transactions on Computational Logic 2, 526–541 (2001)
10. Lifschitz, V., Pearce, D., Valverde, A.: A characterization of strong equivalence for logic programs with variables. In: Baral, C., Brewka, G., Schlipf, J. (eds.) LPNMR 2007. LNCS (LNAI), vol. 4483, pp. 188–200. Springer, Heidelberg (2007)
11. Marek, V., Truszczyński, M.: Stable models and an alternative logic programming paradigm. In: The Logic Programming Paradigm: a 25-Year Perspective, pp. 375–398. Springer, Heidelberg (1999)
12. McCarthy, J.: Applications of circumscription to formalizing common sense knowledge. Artificial Intelligence 26(3), 89–116 (1986)
13. Moschovakis, J.: Intuitionistic logic. In: Zalta, E.N. (ed.) The Stanford Encyclopedia of Philosophy. Fall 2008 edn. (2008), http://plato.stanford.edu/archives/fall2008/entries/logic-intuitionistic
14. Niemelä, I.: Logic programs with stable model semantics as a constraint programming paradigm. Annals of Mathematics and Artificial Intelligence 25, 241–273 (1999)
15. Pearce, D.: A new logical characterization of stable models and answer sets. In: Dix, J., Przymusinski, T.C., Moniz Pereira, L. (eds.) NMELP 1996. LNCS, vol. 1216, pp. 57–70. Springer, Heidelberg (1997)

---

[10] http://userweb.cs.utexas.edu/users/vl/papers/smaf.pdf

# Exploiting Bounded Treewidth with Datalog (A Survey)*

Reinhard Pichler

Technische Universität Wien, Austria
pichler@dbai.tuwien.ac.at

**Abstract.** Many intractable problems have been shown to become tractable if the treewidth of the underlying structure is bounded by a constant. An important tool for deriving such results is Courcelle's Theorem, which states that all properties definable by Monadic Second Order (MSO) sentences are fixed-parameter tractable with respect to the treewidth. In principle, algorithms can be generated automatically from the MSO definition of a problem by exploiting the correspondence between MSO and finite tree automata (FTA). However, this approach has turned out to be problematic, since even relatively simple MSO formulae may lead to a "state explosion" of the FTA.

Recently, monadic datalog (i.e., datalog where all intensional predicate symbols are unary) has been proposed as an alternative method to tackle this class of fixed-parameter tractable problems. On the one hand, if some property of finite structures is expressible in MSO then this property can also be expressed by means of a monadic datalog program. Moreover, the resulting fragment of datalog can be evaluated in linear time (both with respect to the program size and with respect to the data size). In this survey, we present the main ideas of this approach and its extension to counting and enumeration problems.

## 1 Introduction

The high inherent complexity of many interesting problems is a common obstacle to the design of efficient algorithms in many areas of computer science. There are several strategies to deal with such situations, like heuristics, approximations, or probabilistic methods. Over the past decade, parameterized complexity and the study of fixed-parameter algorithms have emerged as another important line of research in response to intractability (see [1,2,3]). In particular, it has been shown that many hard problems become tractable if some problem parameter is fixed or bounded by a constant. For graphs and, more generally, for finite structures, the treewidth is one such parameter which has served as the key to many fixed-parameter tractability (FPT) results. The most prominent method for establishing the FPT in case of bounded treewidth is via Courcelle's Theorem [4,5]: any property of finite structures which is expressible by a Monadic Second Order (MSO) sentence, can be decided in linear time (data complexity) if the treewidth of the structures is bounded by a fixed constant.

In principle, Courcelle's Theorem can be applied directly to construct concrete algorithms by transforming the MSO evaluation problem into a tree language recognition

---

* This work was supported by the Austrian Science Fund (FWF), project P20704-N18.

O. de Moor et al. (Eds.): Datalog 2010, LNCS 6702, pp. 88–105, 2011.

problem (see [6,7]). The latter can then be solved via a finite tree automaton (FTA) (see [8,9]). However, this approach has turned out to be problematic, since even relatively simple MSO formulae may lead to a "state explosion" of the FTA see [10,11]. Consequently, it was already stated in [12] (and similarly in [3]) that the algorithms derived via Courcelle's Theorem are "useless for practical applications". The main benefit of Courcelle's Theorem is that it provides "a simple way to recognize a property as being linear time computable". In other words, proving the FPT of some problem by showing that it is MSO expressible is the starting point (rather than the end point) of the search for an efficient algorithm.

Recently [13], monadic datalog (i.e., datalog where all intensional predicate symbols are unary) has been proposed as a practical tool for devising efficient algorithms in situations where the FPT has been shown via Courcelle's Theorem. Above all, it was proved that if some property of finite structures is expressible in MSO then this property can also be expressed by means of a monadic datalog program over the structure plus the tree decomposition. Hence, in the first place, this is an *expressivity result* rather than a mere complexity result. However, it was also shown that the resulting fragment of datalog can be evaluated in linear time both w.r.t. the program size and w.r.t. the data size. Hence, the corresponding *complexity result* (i.e., Courcelle's Theorem) is obtained as a corollary of this MSO-to-datalog transformation.

This monadic datalog approach has been applied to several problems in the area of database design as well as knowledge representation and reasoning [13,14]. Moreover, it has also been extended to counting and enumeration problems [15,16]. In this survey, we present the main ideas of the monadic datalog approach and its extension to counting and enumeration problems. Moreover, we illustrate the concrete realization of this approach by discussing its application to the SAT problem (i.e., does a given propositional formula have *at least one* satisfying assignment) and the #SAT problem (i.e., *how many* satisfying assignments does a given propositional formula have).

**Organization.** The remainder of this paper is organized as follows. In Section 2, we recall some basic notions and results concerning treewidth and MSO. The main results of the monadic datalog approach (in particular, comparing the expressive power of monadic datalog and MSO over structures of bounded treewidth) are presented in Section 3. In Section 4, this approach is applied to the SAT problem. The extension to counting and enumeration problems is discussed in Section 5. In Section 6, we conclude with a brief summary and an outlook to future work.

## 2 Basic Definitions and Results

**Finite Structures and Treewidth.** Let $\tau = \{R_1, \ldots, R_K\}$ be a set of predicate symbols. A *finite structure* $\mathcal{A}$ over $\tau$ (a $\tau$-*structure*, for short) is given by a finite domain $A = dom(\mathcal{A})$ and relations $R_i^{\mathcal{A}} \subseteq A^{\alpha_i}$, where $\alpha_i \geq 0$ denotes the arity of $R_i \in \tau$. It is convenient to represent a finite structure as a set of ground atoms. All structures and trees considered in this work are assumed to be *finite*. Hence, in the sequel, the finiteness will usually not be explicitly mentioned.

A *tree decomposition* $\mathcal{T}$ of a $\tau$-structure $\mathcal{A}$ is defined as a pair $\langle T, (A_t)_{t \in T} \rangle$ where $T$ is a *rooted* tree and each $A_t$ is a subset of $A$ with the following properties: (1) every

$a \in A$ is contained in some $A_t$; (2) for every $R_i \in \tau$ and every tuple $(a_1, \ldots, a_{\alpha_i}) \in R_i^A$, there exists some node $t \in T$ with $\{a_1, \ldots, a_{\alpha_i}\} \subseteq A_t$; (3) for every $a \in A$, the set $\{t \mid a \in A_t\}$ induces a subtree of $T$.

The set $A_t$ with $t \in T$ is called the *bag* at node $t$. The *width* of a tree decomposition $\langle T, (A_t)_{t \in T} \rangle$ is defined as $max\{|A_t|: t \in T\} - 1$. The *treewidth* $tw(A)$ of $A$ is defined as the minimal width of all tree decompositions of $A$. For a fixed $w \geq 1$, it can be decided in linear time w.r.t. the size of $A$ if $tw(A) \leq w$. Moreover, in case of a positive answer, a tree decomposition of width $w$ can also be computed in linear time [17]. Unfortunately, it has been shown that this linear time algorithm is mainly of theoretical interest and its practical usefulness is limited [18]. Recently, considerable progress has been made in developing heuristic-based tree decomposition algorithms which can handle graphs with moderate size of several hundreds of vertices [18,19,20,21].

For our purposes a normal form of tree decompositions is convenient. In [22], so-called *nice* tree decompositions were introduced, whose definition is recalled below. It is possible to transform any tree decomposition in linear time into a *nice* tree decomposition of the same width.

**Definition 1.** *A tree decomposition $\langle T, (A_t)_{t \in T} \rangle$ is called "nice" if (a) each node in $T$ has at most two children; (b) for each node $t$ with two children $t_1, t_2$, we have $A_t = A_{t_1} = A_{t_2}$; (c) for each node $t$ with one child $t'$, the bags of $t$ and $t'$ differ in at most one element, i.e., $|A_t \Delta A_{t'}| \leq 1$, where $\Delta$ denotes symmetric set difference.*

In this paper, we shall use the SAT problem to illustrate some of the main ideas. Note that a propositional formula $F$ in CNF (or, equivalently, a clause set $F$) can be represented as a structure $A$ over the alphabet $\tau = \{cl(.), var(.), pos(.,.), neg(.,.)\}$ where $cl(z)$ (resp. $var(z)$) means that $z$ is a clause (resp. a variable) in $F$ and $pos(x, c)$ (resp. $neg(x, c)$) means that $x$ occurs unnegated (resp. negated) in the clause $c$. We define the treewidth of $F$ as the treewidth of this structure $A$, i.e., $tw(F) = tw(A)$. Note that the predicate symbols $cl(.)$ and $var(.)$ are contained in $\tau$ for convenience only. They could also be omitted since the information on the variables and clauses in a formula is implicitly given by the predicates $pos(.,.)$ and $neg(.,.)$.

*Example 1.* The propositional formula $F = (x_1 \vee \neg x_2 \vee x_3) \wedge (\neg x_1 \vee x_4 \vee \neg x_5) \wedge (x_2 \vee \neg x_4 \vee x_6)$ in CNF can be represented by the structure $A$ consisting of the following ground atoms: $A = \{var(x_1), var(x_2), var(x_3), var(x_4), var(x_5), var(x_6), cl(c_1), cl(c_2), cl(c_3), pos(x_1, c_1), pos(x_3, c_1), pos(x_4, c_2), pos(x_2, c_3), pos(x_6, c_3), neg(x_2, c_1), neg(x_1, c_2), neg(x_5, c_2), neg(x_4, c_3)\}$.

Two tree decompositions $T_1$ and $T_2$ of this structure are given in Figure 1. Note that $T_2$ is "nice" while $T_1$ is not. The width of both $T_1$ and $T_2$ is 2 since the maximal size of the bags in $T_1$ and in $T_2$ is 3. Actually, the treewidth of $A$ cannot be smaller than 2, which can be seen as follows: when considering the binary predicates $pos$ and $neg$ as edges of a graph, then $A$ gives rise to a cyclic graph. But only cycle-free graphs may have treewidth = 1. Hence, the tree decompositions in Figure 1 are of minimal width and we have $tw(F) = tw(A) = 2$.                                          $\square$

**Monadic Second Order Logic (MSO).** *Monadic Second Order* logic (MSO) extends First Order logic (FO) by the use of *set variables* (usually denoted by upper case letters),

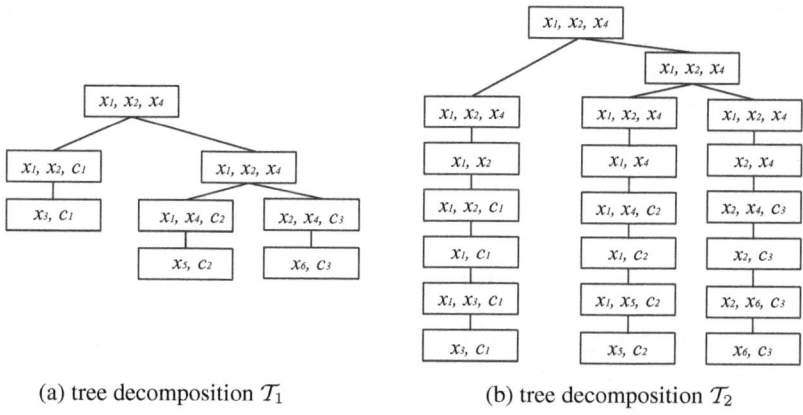

(a) tree decomposition $T_1$          (b) tree decomposition $T_2$

**Fig. 1.** Tree decompositions of formula $F$ of Example 1

which range over sets of domain elements. In contrast, the *individual variables* (which are usually denoted by lower case letters) range over single domain elements. Atomic formulae in an MSO-formula $\varphi$ over a $\tau$-structure have one of the following forms: (1) atoms with some predicate symbol from $\tau$, (2) atoms whose predicate symbol is a monadic second order variable (i.e., a set variable), or (3) equality atoms. An MSO formula $\varphi(x)$ with exactly one free individual variable is called a *unary query*. It is convenient to use set operators such as $\subseteq$, $\subset$, $\cap$, $\cup$, $\in$, and $\notin$ with the obvious meaning. For instance, $X \subseteq Y$ is short for $(\forall u)X(u) \rightarrow Y(u)$. Likewise, $X = Y \cap Z$ is short for $(\forall u)(X(u) \leftrightarrow (Y(u) \wedge Z(u)))$. Moreover, we use $u \in X$ and $X(u)$ interchangeably.

MSO is a useful query language due to its high expressive power. It allows one to express many relevant problems in reasoning, artificial intelligence, graph theory, operations research, etc. For instance, the SAT problem, propositional abduction, closed-world reasoning, answer-set programming, but also database design problems such as primality, BCNF, 3NF, etc. can be nicely expressed by MSO sentences [13,14,23].

*Example 2.* Truth assignments in propositional logic can be represented as sets of variables (namely those variables which are set to true). The following MSO-formula expresses that the assignment $X$ (represented as a set of variables) is a model of some formula $F$ given as a finite structure over signature $\tau = \{cl(.), var(.), pos(.,.), neg(.,.)\}$:

$$model(X, F) := (\forall c)cl(c) \rightarrow (\exists z)[(pos(z, c) \wedge z \in X) \vee (neg(z, c) \wedge z \notin X)].$$

The SAT problem can thus be expressed by the MSO-sentence $(\exists X)model(X, F)$. □

The importance of MSO formulae in the context of parameterized complexity comes from the following result – referred to as *Courcelle's Theorem* [4,5]:

**Theorem 1.** *Let $\varphi$ be an MSO-sentence over some signature $\tau$ and let $\mathcal{A}$ be a $\tau$-structure of treewidth $w$. Evaluating the sentence $\varphi$ over the structure $\mathcal{A}$ can be done in time $\mathcal{O}(f(|\varphi|, w) * |\mathcal{A}|)$ for some function $f$ which only depends on $\varphi$ and $w$ but not on the structure $\mathcal{A}$.*

Courcelle's Theorem means that the evaluation of an MSO sentence over structures of bounded treewidth only requires *linear time* w.r.t. the size of the structure. For instance, the SAT problem is solvable in linear time over propositional formulae of bounded treewidth due to the MSO-encoding of SAT given in Example 2. However, the expression $f(|\varphi|, w)$ in the above theorem can be multiple-exponential in the size of $\varphi$ and $w$. Hence, the search for a feasible algorithm is a non-trivial task even if in theory the linear time upper bound over structures of bounded treewidth can be easily established via Courcelle's Theorem. As far as the SAT problem is concerned, the datalog algorithm presented in Section 4 works in single-exponential time w.r.t. the treewidth.

## 3   Expressive Power of Monadic Datalog

We assume some familiarity with datalog, see e.g. [24,25]. *Monadic datalog* refers to the special case where all intensional predicates (i.e., those occurring in the head of some rule) are unary.

Let $\mathcal{A}$ be a $\tau$-structure with domain $A$ and relations $R_1^{\mathcal{A}}, \ldots, R_K^{\mathcal{A}}$ with $R_i^{\mathcal{A}} \subseteq A^{\alpha_i}$, where $\alpha_i \geq 0$ denotes the arity of $R_i \in \tau$. In order to evaluate a datalog program $\mathcal{P}$ over a structure $\mathcal{A}$, we consider the atoms in $\mathcal{A}$ as additional facts of the program. The result of this evaluation is the set of those (ground) facts which are logically implied by the formula $\mathcal{P} \wedge \mathcal{A}$. The semantics thus obtained is the *minimal model semantics*. Alternatively, datalog has an *operational semantics* defined in terms of the *immediate consequence operator* by viewing the rules of a program as *inference rules*.

In order to apply datalog programs to finite structures of some treewidth $w \geq 1$, we have to extend the finite structure so as to represent also a tree decomposition $\langle T, (A_t)_{t \in T} \rangle$. W.l.o.g., we may assume that $T$ is a binary tree since one can always transform an arbitrary tree decomposition in linear time into a "nice" one according to Definition 1 [22]. We thus define the following extended signature $\tau_{td}$.

$$\tau_{td} = \tau \cup \{root, leaf, child_1, child_2, bag\}$$

where the unary predicates *root*, and *leaf* as well as the binary predicates $child_1$ and $child_2$ are used to represent the tree $T$ in the obvious way. For instance, we write $child_1(t_1, t)$ to denote that $t_1$ is either the first child or the only child of $t$. Finally, *bag* has arity $w + 2$, where $bag(t, a_0, \ldots, a_w)$ means that the bag at node $t$ is $(a_0, \ldots, a_w)$. For a given structure $\mathcal{A}$ with tree decomposition $\mathcal{T}$, we write $\mathcal{A}_{td}$ to denote the structure consisting of $\mathcal{A}$ plus appropriate atoms with predicates *root*, *leaf*, $child_1$, $child_2$, and *bag* to represent $\mathcal{T}$. The domain of $\mathcal{A}_{td}$ consists of the "original" domain elements $a_i$ of $\mathcal{A}$ plus the nodes $t$ of the tree decomposition.

The combined complexity (i.e., the complexity w.r.t. the size of the program $\mathcal{P}$ and the size of the data $\mathcal{A}$) of datalog is EXPTIME-complete (implicit in [26]). However, there are some fragments which can be evaluated much more efficiently. For instance, *monadic datalog* (i.e., all intensional predicates are unary) is NP-complete (combined complexity) [27]. *Propositional datalog* (i.e., all rules are ground) can be evaluated in linear time (combined complexity) [28,29]. The *guarded fragment* of datalog (i.e., every rule $r$ contains an extensional atom $B$ in the body, s.t. all variables occurring in $r$ also occur in $B$) can be evaluated in time $\mathcal{O}(|\mathcal{P}| * |\mathcal{A}|)$ [30]. This upper bound on the time complexity follows easily from the observation that the "guard" $B$ in a rule $r$ admits at most $|\mathcal{A}|$ possible instantiations that are contained in the extensional database $\mathcal{A}$. Since all variables in $r$ occur in $B$, also the number of possible ground instantiations (whose body does not contain an extensional atom outside $\mathcal{A}$) of every rule is bounded by $|\mathcal{A}|$. For the correspondence between MSO and monadic datalog over finite structures of bounded treewidth, a slight relaxation of guarded datalog (namely "quasi-guarded" datalog) is needed, which is defined as follows:

**Definition 2.** *Let $\tau_{td}$ be the extension of a signature $\tau$ and let $\mathcal{P}$ be a datalog program over $\tau_{td}$. Moreover, let $r$ be a rule in $\mathcal{P}$ and let $x, y$ be variables in $r$. We say that $y$ is* functionally dependent on $x$ in one step, *if the body of $r$ contains an atom of one of the following forms: $child_1(x, y)$, $child_1(y, x)$, $child_2(x, y)$, $child_2(y, x)$, or $bag(x, a_0, \ldots, a_k)$ with $y = a_i$ for some $i \in \{1, \ldots, k\}$.*

*We say that $y$ is* functionally dependent on $x$ *if there exists some $n \geq 1$ and variables $z_0, \ldots, z_n$ in $r$ with $z_0 = x, z_n = y$ and, for every $i \in \{1, \ldots, n\}$, $z_i$ is functionally dependent on $z_{i-1}$ in one step.*

*Furthermore, we call a datalog program $\mathcal{P}$ over $\tau_{td}$* quasi-guarded *if every rule $r$ in $\mathcal{P}$ contains an extensional atom $B$, s.t. every variable occurring in $r$ either occurs in $B$ or is functionally dependent on some variable in $B$. If this is the case, we call $B$ a* quasi-guard *of $r$.*

It can be easily verified that, a quasi-guarded program $\mathcal{P}$ can be evaluated over a structure $\mathcal{A}$ in time $\mathcal{O}(|\mathcal{P}| * |\mathcal{A}|)$. Analogously to guarded datalog programs, this is due to the fact that also in quasi-guarded programs, every rule $r$ has at most $|\mathcal{A}|$ possible ground instantiations s.t. the extensional atoms of $r$ are instantiated to atoms in $\mathcal{A}$.

The main result from [13] on the correspondence between MSO and monadic datalog is as follows:

**Theorem 2.** *Let the signature $\tau$ and the integer $w \geq 1$ be arbitrary but fixed. Every MSO-definable unary query over $\tau$-structures of treewidth $w$ is also computable by a quasi-guarded monadic datalog program over $\tau_{td}$.*

Before giving a rough proof sketch, we recall some basic notion and result from finite model theory [31,32]. The *quantifier depth* of an MSO-formula $\varphi$ is defined as the maximum degree of nesting of quantifiers (both for individual variables and set variables) in $\varphi$. Let $\varphi(\boldsymbol{x})$ with $\boldsymbol{x} = (x_0, \ldots, x_w)$ for some $w \geq 0$ be an MSO formula with free individual variables $\boldsymbol{x}$. Furthermore, let $\mathcal{A}$ be a $\tau$-structure and $\boldsymbol{a} = (a_0, \ldots, a_w)$ be distinguished domain elements. We write $(\mathcal{A}, \boldsymbol{a}) \models \varphi(\boldsymbol{x})$ to denote that $\varphi(\boldsymbol{a})$ evaluates to true in $\mathcal{A}$. We call two structures $(\mathcal{A}, \boldsymbol{a})$ and $(\mathcal{B}, \boldsymbol{b})$ *k-equivalent* and write $(\mathcal{A}, \boldsymbol{a}) \equiv_k^{MSO} (\mathcal{B}, \boldsymbol{b})$ if and only if for every MSO-formula $\varphi$ of quantifier depth at most $k$, the equivalence $(\mathcal{A}, \boldsymbol{a}) \models \varphi \Leftrightarrow (\mathcal{B}, \boldsymbol{b}) \models \varphi$ holds. By definition, $\equiv_k^{MSO}$ is an equivalence relation. For any $k$, the relation $\equiv_k^{MSO}$ has only finitely many equivalence classes. These equivalence classes are referred to as *k-types* or simply as *types*. The $\equiv_k^{MSO}$-equivalence between two structures can be effectively decided [31,32].

*Proof Sketch of Theorem 2.* The proof proceeds in three steps:

(1) *Modification of the normal form of tree decompositions.* Recall from Definition 1 the concept of *nice* tree decompositions. For the proof of Theorem 2 it is convenient to slightly modify nice tree decompositions to a normal form where all bags have size

$w + 1$ (with $w$ denoting the width). Moreover, the bags are considered as $(w + 1)$-*tuples* of elements (rather than sets). To this end, condition (c) in Definition 1 is modified as follows: for each node $t$ with one child $t'$, the bag of $t$ is obtained from the bag of $t'$ either by permuting the arguments or by some replacement of the first argument. The advantage of this normal form is that we indeed have $w + 2$ arguments of the bag-predicate in $\tau_{td}$ and do not need to fill in positions with some dummy argument. Any tree decomposition can be normalized in linear time without increasing the width.

Since we are considering bags as tuples of elements, we shall use the notation $\boldsymbol{a}_t$ synonymously for $A_t$ if we want to stress that the elements in the bag $A_t$ are ordered.

(2) *Types of certain induced substructures.* In the construction of the datalog program sketched in step (3) below, we have to deal with those parts of a tree decomposition which have already been visited along a bottom-up or top-down traversal of a tree decomposition. We only discuss the bottom-up case here. Let $\mathcal{T} = \langle T, (A_s)_{s \in T} \rangle$ be a tree decomposition of a structure and let $t$ denote a node of $T$. We write $\mathcal{T}_t$ to denote the part of $\mathcal{T}$ which has been visited along the bottom-up traversal when $t$ is the current node. Formally, we write $T_t$ to denote the *subtree rooted at $t$* and we set $\mathcal{T}_t = \langle T_t, (A_s)_{s \in T_t} \rangle$. Now let $\mathcal{A}$ be a finite structure with tree decomposition $\mathcal{T}$ and let $t$ be a node in $\mathcal{T}$. Moreover, we write $\mathcal{A}_t$ to denote the substructure of $\mathcal{A}$ induced by (the elements in the bags of) $\mathcal{T}_t$. It can be shown that the $k$-type (for arbitrary but fixed $k$) of $(\mathcal{A}_t, \boldsymbol{a}_t)$ is fully determined by (i) the $k$-type of the substructure induced by the subtree rooted at the child node(s) of $t$ and (ii) the relations between elements in the bag at node $t$.

(3) *Construction of the datalog program.* We construct a quasi-guarded datalog program $\mathcal{P}$ over $\tau_{td}$ as follows: suppose that the given MSO formula has quantifier-depth $k$. Thus the intensional predicates of $\mathcal{P}$ correspond to $k$-types of three kinds of structures: (a) we generate all possible $k$-types of structures obtained by a *bottom-up* construction of the tree decomposition; (b) we generate all possible $k$-types of structures obtained by a *top-down* construction of the tree decomposition; and (c) we consider all structures obtained by identifying the root of one tree decomposition with the leaf of another tree decomposition. We only discuss case (a) here, namely the bottom-up construction: depending on whether the root node of the resulting tree decomposition has one or two child nodes, we distinguish two cases:

Case 1. (the root has one child node). We start off with some structure $\mathcal{A}$ plus tree decomposition $\mathcal{T}$ whose root is $t$ and we extend $\mathcal{A}$ and $\mathcal{T}$ in all possible ways to $\mathcal{A}'$ and $\mathcal{T}'$ with root $t'$, s.t. $\mathcal{T} = \mathcal{T}'_t$. By the above considerations, we know that the $k$-type $\vartheta'$ of $(\mathcal{A}', \boldsymbol{a}_{t'})$ is fully determined by the $k$-type $\vartheta$ of $(\mathcal{A}, \boldsymbol{a}_t)$ and the relations between elements in the bag at node $t'$. This correspondence can be expressed by a datalog rule with head atom $\vartheta'(t')$ and with an atom $\vartheta(t)$ occurring in the body. The remaining atoms in the body express the relations which hold between the elements in the bag at node $t$ and information on the relevant part of the tree decomposition like $child_1(t, t')$.

Case 2. (the root has two child nodes). Now we start off with two structures $\mathcal{A}_1$ and $\mathcal{A}_2$ plus tree decompositions $\mathcal{T}_1$ $\mathcal{T}_2$ whose roots are $t_1$ and $t_2$, respectively. We identify the elements in the bag at $t_1$ with the elements in the bag of $t_2$ and consider the set of all remaining elements in $\mathcal{T}_1$ and the set of all remaining elements in $\mathcal{T}_2$ as disjoint. $\mathcal{A}_1$ and

$\mathcal{A}_2$ must have been chosen in such a way that the relations which hold in $\mathcal{A}_1$ between the elements in the bag of $t_1$ and the relations which hold in $\mathcal{A}_2$ between the elements in the bag of $t_2$ are exactly the same. We construct $\mathcal{A}'$ and $\mathcal{T}'$ with root $t'$ such that $\mathcal{T}_1 = \mathcal{T}'_{t_1}$ and $\mathcal{T}_2 = \mathcal{T}'_{t_2}$. By the above considerations, we know that the $k$-type $\vartheta'$ of $(\mathcal{A}', \boldsymbol{a}_{t'})$ is fully determined by the $k$-type $\vartheta_1$ of $(\mathcal{A}_1, \boldsymbol{a}_{t_1})$, the $k$-type $\vartheta_2$ of $(\mathcal{A}_2, \boldsymbol{a}_{t_2})$, and the relations between elements in the bag at node $t'$. Again, this correspondence can be expressed by an appropriate datalog rule with head atom $\vartheta'(t')$.

We conclude this proof by giving an example of what the resulting datalog rules look like. In case of a root node with two child nodes, we get rules of the following form:[1]

$$\vartheta(v) \leftarrow child_1(v_1, v), \vartheta_1(v_1), child_2(v_2, v), \vartheta_2(v_2). \qquad \square$$

Above all, Theorem 2 is an expressivity result. However, by exploiting the low complexity of evaluating quasi-guarded datalog programs, one can immediately derive a complexity result. We thus get a slightly extended version of Courcelle's Theorem as a corollary (which is in turn a special case of Theorem 4.12 in [7]).

**Corollary 1.** *The evaluation problem of unary MSO-queries $\varphi(x)$ over $\tau$-structures $\mathcal{A}$ of treewidth $w$ can be solved in time $\mathcal{O}(f(|\varphi(x)|, w) * |\mathcal{A}|)$ for some function $f$ which only depends on $\varphi(x)$ and $w$ but not on the structure $\mathcal{A}$.*

## 4    Putting Monadic Datalog to Work

We now illustrate the monadic datalog approach at work by applying it to the SAT problem. Suppose that a clause set $\mathcal{C}$ together with a tree decomposition $\mathcal{T}$ of width $w$ is represented by a $\tau_{td}$-structure $\mathcal{A}_{td}$ with $\tau_{td} = \{cl, var, pos, neg, root, leaf, child_1, child_2, bag\}$. W.l.o.g., we may assume that $\mathcal{T}$ fulfills the properties of "nice" tree decompositions [22] recalled in Definition 1. Note that elements in the bags of $\mathcal{T}$ correspond to variables or clauses in $\mathcal{C}$. Hence, if a node $t$ has a single child node $t'$, then the one element by which $A_t$ differs from $A_{t'}$ is either a variable or a clause. In total, we thus distinguish 5 kinds of internal nodes in $\mathcal{T}$: a node $t$ is a *variable removal node* resp. *clause removal node*, if the bag $A_t$ is obtained from $A_{t'}$ by removing a variable resp. a clause; $t$ is a *variable introduction node* resp. a *clause introduction node*, if $A_t$ is obtained from $A_{t'}$ by introducing a new variable resp. clause; finally, if a node $t$ has two children, then $t$ is referred to as a *branch node*. The SAT program in Figure 2 has appropriate rules for leaf nodes and exactly these 5 kinds of internal nodes (cf. [14]).

The program adopts the following notational conventions: lower case letters $v$, $c$, and $x$ (possibly with subscripts) are used as datalog variables for a single node in $\mathcal{T}$, for a single clause, or for a single propositional variable, respectively. In contrast, upper case letters are used as datalog variables denoting sets of variables (in the case of $X, P, N$) or sets of clauses (in the case of $C$). Note that the sets are not sets in the general sense, since their cardinality is restricted by the maximal size $w + 1$ of the bags, where $w$ is a fixed constant. The SAT program in Figure 2 can therefore be seen as a shorthand

---

[1] In the program construction in [13], additional atoms referring to the bags at the nodes $v$, $v_1$, and $v_2$ are contained in the body of the rule. It can be easily checked that they are not needed.

---

**Program** SAT

/* leaf node. */
$solve(v, P, N, C_1) \leftarrow leaf(v), bag(v, X, C), P \cup N = X, P \cap N = \emptyset,$
    $true(P, N, C_1, C).$

/* variable removal node. */
$solve(v, P, N, C_1) \leftarrow bag(v, X, C), child_1(v_1, v), bag(v_1, X \uplus \{x\}, C),$
    $solve(v_1, P \uplus \{x\}, N, C_1).$

$solve(v, P, N, C_1) \leftarrow bag(v, X, C), child_1(v_1, v), bag(v_1, X \uplus \{x\}, C),$
    $solve(v_1, P, N \uplus \{x\}, C_1).$

/* clause removal node. */
$solve(v, P, N, C_1) \leftarrow bag(v, X, C), child_1(v_1, v), bag(v_1, X, C \uplus \{c\}),$
    $solve(v_1, P, N, C_1 \uplus \{c\}).$

/* variable introduction node. */
$solve(v, P \uplus \{x\}, N, C_1 \cup C_2) \leftarrow bag(v, X \uplus \{x\}, C), child_1(v_1, v),$
    $bag(v_1, X, C), solve(v_1, P, N, C_1), true(\{x\}, \emptyset, C_2, C).$

$solve(v, P, N \uplus \{x\}, C_1 \cup C_2) \leftarrow bag(v, X \uplus \{x\}, C), child_1(v_1, v),$
    $bag(v_1, X, C), solve(v_1, P, N, C_1), true(\emptyset, \{x\}, C_2, C).$

/* clause introduction node. */
$solve(v, P, N, C_1 \cup C_2) \leftarrow bag(v, X, C \uplus \{c\}), child_1(v_1, v), bag(v_1, X, C),$
    $solve(v_1, P, N, C_1), true(P, N, C_2, \{c\}).$

/* branch node. */
$solve(v, P, N, C_1 \cup C_2) \leftarrow child_1(v_1, v), solve(v_1, P, N, C_1), child_2(v_2, v),$
    $solve(v_2, P, N, C_2).$

/* result (at the root node). */
$success \leftarrow root(v), bag(v, X, C), solve(v, P, N, C).$

---

**Fig. 2.** SAT decision procedure

for a monadic program, since all but one variable in the head atoms have bounded instantiations. For instance, in the atom $solve(v, P, N, C)$, the sets $P, N, C$ are subsets of the bag of $v$. Hence, each combination $P, N, C$ could be represented by 3 subsets $r_1, r_2, r_3$ of $\{0, \ldots, w\}$ referring to indices of elements in the bag of $v$. Since $w$ is considered as a fixed constant, $solve(v, P, N, C)$ is simply a succinct representation of constantly many monadic predicates of the form $solve_{\langle r_1, r_2, r_3 \rangle}(v)$.

For the sake of readability, we are using non-datalog expressions involving the set operators $\uplus$ (disjoint union), $\cup$, and $\cap$. Of course, they could be easily replaced by "proper" datalog expressions, e.g., $P \cup N = X$ could be replaced by $union(P, N, X)$. In order to facilitate the discussion, we introduce the following notation. Let $\mathcal{C}$ denote the input clause set with variables in $V$ and tree decomposition $\mathcal{T}$. For any node $v$ in $\mathcal{T}$, we write $\mathcal{T}_v$ to denote the subtree of $\mathcal{T}$ rooted at $v$. By $Cl(v)$ we denote the set of clauses in the bag of $v$ while $Cl(\mathcal{T}_v)$ denotes the set of clauses that occur in any bag in $\mathcal{T}_v$. Analogously, we write $Var(v)$ and $Var(\mathcal{T}_v)$ as a shorthand for the set of variables occurring in the bag of $v$ respectively in any bag in $\mathcal{T}_v$. Finally, the restriction of a clause $c$ to the variables in some set $U \subseteq V$ will be denoted by $c|_U$.

The SAT program contains three intensional predicates *solve*, *true*, and *success*. The crucial predicate is $solve(v, P, N, C)$ with the following intended meaning: $v$ denotes a node in $\mathcal{T}$. $P$ and $N$ form a partition of $Var(v)$ representing a truth value assignment on $Var(v)$, s.t. all variables in $P$ take the value true and all variables in $N$ take the value false. $C$ denotes a subset of $Cl(v)$. For all values of $v, P, N, C$, the ground fact $solve(v, P, N, C)$ shall be true in the minimal model of the program plus the structure if and only if the following condition holds:

**Property A.** There exists an assignment $J$ on the variables in $Var(\mathcal{T}_v)$, s.t.

(a) On $Var(v)$, the assignment represented by $(P, N)$ coincides with $J$,
(b) $(Cl(\mathcal{T}_v) \setminus Cl(v)) \cup C$ is true in $J$, and
(c) for every clause $c \in Cl(v) \setminus C$, the restriction $c|_{Var(\mathcal{T}_v)}$ is false in $J$.

The main task of the SAT program is the computation of all facts $solve(v, P, N, C)$ by means of a bottom-up traversal of the tree decomposition. The other predicates have the following meaning: $true(P, N, C_1, C)$ means that $C_1$ contains precisely those clauses from $C$ which are true in the (partial) assignment given by $(P, N)$. We do not specify the implementation of this predicate here. It can be easily achieved via the extensional predicates *pos* and *neg*. The 0-ary predicate *success* indicates if the input structure is the encoding of a satisfiable clause set. In [14], a detailed proof of the correctness and of a precise upper bound (which is linear in the size of the formula and single-exponential in the tree-width) on the time complexity of the SAT program is given. The correctness of the SAT program easily follows from the following lemma [14]:

**Lemma 1.** *The solve-predicate has the intended meaning described above, i.e., for all values $v, P, N$, and $C$, the ground fact $solve(v, P, N, C)$ is true in the minimal model of the program plus the structure if and only if Property A holds.*

*Proof Sketch.* The lemma is shown by structural induction on $\mathcal{T}$. The induction step goes via a case distinction over all possible types of nodes. The proof is lengthy but straightforward. We restrict ourselves here to a brief discussion of the rules in Figure 2 for the various types of nodes. The rule for a *leaf node* $v$ determines all possible assignments $(P, N)$ on $Var(v)$ and checks for each assignment and each clause $c \in Cl(v)$ if $c|_{Var(v)}$ is true. For a *variable removal node* $v$, we distinguish two cases depending on whether the removed variable $x$ had the truth value true or false in the considered truth assignment at the child node $v_1$. In case of a *clause removal node* $v$, we have to check that the removed clause $c$ had the truth value true in the considered truth assignment. In other words, *solve*-facts at node $v_1$ which fail to satisfy the clause $c$ do not give rise to any *solve*-facts at the node $v$. Indeed, by conditions (2) and (3) of the definition of tree decompositions (see Section 2), there is no way to extend such a truth assignment to the variables occurring "above" $v$ to a model of $c$. At a *variable introduction node* $v$, we can extend the truth assignments $(P, N)$ at node $v_1$ in two ways to a truth assignment on $Var(v)$, namely we can set $x$ to true or to false. Consequently, there are two rules for this node type. At a *clause introduction node* $v$, we just have to determine the truth value of $c|_{Var(v)}$ for the truth assignment $(P, N)$. At a *branch node*, we combine those assignments on $Var(\mathcal{T}_{v_1})$ and $Var(\mathcal{T}_{v_2})$ which coincide on $Var(v)$. □

We conclude this section with a brief comparison of the SAT program with the program $\mathcal{P}$ in the proof of Theorem 2. The definition of a monadic datalog program $\mathcal{P}$ from some MSO-formula $\varphi$ in the proof of Theorem 2 is "constructive" in theory. Of course, it would also be applicable to the MSO encoding of the SAT problem. However, we would thus end up with a monadic datalog program $\mathcal{P}$ that is multiple-exponential w.r.t. to the treewidth, where the tower of exponentials essentially corresponds to the quantifier depth of the MSO sentence. In contrast, the SAT program in Figure 2 can be executed in single-exponential time w.r.t. the treewidth. The SAT program follows the intuition of the generic program $\mathcal{P}$ but incorporates several shortcuts: above all, as the Property A of the *solve*-predicate suggests, we only propagate those "types" (represented by the *solve*-facts) which can possibly be extended in bottom-up direction to a solution (i.e., a truth assignment that satisfies all clauses). Moreover, the *solve*-facts do not exactly correspond to the types in Theorem 2 but only describe the properties of each type which are crucial for the concrete target formula $\varphi$. Finally, as has already been explained above, we are using datalog extended by sets of bounded cardinality as a succinct representation of a much bigger monadic datalog program.

## 5  Counting and Enumeration

The predominant class of problems studied in algorithms and complexity theory is the class of decision problems, which normally ask if *at least one solution* to a given problem instance exists, e.g., a satisfying truth assignment of a given formula. However, in many areas such as databases it would be more interesting to know all solutions, e.g., all variable bindings which make a given query over a given database true. If the number of solutions is very big, then it may be sufficient to output just a few solutions plus information as to how many solutions exist in total. Problems which ask for the computation of *all solutions* are referred to as enumeration problems. Problems which ask for the *total number of solutions* are referred to as counting problems.

As far as the complexity is concerned, counting and enumeration problems are clearly at least as hard as the corresponding decision problems. Hence, the intractability of a decision problem carries over to the corresponding counting and enumeration version. In this section, we show how the monadic datalog approach can be extended to counting and enumeration problems so as to devise also for these problems efficient algorithms (based on datalog) in case of bounded treewidth [15,16].

**MSO counting and enumeration problems.** First of all, we have to recall how counting and enumeration problems can be defined by an MSO formula. Let $\varphi(X_1, \ldots, X_m)$ be an MSO formula over some signature $\tau$, s.t. $m \geq 1$ and $X_1, \ldots, X_m$ denote the free variables of this formula. W.l.o.g., we may assume that all variables $X_1, \ldots, X_m$ are *set* variables (since we can always replace individual variables by set variables which may only be instantiated to singletons).

The *counting problem* defined by $\varphi(X_1, \ldots, X_m)$ is the following problem: given a $\tau$-structure $\mathcal{A}$ with domain $dom(\mathcal{A})$, what is the number $|\{(A_1, \ldots, A_m) \mid A_i \subseteq dom(\mathcal{A})$ for every $i$ and $\mathcal{A} \models \varphi(A_1, \ldots, A_m)\}|$?

The *enumeration problem* defined by $\varphi(X_1, \ldots, X_m)$ is the following problem: given a $\tau$-structure $\mathcal{A}$ with domain $dom(\mathcal{A})$, compute the set $\{(A_1, \ldots, A_m) \mid A_i \subseteq dom(\mathcal{A})$ for every $i$ and $\mathcal{A} \models \varphi(A_1, \ldots, A_m)\}$.

**Solving MSO counting problems.** In order to extend the monadic datalog approach to counting problems, we have to extend datalog in two ways, i.e., we need *counter variables* and a SUM-*operator*: intensional predicates are allowed to contain a counter variable as an additional argument. A predicate $p$ having $n$ arguments plus a counter is denoted by $p(t_1, \ldots, t_n, j)$. For a rule $r$, a constant $c$ and counter variables $j, j_1$ and $j_2$ occurring in predicates of $r$, the relations $j = c$, $j = j_1 + j_2$, and $j = j_1 * j_2$ are allowed in $r$. We require that, for every value $\hat{t}_1, \ldots, \hat{t}_n$ of $t_1, \ldots, t_n$, at most one value $\hat{j}$ of $j$ exists, s.t. the fact $p(\hat{t}_1, \ldots, \hat{t}_n, \hat{j})$ is derivable from the datalog program and a given structure $\mathcal{A}$. Furthermore, we allow the expression $\text{SUM}(j)$ in place of a counter variable in the head of a rule. Its semantics is like the SUM aggregate function in ordinary SQL, where we first apply a GROUP BY over all remaining head variables to the result of evaluating the conjunctive query in the body of the rule. For a formal definition of the semantics of SUM, see [33]. Analogously to Definition 2, we say that a program is in *quasi-guarded* extended datalog if every rule $r$ contains an extensional atom $B$, s.t. each non-counter variable in $r$ either occurs in $B$ or is functionally dependent on some variable in $B$. In [16], Theorem 2 was extended to MSO counting problems as follows.

**Theorem 3.** *Let the signature $\tau$, the integer $w \geq 1$, and the MSO-formula $\varphi(X_1, \ldots, X_m)$ over $\tau$ with $m \geq 1$ be arbitrary but fixed. The counting problem defined by $\varphi(X_1, \ldots, X_m)$ over $\tau$-structures of treewidth $w$ can be solved by a quasi-guarded extended datalog program over $\tau_{td}$.*

*Proof Sketch.* Similarly to the proof of Theorem 2 we proceed in three steps.

(1) We again modify the normal form of tree decompositions by considering the bags as tuples rather than sets.

(2) We have to establish the relationship between the $k$-types of certain substructures induced by the elements occurring in some subtrees of a tree decomposition. In the proof of Theorem 2 we considered the $k$-type of structures of the form $(\mathcal{A}_t, \boldsymbol{a}_t)$ where $\mathcal{A}_t$ is such an induced substructure and $\boldsymbol{a}_t$ denotes the bag at some node $t$. For counting problems, we have to handle MSO formulae $\varphi(X_1, \ldots, X_m)$ with free set variables $X_1, \ldots, X_m$. Hence, we now have to deal with the $k$-type of structures of the form $(\mathcal{A}_t, \boldsymbol{a}_t, \boldsymbol{B}_t)$, where $\boldsymbol{B}_t = (B_{t1}, \ldots, B_{tm})$ is an $m$-tuple of sets of domain elements.

(3) Finally, we construct an extended datalog program by again using intensional predicates $\vartheta$ corresponding to certain $k$-types. In contrast to the proof of Theorem 2, these atoms now take the form $\vartheta(t, j)$, where the second argument is a counter variable indicating in how many ways the type $\vartheta$ can be generated at node $t$ by the bottom-up construction in the proof of Theorem 2. Thus for the rules defining the predicates $\vartheta(t, j)$, it no longer suffices to establish *how* type $\vartheta$ at node $t$ can be obtained from possible types at the child node(s) of $t$. In addition, we also have to keep track *in how many ways* type $\vartheta$ at node $t$ can be obtained from possible types at the child node(s) of $t$. To this end, we have to introduce an auxiliary, intensional predicate which is used to collect all possible

ways of generating a certain type at node $t$. The value of $j$ in $\vartheta(t, j)$ is then obtained as the sum over all possible ways of obtaining type $\vartheta$. For instance, in case of a branch node, we thus get the following two kinds of rules:

$$aux(v, \vartheta, \vartheta_1, \vartheta_2, j_1 * j_2) \leftarrow child_1(v_1, v), child_2(v_2, v), \vartheta_1(v_1, j_1), \vartheta_2(v_2, j_2).$$

$$\vartheta(v, \text{SUM}(j)) \qquad\qquad \leftarrow aux(v, \vartheta, \_, \_, j).$$

By slight abuse of notation, we use the symbols $\vartheta, \vartheta_1, \vartheta_2$ as constant symbols (occurring as arguments of the $aux$-predicate) and as predicate symbols. Of course, this could be easily avoided by inventing a constant symbol $c_\vartheta$ for every type $\vartheta$. The multiplication $j_1 * j_2$ in the head of the first rule reflects the fact that all possible ways of obtaining type $\vartheta_1$ at node $t_1$ can be combined with all possible ways of obtaining type $\vartheta_2$ at node $t_2$ to get type $\vartheta$ at node $t$. The rule with head $\vartheta(v, \text{SUM}(j))$ sums up the counter for all derivable facts of the form $aux(v, \vartheta, \_, \_, j)$. $\qquad\square$

For the complexity of solving MSO definable counting problems, we get a similar upper bound as in Corollary 1. More specifically, let us assume unit cost for arithmetic operations. It was shown in [16] that then a quasi-guarded, extended datalog program $\mathcal{P}$ can be evaluated over a structure $\mathcal{A}$ in time $\mathcal{O}(|\mathcal{P}| * |\mathcal{A}|)$. Hence, for structures whose treewidth is bounded by $w$, we can solve the counting problem defined by an MSO formula $\varphi(\boldsymbol{X})$ in time $\mathcal{O}(f(|\varphi(\boldsymbol{X})|, w) * |\mathcal{A}|)$ for some function $f$ which depends on the MSO formula $\varphi(\boldsymbol{X})$ and the treewidth $w$ but not on the input structure $\mathcal{A}$.

**The #SAT problem.** In [15], the datalog program presented in Figure 2, was extended to a program for the #SAT problem (i.e., the problem of counting the number of satisfying truth assignments of a given propositional formula), see Figure 3. The structure of this program is very similar to the decision procedure in Figure 2. We only point out two important differences between the two programs, namely the handling of counter variables and the need for additional datalog rules:

In the counting procedure, the $solve$-predicate has a counter variable as an additional argument. The program evaluation again corresponds to a bottom-up traversal of the tree decomposition. At the root node, we now have to sum up all the counter variables for all derivable $solve$-facts (rather than just asking if at least one such $solve$-fact exists for the root).

For some of the node types, the counting procedure has more rules than the decision procedure. For instance, for variable removal nodes, we now have 3 rather than 2 rules. Let $d_1, d_2$ denote the two rules in case of the decision procedure and $c_1, c_2, c_3$ denote the three rules in case of the counting procedure. Intuitively, we need three rules $c_1, c_2, c_3$ in the counting procedure in order to distinguish the three possible cases how a new fact $solve(v, P, N, C_u)$ may be derived by the decision procedure, namely: $solve(v, P, N, C_u)$ may be derived via a fact $solve(v_1, P \uplus \{x\}, N, C_u)$ (i.e., by firing rule $d_1$) or via a fact $solve(v_1, P, N \uplus \{x\}, C_u, j_2)$ (i.e., by firing rule $d_2$) or via both (i.e., by firing rules $d_1$ $and$ $d_2$). Of course, in case of the decision procedure, it only matters $if$ a fact $solve(v, P, N, C_u)$ can be derived. In contrast, for counting, we need to keep track $in$ $how$ $many$ $ways$ it can be derived. So rule $c_1$ (resp. $c_2$ resp. $c_3$) corresponds to the case that both $d_1$ and $d_2$ (resp. $d_1$ only resp. $d_2$ only) fire.

As mentioned at the end of Section 4, the $solve$-facts in the SAT program (and also in the #SAT program) essentially represent the $k$-types in the generic construction

---

**Program #SAT**

/* leaf node. */
$solve(v, P, N, C_u, 1) \leftarrow leaf(v), bag(v, X, C), P \cup N = X, P \cap N = \emptyset,$
$\quad true(P, N, C_1, C).$

/* variable removal node. */
$solve(v, P, N, C_u, j_1 + j_2) \leftarrow bag(v, X, C), child_1(v_1, v), bag(v_1, X \uplus \{x\}, C),$
$\quad solve(v_1, P \uplus \{x\}, N, C_u, j_1), solve(v_1, P, N \uplus \{x\}, C_u, j_2).$
$solve(v, P, N, C_u, j) \leftarrow bag(v, X, C), child_1(v_1, v), bag(v_1, X \uplus \{x\}, C),$
$\quad solve(v_1, P \uplus \{x\}, N, C_u, j), not\ solve(v_1, P, N \uplus \{x\}, C_u, \_).$
$solve(v, P, N, C_u, j) \leftarrow bag(v, X, C), child_1(v_1, v), bag(v_1, X \uplus \{x\}, C),$
$\quad solve(v_1, P, N \uplus \{x\}, C_u, j), not\ solve(v_1, P \uplus \{x\}, N, C_u, \_).$

/* clause removal node. */
$solve(v, P, N, C_u, j) \leftarrow bag(v, X, C), child_1(v_1, v), bag(v_1, X, C \uplus \{c\}),$
$\quad solve(v_1, P, N, C_u \uplus \{c\}, j).$

/* variable introduction node. */
$solve(v, P \uplus \{x\}, N, C_u, \mathrm{SUM}(j)) \leftarrow bag(v, X \uplus \{x\}, C), child_1(v_1, v), bag(v_1, X, C),$
$\quad solve(v_1, P, N, C_1, j), true(\{x\}, \emptyset, C_2, C), C_1 \cup C_2 = C_u.$
$solve(v, P, N \uplus \{x\}, C_u, \mathrm{SUM}(j)) \leftarrow bag(v, X \uplus \{x\}, C), child_1(v_1, v), bag(v_1, X, C),$
$\quad solve(v_1, P, N, C_1, j), true(\emptyset, \{x\}, C_2, C), C_1 \cup C_2 = C_u.$

/* clause introduction node. */
$solve(v, P, N, C_u, j) \leftarrow bag(v, X, C \uplus \{c\}), child_1(v_1, v), bag(v_1, X, C),$
$\quad solve(v_1, P, N, C_1, j), true(P, N, C_2, \{c\}), C_1 \cup C_2 = C_u.$

/* branch node. */
$solve(v, P, N, C_u, \mathrm{SUM}(j)) \leftarrow child_1(v_1, v), solve(v_1, P, N, C_1, j_1), child_2(v_2, v),$
$\quad solve(v_2, P, N, C_2, j_2), C_1 \cup C_2 = C_u, j_1 * j_2 = j.$

/* result (at the root node). */
$count(\mathrm{SUM}(j)) \leftarrow root(v), bag(v, X, C), solve(v, P, N, C, j).$

---

**Fig. 3.** #SAT counting procedure

according to Theorem 2 (and likewise Theorem 3). However, the SAT- and #SAT program do this in a succinct way by exploiting "domain knowledge" on the SAT-problem, so to speak. By the same token, the #SAT program in Figure 3 does not require auxiliary, intensional predicates as in the proof sketch of Theorem 3. Instead, the rules in Figure 3 compute the required sums directly in the rules with head-predicate *solve*.

**Solving MSO enumeration problems.** In order to solve enumeration problems by datalog programs, we would have to extend datalog by set variables which may be instantiated to sets of *arbitrary* cardinality. In order to better control the *delay* (i.e, the time needed for computing the first respectively next solution), an enumeration method based on post-processing after the execution of the counting-program was proposed in [16]. This enumeration method works as follows. Let an enumeration problem be defined by the MSO formula $\varphi(\boldsymbol{X})$ with $\boldsymbol{X} = (X_1, \ldots, X_m)$. Recall from the proof sketch of Theorem 3 that our extended datalog program keeps track of $k$-types $\vartheta$ of structures $(\mathcal{A}_t, \boldsymbol{a}_t, \boldsymbol{B}_t)$, where $\boldsymbol{B}_t = (B_{t1}, \ldots, B_{tm})$ is an $m$-tuple of sets of domain elements. The relationship between such $k$-types for some node $t$ and its child node $t'$ resp. its child nodes $t_1, t_2$ is represented by facts $aux(t, \vartheta, \vartheta', j)$ resp. $aux(t, \vartheta, \vartheta_1, \vartheta_2, j)$. The enumeration of all solutions of $\varphi(\boldsymbol{X})$ proceeds by iterated top-down traversals of the tree decomposition $\mathcal{T} = \langle T, (A_t)_{t \in T} \rangle$ – one traversal for each solution. The starting points (at the root node $r$) of these traversals are facts $aux(r, \vartheta, \dots)$, s.t. $\vartheta$ is the type of a structure $(\mathcal{A}_r, \boldsymbol{a}_r, \boldsymbol{B}_r)$ with $\mathcal{A}_r \models \varphi(\boldsymbol{B}_r)$. Note that the $aux$-facts at each node contain the information how each type at a node $t$ can be obtained from type(s) at the child node(s) of $t$. Thus each solution of $\varphi(\boldsymbol{X})$ corresponds to the selection of exactly one type $\vartheta_t$ at each node $t \in T$, s.t. for every $t \in T$, a fact of the form $aux(t, \vartheta_t, \dots)$ has been derived and the following conditions are fulfilled. (1) If $t$ is a node with a single child $t'$, then some fact of the form $aux(t, \vartheta_t, \vartheta_{t'}, \dots)$ has been derived. (2) If $t$ is a node with two child nodes $t_1$ and $t_2$, then some fact of the form $aux(t, \vartheta_t, \vartheta_{t_1}, \vartheta_{t_2}, \dots)$ has been derived. Let us refer to such a selection of one type $\vartheta_t$ at each node $t \in T$ as a *derivation tree* since, intuitively, it reflects the derivation of the type $\vartheta_r$ at the root node $r$. Let $\{(\mathcal{A}_t, \boldsymbol{a}_t, \boldsymbol{B}_t) \mid t \in T\}$ be the set of substructures corresponding to the types $\{\vartheta_t \mid t \in T\}$ of such a derivation tree. Then we obtain a solution $\boldsymbol{B}$ of $\varphi(\boldsymbol{X})$ by computing the pointwise union of these vectors $\boldsymbol{B}_t$ of sets, i.e., $\boldsymbol{B} = (B_1, \dots, B_m)$ with $B_i = \bigcup_{t \in T} B_{ti}$. Given a derivation tree, the corresponding solution $\boldsymbol{B}$ can thus be easily obtained. Moreover, in [16], appropriate pointer structures were introduced which allow one to compute all derivation trees of a type $\vartheta_r$ with linear delay.

In total, we thus get an enumeration procedure which, for structures $\mathcal{A}$ of treewidth $\leq w$, computes all solutions of the enumeration problem defined by the MSO formula $\varphi(\boldsymbol{X})$ with delay $\mathcal{O}(f(|\varphi(\boldsymbol{X})|, w) * |\mathcal{A}|)$ for some function $f$ which depends on the MSO formula $\varphi(\boldsymbol{X})$ and the treewidth $w$ but not on the input structure $\mathcal{A}$.

## 6   Conclusion

In this paper, we have recalled the main ideas of the monadic datalog approach from [13], which was originally designed for the evaluation of unary MSO queries over structures with bounded treewidth. Note that decision problems correspond to the special case where the MSO query is 0-ary. We have also looked at the application of this approach to the SAT problem and at the extension to counting and enumeration problems. In [15], experimental results were reported for the #SAT program recalled here. The implementation was built on top of the datalog engine DLV [34]. In summary, the datalog approach scales reasonably well for instances of medium size. Therefore, (extended) datalog programs as the ones presented here can be employed for rapid prototyping and to verify specifications which are possibly planned to be realized in another language. Nevertheless, there is still plenty of work left for further improving the performance of the implementation of such programs.

Two kinds of directions for such improvements were identified in [15]: one has to do with the elimination of extensions to the datalog language used in these programs: recall that we used set-variables and arithmetic on sets whose size is bounded by the treewidth of the input structure. As was discussed in [15], the way how these programs are (automatically) converted into proper DLV-syntax has a huge impact on the performance. The ideal method has to be found yet. The other direction for performance improvement has to do with the datalog engine itself. Integrating some of the extensions used in the programs presented here into the datalog system itself would clearly help to improve the performance. In fact, the direct support of sets and set-arithmetic (as is the case in the extension of DLV called DLV-Complex, see `http://www.mat.unical.it/dlv-complex`) can be seen as a step in this direction.

Other directions of future work are concerned with the identification of appropriate extensions of datalog so as to handle further extensions of Courcelle's Theorem. We have already seen the extension to counting and enumeration problems. In [6], also the extension of MSO with the sum-, minimum-, and maximum-operator were studied over structures of bounded treewidth. It would be interesting to integrate also these extensions into the datalog approach.

Finally, it should be stressed that the datalog approach discussed here is only *one* line of research in the quest for turning theoretical tractability results due to Courcelle's Theorem into efficient algorithms. There are also other approaches. In particular, dynamic programming algorithms are a natural candidate for this kind of problems. For instance, [35] gives a dynamic programming algorithm for the #SAT problem. A completely different approach is proposed in [36]: we have already mentioned that the MSO-to-FTA approach usually fails because of the state explosion in the FTA-construction. This state explosion may occur on two levels: either in the form of big intermediate automata (even though the final automaton is not that big) or in the form of a big final automaton. In [36], the authors propose solutions to both problems by a direct construction of the final automaton (to address the first problem) or by representing the transition function of the FTA as a functional program (rather than explicitly computing all transitions). Further research efforts for the construction of efficient algorithms of MSO-definable problems are clearly needed.

**Acknowledgments.** The work reported here is the result of joint research with my colleagues Georg Gottlob, Michael Jakl, Stefan Rümmele, Fang Wei, and Stefan Woltran. I am very grateful to them for the enjoyable and fruitful collaboration.

# References

1. Downey, R.G., Fellows, M.R.: Parameterized Complexity. Springer, New York (1999)
2. Flum, J., Grohe, M.: Parameterized Complexity Theory. Texts in Theoretical Computer Science. Springer, Heidelberg (2006)
3. Niedermeier, R.: Invitation to Fixed-Parameter Algorithms. Oxford University Press, Oxford (2006)
4. Courcelle, B.: Graph Rewriting: An Algebraic and Logic Approach. In: Handbook of Theoretical Computer Science, vol. B, pp. 193–242. Elsevier Science Publishers, Amsterdam (1990)
5. Courcelle, B.: The monadic second-order logic of graphs. I. Recognizable sets of finite graphs. Inf. Comput. 85, 12–75 (1990)
6. Arnborg, S., Lagergren, J., Seese, D.: Easy Problems for Tree-Decomposable Graphs. J. Algorithms 12, 308–340 (1991)
7. Flum, J., Frick, M., Grohe, M.: Query evaluation via tree-decompositions. J. ACM 49, 716–752 (2002)
8. Doner, J.: Tree acceptors and some of their applications. J. Comput. Syst. Sci. 4, 406–451 (1970)

9. Thatcher, J.W., Wright, J.B.: Generalized Finite Automata Theory with an Application to a Decision Problem of Second-Order Logic. Mathematical Systems Theory 2, 57–81 (1968)
10. Frick, M., Grohe, M.: The complexity of first-order and monadic second-order logic revisited. Ann. Pure Appl. Logic 130, 3–31 (2004)
11. Maryns, H.: On the Implementation of Tree Automata: Limitations of the Naive Approach. In: Proc. TLT 2006: 5th Int. Treebanks and Linguistic Theories Conference, pp. 235–246 (2006)
12. Grohe, M.: Descriptive and Parameterized Complexity. In: Flum, J., Rodríguez-Artalejo, M. (eds.) CSL 1999. LNCS, vol. 1683, pp. 14–31. Springer, Heidelberg (1999)
13. Gottlob, G., Pichler, R., Wei, F.: Monadic datalog over finite structures with bounded treewidth. In: Proc. PODS 2007, pp. 165–174. ACM, New York (2007); Full version to appear in ACM Trans. Comput. Log.
14. Gottlob, G., Pichler, R., Wei, F.: Bounded treewidth as a key to tractability of knowledge representation and reasoning. Artif. Intell. 174, 105–132 (2010)
15. Jakl, M., Pichler, R., Rümmele, S., Woltran, S.: Fast counting with bounded treewidth. In: Cervesato, I., Veith, H., Voronkov, A. (eds.) LPAR 2008. LNCS (LNAI), vol. 5330, pp. 436–450. Springer, Heidelberg (2008)
16. Pichler, R., Rümmele, S., Woltran, S.: Counting and enumeration problems with bounded treewidth. In: Clarke, E.M., Voronkov, A. (eds.) LPAR-16 2010. LNCS, vol. 6355, pp. 387–404. Springer, Heidelberg (2010) (to appear)
17. Bodlaender, H.L.: A Linear-Time Algorithm for Finding Tree-Decompositions of Small Treewidth. SIAM J. Comput. 25, 1305–1317 (1996)
18. Koster, A.M.C.A., Bodlaender, H.L., van Hoesel, S.P.M.: Treewidth: Computational experiments. Electronic Notes in Discrete Mathematics 8, 54–57 (2001)
19. Bodlaender, H.L., Koster, A.M.C.A.: Safe separators for treewidth. Discrete Mathematics 306, 337–350 (2006)
20. Bodlaender, H.L., Koster, A.M.C.A.: Combinatorial optimization on graphs of bounded treewidth. Comput. J. 51, 255–269 (2008)
21. van den Eijkhof, F., Bodlaender, H.L., Koster, A.M.C.A.: Safe reduction rules for weighted treewidth. Algorithmica 47, 139–158 (2007)
22. Kloks, T.: Treewidth: Computations and Approximations. Springer, Berlin (1994)
23. Courcelle, B., Makowsky, J.A., Rotics, U.: On the fixed parameter complexity of graph enumeration problems definable in monadic second-order logic. Discrete Applied Mathematics 108, 23–52 (2001)
24. Abiteboul, S., Hull, R., Vianu, V.: Foundations of databases. Addison-Wesley, Reading (1995)
25. Ceri, S., Gottlob, G., Tanca, L.: Logic Programming and Databases. Springer, Heidelberg (1990)
26. Vardi, M.Y.: The complexity of relational query languages (extended abstract). In: Proc. STOC 1982, pp. 137–146. ACM, New York (1982)
27. Gottlob, G., Koch, C.: Monadic datalog and the expressive power of languages for Web information extraction. J. ACM 51, 74–113 (2004)
28. Dowling, W.F., Gallier, J.H.: Linear-Time Algorithms for Testing the Satisfiability of Propositional Horn Formulae. J. Log. Program. 1, 267–284 (1984)
29. Minoux, M.: LTUR: A Simplified Linear-Time Unit Resolution Algorithm for Horn Formulae and Computer Implementation. Inf. Process. Lett. 29, 1–12 (1988)
30. Gottlob, G., Grädel, E., Veith, H.: Datalog lite: a deductive query language with linear time model checking. ACM Trans. Comput. Log. 3, 42–79 (2002)
31. Ebbinghaus, H.D., Flum, J.: Finite Model Theory, 2nd edn. Springer Monographs in Mathematics. Springer, Heidelberg (1999)

32. Libkin, L.: Elements of Finite Model Theory. Texts in Theoretical Computer Science. Springer, Heidelberg (2004)
33. Kemp, D.B., Stuckey, P.J.: Semantics of logic programs with aggregates. In: Proc. ISLP, pp. 387–401 (1991)
34. Leone, N., Pfeifer, G., Faber, W., Eiter, T., Gottlob, G., Perri, S., Scarcello, F.: The DLV system for knowledge representation and reasoning. ACM Trans. Comput. Log. 7, 499–562 (2006)
35. Samer, M., Szeider, S.: Algorithms for propositional model counting. J. Discrete Algorithms 8, 50–64 (2010)
36. Courcelle, B., Durand, I.A.: Verifying monadic second order graph properties with tree automata. In: European LISP Symposium, pp. 7–21 (2010)

# Equivalence between Extended Datalog Programs — A Brief Survey

Stefan Woltran

Technische Universität Wien, Institute of Information Systems 184/2
Favoritenstrasse 9-11, 1040 Vienna, Austria
woltran@dbai.tuwien.ac.at

**Abstract.** This paper gives a brief overview about the research field on equivalences in Answer-Set Programming. More precisely, we are concerned here with disjunctive logic programs under the stable-model semantics. Such programs can be understood as extended datalog queries (i.e., datalog augmented by default negation and disjunction). In particular, we shall report on characterizations and complexity results for the notions of strong and respectively uniform equivalence. Most notably, uniform equivalence becomes undecidable in the presence of default negation, while strong equivalence remains decidable for full disjunctive datalog. We also consider a restricted setting where the arity of predicates is bounded by a fixed constant.

## 1 Introduction

*Answer Set Programming* (ASP) [23,31,38,40], also known as A-Prolog [1,22], has emerged as a declarative programming paradigm which has its roots in logic programming and non-monotonic reasoning and is nowadays a well-acknowledged method for solving intractable problems. Many successful applications of ASP, in particular in the areas of Artificial Intelligence (AI) and Knowledge Representation (KR) have been presented over the past decade. As most prominent application, one has to mention the use of ASP techniques in a decision support system for the space shuttle [41].

The ASP core language of logic programs, which goes back to the seminal paper by Gelfond and Lifschitz [24], can be seen as datalog enhanced by default negation and has later been extended to rules with disjunctive heads [25,39]. Consequently, this formalism was also studied under the term *disjunctive datalog* (see, e.g. [14]). However, in contrast to standard datalog these extensions lead to the fact that a query does not necessarily provide a unique answer, but yields several so-called *answer sets* or *stable models*. This resulted in a shift of paradigm where programs are understood as declarative problem descriptions, such that the query results represent *all* solutions of the given problem. For instance, a program representing the 3-colorability problem for graphs should return as answers all possible 3-colorings for the graph which is provided as the input database. Although the introduction of concepts as negation or disjunction to datalog also comes with the price of an increased complexity, dedicated disjunctive datalog systems as DLV [29], which was first released in 1996, were developed and boosted the success of ASP.

O. de Moor et al. (Eds.): Datalog 2010, LNCS 6702, pp. 106–119, 2011.

The higher complexity of disjunctive datalog compared to standard datalog is also mirrored in the typical architecture of ASP systems. In fact, such systems usually consist of two parts (often these are even separate systems): (i) the *grounding* which instantiates the variables of the given program resulting in a set of ground (i.e. propositional) rules; (ii) the *solving* itself then evaluates the ground program and computes its set of stable models which are also the answers to the original non-ground program. Reports on the latest ASP system evaluations [4,21] provide a good overview about the different grounders and solvers which are now available and give respective pointers to the literature.

For programs without negation or disjunction (i.e. standard datalog queries), the grounding process directly provides the query answer. For general ASP programs the performance of the second step, i.e. solving the ground program, turns out to be crucial, since the grounded programs tend to get very large (in general they are of exponential size w.r.t. the original program). Thus, these solvers often rely on techniques stemming from SAT or CSP, although the rule-based language of logic programs requires further dedicated methodologies (see, e.g. [47] for a short discussion on that topic). Another difference when talking about ASP on the one hand and disjunctive datalog on the other hand is the fact that ASP (similar as in prolog convention) not necessarily separates the database from the query, while in the datalog world this separation is tacitly assumed.[1]

Due to this focus on ground programs, theoretical research on ASP often was addressed only for the propositional case. In fact, also the research on equivalence was carried out first for propositional programs. The earliest notion of equivalence studied in the ASP literature dates back to 2001 and was not on query equivalence (which one might expect from the datalog point of view) but on equivalence for (sub-)program replacement, which was named *strong equivalence* [32]. To be a bit more formal, strong equivalence between programs $P$ and $Q$ holds, if for any further program $R$, $P \cup R$ and $Q \cup R$ possess the same stable models. In their seminal paper, Lifschitz, Pearce and Valverde [32] showed that strong equivalence can be decided by checking whether $P$ and $Q$ are equivalent in the logic of here-and-there (also known as Gödel's three-valued logic). A different yet equivalent (for logic programs) characterization in terms of program reducts was given by Turner [50], nowadays known as *SE-models*. Strong equivalence was then deeply investigated for the propositional case (see e.g. [3,35,44,55]) and also further notions of equivalence (see, e.g. [6,12,28,43,45]) have been thoroughly studied for the propositional case with *uniform equivalence* being the most prominent one. Hereby, the task is to decide whether $P \cup F$ and $Q \cup F$ are equivalent for any set $F$ of facts (rather than rules). Lin [34] was the first to discuss the non-ground variant of strong equivalence and gave a translation into first-order logic as a decision procedure. The model-theoretic characterization in terms of SE-models was finally lifted to the non-ground case in [10]. In that paper also first complexity and undecidability results were presented which were then complemented in [11]. Using first-order variants of the aforementioned logic of here-and-there to decide strong equivalence was later discussed in [33].

---

[1] As a convention for this survey, we use the word *program*, for a set of rules which already contains the database as facts, while by a *query* we understand a set of rules considered to be conjoined with some input database.

In the standard datalog setting the research line was rather different. Starting with the undecidability result by Shmueli [48] on *query equivalence* from 1987, research focused on the one hand on identifying the exact frontier between decidable and undecidable language fragments, and on the other hand, on sound approximations to query equivalence. Uniform equivalence was introduced by Sagiv [46] as one such approach. *Equivalence of program segments* (which is the pendant to strong equivalence introduced above) was introduced by Maher [37] but coincides with uniform equivalence for datalog queries. As we will see later, the presence of negation makes uniform and strong equivalence different concepts.

In this survey, we review the main results for strong and uniform equivalence for disjunctive datalog and several syntactical subclasses thereof. The results are mainly collected from the work by Eiter *et al.* [5,10,11]. The organization of the paper is as follows. In the next section, we provide some formal preliminaries to define the discussed problems in sufficient accuracy. Section 3 contains the overview on the results: we exactly define the notions of strong and uniform equivalence for disjunctive datalog and provide model-theoretic characterizations. Then, we present the central complexity results for the problems in question for full disjunctive datalog as well as for subclasses where negation or disjunction is omitted. We also consider the setting of programs where the arities of the (intensional) predicates are bounded [5]. Finally, we discuss some further results which deal with stratified negation, relativized notions of equivalences, and program rewritings. We conclude the paper with a brief summary and a list of important issues which still remain open.

## 2  Background

We recall the basic formal concepts for disjunctive logic programming [25] under the stable semantics and give a brief review on the main complexity results for reasoning tasks [2]. For further details, the reader is referred to [14,29].

Logic programs are formulated in a language containing a set $\mathcal{A}$ of *predicate symbols*, a set $\mathcal{V}$ of *variables*, and a set $\mathcal{U}$ of *constants*. Unless stated otherwise, we assume these sets to be infinite. Each predicate symbol has an associated *arity* $n \geq 0$; the set $\mathcal{U}$ is also referred to as the *domain*. An *atom* is an expression of form $p(t_1, \ldots, t_n)$, where $p \in \mathcal{A}$ is a predicate of arity $n$ and $t_i \in \mathcal{U} \cup \mathcal{V}$, for $1 \leq i \leq n$. An atom is *ground* if no variable occurs in it. For a set $A \subseteq \mathcal{A}$ of predicate symbols and a set $C \subseteq \mathcal{U}$ of constants, we write $B_{A,C}$ to denote the set of all ground atoms constructed from the predicate symbols from $A$ and the constants from $C$.

A *(disjunctive) rule* $r$ is of the form

$$a_1 \vee \cdots \vee a_n \leftarrow b_1, \ldots, b_k, \text{ not } b_{k+1}, \ldots, \text{ not } b_m, \tag{1}$$

where $a_1, \ldots, a_n, b_1, \ldots, b_m$ are atoms, with $n \geq 0$, $m \geq k \geq 0$, and $n + m > 0$, and "*not*" is *default negation*. The *head* of $r$ is the set $H(r) = \{a_1, \ldots, a_n\}$, and the *body* of $r$ is $B(r) = \{b_1, \ldots, b_k, \text{ not } b_{k+1}, \ldots, \text{ not } b_m\}$. Furthermore, we define $B^+(r) = \{b_1, \ldots, b_k\}$ and $B^-(r) = \{b_{k+1}, \ldots, b_m\}$. A rule of form (1) is called (i) a *fact*, if $m = 0$ and $n = 1$ (in which case the symbol $\leftarrow$ is usually omitted), (ii) a *constraint*, if $n = 0$, (iii) *normal*, if $n \leq 1$, (iv) *positive*, if $k = m$, and (v) *Horn*, if $k = m$ and $n \leq 1$.

A rule $r$ is *safe* if each variable occurring in $H(r) \cup B^-(r)$ also occurs in $B^+(r)$; $r$ is *ground*, if all atoms occurring in $r$ are ground.

By a *program* we understand a set of rules. The set of variables (resp., constants, predicate symbols) occurring in an expression $e$ (atom, rule, program, etc.) is denoted by $\mathcal{V}_e$, (resp., $\mathcal{U}_e$, $\mathcal{A}_e$). If no constant appears in a program $P$, then $\mathcal{U}_P = \{c\}$, for an arbitrary constant $c$. Moreover, $B_P = B_{\mathcal{A}_P, \mathcal{U}_P}$ is the Herbrand base of $P$. Given a rule $r$ and $C \subseteq \mathcal{U}$, we define $Gr(r, C)$ as the set of all rules obtained from $r$ by all possible substitutions of elements of $C$ for the variables in $r$. Moreover, we define $Gr(P, C) = \bigcup_{r \in P} Gr(r, C)$. In particular, $Gr(P, \mathcal{U}_P)$ is referred to as the *grounding* of $P$, written $Gr(P)$. A predicate $p \in \mathcal{A}_P$ is called *extensional* (in $P$) iff there is no $r \in P$ with $p \in H(r)$, otherwise it is *intensional* (in $P$).

Programs are normal (resp., positive, Horn, ground, safe) if all of their rules enjoy this property. Thus a Horn program amounts to a standard datalog query. Unless stated otherwise, we assume that programs are finite and safe. A normal program $P$ is called *stratified* iff there is a function $f : \mathcal{A} \to N$ such that, for each $r \in P$ with $H(r) = \{h\}$ being nonempty, (i) $f(\mathcal{A}_b) < f(\mathcal{A}_h)$, for each $b \in B^-(r)$, and (ii) $f(\mathcal{A}_b) \leq f(\mathcal{A}_h)$, for each $b \in B^+(r)$.

By an *interpretation* we understand a set of ground atoms. A ground rule $r$ is *satisfied* by an interpretation $I$ iff $H(r) \cap I \neq \emptyset$ whenever $B^+(r) \subseteq I$ and $B^-(r) \cap I = \emptyset$. $I$ satisfies a ground program $P$ iff each $r \in P$ is satisfied by $I$ ($I$ is then also called a model of $P$). The *Gelfond-Lifschitz reduct* [25] of a ground program $P$ (with respect to an interpretation $I$) is given by the positive program

$$P^I = \{H(r) \leftarrow B^+(r) \mid r \in P, \; I \cap B^-(r) = \emptyset\}.$$

A set $I$ of ground atoms is an *answer set* (or stable model) of $P$ iff $I$ is a subset-minimal set satisfying $Gr(P)^I$. The set of all answer sets of $P$ is denoted by $\mathcal{AS}(P)$. Note that for each $I \in \mathcal{AS}(P)$, $I \subseteq B_P$ holds by minimality. As is well known, a program $P$ might possess multiple or no answer set, while every stratified program (and thus every Horn program) has at most one answer sets.

We finally review a few complexity results compiled from the surveys [2,14]; see the references therein for further pointers to the original results. In fact, we give the results for both combined and data complexity [51]; recall that for data complexity the query is assumed fixed and only the database is part of the input. Moreover, we consider the typical two reasoning modes which arise from the fact that programs may possess multiple answer sets: for a program $P$ and a ground atom $a$, we define

- $P \models_c a$ if $a \in I$ for at least one $I \in \mathcal{AS}(P)$ (credulous reasoning);
- $P \models_s a$ if $a \in I$ for all $I \in \mathcal{AS}(P)$ (skeptical reasoning).

For programs which have a unique answer set, $\models_c$ and $\models_s$ thus coincide.

**Proposition 1.** *Combined and data complexity for reasoning in disjunctive datalog (and fragments thereof) is given as in Table 1 (all entries in the table are completeness results).*

We will later compare these results with the complexity for equivalence checking.

**Table 1.** Combined/data complexity for disjunctive datalog

|  | Horn programs | normal programs | positive programs | general case |
|---|---|---|---|---|
| $\models_c$ | EXPTIME / P | NEXPTIME / NP | NEXPTIME$^{NP}$/ $\Sigma_2^P$ | NEXPTIME$^{NP}$ / $\Sigma_2^P$ |
| $\models_s$ | EXPTIME / P | co-NEXPTIME / coNP | NEXPTIME/ coNP | co-NEXPTIME$^{NP}$ / $\Pi_2^P$ |

## 3  Results for Strong and Uniform Equivalence

We consider the following notions of equivalence between two programs $P$ and $Q$:

- ordinary equivalence, $P \equiv_o Q$: $\mathcal{AS}(P) = \mathcal{AS}(Q)$;
- uniform equivalence, $P \equiv_u Q$: for each finite set $F$ of facts, $\mathcal{AS}(P \cup F) = \mathcal{AS}(Q \cup F)$; and
- strong equivalence, $P \equiv_s Q$: for each program $R$, $\mathcal{AS}(P \cup R) = \mathcal{AS}(Q \cup R)$.

By definition, we have that $P \equiv_s Q$ implies $P \equiv_u Q$ and that $P \equiv_u Q$ implies $P \equiv_o Q$. Moreover, all three notions are different concepts.

*Example 1.* For queries $P = \{p \leftarrow q\}$ and $Q = \{p \leftarrow r\}$, we have $\mathcal{AS}(P) = \mathcal{AS}(Q) = \{\emptyset\}$ and thus $P \equiv_o Q$. However, $P \not\equiv_u Q$ is derived by adding fact $q$, where we get $\mathcal{AS}(P \cup \{q\}) = \{\{p, q\}\} \neq \{\{q\}\} = \mathcal{AS}(Q \cup \{q\})$.    ◊

Let us next recall canonical examples which show that uniform and strong equivalence do not coincide as soon as negation comes into play.

*Example 2.*  Consider

$$P = \{p \vee q \leftarrow\}; \qquad Q = \{p \leftarrow not\ q;\ q \leftarrow not\ p\}.$$

Both, $P$ and $Q$ have the same answer sets, $\{p\}$ and $\{q\}$. Moreover, for any set $F$ of facts such that $F \cap \{p, q\} = \emptyset$, $\mathcal{AS}(P \cup F) = \mathcal{AS}(Q \cup F) = \{F \cup \{p\}, F \cup \{q\}\}$. Moreover, for any set $G$ of facts such that $G \cap \{p, q\} \neq \emptyset$, $\mathcal{AS}(P \cup G) = \mathcal{AS}(Q \cup G) = \{G\}$. Thus, $P \equiv_u Q$. On the other hand, for $R = \{p \leftarrow q;\ q \leftarrow p\}$, we get that $P \cup R$ has a unique answer set, $\{p, q\}$ (the minimal interpretation satisfying the positive program $P \cup R$), while $Q \cup R$ has no answer set; in particular, $I = \{p, q\}$ is not an answer set of $Q \cup R$, since $I$ is not minimal in satisfying $(Q \cup R)^I = R$. Thus, $P \not\equiv_s Q$.    ◊

*Example 3.*  Another such example but without disjunction involved is

$$P = \{p \leftarrow q;\ p \leftarrow not\ q\}; \qquad Q = \{p \leftarrow r;\ p \leftarrow not\ r\};$$

where $P \equiv_u Q$ holds, but $P$ and $Q$ are not strongly equivalent (take $R = \{q \leftarrow p\}$ as a counter example).    ◊

Note that in the last example $P$ and $Q$ are both stratified programs; however conjoining $P$ with the counter example $R$ (which itself is stratified) leads to an unstratified program $P \cup R$. Thus, the correct definition of strong equivalence for the case of stratified programs is not so clear (see [11] for a discussion on this issue). However, as shown in [10], strong and uniform equivalence coincide not only for Horn programs (as was already observed by Maher [37]) but also for positive disjunctive programs; we will give a proof sketch for this result in the next section.

We remark that the difficulty to deal with uniform or strong equivalence (in contrast to ordinary equivalence) in the non-ground case has its origin in the extended programs $P \cup R$ and $Q \cup R$ which naturally enlarge the active domains $\mathcal{U}_P$, resp. $\mathcal{U}_Q$. Thus the original Herbrand bases of the compared programs $P$ and $Q$ are not useful anymore.

## 3.1 Characterizations

Several characterizations to decide strong and uniform equivalence between ground (i.e. propositional) programs have been presented in the literature. We use here the characterization by Turner [50] which simplifies the original result from [32] by using the notion of the reduct instead of a full logic.[2] Within our language, the result by Turner can be formulated as follows: Let an SE-model of a ground program $P$ be any pair $(X, Y)$ such that $X \subseteq Y \subseteq B_{\mathcal{A}, \mathcal{U}}$, $Y$ satisfies $P$, and $X$ satisfies $P^Y$.

**Proposition 2.** *Two propositional programs are strongly equivalent, i.e. $P \equiv_s Q$, if and only if $P$ and $Q$ possess the same SE-models.*

Given two ground programs $P$ and $Q$ it is sufficient to restrict this test to pairs $(X, Y)$ where $X$ and $Y$ are subsets of the ground atoms occurring in $P$ or $Q$. Let us illustrate the basic idea using the programs from Example 2.

*Example 4.* Consider

$$P = \{p \vee q \leftarrow\}; \qquad Q = \{p \leftarrow not\ q;\ q \leftarrow not\ p\}.$$

It is sufficient to compute SE-models over atoms $\{p, q\}$. Since $P$ is positive we just have to form all pairs $(X, Y)$ such that $X \subseteq Y$ and where $X$ and $Y$ are models of $P$. This yields[3]

$$(p, p),\ (q, q),\ (p, pq),\ (q, pq),\ (pq, pq).$$

On the other hand, observe that the reduct of $Q$ with respect to interpretation $\{p, q\}$ yields the empty program, thus in particular also the pair $(\emptyset, pq)$ is SE-model of $Q$. In fact, the SE-models of $Q$ are given by

$$(p, p),\ (q, q),\ (\emptyset, pq),\ (p, pq),\ (q, pq),\ (pq, pq)$$

and thus differ from the SE-models of $P$. By Proposition 2, we thus get $P \not\equiv_s Q$ directly (we already have seen before that adding $R = \{p \leftarrow q\quad q \leftarrow p\}$ yields a counter example).    ◊

---

[2] Undoubtedly, using a pure logical characterization has numerous advantages and the result from [32] moreover goes beyond the notion of logic programs. However, for the sake of the survey we use the simpler notion of SE-models which circumvents the introduction of further formal machinery.

[3] We omit parentheses "{","}" within SE-models for better readability.

For uniform equivalence (being a weaker concept than strong equivalence), characterizations first aimed to select subsets of SE-models in order to decide uniform equivalence. The concept of UE-models, introduced in [6], is defined as follows: an SE-model $(X,Y)$ of a program $P$ is also an UE-model of $P$ iff there is no $X'$ of the form $X \subset X' \subset Y$, such that $(X',Y)$ is also SE-model of $P$.

**Proposition 3.** *Two propositional programs are uniformly equivalent, i.e. $P \equiv_u Q$, if and only if $P$ and $Q$ possess the same UE-models.*

*Example 5.* Recall programs $P$ and $Q$ and their SE-models from Example 4. By definition of UE-models, each SE-model of $P$ is also UE-model $P$, while all SE-models of $Q$ *except* $(\emptyset, pq)$ are also UE-models of $Q$. Thus $P$ and $Q$ possess the same UE-models. We conclude that $P \equiv_u Q$ holds. ◇

One more remark is in order about uniform equivalence: in case of infinite programs, UE-models do not yield a suitable characterization. Recent work by Fink [18] discusses this issue in detail.

For the case of non-ground programs which we are interested here, these characterizations can be lifted in a straight forward way to compare the SE-models, resp. UE-models, for all possible groundings of the compared programs. More formally, $P \equiv_s Q$ holds iff $Gr(P,C) \equiv_s Gr(Q,C)$, for all $C \subseteq \mathcal{U}$, and likewise, $P \equiv_u Q$ holds iff $Gr(P,C) \equiv_u Gr(Q,C)$, for all $C \subseteq \mathcal{U}$. However, as shown in [10], there exists a certain short-cut for strong equivalence.

**Proposition 4.** *Let $\mathcal{U}_{P,Q}^+ = \mathcal{U}_P \cup \mathcal{U}_Q \cup U$ where $U = \{c_1, \ldots, c_m\}$ is a set of $m$ distinct constants disjoint from $\mathcal{U}_P \cup \mathcal{U}_Q$ and $m$ is the maximal number of variables occurring in a rule of $P \cup Q$. Then, $P \equiv_s Q$ iff $Gr(P, \mathcal{U}_{P,Q}^+) \equiv_s Gr(Q, \mathcal{U}_{P,Q}^+)$.*

*Proof.* (Sketch) The only-if direction follows from the already mentioned relation that $P \equiv_s Q$ holds iff $Gr(P,C) \equiv_s Gr(Q,C)$, for all $C \subseteq \mathcal{U}$. For the other direction one can reason as follows: Suppose $Gr(P,C) \not\equiv_s Gr(Q,C)$ for some $C \subseteq \mathcal{U}$. Then, there is a pair $(X,Y) \in B_{\mathcal{A},\mathcal{U}}$ which is SE-model of exactly one out of $Gr(P,C)$ and $Gr(Q,C)$. Assume $(X,Y)$ is not SE-model of $Gr(P,C)$, i.e. there is a ground rule $r \in Gr(P,C)$ such $(X,Y)$ is not SE-model of $\{r\}$. Let $D$ be the set of constants occurring in $r$. Then $D \subseteq C$ and w.l.o.g. we can assume that $D \subseteq \mathcal{U}_{P,Q}^+$. Since $(X,Y)$ is not SE-model of $\{r\}$, $(X,Y)$ is not SE-model of $Gr(P,D)$. On the other, $(X,Y)$ being SE-model of $Gr(Q,C)$ implies that $(X,Y)$ is SE-model of $Gr(Q,D)$, since $D \subseteq C$. From these observations, $Gr(P,\mathcal{U}_{P,Q}^+) \equiv_s Gr(Q,\mathcal{U}_{P,Q}^+)$ then follows. □

*Example 6.* As a simple example consider queries

$$P = \{q(X) \leftarrow e(X,Y)\}; \qquad Q = \{q(X) \leftarrow e(X,X)\}.$$

It is obvious that $P$ and $Q$ are not strongly equivalent, since adding a fact like $e(a,b)$ already yields $\mathcal{AS}(P \cup \{e(a,b)\}) = \{\{q(a), e(a,b)\}\} \neq \{\{e(a,b)\}\} = \mathcal{AS}(Q \cup \{e(a,b)\})$. To recognize this difference by just inspecting $P$ and $Q$, it is rather straight forward to see that one has to compare groundings $Gr(P,C)$ and $Gr(Q,C)$ where $C$ contains at least two elements from $\mathcal{U}$. Note that $\mathcal{U}_{P,Q}^+$ contains exactly two such elements. ◇

**Table 2.** Complexity results for equivalence checking (general case/bounded arity)

|   | Horn programs | normal programs | positive programs | general case |
|---|---|---|---|---|
| SE | EXPTIME/coNP | co-NEXPTIME/$\Pi_2^P$ | co-NEXPTIME/$\Pi_2^P$ | co-NEXPTIME/$\Pi_2^P$ |
| UE | EXPTIME/coNP | undec./ ? | co-NEXPTIME/$\Pi_2^P$ | undec./undec. |
| OE | EXPTIME/coNP | co-NEXPTIME/$\Pi_2^P$ | co-NEXPTIME$^{\mathrm{NP}}$/$\Pi_3^P$ | co-NEXPTIME$^{\mathrm{NP}}$/$\Pi_3^P$ |

In other words, strong equivalence between non-ground programs can be decided by a single test for strong equivalence between two ground programs. For the latter test we can make use of the concept of SE-models introduced above. For uniform equivalence, no such short-cut is possible due to the undecidability results we will present in the following subsection. For positive programs, decidability for uniform equivalence however holds.

**Proposition 5.** *For positive programs $P$, $Q$, strong and uniform equivalence coincide, i.e. we have $P \equiv_s Q$ iff $P \equiv_u Q$.*

*Proof.* (Sketch) The only-if direction is by definition. The if-direction follows from the observation that for any program $R$, any $C \subseteq \mathcal{U}$ and any interpretation $I$, it holds that $(Gr(R,C)^I) = Gr(R,C)$. Thus any non-total SE-model $(X,Y)$ of a grounding of positive program $Gr(R,C)$ is reflected by a total SE-model $(X,X)$ of the same program. Since each total SE-model is also an UE-model, the claim then follows quite easily. $\qquad\square$

Let us finally mention that the characterizations we have introduced here, slightly reformulate the corresponding results from [10]. In fact, [10] explictly defined SE-models (resp. UE-models) for non-ground programs, while we only made use of SE-models (resp. UE-models) for groundings of the compared programs.

## 3.2 Complexity

We now present the main results for deciding strong equivalence (SE), uniform equivalence (UE), and ordinary equivalence (OE). Besides the general case, we also provide the results for programs having the arities of their (intensional) predicates bounded [5] (bounding the arity has also been studied in the datalog world, see e.g. [27]). Similar results can be obtained by bounding the number of variables in rules (see also [52]).

**Proposition 6.** *Complexity for deciding strong, uniform and ordinary equivalence in disjunctive datalog (and fragments thereof) is given as in Table 2 (where "undec." refers to undecidable problems, "?" marks an open problem, while all remaining entries in the table refer to completeness results for the given complexity class).*

The results for uniform and respectively strong equivalence in the disjunctive, positive, and normal case are compiled from [10,11]. The case of ordinary equivalence as well as the results for Horn programs (i.e. the standard datalog case) have been established earlier (again, we refer to the survey [2] for the respective pointers to the literature).

We now give a few hints how the results for strong and uniform equivalence have been established. Let us start with strong equivalence. Indeed, decidability for strong equivalence is based on Proposition 4, which showed that a single check for strong equivalence between finite ground programs is sufficient. The co-NEXPTIME$^{\text{NP}}$ hardness for strong equivalence can be shown via a reduction from a certain class of second-order formulas [13]; this holds also for the other hardness results in Table 2. We emphasize that for full disjunctive datalog, deciding strong equivalence is easier than deciding ordinary equivalence. To put it in other words, for the problem of strong equivalence, disjunction does not increase the complexity (as it is the case for other reasoning problems). Also recall that for programs without negation, strong and uniform equivalence coincide (cf. Proposition 5). Thus for positive programs, the results for uniform equivalence come for free.

As soon as negation is involved, uniform equivalence becomes undecidable. In [10], this result was shown for disjunctive programs by making use of the undecidability result due to Shmueli [48]. We briefly sketch the idea of the reduction: In fact, [10] reduces the notion of program equivalence (which is easily shown to be undecidable by a reduction from query equivalence, see e.g. [10]) between Horn programs to uniform equivalence between disjunctive programs (programs $P$ and $Q$ are program equivalent, if for any finite set $F$ of ground atoms over extensional predicates[4], $\mathcal{AS}(P \cup F) = \mathcal{AS}(Q \cup F)$ holds). Basically, the idea is to rewrite the programs in such a way that SE-models $(X, Y)$ of the groundings carry the counter models of the original programs. More precisely, given a program $P$ and a set $C \subseteq \mathcal{U}$, we want to define a program $P^{\rightarrow}$, such that $(X, Y) \in SE(Gr(P^{\rightarrow}, C))$, $X \neq Y$, if and only if $X$ does not satisfy $Gr(P, C)$. Then, minimal models of $Gr(P, C)$ correlate to certain maximal SE-models of $Gr(P^{\rightarrow}, C)$, and thus to the UE-models of $Gr(P^{\rightarrow}, C)$. Since $P$ and $Q$ are Horn, it can be shown that $P$ and $Q$ are program equivalent iff $P^{\rightarrow} \equiv_u Q^{\rightarrow}$. $P^{\rightarrow}$ (likewise, $Q^{\rightarrow}$) can be defined by "reversing" the rules of $P$ and to allow only certain saturated models to satisfy $P^{\rightarrow}$. The "reversing" of rules requires disjunctions in the head, while for the restriction to saturated models a single negative constraint is sufficient. Moreover, the construction of $P^{\rightarrow}$ shows that undecidability holds already for programs where all predicates have bounded arity (this follows from the reduction of the original result by Shmueli [48] which requires predicates having their arities bounded by 3).

In [11], the undecidability result for uniform equivalence in disjunctive datalog was strengthened by using a similar idea but starting from a different undecidability result for datalog query equivalence, namely due to Feder and Saraiya [17]. They showed that query equivalence remains undecidable for linear programs (programs with at most one intensional predicate in the rule bodies). This allows to adapt the construction of the reversed programs $P^{\rightarrow}$ in such a way that no disjunction is required. However, applying this alternative reduction does not directly lead to a result which takes bounded predicate arity into account. Indeed, it is an open question whether undecidability of uniform equivalence for normal programs still holds in case the predicate arities are bounded. We also remark that the problem of uniform equivalence becomes decidable if only one of the compared programs contains negation.

---

[4] One can assume here w.l.o.g. that $P$ and $Q$ share the same extensional predicates.

We finally comment on the decrease of complexity for the decidable problems in case we consider the arities bounded (for the decrease it is sufficient to have this restriction only on the intensional predicates). Basically, the reason why these problems then become easier is that we now are able to guess a counter-example (for instance a pair $(X, Y)$ which is SE-model of either $Gr(P, \mathcal{U}_{P \cup Q}^{+})$ or $Gr(Q, \mathcal{U}_{P \cup Q}^{+})$) in polynomial space. Hardness results are shown by suitable reductions from QSAT problems, see [5].

### 3.3 Further Issues

*Stratification.* In Table 1, the reported complexity results for Horn programs also carry over the stratified programs, but the same does not hold for equivalence checking. In fact, not all problems are solved for stratified programs yet. While strong equivalence can be shown to be co-NEXPTIME complete [11], it is, to the best of our knowledge, still an open question whether uniform equivalence between stratified programs is, in general, decidable (decidability holds for monadic programs (follows from [26]) and in case the compared programs possess a joint stratification [30]). Interestingly, for the ground case, it was shown in [11] that deciding strong or uniform equivalence becomes intractable for stratified programs (and thus becomes harder as the corresponding problems for Horn programs).

*Finite Domains.* In the previous section, the undecidability results are clearly due to the fact that the domain of constants was considered to be infinite; in case of a finite domain $\mathcal{U}$, all discussed problems become obviously decidable; exact complexity bounds range from EXPTIME to co-NEXPTIME$^{\mathrm{NP}}$, see [10] for the details.

*Rewritings.* Based on the different equivalence notions, several papers studied rewriting rules in order to faithfully simplify a program. In particular, known results from the ground case [9] were lifted to the non-ground case in [7]. Most notably, deciding the applicability of such rewritings (i.e., whether a rule is subsumed by another rule) is intractable and even higher complexity is involved in the case of finite domains, see [19]. A slightly different approach is to re-cast programs. Hereby the question is for a given program $P$, whether there exists a program $Q$ from a different class such that $P$ and $Q$ are equivalent under a certain equivalence notion. Results for such re-casts in the propositional case can be found, for instance, in [8,9].

*Relativized Notions of Equivalence.* There is a huge gap between the notions of strong equivalence (equivalence for substitution) and ordinary equivalence (the compared programs only have to possess the same stable models; no addition of programs is considered). Uniform equivalence can be seen as one notion in between strong and ordinary equivalence by restricting the syntactic structure of the possibly added programs (i.e., restricting them to facts); in fact, it was shown that rule-wise restrictions of the syntax either results in strong, uniform or ordinary equivalence [45]. Another option is to bound the language of the the added programs. The latter approach has been introduced as relativized strong equivalence and has been investigated for ground programs in [12,28,53]. Similarly, a notion of relativized uniform equivalence was investigated in these papers.

Later, a more fine-grained parameterized notion of equivalence was investigated where the rules which might be added can be specified in terms of two alphabets, one for their heads and one for their bodies [54]. This concept, also termed hyperequivalence [49], allows for a common characterization of strong and uniform equivalence and thus to understand the difference between these notions on a model-theoretical side (recall the conceptual difference between SE- and UE-models sketched in Section 3.1). Another line of research considered equivalence notions where the comparison only takes place over projected answer sets, see e.g. [15]. Recently, all these notions have been introduced to non-ground programs [42] as well.

## 4  Conclusion

In this paper, we summarized the current state of research about deciding equivalence (with an emphasis on strong and respectively uniform equivalence) between queries formulated in an extended datalog language. In particular, we considered here disjunctive datalog which allows queries to contain negation in rule bodies and disjunction in rule heads. Nowadays such programs are usually referred to when talking about the answer-set programming (ASP) paradigm. We have seen that the notion of strong equivalence remains decidable for this language, while negation causes uniform equivalence to become an undecidable problem (which is in strong contrast to the classical datalog world, where uniform equivalence was introduced as a decidable and sound approximation for query equivalence).

The exact frontier between decidable and undecidable problems is not fully explored yet (for standard datalog a huge body of such results can be found, e.g. in [26]). In particular, the case of stratified negation still leaves some open questions. Similarly, for the undecidable problems presented here, decidable fragments still have to be explored. As well, the complexity of deciding whether a program falls into a decidable fragment has not been investigated for disjunctive datalog (see e.g., [20,27] for such work in the standard datalog area).

Another open issue concerns the question how further language extensions like aggregates (see e.g., [16]) effect decision procedures for strong or uniform equivalence; in the propositional setting, preliminary work in this direction has been already conducted, for instance, in [36]. Finally, on the practical side, it turned out that the theoretical results on equivalence have not found their way to ASP systems in order to optimize the grounders or solvers. A closer collaboration between theoreticians and system developers is necessary to put the whole body of theoretical work to practice, and moreover, to guide future directions of research in the area of equivalence for ASP programs.

## References

1. Baral, C.: Knowledge Representation, Reasoning and Declarative Problem Solving. Cambridge University Press, Cambridge (2002)
2. Dantsin, E., Eiter, T., Gottlob, G., Voronkov, A.: Complexity and Expressive Power of Logic Programming. ACM Computing Surveys 33(3), 374–425 (2001)
3. de Jongh, D., Hendriks, L.: Characterizations of Strongly Equivalent Logic Programs in Intermediate Logics. Theory and Practice of Logic Programming 3(3), 259–270 (2003)

4. Denecker, M., Vennekens, J., Bond, S., Gebser, M., Truszczynski, M.: The Second Answer Set Programming Competition. In: Erdem, E., Lin, F., Schaub, T. (eds.) LPNMR 2009. LNCS, vol. 5753, pp. 637–654. Springer, Heidelberg (2009)
5. Eiter, T., Faber, W., Fink, M., Woltran, S.: Complexity Results for Answer Set Programming with Bounded Predicate Arities and Implications. Annals of Mathematics and Artificial Intelligence 51(2-4), 123–165 (2007)
6. Eiter, T., Fink, M.: Uniform Equivalence of Logic Programs under the Stable Model Semantics. In: Palamidessi, C. (ed.) ICLP 2003. LNCS, vol. 2916, pp. 224–238. Springer, Heidelberg (2003)
7. Eiter, T., Fink, M., Tompits, H., Traxler, P., Woltran, S.: Replacements in Non-Ground Answer-Set Programming. In: Proc. KR 2006, pp. 340–351. AAAI Press, Menlo Park (2006)
8. Eiter, T., Fink, M., Tompits, H., Woltran, S.: On Eliminating Disjunctions in Stable Logic Programming. In: Proc. KR 2004, pp. 447–458. AAAI Press, Menlo Park (2004)
9. Eiter, T., Fink, M., Tompits, H., Woltran, S.: Simplifying Logic Programs Under Uniform and Strong Equivalence. In: Lifschitz, V., Niemelä, I. (eds.) LPNMR 2004. LNCS (LNAI), vol. 2923, pp. 87–99. Springer, Heidelberg (2003)
10. Eiter, T., Fink, M., Tompits, H., Woltran, S.: Strong and Uniform Equivalence in Answer-Set Programming: Characterizations and Complexity Results for the Non-Ground Case. In: Proc. AAAI 2005, pp. 695–700. AAAI Press, Menlo Park (2005)
11. Eiter, T., Fink, M., Tompits, H., Woltran, S.: Complexity Results for Checking Equivalence of Stratified Logic Programs. In: Proc. IJCAI 2007, pp. 330–335. AAAI Press, Menlo Park (2007)
12. Eiter, T., Fink, M., Woltran, S.: Semantical Characterizations and Complexity of Equivalences in Answer Set Programming. ACM Transactions on Computational Logic 8(3), pages 53 (2007)
13. Eiter, T., Gottlob, G., Gurevich, Y.: Normal Forms for Second-Order Logic over Finite Structures, and Classification of NP Optimization Problems. Annals of Pure and Applied Logic 78(1-3), 111–125 (1996)
14. Eiter, T., Gottlob, G., Mannila, H.: Disjunctive Datalog. ACM Transactions on Database Systems 22(3), 364–418 (1997)
15. Eiter, T., Tompits, H., Woltran, S.: On Solution Correspondences in Answer Set Programming. In: Proc. IJCAI 2005, pp. 97–102. Professional Book Center (2005)
16. Faber, W., Pfeifer, G., Leone, N., Dell'Armi, T., Ielpa, G.: Design and Implementation of Aggregate Functions in the DLV System. Theory and Practice of Logic Programming 8(5-6), 545–580 (2008)
17. Feder, T., Saraiya, Y.: Decidability and Undecidability of Equivalence for Linear Datalog with Applications to Normal-Form Optimizations. In: Hull, R., Biskup, J. (eds.) ICDT 1992. LNCS, vol. 646, pp. 297–311. Springer, Heidelberg (1992)
18. Fink, M.: A General Framework for Equivalences in Answer-Set Programming by Countermodels in the Logic of Here-and-There. CoRR, abs/1006.3021 (2010) (to appear); Theory and Practice of Logic Programming
19. Fink, M., Pichler, R., Tompits, H., Woltran, S.: Complexity of Rule Redundancy in Non-Ground Answer-Set Programming over Finite Domains. In: Baral, C., Brewka, G., Schlipf, J. (eds.) LPNMR 2007. LNCS (LNAI), vol. 4483, pp. 123–135. Springer, Heidelberg (2007)
20. Gaifman, H., Mairson, H., Sagiv, Y., Vardi, M.: Undecidable Optimization Problems for Database Logic Programs. Journal of the ACM 40(3), 683–713 (1993)
21. Gebser, M., Liu, L., Namasivayam, G., Neumann, A., Schaub, T., Truszczynski, M.: The First Answer Set Programming System Competition. In: Baral, C., Brewka, G., Schlipf, J. (eds.) LPNMR 2007. LNCS (LNAI), vol. 4483, pp. 3–17. Springer, Heidelberg (2007)

22. Gelfond, M.: Representing Knowledge in A-Prolog. In: Kakas, A.C., Sadri, F. (eds.) Computational Logic: Logic Programming and Beyond. LNCS (LNAI), vol. 2408, pp. 413–451. Springer, Heidelberg (2002)
23. Gelfond, M., Leone, N.: Logic Programming and Knowledge Representation - The A-Prolog Perspective. Artificial Intelligence 138(1-2), 3–38 (2002)
24. Gelfond, M., Lifschitz, V.: The Stable Model Semantics for Logic Programming. In: Proc. ICLP 1988, pp. 1070–1080. MIT Press, Cambridge (1988)
25. Gelfond, M., Lifschitz, V.: Classical Negation in Logic Programs and Disjunctive Databases. New Generation Computing 9, 365–385 (1991)
26. Halevy, A., Mumick, I., Sagiv, Y., Shmueli, O.: Static Analysis in Datalog Extensions. Journal of the ACM 48(5), 971–1012 (2001)
27. Hillebrand, G., Kanellakis, P., Mairson, H., Vardi, M.: Tools for Datalog Boundedness. In: Proc. PODS 1991, pp. 1–12. ACM Press, New York (1991)
28. Inoue, K., Sakama, C.: Equivalence of Logic Programs Under Updates. In: Alferes, J.J., Leite, J. (eds.) JELIA 2004. LNCS (LNAI), vol. 3229, pp. 174–186. Springer, Heidelberg (2004)
29. Leone, N., Pfeifer, G., Faber, W., Eiter, T., Gottlob, G., Perri, S., Scarcello, F.: The DLV System for Knowledge Representation and Reasoning. ACM Transactions on Computational Logic 7(3), 499–562 (2006)
30. Levy, A., Sagiv, Y.: Queries Independent of Updates. In: Proc. VLDB 1993, pp. 171–181. Morgan Kaufmann, San Francisco (1993)
31. Lifschitz, V.: Answer Set Programming and Plan Generation. Artificial Intelligence 138, 39–54 (2002)
32. Lifschitz, V., Pearce, D., Valverde, A.: Strongly Equivalent Logic Programs. ACM Transactions on Computational Logic 2(4), 526–541 (2001)
33. Lifschitz, V., Pearce, D., Valverde, A.: A Characterization of Strong Equivalence for Logic Programs with Variables. In: Baral, C., Brewka, G., Schlipf, J. (eds.) LPNMR 2007. LNCS (LNAI), vol. 4483, pp. 188–200. Springer, Heidelberg (2007)
34. Lin, F.: Reducing Strong Equivalence of Logic Programs to Entailment in Classical Propositional Logic. In: Proc. KR 2002, pp. 170–176. Morgan Kaufmann, San Francisco (2002)
35. Lin, F., Chen, Y.: Discovering Classes of Strongly Equivalent Logic Programs. Journal of Artificial Intelligence Research 28, 431–451 (2007)
36. Liu, L., Truszczynski, M.: Properties and Applications of Programs with Monotone and Convex Constraints. Journal of Artificial Intelligence Research 27, 299–334 (2006)
37. Maher, M.: Equivalences of Logic Programs. In: Minker, J. (ed.) Foundations of Deductive Databases and Logic Programming, pp. 627–658. Morgan Kaufmann, San Francisco (1988)
38. Marek, V., Truszczyński, M.: Stable Models and an Alternative Logic Programming Paradigm. In: Apt, K., Marek, V.W., Truszczyński, M., Warren, D.S. (eds.) The Logic Programming Paradigm – A 25-Year Perspective, pp. 375–398. Springer, Heidelberg (1999)
39. Minker, J.: Overview of Disjunctive Logic Programming. Annals of Mathematics and Artificial Intelligence 12, 1–24 (1994)
40. Niemelä, I.: Logic Programming with Stable Model Semantics as Constraint Programming Paradigm. Annals of Mathematics and Artificial Intelligence 25(3-4), 241–273 (1999)
41. Nogueira, M., Balduccini, M., Gelfond, M., Watson, R., Barry, M.: An A-Prolog Decision Support System for the Space Shuttle. In: Gupta, G. (ed.) PADL 1999. LNCS, vol. 1551, pp. 169–183. Springer, Heidelberg (1999)
42. Oetsch, J., Tompits, H.: Program Correspondence under the Answer-Set Semantics: The Non-ground Case. In: Garcia de la Banda, M., Pontelli, E. (eds.) ICLP 2008. LNCS, vol. 5366, pp. 591–605. Springer, Heidelberg (2008)
43. Oikarinen, E., Janhunen, T.: Modular Equivalence for Normal Logic Programs. In: Proc. ECAI 2006, pp. 412–416. IOS Press, Amsterdam (2006)

44. Pearce, D., Tompits, H., Woltran, S.: Characterising Equilibrium Logic and Nested Logic Programs: Reductions and Complexity. Theory and Practice of Logic Programming 9(5), 565–616 (2009)
45. Pearce, D., Valverde, A.: Uniform Equivalence for Equilibrium Logic and Logic Programs. In: Lifschitz, V., Niemelä, I. (eds.) LPNMR 2004. LNCS (LNAI), vol. 2923, pp. 194–206. Springer, Heidelberg (2003)
46. Sagiv, Y.: Optimising DATALOG Programs. In: Minker, J. (ed.) Foundations of Deductive Databases and Logic Programming, pp. 659–698. Morgan Kaufmann, San Francisco (1988)
47. Schaub, T.: Making Your Hands Dirty Inspires Your Brain! Or How to Switch ASP into Production Mode. In: Erdem, E., Lin, F., Schaub, T. (eds.) LPNMR 2009. LNCS (LNAI), vol. 5753, pp. 631–633. Springer, Heidelberg (2009)
48. Shmueli, O.: Decidability and Expressiveness Aspects of Logic Queries. In: Proc. PODS 1987, pp. 237–249. ACM Press, New York (1987)
49. Truszczynski, M., Woltran, S.: Relativized Hyperequivalence of Logic Programs for Modular Programming. Theory and Practice of Logic Programming 9(6), 781–819 (2009)
50. Turner, H.: Strong Equivalence Made Easy: Nested Expressions and Weight Constraints. Theory and Practice of Logic Programming 3(4-5), 602–622 (2003)
51. Vardi, M.: The Complexity of Relational Query Languages (Extended Abstract). In: Proc. STOC 1982, pp. 137–146. ACM, New York (1982)
52. Vardi, M.: On the Complexity of Bounded-Variable Queries. In: Proc. PODS 1995, pp. 266–276. ACM Press, New York (1995)
53. Woltran, S.: Characterizations for Relativized Notions of Equivalence in Answer Set Programming. In: Alferes, J.J., Leite, J. (eds.) JELIA 2004. LNCS (LNAI), vol. 3229, pp. 161–173. Springer, Heidelberg (2004)
54. Woltran, S.: A common view on Strong, Uniform, and other Notions of Equivalence in Answer-Set Programming. Theory and Practice of Logic Programming 8(2), 217–234 (2008)
55. Wong, K.-S.: Sound and Complete Inference Rules for SE-Consequence. Journal of Artificial Intelligence Research 31, 205–216 (2008)

# Cluster Computing, Recursion and Datalog

Foto N. Afrati[1], Vinayak Borkar[2], Michael Carey[2],
Neoklis Polyzotis[3], and Jeffrey D. Ullman[4]

[1] National Technical University of Athens
[2] UC Irvine
[3] UC Santa Cruz
[4] Stanford University

**Abstract.** The cluster-computing environment typified by Hadoop, the open-source implementation of map-reduce, is receiving serious attention as the way to execute queries and other operations on very large-scale data. Datalog execution presents several unusual issues for this enviroment. We discuss the best way to execute a round of seminaive evaluation on a computing cluster using the map-reduce. Using transitive closure as an example, we examine the cost of executing recursions in several different ways. Recursive processes such as evaluation of a recursive Datalog program do not fit the key map-reduce assumption that tasks deliver output only when they are completed. As a result, the resilience under compute-node failure that is a key element of the map-reduce framework is not supported for recursive programs. We discuss extensions to this framework that are suitable for executing recursive Datalog programs on very large-scale data in a way that allows progress to continue after node failures, without restarting the entire job.

## 1 Background

There has been a surprising resurgence of interest in Datalog for large-scale data-processing applications, including networking [14], analysis of very large programs [19], and distributed (social) networking [23]. The subject of this paper is implementing Datalog in a cloud-computing environment, where there is a cluster of compute-nodes, and parallel computation is performed using Hadoop or a similar tool. We assume the reader has exposure to this technology, and we give only a summary of references for cluster computing systems and for Datalog.

### 1.1 Datalog Concepts and Seminaive Evaluation

We assume the reader is familiar with Datalog and the notation found in [24], which we use here. Important issues include the distinction between IDB relations/predicates (those defined by rules) and EDB relations/predicates (those stored in the database).

We also assume familiarity with seminaive evaluation, where recursive rules are evaluated incrementally. At each round, for each recursive predicate $p$, a

O. de Moor et al. (Eds.): Datalog 2010, LNCS 6702, pp. 120–144, 2011.

*delta-relation*, denoted $p'$ is computed, consisting of all those $p$-tuples that are discovered for the first time at that round. Each round is computed in a restricted way, where only evaluations of the body in which at least one tuple comes from the delta relation of the previous round are allowed.

*Example 1.* If the rule is

```
p(X,Y)  :- q(X,Z) & r(Z,W) & s(W,Y)
```

then we compute

$$\pi_{X,Y}\big(q'(X,Z) \bowtie r(Z,W) \bowtie s(W,Y) \cup$$
$$q(X,Z) \bowtie r'(Z,W) \bowtie s(W,Y) \cup$$
$$q(X,Z) \bowtie r(Z,W) \bowtie s'(W,Y)\big)$$

The tuples of this relation that were not placed in $p$ prior to the previous round are added to $p$ and are also in the delta-relation $p'$ for this round only.

Seminaive evaluation often computes tuples more than once. In this paper, we shall several times argue that the work done in a parallel evaluation of Datalog is no greater than what we would need for any implementation of seminaive evaluation. A *derivation* of a tuple $t$ is a substitution of values for variables in some rule that makes all the subgoals true and makes the head be $t$. Thus, there are as many derivations as there are such substitutions. The number of derivations of tuples is a measure of the performance of seminaive evaluation on a given Datalog program.

*Example 2.* Consider the Datalog rule

```
p(X,Y)  :- e(X,Z) & p(Z,Y)
```

Think of this rule as the right-linear method for computing paths in a graph from its arcs. A path tuple $p(x,y)$ has many different derivations. In particular, whenever there is a node $z$ such that $e(x,z)$ is a given arc and path $p(z,y)$ is discovered during the recursive evaluation of this rule, there is a derivation of $p(x,y)$ using the set of facts $\{e(x,z),\ p(z,y)\}$. Thus, whenever there is an arc $e(x,z)$ and at least one path from $z$ to $y$ there is one derivation of fact $p(x,y)$. Note that because we are using seminaive, even if there are more than one paths from $z$ to $y$ going through $z$, the number of derivations of $p(x,y)$ due to $z$ is not more than one. However, $z$ may contribute to the creation of derivations for other tuples $p(x',y')$ as long as there is an arc $e(x',z)$ and a path $(z,y')$.

Thus each $z$ causes a number of derivations, say $d_z$, which is equal to the number of nodes that $z$ can reach times the in-degree of $z$. Hence, the total number of derivations ever created by applying seminaive is the sum over all nodes $z$ of $d_z$. Were we to rewrite the rule in its left-linear form

```
p(X,Y)  :- p(X,Z) & e(Z,Y)
```

we get a somewhat different computation for the number of derivations: the sum over all nodes $z$ of $d'_z$, where $d'_z$ is equal to the number of nodes that can reach $z$ times the out-degree of $z$. And if we use the nonlinear formulation

```
p(X,Y) :- p(X,Z) & p(Z,Y)
```

we get a larger number of derivations: the sum over all nodes $z$ of $d_z''$, where $d_z''$ is the the product of the number of nodes $z$ reaches times the number of nodes that reach $z$.

The following theorem states that seminaive evaluation performs each derivation exactly once. Thus the number of duplicates produced during seminaive evaluation depends only on the number of derivations and not on the number of iterations.

**Theorem 1.** *The number of times a tuple $t$ is produced during seminaive evaluation is equal to the number of derivations of $t$.*

*Proof.* Consider a derivation of $t$. We need to prove two things:

a) That this derivation will be fired at least once during seminaive evaluation and
b) That this derivation will not be fired more than once.

To prove (a): let $S_d$ be the set of tuples used in some derivation of $t$. Let $i$ be the earliest round where all the facts in $S_d$ are available. Since it is the earliest, one of the facts in $S_d$ will be in the delta-relation at this iteration. Thus, this derivation will be fired.

   To prove (b): in subsequent iterations after round $i$ none of the facts in $S_d$ will be in the delta-relation. Thus this derivation will not be fired again. Also in previous rounds, the derivation could not have been fired since at least one of the facts in $S_d$ was not available.

## 1.2   Cluster Computing

We assume the reader is familiar with the concept of a map-reduce algorithm. The original Google implementation is in [10], and the concept has been popularized through the open-source Hadoop implementation [4]. Both are built on top of a *distributed file system* [13], which manages huge files in *chunks* typically 64MB in size, replicating each chunk about three times (typically) at three separate nodes of a computing cluster. A synopsis of the technology behind map-reduce, including implementation of the core relational-algebra operations, such as join, in map-reduce can be found in [22].

   Computing by map-reduce involves the interaction of two functions, called Map and Reduce, each of which is typically implemented by spawning many tasks that execute one of these functions on a portion of the data. Typically, Map tasks are each given a chunk of the input file, from which they produce "key-value pairs." The keys are hashed, and each bucket of keys is assigned to one of the Reduce tasks. We may think of map-reduce as a simple workflow, in which one function, Map, feeds a second function, Reduce, and each is implemented by many tasks. This idea naturally generalizes to any acyclic graph as a workflow. Some recent research systems that make this leap are:

1. Dryad [16] and its extension DryadLINQ [26] from Microsoft,
2. Clustera [11] from the University of Wisconsin,
3. Hyracks [6] from the U. C. Irvine,
4. Boom [3] from the U.C. Berkeley, and
5. Nephele/PACT [5] from T. U. Berlin.

### 1.3  Dealing with Node Failures

There is a critical property of the functions supported by systems such as Hadoop or its extensions mentioned above: *all tasks read their input at the beginning and write their output at the end.* The reason this property is essential is that these systems not only implement parallelism; they do so in a way that allows failure of a task without the need to restart the entire computation. In systems such as these, when a task fails, a *master controller* detects the failure and starts the same task at a different compute-node. The input to the task is available, either through the distributed file system or through an ad-hoc replication of files during the execution of the program.

If a task $T$ produced output that other tasks consumed, and $T$ later failed, we could not simply restart $T$ and let it produce its output again. If we did, some tasks would receive duplicate data and might produce an incorrect result. It is therefore unfortunate that recursion, as found in Datalog programs, solutions to differential equations, and many other problem domains, do not allow tasks to obey the critical constraint that all output occurs at the end of a task. In this paper, we concentrate on Datalog recursion. A typical task has the responsibility for applying a logical rule, say

    p(X,Y) :- q(X,Z) & r(Z,Y)

to a subset of the tuples that are known for each relation mentioned in its body, $q$ and $r$ in this example. However if $q$ is a recursive predicate the tuples that belong to this predicate and are supposed to be hashed in this task may not be available right in the beginning but are expected to be in the output of some other task and will be shipped in the former task after some computation is done. If all tasks refrain from shipping their output to some other task until they have done all their work, then this task may not produce any tuples ever. The reason is that it cannot be sure some other task will not produce $q$ or $r$ tuples later (assuming these are recursive IDB predicates). Thus, nothing ever gets done if a task is not allowed to produce some tuples and then receive some additional inputs and work on those inputs, possibly producing more $p$-tuples later. For example, in Section 4.3, there are join tasks that are responsible for joining certain tuples (according to the hashing function) and some of those tuples will be available from some other tasks after they have worked through a part of their input.

### 1.4  Join Implemented by Map-Reduce

We shall discuss briefly how a join is implemented in map-reduce. The join $R(A, B) \bowtie S(B, C)$ will serve to explain how any equijoin could be executed.

The idea is essentially a distributed hash join. Map tasks each take a chunk of the file in which $R$ is stored or the file in which $S$ is stored. If there are $k$ Reduce tasks, then tuples of $R$ or $S$ are hashed to one of $k$ buckets, with the hash function depending only on the $B$-value, and a bit is attached to them indicating whether the tuple came from $R$ or $S$. Each Reduce task is responsible for one of the buckets. Any pair of tuples that join are surely sent to the same Reduce task, since their $B$-values are identical and therefore hash to the same bucket. The Reduce tasks thus execute any join algorithm locally and produce the result of that local join. The union of the results of all the Reduce tasks is the output of the entire join algorithm.

A different approach to the joining of several relations was proposed in [1]. Instead of a cascade of two-way joins, each tuple of the relations that participate in the join can be distributed by the Map tasks to several of the Reduce tasks. As for the two-way join described above, the result of the join algorithm is the union of the tuples produced by each Reduce task.

*Example 3.* Consider the three-way chain join $R(A, B) \bowtie S(B, C) \bowtie T(C, D)$. If we have $k$ Reduce tasks, we can use two hash functions $h(B)$ and $g(C)$, that map $B$-values and $C$-values, respectively, to $\sqrt{k}$ buckets each. Then, a Reduce task corresponds to a pair of buckets, one for $h$ and the other for $g$. A tuple of $S$ can be sent by its Map task to one Reduce task, since we know both its $B$- and $C$-values. However, a tuple of $R$ must be sent to $\sqrt{k}$ Reduce tasks, since although we know its $B$-value, we know nothing about the bucket $g(C)$ would choose. That is, the tuple $r(a, b)$ must be sent to all the Reduce tasks corresponding to the bucket pair $(h(b), x)$ for any of the $\sqrt{k}$ possible values of $x$. Similarly, every tuple of $T$ must be sent to $\sqrt{k}$ Reduce tasks, since we know the bucket $g(C)$ but not the bucket for $h$. Depending on the sizes of $R$ and $T$, it may not be optimal to use the same number of buckets for $h$ and $g$, but this optimization will have to wait until we discuss cost measures in Section 2.1.

## 2   The Computation Model

There are two issues that we need to address.

1. The cost of executing a program on a computing cluster depends on many factors. When the operations performed by the tasks are relatively simple, such as the operations of relational algebra that we shall discuss in connection with Datalog execution, communication tends to dominate. We shall thus introduce cost measures based on communication.
2. We must model the cost of failures. In particular, while it is desired that when a failure occurs, the computation is able to proceed without restart, all systems under discussion have single points of failure. We must evaluate different approaches to recovery by their expected running time, including both task restart and restart of the entire job.

## 2.1   Communication Cost

We shall assume that the computation performed at a node is relatively efficient and typically will be performed in main memory. An example would be a
hash join of two 64MB chunks from two relations. Given that communication is
typically performed over gigabit Ethernet, it is reasonable to suppose that the
bottleneck is in getting the data to the node. Even if the data is stored locally
at the node, it must still be read from disk, and that often takes more time that
simple main-memory processing of the data.

Thus, we shall measure the cost of a task by the amount of data in its input.
The cost of a job is the sum of the costs of all the tasks involved in performing
the job. Since this cost measures the time it takes to make the input available
for computation, we refer to it as *communication cost*.

*Example 4.* In Example 3 we discussed the join $R(A, B) \bowtie S(B, C) \bowtie T(C, D)$.
There, we observed that if we used $k$ Reduce tasks, and we hashed both $B$ and
$C$ to $\sqrt{k}$ buckets, we could ship each tuple of $R$ and $T$ to $\sqrt{k}$ nodes and ship
each tuple of $S$ to only one node. If we use $r$, $s$, and $t$ to represent the sizes of $R$,
$S$, and $T$, respectively, then the communication cost of this join is $s + \sqrt{k}(r + t)$.

However, if $r \neq t$, we can use less communication. In [1] it is shown that by
hashing $B$ to $\sqrt{kt/r}$ buckets and hashing $C$ to $\sqrt{kr/t}$ buckets, we can obtain
the optimum communication cost[1] This communication is equal to $s + t\sqrt{kr/t} +$
$r\sqrt{kt/r} = s + 2\sqrt{krt}$. This figure may or may not be better than the communication cost of taking the join of $R$ and $S$ first and then joining the result with $T$
(or similarly starting with the join of $S$ and $T$). However, it beats the cascade
of two-way joins in two important cases:

1. When $R$, $S$, and $T$ have a high fan-out, e.g., when they are each the "friends"
   relation of a social-networking site or they are each the link relation of the
   Web. In these cases, communicating the intermediate result is more expen-
   sive than communicating tuples of $R$ and $S$ several times.
2. When $S$ is a fact table and $R$ and $T$ are much smaller dimension tables of a
   star join.

The technique for finding the correct number of buckets to hash each variable
was solved in its generality in [1]; it is not restricted to chain joins. Of course
the optimum numbers of buckets often comes out nonintegral, in which case
rounding must be applied, and the value of $k$ (the number of Reduce tasks)
must be adjusted up or down accordingly.

One might be concerned that counting only input size for tasks, and not output size, gives a false reading of the true cost of communication. However, each
output is either input to at least one other task, in which case the cost of communication will be counted at the receiving task, or it is output of the entire

---

[1] Intuitively, the larger relation $R$ is, the fewer the number of buckets its tuples should
   be hashed to for the communication to be minimized. The same holds for relation
   $T$.

job. In practice, outputs that are query results, as would be the case for Datalog programs, are not too large, because an immense output file cannot be used by a human observer; it would have to be input to yet another process, and its cost could be accounted for there. For example, star joins [12] produce huge output, but in the typical analytic query the join result is aggregated and thus reduced significantly in size — far below the size of the typical fact table. We thus neglect the cost of storing the output of a job.

## 2.2   Cost of Restarts

When a large job is executed on a computing cluster, it is common for there to be failures during the computation. If there are thousands of compute-nodes working for hours on a job, it is not uncommon for one or more to fail; e.g., a disk at one of the nodes could crash. It is also conceivable that part of the communication network will fail, perhaps taking a whole rack of nodes out of the computation. Curiously, there are situations where the greatest probability of failure comes from a software problem. For example, a task could be written in the latest version of Java, while some nodes have an earlier version of Java installed, and the task fails when run at one of these nodes.

Our computing model must distinguish between *catastrophic failures*, where there is no solution but to restart the entire job, and *local failures*, where a task cannot complete, but all or most other tasks can continue. For example, Hadoop has a *master controller* that runs at a single node and is responsible for managing all the tasks of a job. If the node with the master fails, the job must be redone. While the probability of *something* going wrong during the execution of a large job is high, the probability of a *particular* failure, such a hardware fault at the node executing the master controller is small, even for the largest jobs being run today.

If the probability of a catastrophic failure is $p$, then a job that would take time $t$ were there no failures will finish in an expected time $t/(1-p)$. As long as $p$ is small, say 1%, we can tolerate these failures. More importantly, if modifying the code in order to convert catastrophic failures into local failures increases the running time of tasks by a factor greater than $1/(1-p)$, then it is unclear why we should perform the modification. However, as there are failure modes in practice that have too great a probability of occurrence, we typically need to manage tasks and their input/output so that restart of only the failed task(s) is feasible.

## 3   Evaluation of Single Datalog Rules

The multiway join algorithm mentioned in Example 4 for the case of a chain-join of three subgoals can be used regardless of the number of subgoals in a rule (provided it is at least three subgoals, since with two subgoals we have no intermediate relations to care about, and the multiway join reduces to a two-way join). There are circumstances, such as when the Datalog rule is computing a star join on a fact table, where the multiway join would be preferable to using supplementary relations and evaluating the rule by a cascade of two-way joins. However, the point where the evaluation of a rule is most impacted by the cluster-computing model is when we use seminaive evaluation to compute the result of a recursive Datalog program.

## 3.1   Seminaive Evaluation on a Cluster

To see the elements of the problem, suppose we are evaluating a rule whose body involves the join $R(A, B) \bowtie S(B, C) \bowtie T(C, D)$, as in Example 4. To evaluate the join incrementally, we use relations $R$, $S$, and $T$, representing the values of these relations prior to the most recent rounds, and we use $R'$, $S'$, and $T'$ for the delta-relations — the new tuples discovered for these three relations at the previous round. To get the new tuples for the current round, we compute the union of seven terms, where we choose one of $R$ and $R'$, one of $S$ and $S'$, and one of $T$ and $T'$, in all combinations except the one where none of the delta-relations are chosen. That is, we must compute

$$RST' + RS'T + R'ST + RS'T' + R'ST' + R'S'T + R'S'T' \qquad (1)$$

where we use concatenation for join and $+$ for union, to simplify the notation.

To make the calculation of communication cost simple, we shall assume that the size of each delta-relation is the same fraction $a$ of the size of its corresponding relation. That is, we shall use $r$, $s$, and $t$ for the sizes of $R$, $S$, and $T$, respectively, and we shall assume that the sizes of $R'$, $S'$, and $T'$ are $ar$, $as$, and $at$, respectively. Note that $a$ may vary from round to round. It would be common for $a$ to be large in early rounds and small in later rounds.

Suppose we have $k$ Reducers and we want to evaluate Equation (1). The obvious approach is to treat $R + R'$ as one relation of size $(1 + a) \times r$, $S + S'$ as one relation of size $(1 + a) \times s$, and $T + T'$ as one relation of size $(1 + a) \times t$. If we do, the formula of Example 4 says the optimum way to distribute these relations will have communication cost $(1 + a) \times s + 2\sqrt{k \times (1 + a) \times r \times (1 + a) \times t}$, or $(1 + a)(s + 2\sqrt{krt})$.[2] However, there are other ways we could use $k$ reducers to evaluate Equation (1).

*Example 5.* We could divide the seven terms into three groups of $k_1$, $k_2$, and $k_3$ reducers, respectively, where $k_1 + k_2 + k_3 = k$. We could use the first group to compute $(S + S')(R + R')T'$, the second to compute $(S + S')R'T$, and the third to compute $S'RT$. The first group requires us to distribute five of the six relations — all but $T$. Using the formula from Example 4 again, the minimum communication for this distribution would be

$$(1 + a) \times s + 2\sqrt{k_1 \times (1 + a) \times r \times a \times t}$$

---

[2] Note that in this approach, we hash attributes $B$ and $C$ for each of the six relations, and choose the number of buckets for each hash according to the formula of Example (4). Doing so makes sure that whatever term of Equation 1 we compute, all sets of three tuples that join will appear together at one reducer.

For the second group, we need to distribute $S$, $S'$, $R'$, and $T$. The same formula tells us the minimum communication cost is

$$(1 + a) \times s + 2\sqrt{k_2 \times a \times r \times 1 \times t}$$

Finally, for the third group, where we distribute $S'$, $R$, and $T$, the minimum cost is

$$a \times s + 2\sqrt{k_3 \times 1 \times r \times 1 \times t}$$

We still have the option to adjust $k_1$, $k_2$, and $k_3$ in Example 5, subject to the constraint that their sum is $k$. More generally, we can have any number of groups, and each group will be assigned $k_i$ compute-nodes, again subject to the constraint that $\sum_i k_i = k$. Note that the cost of distributing $s$ will be at least $s(1 + a)$, and therefore can only increase as the number of groups increases. Moreover, for large $k$, we can neglect the cost of distributing $s$, so we shall say no more about its cost.

In order to minimize the finishing time, we must choose the $k_i$'s proportional to the work for each group. Recall that we take the measure of work to be the communication cost for that group, and by Example 4 the cost of distributing $R$, $R'$, $T$, and $T'$ to a group, as necessary, is $2\sqrt{k_i r_i t_i}$, where:

1. $r_i$ is the cost of distributing $R$ and/or $R'$, that is, one of $r$, $ar$, or $(1 + a)r$, depending on whether $R$, $R'$, or both are needed by the group.
2. $t_i$ is likewise related to $T$ and $T'$.

If $2\sqrt{k_i r_i t_i}/k_i$ is a constant independent of $i$, it follows that for some constant $\alpha$, $k_i = \alpha r_i t_i$. Further, if $\sum_i k_i = k$, then $\alpha = k/\sum_i r_i t_i$. Now the communication cost for all the groups (neglecting $S$, as before) is $\sum_i 2\sqrt{k_i r_i t_i}$. Substitute $\alpha r_i t_i$ for $k_i$, giving us a cost of $2\sqrt{\alpha}\sum_i r_i t_i$. Finally, substitute $k/\sum_i r_i t_i$ for $\alpha$, giving the formula for communication cost:

$$2\sqrt{k}\sqrt{\sum_i r_i t_i}$$

Some group, say group $i$, covers the term $RS'T$, and in this group we have the term $rt$ in $r_i t_i$. Another group (possibly the same), say group $j$, covers $R'ST$, and for this group there is a term $art$ in $r_j t_j$. Likewise, the group that covers $RST'$ has a term $art$, and the group that covers $R'ST'$ has a term $a^2 rt$. When we sum $\sum_i r_i t_i$ we therefore get at least $(1 + a)^2 rt$. Thus, a lower bound on the cost $2\sqrt{k}\sqrt{\sum_i r_i t_i}$ is $2(1 + a)\sqrt{krt}$, which is the same as the term not involving $s$ in the cost of the single-group method: $(1 + a)(s + 2\sqrt{krt})$. Since $S$ and $S'$ must each appear in at least one group, the cost of distributing $S$ will be at least $(1+a)s$. Thus, for this particular example of seminaive evaluation, we have proved that the single-group method has the least communication cost.

**Conjecture:** *The above generalizes to the seminaive evaluation of any join of any number of terms. That is, one can never both finish faster and use less* *communication than by considering all the necessary terms to be in one group and hashing each relation and its corresponding delta-relation in the same way.*

It is important to note that if we do not require that communication cost be minimized under the constraint that the groups finish at the same time, then an extreme distribution of the work can technically minimize communication. For example, we could put only $R'ST'$ in one group, and use $k_1 = k - 1$ for this group, while putting the other six terms into a second group, with $k_2 = 1$. That group, which does almost all the work, has minimal communication cost $(1 + a)(r + s + t)$, while the first group has cost $s + 2a^2\sqrt{(k-1)rt}$. The sum of these costs is much less than $(1 + a)(s + 2\sqrt{krt})$ under many situations: as long as $s$ is not too much larger than $r$ and $t$, and $a < 1$.

# 4   Recursive Datalog

Our general strategy for evaluating recursive Datalog programs is to distribute the responsibility for each rule among some number of tasks, with the division based on hashing the values corresponding to one or more of the variables in the body of the rule. The evaluation of a rule body is essentially a join of relations, so we shall use the strategy of [1] to decide which variables to use as part of the hash key and how many values to use when hashing each variable. However, for a single join, we assume it is possible to know or estimate the size of the relations being joined. When a join participant is actually an IDB relation, we don't know its size when we plan the evaluation strategy, so the estimate of its size must necessarily be something of a conjecture. It is possible, as we evaluate the recursive relations, that we shall get a better estimate of size. That would motivate us to recalculate the numbers of buckets for each variable, but we shall not consider this issue here.

In this section, we shall consider the matter of algorithms for implementing recursive Datalog as a collection of recursive tasks running on a cluster. Section 5 will address the equally important issue of what can be done to recover from node failures without restarting all the tasks. Our goal is to use an amount of communication that is at most proportional to the number of derivations in a seminaive evaluation of the same program, as given by Theorem 1. However, we shall begin with a simple example where the communication is much less than the number of derivations.

## 4.1   Linear Transitive Closure

Consider the right-linear recursion for paths in a graph:

```
p(X,Y) :- e(X,Y)
p(X,Y) :- e(X,Z) & p(Z,Y)
```

Here, $e$ is an EDB predicate representing the arcs in a graph, and $p$ is the corresponding path predicate for that graph. Suppose that the relation $e$ is small enough that we are willing to distribute it to every compute-node. Perhaps it

```
for (each tuple p(a,b))
    for (each tuple e(x,a))
        if (p(x,b) was not previously generated)
            add (p(x,b) to the set of generated tuples;
```

**Fig. 1.** Evaluation of right-linear transitive closure

fits in main memory, or perhaps it requires disk but we are willing to store it at each node and retrieve parts of it as needed.

Suppose we use $k$ tasks to compute $p$, and we determine responsibility for a tuple $p(X, Y)$ by hashing the value of $Y$ into $k$ buckets, using some hash function $h$. Initially, the task numbered $i$ is given all tuples of $e$, and those tuples $p(a, b)$ such that $e(a, b)$ is an EDB tuple and $h(b) = i$. Task $i$ then does the steps outlined in Fig. 1. Notice that each generated $p(x, b)$ will hash to the task that generated it, since the $B$-values are the same. We thus have the pleasant situation that, after replicating $e$ at each compute-node, there is no further communication. The answer is the union of the $p$-facts generated at each of the $k$ compute-nodes.

For this method of computation, we have communication cost $k|e|$, that is, $k$ times the size of the relation $e$. The number of derivations in a seminaive evaluation can be much larger; it is the sum over all nodes $z$ of the number of the number $d_z$ that was computed in Example 2. In some cases, the number of derivations can be less than $k|e|$. For instance, suppose the graph consists of disconnected edges, so the number of derivations is 0. However, if $k$ is not too large, and the graph is complex, we expect the communication cost to be much less than the number of derivations.

*Example 6.* Based on the study of [7], suppose the graph is the Web. A typical page can reach about half the Web and has an in-degree of 10. On that basis, a Web graph with $n$ nodes would have $|e| = 10n$ and a number of derivations $5n^2$. Thus, as long as $k \ll n/2$, this approach uses much less communication than the number of derivations.

Of course the derivations that occur in a seminaive evaluation still occur at the various nodes, so the computation time at the nodes will be proportional to the number of derivations. That observation suggests that communication cost may not be the best measure of running time for this example. While that is undoubtedly true when the number of derivations is huge, we can do a lot of main-memory calculation in the time it takes to communicate $e$ over a gigabit line, so in at least some cases, the true cost will still be primarily the cost needed to replicate $e$.

Whether or not the number of derivations dominates the running time of the recursion, we should verify that the total execution time of the compute-nodes is at most proportional to this quantity. The argument is simple and depends on two observations:

1. A tuple $p(a, b)$ can only be derived by the task $h(b)$.
2. A tuple $p(a, b)$ is considered only once for matching $e$-tuples.

Thus, an assignment $(x, a, b)$ to the variables $(X, Z, Y)$ of the recursive rule is made only once in Fig. 1: at the task $h(b)$ when $p(a, b)$ is considered and matched with $e(x, a)$.

## 4.2   Nonlinear Transitive Closure

The nonlinear version of transitive closure:

```
p(X,Y)  :- e(X,Y)
p(X,Y)  :- p(X,Z) & p(Z,Y)
```

does not allow us to avoid communication among the tasks that apply the recursive rule. We can, however, use communication that is on the order of the number of derivations in a seminaive evaluation of this program. We shall give two different approaches, depending on whether we use separate tasks for duplicate-elimination or combine the join and duplicate-elimination steps.

To begin, recall from Example 2 that the number of derivations for the nonlinear transitive closure is the sum over all nodes $z$ in the graph of the number $d_z''$. Recall that $d_z''$ is the product of the number of predecessors (nodes that can reach $z$ by a path of length one or more) times the number of successors (nodes that $z$ reaches by paths of length one or more). In comparison, the right-linear version of Section 4.1 has a number of derivations equal to the sum over nodes $z$ of the in-degree of $z$ times the number of successors of $z$. For the left-linear version, where the body of the recursive rule is `p(X,Z) & e(Z,Y)`, the number of derivations is the sum over nodes $z$ of the number of predecessors of $z$ times the out-degree of $z$. Thus, the numbers of derivations of the left- and right- linear versions are incomparable, but each is less than the number of derivations for the nonlinear rules.

Nevertheless, there is some reason why we might want to use the nonlinear version. The number of iterations for the linear versions is equal to the length of the longest path in the graph, while for the nonlinear version it is the log of that length. There is overhead involved in iteration, as we must pass many files among the tasks at each iteration. The overhead becomes a severe problem when there are a few long paths in the graph, and later iterations discover few new path facts, resulting in short files that must be passed among tasks. We shall discuss ways to minimize overhead of data distribution in Section 4.9. Moreover, there is a simple rewriting of the nonlinear transitive closure that maintains the logarithmic number of iterations, yet significantly reduces the number of derivations. We shall discuss this improvement in Section 4.7.

## 4.3   Using Join Tasks to Compute the Transitive Closure

Our first method uses $k$ tasks, which we call *join tasks* to compute the nonlinear transitive closure Datalog program from Section 4.2. We use a hash function $h$ that maps values of the variable $Z$ to $k$ buckets. We begin by applying the basis rule. Each EDB tuple $e(a, b)$ is sent to two tasks, those corresponding to buckets $h(a)$ and $h(b)$, as the $p$-tuple $p(a, b)$. Each task stores all the $p$-tuples it

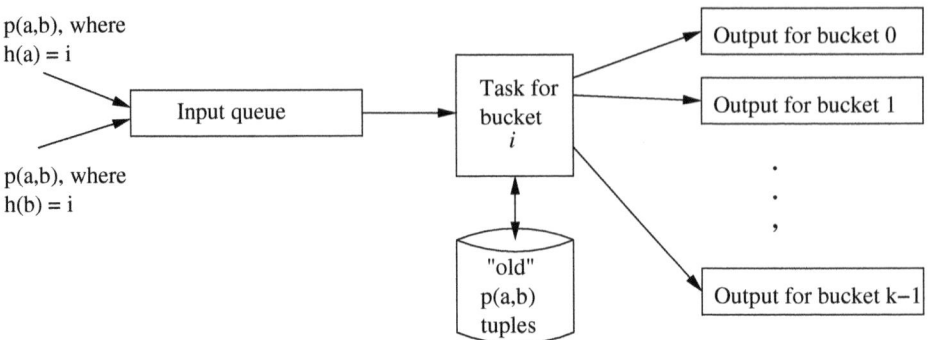

**Fig. 2.** A join task

receives, so it can tell whether what it receives is a duplicate and therefore can be ignored. The structure of a join task is suggested by Fig. 2.

When $p(a, b)$ is received by a task for the first time, the task:

1. If this task is $h(b)$, it searches for previously received tuples $p(b, x)$ for any $x$. For each such tuple, it sends $p(a, x)$ to two tasks: $h(a)$ and $h(x)$.
2. If this task is $h(a)$, it searches for previously received tuples $p(y, a)$ for any $y$. For each such tuple, it sends $p(y, b)$ to the tasks $h(y)$ and $h(b)$.
3. The tuple $p(a, b)$ is stored locally as an already seen tuple.

Note that in the rare case that $h(a) = h(b)$, both (1) and (2) are performed, but there is no need for this task to send the discovered tuple to itself. It will, however, treat the discovered tuples as if they were input arrived from another task.

**Theorem 2.** *The number of tuples communicated by the tasks described above is at most twice the number of derivations of the nonlinear transitive-closure program.*

*Proof.* First, consider the derivations in the basis rule $\texttt{p(X,Y)} \ \texttt{:-} \ \texttt{e(X,Y)}$. Each derivation consists of instantiating $X$ and $Y$ to constants $x$ and $y$ such that $e(x, y)$ is a given tuple. The initial step sends $p(x, y)$ to at most two tasks, $h(x)$ and $h(y)$, and this rule is never again used.

For the recursive rule, consider an instantiation $(x, z, y)$ for variables $X$, $Z$, and $Y$. This instantiation can only take place at the task $h(z)$, because only that task considers joining tuples $p(x, z)$ with $p(z, y)$. Moreover, this join only occurs when the second of $p(x, z)$ and $p(z, y)$ is processed from the input of that task. After that time, both tuples are considered "old," and if they appear on the input a second time, they will not be considered for a join. Thus, this derivation occurs only once among all the tasks, and it results in at most two communications of the resulting tuple.

## 4.4    File Management for the Nonlinear Recursion

From the discussion of Section 4.3, you might imagine that tuples are passed among tasks as soon as they are generated. However, passing single tuples incurs severe overhead. Roughly, it is only economical to send tuples in packages of thousands. We assume that each task has an input queue of tuples, which from time to time is passed new input tuples by other tasks, or (rarely) by itself. Each task maintains one output file for each of the other tasks, into which it places discovered tuples destined for that task. There are some options regarding when these files are transmitted.

1. *Operation in Rounds.* We can wait until each task has exhausted its input. At that time, all tasks transmit all their files to the proper destination task. This approach treats the recursion as an iteration. It is commonly used in map-reduce implementations. For example, we can see the common Page-Rank calculation, which is technically a recursion, as an iteration in which each step is carried out by a separate map-reduce job, with distribution of data interspersed. It is also the approach used by [21], called *supersteps*, for implementing recursive graph algorithms. The disadvantage is that some tasks may finish early and must idle while other tasks finish.

2. *Tasks Choose to Send Data.* An alternative is to allow each task to decide when it is ready to send a file. It might send a file as soon as it has reached a certain size, or send all its files after the total amount of output it has generated has reached a limit. There are two advantages of this approach. First, it makes it more likely that each task will have some input available at all times. Second, it keeps the communication network busy most of the time, instead of letting it idle between rounds.

3. *A Global Decision.* We can allow the controller for the tasks (the *master* in the parlance of Hadoop or similar systems) to decide when to pass data. It could call for data to be sent at regular time intervals, or it could monitor the total amount of data generated and call for transmission when the total amount of data reaches a set limit.

Regardless of the method used, there is a problem that must be solved in some manner: at the end of the recursion, where files are small, it is possible that no task will have generated enough output to be worth sending. We discuss management of the "endgame" in Section 4.9.

## 4.5    Join/Duplicate-Elimination Method for Nonlinear TC

A somewhat different approach to the nonlinear transitive-closure recursion is to use two sets of tasks:

1. *Join tasks*, which perform the join of tuples as in Section 4.3. Join tasks correspond to a bucket of a hash function $h$ that is used to hash $Z$-values in the recursive rule. As before, a join task receives all tuples $p(a, b)$ such that either $h(a)$ or $h(b)$ is its bucket number. Received tuples are joined with all

previously received tuples, but there is no need to check whether the received tuple itself is a duplicate.

2. *Dup-elim tasks*, whose job is to catch duplicate $p$-tuples before they can propagate. These tasks correspond to buckets of a hash function $g$ that hashes pairs consisting of an $X$-value and a $Y$-value in the recursive rule. That is, tuple $p(a, b)$ is the responsibility of dup-elim task $g(a, b)$, which stores all such tuples that it has seen.

Initially, each EDB tuple $e(a, b)$ is sent to the join tasks $h(a)$ and $h(b)$ as a $p$-tuple, as in the previously described method, and it is also sent to the dup-elim task $g(a, b)$ to be recorded as a previously seen $p$-tuple. When a join task produces a tuple $p(a, b)$, it sends it to dup-elim task $g(a, b)$. If that task has seen this tuple before, it does nothing. If $p(a, b)$ has not been seen before, it stores it locally and sends a copy to the two join tasks $h(a)$ and $h(b)$. As we shall see, this method has a small advantage over the method of Section 4.3 in communication cost, and it also supports failure recovery in a way that the latter does not (see Section 5.2). Figure 3 suggests the two-rank structure of tasks when duplicate elimination is separated from the join operation.

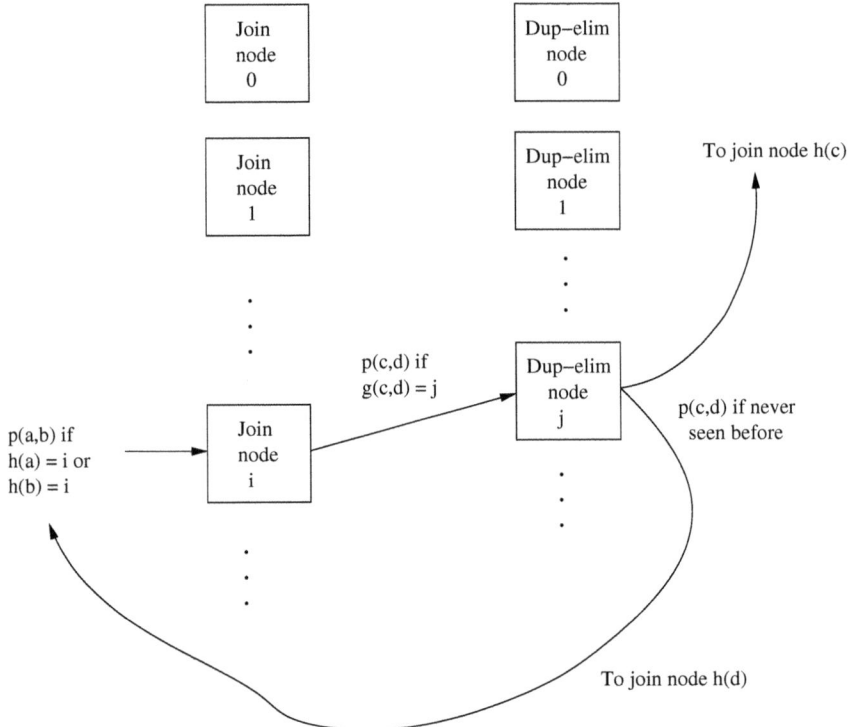

**Fig. 3.** Relationship between join and dup-elim tasks

**Theorem 3.** *The method described above for combining join and duplicate-elimination tasks communicates a number of tuples that is at most the sum of:*

1. *The number of derivations plus*
2. *Twice the number of distinct IDB tuples derived plus*
3. *Three times the number of EDB tuples.*

*Proof.* The initial distribution of the EDB tuples, each to three tasks (one dup-elim task and two join tasks) accounts for term (3) in the statement of the theorem. As in Theorem 2, the join tasks can only use a derivation once, since after that, both joined tuples are "old," and therefore will not be considered as a joining pair again. However, unlike in the previous theorem, here each derivation causes only one copy of its result to be communicated; this copy goes to a single dup-elim task. This observation accounts for term (1).

Each dup-elim node communicates a tuple only once, as it remembers it has been seen if it appears again on its input. That tuple is communicated to two different join tasks. It is easy to see that no two dup-elim tasks can communicate the same tuple, since they can communicate only tuples in their own bucket.

### 4.6   Generalization to All Recursive Datalog

The two strategies we outlined for nonlinear transitive closure can be used for any recursive Datalog program. First, consider the simpler method in Section 4.3. In analogy to the join tasks, we can have one set of tasks for the body of each rule. Note that a single predicate with several recursive rules will have more than one group of tasks, one group for each rule. When a task from any group produces a tuple for the head of its rule, it must be delivered to all groups that use the head predicate. Which task in a group receives the new tuple depends on the hashing scheme used for that group.

The job of the tasks for a rule is to take the join of all the subgoals in the body. If a body consists of two subgoals, the tuples from these subgoals are hashed on the common variables to determine to which task they must be sent when generated. Each task stores previously received tuples, so it can avoid repeating work, and thus will communicate no more tuples than the number of derivations performed at that task (i.e., the communication cost is proportional to the number of derivations).

If there is a body with more than two subgoals, we have two choices:

1. Split the bodies of rules, so there are only two subgoals per rule.
2. Use a multiway join, as in [1].

Splitting makes sense unless the intermediate relations created by the splitting are much larger than the relations of the original predicates. The multiway join requires replication of tuples to many join tasks, and will always have a communication cost above the bound given in Theorem 1. However, it avoids the creation of large intermediates, and is sometimes preferable.

The second approach to nonlinear TC, from Section 4.5, also generalizes to any recursive Datalog program. The difference is that the responsibility for detecting duplicates is given to a separate set of tasks associated with each recursive predicate. Note there is only one set of dup-elim tasks per predicate, regardless of how many rules that predicate has. Also note that the join tasks for a rule still need to store the received tuples, in order to join them later with newly received tuples. However, when a tuple is received at a join task, it can be stored without checking whether it is a duplicate.

## 4.7   Nonlinear TC via Recursive Doubling

We shall now take up a method for implementing the nonlinear transitive closure that typically makes fewer deductions than the direct implementations described previously. The algorithm that we shall discuss has been called *Smart Transitive Closure*. It appears originally in [25] and [15]. In [17] it was shown to be highly efficient as a serial algorithm.

The key idea is to find pairs of nodes $(x, y)$ such that the shortest path from $x$ to $y$ has a length that is a power of 2. Since any path from $x$ to $y$ can be broken into a path of length $2^i$ from $x$ to some node $z$, followed by a path of length at most $2^i$ from $z$ to $y$, we can allow one of the $p$ predicates in the nonlinear recursion to be restricted to powers of 2, and still converge in a number of rounds that is logarithmic in the length of the longest path. To simplify the algorithm, we shall assume that the graph is first made acyclic by collapsing strong components into single nodes, as was suggested in the analysis of TC algorithms [9].

The smart TC algorithm is best described as an iteration, where in round $i \geq 0$ we compute:

1. $p_i(X, Y)$ = the set of pairs of nodes $(x, y)$ such that there is a path from $x$ to $y$ of length between 0 and $2^i - 1$.
2. $q_i(X, Y)$ = the set of pairs of nodes $(x, y)$ such that the shortest path from $x$ to $y$ is of length exactly $2^i$.

Smart TC is sketched in Fig. 4. Note that we use :- to represent nonrecursive Datalog rule evaluation, contrasted with :=, which represents conventional assignment.

The basis is lines (1) through (3). Line (1) initializes $q_0$ to be the edges of the graph, i.e., those pairs of nodes whose shortest path is of length $2^0 = 1$. Note that we assume the graph is acyclic, and thus has no loops. If not, we would have to remove $q_0(x, x)$ where there a loop from $x$ to itself. Line (2) initializes $p_0$ to be the paths of length 0, that is, all tuples $p_0(x, x)$. Finally, line (3) sets $i$, the iteration counter, to 0.

Lines (4) through (10) are a loop that iterates until at some stage we discover no more $q$-tuples have been uncovered. After incrementing $i$ at line (5), we compute $p_i$ at lines (6) and (7). Line (6) joins $q_{i-1}$ and $p_{i-1}$, thereby discovering all paths of length between $2^{i-1}$ and $2^i - 1$. Line (7) then adds in the $p$-facts discovered on previous rounds, i.e., those paths of length less than $2^{i-1}$. Line (8)

```
1)  q₀(X,Y) :- e(X,Y);
2)  p₀(X,X) :- ;
3)  i := 0;
4)  repeat {
5)  i := i + 1;
6)          pᵢ(X,Y) :- qᵢ₋₁(X,Z) & pᵢ₋₁(Z,Y);
7)          pᵢ(X,Y) := pᵢ(X,Y) ∪ pᵢ₋₁(X,Y);
8)          qᵢ(X,Y) :- qᵢ₋₁(X,Z) & qᵢ₋₁(Z,Y);
9)          qᵢ(X,Y) := qᵢ(X,Y) − pᵢ(X,Y);
    }
10) until (qᵢ == ∅)
```

**Fig. 4.** Transitive closure by recursive doubling

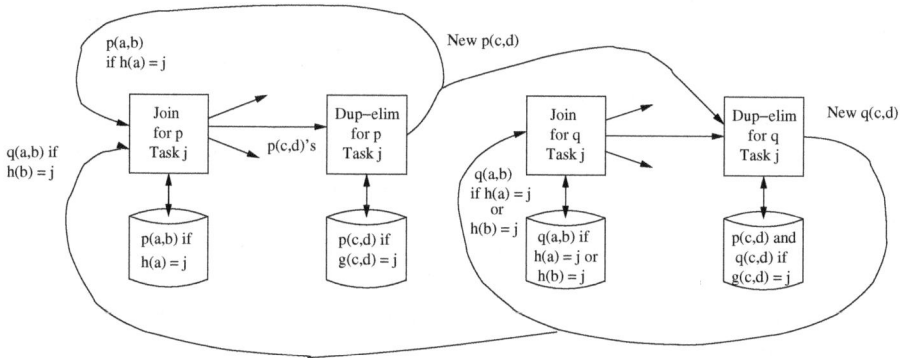

**Fig. 5.** Computing the transitive closure by recursive doubling

computes $q_i$ to be the join of $q_{i-1}$ with itself. That will surely discover all paths of length $2^i$. However, it also will include some pairs that have a path of length $2^i$ but also have a shorter path. These pairs are eliminated by line (9).

To implement this algorithm, we shall use join and dup-elim tasks, as in Section 4.5. The responsibility for tuples is divided among these tasks using hash functions $h$ and $g$, also as described in that section. The tasks must operate in rounds; i.e., we assume the first of the approaches discussed in Section 4.4. There are two groups of join tasks and two groups of dup-elim tasks, as suggested by Fig. 5.

The network of tasks that implement Fig. 5 consists of four groups of tasks. In the figure, each group is represented by a single task, referred to as "task $j$" for that group. The four groups, from the left, implement steps (6), through (9), respectively. To begin the $i$th round, the first group of tasks, the join tasks for $p$, will have received all tuples $p(a, b)$ generated on round $i - 1$, with the $j$th task of the group receiving those $p(a, b)$ such that $a$ hashes to $j$. $p$-tuples generated on previous rounds will have been received and stored at those rounds, so they too are available for the join. In addition, this task $j$ will just have received all $q(a, b)$ tuples such that $b$ hashes to $j$. These are exactly the tuples in $q_{i-1}$. They are joined with all the received and stored $p$-tuples, and all resulting tuples are shipped to the appropriate task in the second group, the dup-elim tasks for $p$. The appropriate dup-elim task for $p(c, d)$ is determined by hashing the $c$-$d$ combination.

The second task shown in Fig. 5 represents the group of tasks that do duplicate elimination for $p$. These tasks store all $p$ tuples received, and pass on only the new tuples. Such a tuple $p(c, d)$ is passed to two other tasks:

1. The appropriate join task for $p$. This task is determined by hashing $c$.
2. The dup-elim task for $q$ with the same index. This tuple will be used in step (9) to eliminate a $q$-tuple if that tuple is found to have a path shorter than $2^i$.

The third group of tasks are join tasks for $q$. These tasks receive all tuples $q(a, b)$ in $q_{i-1}$ from the previous round. The task numbered $j$ receives $q(a, b)$ if either $a$ or $b$ hashes to $j$. The result of these tasks are candidate tuples for $q_i$, so $q(c, d)$ is passed to one of the fourth group of tasks: the dup-elim task for $q$ whose index is the result of hashing the $c$-$d$ combination.

The fourth group of tasks store all the $q$- and $p$-tuples that have been generated on rounds up to $i - 1$, and on the $i$th round they receive the newly generated $p$-tuples. Thus, they are prepared to eliminate those tuples $q(c, d)$ such that there is a path of length less than $2^i$ from $c$ to $d$. Tuples that are not eliminated are fed back to the first and third group, the join tasks for $q$ and $p$, for use in round $i + 1$. Notice that each such tuple goes to two tasks of group three, but only one task of group one.

## 4.8   Communication Cost of TC Using Recursive Doubling

Recall that we considered nonlinear TC not because it yielded less communication than the linear methods, but because it reduced the number of rounds and therefore might reduce the overhead inherent in large numbers of rounds. It is nevertheless important that the recursive-doubling approach to nonlinear TC reduces the communication cost significantly below that of the conventional nonlinear TC. In this section we provide an upper bound on the communication cost for implementing the algorithm of Fig. 4. Line (1) has cost at most equal to the number of EDB facts. Line (2) is implemented with no communication; each join task for $p$ implicitly generates all $(x, x)$ such that $h(x)$ is the index of that task.

The joining and generation of tuples that may or may not be duplicates occurs at lines (6) and (8). At line (6), the number of tuples generated by a $Z$-value $z$ at the $i$-th round is the number of predecessors that $z$ has at distance exactly $2^{i-1}$ times the number of successors of $z$ at distance less than $2^{i-1}$. At line (8), the number of tuples generated by $z$ at the $i$-th round is the number of predecessors that $z$ has at distance exactly $2^{i-1}$ times the number of successors of $z$ at distance exactly $2^{i-1}$. Thus, between the two of these join operations, the number of tuples generated by $z$ at the $i$-th round is the number of predecessors that $z$ has at distance exactly $2^{i-1}$ times the number of successors of $z$ at distance up to and including $2^{i-1}$. The total number of tuples communicated out of the two groups of join tasks is the sum of this quantity over all nodes and all $i$. It is hard to give a more succinct statement of the amount of communication, but it is easy to observe that this quantity is surely less than that of Theorem 3 for the straightforward implementation of nonlinear TC.

There is also communication out of the dup-elim tasks, but this cost can be neglected. That is, each $p$ fact can leave only one task in the second group, and it is sent to exactly two tasks — one in group one and one in group four. Each $q$ fact likewise leaves only one task in group four, and it is communicated three times — once to group one and twice to group three.

### 4.9   The Endgame: Dealing with Small Files

In later rounds of a recursion, it is possible that the number of new facts derived at a round drops considerably. Recall that there is significant overhead involved in transmitting files, so it is desired that each of the recursive tasks have thousands of tuples for each of the other tasks whenever we distribute data among the tasks. However, the large number of tasks suitable for early rounds of the recursion may lead to very small files at later rounds. Thus, in at least some instances, there will be need for an "endgame" strategy, where as the sizes of files shrink, the algorithm used to implement the recursion changes. Two possibilities are:

1. Reduce the number of compute-nodes used for the tasks and therefore cause many tasks to execute at the same node. Collect all the tuples at a compute-node that are destined for tasks at a single other compute-node into a single file. Ship that file to the destination and have that node sort the input into separate files for each of the tasks at that node.

2. Create one or more additional *hub tasks* whose only job is to receive files from the join and dup-elim tasks and consolidate them into files destined for each task. As in the first strategy, each task can bundle the tuples destined for each other task (labeling the tuples by destination, of course) into a single file and ship them as one file to a hub task.

## 5   Recovery from Node Failures

To this point, we have assumed that computations proceed to completion with no failures. In reality, several kinds of failures can occur. These include single-node failures (e.g., a disk crash), failures of the communication network belonging to a rack of nodes, and software failures due to missing or out-of-date system components at a node. In this section, we shall discuss some options for modifying the execution strategies we have discussed in order to allow computation to proceed in the face of most node failures.

## 5.1   Existing Recursive Systems

Recall that if a task fails, it is important that it has not delivered any output to other tasks. That way, the failed task can be restarted as in Hadoop or its generalizations, without affecting any other task. But when a task is recursive, we cannot wait until it completes to deliver its output. There are two recent systems that implement recursive tasks and deal with this problem in their own way.

1. HaLoop [8] implements recursion as an iteration of map-reduce jobs, trying hard to make sure that tasks for one round are located at the node where its input was created by the previous round. Since all tasks exist for only a single iteration, they are not really recursive, and no problem of dealing with failure arises.
2. Pregel [20] implements true recursion, but checkpoints all tasks at intervals. If any task fails, all tasks are rolled back to the previous checkpoint.

## 5.2   Use of Idempotence

Pure Datalog, unlike most forms of recursion, has an idempotence property due to its reliance on the set model of data. That is, generating a tuple a second time has no effect on the eventual outcome of the recursion. Thus, if a node fails, we can restart its task(s) at a different node without affecting the global computation. There are, however, some mechanisms necessary to allow a task to run from the beginning, without forcing the tasks that supplied its input to repeat those inputs. Here are the options:

1. When each task produces output files, they can be stored in the supporting distributed file system, replicated several times. For each task, the DFS must maintain one file containing all its inputs generated by any task, including itself. If a task needs to restart, it gets previously generated tuples that were sent to the failed version of the same task from the DFS.
2. The master controller for the job can store each file that a task generates at another node or at several nodes. This approach may be better than storing files in the DFS, because each of the files is (comparatively) short, and there are many files. If a task needs to restart, we hope that there is a surviving node holding all its previous inputs.
3. If we use the two-stage approach typified by the join/dup-elim tasks of Section 4.5, we have an additional option. Suppose we keep the join tasks on different racks from the dup-elim tasks. Each task of one kind is capable of supplying all the inputs to a task of the other kind, if it stores locally the output files it generates at each round. This structure can survive any single failure, even a rack failure. Only if a join task and a dup-elim task fail at (roughly) the same time, will the entire job have to be restarted. Thus, the probability of having to restart is the probability of two independent failures at the same time.

## 5.3   When Idempotence Cannot Be Used

Many recursions involve nonidempotent operations. For example, we may want to compute relations recursively, using the normal bag-model semantics of SQL. Or we may have an aggregation involved in a Datalog recursion, such as counting the number of paths in a graph or the number of nodes reachable from each node in a graph. If so, we not only need to reconstruct the inputs to a restarted task. We need to know which output files from the corresponding failed task were delivered to their destination, so we do not send the same data again. There are again several approaches worth consideration.

1. The master controller must record each file ever shipped from one task to another. The file itself can be stored in a number of ways, such as in the DFS or in a replication system managed by the master. A restarted task is told by the master which files the original task received as input. There must be a way to reproduce the timing of the generation of output files; for example, if output files are generated in rounds, the restarted task can produce the same output files as the original version of the task, since it is given the same input files in the same sequence. The restarted task must execute the same steps as the original, in order to develop the same internal state as the original. However, when it generates an output file that was previously received from the original version of the restarted task, the master does not deliver it; this file is "thrown away."

2. Instead of giving the master the responsibility for throwing away repeated output files, the recipient can be given that responsibility. Each task records all the files it ever receives. It may not be necessary to record the file contents, but certainly it must record enough information to know if it receives an identical file: an identifier of the task and the round at which that file was sent. More specifically:

   (a) A task identifier must be the same for an original task and a restarted task. For example, in the nonlinear TC implementation of Section 4.3, it would be appropriate to identify a join task by the hash value to which it corresponds.

   (b) The "round" at which a file was sent makes sense even if there aren't strict rounds. For instance, if we use approach (2) mentioned in Section 4.4 (deliver files when a size limit is reached), files from one task to another are still delivered in the same order and will have the same contents. A simple serial number for the file will serve to identify the "round."

## 5.4   Checkpointing

A different approach to task restart involves checkpointing — storing the state of all tasks periodically, so they can be restarted from the previous checkpoint. This approach has been studied for parallel/distributed computation by many: [21], [2], [18], and is the strategy used by Pregel mentioned in Section 5.1. However, our goal is to be able to use checkpoint information to restart a task from the last checkpoint without affecting other tasks (unlike Pregel, which *does* affect other tasks). In order to allow restart of a single task from its prior checkpointed state, there are several conditions that must be met:

1. As discussed in Section 1.3, simple restart depends on the failed task having made no output that has been consumed elsewhere. In the context of checkpointing, that means a task must be checkpointed any time it delivers output files. More precisely:
   (a) The task must tell the master it is ready to deliver output (or vice-versa — the master tells the task to deliver output).
   (b) The master delivers the output to its destination(s), but does not tell the recipients they can use the files as input.
   (c) The checkpoint is made.
   (d) The master tells the recipients they can use the input.
   Note that with regard to step 1d, we assume that the master does not fail, or else the whole job fails. In addition, we assume the files delivered by the master are replicated sufficiently that they will not be lost once they are delivered at step 1a.

2. A checkpoint includes the entire internal state of the task, including all the data that has been stored by the task. For example, a join task in the TC algorithm of Section 4.3 would need to have all the tuples it has received and stored be part of the checkpoint. It may make sense to include output files in the checkpoint, as it would assure replication if needed. This strategy would negate the risk of losing a delivered file discussed just above.

3. In general, tasks are instantiations of a prototype function. If we are to allow restart from a checkpoint, each such function must be written to take a checkpointed state and re-establish this state locally. In the vast majority of cases, where a task is not a restart but is running ab-initio, the empty state must be provided as a dummy "checkpoint," and the code must work correctly from that state.

## 6  Summary

Implementing Datalog on a computing cluster presents a number of interesting challenges. Some of these are:

– The cost of transporting data to the compute-node(s) that need it is an important factor for the evaluation of algorithms. When communication cost is considered, multiway joins sometimes make sense as a way to implement Datalog rules. We also conjecture that seminaive evaluation is best computed by distributing the previous and incremental parts of a given relation in the same way.

– Because of the overhead of transporting files in a cluster environment, we must manage files carefully, especially in later rounds of a recursion, where few new facts are being discovered in one round. We have suggested several ways that small files can be combined into larger ones in later rounds.

- Another response to the problem of unproductive later rounds is to replace linear recursions by nonlinear recursions. We have examined transitive closure in particular. While the communication cost of a nonlinear TC is typically much greater than that of the linear versions of TC, a variant of nonlinear TC developed a generation ago can make the communication cost much closer to that of the linear versions.
- Map-reduce manages failures at run-time by using tasks that have an important property: their output is not delivered until they have completed successfully. Recursive tasks cannot have that property. We have suggested several strategies for allowing recursive tasks to be restarted correctly, even though they have delivered some of their output, and that output has been consumed by other tasks.

# References

1. Afrati, F.N., Ullman, J.D.: Optimizing joins in a map-reduce environment. In: EDBT (2010)
2. Al-Kiswany, S., Ripeanu, M., Vazhkudai, S.S., Gharaibeh, A.: stdchk: A checkpoint storage system for desktop grid computing. In: ICDCS, pp. 613–624 (2008)
3. Alvaro, P., Condie, T., Conway, N., Elmeleegy, K., Hellerstein, J.M., Sears, R.: Boom analytics: exploring data-centric, declarative programming for the cloud. In: EuroSys, pp. 223–236 (2010)
4. Apache. Hadoop (2006), http://hadoop.apache.org/
5. Battré, D., Ewen, S., Hueske, F., Kao, O., Markl, V., Warneke, D.: Nephele/pacts: a programming model and execution framework for web-scale analytical processing. In: SoCC 2010: Proceedings of the 1st ACM Symposium on Cloud Computing, pp. 119–130. ACM, New York (2010)
6. Borkar, V., Carey, M., Grover, R., Onose, N., Vernica, R.: Hyracks: A flexible and extensible foundation for data-intensive computing. In: Proceedings of the IEEE International Conference on Data Engineering (to appear, 2011)
7. Broder, A.Z., Kumar, R., Maghoul, F., Raghavan, P., Rajagopalan, S., Stata, R., Tomkins, A., Wiener, J.L.: Graph structure in the web. Computer Networks 33(1-6), 309–320 (2000)
8. Bu, Y., Howe, B., Balazinska, M., Ernst, M.: Haloop: efficient iterative data processing on large clusters. In: VLDB Conference (2010)
9. Dar, S., Ramakrishnan, R.: A performance study of transitive closure algorithms. In: SIGMOD Conference, pp. 454–465 (1994)
10. Dean, J., Ghemawat, S.: Mapreduce: simplified data processing on large clusters. Commun. ACM 51(1), 107–113 (2008)
11. DeWitt, D.J., Paulson, E., Robinson, E., Naughton, J.F., Royalty, J., Shankar, S., Krioukov, A.: Clustera: an integrated computation and data management system. PVLDB 1(1), 28–41 (2008)
12. Garcia-Molina, H., Ullman, J.D., Widom, J.: Database Systems: The complete book (2009)
13. Ghemawat, S., Gobioff, H., Leung, S.-T.: The google file system. In: 19th ACM Symposium on Operating Systems Principles (2003)
14. Hellerstein, J.M.: The declarative imperative: experiences and conjectures in distributed logic. SIGMOD Rec. 39, 1, 5–19 (2010)

15. Ioannidis, Y.E.: On the computation of the transitive closure of relational operators. In: Proceedings of the 12th International Conference on Very Large Data Bases, VLDB 1986, pp. 403–411. Morgan Kaufmann Publishers Inc., San Francisco (1986)
16. Isard, M., Budiu, M., Yu, Y., Birrell, A., Fetterly, D.: Dryad: distributed data-parallel programs from sequential building blocks. In: EuroSys 2007 (2007)
17. Kabler, R., Ioannidis, Y.E., Carey, M.J.: Performance evaluation of algorithms for transitive closure. Inf. Syst. 17(5), 415–441 (1992)
18. Kontogiannis, S.C., Pantziou, G.E., Spirakis, P.G., Yung, M.: Robust parallel computations through randomization. Theory Comput. Syst. 33(5/6), 427–464 (2000)
19. Lam, M., et al.: Bdd-based deductive database. bddbddb.sourceforge.net (2008)
20. Malewicz, G., Austern, M., Bik, A., Dehnert, J., Horn, I., Leiser, N., Czajkowski, G.: Pregel: A system for large-scale graph processing. In: SIGMOD Conference (2010)
21. Malewicz, G., Austern, M.H., Bik, A.J.C., Dehnert, J.C., Horn, I., Leiser, N., Czajkowski, G.: Pregel: a system for large-scale graph processing. In: SIGMOD 2010: Proceedings of the 2010 International Conference on Management of Data, pp. 135–146. ACM, New York (2010)
22. Rajaraman, A., Ullman, J.D.: Mining of Massive Datasets (2010)
23. Seong, S.-W., Nasielski, M., Seo, J., Sengupta, D., Hangal, S., Teh, S.K., Chu, R., Dodson, B., Lam, M.S.: The architecture and implementation of a decentralized social networking platform (2009), http://prpl.stanford.edu/papers/prpl09.pdf
24. Ullman, J.D.: Principles of Database and Knowledge-Base Systems (1989)
25. Valduriez, P., Boral, H.: Evaluation of recursive queries using join indices. In: Expert Database Conf., pp. 271–293 (1986)
26. Yu, Y., Isard, M., Fetterly, D., Budiu, M., Erlingsson, L., Gunda, P.K., Currey, J.: Dryadlinq: A system for general-purpose distributed data-parallel computing using a high-level language. In: Draves, R., van Renesse, R. (eds.) OSDI, pp. 1–14. USENIX Association (2008)

# Datalog-Related Aspects in Lixto Visual Developer

Robert Baumgartner

Lixto Software GmbH,
Favoritenstr. 16, Vienna, Austria

**Abstract.** Lixto Visual Developer is an integrated development environment specifically geared towards the visual development of Web data extraction programs, supporting complex navigation and extraction tasks on highly dynamic Web applications. Internally, created extraction rules are reflected in a declarative extraction language called Elog, which relies on a datalog syntax and semantics. It is ideally suited for representing and successively incrementing the knowledge about patterns described by application designers. In this paper, we illustrate aspects of the Visual Developer and the Elog language exploiting some examples.

**Keywords:** Datalog, Data Extraction, Tree Structures, Web, Wrapper Generation.

## 1   Introduction

The World Wide Web comprises a vast amount of data and can be considered as the "largest database" of the world. Unfortunately, it is not straightforward to query and access the desired information due to the heterogeneous nature of the Web. Languages for accessing, extracting, transforming, and syndicating the desired information are required. On the top, user-friendly tools based on expressive languages for extracting and integrating information from various different Web sources, or in general, various heterogeneous sources are essential to create, execute and monitor Web extraction scenarios. In case of semi-structured data, understanding the tree structure and the visual presentation on the one hand, and understanding the application logic of Web 2.0 applications and deep Web navigations on the other hand, are the key to collect ample sets of data from deep Web databases and from state-of-the-art web sites with rich user interfaces.

As defined in [5], a web data extraction system is a *"software system that automatically and repeatedly extracts data from Web pages with changing content and delivers the extracted data to a database or some other application"*. Over the time, a number of approaches, academic, commercial and open-source systems have been proposed (refer to [9,15,16,17]).

The task of web data extraction performed by such a system is usually divided into a number of functions, comprising deep Web interaction and data extraction, as well as scheduling, data transformation and system connectivity. In this paper, we focus especially on the task of data extraction from tree structures

O. de Moor et al. (Eds.): Datalog 2010, LNCS 6702, pp. 145–160, 2011.

and describe the Lixto Visual Developer, a tool for visually and interactively creating data extraction programs (also referred to as *wrappers*). In particular, we elaborate the foundations of its internal extraction language, which adheres to the *logical approach* to Web data extraction.

As described in [5], the logical approach consists of the specification of a finite number of monadic predicates, i.e., predicates, that define sets of parse-tree nodes and that evaluate to true or false on each node of a tree-structured document. The predicates can be defined either by logical formulas, or by logic programs such as monadic datalog, which was shown to be equivalent in expressive power to monadic second-order logic (MSO) ([12], rf. to Section 4.6).

In this spirit, four desiderata to a Web wrapping language have been postulated in [13]:

1. The language has a solid and well understood theoretical foundation;
2. it provides a good trade-of between complexity and the number of practical wrappers that can be expressed;
3. it is easy to use as a wrapper programming language, and
4. it is suitable for being incorporated into visual tools, since ideally all constructs of a wrapping language can be realized through corresponding visual primitives.

As we describe here, the data extraction language *Elog* satisfies all criteria.

Considering data extraction from a functional point of view, a wrapper can be considered as a function from the DOM (W3C Document Object Model) tree to the set of all subtrees; in particular, the leaves of the subtrees are among the leaves of the original tree. In practice, this is a limitation in the sense that merely tree nodes are extracted, and other objects such as strings or CSS boxes are neglected. However, please note that this restriction is useful for theoretical considerations on the complexity and expressiveness of wrapper languages over particular structures (as done with datalog over trees in [12]). In practice, Lixto Visual Developer can also extract other kind of objects, and one can define a wrapper to be a mapping to a different set of objects as well.

Please note that usually a wrapper is not responsible for re-formating or re-structuring Web documents, but for extracting/labelling selected information. This restriction gives considerable advantages regarding complexity. One is interested in maximizing the expressiveness (while at the same time keeping the complexity low), e.g. being able to pose all kind of tree queries (like to extract all nodes that have an even number of descendants), and understanding the expressiveness of such a fragment of a wrapper language. In practice, tools such as the Visual Developer allow also the re-structuring of information to a certain amount (e.g. if a date is given once on the page, but valid for all items, the date should be given in the context of each item in the output).

One goal is to visually define extraction functions and we will illustrate how this is done in the Visual Developer, and how nicely the declarative and/or semantics of datalog matches the narrowing and broadening steps of the pattern generation process.

This paper in particular summarizes datalog-related aspects of the Visual Developer that have been introduced in the recent ten years by several authors and implemented in the Lixto solution. The rest of the paper is structured as follows. In Section 2, we give a brief overview of the Lixto architecture and components. In Section 3 we survey the processes of visually creating a wrapper. In Section 4 we describe the logical fundaments of the data extraction language Elog used in Lixto. Finally, some brief concluding remarks, application scenarios and research directions are given in Section 5.

## 2   Lixto Overview and Architecture

Lixto (http://www.lixto.com), is a company based in Vienna offering data extraction tools and services. Lixto provides solutions for Price Intelligence, Web Process Integration, SOA Enablement, Vertical Search, and Web Application Testing. Lixto was first presented to the academical community in 2001 [3]. Lixto's Web data extraction technology has been designed to access, augment and deliver content and data from web applications that utilize client-side processing techniques such as JavaScript, AJAX and dynamic HTML.

In its *Price Intelligence Solution*, Lixto uses enterprise-class reporting infrastructure to provide all necessary reports and analytics based on extracted price and market data. Important market events are highlighted and reports customized to show exactly the data items that are of most interest to individual users, e.g. product prices compared to competitor offers. Lixto uses Cloud Computing to dynamically scale its extractions on demand [6]. A second different use case is covered by Lixto's *Web Process Integration Solutions*: Lixto integrates Web applications seamlessly into a corporate infrastructure or service oriented landscape [4] by generating Web services from given Web sites. This "front-end integration" integrates cooperative and non-cooperative sources without the need for information providers to change their backend.

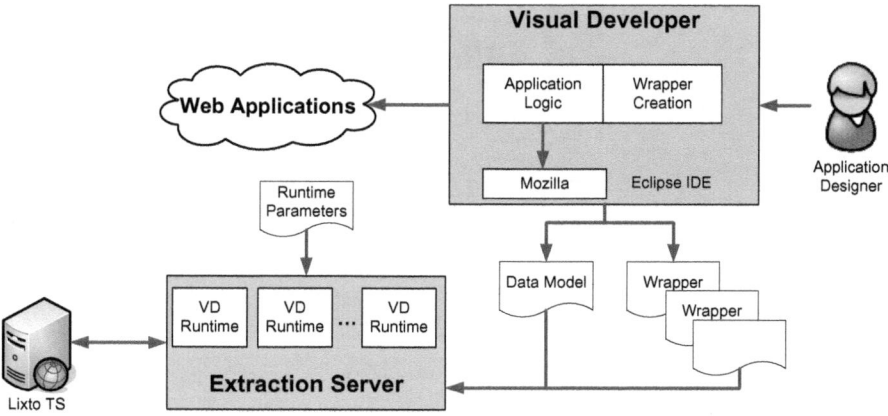

**Fig. 1.** Visual Developer Architecture

With the Lixto Visual Developer (VD), wrappers are created in an entirely visual and interactive fashion. Figure 1 sketches the architecture of VD and its runtime components. The VD is an Eclipse-based visual integrated development environment (IDE). It embeds the *Firefox* browser and interacts with it on various levels, e.g. for highlighting web objects, interpreting mouse clicks or interacting with the document object model (DOM). Usually, the application designer creates or imports a *data model* as a first step. The data model is an XML schema-based representation of the application domain. For instance, in a retail scenario, this comprises product name, price, EAN (European Article Number) and product attributes. The data model is a shared entity throughout a project. Robustness algorithms partly rely on properties of the data model.

Visual Developer supports recording of deep Web macros on the user interface level, supports dynamically changing Web 2.0 pages, understands complex application flows including to follow "detail" and "next" pages, handles pop-up windows, authentications, is robust to structural changes on the Web page, and features the expressive declarative logic-based extraction language Elog.

Figure 2 shows a screenshot of the GUI of the Visual Developer. On the left-hand side, the project overview and the outline view of the currently active wrapper are illustrated. In the center, the embedded browser is shown. At the bottom, in the Property View, navigation and extraction actions can be inspected and configured. In this screenshot, a before condition is created.

During *wrapper creation*, the application designer visually creates deep web navigations (e.g. form filling), logical elements (e.g. click if exists), and extraction rules. The system supports this process with automatic recording, immediate feedback mechanisms, generalization heuristics, domain-independent and retail-specific templates. The application designer creates the wrapper based on

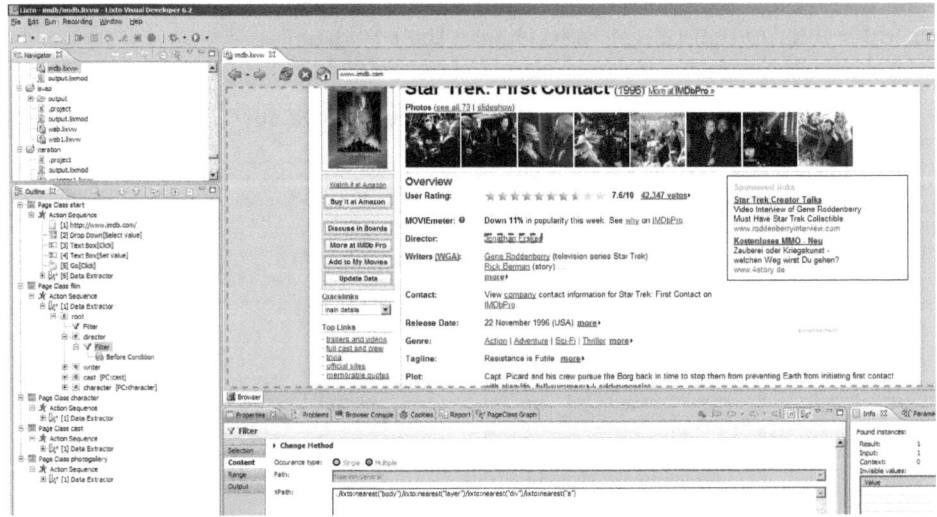

**Fig. 2.** Visual Developer GUI

samples, both in the case of navigation steps (e.g. use a particular product category) and in the case of extraction steps.

The language *Elog* [2,11], the web object detections based on XPath2, token grammars and regular expressions are part of the *application logic*. In addition, this comprises deep Web navigation and workflow elements for understanding Web processes, as well as technical aspects such as dialogue handling.

For sake of completeness, though not relevant for aspects of the Elog language described next, further components of the Lixto architecture are shortly summarized here (these are not depicted in Figure 1, however, are described in detail e.g. in [6]): Lixto wrappers are executed on a scalable server environment. Lixto Server products are clustered Glassfish (an open source application server project led by Sun Microsystems for the Java EE platform) applications. In the *Lixto Transformation Server* [14], large extraction scenarios are managed, scheduled and executed, and an extraction plan in case of larger scenarios with time and resource constraints is generated. The *Lixto Load Balancer* acts as service that distributes extraction requests to the most adequate Extraction Server and automatically starts and manages additional server instances from Cloud in times of high peak load. Each Extraction Server (Figure 1) manages a number of parallel Visual Developer runtime processes. The *Lixto Price Intelligence Panel* [6] is geared towards the consumer who defines tailor-made queries and inspects the status of running extraction jobs, and is the entry point to viewing the reports that have been created based on the extracted Web data.

## 3   Visual Wrapper Generation with Visual Developer

### 3.1   Page Class Concept and Pattern Structure

In Visual Developer, a wrapper comprises a list of *page classes* as depicted in Figure 3. A page class is a template that contains a procedure of actions and default responses (referred to as navigation sequence). Two primitive actions are *Mouse Actions* and *Key Actions*. Mouse actions include mouse move and mouse click elements, whereas key actions enter textual data in fields. The navigation and process flow language of the VD was first described in [1]. Examples of further supported actions include the *DropDown* and *TextBox* action. The latter

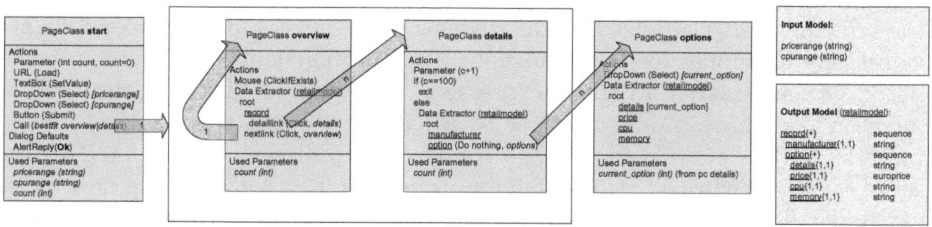

**Fig. 3.** Page Class Concept and Input/Output Model

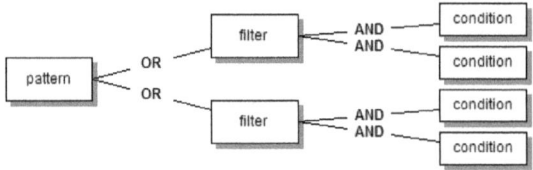

**Fig. 4.** Pattern and Filter Structure

for instance supports the following operations: *Click, Click if exists, Submit, SetValue, AppendValue,* and *GetValue*.

A *data extractor* is a special action applied during the navigation flow. It freezes the DOM tree, and applies rules for extracting a nested data structure. Each wrapper comprises a hierarchical structure of *patterns*. Each pattern matches one kind of information on a Web page (e.g. prices). Patterns are usually constructed and structured hierarchically, and usually the extraction is created top-down. The application designer can decide to create patterns on the fly, or refer to existing model patterns; the latter is especially useful in case many wrappers have to map to the same data structure. On the right-hand side of Figure 3, an output model and its constraints are specified; in the data extractors of Figure 3 model patterns are underlined; by default only model pattern instances are reflected in the output.

A page class can be considered as a declarative template that comprises

- a procedural and imperative navigation action sequence (e.g. form fillout). These actions are either recorded or manually generated in the GUI.
- a declarative extraction program that extracts and labels objects from the page (depicted in blue colour in Figure 3). Its example-based step-by-step creation process creates a declarative program (the *data extractor* action). The extraction program is capable of triggering events on extracted nodes, and hence can either branch to other page classes, or call itself in case of "Next" links to pages with a similar structure.

## 3.2   Visual Pattern and Filter Generation

Each pattern comprises a set of filters. Application designers create filters in a visual and example-based way. Usually, first one example is selected directly in the browser, and generalized by the system. In the next step a wrapper designer can decide to impose further conditions, e.g. that particular attributes need to be present and match a regular expression, something is directly before, or an image is contained. Adding a filter to a pattern extends the set of extracted targets ("OR"), whereas imposing a condition to a filter restricts ("AND") the set of targets (Figure 4). Alternately imposing conditions and adding new filters can perfectly characterize the desired information. The iterative refining process of how to characterize pattern instances with filters and conditions is given in Figure 5. It is ideally suited for representing and successively incrementing

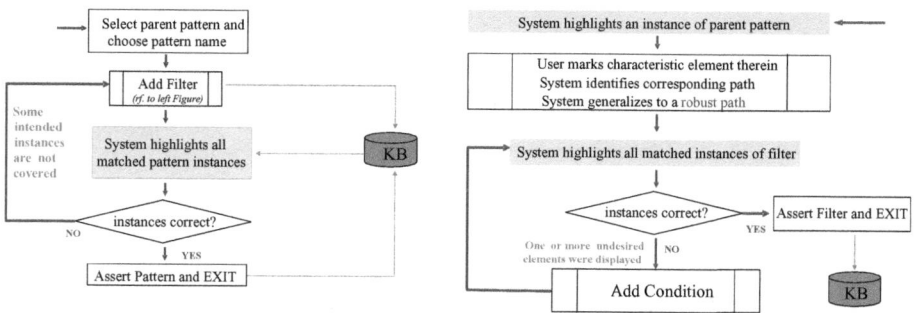

**Fig. 5.** Pattern and Filter Generation Process

the knowledge about patterns described by application designers. During this interactive process, the system also generalizes the identification of elements to robust criteria. In particular, such criteria are different if the application designer intends to match a single item or multiple items in one selection.

### 3.3 Pattern Graph

Usually, patterns are hierarchically structured and hence can be considered as tree. However, in some cases, an extraction program can only be described with a pattern graph. A filter extracts instances in relation to a particular parent pattern (e.g. extract a price within a hotel record). Hence, each filter refers to at least one pattern. The extracted instances are labelled with the pattern name from the pattern to which the filter belongs. However, in a pattern that comprises more than one filter, each filter might point to a different parent, and as a consequence, the pattern points to two patterns. Also, there can be cycles in the pattern structure (like: in a document a next link is extracted, and from a next link a further document is extracted), even in case of single filters per pattern. In case the pattern structure forms a tree it is classified as *homogeneous*, if it is a graph as *heterogeneous*.

Figure 6 illustrates a sample pattern graph. Each node is either a pattern or a page class. The one with rounded edges contain filters extracting tree instances, the trapezoid ones extract textual data, and the angle ones reflect page classes. Dotted lines indicate temporary patterns, whereas continuous lines indicate model patterns. Integrity constraints of the data model are given above the nodes. The "overview" node resembles a page class, whose data extractor pattern is called "root". It receives the initial input from a navigation sequence. Instances of "next" links, which are children of the root pattern instance, are traversed producing new instances of the "overview" page class. This kind of recursion can be visually specified and can be nicely captured by a datalog program. In Visual Developer, visualization of pattern structures are always serialized as trees. In Section 4, we show the corresponding Elog program to the pattern graph and we illustrate that this serialization is the ground program (and this one is stratified,

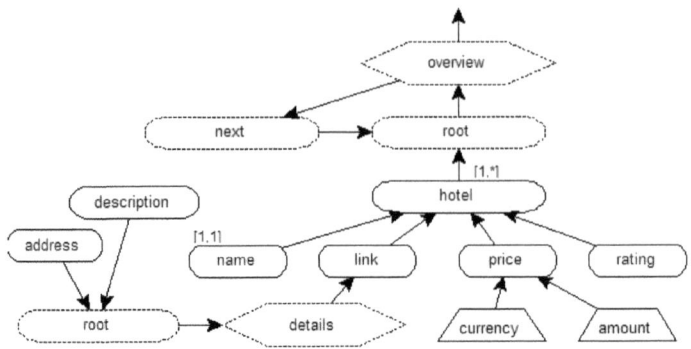

**Fig. 6.** A sample pattern graph

i.e. recursion-free). Please note that the Elog program itself is invisible to the wrapper designer (who can inspect it though, if desired).

## 3.4   Object Model

Patterns extract objects from Web pages. In most cases, such objects are nodes from a labeled unranked tree (in our case, a DOM tree). However, the extraction language is capable of considering different objects as well; these comprise:

- Lists of nodes;
- Attribute values;
- Text fragments;
- Transformed text values (such as checksums);
- Binary objects (such as images);
- CSS Boxes;
- Visual fragments based on the rendition of a page.

In case of visual fragments and CSS boxes, spatial relations are exploited (such as "is left") [10]. In case of tree structures (and flat strings), conditions are based on relations such as "after", "before", "contains", and "n-th child". These relations can be derived from primitive relations "next-sibling" and "first-child" predicates. In this regional algebra further relations can be created such as "immediatelybefore" or "overlaps". Comparison is a partial order, as some elements can not be compared to each other.

It is important to specify upon which objects an extraction language works. The objects form the Herbrand Universe on which the Elog program operates. In the next section we describe the theoretical fundaments of Elog over tree structures. In practice, VD has a defined semantics on other kind of objects as well; however, the Visual Developer limits interaction between different types of objects (e.g. if a text fragment is extracted, one can not go back to the node level in child patterns).

# 4   The Elog Data Extraction Language

## 4.1   Motivation and Example

The idea of Elog is to create an expressive rule language to extract factual data
from the Web that at the same time can be created in a visual and intuitive way.
Elog was introduced at VLDB 2001 [3] and further elaborated in [2]. Complexity
and expressiveness results have been proven by Gottlob and Koch in [11].

Figure 7 illustrates a set of Elog rules that correspond to parts of the pattern
graph given in Figure 6. Each rule head contains an intensional database (IDB)
predicate with two variables as arguments. The instances of the variable $X_0$ are
the parent pattern instances, whereas the instances of the variable $X_1$ are the
instances extracted by the rule. The body contains predicates that evaluate to
true in case particular objects of the Herbrand universe are in relation with each
other (e.g. before, contains). If all body atoms of an assignment to all variables
evaluate to true for a given rule, the head predicate evaluates to true. Hence, an
instance of $X_1$ is extracted and labelled with the predicate name.

The triple dots in Figure 7 merely indicate that the full path expression in
the program has be shortened for the sake of readability. The function "nearest"
is an extension to avoid the usage of the costly "//" for descendant traversal
and is at the same time quite useful for *hierarchical* data extraction: "nearest"
returns the closest node with particular properties in each branch.

```
overview(X0,X1) :-
  getDocumentFromNavigation(X0=$1,X1).

root(X0,X1) :-
  overview(_,X0),
  subelem(X0,(.,[]),X1).

hotel(X0,X1) :-
  root(_,X0),
  subelem(X0,(...lixto:nearest("tr"),[]),X1),
  contains(X1,(./td[1]/a[1],[]),X2),
  before(X0,X1,(...strong[1],[('text','Sortieren',CONTAINS)]),0,-1,X3,X4).

link(X0,X1) :-
  hotel(_,X0), subelem(X0,(...lixto:nearest("a"),[('class','.*url',REGEXP)]),X1).

detail(X0,X1) :-
  link(_,X0), getDocumentbyClick(X0,X1).

price(X0,X1) :-
  hotel(_,X0),
  subelem(X0,(...lixto:nearest("div")/lixto:nearest("strong"),[]),X1)
  [1,1].

next(X0,X1) :-
  root(_,X0),
  subelem(X0,(...lixto:nearest("a"),[('text','Nächste Seite',CONTAINS)]),X1).

overview(X0,X1) :-
  next(_,X0), getDocumentbyClick(X0,X1).
```

**Fig. 7.** Elog Example Program in Visual Developer

## 4.2  Elog Rules

The pattern and filter terminology used from the wrapper designer's perspective maps to logic program constructs as follows:

- Wrapper: Elog Program
- Pattern: IDB-Predicate
- Filter : Rule
- Condition: Atom of rule body, EDB-predicate
- Parent Pattern: Special body atom
- Object Identification (such as XPath): Special body atom

The declarative *and/or* semantics of datalog nicely matches the narrowing and broadening steps of the pattern generation process. Datalog (and Elog) has a nice operational semantics, giving not only means to describe the problem, but also showing up how to solve it (unlike other mechanisms like MSO which lack this kind of operational semantics). Elog differs from datalog in some aspects described below, however, can be mapped to datalog syntax and semantics.

A *standard extraction* rule looks as follows:

$$\texttt{New}(\texttt{S},\texttt{X}) \leftarrow \texttt{Parent}(\_,\texttt{S}), \texttt{Extract}(\texttt{S},\texttt{X}), \texttt{Constraints}(\texttt{S},\texttt{X},\ldots).[\texttt{a},\texttt{b}]$$

where $S$ is the parent instance variable, $X$ is the pattern instance variable, $Extract(S,X)$ is an extraction definition predicate, and the optional predicates $Constraints(S,X,\ldots)$ are further imposed conditions. A tree (string) extraction rule uses a tree (string) extraction definition atom and possibly some tree (string) conditions and general conditions. The numbers $a$ and $b$ are optional and serve as range parameters restricting which instances are extracted. *New* and *Parent* are pattern predicates referring to the parent pattern and defining the new pattern, respectively. This standard rule reflects the principle of aggregation. Other types of rules such as specialization rules have been introduced in [2].

The semantics of a rule is given as the set of matched targets $x$: A substitution $s$, $x$ for $S$ and $X$ evaluates $New(s,x)$ to *true* iff all atoms of the body are true for this substitution. Only those targets are extracted for which the head of the rule resolves to true. For evaluation, one creates a graph of predicates, computes dependencies and which predicates have to be evaluated first.

Moreover, if a pattern contains multiple filters, only minimal instances are matched (i.e. instances that do not contain any other instances) – real-life use cases created this requirement. Range condition are a speciality of Elog rules (and have been introduced since they are very helpful in the creation of a wrapper). Note that range conditions are well-defined only in the case of no reference recursion (cf. to Section 4.5 for details). Maintenance in Elog Wrappers is local to the changed criteria and hence simple – usually, in case something changes on a Web page, only a single rule or a single predicate have to be modified.

## 4.3  Built-in Predicates

Elog features a rich set of built-In predicates, each with a particular binding schema. Some predicates are given below:

- $subelem(S, path, X)$: subelem(s,path,x) evaluates to true iff s is a node, path is a relative XPath and x is a node contained in s where x matches path.
- On textual level: $subtext$, $subatt$
- On document level: $getDocument(X, Y)$ (where instances of $X$ are URLs), $getDocumentbyClick(X, Y)$, ...
- Contextual: $before(S, X, path, d1, d2, Y, D)$ (where $d1$ and $d2$ are minimum and maximum distance, and the variable $D$ stores the actual difference), $after$, $notbefore$, $notafter$
- Internal: $contains$, $nthchild$, ...
- Concepts: $isDate(X, Y)$, $isNumber(X)$, $isCity$, ...
- Comparisons: $<$, $>$, ... (e.g. compare distances or dates)
- Pattern References: refer to any IDB predicate (e.g.: before something there is an instance of price)

## 4.4   Elog Programs

An *Elog pattern* $p$ is a set of *Elog* rules with the same head predicate symbol. It is forbidden to combine tree, string or document filters with each other within one pattern. The head predicate is visually defined with *Lixto* and named by the wrapper designer. This name is also used as XML tag in the output.

Let us consider another small example program:

```
document(S, X) ← getDocument($1, X).
    table(S, X) ← document(_, S), subelem(S, nearest(table), X).
    table(S, X) ← table(_, S), subelem(S, nearest(table), X).
```

It extracts all nested tables within one page, starting with the outermost, and stores them in this hierarchical order in the pattern instance base. The second rule of <table> is iteratively called, until no further table can be extracted.

Based on the definition of homogeneous and heterogeneous pattern graphs above, an Elog program is considered to be homogeneous iff all Filters that define the same IDB predicate refer to the same parent pattern and the relationship is strictly hierarchical. In case of a homogeneous pattern, the notion of "parent pattern" can be associated with a pattern rather than with its filters. An Elog program is heterogeneous if at least two filters that define the same IDB predicate refer to different parent patterns or if the pattern structure is cyclic. However, the ground instantiation of a heterogenous Elog program does not contain any cycles, i.e. a heterogeneous Elog program is locally stratified – at least if particular limitations are obeyed (such as not mixing range and pattern references, see below). A formal semantics of Elog programs is defined below by mapping Elog programs to datalog programs.

Please note that we distinguish two sources of recursions in Elog programs:

- The first one is the one that results in cyclic pattern graphs (e.g. next page recursions), like a typical transitive closure. A standard operational semantics using a fixpoint computation can be applied: evaluate all rules again and again considering the new facts until no more instances can be derived. The ground program is not recursive.

– A second kind of recursion can result due to pattern references. I.e., additional references that are not only pointing to parents, but to other extracted instances; e.g. extract something if before there is an instance of something. Mixing this with range conditions can result in a non-monotonic program, since range, as will be seen below, introduces negation when mapping to Datalog. It is necessary to check for stratification and generate the strata for evaluation (in practice, we introduce certain limitations that force a program to be locally stratified).

In case of homogeneous programs the evaluation can be further simplified to a hierarchical top-down evaluation.

## 4.5 Datalog Representation

We describe the semantics of Elog by mapping Elog rules to Datalog rules and applying the standard Datalog semantics. Elog rules exhibit some specialities compared to datalog. Without pattern references, range conditions and minimization of rule results the semantics is straightforward. However, to express range conditions and minimization in Datalog and apply the standard semantics, one needs to transform Elog rules containing range conditions and rules that return objects contained within other objects, into datalog rules.

*Constants*: To formally use datalog over tree structures, we need to be conform to the standard signature of datalog over unranked ordered trees (using the child and nextsibling relations). Labels are reflected as indices on a predicate, and new predicates that describe that two objects are in relation based on a particular path are iteratively derived. One example is given below:

$$\text{subelem}_\epsilon(X, Y) \leftarrow X = Y$$
$$\text{subelem}_{\_path}(X, Y) \leftarrow \text{child}(X, Z), \text{subelem}_{path}(Z, Y).$$
$$\text{subelem}_{a.path}(X, Y) \leftarrow \text{child}(X, Z), \text{label}_a(Z), \text{subelem}_{path}(Z, Y).$$

Please note: For object identification, in practice, full XPath2 is supported in Visual Developer as a commitment to state-of-the-art technologies (these are evaluated by calling an XPath processor during evaluation). Moreover, rules can operate over different object structures (e.g. plain strings) as well. Please note that the favorable complexity results described below only hold if working with tree structures only, and for path expressions that can be rewritten using the firstchild and nextsibling relations as described in Section 4.6.

*Pattern minimization* can be expressed in *Datalog* extended with stratified negation and a suitable built-in predicate *contained_in(X, Y)* expressing offset-wise containment of $X$ in $Y$. In particular, a set of filters of $p(S, X)$ defining the pattern $p$ is rewritten in the following way. Consider the initial pattern definition (where $Ex$ is the main extraction atom and $Co$ a set of conditional atoms):

$$p(S, X) \leftarrow \text{par}_1(\_, S), Ex_1(S, X), Co_1(S, X, \ldots).$$
$$p(S, X) \leftarrow \cdots$$
$$p(S, X) \leftarrow \text{par}_n(\_, S), Ex_n(S, X), Co_n(S, X, \ldots).$$

The pattern name is renamed to $p'$ and additional rules are added:

$$\texttt{p}'(\texttt{S}, \texttt{X}) \leftarrow \texttt{par}_1(\_, \texttt{S}), \texttt{Ex}_1(\texttt{S}, \texttt{X}), \texttt{Co}_1(\texttt{S}, \texttt{X}, \ldots).$$
$$\texttt{p}'(\texttt{S}, \texttt{X}) \leftarrow \cdots$$
$$\texttt{p}'(\texttt{S}, \texttt{X}) \leftarrow \texttt{par}_n(\_, \texttt{S}), \texttt{Ex}_n(\texttt{S}, \texttt{X}), \texttt{Co}_n(\texttt{S}, \texttt{X}, \ldots).$$
$$\texttt{p}''(\texttt{S}, \texttt{X}) \leftarrow \texttt{p}'(\texttt{S}, \texttt{X}), \texttt{p}'(\texttt{S}, \texttt{X}_1), \texttt{contained\_in}(\texttt{X}_1, \texttt{X})$$
$$\texttt{p}(\texttt{S}, \texttt{X}) \leftarrow \texttt{p}'(\texttt{S}, \texttt{X}), \texttt{not } \texttt{p}''(\texttt{S}, \texttt{X}).$$

The final two rules require that instances of $X$ and $X_1$ are both from the same parent pattern instance (otherwise, if they stem from different parent-pattern instances, minimization is usually undesired). In the rewriting, $p'$ is the pattern predicate initially being built by different filters. Each instance $p(s, x)$, which is non-minimal, i.e. for which there exists a smaller valid $p''(s, x)$, is not derived. Only minimal instances are derived.

*Ranges.* The semantics of range criteria $[a, b]$ of a filter rule $NewPat(S, X) \leftarrow filterbody[a, b]$ can also be expressed by a suitable rewriting of the rule. A range condition assumes that an order relation is defined among pattern instances extracted by the same parent pattern instance, thus in the rewriting, we assume the presence of a successor predicate (using character offsets for comparison). The first step of rewriting consists of adding a new predicate $NewPat$ that is defined by a unique filter $NewPat'(S, X) \leftarrow filterbody$.

$$\texttt{NewPat}(\texttt{S}, \texttt{X}) \leftarrow \texttt{NewPat}'(\texttt{S}, \texttt{X}), \texttt{Solposition}(\texttt{S}, \texttt{X}, \texttt{P}), \texttt{a} \leq \texttt{P} \leq \texttt{b}.$$
$$\texttt{Solposition}(\texttt{S}, \texttt{X}, 1) \leftarrow \texttt{NewPat}'(\texttt{S}, \texttt{X}), \texttt{not } \texttt{succ}(\texttt{S}, \texttt{X}', \texttt{X}).$$
$$\texttt{Solposition}(\texttt{S}, \texttt{X}, \texttt{P}) \leftarrow \texttt{Solposition}(\texttt{S}, \texttt{X}', \texttt{P}'), \texttt{NewPat}'(\texttt{S}, \texttt{X}), \texttt{succ}(\texttt{S}, \texttt{X}', \texttt{X}), \texttt{P} = \texttt{P}' + 1.$$

Due to this, $NewPat$ depends on negation of predicates in its body. In case no pattern references are involved, this negation is stratified.

*Pattern Reference Recursion and Ranges.* Using ranges together with pattern references might introduce unstratified negation. Using pattern references can introduce *reference recursion*. Still, without ranges, a unique model is returned. However, additionally allowing range conditions to occur in such recursive rules requires to use a semantics akin to the stable model semantics (returning multiple models) or well-founded semantics (returning a minimal model) as this introduces unstratified negation into the program (considering the above rewriting). For the following example (possibly containing additional filters for $p$ and $q$), a nonmonotonic semantics is required. In practice we limit pattern references to rules without ranges.

$$\texttt{p}(\texttt{S}, \texttt{X}) \leftarrow \texttt{par}(\_, \texttt{S}), \texttt{subelem}(\texttt{S}, \texttt{epd}, \texttt{X}), \texttt{before}(\texttt{S}, \texttt{X}, \ldots, \texttt{Y}), \texttt{q}(\texttt{S}, \texttt{Y}).[\texttt{a}, \texttt{b}]$$
$$\texttt{q}(\texttt{S}, \texttt{X}) \leftarrow \texttt{par}(\_, \texttt{S}), \texttt{subelem}(\texttt{S}, \texttt{epd}, \texttt{X}), \texttt{before}(\texttt{S}, \texttt{X}, \ldots, \texttt{Y}), \texttt{p}(\texttt{S}, \texttt{Y}).[\texttt{c}, \texttt{d}]$$

## 4.6   Expressiveness and Complexity

Gottlob and Koch [11,12] studied the expressiveness and complexity of a core fragment of Elog. $Elog_2^-$ focusses on extraction from unranked ordered labelled trees (and ignores some features of Elog, such as extraction on textual structures and distances). It operates on a DOM Tree and uses the firstchild, nextsibling and lastsibling relations. All built-in predicates of Elog can be derived as illustrated in Section 4.5. The $Elog^-$ fragment furthermore makes all IDB predicates unary by rewriting rules. This is no problem, since the rational of having this binary in Elog is just to build a child relation for an output XML graph. $Elog^-$ and $Elog_2^-$ characterize the same tree language.

Unary queries in MSO over trees serve as expressiveness yardstick for information extraction functions. However, MSO is hard to use as wrapping language due to the lack of an operational semantics. Additionally, monadic Datalog over trees has very low computational complexity, and programs have a simple normal form, so rules never have to be very long. The following theorems are proven in [11]:

**Theorem 1.** *(Gottlob and Koch) Monadic Datalog over unranked ordered trees has combined complexity: $O(|dom| * |program|)$.*

**Theorem 2.** *(Gottlob and Koch) Over unranked ordered trees, Monadic Datalog = MSO.*

As a consequence, a unary query is definable in MSO iff it is definable via a monadic datalog program. Since $Elog^-$ expresses monadic datalog plus child relation, and all of $Elog^-$ is graphically programmable via Lixto, the following corollary can be derived. This formally verifies that Elog and Lixto satisfy the four desiderata of Section 1.

**Corollary 1.** *(Gottlob and Koch) Lixto expresses all MSO wrapping tasks.*

Comparing the expressiveness of Elog to other wrapper languages is problematic, as most wrapper generation frameworks lack or do not make available a formal definition of their extraction language. Moreover, in real-life data extraction scenarios other aspects such as extraction from visual rendition play a role in addition to tree structures. In [5], a high-level description of some state-of-the-art wrapper generation tools is given; in [11], Elog is compared to selected wrapping languages such as HEL.

# 5    Conclusion

Application areas of Web data extraction are manifold. Today they include mashup enablement, Web process integration, vertical search, Web application testing, and Web accessibility. One of the most important application areas is Competitive Intelligence. Nowadays, a lot of basic information about competitors can be retrieved from public sources on the Web, such as annual reports, press releases or public data bases. There is a growing economic need to efficiently integrate external data, such as market and competitor information, into internal BI systems as well. Key factors in this application area include scalable environments to extract and schedule processing of very large data sets efficiently, capabilities to pick representative data samples, cleaning extracted data to make it comparable, and connectivity to data warehouses. The Lixto Online Market Intelligence solution addresses this scenario and is described in [6].

Current research directions include declarative data extraction from PDF and visual structures. Whereas Web wrappers today dominantly focus on either the flat HTML code or the DOM tree representation of Web pages, recent approaches aim at extracting data from the CSS box model and the visual representation of Web pages [10]. This method can be particularly useful in recent times where the DOM tree does not accurately reflect how the user perceives a Web page and will be supported in future versions of the Lixto Visual Developer.

In the ongoing ABBA project [8] an abstract model of a Web page is generated. A Web page is transformed into a formal multi-axial semantic model; the different axes offer means to reason on and serialize the document by topological, layout, functional, content, genre and saliency properties. One usecase is that a blind person can navigate along and jump between these axes to skip to the relevant parts of a page. E.g., the presentational axis contains transformed visual cues, allowing the user to list information in the order of visual saliency. Internally, SPARQL is used to define extraction queries.

Key factors in the area of mashup scenarios include efficient real-time extraction capabilities for a large number of concurrent queries and detailed understanding of how to map queries to particular Web forms. Other challenges include to use focused spidering techniques for crawling into the application logic of Web 2.0 applications, and product matching and record linkage techniques.

One other important challenge is automatic and generic Web wrapping. On the one hand, this includes to evolve from site-specific wrappers to domain-specific wrappers by using semantic knowledge in addition to the structural and presentational information available. On the other hand, however, it is essential that wrappers still are sufficiently robust to provide meaningful data. Hence, techniques for making wrappers more robust and automatically adapt wrappers to new situations will contribute to this challenge. The fully automatic generation of wrappers for restricted domains such as real estate is a challenge tackled by the DIADEM at Oxford University. The DIADEM project uses $Datalog^{\pm}$ [7] as extraction language. $Datalog^{\pm}$ uses existential quantification in rule heads. This allows the creation of new objects concatenated of other simple objects during data extraction. $Datalog^{\pm}$ furthermore imposes some restrictions to maintain the good data complexity of plain Datalog.

# References

1. Baumgartner, R., Ceresna, M., Ledermüller, G.: Deep web navigation in web data extraction. In: Proc. of IAWTIC (2005)
2. Baumgartner, R., Flesca, S., Gottlob, G.: Declarative Information Extraction, Web Crawling and Recursive Wrapping with Lixto. In: Eiter, T., Faber, W., Truszczyński, M. (eds.) LPNMR 2001. LNCS (LNAI), vol. 2173, p. 21. Springer, Heidelberg (2001)
3. Baumgartner, R., Flesca, S., Gottlob, G.: Visual Web Information Extraction with Lixto. In: Proc. of VLDB (2001)

4. Baumgartner, R., Campi, A., Gottlob, G., Herzog, M.: Web data extraction for service creation. In: SeCO Workshop, pp. 94–113 (2009)
5. Baumgartner, R., Gatterbauer, W., Gottlob, G.: Web Data Extraction System. In: Encyclopedia of Database Systems. Springer-Verlag New York, Inc., New York (2009)
6. Baumgartner, R., Gottlob, G., Herzog, M.: Scalable web data extraction for online market intelligence. PVLDB 2(2), 1512–1523 (2009)
7. Calì, A., Gottlob, G., Lukasiewicz, T.: Datalog$^\pm$: a unified approach to ontologies and integrity constraints. In: ICDT, pp. 14–30 (2009)
8. Fayzrakhmanov, R., Goebel, M., Holzinger, W., Kruepl, B., Mager, A., Baumgartner, R.: Modelling web navigation with the user in mind. In: Proc. of the 7th International Cross-Disciplinary Conference on Web Accessibility (2010)
9. Flesca, S., Manco, G., Masciari, E., Rende, E., Tagarelli, A.: Web wrapper induction: a brief survey. AI Communications 17(2) (2004)
10. Gatterbauer, W., Bohunsky, P., Herzog, M., Krüpl, B., Pollak, B.: Towards domain-independent information extraction from web tables. In: Proc. of WWW, May 8-12 (2007)
11. Gottlob, G., Koch, C.: Monadic datalog and the expressive power of languages for Web Information Extraction. In: Proc. of PODS (2002)
12. Gottlob, G., Koch, C.: Monadic Datalog and the Expressive Power of Web Information Extraction Languages. Journal of the ACM 51(1) (2004)
13. Gottlob, G., Koch, C., Baumgartner, R., Herzog, M., Flesca, S.: The Lixto data extraction project - back and forth between theory and practice. In: PODS, pp. 1–12 (2004)
14. Herzog, M., Gottlob, G.: InfoPipes: A flexible framework for M-Commerce applications. In: Proc. of TES Workshop at VLDB (2001)
15. Kuhlins, S., Tredwell, R.: Toolkits for generating wrappers. In: Net.ObjectDays (2002)
16. Laender, A.H.F., Ribeiro-Neto, B.A., da Silva, A.S., Teixeira, J.S.: A brief survey of web data extraction tools. Sigmod Record 31(2) (2002)
17. Liu, B.: Web Content Mining. In: Proc. of WWW, Tutorial (2005)

# Informing Datalog through Language Intelligence – A Personal Perspective

Veronica Dahl[1,2]

[1] GRLMC-Research Group on Mathematical Linguistics
Rovira i Virgili University
43002 Tarragona, Spain
[2] Department of Computer Science and Logic and Functional Programming Group
Simon Fraser University
Burnaby, B.C., Canada
veronica@cs.sfu.ca

**Abstract.** Despite AI's paramount aim of developing convincing similes of true natural language "understanding", crucial knowledge that is increasingly becoming available to computers in text form on web repositories remains in fact decipherable only by humans. In this position paper, we present our views on the reasons for this failure, and we argue that for bringing computers closer to becoming true extensions of the human brain, we need to endow them with a cognitively-informed web by integrating new methodologies in the inter-disciplines involved, around the pivot of Logic Programming and Datalog.

**Keywords:** Datalog, logic programming, logic grammars, web search, semantic web, knowledge extraction, computational linguistics, cognitive sciences.

## 1 Introduction

AI, despite impressive specialized accomplishments, still falls quite short of its original aim of endowing computers with human-like reasoning skills, including the ability to make useful sense of human languages.

Glaringly lacking is a generally useful manner for computers to decode text in human languages. In general, we cannot even reliably ask a computer simple questions that require little or no inference, such as "Who won the Formula 1 race last year": whether with key-word based or linguistically informed systems (Hakia, Powerset), the best answer we can hope for is a deluge of documents that the user must wade through, and which may or may not contain the answer.

Thus, crucial knowledge that is increasingly becoming available to computers in text form on web repositories, remains in fact decipherable only by humans, while the world's need for computers to correctly interpret, and to draw specialized inferences from, text sources, has never been greater. Natural language techniques for information retrieval and for some kind of language understanding have long been explored, and have led to even spectacular but always partial

O. de Moor et al. (Eds.): Datalog 2010, LNCS 6702, pp. 161–180, 2011.

successes, made possible through severely delimiting a specific domain of application and corresponding language coverage.

In this article we analyse the reasons for AI's failure to deliver where language intelligence is concerned, and we argue that a fuller integration between logic, natural language understanding and knowledge-based systems is needed, around the axis of intelligent web mining. We examine relevant and still underexploited possible connections between the disciplines in play , which could be exploited around the pivot of Logic Programming, to help develop an executable theory of Language Intelligence (LI). This theory will give computers the ability to decode text into knowledge bases, and even to form new concepts and ideas, along explicit guidelines and principles, from those extracted through analyzing text from heterogeneous sources. In the long run, we expect it to evolve into an executable theory of machine-informed human cognition which can bring computers closer to becoming true human brain extensions- and thus, humanistic agents of change-, by informing us along accurate, principled-relevant lines of thought.

## 2    Background - What Is Lacking

In our view, the reasons why we don't yet have true language intelligence at our computers' disposal can be summarized as lack or under-utilization of flexible enough, sophisticated methodologies, and perhaps more importantly, as lack of integration between the various disciplines involved, namely: a) web-based knowledge acquisition techniques, since the information deluge is pouring mostly as web documents; b) natural language understanding (NLU) skills, since much of the information to be processed is in human language text form, and; c) higher level inference mechanisms both to help interpret language correctly and to draw reliable inferences as needed from the knowledge it expresses.

While two-way integrations between these needed elements are actively being pursued, what has never been attempted is the simultaneous integration of all of them. As a result, for instance, web-mining agents that include sophisticated parsers in order to admit English queries exhibit, surprisingly, similar elementary logic flaws as those documented in [36] for plain, keyword-based Google (e.g., incorrect answers to questions containing conjunctions and disjunctions). The parsing ability they incorporate has not been integrated with elementary logic ability, despite the fact that logical inference, being crucial for natural language understanding (NLU), should be flexibly available for computing answers as well as for parsing purposes. As another example, evaluation metrics that were adequate for parser development within linguistics are no longer enough when applied to web mining for bioinformatics (documented e.g. in [41] for the case of protein-protein interaction).

We next look at the status quo in each of the areas involved, before proposing our own perspective of how they could be fruitfully integrated towards providing true language intelligence.

## 2.1   Web Search Engines

The state-of-the-art in web search engines, despite recent prodigious expenditures of talent, time, and money meant to bring it up to human-acceptable standards, remains by-and-large keyword based, with little more coming to its aid than document ranking through links. As any user of search engines knows, the result is often frustrating in terms of silence (the document queried for exists but is not found) and noise (the user is drowned in "results" that are irrelevant to the query).

Much effort is being poured into trying to remediate this situation through the Semantic Web , an ambitious undertaking for encoding some of the semantics of resources in a machine-processable form. It consists of design principles, collaborative working groups, and a variety of enabling technologies such as Resource Description Framework (RDF), the RDF query language SPARQL, Rule Interchange Format (RIF) and the Web Ontology family of languages for representing ontologies. It focusses on informing documents beyond their literal expression through semantic annotations, so that they can be associated with concepts, terms and relationships useful when searching them. The Web Ontology language family is based on Description Logics, and in its most recent incarnation, OWL 2, it provides classes, properties, individuals, and data values which are stored as Semantic Web documents (http://www.w3.org/TR/owl2-overview/). OWL 2 ontologies can be used along with information written in RDF, and OWL 2 ontologies themselves are primarily exchanged as RDF documents, while the RIF component, originally thought out as a "rules layer" for the semantic web, provides the means to exchange rules between rule-based languages in existence. SPARQL as a query language comes perhaps the closest to our aims among Semantic Web technologies, but is still quite distant from human language processing, being based on simple patterns such as triples. While a helpful extension of the idea of simple markup languages, this line of research is still based on marking codes- albeit more complex than HTML, and often includes serious tradeoffs in design that result in a proliferation of dialects (for instance the RIF dialects Core, BLD, PRD, each of which is a standard rule language).

There are two main ways in which this research is proceeding: the majority of the work tries to develop new forms of search for making sense of the new representation formalisms of the Semantic Web. A less explored but very interesting approach, followed in [35], is to mine (using existing search engines) the data and knowledge already present in the Semantic Web in order to add some semantics that can better guide the Web search. This extra information assists in retrieving documents that can answer the user's query, stated in terms of a tractable extension of Datalog. Such queries are transformed by a specialized search engine into subqueries that can be independently submitted to a standard Web search engine, such as Google. The results of these subqueries are then combined to produce an answer in many cases more accurate than was possible with previous methods. For instance, it correctly answers queries containing conjunctions and disjunctions which other systems- including, surprisingly, some that incorporate language processing skills, such as Powerset- fail to understand. If it also incorporated natural language understanding- albeit in deeper forms than the existing counterparts such as Powerset- the range of useful results could be expanded even more. This very promising approach could be complemented with a language interface capable of transforming human language queries into the complex query form required by the subset of Datalog concerned, and of enhancing their very retrieval tasks whenever possible, through the language analyser informing the retrieval methods.

All these efforts aim at ultimately bridging the gap between the intended meaning of a user's query (which in many cases is just a plea for the answer to a question), and the "meaning" contemporary systems give it, namely, a flood of documents which may or may not contain the answer.

## 2.2   Natural Language Understanding

While natural Language Understanding traditionally tackles punctual applications within well-delimited domains, endowing computers with a true simile of language intelligence would amount to giving humans the power to indirectly program a query with human language words, and to receive sensible answers in the same language.

The advent of Semantic Web languages, with their focus on meaning, which is also crucial to natural language, seemed to propitiate a better integration between web consultation and human languages, yet most of their efforts are very technical and thus not too friendly to users with no background on formal methods. Recently, controlled English has been argued as a panacea in this area [15]. Controlled languages are subsets of language obtained by restricting the grammar and vocabulary to computer-manageable scope, while maintaining naturalness and correctness (as opposed to telegraphic or pidgin languages). The ACE subset of English is used in [15] to exemplify translatability into various logic based languages, including Semantic Web ones, and to conclude that controlled natural languages can make the Semantic Web more understandable and usable. While this is true, this approach relies on texts having been semantically annotated as per Semantic Web requirements, and thus cannot provide true language intelligence where fairly arbitrary texts- which is what the Web is most prolific at- are concerned.

Query answering is a well studied topic within Knowledge Based systems, but these expect the information to be presented in even more formal ways than semantically annotated web documents can. Natural Language Understanding techniques can help bridge the gap, but even in language processing based systems for web search, they are not exploited to their full potential, e.g. because of logical flaws in interpreting the coordinating elements (i.e., in interpreting the logically corresponding conjunctive and disjunctive connectors). In [16] it is rightly mentioned that the use of ontological conjunctive queries in a convenient extension of Datalog can pave the way for accepting natural language, but in practice they are only used to provide easier ways of querying, while logic based NLU techniques combined with ontologies have been for many years now used to nail down useful meaning representations of NL sentences for question-answering purposes.

It is our view that Semantic Web cross-fertilizations with the various disciplines involved, utilizing the full extent of their state-of-the-art, and in particular that of the language processing field, stands to provide the most substantial breakthroughs where reliable search is concerned.

### 2.3   Computational Logic

Within *computational logic*, logic programming has become quite ubiquituous during the past decade due to the re-discovery or re-elaboration of some of its concepts within the database and the semantic web communities: a) the *database* community re-elaborated in a sense logic programming by developing Datalog as a subset of Prolog, in which query evaluation is sound and complete. Efforts to extend Datalog while preserving good computational features have been underway since [29] and several interesting subsets have been thoroughly studied recently from the complexity point of view [16]; b) the *Semantic Web* scene, in particular, is approaching logic programming in many respects through Description Logics having become its cornerstone for the design of ontologies [6,47]. Description Logic programs have been introduced [14] to combine description logics and logic programs, as part of the attempt to combine rules and ontologies for the Semantic Web, and consist roughly of a normal logic program plus a description logic knowledge base. Their computational complexity is however greater (although not dramatically so) than that of normal logic programs [7]. Of particular interest is a recent extension of Datalog which embeds Description Logics, thus bridging the apparent gap between the latter and database query languages; and which extends Description Logics with some ontological reasoning [16]. This approach represents ontological axioms in the form of integrity constraints in terms of which both the DL-Lite and the F-logic Lite families of Description Logics can be expressed. It is derived from Datalog by allowing existentially quantified variables in rule heads, and enforcing suitable properties in rule bodies, to ensure decidable and efficient query answering. If complemented with tailored modern inference and NLU techniques, this extension could become the missing link towards endowing web knowledge mining with unprecedented accuracy and discriminative power given that Datalog queries are already sufficiently close to natural language to promote conversion from one to the other and that Description Logics underlie ontology languages, key players in semantic web research; c) Another important recent breakthrough in computational logic has been the *executable formalization of non-classical inference*. Of particular interest to this article, are hypothetical reasoning and constraint-based reasoning, important both for NLU and knowledge extraction, and argumentation theory, crucial for obtaining and justifying good quality answers. *Hypothetical reasoning* involves a logic system in which a set of facts and a set of possible hypotheses whose instances can be assumed if they are consistent with the facts. Both abduction (the unsound but useful inference of p as a possible explanation for q given that p implies q) and assumptions (resources that are globally available as from their inception while being backtrackable) fall into that general category. Their formalization within Abductive Logic Programming [9] and Assumptive Logic Programming [8], respectively, refines this general notion by, for instance, requiring in the first case consistency with a special type of facts: integrity constraints. Both allow us to move beyond the limits of classical logic to explore possible cause and what-if scenarios. They have proved useful for diagnosis, recognition, sophisticated human language processing problems, and many other applications. However in practice, abduction in particular, has not been used to its full potential in mainstream research owing to implementation indirections which have only recently been solved [10]. *Constraint-based reasoning* is less explored because the efficient handling of linguistic constraints in LP is a very new phenomenon. Constraints can now be described in terms of CHR, an extension of logic programming which can also stand alone or extend other paradigms [11] and has quickly become a leading technology for automating and optimizing resource based tasks among other things. It rejoins Datalog in that it operates bottom-up while interacting with top-down program fragments as needed, within Prolog. *Argumentation theory*, or the study of how humans can reach conclusions through logical reasoning has spawned a recent surge of computational argumentation systems surveyed in [12]. An important component of argumentation is defeasible reasoning, useful to derive plausible conclusions from partial and sometimes conflicting information. It plays a major role within constructivist decision theories, and has moreover, been maturing within logic programming in recent years.

The computational logic community, the database and semantic web communities are recognizing their commonality of interests and joining forces more consciously than ever- e.g. a special issue of the journal Theory and Practice of Logic Programming has appeared this year on the theme: Logic Programming in Databases: from Datalog to Semantic-Web Rules.

An interesting new development is the application of these methods to bioinformatics and molecular biology. As well, methodologies that pertain to the NLU field of AI are now being exploited to analyze biological sequences, which is uncovering similarities between the languages of molecular biology and human languages. Such similarities might help explain the curious fact discussed in [44], that many techniques used in bioinformatics, even if developed independently, may be seen to be grounded in linguistics. Some are even starting to be explicitly adapted to provide in turn fresh insights into linguistic theory ([26]) and into NLU [22].

## 3   LI vs. NLU

Natural Language Understanding studies techniques by which written text can be translated into various representations, including what the field calls *meaning* representations. Such "meanings" however, have been criticized as constituting in fact "the other syntax", i.e., formalized paraphrases of natural language constructs that might come in handy for processing by computers but whose claim to constituting any "meaning" is rather weak [42]. In our view, "other syntax" approaches work reasonably well for for tailored questioning within specific domains, but do not work so well for translating text. We believe that the full power of knowledge bases, which can represent inference executably, is needed to represent the meaning of textual passages. Another difference is that written text subjected to NLU techniques is most often restricted, whereas our focus on Web texts, where their very processing is moreover also Web based, entails the need for arbitrary text to be treated.

So by Language Intelligence, or LI, we mean the art of endowing computers with the ability to decode human text from non-predefined sources, into either knowledge bases or commands as may be required, perhaps forming new concepts as needed, and incorporating the web itself as a useful extension. In our opinion, this involves developing the cutting-edge theories and methods needed to integrate the now established disciplines of computational logic and computational linguistics with the emerging disciplines of web-based knowledge acquisition, for endowing computers with the ability to decode text in human languages. One promising avenue would be to integrate state-of-the-art, ontology-enriched, semantic web mining methods with novel logic grammar methods that can process even incomplete input and blend linguistic and meaning representation capabilities within the same process, so that their interaction can fine-tune the resulting knowledge bases in ways warranted by the linguistic information, thus going beyond the state of the art capabilities in text mining.

We believe that each community involved in achieving LI has something the other does not have, or not as completely, and should be shared for mutual benefit:

- The semantic web community has contributed a square but nevertheless useful wheel for gleaning info from web sources
- The database community has contributed efficiency and theoretical property gains from experimenting with variants of logic programming
- The computational logic community has provided the scientific results on which semantic web research could have been based all along.

We shall next discuss concrete under-exploited connections between this disciplines which stand to provide, in our view, great gains by being shared and developed multi-disciplinarily.

## 4   Ontological Parsing

Text and knowledge can simultaneously inform each other, for mutual benefit. We can use semantic types present in specialized lexicons for completing queries with information such as set membership and roles as a result of parsing.

E.g., the automated analysis of *Who works for Oxford University and is author of "Semantic Web Search"?* using an ontological grammar lexicon (which marks terms with their expected types in an embedded ontology) can yield the type-annotated query:

```
q(Xscientist&human):-works_for(X-scientist&human,
    Oxford University-university&academic_institution),
    author_of(Semantic Web Search-thesis&publication,
    X-scientist&human).
```

This expresses more than the ontological Datalog query one would come up with by hand, namely:

```
Q(X):- (Scientist(X) & worksFor(X,Oxford University) &
isAuthorOf(X,Semantic Web Search))
```

Established methods exist for encoding semantic types in such a way that type inclusion relationships can be computed on the fly largely via unification [34]. As an example, use of such types for the problem of de-identification of medical texts has recently been proposed [33], based on a rigorous logical system for incomplete types which we present below in the Appendix, including in particular a definition of incomplete types and examples of their use. Other than allowing for many implicit parts of the query to become explicit, they induce drastic reductions of the search space and may even serve for deriving relevant novel hypotheses in certain restricted fields (reported e.g. in [40]).

## 5  Logic Grammars

The parsing model needed for Language Intelligence as we understand it must satisfy three main requirements: ability to decode text into knowledge bases, flexibility to accommodate the imperfections and imprecision typical of spontaneous human language use, while exploiting its rich expressive power to good advantage, and good potential to blend in, and cooperate with, the semantic web technologies chosen. Since the latter are built around logic programming, which is also my proposed axis because inference is key to our objectives, logic grammars [AD89] stand out as natural candidates to be considered. In particular, adapting the new family of Abductive Grammars [21,28] holds great promise, because of their built-in ability to construct knowledge bases from language sentences. As well, a constraint-based rendition of Property Grammars [24]) holds great promise because of their focus on yielding useful results even for imperfect input. The types of imperfection to be addressed will involve noise, incorrect input, and incomplete input.

In this section we informally describe the most common types of logic grammars [1] for completeness, and also newer types which could be blended with each other as well as with Datalog, in view of combining the features of efficiency, termination, robust parsing, parsing despite incomplete or erroneous input, and flexible, high level inference mechanisms which can also be exploited in view of logically correct text interpretations.

### 5.1  DCGs

The most popular logic grammars are MG, or Metamorphosis Grammars ([18], popularized by Warren and Pereira as DCG (Definite Clause grammars, [46]) and currently included in every modern Prolog version. Informally, DCGs have a context-free rule format, except that symbols can be logic terms (noted as in Prolog) rather than simple identifiers, and Prolog calls (noted between curly brackets) are allowed. They become executable for either analysis or synthesis of sentences in the language they describe, by re-expression into Prolog; for instance:

```
s - -> noun (N1), verb (N2), {agree(N1,N2}.

noun(plural) - -> [lions].
verb(plural) - -> [sleep].
```

compiles into Prolog usually by adding two variables to each symbol: one that carries the string to be analysed, and a second one which returns the substring left over after the front of the string has been analyzed (by the rule's successful application). Calls to Prolog compile to themselves. Thus, the above grammar can translate into Prolog as:

```
s(P1,P2):- noun(N1,P1,P), verb(N2,P,P2), agree(N1,N2).

noun(plural,[lions|X],X).
verb(plural,[sleep|X],X]).
```

### 5.2   Logic Grammars and Datalog

Interestingly, one can simply note input sentences as assertions rather than lists, as first proposed in [39], and restrict terms as in Datalog by allowing no functional symbols, and presto, we inherit all the good computational properties and processing methodologies of Datalog. The resulting formalism was proposed in [30], where it was named Datalog Grammars. They relate to Chain Datalog grammars, independently proposed one year later by Dong and Ginsburg [31]. Tableaux based implementations have been extensively studied around David Scott Warren's very efficient XSB system [49].

The new notation (which can of course be easily obtained by compilation from the list notation) would describe an input sentence "lions sleep" as

```
connects(lions,1,2).
connects(sleep,2,3).
```

Non-lexical grammar rules need not be touched, e.g.

```
s(P1,P):- np(P1,P2), vp(P2,P).
```

is simply reinterpreted: the Pis are now word boundary points rather than lists of words, e.g. the following rule instance would be used for parsing "lions sleep":

```
s(1,3):- np(1,2), vp(2,3).
```

Datalog Grammars' main advantages, inherited from Datalog, are efficiency, termination, and incremental techniques allowing the grammar to guess partially unknown input. They have been shown appropriate for sophisticated applications, e.g. for treating natural language sentence coordination [32] and for syntactic error diagnosis and repair [4].

It is also interesting that the Prolog implementation of DCGs can be adapted to Datalog grammars quite readily, by replacing the usual list-based connection predicate present in most DCG compilers by the assertional equivalent: connects(Word,N1,N2):- N2 is N1+1.

Connections with Semantic Web and Datalog have been studied in the Semantic Web community with interesting results, e.g. extensions of Datalog rules to accommodate ontologies have been developed and formally studied that propitiate interaction with standard ontology languages such as RDFs and OWL. A survey of efforts in this direction, with a classification of different approaches, can be found in [7], which concludes with an analysis of the reasons why despite the great need for such integrations, none has significantly materialized so far: none of the existing approaches is regarded as completely satisfactory, including where efficiency is concerned; there is a lack of extended case studies and large scale examples; there is need to combine knowledge sources beyond rules and ontologies; and -most importantly from our point of view- there is a need for complex data structures beyond the Datalog fragment, such as can be modeled by logic programs using function symbols. Alternative efforts for modeling complex data structures, such as the hybrid well-founded semantics [13] work in theory, but in the current solvers for stable model and answer set semantics, function symbols are largely banned. Despite decades of trying to purge logic programming from complex structures in order to maintain good computational properties, it seems that function symbols are making a comeback, with recent systems being proposed to provide function symbols in decidable settings (e.g. [19]).

### 5.3    Contemporary Logic Grammars

For an informal idea of the expressive power of the logic grammars we can build on, we show in this section a sample Constraint Handling Rule grammar [17] (based on CHR [20]) and consultation for detecting tandem repeats in DNA strings, where results show the boundaries, e.g. ACCGT repeats within positions 0 and 10; next we show our Property Grammar analysis [24] of an incorrect noun phrase in French, where the last list output shows what property was violated (unicity of determiner between word boundaries 0 and 3); and finally, a sample member of the Abductive Logic Grammar family ([21,28], capable of abducing semantic types for named entities. We then discuss how these formalisms can aid our final aim of language intelligence.

## A CHRG Grammar for Detecting Tandem Repeats, and a Consultation Session Example

```
[X], string(Y) ::> string([X|Y]).
[X] ::>string([X]).


string(X),string(X)::> tandem_repeat(X).


?- parse([a,c,c,g,t,a,c,c,g,t]).

tandem_repeat(0,10, [a,c,c,g,t]);
tandem_repeat(1,3,[c]).
tandem_repeat(6,8,[c]).
```

**A Property Grammar's Output for a Mistyped Noun Phrase with Repeated Determiner.** For the input string " le le livre", we obtain the following output:

```
cat(0,3,sn,[sing,masc],np(det(le),det(le),n(livre)),
    [prec(1,det,2,n,3),dep(1,det,2,n,3),unicity(det,1,3),
     exige(n,det,1,3),prec(0,det,1,n,3),dep(0,det,1,n,3),
     exige(n,det,0,3)],[unicity(det,0,3)]) ?
yes
```

A noun phrase (sn )is recognized between word boundaries 0 and 3, singular and masculine, with parse tree (det(le),det(le),n(livre)), satisfying properties such as precedence (prec) and dependency (dep) between determiner and noun, and violating the unicity of determiner property.

## A sample Abductive Logic Grammar with Fixed Knowledge-Base

```
G1 = <<N1, T1, R1,d>, C1>, where
N1 = {d/0,s/0, np/1,vp/2}
T1 = {thinks, stands, curie, marie, pierre, the, sofa,...}
R1 = {d ->s| s d
s -> np(X) vp(X,Knowledge)
                        {Knowledge},
 np(Marie_curie) -> marie curie,
 np(sofa7) -> the sofa,
 vp(X, thinks(X)) -> thinks,
 vp(X, stands(X)) -> stands}


C1 =<A1, Kbg1>, where A1 =  {human/1,thing/1}
Kbg1= {thinks(X) <->human(X),
    stands(X) <->human(X) or
    thing(X)),not(human(X) and thing(X))}}
```

Informally: N1, T1, R1,d are as in traditional grammars (non terminals, terminals, productions, start symbol d, for discourse); C1 is a constraint system for abduction where A1 are the abducibles, Kbg1 the background knowledge base. From Marie Curie thinks, $\{human(marie\_curie)\}$ is abduced by the grammar; the sentence Marie Curie stands has two minimal explanations, $\{human(marie\_curie)\}$ and $\{thing(marie\_curie)\}$; the discourse containing both sentences has exactly $\{human(marie\_curie)\}$ as its minimal substantiated explanation.

N.B. Dynamic abductive grammars (not shown here) go further by allowing for explicit knowledge update terms within grammar rules to modify the knowledge base upon rule application, maintaining its consistency.

## 5.4   Discussion: Possible Cross-Fertilizations

In the Property Grammar approach, as exemplified above, grammars are described through properties between constituents plus conditions under which some can be relaxed. Faced with incomplete or incorrect input, the parser still delivers results rather than failing and indicates the reasons of anomaly through a list of satisfied and a list of violated properties. Hypothetical and abductive reasoning capabilities can complete some of the missing parts by intelligently gleaning relevant information from the web (e.g. on semantic roles and ontologies), both for parsing and for inferential purposes. Since Abductive Grammars already include such capabilities, an obvious first choice is to extend them with property checking mechanisms allowing us to parse imperfect input a la Property Grammars. As well, they can be extended with semantic role labeling techniques gleaned through ontologies, such as found in OWL and OWL2 repositories [47] or through NLU techniques (surveyed in [48]) for quick disambiguation and semantic role compatibility checkups, as well as search-reduction side effect. It is possible also to extend our Property Grammar parsing techniques [24] into a model of Concept Formation [25]. This model has been applied to mining linguistics and molecular biology texts [2], to diagnosing lung cancer [5], and to knowledge extraction from biomedical text [27], leading to a Concept Formation model for Molecular Biology [23].

Abductive logic grammars [21] evolve from [28] and relate to abductive logic programming [38] by implementing knowledge-base extraction through constraint-based abduction- a paradigm used, e.g., for abducing molecular acid strings from RNA secondary structure [3]- with the novel feature that they allow abducibles to appear in heads of clauses through the notion of substantiated answers. Secondly, they relate to knowledge extraction from texts with the novelty that they allow us to blend linguistic and meaning representation capabilities within the same process, so that their interaction can fine-tune the resulting knowledge bases in ways warranted by the linguistic information, thus going beyond the state of the art capabilities in text mining. A precedent exists of work which couples a syntactico-semantic grammar and a knowledge base implemented in Description Logic which is consulted by the grammar to ensure that only semantically acceptable parses are built [45]. While the knowledge base can also learn new information from the parser's calls (i.e. from a new sentence being analysed), this information focusses mostly on lexical semantics given that this approach's main aim is semantic correctness. In contrast, Abductive Logic Grammars can infer full knowledge bases from their description in human language with semantic correctness being only one of its possible applications. Another related approach [37] uses abduction for obtaining a minimal explanation of why the text could be true, but results in combinatorial explosion needing various techniques to control it. Constraints, present in all of the above described formalisms, constitute an obvious axis for cross-fertilization, since they are crucial both for implementing robust parsing around properties between constituents [25,27] and for constructing knowledge from text. These types of grammars can provide good starting points, particularly in view of integrations with Web mining. There are also interesting possible cross-fertilizations with ontological query answering, in that an interaction with semantic role labeling techniques and ontologies, such as found in OWL repositories [47] would allow for quick disambiguation and semantic role compatibility checkups (along the lines exemplified in the Appendix); for uncovering implicit parts of sentences; and for a two way interaction: a) gleaning semantic types from outside sources, and b) contributing to them any missing info gleaned from text analysis. As well, an abductive grammar's use of ontological lexicons can inform the web search methods enough to not need annotating each and every document to be used, before a query is attempted; and semantic role and type inference at the parsing stage may help Datalog's negated queries by converting them into safe ones if they are not safe to begin with, as they may not be if produced from certain natural language phrasings, or by a careless Datalog expert. A most interesting possible cross-fertilization in this respect would be to complement the approach of [35] with new NLU and unconventional inference techniques suitably adapted, to make it language informed. Its arquitecture is shown in Figure 1, complemented as here proposed, by adding in particular a language interface capable of transforming human language queries into the complex query form required by the subset of Datalog concerned. The cost associated with [35] 's present approach of completing with annotations each and every document to be used, before a query is attempted, can be decreased in two ways. Their approach is quite costly even if done as a preprocessing stage, since accessing a web source is very costly in terms of response time. Instead, we can 1) use the NL interfaces ontological lexicons not only to parse but also to inform the web search methods, and 2) use an abductive logic grammar component (the Knowledge Abducer) to glean knowledge bases by examining not the entire documents returned, but just the answers proposed by existing engines.

For a proof-of-concept within a specific domain, bioinformatics and molecular biology hold the most promise as candidate domains due to their great cross-fertilization potential with linguistic theories and methods. Quick results can be obtained through partial analyses for punctual tasks such as gleaning punctual knowledge of interest, e.g. determining from context whether an expression such as binding site refers to a protein domain or a DNA domain, or whether two

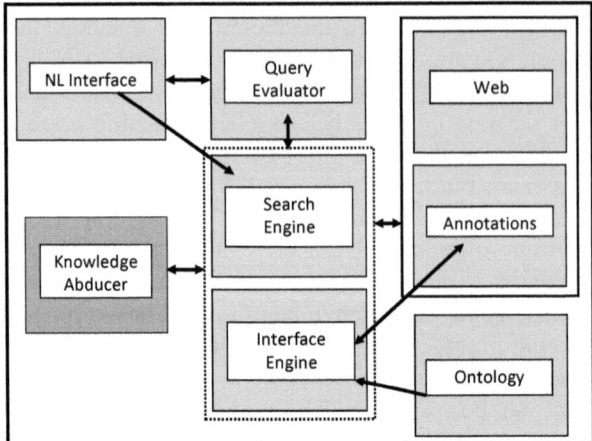

**Fig. 1.** System Architecture

entities of interest interact. In a second stage, further connections can be attempted, always in interaction between parsing and knowledge-based web mining methodologies. Recently proposed models of biological concept formation [8] can aid in such attempts. This domain as a specific pivot of study is fascinating because it implies including among the study of human languages those not conventionally regarded as such in the field, namely the languages of molecular biology. This choice is not only for the altruistic goal of providing molecular biologists with the ground-breaking tools they desperately need (since e.g. nucleic acid sequences of crucial interest are being produced much faster than they can be analyzed by traditional methods), but also importantly, because it is becoming apparent that many fascinating cross-fertilizations can ensue from this expanded view of linguistics which have enormous potential for inducing a qualitative leap in linguistics sciences themselves [26]. To develop an executable theory of Language Intelligence that incorporates the Web as a useful extension, however, we need to move into searching for answers within unrestricted web documents (not just Semantic Web documents), and into more arbitrary domains. This is admittedly higher risk, but if such scaling-up proves unfeasible, a good alternative approach would be to explore which minimal machinery (e.g. perhaps using only semantic role labeling, or that plus generalized ontologies) might capture enough nuanced meaning from arbitrary web documents to correctly answer queries. Else we can at least delimit a few sub-domains in which we can reign through dividing.

## 6    Conclusion: LP, Datalog as the Connective Tissue, the Universal Glue

True Language Intelligence stands to elicit a major shift in the way science, technology, scholarly work and even societal transactions are conducted, by providing instantaneous intelligent access, without the mediation of a computer expert, to the wealth of permanently updated information available through the worlds computers. E.g. biologists will be able to command computers directly through their own human language such as English, for tasks such as extracting genetic information of their interest which is encoded in DNA strings, or gleaning relationships between biological entities of interest mentioned in a large number of written documents, or simply to retrieve the answer to a question. This will free them from having to rely, with no real proof that their trust is justified, on computer specialists interpretations of their stated problems- a situation which Dr. A. Levesque, in his invited speech at UNESCOs Biodiversity meeting in Paris (January 2010, personal communication), equated with that of an airplane being conducted with no map and no navigation system, by an inexperienced pilot. In our opinion, in order to achieve it we might as well admit we are using LP already in various guises, and integrate it more consciously into various paradigms that have been evolving into forms that are close to LP and to Datalog, while taking inspiration as well from logic programming techniques for natural language. This uniformity of methodology will cut down on interfaces and indirections, getting us closer to giving humans the power to program with words, i.e., to command computers directly through their own language, and at the same time giving computers the ability to decode text into knowledge bases, and even to form new concepts and ideas, along explicit guidelines and principles, from those extracted through analyzing text from heterogeneous sources.

**Acknowledgement.** Support from the European Commission in the form of V. Dahl's Marie Curie Chair of Excellence, and from both universities as well as from the Canadian National Sciences Research Council, is gratefully acknowledged. We also thank the anonymous referees for very useful comments on this article's first draft.

# References

1. Abramson, H., Dahl, V.: Logic Grammars. Springer, Berlin (1989)
2. Bel Enguix, G., Jimenez-Lopez, M.D., Dahl, V.: DNA and Natural Languages: Text Mining. In: IC3K 2009, pp. 140–145. INSTICC, Madeira (2009)
3. Bavarian, M., Dahl, V.: Constraint-Based Methods for Biological Sequence Analysis. Journal of Universal Computing Science 12, 1500–1520 (2006)
4. Balsa, J., Dahl, V., Pereira Lopes, J.G.: Datalog Grammars for Abductive Syntactic Error Diagnosis and Repair. In: Natural Language Understanding and Logic Programming Workshop, Lisbon (1995)
5. Barranco-Mendoza, A., Persaud, D.R., Dahl, V.: A Property-Based Model for Lung Cancer Diagnosis. In: RECOMB 2004, San Diego, Poster (2004)
6. Calvanese, D., De Giacomo, G., Lembo, D., Lenzerini, M., Rosati, R.: Tractable Reasoning and Efficient Query Answering in Description Logics: the DL-Lite Family. JAR 39, 385–429 (2007)
7. Drabent, W., Eiter, T., Ianni, G., Krennwallner, T., Lukasiewicz, T., Maluszynski, J.: Hybrid Reasoning with Rules and Ontologies. In: Bry, F., Małuszyński, J. (eds.) Semantic Techniques for the Web. LNCS, vol. 5500, pp. 1–49. Springer, Heidelberg (2009)

8. Dahl, V., Tarau, P.: Assumptive Logic Programming. In: Proc. ASAI 2004, Cordoba (2004)
9. Endriss, U., Mancarella, P., Sadri, F., Terreni, G., Toni, F.: The CIFF Proof Procedure for Abductive Logic Programming with Constraints. In: Alferes, J.J., Leite, J. (eds.) JELIA 2004. LNCS (LNAI), vol. 3229, pp. 31–43. Springer, Heidelberg (2004)
10. Christiansen, H., Dahl, V.: HYPROLOG: a New Logic Programming Language with Assumptions and Abduction. In: Gabbrielli, M., Gupta, G. (eds.) ICLP 2005. LNCS, vol. 3668, pp. 159–173. Springer, Heidelberg (2005)
11. Fruhwirth, T.W.: Theory and Practice of Constraint Handling Rules. Journal of Logic Programming 37(1-3), 95–138 (1998)
12. Rahwan, Simari, G.R. (eds.): Argumentation in Artificial Intelligence. Springer, Heidelberg (2009)
13. Drabent, W.T., Maluszynski, J.: Well-Founded Semantics for Hybrid Rules. In: Marchiori, M., Pan, J.Z., de Sainte Marie, C. (eds.) RR 2007. LNCS, vol. 4524, pp. 1–15. Springer, Heidelberg (2007)
14. Eiter, T., Lukasiewicz, S.R., Tompits, H.: Combining Answer-Set Programming with Description Logics for the Semantic Web. In: Dubois, D., Welty, C., Williams, M.A. (eds.) Ninth International Conference on Principles of Knowledge Representation and Reasoning, B.C., Canada, pp. 141–151 (2004)
15. De Coi, J.L., Fuchs, N.E., Kaljurand, K., Kuhn, T.: Controlled English for Reasoning on the Semantic Web. In: Bry, F., Małuszyński, J. (eds.) Semantic Techniques for the Web. LNCS, vol. 5500, pp. 276–308. Springer, Heidelberg (2009)
16. Cali, A., Gottlob, G., Lukasiewicz, T.: A General Datalog-based Framework for Tractable Query Answering over Ontologies. In: 28th ACM SIGMOD-SIGACT-SIGART Symposium on Principles of Database Systems, Providence (2009)
17. Christiansen, H.: CHR Grammars. Journal on Theory and Practice of Logic Programming 5, 467–501 (2005)
18. Colmerauer, A.: Metamorphosis Grammars. In: Bolc, L. (ed.) Natural Language Communication with Computers. LNCS, vol. 63, pp. 133–189. Springer, Heidelberg (1978)
19. Calimeri, F., Cozza, S., Ianni, G., Leone, N.: Computable Functions in ASP: Theory and implementation. In: Garcia de la Banda, M., Pontelli, E. (eds.) ICLP 2008. LNCS, vol. 5366, pp. 407–424. Springer, Heidelberg (2008)
20. Fruhwirth, T.: Theory and Practice of Constraint Handling Rules. Journal of Logic Programming, Special Issue on Constraint Logic Programming 37, 95–138 (1998); Stuckey, P., Marriot, K. (eds.)
21. Christiansen, H., Dahl, V.: Abductive Logic Grammars. In: Ono, H., Kanazawa, M., de Queiroz, R. (eds.) WoLLIC 2009. LNCS, vol. 5514, pp. 170–181. Springer, Heidelberg (2009)
22. Dahl, V.: Decoding Nucleic Acid Strings through Human Language. In: Bel-Enguix, G., Jiménez-López, M.D. (eds.) Language as a Complex System: Interdisciplinary Approaches, Cambridge Scholars Publishing (2010)
23. Dahl, V., Barahona, P., Bel-Enguix, G., Kriphal, L.: Biological Concept Formation Grammars- A Flexible, Multiagent Linguistic Tool for Biological Processes. LAMAS (2010)
24. Dahl, V., Blache, P.: Directly Executable Constraint Based Grammars. In: Journées Francophones de Programmation en Logique avec Contraintes, Angers, France (2004)

25. Dahl, V., Voll, K.: Concept Formation Rules: An Executable Cognitive Model of Knowledge Construction. In: 1st International Workshop on Natural Language Understanding and Cognitive Sciences, Porto, Portugal (2004)
26. Dahl, V., Maharshak, E.: DNA Replication as a Model for Computational Linguistics. In: Mira, J., Ferrández, J.M., Álvarez, J.R., de la Paz, F., Toledo, F.J. (eds.) IWINAC 2009. LNCS, vol. 5601, pp. 346–355. Springer, Heidelberg (2009)
27. Dahl, V., Gu, B.: Semantic Property Grammars for Knowledge Extraction from Biomedical Text. In: 22nd International Conference on Logic Programming (2006)
28. Dahl, V.: From Speech to Knowledge. In: Pazienza, M.T. (ed.) SCIE 1999. LNCS (LNAI), vol. 1714, pp. 49–75. Springer, Heidelberg (1999)
29. Dahl. V., Tarau, P., Andrews, J.: Extending Datalog Grammars. In: NLDB 1995, Paris (1995)
30. Dahl, V., Tarau, P., Huang, Y.N.: Datalog Grammars. In: 1994 Joint Conference on Declarative Programming, Peniscola, Spain, pp. 268–282 (1994)
31. Dong, G., Ginsburg, S.: On decompositions of chain datalog programs into P (left)-linear 1-rule components. Journal of Logic Programming (JLP) 23(3), 203–236 (1995)
32. Dahl. V., Tarau, P., Moreno, L., Palomar, M.: Treating Coordination with Datalog Grammars. In: The Joint COMPULOGNET/ELSNET/EAGLES Workshop on Computational Logic For Natural Language Processing, Edinburgh (1995)
33. Dahl, V., Saghaei, S., Schulte, O.: Parsing Medical Text into De-identified Databases. In: 1st International Workshop on AI Methods for Interdisciplinary Research in Language and Biology, Rome (2011) (in press)
34. Fall, A.: The Foundations of Taxonomic Encoding. Computational Intelligence 14, 598–642 (1998)
35. Fazzinga, B., Gianforme, G., Gottlob, G., Lukasiewicz, T.: Semantic Web Search Based on Ontological Conjunctive Queries. In: Link, S., Prade, H. (eds.) FoIKS 2010. LNCS, vol. 5956, pp. 153–172. Springer, Heidelberg (2010)
36. Gottlob, G.: Computer Science as the Continuation of Logic by other Means. In: Keynote Address, European Computer Science Summit 2009, Paris (2009)
37. Hobbs, J.: Abduction in Natural Language Understanding. In: Horn, L., Ward, G. (eds.) Handbook of Pragmatics, pp. 724–741. Blackwell, Malden (2004)
38. Kakas, A., Kowalski, R., Toni, F.: The Role of Abduction in Logic Programming. In: Gabbay, D.M., Hogger, C.J., Robinson, J.A. (eds.) Handbook in Logic in AI and LP, vol. 5. Oxford University Press, Oxford (1998)
39. Kowalski, R.A.K.: Logic for Problem Solving. Elsevier, Amsterdam (1998)
40. Li, G., Huang, C., Zhang, X., Xu, X., Hu, X.: A New Method for Mining Biomedical Knowledge Using Biomedical Ontology. Wuhan University Journal of Natural Sciences 14(2), 134–136 (2009)
41. Miyao, Y., Sagae, K., Saetre, R., Matsuzaki, T., Tsujii, J.: Evaluating Contributions of NL Parsers to Protein-Protein Interaction Extraction. Bioinformatics 25, 394–400 (2009)
42. Penn, G., Richter, F.: The Other Syntax: Approaching Natural Language Semantics through Logical Form Composition. In: Christiansen, H., Skadhauge, P.R., Villadsen, J. (eds.) CSLP 2005. LNCS (LNAI), vol. 3438, pp. 48–73. Springer, Heidelberg (2005)
43. Roussel, P.: Prolog, Manuel de Reference et d'Utilisation. Groupe Intelligence Artificielle, Faculte des Sciences de Luminy, Universite Aix-Marseille II, France (1975)
44. Searls, D.: The Language of Genes. Nature 420, 211–217 (2002)

45. Sargot, B., Ghali, A.E.: Coupling Grammar and Knowledge Base: Range Concatenation Grammars and Description Logics. In: Sojka, P., Kopeček, I., Pala, K. (eds.) TSD 2004. LNCS (LNAI), vol. 3206, pp. 195–202. Springer, Heidelberg (2004)
46. Warren, D.H.D., Pereira, F.: Definite Clause Grammars for Language Analysis - A Survey of the Formalism and a Comparison with Augmented Transition Networks. Artificial Intelligence Journal 13(3), 231–278 (1980)
47. OWL Web Ontology Language Guide- W3C Recommendation (2004)
48. Wu, W.: A Study on the Fundamentals of Semantic Role Labeling. Masters Thesis Report. Simon Fraser University (2009)
49. Warren, D.S.: Programming in tabled Prolog (in preparation), http://www.cs.sunysb.edu/~warren/xsbbook/book.html

# Appendix: An Example of Semantic Types as Incomplete Types

### Formal definition of an incomplete-type system for de-identification in medical texts

We define as follows:

— Let $K$ be a finite set of symbols called *proper names*.
— Let $T$ be a finite set of symbols called *types*.
— Let $R$ be a finite set of symbols called *relational symbols*.
— Let $X$ be a set of first-order variables.
— Let $IdK$, $IdT$, $IdR$ and $IdX$ be subsets of, respectively, $K$ (called *identifying proper names*), $T$ (called *identifying types*), $R$ (called *identifying relational symbols*) and $X$ (called *identifying variables*).
— To each symbol $k \in K$ corresponds a symbol $t = \text{type}(k)$, with $t \in T$.
— To each variable $x \in X$ corresponds a symbol $t = \text{type}(x)$, with $t \in T$.
— To each symbol $r \in R$ we associate:
  - a positive integer $n = \text{degree}(r)$.
  - a list $[t_1, \ldots, t_n] = \text{domain}(r)$, where $t_i \in T$.
— Let $E(t)$ represent the set of proper names whose type is $t$.
— Let $L = \{E(t) \mid t \in T\}$.
— Let $U = \bigcup_{t \in T} E(t)$.

Then a lattice is defined by $L$, the partial ordering relation of set inclusion ($\subset$), and the binary operators of set union ($\cup$) and intersection ($\cap$). It is bounded by the top $U$ and the bottom $\{\ \}$.

**Definition.** A *de-identification database* $g$ is an application which associates, to each relational symbol $r \in R$ of degree $n$ and domain $[t_1, \ldots, t_n]$, an $n$-ary relation $\rho = g(r)$, which maps $E(t_1) \times \cdots \times E(t_n) \rightarrow \{\text{true}, \text{false}\}$.

**Definition.** A tuple in a relation is an *identifying tuple* if its relational symbol belongs to $IdR$, or if it contains any identifying proper names, types, or variables.

**Corollary.** All tuples in an identifying relation are identifying tuples.

**Notation.** All identifying tuples $r(t1, ..., tn)$ will be noted $+r(t1, ..., tn)$.

In logic programming terms, a de-identification database $g$ is a logic program in which some tuples (intuitively, those that contain identifying elements which de-identification needs to disguise) are hypothesized rather than taken as factual; in which variables and constants are typed e.g. A $\in$ `patient`; and in which the set inclusion relationships between these types have been declared through clauses of the form[1]

$t_i \subset tj \ k \in_i$

where `ti, tj` $\in T$ and k $\in K$.

**Definition.** An *incomplete type* for $t$, noted $h(t)$, is a term of the form: $[t_1, \ldots, t_{n-1}, t \mid V]$, where the $t_i \in T$, V is a variable ranging over incomplete types, $t \subset t_{n-1} \subset \cdots \subset t_1$ and there exists no $t_0 \in T$ such that $t_1 \subset t_0$. | is a binary operator in infix notation that separates the head from the rest of a list.

**Property.** Let $s, t \in T$. Then $s \subset t \Leftrightarrow \exists h(t), h(s)$ and a substitution $\Theta$ such that $h(s) = h(t)\,\Theta$.

**Remark.** As a practical consequence of this property a type $s$ can be proven to be a subtype of $t$ simply by unifying $h(s)$ and $h(t)$, and checking that $t$'s tail variable has become instantiated.

## Uses for disambiguation

By using a grammar where each term is marked by its semantic type with respect to a given hierarchy, we can perform a quick semantic compatibility check which ensures disambiguation on the fly. For instance in an application for de-identification of records of admission to a hospital-, given that "enter" is a synonym for "admitted", there will be at least two lexical entries for that verb, e.g.

```
enter(patient-X,hospital-Y)
enter(patient-X,state-Y)
      (as in ''entered into a comma")
```

resulting for instance in the following analyses for the sentences shown below:

1. Huntington entered the hospital on April 16, 2010.
2. Smith should be tested for Huntington.

 

1. entered(patient-huntington,hospital-X,date-16-04-2010).
2. must(test-for(patient-smith,disease-huntington))

Notice as well that disambiguation and anaphora resolution can cooperate with each other, as the following discourse and corresponding initial representations exemplify.

Huntington entered the hospital on April 16, 2010. This patient should be tested for Huntington.

---

[1] In practice, the symbols $\subset$, $\in$ are replaced by available keyboard symbols, such as < and :. These are declared as binary operators in infix notation.

```
+entered(patient-id(huntington),
    hospital-id(universalcures),
    date-id(16-04-2010)).
must-test-for(patient-P,disease-huntington).
```

Our parser's anaphora resolution system will instantiate P into id(huntington) and correspondingly mark the tuple for "must-test-for" as an assumption. Note that the explicit mention of a type ("patient") in the subject of the second sentence serves as a corroboration to the anaphora resolution system that we are referring indeed to the Huntington typed as a patient by the first sentence's analysis (or the two types would not match). However if the second sentence had been "He should be tested for Huntington", the type gleaned from the first sentence for this individual would simply carry over, together with his name, into the term representing it.

Of course, even for humans there will be cases in which even context leaves us clueless, as in "Huntington won". We are content if our proposed methodology allows us to deal with ambiguity with at least as much success as humans can.

# Dyna: Extending Datalog for Modern AI*

Jason Eisner and Nathaniel W. Filardo

Johns Hopkins University
Computer Science Department
3400 N. Charles Ave.
Baltimore, MD 21218, USA
http://www.cs.jhu.edu/~{jason,nwf}/
{jason,nwf}@cs.jhu.edu

**Abstract.** Modern statistical AI systems are quite large and complex; this interferes with research, development, and education. We point out that most of the computation involves database-like queries and updates on complex views of the data. Specifically, recursive *queries* look up and aggregate relevant or potentially relevant values. If the results of these queries are memoized for reuse, the memos may need to be *updated* through change propagation. We propose a declarative language, which generalizes Datalog, to support this work in a generic way. Through examples, we show that a broad spectrum of AI algorithms can be concisely captured by writing down systems of equations in our notation. Many strategies could be used to actually solve those systems. Our examples motivate certain extensions to Datalog, which are connected to functional and object-oriented programming paradigms.

## 1   Why a New Data-Oriented Language for AI?

Modern AI systems are frustratingly big, making them time-consuming to engineer and difficult to modify. In this chapter, we describe our work toward a declarative language that was motivated originally by various use cases in AI. Our goal is to make it easier to specify a wide range of new systems that are more or less in the mold of existing AI systems. Our declarative language should simplify inferential computation in the same way that the declarative language of regular expressions has simplified string pattern matching and transduction.

All areas of AI have become data-intensive, owing to the flood of data and the pervasiveness of statistical modeling and machine learning. A system's **extensional data** (inputs) include not only current sensory input but also background

* This chapter has been condensed for publication; the full version is available as [22]. This material is based on work supported by the National Science Foundation under Grants No. 0347822 and 0964681 to the first author, and by a graduate fellowship to the second author from the Human Language Technology Center of Excellence, Johns Hopkins University. We thank Wren N. G. Thornton and John Blatz for many stimulating discussions. We also thank Yanif Ahmad, Adam Teichert, Jason Smith, Nicholas Andrews, and Veselin Stoyanov for timely comments on the writing.

O. de Moor et al. (Eds.): Datalog 2010, LNCS 6702, pp. 181–220, 2011.

knowledge, large collections of training examples, and parameters trained from past experience. The **intensional data** (intermediate results and outputs) include combinatorially many possible analyses and conclusions derived from the inputs.

Each AI system usually builds and maintains its own custom data structures, so that it can efficiently query and update the current state of the system. Although many conceptual ideas are reused across AI, each implemented system tends to include its own specialized code for storage and inference, specialized to the data and computations used by that system. This turns a small mathematical abstraction into a large optimized implementation. It is difficult to change either the abstract computation or the storage and execution strategy because they are intertwined throughout the codebase. This also means that reusable general strategies have to be instantiated anew for each implemented system, and cannot even be easily described in an abstract way.

As an alternative, we are working to develop an appealing declarative language, Dyna, for concise specification of algorithms, with a compiler that turns such specifications into efficient code for storage and inference. Our goal is to produce a language that practitioners will actually use.

The heart of this long paper is the collection of suggestive Dyna code examples in §3.1. Readers are thus encouraged to browse at their leisure through Figures 1–12, which are relatively self-contained. Readers are also welcome to concentrate on the main flow of the paper, skipping over details that have been relegated for this reason to footnotes and figures.

## 1.1   AI and Databases Today

Is a new language necessary? That is, why don't AI researchers already use database systems to manage their data [8]? After all, any procedural AI program is free to store its data in an external database. It could use Datalog or SQL to express queries against the current state of a database, perform some procedural computation on the results, and then store the results back to the database.

Unfortunately, there is rather little in most AI systems that looks like typical database queries:

– Queries in a standard language like Datalog or SQL are not expressive enough for any one query to capture the entire AI computation. The restrictions are intended to guarantee that each query terminates in polynomial time and has a single well-defined answer. Yet the overall AI algorithm may not be able to make those guarantees anyway—so the effect of the restrictions is only to partition the algorithm artificially into many smaller queries. This limits the opportunities for the database system itself to plan, rearrange, and parallelize computations.

– It may be inefficient to implement the algorithm in terms of database queries. AI systems typically work with lots of smaller, in-memory, ephemeral, write-heavy data sets often accessed at the level of individual records. For example, upon creating a promising hypothesis, the AI system might try to score it or extend it or compute its consequences, which involves looking up and storing *individual* records related to that specific hypothesis. Channeling these record-at-a-time queries and updates through a standard database would have considerable overhead.

– Standard database languages do not support features for programming-in-the-large, such as modules, structured objects, or inheritance.

In this setting, switching from a data structure library to a relational database is likely to hurt performance without significantly easing implementation.

## 1.2   A Declarative Alternative

Our approach instead eliminates most of the procedural program, instead specifying its computations *declaratively*. We build on Datalog to propose a convenient, elegantly concise notation for specifying the systems of equations that relate intensional and extensional data. This is the focus of §2, beginning with a review of ordinary Datalog in §2.1.

A program in our Dyna language specifies what we call a **dynabase**. Recall that a **deductive database** [11,56] contains not only extensional relations but also rules (usually Datalog rules or some other variant on Horn clauses) that define additional intensional relations, similar to views. Our term "dynabase" emphasizes that our deductive databases are *dynamic*: they can be declaratively extended into new dynabases that have modified extensional data, with consequent differences in the intensional data.

Because a Dyna program merely specifies a dynabase, it has no serial I/O or side effects. How, then, are dynabases used in a procedural environment? A running process, written in one's favorite procedural language, which does have I/O and side effects, can create a dynabase and update it serially by adding extensional data. At any time, the process can *query* the dynabase to retrieve either the current extensional data, or intensional data that are defined in terms of the extensional data. As the process *updates* the extensional data, the intensional data that depend on it (possibly in other dynabases) are automatically maintained, as in a spreadsheet. Carrying out the query and update operations requires the "heavy computational lifting" needed in AI for search, deduction, abduction, message passing, etc. However, the needed computations are specified only declaratively and at a high level of abstraction. They are carried out by the Dyna execution engine (eagerly or lazily) as needed to serve the process.

Essentially, a Dyna program is a set of equational schemata, which are similar to Datalog rules with (non-stratified) negation and aggregation. These schemata together with the extensional data define a possibly infinite system of equations, and the queriable "contents" of the dynabase come from a solution to this system. We give a gentle introduction in §2.3, and sketch a provisional semantics in an appendix to the full version [22].

Dyna does extend Datalog in several ways, in part by relaxing restrictions (§2.4). It is Turing-complete, so that the full computation needed by an AI system can be triggered by a single query against a dynabase. Thus it is not necessary to specify which data to look up when, or whether or where to store the results. The resulting Turing-completeness gives greater freedom to both the Dyna programmer and the execution model, along with greater responsibility. Dyna also includes programming language features that improve its usability, such as typing, function evaluation, encapsulation, inheritance, and reflection.

Finally, Dyna's syntax for aggregation is very concise (even compared to other logic notations, let alone explicit loops) because its provable items have arbitrary values, not just truth values. Evaluating items in place makes it possible to write equations quite directly, with arithmetic and nested function evaluation.

We show and justify some of our extensions by way of various examples from AI in §3. As Figures 1–12 illustrate, Dyna programs are startlingly short relative to more traditional, procedural versions. They naturally support record-at-a-time execution strategies (§2.6), as well as automatic differentiation (§3.1) and change propagation (§4.3), which are practically very important. Dynabases are modular and can be easily integrated with one another into larger programs (§2.7). Finally, they do not specify any particular storage or execution strategies, leaving opportunities for both automatic and user-directed optimizations that preserve correctness.

### 1.3    Storage and Execution Strategies

In this paper, we focus on the *expressivity* and *uses* of the Dyna language, as a user of Dyna would. From this point of view, the underlying computation order, indexing, and storage are distractions from a Dyna program's fundamentally declarative specification, and are relegated to an execution model—just as ordinary Datalog or SQL is a declarative language that leaves query optimization up to the database engine.

Actually computing and updating intensional data under a Dyna program may involve recursive internal queries and other work. However, this happens in some implementation-dependent order that can be tuned manually or automatically without affecting correctness.

The natural next questions concern this query and update planning, as well as physical design. How do we systematize the space of execution strategies and optimizations? Given a particular Dyna program and workload, can a generic Dyna engine discover the algorithms and data structures that an expert would choose by hand?

By showing in this paper that Dyna is capable of describing a wide range of computations, we mean to argue that finding efficient execution strategies for Dyna constitutes a substantial general program of research on *algorithms for AI and logic programming*.[1] After all, one would like a declarative solution of a given problem to exploit the relevant tricks used by the state-of-the-art procedural solutions. But then it is necessary to generalize these tricks into strategies that can be incorporated more generally into the Dyna runtime engine or encapsulated

---

[1] More restricted declarative formalisms have developed substantial communities that work on efficient execution: propositional satisfiability, integer linear programming, queries and physical design in relational databases, etc.

as general Dyna-to-Dyna program transformations [21,13]. These strategies may then be applied in new contexts. Building a wide range of tricks and strategies into the Dyna environment also raises the issue of how to manually specify and automatically tune strategies that work well on a particular workload.

Algorithms and pseudocode for a fragment of Dyna—the Dyna 1 prototype—appeared in [23]. We are now considering a much larger space of execution strategies, supported by type and mode systems (cf. [53]). Again, the present paper has a different focus; but a high-level discussion of some of the many interesting issues can be found in the final sections of the full version [22].

## 2 Basic Features of the Language

Our goal in this section is to sketch just enough of Dyna that readers will be able to follow our AI examples in the next section. After quickly reviewing Datalog, we explain how Dyna augments Datalog by proving that terms have particular values, rather than merely proving that they are true; by relaxing certain restrictions; and by introducing useful notions of encapsulation and inheritance. (Formal semantics are outlined in an appendix to the full version [22].)

### 2.1 Background: Datalog

Datalog [10] is a language—a concrete syntax—for defining named, flat relations. The (slightly incorrect) statement "Two people are siblings if they share a parent" can be precisely captured by a **rule** such as

$$\| \texttt{sibling(A,B) :- parent(C,A), parent(C,B).} \tag{1}$$

which may be read as "A is a sibling of B *if*, for some C, C is a parent of A *and* C is a parent of B." Formally, capitalized identifiers such as A,B,C denote universally quantified **variables**,[2] and the above rule is really a schema that defines infinitely many propositional implications such as

$$\| \texttt{sibling(alice,bob) :- parent(charlie,alice),} \\ \texttt{parent(charlie,bob).} \tag{2}$$

where alice, bob, and charlie are constants. (Thus, (2) is one of many possible implications that could be used to prove sibling(alice,bob).) Rules can also mention constants directly, as in

$$\| \begin{array}{l} \texttt{parent(charlie,alice).} \\ \texttt{parent(charlie,bob).} \end{array} \tag{3}$$

Since the rules (3) also happen to have no conditions (no ":- ..." part), they are simply **facts** that directly specify part of the binary relation parent, which

---

[2] A, B, C can have *any* value. The full version of this paper [22] (both at this point and in §2.4) discusses optional type declarations that can aid correctness and efficiency.

may be regarded as a two-column table in a relational database. The rule (1) defines another two-column table, `sibling`, by joining `parent` to itself on its first column and projecting that column out of the result.

Informally, we may regard `parent` (3) as extensional and `sibling` (1) as intensional, but Datalog as a language does not have to distinguish these cases. Datalog also does not specify whether the `sibling` relation should be materialized or whether its individual records should merely be computed as needed.

As this example suggests, it is simple in Datalog to construct new relations from old ones. Just as (1) describes a join, Datalog rules can easily describe other relational algebra operations such as project and select. They also permit recursive definitions. Datalog imposes the following syntactic restrictions to ensure that the defined relations are finite [10]:

- **Flatness:** Terms in a rule must include exactly one level of parentheses. This prevents recursive structure-building rules like

$$\left\|\begin{array}{l} \texttt{is\_integer(zero).} \\ \texttt{is\_integer(oneplus(X))\ :-\ is\_integer(X).} \end{array}\right. \tag{4}$$

which would define an infinite number of facts such as
`is_integer(oneplus(oneplus(oneplus(zero))))`.

- **Range restriction:** Any variables that occur in a rule's **head** (to the left of `:-`) must also appear in its **body** (to the right of `:-`). This prevents rules like

$$\left\| \texttt{equal(X,X).} \right. \tag{5}$$

which would define an infinite number of facts such as `equal(31,31)`.

Pure Datalog also disallows built-in infinite relations, such as $<$ on the integers. We will drop all these restrictions below.

## 2.2   Background: Datalog with Stratified Aggregation

Relations may range over numbers: for example, the variable `S` in `salary(alice,S)` has numeric type. Some Datalog dialects (e.g., [55,70]) support numeric **aggregation**, which combines numbers across multiple proofs of the same statement. As an example, if $w_{\mathrm{parent}}(\texttt{charlie},\texttt{alice}) = 0.75$ means that `charlie` is 75% likely to be a parent of `alice`, we might wish to define a soft measure of siblinghood by summing over possible parents:[3]

$$w_{\mathrm{sibling}}(A, B) = \sum_C w_{\mathrm{parent}}(C, A) \cdot w_{\mathrm{parent}}(C, B). \tag{6}$$

The sum over `C` is a kind of aggregation. The syntax for writing this in Datalog varies by dialect; as an example, [14] would write the above fact and rule (6) as

---

[3] This sum cannot necessarily be interpreted as the probability of siblinghood (for that, see related work in §2.5). We use definition (6) only to illustrate aggregation.

```
parent(charlie,alice;0.75).
sibling(A,B;sum(Ma*Mb))  :- parent(C,A;Ma),                (7)
                             parent(C,B;Mb).
```

Datalog dialects with aggregation (or negation) often impose a further requirement to ensure that the relations are well-defined [4,49]:

– **Stratification:** A relation that is defined using aggregation (or negation) must not be defined in terms of itself. This prevents cyclic systems of equations that have no consistent solution (e.g., a :- not a) or multiple consistent solutions (e.g., a :- not b and b :- not a).

We omit details here, as we will drop this restriction below.

### 2.3 Dyna

Our language, Dyna, aims to readily capture *equational* relationships with a minimum of fuss. In place of (7) for (6), we write more simply

```
parent(charlie,alice) = 0.75.
sibling(A,B) += parent(C,A) * parent(C,B).                 (8)
```

The += carries out summation over variables in the body which are not in the head, in this case C. For *each* A and B, the value of sibling(A,B) is being defined via a sum over values of the other variables in the rule, namely C.

The key point is that a Datalog program proves **items**, such as sibling(alice,bob), but a Dyna program also proves a **value** for each provable item (cf. [38]). Thus, a Dyna program defines a partial function from items to values. Values are numeric in this example, but in general may be arbitrary ground terms.[4]

Non-provable items have no value and are said to be **null**. In general, null items do not contribute to proofs of other items, nor are they retrieved by queries.[5]

Importantly, only **ground terms** (variable-free terms) can be items (or values), so sibling(A,B) is not itself an item and cannot have values. Rather, the += rule above is a schema that defines infinitely many grounded rules such as

```
sibling(alice,bob) += parent(charlie,alice)               (9)
                    * parent(charlie,bob).
```

which contributes a summand to sibling(alice,bob) iff parent(charlie,bob) and parent(charlie,alice) are both provable (i.e., have values).

The Dyna program may include additional rules beyond (8) that contribute additional summands to sibling(alice,bob). All rules for the same item must

---

[4] Abstractly, the value could be regarded as an additional argument with a functional dependency; see the full version of this paper [22] for more discussion.

[5] Dyna's support for non-monotonic reasoning (e.g., Figure 5) does enable rules to determine whether an item is null, or to look up such items. This is rarely necessary.

specify the same **aggregation operator** (or **aggregator** for short). In this case that operator is += (summation), so sibling(alice,bob) is defined by summing the value of $\gamma$ over *all* grounded rules of the form sibling(alice,bob) += $\gamma$ such that $\gamma$ is provable (non-null). If there are no such rules, then sibling(alice,bob) is null (note that it is not 0).[6]

In the first line of (8), the aggregation operator is =, which simply returns its single aggregand, if any (or gives an error if there are multiple aggregands). It should be used for clarity and safety if only one aggregand is expected. Another special aggregator we will see is :=, which chooses its *latest* aggregand; so the value of a := item is determined by the *last* rule (in program order) to contribute an aggregand to it (it is an error for that rule to contribute multiple aggregands).

However, most aggregators are like +=, in that they do not care about the order of aggregands or whether there is more than one, but simply reduce the multiset of aggregands with some associative and commutative binary operator (e.g, +).[7]

Ordinary Datalog as in (1) can be regarded as the simple case where all provable items have value **true**, the comma operator denotes boolean conjunction (over the subgoals of a proof), and the aggregator :- denotes boolean disjunction (over possible proofs). Thus, **true** and null effectively form a 2-valued logic. Semiring-weighted Datalog programs [30,23,31] correspond to rules like (8) where + and * denote the operations of a semiring.

## 2.4   Restoring Expressivity

Although our motivation comes from deductive databases, Dyna relaxes the restrictions that Datalog usually imposes, making it less like Datalog and more like the pure declarative fragment of Datalog's ancestor Prolog (cf. Mercury [46]).[8] As we will see in §3.1, relaxing these restrictions is important to support our AI use cases.

- **Flatness:** We drop this requirement so that Dyna can work with lists and other nested terms and perform unbounded computations.[9] However, this makes it Turing-complete, so we cannot guarantee that Dyna programs will terminate. That is the programmer's responsibility.
- **Range restriction:** We drop this requirement primarily so that Dyna can do default and non-monotonic reasoning, to support general function

---

[6] This language design choice naturally extends completion semantics [12]. One can still force a default 0 by adding the explicit rule sibling(A,B) += 0 to (8). See the full version of this paper [22] for further discussion.

[7] See the full version of this paper [22] for more discussion of aggregation operators.

[8] Of course, Dyna goes beyond pure Prolog, most importantly by augmenting items with values and by adding declarative mechanisms for situations that Prolog would handle non-declaratively with the cut operator. We also consider a wider space of execution strategies than Prolog's SLD resolution.

[9] For example, in computational linguistics, a parser's hypotheses may be represented by arbitrarily deep terms that are subject to unification. See the full version of this paper [22] for discussion and references.

definitions, and to simplify certain source-to-source program transformations [21]. However, this complicates Dyna's execution model.

- **Stratification:** We drop this requirement because Dyna's core uses include many non-stratified design patterns such as recurrent neural networks, message passing, iterative optimization, and dynamic programming. Indeed, the examples in §3.1 are mainly non-stratified. These domains inherently rely on cyclic systems of equations. However, as a result, some Dyna programs may not converge to a unique solution (partial map from items to values) or even to any solution.

The difficulties mentioned above are inevitable given our use cases. For example, an iterative learning or optimization procedure in AI[10] will often get stuck in a local optimum, or fail to converge. The procedure makes no attempt to find the global optimum, which may be intractable. Translating it to Dyna, we get a non-stratified Dyna program with multiple supported models[11] that correspond to the local optima. Our goal for the Dyna engine is merely to mimic the original AI method; hence we are willing to return any supported model, accepting that the particular one we find (if any) will be sensitive to initial conditions and procedural choices, as before. This is quite different from usual practice in the logic programming community (see [54] for a review and synthesis), which when it permits non-stratified programs at all, typically identifies their semantics with one [29] or more [44] "stable models" or the intersection thereof [63,37], although in general the stable models are computationally intractable to find.

A simple example of a non-stratified program (with at most one supported model [58]) is single-source shortest paths,[12] which defines the total cost from the **start** vertex to each vertex V:

$$\left\|\begin{array}{ll} \texttt{cost\_to(start)} & \texttt{min= 0.} \\ \texttt{cost\_to(V)} & \texttt{min= cost\_to(U) + edge\_cost(U,V).} \end{array}\right. \tag{10}$$

The aggregator here is **min=** (analogous to **+=** earlier) and the second rule aggregates over values of U, for each V. The weighted directed graph is specified by the **edge_cost** items. These are to be provided as extensional input or defined by additional rules (which could specify a very large or infinite graph).

**Evaluation.** The above example (10) also illustrates **evaluation**. The **start** item refers to the start vertex and is evaluated in place, i.e., replaced by its value,

---

[10] Such as expectation-maximization, gradient descent, mean-field inference, or loopy belief propagation (see Figure 7).

[11] A **model** (or interpretation) of a logic program $P$ is a partial map $[\![\cdot]\!]$ from items to values. A **supported model** [4] is a fixpoint of the "immediate consequence" operator $T_P$ associated with that program [62]. In our setting, this means that for each item $\alpha$, the value $[\![\alpha]\!]$ (according to the model) equals the value that would be computed for $\alpha$ (given the program rules defining $\alpha$ from other items and the values of those items according to the model).

[12] See the full version of this paper [22] for why it is hard to stratify this program.

as in a functional language.[13] The items in the body of line 2 are also evaluated in place: e.g., `cost_to("bal")` evaluates to 20, `edge_cost("bal","nyc")` evaluates to 100, and finally 20+100 evaluates to 120 (the evaluation mechanism is explained in the full version of this paper [22]). This notational convention is not deep, but to our knowledge, it has not been used before in logic programming languages.[14] We find the ability to write in a style close to traditional mathematics quite compelling.

## 2.5   Related Work

Several recent AI projects have developed attractive probabilistic programming languages (for space reasons, references are in the full version of this paper [22]).

By contrast, Dyna is not specifically probabilistic. Why? Our full paper [22] lists a wide variety of other numeric and non-numeric objects that are commonly manipulated by AI programs. Of course, Dyna items *may* take probabilities (or approximate probabilities) as their values, and the rules of the program *may* enforce a probabilistic semantics. However, the value of a Dyna item can be any term (including another dynabase). We will see examples in §3.1.

There are other logic programming formalisms in which provable terms are annotated by general values that need not be probabilities (some styles are exemplified by [38,30,26]). However, to our knowledge, all of these formalisms are too restrictive for our purposes.

In general, AI languages or toolkits have usually been designed to enforce the semantics of some *particular* modeling or algorithmic paradigm within AI.[15] Dyna, by contrast, is a more relaxed and general-purpose language that aims to accommodate all these paradigms. It is essentially a general infrastructure layer: specific systems or toolkits could be written in Dyna, or more focused languages could be compiled to Dyna. Dyna focuses on defining relationships among data items and supporting efficient storage, queries, and updates given these relationships. We believe that this work is actually responsible for the bulk of the implementation and optimization effort in today's AI systems.

---

[13] Notice that items and their values occupy the same universe of terms—they are not segregated as in §2.2. Thus, the value of one item can be another item (a kind of pointer) or a subterm of another item. For example, the value of **start** is used as a subterm of `cost_to(...)`. As another example, extending (10) to actually extract a shortest path, we define `best_path(V)` to have as its value a list of vertices:

```
best_path(V) ?= [U | best_path(U)]
               whenever cost_to(V) == cost_to(U)
                                     + edge_cost(U,V).
```

(Here the construction [First | Rest] prepends an element to a list, as in Prolog. The "free-choice" aggregator ?= allows the system to arbitrarily select any one of the aggregands, hence arbitrarily breaks ties among equally short paths.)

[14] With the exception of the hybrid functional-logic language Curry [17]. Curry is closer to functional programming than to Datalog. Its logical features focus on nondeterminism in lazy evaluation, and it does not have aggregation.

[15] Again, see the full paper for references.

## 2.6   A First Execution Strategy

Before we turn to our AI examples, some readers may be wondering how programs might be executed. Consider the shortest-path program in (10). We wish to find a fixed point of the system of equations that is given by those rules (grounding their variables in all possible ways) plus the extensional data.

Here we can employ a simple **forward chaining** strategy (see [23] for details and pseudocode). The basic idea is to propagate updates from rule bodies to rule heads, until the values of all items converge.[16] We refer to items in a rule's body as **antecedents** and to the item in the rule's head as the **consequent**.

At all times, we maintain a **chart** that maps the items proved so far to their current values, and an **agenda** (or worklist) of updates that have not yet been applied to the chart. Any changes to the extensional data are initially placed on the agenda: in particular, the initial definitions of `start` and `edge_cost` items.

A step of the algorithm consists of popping an update from the agenda, applying it to the chart, and computing the effect that will have on other items. For example, finding a new, shorter path to Baltimore may cause us to discover a new, shorter path to other cities such as New York City.

Concretely, when updating `cost_to("bal")` to 20, we see that this item pattern-matches one of the antecedents in the rule

$$\| \text{cost\_to(V) min= cost\_to(U) + edge\_cost(U,V)} . \qquad (11)$$

with the binding `U="bal"`, and must therefore drive an update through this rule. However, since the rule has two antecedents, the **driver** of the update, `cost_to("bal")`, needs a **passenger** of the form `edge_cost("bal",V)` to complete the update. We query the chart to find all such passengers. Suppose one result of our query `edge_cost("bal",V)` is `edge_cost("bal","nyc")=100`, which binds `V="nyc"`. We conclude that one of the aggregands of the consequent, `cost_to("nyc")`, has been updated to 120. If that *changes* the consequent's value, we place an update to the consequent on the agenda.

This simple update propagation method will be helpful to keep in mind when studying the examples in Figures 1–12. We note, however, that there is a rich space of execution strategies, as alluded to in §1.3.

## 2.7   Multiple Interacting Dynabases

So far we have considered only one dynabase at a time. However, using multiple interacting dynabases is useful for encapsulation, inheritance, and "what if" analysis where one queries a dynabase under changes to its input items.

Readers interested mainly in AI will want to skip the artificial example in this section and move ahead to §3, returning here if needed when multiple dynabases come into play partway through §3.1 (in Figures 7, 11 and 12).

All code fragments in this section are part of the definition of a dynabase that we call $\delta$. We begin by defining some ordinary items of $\delta$:

---

[16] This is a record-at-a-time variant of semi-naive bottom-up evaluation.

```
three = 3.
e = { pigs += 100.      % we have 100 adult pigs
      pigs += piglets.  % and any piglets we have are also pigs
    }.
```
$$(12)$$

In $\delta$, the value of **three** is 3 and the value of **e** is a particular dynabase $\varepsilon$. Just as 3 is a **numeric literal** in the program that specifies a number, the string {...} is an **dynabase literal** that specifies a **literal dynabase** $\varepsilon$.[17]

Since $\varepsilon$ does not declare its items **pigs** and **piglets** to be private, our rules in $\delta$ can refer to them as **e.pigs** and **e.piglets**, which evaluate to 100 and null. (More precisely, **e** evaluates to $\varepsilon$ within the expression **e.pigs**, and the resulting expression $\varepsilon$.**pigs** looks up the value of item **pigs** in dynabase $\varepsilon$.)

Storing related items like **pigs** and **piglets** in their own dynabase $\varepsilon$ can be a convenient way to organize them. Dynabases are first-class terms of the language, so one may use them in item names and values. For example, this definition of matrix transposition

```
transpose(Matrix) = { element(I,J) = Matrix.element(J,I). }.
```
$$(13)$$

defines for each dynabase $\mu$ an item **transpose($\mu$)** whose value is also a dynabase. Each of these dynabases is an encapsulated collection of many elements. Notice that **transpose** resembles an object-oriented function that takes an object as an argument and returns an object.

However, the real power of dynabases comes from the ability to **extend** them. Remember that a dynabase is a *dynamic* deductive database: $\varepsilon$.**pigs** is defined in terms of $\varepsilon$.**piglets** and should increase when $\varepsilon$.**piglets** does. However, $\varepsilon$.**piglets** cannot actually change because $\varepsilon$ in our example is an immutable constant. So where does the dynamism come in? How can a procedural program, or another dynabase, supply new input to $\varepsilon$ once it has defined or loaded it?

A procedural program can create a new **extension** of $\varepsilon$: a modifiable copy $\varepsilon'$. As the **owner** of $\varepsilon'$, the program can freely specify new aggregands to its writeable items. That serves to *increment* $\varepsilon'$.**pigs** and *replace* $\varepsilon'$.**piglets** (assuming that their aggregators are respectively **+=** and **:=**; see §2.3). These updates affect only $\varepsilon'$ and so are not visible to other users of $\varepsilon$.[18] The procedural program can interleave updates to $\varepsilon'$ with queries against the updated versions (see §1).

A Dyna program with access to $\varepsilon$ can similarly extend $\varepsilon$ with new aggregands; here too, changes to **piglets** will feed into **pigs**. Continuing our definition of $\delta$:

```
f = new e.         % f is a new pigpen φ that inherits all rules of ε
f.pigs      += 20.     % but has 20 extra adult pigs
f.piglets := three.    % and exactly three piglets
```
$$(14)$$

---

[17] One could equivalently define **e** = **$load("pigpen")**, where the file **pigpen.dyna** consists of "**pigs += 100. pigs += piglets.**" or a compiled equivalent. Then **$load("pigpen")** will evaluate to $\varepsilon$ (until the file changes). (Note: Reserved-word functors such as **$load** start with **$**, to avoid interference with user names of items.)

[18] The converse is not true: any updates to $\varepsilon$ would be inherited by its extension $\varepsilon'$.

These rules are written as part of the definition of $\delta$ (the owner[19] of the new dynabase $\varphi$) and supply new aggregands 20 and 3 to $\varphi$'s versions of `pigs` and `piglets`.

The **parent** dynabase $\varepsilon$ remains unchanged, but its extension $\varphi$ has items `pigs` and `piglets` with values 123 and 3, just as if it had been defined in the first place by combining (12) and (14) into[20]

$$
\begin{Vmatrix}
\texttt{f = \{ pigs} & \texttt{+= 100.} \\
\texttt{pigs} & \texttt{+= piglets.} \\
\texttt{pigs} & \texttt{+= 20.} \\
\texttt{piglets := \$owner.three. \}} & \textit{\% where \$owner refers to } \delta
\end{Vmatrix}
\tag{15}
$$

The important point is that setting `f.piglets` to have the same value as `three` also affected `f.pigs`, since $\varepsilon$ defined `pigs` in terms of `piglets` and this relationship remains operative in any extension of $\varepsilon$, such as `f`'s value $\varphi$.

Interactions among dynabases can be quite flexible. Some readers may wish to see a final example. Let us complete the definition of $\delta$ with additional rules

$$
\begin{Vmatrix}
\texttt{g = new e.} & \\
\texttt{offspring = g.pigs / three.} & \textit{\% all pigs have babies} \\
\texttt{g.piglets := offspring.} & \textit{\% who are piglets}
\end{Vmatrix}
\tag{16}
$$

This creates a loop by feeding $\frac{1}{3}$ of g's "output item" `pigs` back into g's "input item" `piglets`, via an intermediate item `offspring` that is not part of g at all. The result is that `g.pigs` and `g.piglets` converge to 150 and 50 (e.g., via the forward chaining algorithm of §2.6). This is a correct solution to the system of equations specified by (12) and (16), which state that there are 100 more pigs than piglets and $\frac{1}{3}$ as many piglets as pigs:

$$
\delta.\texttt{three} = 3 \qquad\qquad \delta.\texttt{offspring} = \gamma.\texttt{pigs}/\delta.\texttt{three} \tag{17}
$$
$$
\gamma.\texttt{pigs} = 100 + \gamma.\texttt{piglets} \qquad \gamma.\texttt{piglets} = \delta.\texttt{offspring}
$$

Dynabases are connected to object-oriented programming. We will see practical uses of multiple dynabases for encapsulation (Figure 7), modularity (Figure 11), and backtracking search (Figure 12). More formal discussion of the overall language semantics, with particular attention to dynabase extension, can be found in an appendix to the full version [22].

## 3   Design Patterns in AI

Given the above sketch, we return to the main argument of the paper, namely that Dyna is an elegant declarative notation for capturing the logical structure of computations in modern statistical AI.

---

[19] Because $\delta$ invoked the **new** operator that created $\varphi$, $\delta$ is said to **own** $\varphi$. This is why $\delta$ is permitted to have rules that extend $\varphi$ with additional aggregands as shown in (14). See the full version of this paper [22] for further discussion of ownership.

[20] Fine points and formal semantics are covered in the full version of this paper [22].

Modern AI systems can generally be thought of as observing some input and recovering some (hidden) structure of interest:

- We observe an image and recover some description of the scene.
- We observe a sentence of English and recover a syntax tree, a meaning representation, a translation into Chinese, etc.
- We are given a goal or reward function and recover a plan to earn rewards.
- We observe some facts expressed in a knowledge representation language and recover some other facts that can be logically deduced or statistically guessed from them.
- We observe a dataset and recover the parameters of the probability distribution that generated it.

Typically, one defines a discrete or continuous space of possible structures, and learns a scoring function or probability distribution over that space. Given a partially observed structure, one either tries to recover the best-scoring completion of that structure, or else queries the probability distribution over all possible completions. Either way, the general problem is sometimes called **structured prediction** or simply **inference**.

### 3.1   Brief AI Examples in Dyna

We will show how to implement several AI patterns in Dyna. All the examples in this section are brief enough that they are primarily pedagogical—they could be used to teach and experiment with these basic versions of well-known methods.

Real systems correspond to considerably larger Dyna programs that modify and combine such techniques. Real systems must also obtain their input by transforming raw datasets (using additional Dyna rules).

*Each of the code examples below is in a self-contained figure, with details in the captions.* Typically the program defines a dynabase in which all items are still null, as it merely defines intensional items in terms of extensional items that have not been supplied yet. One may however extend this dynabase (see §2.7), adding observed structure (the input) and the parameters of the scoring function (the model) as extensional data. Results now appear in the extended dynabase as intensional data defined by the rules, and one may read them out.

**Arithmetic Circuits.** One simple kind of system is an arithmetic circuit. A classic AI example is a neural net (Figure 1). In the Dyna implementation (Figure 2), the network topology is specified by defining values for the `weight` items.

As in the shortest-path program (10), the items that specify the topology may be either provided directly at runtime (as extensional data), or defined by additional Dyna rules (as intensional data: Figure 3 gives an attractive example).

Notice that line 3 of Figure 2 is a matrix-vector product. It is sparse because the neural-network topology is typically a sparse graph (Figure 1). Sparse products are very common in AI. For example, sparse dot products are used both in computing similarity and in linear or log-linear models [15]. A dot product like `score(Structure) += weight(Feature)*strength(Feature,Structure)`

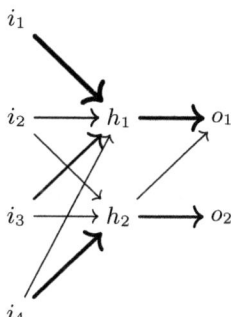

**Fig. 1.** A small acyclic neural network. The activation $x_n$ at each node $n$ is a nonlinear function $f$, such as a sigmoid or threshold function, of a weighted sum of activations at $n$'s parent nodes: $x_n \overset{\text{def}}{=} f\left(\sum_{(n',n) \in E} x_{n'} w_{n',n}\right)$. The three layers shown here are the traditional input, hidden, and output nodes, with $w_{n',n}$ values represented by arrow thickness.

```
sigmoid(X) = 1 / (1 + exp(-X)).
output(Node) = sigmoid(input(Node)).
input(Node) += output(Child) * weight(Child,Node).
error += (output(Node) - target(Node))**2.
```

**Fig. 2.** A general neural network in Dyna. Line 1 defines the sigmoid function over all real numbers X. In Line 2, that function is applied to the *value* of input(Node), which is evaluated in place. Line 3 sums over all incoming edges to Node. Those edges are simply the (Child,Node) pairs for which weight(Child,Node) is defined. Additional summands to some of the input(Node) items may be supplied to this dynabase at runtime; this is how $i_1, i_2, i_3, i_4$ in Figure 1 would get their outside input. Finally, Line 4 evaluates error by summing over just those nodes for which target(Node) has been defined (i.e., is non-null), presumably the output nodes $o_j$.

```
weight(pixel(X+I,Y+J), hidden(X,Y)) = shared_weight(I,J).
```

**Fig. 3.** One layer of a neural network topology for vision, to be used with Figure 2. Each hidden node hidden(X,Y) is connected to a $5 \times 5$ rectangle of input nodes pixel(X+I,Y+J) for $I, J \in \{-2, -1, 0, 1, 2\}$, using a collection of 25 weights that are reused across spatial positions (X,Y). The shared_weight(I,J) items should be defined (non-null) only for $I, J \in \{-2, -1, 0, 1, 2\}$. This rule then connects nodes with related names, such as such as hidden(75,95) and pixel(74,97).

This rule exploits the fact that the node names are structured objects.[21] By using structured names, we have managed to specify an *infinite* network in a single line (plus 25 weight definitions). Only a finite portion of this network will actually be used by Figure 2, assuming that the image (the collection of pixel items) is finite.

---

[21] These names are not items but appear in the rule as *unevaluated* terms. However, the expressions X+I and Y+J are evaluated in place, so that the rule is equivalent to

```
weight(pixel(X2,Y2), hidden(X,Y)) = shared_weight(I,J)
                          whenever X2 is X+I, Y2 is Y+I.
```

where in general, the condition $\gamma$ is $\alpha$ has value true if $\gamma$ is the value of item $\alpha$, and is null otherwise. For example, 97 is 95+2 has value true.

```
count(X,Y) += 0 whenever is_event(X), is_event(Y).   % default
count(X)   += count(X,Y).
count      += count(X).

% Maximum likelihood estimates
mle_prob(X)   = count(X)   / count.
mle_prob(X,Y) = count(X,Y) / count(Y).

% Good-Turing smoothed estimates [50]
gt_prob(X)   = total_mle_prob(count(X)+1)   / n(count(X)).
gt_prob(X,Y) = total_mle_prob(count(X)+1,Y) / n(count(X),Y).

% Used by Good-Turing: How many events X occurred R times, or
% cooccurred R times with Y, and what is their total probability?
n(R) += 0.                    n(R)   += 1 whenever R==count(X).
n(R,Y) += 0.                  n(R,Y) += 1 whenever R==count(X,Y).
total_mle_prob(R)   += mle_prob(X)   whenever R==count(X).
total_mle_prob(R,Y) += mle_prob(X,Y) whenever R==count(X,Y).
```

**Fig. 4.** Estimating conditional probabilities $p(x)$ and $p(x \mid y)$, based on counts of $x$ with $y$. The user can simply increment count$(x,y)$ whenever $x$ is observed together with $y$, and the probability estimates will update (see §4.3). See the full version of this paper [22] for more detailed discussion of this code.

resembles line 3, and can benefit from using complex feature names, just as Figure 3 used complex node names.

A rather different example of arithmetic computation is shown in Figure 4, a dynabase that maintains probability estimates based on the counts of events. Some other commonly used arithmetic formulas in AI include distances, kernel functions, and probability densities.

**Training of Arithmetic Circuits.** To train a neural network or log-linear model, one must adjust the weight parameters to reduce error. Common optimization methods need to consult more than just the current error: they need to query the gradient of error with respect to the parameters. How can they obtain the gradient? **Automatic differentiation** can be written very naturally as a source-to-source transformation on Dyna programs, automatically augmenting Figure 2 with rules that compute the gradient by back-propagation [23]. The gradient can then be used by other Dyna rules or queried by a procedural optimizer. Alternatively, the execution engine of our prototype Dyna implementation natively supports [23] computing gradients, via tape-based automatic differentiation in the reverse mode [32]. It is designed to produce exact gradients even of incomplete computations.

An optimizer written in a conventional procedural language can iteratively update the weight items in the dynabase of Figure 2, observing at each step how the output, error, and gradient change in response. Or the optimizer could be written in Dyna itself, via rules that define the weights at time step T+1 in

```
fly(X) := false.
fly(X) := true if bird(X).
fly(X) := false if penguin(X).
fly(bigbird) := false.
```

**Fig. 5.** An example of non-monotonic reasoning: all birds fly, other than Sesame Street's Big Bird, until such time as they are proved or asserted to be penguins. Recall from §2.3 that the := aggregator is sensitive to rule ordering, so that where the later rules apply at all, they override the earlier rules. The first rule is a "default rule" that is not range-restricted (see §2.1): it proves infinitely many items that unify with a pattern (here the very simple pattern X).

terms of items (e.g., gradient) computed at time step T. This requires adding an explicit time argument T to all terms (another source-to-source transformation).

**Theorem Proving.** Of course, logic and logic programming have a long history in symbolic AI. Traditional systems for knowledge representation and reasoning (KRR) are all automated theorem provers (see the full version of this paper [22] for some references). They compute the entailments of a set of axioms obtained from human input or derived by other theorem provers (e.g., OWL web services).

Logical languages like Dyna support these patterns naturally. The extensional items are axioms, the intensional ones are theorems, and the inference rules are the rules of the program. A simple example appears in our full paper.

Dyna also naturally handles some forms of default and non-monotonic reasoning [6], via := rules like those in Figure 5. A related important use of default patterns in AI is "lifted inference" [61] in probabilistic settings like Markov Logic Networks [57], where additional (non-default) computation is necessary only for individuals about whom additional (non-default) facts are known. Yet another use in AI is default arcs of various kinds in deterministic finite-state automata over large or unbounded alphabets [3,52].[22]

Some emerging KRR systems embrace statistics and draw probabilistic inferences rather than certain ones (again, see our full paper for references). Their computations can typically be described in Dyna by using real-valued items.

**Message Passing.** Many AI algorithms come down to solving (or approximately solving) a system of simultaneous equations, often by iterating to convergence. In fact, the neural network program of Figure 2 already requires iteration to convergence in the case of a cyclic ("recurrent") network topology [64].

Such iterative algorithms are often known as "message passing" algorithms. They can be regarded as *negotiating* a stable configuration of the items' values. Updates to one item trigger updates to related items—easily handled in Dyna since update propagation is exactly what a basic forward-chaining algorithm does

---

[22] Dyna rules illustrating this are given in the full version of this paper [22].

(§2.6). When the updates can flow around cycles, the system is not stratified and sometimes has no guarantee of a unique fixed point, as warned in §2.4.

Message passing algorithms seek possible, likely, or optimal values of random variables under a complex set of hard or soft constraints. Figure 6 and Figure 7 show two interesting examples in Dyna: arc consistency (with boolean values) and loopy belief propagation (with unnormalized probabilities as the values).[23] Other important examples include alternating optimization algorithms such as expectation-maximization and mean-field. Markov chain Monte Carlo (MCMC) and simulated annealing algorithms can also be regarded as message passing algorithms, although in this case the updates are randomized; Dyna code for a simple random walk appears in the full version of this paper [22].

**Dynamic Programming.** Dyna began [23] as a language for dynamic programming (hence the name). The connection of dynamic programming to logic programming has been noted before (e.g., [33]). Fundamentally, dynamic programming is about solving subproblems and reusing stored copies of those solutions to solve various larger subproblems. In Dyna, the subproblems are typically named by items, whose values are their solutions. An efficient implementation of Dyna will typically store these solutions for reuse,[24] whether by backward chaining that lazily memoizes values in a table (as in XSB [65] and other tabled Prologs), or by forward chaining that eagerly accumulates values into a chart (as in §2.6 and the Dyna prototype [23]).

A traditional dynamic programming algorithm can be written directly in Dyna as a set of recurrence equations. A standard first example is the Fibonacci sequence, whose runtime goes from exponential to linear in N if one stores enough of the intermediate values:

$$
\begin{array}{ll}
\texttt{fib(N) := fib(N-1) + fib(N-2).} & \textit{\% general rule} \\
\texttt{fib(0) := 1.} & \textit{\% exceptions for base cases} \quad (18) \\
\texttt{fib(1) := 1.} &
\end{array}
$$

As a basic AI example, consider context-free parsing with a CKY-style algorithm [67]. The Dyna program in Figure 8 consists of 3 rules that directly and intuitively express how a parse tree is recursively built up by combining adjacent phrases into larger phrases, under the guidance of a grammar. The forward-chaining algorithm of §2.6 here yields "agenda-based parsing" [60]: when a recently built or updated phrase pops off the agenda into the chart, it tries to combine with adjacent phrases in the chart.

---

[23] Twists on these programs give rise to other popular local consistency algorithms (bounds consistency, $i$-consistency) and propagation algorithms (generalized belief propagation, survey propagation).

[24] This support for reuse is already evident in our earlier examples, even though they would not traditionally be regarded as dynamic programming. The activation of node $h_1$ in Figure 1 (represented by some output item in Figure 2) takes some work to compute, but once computed, it is reused in computing each node $o_j$. Similarly, each count n(R) or n(R,Y) in Figure 4 is reused to compute many smoothed probabilities.

```
% For Var:Val to be possible, Val must be in-domain, and
% also supported by each Var2 that is co-constrained with Var.
% The conjunctive aggregator &= is like universal quantification over Var2.
possible(Var:Val) &= in_domain(Var:Val).
possible(Var:Val) &= supported(Var:Val, Var2).
p
% Var:Val is supported by Var2 only if it is still possible
% for Var2 to take some value that is compatible with Val.
% The disjunctive aggregator |= is like existential quantification over Val2.
supported(Var:Val, Var2)
    |= compatible(Var:Val, Var2:Val2) & possible(Var2:Val2).

% If consistent ever becomes false, we have detected unsatisfiability:
% some variable has no possible value.
non_empty(Var) |= false.              % default (if there are no possible values)
non_empty(Var) |= possible(Var:Val). % Var has a possible value
consistent &= non_empty(Var) whenever is_var(Var).
                        % each Var in the system has a possible value
```

**Fig. 6.** Arc consistency for constraint programming [19]. The goal is to rule out some impossible values for some variables, using a collection of unary constraints (`in_domain`) and binary constraints (`compatible`) that are given by the problem and/or tested during backtracking search (see Figure 12). The "natural" forward-chaining execution strategy for this Dyna program corresponds to the classical, asymptotically optimal AC-4 algorithm [48].

Variables and constraints can be named by arbitrary terms. `Var:Val` is syntactic sugar for an ordered pair, similar to `pair(Var,Val)` (the : has been declared as an infix functor). The program determines whether `possible(Var:Val)`. The user should define `is_var(Var)` as `true` for each variable, and `in_domain(Var:Val)` as `true` for each value `Val` that `Var` should consider. To express a binary constraint between the variables `Var` and `Var2`, the user should define `compatible(Var:Val, Var2:Val2)` to be `true` or `false` for each value pair `Val` and `Val2`, according to whether the constraint lets these variables simultaneously take these values. This ensures that `supported(Var:Val,Var2)` will be `true` or `false` (not null) and so will contribute a conjunct to line 2.

We will return to this example in §3.2. Meanwhile, the reader is encouraged to figure out why it is not a stratified program (§2.2), despite being based on the stratified CKY algorithm.[25] Replacing the += aggregator with `max=` (compare (10)) would make it find the probability of the single best parse, instead of the total probability of all parses [30].

This example also serves as a starting point for more complicated algorithms in syntactic natural-language parsing and syntax-directed translation.[26] The uses

---

[25] See the full version of this paper [22] for a detailed answer.

[26] The connection of these areas to deductive inference and logic programming has been well explored. See the full version of this paper [22] for discussion and references.

```
% Belief at each variable based on the messages it receives from constraints.
belief(Var:Val) *= message(Con, Var:Val).


% Belief at each constraint based on the messages it receives from variables
% and the preferences of the constraint itself.
belief(Con:Asst) = messages_to(Con:Asst) * constraint(Con:Asst).


% To evaluate a possible assignment Asst to several variables, look at messages
% to see how well each variable Var likes its assigned value Asst.Var.
messages_to(Con:Asst) *= message(Var:(Asst.Var), Con).


% Message from a variable Var to a constraint Con. Var says that it plausibly
% has value Val if Var independently believes in that value (thanks to other
% constraints, with Con's own influence removed via division).
message(Var:Val, Con) := 1.   % initial value, will be overridden
message(Var:Val, Con) := belief(Var:Val) / message(Con, Var:Val).


% Messages from a constraint Con to a variable Var.
% Con says that Var plausibly has value Val if Con independently
% believes in one or more assignments Asst in which this is the case.
message(Con, Var:Val) += belief(Con:Asst) / message(Var:Val, Con)
                         whenever Asst.Var == Val.
```

**Fig. 7.** Loopy belief propagation on a factor graph [66]. The constraints together define a Markov Random Field joint probability distribution over the variables. We seek to approximate the marginals of that distribution: at each variable Var we will deduce a belief about its value, in the form of relative probabilities of the possible values Val. Similarly, at each constraint Con over a *set* of variables, we will deduce a belief about the correct *joint assignment* of values to *just those* variables, in the form of relative probabilities of the possible assignments Asst.

Assignments are slightly complicated because we allow a single constraint to refer to arbitrarily many variables (in contrast to Figure 6, which assumed binary constraints). A specific assignment is a map from variable names (terms such as color, size) to their values (e.g., red, 3). It is convenient to represent this map as a small sub-dynabase, Asst, whose elements are accessed by the . operator: for example, Asst.color == red and Asst.size == 3.

As input, the user must define constraint so that each constraint ("factor" or "potential function") gives a non-negative value to each assignment, giving larger values to its preferred assignments. Each variable should be subject to at least one constraint, to specify its domain (analogous to in_domain in Figure 6).

A *message* to or from a variable specifies a relative probability for each value of that variable. Since messages are proved circularly from one another, we need to initialize some messages to 1 in order to start propagation; but these initial values are overridden thanks to the := aggregator, which selects its "latest" aggregand and hence prefers the aggregand from line 5 (once defined) to the initial aggregand from line 4. *Note:* For simplicity, this version of the program glosses over minor issues of message normalization and division by 0.

```
% A single word is a phrase (given an appropriate grammar rule).
phrase(X,I,J) += rewrite(X,W) * word(W,I,J).
% Two adjacent phrases make a wider phrase (given an appropriate rule).
phrase(X,I,J) += rewrite(X,Y,Z) * phrase(Y,I,Mid) * phrase(Z,Mid,J).
% An phrase of the appropriate type covering the whole sentence is a parse.
goal          += phrase(start_nonterminal,0,length).
```

**Fig. 8.** Probabilistic context-free parsing in Dyna (the "inside algorithm"). `phrase(X,I,J)` is provable if there might be a constituent of type X from position I to position J of the input sentence. More specifically, the *value* of `phrase(X,I,J)` is the probability that nonterminal symbol X would expand into the substring that stretches from I to J. It is defined using `+=` to sum over all ways of generating that substring (considering choices of Y, Z, Mid). Thus, `goal` is the probability of generating the input sentence, summing over all parses.

The extensional input consists of a sentence and a grammar. `word("spring",5,6)=1` means that `"spring"` is the sixth word of the sentence; while `length=30` specifies the number of words. `rewrite("S","NP","VP")=0.9` means that any copy of nonterminal S has a priori probability 0.9 of expanding via the binary grammar production S → NP VP; while `start_nonterminal="S"` specifies the start symbol of the grammar.

of the Dyna prototype (listed in a section of [22]) have been mainly in this domain; see [21,23] for code examples. In natural language processing, active areas of research that make heavy use of parsing-like dynamic programs include machine translation, information extraction, and question answering.[27] There is a tremendous amount of experimentation with models and algorithms in these areas and in parsing itself. The machine vision community has also begun to explore recursive parsing of images [69,27]. Dyna is potentially helpful on all of these fronts.

Other dynamic programming algorithms are also straightforward in Dyna, such as the optimal strategy in a game tree or a Markov Decision Process (Figure 9), variations from bioinformatics on weighted edit distance (Figure 10) and multiple sequence alignment, or the intersection or composition of two finite-state automata (see [13] for Dyna code).

**Processing Pipelines.** It is common for several algorithms and models to work together in a larger AI system. Connecting them is easy in Dyna: one algorithm's input items can be defined by the output of another algorithm or model, rather than as extensional input. The various code and data resources can be provided in separate dynabases (§2.7), which facilitates sharing, distribution, and reuse.

For example, Figure 11a gives a version of Figure 8's parser that conveniently accepts its **grammar** and **input** in the form of other dynabases. Figure 11b illustrates how this setup allows painless scripting.

Figure 11c shows how the provided **grammar** may be an interesting component in its own right if it does not merely *list* weighted productions but *computes*

---

[27] Again, see our full paper [22] for references.

```
% The optimal value function V.
value(State)          max= value(State,Action).

% The optimal action-value function Q.
% Note: The value of p(s,a,s') is a conditional transition probability, P(s' | s,a).
value(State,Action) += reward(State,Action).
value(State,Action) += γ * p(State,Action,NewState) * value(NewState).

% The optimal policy function π. The free-choice aggregator ?= is used
% merely to break ties as in footnote 13.
best_action(State)   ?= Action if value(State) == value(State,Action).
```

**Fig. 9.** Finding the optimal policy in an infinite-horizon Markov decision process, using value iteration. The reward and transition probability functions can be sensitive to properties of the states, or to their structured names as in Figure 3. The optimal value of a `State` is the expected total reward that an agent will earn if it follows the optimal policy from that `State` (where the reward at $t$ steps in the future is discounted by a factor of $\gamma^t$). The optimal value of a `(State,Action)` pair is the expected total reward that the agent will earn by first taking the given `Action`—thereby earning a specified reward and stochastically transitioning to a new state—and thereafter following the optimal policy to earn further reward.

The mutual recurrence between $V$ and $Q$ interleaves two different aggregators: `max=` treats optimization by the agent, while `+=` computes an expectation to treat randomness in the environment. This "expectimax" strategy is appropriate for acting in a random environment, in contrast to the "minimax" strategy using `max=` and `min=` that is appropriate when acting against an adversarial opponent. The final line with `?=` merely extracts the optimal policy once its value is known.

them using additional Dyna rules (analogous to the neural network example in Figure 3). The particular example in Figure 11c constructs a context-free grammar from weights. It is equally easy to write Dyna rules that construct a grammar's productions by transforming another grammar,[28] or that specify an infinitely large grammar.[29]

Not only `grammar` but also `input` may be defined using rules. For example, the input sequence of words may be derived from raw text or speech signal using a structured prediction system—a tokenizer, morphological analyzer, or automatic speech recognizer. A generalization is that such a system, instead of just producing a single "best guess" word sequence, can often be made to produce a *probability distribution* over possible word sequences, which is more informative.

---

[28] E.g., one can transform a weighted context-free grammar into Chomsky Normal Form for use with Figure 11a, or coarsen a grammar for use as an A$^*$ heuristic [39].

[29] E.g., the non-range-restricted rule `rewrite(X/Z,X/Y,Y/Z).` encodes the infinitely many "composition" rules of combinatory categorial grammar [60], in which a complex nonterminal such as `s/(pp/np)` denotes an incomplete sentence (`s`) missing an incomplete prepositional phrase (`pp`) that is in turn missing a noun phrase (`np`).

```
% Base case: distance between two empty strings.
dist([],[]) = 0.

% Recursive cases.
dist([X|Xs],   Ys ) min= delete_cost(X)   + dist(Xs,Ys).
dist(   Xs, [Y|Ys]) min= insert_cost(Y)   + dist(Xs,Ys).
dist([X|Xs],[Y|Ys]) min=  subst_cost(X,Y) + dist(Xs,Ys).

% Part of the cost function.
substcost(L,L) = 0.    % cost of 0 to align any letter to itself
```

**Fig. 10.** Weighted edit distance between two strings. This example illustrates items whose names are arbitrarily deep terms: each `dist` name encodes two strings, each being an list of letters. As in Prolog, the syntactic sugar `[X|Xs]` denotes a list of length $> 0$ that is composed of a first element `X` and a remainder list `Xs`.

We pay some cost for aligning the first 0 or 1 letters from one string with the first 0 or 1 letters from the other string, and then recurse to find the total cost of aligning what is left of the two strings. The choice of how many initial letters to align is at lines 2–4: the program tries all three choices and picks the one with the minimum cost. Reuse of recursive subproblems keeps the runtime quadratic. For example, if all costs not shown are 1, then `dist([a,b,c,d], [s,b,c,t,d])` has value 2. This is obtained by optimally choosing the line with `subst_cost(a,s)` at the first recursive step, then `subst_cost(b,b)`, `subst_cost(c,c)`, `insert_cost(t)`, `subst_cost(d,d)`, for a total cost of 1+0+0+1+0.

This distribution is usually represented as a "hypothesis lattice"—a probabilistic finite-state automaton that may generate exponentially or infinitely many possible sequences, assigning some probability to each sequence. The parser of Figure 11a can handle this kind of nondeterministic input without modification. The only effect on the parser is that I, J, and `Mid` in Figure 11a now range over states in an automaton instead of positions in a sentence.[30]

At the other end of the parsing process, the parse output can be passed downstream to subsequent modules such as information extraction. Again, it is not necessary to use only the single most likely output (parse tree). The downstream customer can analyze *all* the **phrase** items in the dynabase of Figure 11a to exploit high-probability patterns in the *distribution* over parse trees [59,68].

As discussed in the caption for Figure 11c, the training of system parameters can be made to feed back through this processing pipeline of dynabases [20]. Thus, in summary, hypotheses can be propagated forward through a pipeline (joint prediction) and gradients can be propagated backward (joint training). Although this is generally understood in the natural language processing community [28], it is surprisingly rare for papers to actually implement joint prediction or joint training, because of the extra design and engineering effort, particularly

---

[30] See the full version of this paper [22] for details.

```
phrase(X,I,J) += grammar.rewrite(X,W) * input.word(W,I,J).
phrase(X,I,J) += grammar.rewrite(X,Y,Z) * phrase(Y,I,Mid)
                                         * phrase(Z,Mid,J).
goal           += phrase(grammar.start_nonterminal,0,input.length).
```

**(a)** A parser like that of Figure 8, except that its input items are two dynabases (denoted by **grammar** and **input**) rather than many separate numbers (denoted by **rewrite**(...), **word**(...), etc.).

```
% Specialize (a) into an English-specific parser.
english_parser = new $load("parser").    % parser.dyna is given in (a)
english_parser.grammar = $load("english_grammar").   % given in (c)

% Parse a collection of English sentences by providing different inputs.
doc = $load("document").
parse(K) = new english_parser.          % extend the abstract parser ...
parse(K).input = doc.sentence(K).       % ... with some actual input

% The total log-probability of the document, ignoring sentences for which
% no parse was found.
logprob += log(parse(K).goal).
```

**(b)** An illustration of how to use the above parser. This declarative "script" does not specify the serial or parallel order in which to parse the sentences, whether to retain or discard the parses, etc. All dynabases **parse(K)** share the same grammar, so the rule probabilities do not have to be recomputed for each sentence. A good grammar will obtain a comparatively high **logprob**; thus, the **logprob** measure can be used for evaluation or training. (Alternative measures that consider the *correct* parses, if known, are almost as easy to compute in Dyna.)

```
% Define the unnormalized probability of the grammar production X → Y Z
% as a product of feature weights.
urewrite(X,Y,Z) *= left_child_weight(X,Y).
urewrite(X,Y,Z) *= right_child_weight(X,Z).
urewrite(X,Y,Z) *= sibling_weight(Y,Z).
urewrite(X,Y,Y) *= twin_weight.         % when the two siblings are identical
urewrite(X,Y,Z) *= 1.                   % default in case no features are defined

% Normalize into probabilities that can be used in PCFG parsing:
% many productions can rewrite X but their probabilities should sum to 1.
urewrite(X) += urewrite(X,Y,Z)
                 whenever nonterminal(Y), nonterminal(Z).
rewrite(X,Y,Z) = urewrite(X,Y,Z) / urewrite(X).
```

**(c)** Constructing a dense grammar for use by the above programs, with probabilities given by a conditional log-linear model. With $k$ grammar nonterminals, this scheme specifies $k^3$ rule probabilities with only $O(k^2)$ feature weights to be learned from limited data [5]. Just as for neural nets, these weights may be trained on observed data. For example, maximum likelihood estimation would try to maximize the resulting **logprob** in 11b.

**Fig. 11.** A modular implementation of parsing

when integrating non-trivial modules by different authors. Under Dyna, doing so should be rather straightforward.

Another advantage to integrating the phases of a processing pipeline is that integration can speed up search. The phases can *interactively negotiate* an exact or approximate solution to the joint prediction problem—various techniques include alternating optimization (hill-climbing), Gibbs sampling, coarse-to-fine inference, and dual decomposition. However, these techniques require systematic modifications to the programs that specify each phase, and are currently underused because of the extra implementation effort.

**Backtracking Search.** Many combinatorial search situations require backtracking exploration of a tree or DAG. Some variants include beam search, game-tree analysis, the DPLL algorithm for propositional satisfiability, and branch-and-bound search in settings such as Integer Linear Programming.

It is possible to construct a search tree *declaratively* in Dyna. Since a node in a search tree shares most properties with its children, a powerful approach is to represent each node as a dynabase, and each of its child nodes as a modified extension of that dynabase (see §2.7).

We illustrate this in Figure 12 with an elegant DPLL-style program for solving NP-hard satisfiability problems. Each node of the search tree runs the arc-consistency program of Figure 6 to eliminate some impossible values for some variables, using a message-passing local consistency checker. It "then" probes a variable `nextvar`, by constructing for *each* of its remaining possible values `Val` a child dynabase in which `nextvar` is constrained to have value `Val`. The child dynabase copies the parent, but thanks to the added constraint, the arc-consistency algorithm can pick up where it left off and make even more progress (eliminate even more values). That reduces the number of grandchildren the child needs to probe. The recursion terminates when all variables are constrained.

One good execution strategy for this Dyna program would resemble the actual DPLL method [18], with

- a reasonable variable ordering strategy to select `nextvar`;
- each child dynabase created by a temporary modification of the parent, which is subsequently undone;
- running arc consistency at a node to completion *before* constructing any children, since quickly eliminating values or proving unsatisfiability can rule out the need to examine some or all children;
- skipping a node's remaining children once `consistent` has been proved `false` (by arc consistency) or `true` (by finding a consistent child).

However, the program itself is purely declarative and admits other strategies, such as parallel ones.

```
% Freely choose an unassigned variable nextvar, if any exists.
% For each of its values Val that is still possible after arc consistency,
% create a clone of the current dynabase, called child(Val).
nextvar ?= Var whenever unassigned(Var).          % free choice of nextvar
child(Val) = new $self if possible(nextvar:Val).  % create several extensions

% Further constrain each child(Val) via additional extensional input,
% so that it will only permit value Val for nextvar,
% and so that it will choose a new unassigned variable to assign next.
child(Val).possible(nextvar:Val2) &= (Val==Val2)
                                    whenever possible(nextvar:Val).
child(Val).unassigned(nextvar) &= false.   % nextvar has been assigned

% We are satisfiable if Figure 6 has not already proved consistent to be false,
% and also at least one of our children (if we have any) is satisfiable.
consistent &= some_child_consistent.
some_child_consistent |= child(Val).consistent.
        % usually is true or false, but is null at a leaf (since nextvar is null)
```

**Fig. 12.** Determining the satisfiability of a set of constraints, using backtracking search interleaved with arc consistency. These rules extend the program of Figure 6—which rules out some impossible values for some variables, and which sometimes detects unsatisfiability by proving that **consistent** is **false**. Here, we strengthen **consistent** with additional conjuncts so that it fully checks for satisfiability. Lines 1–2 choose a single variable **nextvar** (using the "free-choice" aggregator **?=**) and guess different values for it in child dynabases. We place constraints into the child at lines 3–4 and read back the result (whether that child is satisfiable) at line 6.

A simple modification to the program will allow it to solve MAX-SAT-style problems using branch-and-bound.[31] In this case, a more breadth-first variant

---

[31] The goal is to find a maximum-scoring joint assignment to the variables, subject to the constraints. The score of a given assignment is found by summing the **subscore** values (as specified by the user) of the several **Var:Val** pairs in the assignment.

In Figure 6 and Figure 12, replace **consistent** (a boolean item aggregated by **&=**) by **score** (a real-valued item aggregated by **min=**). In Figure 6, just as **consistent** computes a boolean upper bound on satisfiability, **score** computes a numeric upper bound on the best achievable score:

```
subscore(Var) max= -∞.
subscore(Var) max= subscore(Var:Val) whenever possible(Var:Val).
upper_bound   +=   subscore(Var) whenever is_var(Var).
score         min= upper_bound.
```

Then in Figure 12, **score** is reduced to the best score actually achieved by any child:

```
score             min= best_child_score.
best_child_score max= child(nextvar:Val).score.
```

such as A$^*$ or iterative deepening will often outperform the pure depth-first DPLL strategy. All these strategies can be proved correct from the form of the Dyna program, so a Dyna query engine is free to adopt them.[32]

**Local Search and Sampling.** While the search tree constructed above was exhaustive, a similar approach can be used for heuristic sequential search strategies: greedy local search, stochastic local search, particle filtering, genetic algorithms, beam search, and survey-inspired decimation. Each configuration considered at time `T` can be described by a dynabase that extends a configuration from time `T-1` with some modifications. As with our arc consistency example, rules in the dynabase will automatically compute any *consequences* of these modifications. Thus, they helpfully update any intensional data, including the score of the configuration and the set of available next moves.

The same remarks apply to Monte Carlo *sampling* methods such as Gibbs sampling and Metropolis-Hastings, which are popular for Bayesian learning and inference. Modifications at time `T` are now randomly sampled from a move distribution computed at time `T-1`. Again, the consequences are automatically computed; this updates the move distribution and any aggregate sample statistics.

### 3.2   Proofs and Proof Forests

It is useful to connect Dyna, whose items have weights or values, to the traditional notion of proofs in unweighted logic programming.

Datalog can be regarded as defining **proof trees**. Figures 13a–13b show a collection of simple inference rules (i.e., a **program**) and two proof trees that can be constructed from them. As a more meaningful example, Figures 14–15 show inference rules for context-free CKY parsing (unweighted versions of the rules in Figure 8) and two proof trees that can be constructed using them.[33] These proof trees are *isomorphic* to the parse trees in Figure 16. In other words, a parser is really trying to prove that the input string can be generated by the grammar. By exploring the proof trees, we can see the useful hidden derivational structures that record how the string could have been generated, i.e., the possible parses.[34]

A Datalog program may specify a great many proof trees, but thanks to shared substructure, the entire collection may be represented as a **packed forest**. The

---

[32] For example, it is easy to see that `upper_bound` at each node $n$ (once it has converged) is indeed an upper bound on the score of the node (so can be used as an admissible heuristic for A$^*$). It can further be proved that as long as this bound is smaller than the current value of `best_child_score` at an ancestor of $n$ whose `score` was queried, then exploring the children of $n$ further cannot affect the query result.

[33] To obtain the CKY proof trees, we must add facts that specify the words and grammar rules. That is, we extend the CKY program with the extensional input.

[34] The mapping from proof trees (**derivation trees**) to syntactic parse trees (**derived trees**) is generally deterministic but is not always as transparent as shown here. For example, a semantics-preserving transformation of the Dyna program [47,21,36] would change the derivation trees but not the derived trees.

hypergraph in Figure 13c shows the packed forest of *all* proofs licensed by the program in Figure 13a. Some vertices here have multiple incoming hyperedges, indicating that some items can be proved in multiple ways. The number of proofs therefore explodes combinatorially with the in-degree of the vertices.[35] In fact, the forest in Figure 13c, being cyclic, contains *infinitely* many proof trees for $b$. Even an acylic forest may contain a number of proof trees that is *exponential* in the size of the hypergraph.

Indeed, a Datalog program can be regarded simply as a finite specification of a proof forest. If the rules in the program do not contain variables, then the program is actually isomorphic to the proof forest, with the items corresponding to nodes and the rules corresponding to hyperedges. Rules with variables, however, give rise to infinitely many nodes (not merely infinitely many proofs).

### 3.3    From Logical Proofs to Generalized Circuits

To get a view of what Dyna is doing, we now augment our proof forests to allow items (vertices) to have values (Figure 13e). This yields what we will call **generalized circuits**. Like an arithmetic (or boolean) circuit, a generalized circuit is a directed graph in which the value at each node $\alpha$ is a specified function of the values at the 0 or more nodes that point to $\alpha$. Finding a consistent solution to these equations (or enough of one to answer particular value queries) is challenging and not always possible, since Dyna makes it possible to define circuits that are cyclic and/or infinite, including infinite fan-in or fan-out from some nodes. (Arithmetic circuits as traditionally defined must be finite and acyclic.)

We emphasize that our generalized circuits are different from weighted proof forests, which attach weights to the individual proof trees of an item and then combine those to get the item's weight. In particular, the common setup of **semiring-weighted deduction** is a special case of weighted proof forests that is strictly less general than our circuits. In semiring-weighted deduction [30], the weight of each proof tree is a product of weights of the individual rules or facts in the tree. The weight of an item is the sum of the weights of all its proofs. It is required that the chosen product operation $\otimes$ distributes over the chosen sum operation $\oplus$, so that the weights form a **semiring** under these operations. This distributive property is what makes it possible to sum over the exponentially many proofs using a compact generalized circuit like Figure 8 (the inside algorithm) that is isomorphic to the proof forest and computes the weight of all items at once.

Our original prototype of Dyna was in fact limited to semiring-weighted deduction (which is indeed quite useful in parsing and related applications). Each program chose a single semiring $(\oplus, \otimes)$; each rule in the program had to multiply its antecedent values with $\otimes$ and aggregate these products using $\oplus=$.

However, notice that most of our useful AI examples in §3.1 actually fall outside this form. They mix several aggregation operators within a program,

---

[35] Although $a$ has only one incoming edge, it has two proof trees, one in which $p$ is proved from $y$ and the other (shown in Figure 13b) in which $p$ is proved from $z$.

$$\frac{x \quad p}{a} \qquad \frac{p}{b} \qquad \frac{b \quad f}{b}$$

$$\frac{y}{p} \qquad \frac{z}{p} \qquad \overline{f}$$

$$\overline{x} \qquad \overline{y} \qquad \overline{z}$$

```
a :- x, p.
b :- p.
b :- b, f.
p :- y.
p :- z.
f.
x.
y.
z.
```

**(a)** A set of inference rules, and their encoding in Datalog. Axioms are written as inference rules with no antecedents.

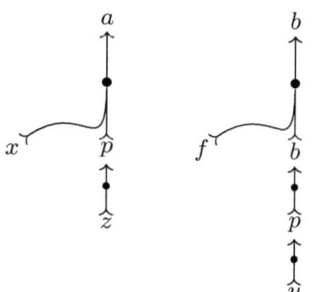

**(b)** Two proof trees using these rules. When an item is proved by an inference rule from 0 or more antecedent items, its vertex has an incoming hyperedge from its antecedents' vertices. Hyperedges with 0 antecedents (to $f, x, y, z$) are not drawn.

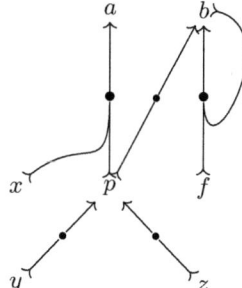

```
a += x + p.
b += p.
b += b / f.
p *= y.
p *= z.
f = 4.
x = 1.
y = 2.
z = 3.
```

**(c)** The proof forest containing all possible proofs. In contrast, each hypergraph in 13b shows only a single proof from this forest, with each copy of an item selecting only a single incoming hyperedge from the forest, and cycles from the forest unrolled to a finite depth.

**(d)** A set of numeric recurrence relations that are analogous to the unweighted inference rule in Figure 13a. We use Dyna's syntax here.

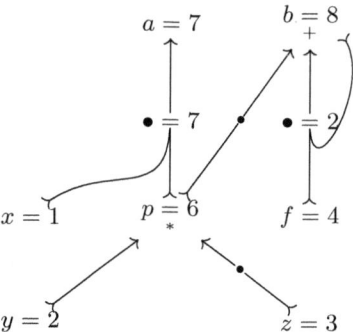

**(e)** A generalized arithmetic circuit with the same shape as the proof forest in Figure 13c. The weight labellings are consistent with 13d. Each node (including the • nodes) is computed from its predecessors.

**Fig. 13.** Some examples of proof trees and proof forests, using hypergraphs (equivalently, AND-OR graphs). Named nodes in the graphs represent items, and • nodes represent intermediate expressions.

$$\frac{{}_iw_j \quad X \to w}{{}_iX_j} \qquad \frac{{}_iY_j \quad {}_jZ_k \quad X \to Y\,Z}{{}_iX_k}$$

**Fig. 14.** The two proof rules necessary to support context-free grammars with unary productions and binary rewrites. $w$ denotes a word from the input sentence and $X$ a symbol of the grammar. Subscripts denote the object's span (which part of the sentence they cover).

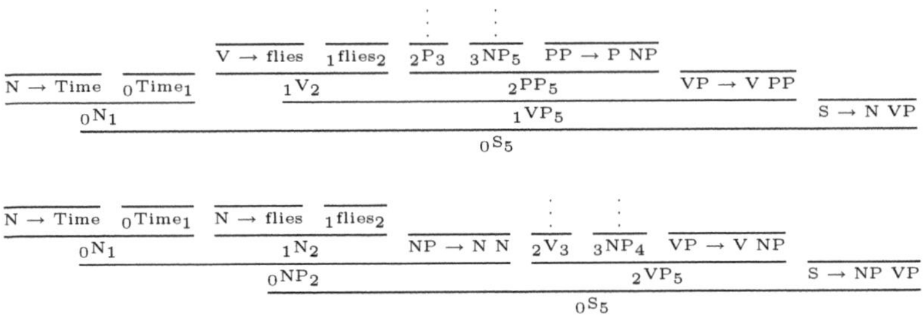

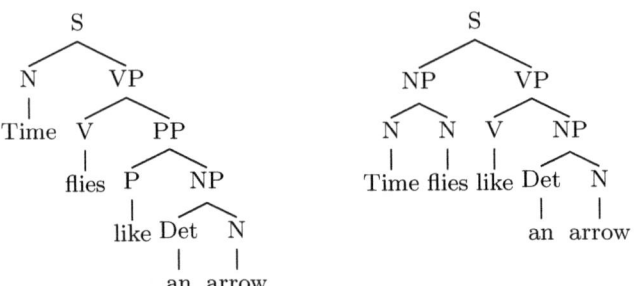

**Fig. 15.** Two example proofs that "Time flies like an arrow." is an English sentence, using the rules in Figure 14. This is traditional notation, but the hypergraphs of Figure 13 are more flexible because they would be able to show reuse of subgoals within a single proof, as well as making it possible to show packed forests of multiple proofs with shared substructure, as in Figure 13c.

**Fig. 16.** Two example parse trees of the sentence "Time flies like an arrow" [40]. These are isomorphic to the proofs in Figure 15 (upside down) and correspond to different meanings of the sentence. The first conveys information about how time passes; the second tree says that flies of a certain species ("time flies") are fond of an arrow.

sometimes including non-commutative aggregators like :=, and it is sometimes important that they define the aggregation of 0 items to be null, rather than requiring the aggregator to have an identity element and using that element. They also use additional non-linear operations like division and exponentiation.

As a result, it is not possible to regard each of our AI examples as simply an efficient way to sum over exponentially many proofs of each output item. For example, because of the sigmoid function in Figure 2, the distributive property from semiring-weighted programs like Figure 8 does not apply there. One *cannot* regard the activation value of an output node in a neural network as a sum over the values of many individual proofs of that output node.[36] That is, a generalized circuit does not necessarily fall apart into disjoint trees the way that a weighted forest does. Rather, the computations are tangled together. In the neural network example, computing intermediate sums at the hidden nodes is important not only for dynamic programming efficiency (as it is in the semiring-weighted program of Figure 8) but also for correctness. The sigmoid function at each node really does need to apply to the sum, not to each summand individually.

We remark that even generalized circuits are not a convenient representation for all Dyna programs. The rule `f(0) += g(1)` generates a single edge in a generalized circuit. However, the rule `f(start) += g(end)`, where `start` and `end` are evaluated, would generate edges to `f`$(x)$ (for *every* $x$ that is a possible value of `start`) from `start`, `end`, and `g`$(y)$ (for *every* $y$ that is a possible value of `end`). Typically this leads to infinitely many edges, only one of which is actually "active" in a given solution to the program.

Despite all this freedom, Dyna circuits remain circuits, and do not seem to present the difficulties of arbitrary systems of equations. A Dyna program cannot impose fiendish constraints such as $x^3 + y^3 = z^3$. (Recall that Fermat's Last Theorem says that there are no postive integer solutions.) Rather, each equation in a Dyna system constrains a *single* item to equal some function of the items in the program. (This arises from Dyna's use of single-headed rules, similar to Horn clauses.) Furthermore, every item has exactly one "defining constraint" of this sort (obtained by aggregating across multiple rules).[37] So one cannot formulate $x^3 + y^3 = z^3$ by writing $u = x^3 + y^3$ and $u = z^3$ (which would give two defining constraints). Nor can one formulate it by writing $s = s + (x^3 + y^3 - z^3)$, a legal Dyna program that might appear to imply $x^3 + y^3 - z^3 = 0$, but whose unique solution is actually that $x, y, z, s$ are all null, since each of $x, y, z$ (having no defining rules) has a defining constraint that it is the aggregation of 0 aggregands.

# 4    Practical AI and Logic Programming

Given an applied AI problem, one would like to experiment with a broad range of models, exact or approximate inference algorithms, decision procedures, training procedures for the model parameters and system heuristics, and storage and execution plans. One must also experiment when developing new general methods.

Dyna supports the common computational core for all this—mechanisms for maintaining a possibly infinite and possibly cyclic network of related items that

---

[36] Each proof of $o_1$ in Figure 1 would be a separate path of length 2, from some input node through some hidden node to $o_1$.

[37] As mentioned earlier, this generalizes the completion semantics of [12], which treats a logic program as defining each boolean item with an "if and only if" constraint.

are named by structured terms. Its job is to store and index an item's value, to query for related items and aggregate their values (including planning of complex queries), to maintain the item's value and propagate changes to related items, and to back-propagate gradient information.

In this section, we expand on our argument from §1 that a fast and scalable implementation of Dyna would be of *practical* use to the AI community. The full version of this paper [22] gives a more detailed argument, with many citations as well an informal survey of current code and data size.

### 4.1    What's Wrong with Current AI Practices

Current AI practices, especially in our target area of natural-language processing and machine learning, suffer from a large distance between specification and implementation. Typical specifications are a handful of recurrence relations (though not as short as the examples in this paper). Creative graduate students can easily dream up innovative systems at the specification level. Implementations, however, are typically imperative and by necessity include storage and inference code.

**Large Extensional Data.** Modern statistical methods mine large corpora of data and produce sizable models. It is not atypical to process billions of words and extract models with millions of constants and hundreds of millions of relations between those constants.

Knowledge bases and information integration pose additional problems of scale. As statistical methods gain popularity in other computational fields, the large-data problem spreads. Storage and indexing structures are becoming extremely relevant, as are approximation and streaming techniques.

**Large Intensional Effort.** As we have seen, even when extensional data is small, modern AI systems often have large computations over intermediate quantities. For many algorithms, the (weighted) proof forests may be exponentially or unboundedly large. Here, efficient inference algorithms, prioritization, and query planning become critical for managing execution time.

Modern AI academic research systems consist of large bodies of imperative code (20,000–100,000 lines), specialized for the purpose at hand. Regardless of programmer intent, there is little cross-system code reuse. Some researchers have aimed to develop reusable code libraries (known as toolkits) to support common development patterns. However, even the best and most flexible of these toolkits are themselves large, and invariably are not general enough for all purposes.[38]

**Uncaught Bugs.** The size of these coding efforts is not only a barrier to entry, to learning, and to progress, but also likely affects correctness. The potential for uncaught bugs was recognized early in statistical AI. Statistical AI systems have many moving parts, and tend to produce some kind of quantitative result that is used to evaluate the method. The results are not expected to be perfect,

---

[38] See the full version of this paper [22] for discussion of an example, and for the code sizes of some AI systems and toolkits.

since the problems are inherently hard and the statistical models usually cannot achieve human-level performance even at their best. This makes it very difficult to detect errors. Methods that appear to be producing "reasonable" results sometimes turn out to work even better (and occasionally worse) when bugs in the implementation are later noticed and fixed.

**Diverse Data Resources.** The AI community is distributed over many geographic locations, and many AI researchers produce data for others to share. The difficulty in using this vast sea of resources is that they tend to be provided in idiosyncratic formats. Trying out a new dataset often requires understanding a new encoding scheme, parsing a new file format, and building one's own data structures for random access.

**Diverse Code Resources.** Many AI resources are in the form of code rather than data. It can be very valuable to build on the systems of others, and there are principled ways to do so. At present, however, software engineering considerations strongly discourage any deep integration of systems that were built in different labs. One would like pipelines (of the kind discussed in §3.1) to agree on a common high-quality output and common parameters, but this requires the ability for components to query one another or pass messages to one another [28]. Similarly, one may wish to combine the strengths of diverse AI systems that are attempting the same task [35]. A recently emerging theme, therefore, is the development of principled methods for coordinating the work of multiple combinatorial algorithms. See references in the full version of this paper [22].

**Ad Hoc Experimental Management.** AI researchers spend considerable time managing computational experiments. It is usual to compare multiple systems, compare variants of a system, tune system parameters, graph performance across different types and amounts of data, and so forth. Common practice is to run programs at the Unix command line and to store results in files, perhaps writing scripts to manage the process. Sometimes one keeps intermediate results in files for reuse or manual analysis. It can be difficult to keep all the files organized, up to date, and track their provenance [7].

## 4.2 Declarative Programming to the Rescue

The above problems are intensifying as AI research grows in size, scope, and sophistication. They have motivated our attempt to design a unified declarative solution that hides some of the complexity. We would like it to be easy again to simply try out good ideas!

Promising declarative languages based on Datalog have recently been built for domains such as sensor networks [43] and business data analytics [41,42].

Why does a declarative approach fit for AI as well? We believe the business of AI is deriving hypotheses and conclusions from data (as discussed in a section of the full version of this paper [22]). These are fundamentally declarative problems: *what* to conclude can be specified without any commitment to *how* to conclude it, e.g., the order of computation. The Dyna approach has something to contribute toward solving each of the challenges of the previous section:

*Large Extensional Data.* We expect that most access by AI programs to large extensional data stores could be supported by traditional on-disk database technology, such as B-trees, index structures, and standard query planning methods. AI programs can automatically exploit this technology if they are written in a Datalog-derived language with an appropriate implementation.

*Large Intensional Effort.* The computational load of AI programs such as those in §3.1 consists mainly of database queries and updates. Dyna provides an executable language for specifying these algorithms, making them concise enough to publish within a paper.

Our hope is that the details left unspecified in these concise programs—the storage and inference policies—can be efficiently handled in a modular, reusable way across problems, eventually with automatic optimization and performance tuning. Even basic strategies like those in §2.6 sometimes correspond closely to current practice, and are often asymptotically optimal [45]. We are deeply interested in systematizing existing tricks of the trade and making them reusable across problems,[39] as well as pushing in new directions (§1.3).

*Quality Control.* Smaller programs should have fewer bugs. We also expect that Dyna will allow some attractive paradigms for inspecting and debugging what a system is doing, as discussed in a section of the full version of this paper [22].

*Diverse Data Resources.* We hope that dynabases can provide a kind of natural interchange format for data resources. They allow flexible representation of typed, structured data, and Dyna offers an attractive query language that can be integrated directly into arbitrary computations. It is conceptually straightforward to convert existing data resources into collections of Dyna facts that can be stored and queried as in Datalog.

*Diverse Code Resources.* Dynabases are a useful format for code resources as well. We do not claim that wrapping Java code (for example) in a dynabase interface will improve its API. However, computational resources that are natively written in the Dyna language do have advantages as components of larger AI systems. First, they can more easily expose their internal hypotheses to be flexibly queried and influenced by another component. Second, query optimization can take place across the dynabase boundary, as can automatic differentiation. Third, we suspect that Dyna programs are simply easier for third parties to understand and modify manually when necessary. They can also be manipulated and combined by program transformation; for example, [13] shows how to combine two Dyna programs into a product-of-experts model.

*Ad Hoc Experimental Management.* Dyna suggests an elegant solution to running collections of experiments. Figure 11b gives a hint of how one could create a parametric family of dynabases that vary input data, training data, experimental parameters, and even the models and algorithms. The dynabases are named by

---

[39] See additional discussion in the full version of this paper [22].

structured terms. Each dynabase holds the results of some experiment, including all intermediate computations, and can track the provenance of all computations (by making the hyperedges of proof forests visible as items). Some computations would be automatically shared across related dynabases.

Using dynabases to store experimental results is quite flexible, since dynabases can be structured and nested, and since the Dyna language can be used to query, aggregate, analyze, and otherwise explore their contents.

In principle, this collection of dynabases may be infinite, representing an infinite variety of parameter settings. However, the contents of a dynabase would be materialized only when queried. Which materialized intermediate and final results are stored for later use, versus being discarded and recreated on demand, would depend on the dynabase's chaining and memoization policies,[40] as declared by the user or chosen by the system to balance storage, latency, and total runtime.

## 4.3   Uses of Change Propagation in AI

Recall that dynabases implement *dynamic algorithms*: their intensional items update automatically in response to changes in their extensional input. This corresponds to "view maintenance" in databases [34], and to "self-adjusting computation" [1] in functional languages.

We observe that this kind of **change propagation** is widely useful in AI algorithms. Internally, many algorithms simply propagate changes until convergence (see the discussion of message passing in §3.1). In addition, AI systems frequently experiment with slight variants of their parameters or inputs for training, validation, or search.

**Optimization of Continuous or Discrete Parameters.** Training a data-driven system typically runs the system on a fixed set of training examples. It explores different parameter settings in order to maximize an objective measure of system performance. A change to an individual parameter may affect relatively few of the training examples. Similarly, adding or removing parameters ("feature selection") may require only incremental changes to feature extractors, automata, or grammars. The ability to quickly recompute the objective function in response to such small changes can significantly speed up training [51].

*k*-**Fold Cross Validation.** The dual situation occurs when the parameters are held fixed and the training data are varied. Systems often use *cross-validation* to tune some high-level parameters of a model. For example, a language model is a probability distribution over the strings of a language, and is usually trained on as much data as possible. "Smoothing parameters" that affect how much probability mass is reserved for events that have not been seen in the training data (cf. Figure 4). To evaluate a particular choice of smoothing parameters, cross-validation partitions the available training data into $k$ "folds," and evaluates the method's performance on *each* fold when the language model is trained on the other $k - 1$ folds. This requires training $k$ different language models. However, it

---

[40] Additional details may be found in a section of the full version of this paper [22].

should not be necessary to build each model from scratch. Rather, one can train a master model on the full dataset, and then create variants by removing each fold in turn. This removal should not require recomputing all counts and probabilities of the model, particularly when $k$ is large. For example, "leave-one-out" training takes each sentence to be a separate fold.

**Search and Sampling.** §3.1 already described how change propagation was useful in backtracking search, local search, and sampling. In all of these cases, some tiny change is made to the configuration of the system, and all the consequences must be computed. For example, in the DPLL backtracking search of Figure 12, constraining a single additional variable may have either small or large effects on reducing the possibilities for other variables, thanks to the arc consistency rules.

**Control and Streaming-Data Systems.** Systems that process real-world data have obvious reasons for their inputs to change: time passes and more data is fed in. Monitoring the results is why commercial database engines such as Oracle have begun to support continuous queries, where the caller is continually notified of any changes to the query result. The Dyna version of continuous queries is discussed in a section of the full version of this paper [22]. Applications include business intelligence (e.g., LogicBlox [41]); stream processing for algorithmic equities trading (e.g., DBToaster [2]); user interfaces (e.g., Dynasty [24] and Fruit [16]); declarative animation (e.g., Fran [25]); query planners and optimizers (see the discussion in the full paper); and even (incremental) compilers [9].

In an AI system—for example, medical decision support—sensors may continuously gather information from the world, users may state new facts or needs, and information integration may keep track of many large, evolving datasets at other locations. We would like a system to absorb such changes and draw conclusions about the state of the world. Furthermore, it should draw conclusions about desirable actions—actions such as notifying a human user of significant changes, controlling physical actuators, seeking more information, or carrying out more intensive computation. A running process can monitor these recommended actions and carry them out.

# 5   Conclusion

We have described our work towards a general-purpose weighted logic programming language that is powerful enough to address the needs of statistical AI. Our claim is that modern AI systems can be cleanly specified using such a language, and that much of the implementation burden can be handled by general mechanisms related to logical deduction, database queries, and change propagation. In our own research in natural language processing, we have found a simple prototype of the language [23] to be very useful, enabling us to try out a range of ideas that we otherwise would have rejected as too time-consuming. The new version aims to support a greater variety of execution strategies across a broader range of programs, including the example programs we have illustrated here.

*Note:* Throughout this book chapter, we have referred to additional material in the full version [22]. The full version also includes sections that sketch execution strategies; how dynabases interact with the world (the form of queries/results/updates, the dynabase API, mode checking, foreign dynabases, debugging); and formal semantics.

# References

1. Acar, U.A., Ley-Wild, R.: Self-adjusting computation with Delta ML. In: Koopman, P.W.M., Plasmeijer, R., Swierstra, S.D. (eds.) AFP 2008. LNCS, vol. 5832, pp. 1–38. Springer, Heidelberg (2009)
2. Ahmad, Y., Koch, C.: DBToaster: A SQL compiler for high-performance delta processing in main-memory databases. In: Proc. of VLDB, pp. 1566–1569 (2009)
3. Allauzen, C., Riley, M., Schalkwyk, J., Skut, W., Mohri, M.: OpenFST: A general and efficient weighted finite-state transducer library. In: Holub, J., Žďárek, J. (eds.) CIAA 2007. LNCS, vol. 4783, pp. 11–23. Springer, Heidelberg (2007)
4. Apt, K.R., Blair, H.A., Walker, A.: Towards a theory of declarative knowledge. In: Minker, J. (ed.) Foundations of Deductive Databases and Logic Programming, ch. 2. Morgan Kaufmann, San Francisco (1988)
5. Berg-Kirkpatrick, T., Bouchard-Côté, A., DeNero, J., Klein, D.: Painless unsupervised learning with features. In: Proc. of NAACL, pp. 582–590. ACL (2010)
6. Bidoit, N., Hull, R.: Minimalism, justification and non-monotonicity in deductive databases. Journal of Computer and System Sciences 38(2), 290–325 (1989)
7. Breck, E.: zymake: A computational workflow system for machine learning and natural language processing. In: Software Engineering, Testing, and Quality Assurance for Natural Language Processing, SETQA-NLP 2008, pp. 5–13. ACL (2008)
8. Brodie, M.L.: Future Intelligent Information Systems: AI and Database Technologies Working Together. Morgan Kaufmann, San Francisco (1988)
9. Burstall, R.M., Collins, J.S., Popplestone, R.J.: Programming in POP-2. Edinburgh University Press, Edinburgh (1971)
10. Ceri, S., Gottlob, G., Tanca, L.: What you always wanted to know about datalog (and never dared to ask). IEEE Transactions on Knowledge and Data Engineering 1, 146–166 (1989)
11. Ceri, S., Gottlob, G., Tanca, L.: Logic Programming and Databases. Springer, Heidelberg (1990)
12. Clark, K.L.: Negation as failure. In: Gallaire, H., Minker, J. (eds.) Logic and Data Bases, pp. 293–322. Plenum, New York (1978)
13. Cohen, S.B., Simmons, R.J., Smith, N.A.: Products of weighted logic programs. Theory and Practice of Logic Programming (2010)
14. Cohen, S., Nutt, W., Serebrenik, A.: Algorithms for rewriting aggregate queries using views. In: Masunaga, Y., Thalheim, B., Štuller, J., Pokorný, J. (eds.) ADBIS 2000 and DASFAA 2000. LNCS, vol. 1884, pp. 65–78. Springer, Heidelberg (2000)
15. Cortes, C., Vapnik, V.: Support-vector networks. Machine Learning 20(3), 273–297 (1995)
16. Courtney, A., Elliott, C.: Genuinely functional user interfaces. In: 2001 Haskell Workshop (2001)
17. The functional logic language Curry, http://www.informatik.uni-kiel.de/~curry/

18. Davis, M., Logemann, G., Loveland, D.: A machine program for theorem-proving. Communications of the ACM 5(7), 394–397 (1962)
19. Dechter, R.: Constraint Processing. Morgan Kaufmann, San Francisco (2003)
20. Eisner, J.: Parameter estimation for probabilistic finite-state transducers. In: Proc. of ACL, pp. 1–8 (2002)
21. Eisner, J., Blatz, J.: Program transformations for optimization of parsing algorithms and other weighted logic programs. In: Wintner, S. (ed.) Proc. of FG 2006: The 11th Conference on Formal Grammar, pp. 45–85. CSLI Publications, Stanford (2007)
22. Eisner, J., Filardo, N.W.: Dyna: Extending Datalog for modern AI (full version). Tech. rep., Johns Hopkins University (2011); Extended version of the present paper, http://dyna.org/Publications
23. Eisner, J., Goldlust, E., Smith, N.A.: Compiling comp ling: Weighted dynamic programming and the Dyna language. In: Proc. of HLT-EMNLP, pp. 281–290. Association for Computational Linguistics (2005)
24. Eisner, J., Kornbluh, M., Woodhull, G., Buse, R., Huang, S., Michael, C., Shafer, G.: Visual navigation through large directed graphs and hypergraphs. In: Proc. of IEEE InfoVis, Poster/Demo Session, pp. 116–117 (2006)
25. Elliott, C., Hudak, P.: Functional reactive animation. In: International Conference on Functional Programming (1997)
26. Felzenszwalb, P.F., McAllester, D.: The generalized A* architecture. J. Artif. Int. Res. 29(1), 153–190 (2007)
27. Fidler, S., Boben, M., Leonardis, A.: Learning hierarchical compositional representations of object structure. In: Dickinson, S., Leonardis, A., Schiele, B., Tarr, M.J. (eds.) Object Categorization: Computer and Human Vision Perspectives, Cambridge University Press, Cambridge (2009)
28. Finkel, J.R., Grenager, T., Manning, C.: Incorporating non-local information into information extraction systems by Gibbs sampling. In: Proc. of ACL, pp. 363–370. ACL (2005)
29. Gelfond, M., Lifschitz, V.: The stable model semantics for logic programming. In: Proc. of the 5th International Conference and Symposium Logic Programming, pp. 1070–1080 (1988)
30. Goodman, J.: Semiring parsing. Computational Linguistics 25(4), 573–605 (1999)
31. Green, T.J., Karvounarakis, G., Tannen, V.: Provenance semirings. In: Proc. of PODS, pp. 31–40 (2007)
32. Griewank, A., Corliss, G. (eds.): Automatic Differentiation of Algorithms. SIAM, Philadelphia (1991)
33. Guo, H.-F., Gupta, G.: Simplifying dynamic programming via tabling. In: Jayaraman, B. (ed.) PADL 2004. LNCS, vol. 3057, pp. 163–177. Springer, Heidelberg (2004)
34. Gupta, A., Mumick, I.S.: Maintenance of materialized views: Problems, techniques, and applications. IEEE Data Eng. Bull. 18(2), 3–18 (1995)
35. Hinton, G.: Products of experts. In: Proc. of ICANN, vol. 1, pp. 1–6 (1999)
36. Johnson, M.: Transforming projective bilexical dependency grammars into efficiently-parsable CFGs with unfold-fold. In: Proc. of ACL, pp. 168–175 (2007)
37. Kemp, D.B., Stuckey, P.J.: Semantics of logic programs with aggregates. In: Proc. of the International Logic Programming Symposium, pp. 338–401 (1991)
38. Kifer, M., Subrahmanian, V.S.: Theory of generalized annotated logic programming and its applications. Journal of Logic Programming 12(4), 335–368 (1992)
39. Klein, D., Manning, C.D.: A* parsing: Fast exact Viterbi parse selection. In: Proc. of HLT-NAACL (2003)

40. Kline, M.: Mathematics in the modern world; readings from Scientific American. With introductions by Morris Kline. W.H. Freeman, San Francisco (1968)
41. LogicBlox: Datalog for enterprise applications: from industrial applications to research (2010), http://www.logicblox.com/research/presentations/arefdatalog20.pdf, presented by Molham Aref at Datalog 2.0 Workshop
42. LogicBlox: Modular and reusable Datalog (2010), http://www.logicblox.com/research/presentations/morebloxdatalog20.pdf, presented by Shan Shan Huang at Datalog 2.0 Workshop
43. Loo, B.T., Condie, T., Garofalakis, M.N., Gay, D.E., Hellerstein, J.M., Maniatis, P., Ramakrishnan, R., Roscoe, T., Stoica, I.: Declarative networking. Commun. ACM 52(11), 87–95 (2009)
44. Marek, V., Truszczyński, M.: Stable models and an alternative logic programming paradigm. In: Apt, K., Marek, V., Truszczyński, M., Warren, D. (eds.) The Logic Programming Paradigm: A 25-Year Perspective, pp. 375–398. Springer, Heidelberg (1999)
45. McAllester, D.A.: On the complexity analysis of static analyses. J. ACM 49(4), 512–537 (2002)
46. The Mercury Project, http://www.cs.mu.oz.au/research/mercury/index.html
47. Minnen, G.: Magic for filter optimization in dynamic bottom-up processing. In: ACL, pp. 247–254 (1996)
48. Mohr, R., Henderson, T.: Arc and path consistency revised. Artificial Intelligence 28, 225–233 (1986)
49. Mumick, I.S., Pirahesh, H., Ramakrishnan, R.: The magic of duplicates and aggregates. In: Proc. of VLDB, pp. 264–277 (1990)
50. Nádas, A.: On Turing's formula for word probabilities. IEEE Transactions on Acoustics, Speech, and Signal Processing ASSP-33(6), 1414–1416 (1985)
51. Ngai, G., Florian, R.: Transformation-based learning in the fast lane. In: Proc. of NAACL-HLT (2001)
52. van Noord, G., Gerdemann, D.: Finite state transducers with predicates and identities. Grammars 4(3) (2001)
53. Overton, D.: Precise and Expressive Mode Systems for Typed Logic Programming Languages. Ph.D. thesis, University of Melbourne (2003)
54. Pelov, N.: Semantics of Logic Programs With Aggregates. Ph.D. thesis, Katholieke Universiteit Leuven (2004)
55. Ramakrishnan, R., Srivastava, D., Sudarshan, S., Seshadri, P.: The coral deductive system. The VLDB Journal 3(2), 161–210 (1994); Special Issue on Prototypes of Deductive Database Systems
56. Ramamohanarao, K.: Special issue on prototypes of deductive database systems. VLDB 3(2) (1994)
57. Richardson, M., Domingos, P.: Markov logic networks. Machine Learning 62(1-2), 107–136 (2006)
58. Ross, K.A., Sagiv, Y.: Monotonic aggregation in deductive databases. In: Proc. of PODS, pp. 114–126 (1992)
59. Schmid, H., Rooth, M.: Parse forest computation of expected governors. In: Proc. of ACL (2001)
60. Shieber, S.M., Schabes, Y., Pereira, F.: Principles and implementation of deductive parsing. Journal of Logic Programming 24(1-2), 3–36 (1995)
61. Singla, P., Domingos, P.: Lifted first-order belief propagation. In: Proc. of AAAI, pp. 1094–1099. AAAI Press, Menlo Park (2008)
62. Van Emden, M.H., Kowalski, R.A.: The semantics of predicate logic as a programming language. JACM 23(4), 733–742 (1976)

63. Van Gelder, A., Ross, K.A., Schlipf, J.S.: The well-founded semantics for general logic programs. Journal of the ACM 38(3), 620–650 (1991)
64. Williams, R., Zipser, D.: A learning algorithm for continually running fully recurrent neural networks. Neural Computation 1(2), 270–280 (1989)
65. XSB, http://xsb.sourceforge.net/
66. Yedidia, J.S., Freeman, W.T., Weiss, Y.: Understanding belief propagation and its generalizations. In: Exploring Artificial Intelligence in the New Millennium, ch. 8. Science & Technology Books (2003)
67. Younger, D.H.: Recognition and parsing of context-free languages in time $n^3$. Information and Control 10(2), 189–208 (1967)
68. Zhang, M., Zhang, H., Li, H.: Convolution kernel over packed parse forest. In: Proc. of ACL, pp. 875–885 (2010)
69. Zhu, S.C., Mumford, D.: A stochastic grammar of images. Foundations and Trends in Computer Graphics and Vision 2(4), 259–362 (2006)
70. Zukowski, U., Freitag, B.: The deductive database system *LOLA*. In: Fuhrbach, U., Dix, J., Nerode, A. (eds.) LPNMR 1997. LNCS (LNAI), vol. 1265, pp. 375–386. Springer, Heidelberg (1997)

# Datalog for the Web 2.0: The Case of Social Network Data Management*

Matteo Magnani[1] and Danilo Montesi[2]

Dept. of Computer Science,
University of Bologna
`magnanim@cs.unibo.it`
[2] Dept. of Computer Science,
University of Bologna
`montesi@cs.unibo.it`

**Abstract.** The clean representation of recursive queries enabled by Datalog makes it a strong candidate to be used as the reference query language for social network data management. In this extended abstract we try to identify the capabilities that should be provided by a language for the manipulation of social data.

## 1 Introduction

Social Network Sites are among the most relevant places where information is created, exchanged and transformed, as witnessed by more than 500.000.000 users on FaceBook (July 2010), more than 350.000.000 on QQ[1] (January 2009), an increasing number of users on Twitter and by their activity during events and campaigns like the terror attack in Mumbai in 2008 or the so-called Twitter revolution in Iran in 2009 [1,2].

Social data are usually stored into relational databases — MySQL, in the case of FaceBook, containing large amounts of information with relevant potential applications: from practical areas like politics and marketing to more theoretical fields like social sciences and psychology. The clean representation of recursive queries enabled by Datalog makes it a strong candidate to be used as the reference query language for these applications. However, social data present many complex features and social query languages should satisfy all the corresponding requirements.

In this extended abstract we try to identify the capabilities that should be provided by a language for the manipulation of modern social data (that we call SocQL), and discuss which features are already provided by Datalog and which extensions are required. It is in fact fundamental for a database query language to be motivated by applications, to move from academia to real applications, and the Web 2.0 within the specific context of social databases seems to be a

---

* This work has been partially funded by Telecom Italia.
[1] The largest Social Network Site in China now reaching more than 100.000.000 users simultaneously on-line.

O. de Moor et al. (Eds.): Datalog 2010, LNCS 6702, pp. 221–224, 2011.

potential candidate to test the applicability of a recursive language to a real and complex scenario.

To this aim, we have extracted a Large Social Database (LSD) from a popular Social Network Site and studied its features to identify query capabilities required by this complex kind of data that should be provided by a Datalog-based system in order to be practically usable in this context.

The social data has been extracted from Friendfeed, a well known SNS recently acquired by FaceBook, which offers features that can be associated both to Twitter (i.e. providing status updates) and FaceBook (i.e., creating complex conversations). In the literature the definition of social query languages has been addressed also with regard to non-conversational social sites [3,4], and Friendfeed has already been the subject of several studies about information diffusion and retrieval [5,6,7,8]. A first example of Datalog-based social query language is described in [9].

## 2   Data Anatomy

The analysis presented in this extended abstract is based on the study of a real LSD extracted by monitoring the Friendfeed SNS. This database is downloadable at the project website (http://larica.uniurb.it/sigsna).

Despite its apparent relational structure, the dataset under analysis contains a mixture of **structured**, **semi-structured** and **unstructured** data, requiring a complex data model. In particular, several **data graphs** can be identified. If we consider the relationships between users, they induce a directed, labeled, weighted graph where nodes represent users, labels the kind of interaction (subscription/like/comment), weights the strength of the interaction, e.g., the number of comments, with additional text annotations. Considering different labels, we can extract sub-graphs about **active** relationships between users (comments and likes), **passive** relationships (subscriptions) and even **implicit** relationships not directly expressed in the data. For example, when Annie subscribes to John, who subscribed to Susan, Annie may see part of the content of Susan through John's feed, without having a direct subscription to her. Finally, part of the data constitutes *conversation graphs* not directly involving users, but their posting activity (entries and comments), and also in this case we can have implicit arcs[2].

In this last case, nodes of the graph represent short pieces of text (posts). Therefore, in addition to semi-structured data, social databases contain a large amount of **unstructured content** (text and other media) attached to different entities (users and posts).

Part of the data consists of the personal data associated to each user. From our sample it appears that although users are asked to insert much personal information at registration time this is rarely accessible because of privacy settings. Therefore, depending on the required analysis it may be necessary to obtain some derived data not directly present in the database.

---

[2] For instance, the @ symbol followed by a user nickname is used inside text comments to indicate the recipient of the message.

A first way to obtain this data is to perform a joint analysis of all public on-line identities of each user. Finding these identities may be simplified by looking at aggregators, like Friendfeed, where users register their *services* (other internet social accounts) from which data should be imported. In addition, some relevant data may be obtained through information extraction activities. In this case, though, data is associated to a degree of **uncertainty**, which may make data analysis complicated. As an example, consider two relevant attributes that are not present in the original database. Age can be imported from other accounts (which may create inconsistencies) and automatically extracted from the Description attribute, and language can be guessed from the analysis of the user's posts. For a more detailed application of a language identification system to SNS analysis see [5].

As a consequence of the complexity of the data model, querying the Social Data Set under examination requires **recursive graph traversal** operators, **text extraction**, with Information Retrieval capabilities to evaluate the **relevance** of single text items or groups of inter-connected items, counting and other **aggregate operators**, both on nodes and on the amount and strength of arcs. In addition, due to the size and the complexity of the data, it seems to be important for the query language to support data analysis. In fact, typical operations on social data require the extraction of groups of entities without exact a priori knowledge of their features, e.g., clusters of users who posted similar comments or with similar descriptions. In our opinion it is essential that this kind of queries involving data mining algorithms are integrated in a system and query language for complex social data. In the next section we discuss in more detail these requirements with regard to Datalog.

# 3   Requirements for a Social Datalog

In our example social data consist of $10^{6-7}$ records per week. Therefore, it will be probably necessary to build social extensions of Datalog over existing relational systems, providing an efficient architecture to deal with large volumes of data. The structured portion of the data that can be stored using the relational model is already supported by Datalog, and the relevance of graph data can be one of the key motivations behind the adoption of Datalog as a social query language. However, it is necessary to be able to manipulate weights, e.g., indicating the strength of a friendship relationship, according to some model to be defined. Similarly, as we have seen in our example data graph, different arcs should be treated differently depending on their labels. Labels may indicate an arc type, but also contain unstructured text.

With regard to the operations we would like to perform on social data, recursive traversal is easily supported by Datalog and could constitute one of its strengths. In addition, dealing with weighted graphs we may need to compute summary metrics of sub-graphs involving the aggregation of floating point numbers. Moreover, it is important to be able to evaluate aggregate metrics concerning labels: for example, counting all arcs of a given type. Data graphs also contain a lot of unstructured text, therefore queries should necessarily provide Information Retrieval capabilities and should also take the structure of the graph under consideration. All these features should be included in a Datalog-based system.

Finally, being very complex, a social data model contains a lot of information not directly exposed using its data structures but hidden inside them. Therefore, to be able to extract the required information it is often necessary to execute *exploratory* queries, based on data analysis functions such as graph clustering or sub-graph matching.

# References

1. Schectman, J.: Iran's twitter revolution? maybe not yet. Business Week (2009)
2. Boyd, D.: Taken Out of Context: American Teen Sociality in Networked Publics. PhD thesis, University of California-Berkeley, School of Information (2008)
3. Amer-Yahia, S., Lakshmanan, L.V.S., Yu, C.: Socialscope: Enabling information discovery on social content sites. In: CIDR (2009)
4. Amer-Yahia, S., Huang, J., Yu, C.: Jelly: A language for building community-centric information exploration applications. In: ICDE, pp. 1588–1594. IEEE, Los Alamitos (2009)
5. Celli, F., Di Lascio, F.M.L., Magnani, M., Pacelli, B., Rossi, L.: Social network data and practices: the case of friendfeed. In: SBP Conference. LNCS, pp. 346–353. Springer, Berlin (2010)
6. Magnani, M., Montesi, D., Rossi, L.: Information propagation analysis in a social network site. In: ASONAM Conference, pp. 296–300. IEEE Computer Society, Los Alamitos (2010)
7. Magnani, M., Montesi, D., Rossi, L.: Friendfeed breaking news: Death of a public figure. In: IEEE SocialCom, pp. 528–533. IEEE Computer Society, Los Alamitos (2010)
8. Magnani, M., Montesi, D.: Toward conversation retrieval. In: Agosti, M., Esposito, F., Thanos, C. (eds.) Italian Research Conference on Digital Libraries - Revised Selected Papers. CCIS, vol. 91. Springer, Heidelberg (2010)
9. Ronen, R., Shmueli, O.: Evaluating very large datalog queries on social networks. In: EDBT Conference, pp. 577–587. ACM, New York (2009)

# Context Modelling and Context-Aware Querying*
## (Can Datalog Be of Help?)

Giorgio Orsi and Letizia Tanca

Dipartimento di Elettronica e Informazione,
Politecnico di Milano,
Piazza Leonardo da Vinci, 32—20133 Milano, Italy
{orsi,tanca}@elet.polimi.it

**Abstract.** Many interpretations of the notion of context have emerged in various fields and context-aware systems are pervading everyday life, becoming an expanding research field. Context has often a significant impact on the way humans (or machines) act, and on how they interpret things; furthermore, a change in context causes a transformation in the experience that is going to be lived. Accordingly, while the computer science community has initially perceived the context simply as a matter of user time and location, in the last few years this notion has been considered not simply as a state, but as part of a process in which users are involved; thus, sophisticated and general context models and systems have been proposed to support context-aware applications. In this paper we propose a foundational framework for the life-cycle of context-aware system, in which the system design and management activities consider context as an orthogonal, first-class citizen. In doing so, we present a Datalog-based formulation for the definition of context-aware databases.

## 1 Introduction

In a modern information system the content is available at different sources and with different formats. Users are integral parts of numerous applications interacting with service and product providers, governmental organisations, friends and colleagues, as well as sensing and actuation devices [1]. Such extensive information constitutes an unprecedented opportunity for users, but at the same time risks to overwhelm them. In the Workshop on *Using Knowledge in its Context* [2] co-located with IJCAI '93, it was already recognised that "knowledge has a contextual component", and that this component may be of use to "extract and present the relevant chunks of knowledge", thus allowing for information *filtering, focusing and reduction*.

Accordingly, context can contribute to the meaning that must be inferred from the adjacent world, ranging from the references intended for indefinite indications such as "take that" to the shared reference frame of ideas and objects that are suggested by a situation. Context has often a significant impact on the way humans (or machines) act, and on how they interpret things; furthermore, a change in context causes a transformation in the experience that is going to be lived. Thus, context goes beyond immediate

---

* This research has been partially funded by the European Commission, Programme IDEAS-ERC, Project 227977-SMScom.

O. de Moor et al. (Eds.): Datalog 2010, LNCS 6702, pp. 225–244, 2011.

binding of variables to the establishment of a framework for knowledge fruition and communication, possibly based on shared experience.

Many interpretations of the notion of context have emerged in various fields of research like psychology, philosophy, and computer science [3,4,5,6,7]. During the IJCAI '93 workshop it was observed that the contextual component is however seldom dealt with *explicitly*: rather, it is often hard-coded in the application and in the representation of information, and not sufficiently exploited in knowledge processing [2]. At that time, one of the reasons for this state of affairs was obviously in the requirement for context-aware systems of sufficient computational and communication capabilities. However, while the power of computing and communication technology has now improved dramatically even for mobile devices, not much has been done to exploit the notion of context explicitly. According to the same source, not recognising – and thus not seizing the opportunity to exploit – the orthogonality of context modelling w.r.t. modelling the application space (the *object knowledge*) provokes "a gap between what is known and what is done".

*Contributions:* Our research aims at defining a foundational, disciplined framework for the life-cycle of context-aware systems, in which the system design and management activities consider context as a first-class citizen. In this paper, starting from the consideration that the Datalog language is conveniently used to formalise both knowledge and its processing, we attempt a Datalog-based, uniform but orthogonal formulation both of context and of the *object knowledge*. By means of this framework we perform *context-aware information access personalisation*, considered as a set of actions that can appropriately tailor the available information (or more in general, *knowledge*) to each particular user in each particular situation.

*Organisation:* The paper is organised as follows: the next section contains a brief analysis of the work on context-aware systems, presenting the different perspectives context is viewed from in the context-related literature in computer science, and some examples thereof. In Section 3 we introduce our methodological point of view on context-aware system design, followed by a quick overview of the *CDT* [8], the conceptual context-model we rely upon. Then, in Section 4 we show how it is possible to model context meta-data using Datalog and its extensions while its exploitation for data tailoring and query processing is described in Section 5. Finally Section 6 draws some concluding remarks.

*Running Example:* Assume we want to design the data structures for a mobile application (in the style of mOX[1]) that offers a personalised information service about courses and seminars held at Oxford University. Assume the needed information is stored inside a standard relational database whose conceptual (E/R) and logical (relational) schemata are represented in Figure 1. The database stores basic information about *students* and their *enrolments* in *courses* along with basic information about the *professors* that serve as *lecturers* for some course or as *speakers* in some *event* such as *meetings* and *seminars*.

---

[1] http://m.ox.ac.uk

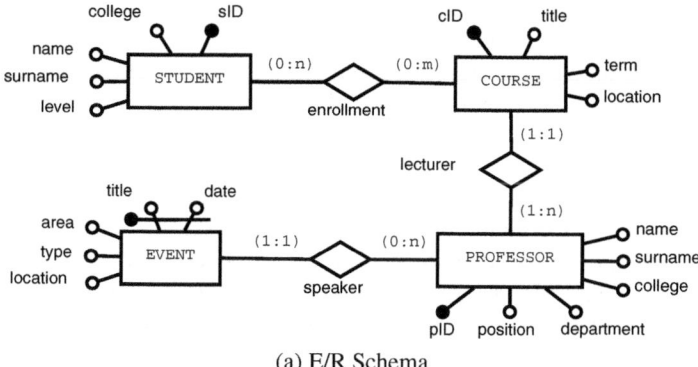

(a) E/R Schema

STUDENT(sID, name, surname, level, college)
COURSE(cID, title, location, term, lecturer)
PROFESSOR(pID, name, surname, position, department, college)
EVENT(title, date, area, type, location, speaker)
ENROLMENT(sID,cID)

(b) Relational Schema

**Fig. 1.** Conceptual and Relational Schemata for the mOX Application

We aim at exploiting Datalog to model the contextual meta-data and to enable context-aware query processing in order to provide the users of the mobile application with personalised information depending on their actual situations.

## 2    Context-Aware Systems' Overview

While, according to the *cognitive-science view*, "context is used to model interactions and situations in a world of infinite breadth, and human behaviour is key in extracting a model" [2], in the subsumed and less ambitious *engineering view* "context is useful for representing and reasoning about a restricted state space within which a problem can be solved". In this work we focus on the latter interpretation.

The computer science community has initially perceived the context simply as a matter of user time and location, thus most context-aware applications offer a notion of context limited to time and location information, which is based on the internal clock of a mobile device and on cellular-network/GPS positioning. Fortunately, in the last few years context is considered not simply as a state, but as part of a process in which users are involved; accordingly, sophisticated and general context-aware applications [9, 10, 11, 12, 13] have been designed. Such applications adopt a context-aware perspective in order to manage:

- **Communication:**
    - capability to adapt content presentation to different channels or to different devices (system communication *with* the users). CC/PP (Composite Capabilities/Preference Profiles) is a W3C recommendation where a profile is a

description of device capabilities and user preferences. Following the CC/PP recommendation, CSCP [14] is a Mobility Portal combining application-spanning media conversion and transcoding with application- specific information filtering. MAIS[2] (Multi Channel Adaptive Information System) has the objective of configuring the software on board of the mobile device, based on presentation, device characteristics and available channel.

- agreement and shared reasoning among peers (communication *among* users or systems). For example, in CoBra [15] an intelligent context broker maintains and manages a shared contextual model on behalf of a community of agents, while [16] provides Web information filtering on a P2P basis.
- building smart environments (the system supports the users' communication *with the environment*). Again, in CoBra an agent-based architecture supports context-aware computing in intelligent spaces, i.e. physical spaces (e.g., living rooms, vehicles, corporate offices and meeting rooms) populated with intelligent systems.

– **Situation-awareness:**
- modelling location and environment aspects (*physical* situation). In CodaMos [17] every device will contain its own context specification with a full description of its provided services, plus pointers to relevant information on the device in its environment.
- modelling what the user is currently doing (*personal* situation). In [18] Activity Theory is used to represent concepts such as roles, rules and tools, which have important impacts on users activities. Activity Theory also maps the relationships amongst the elements that it identifies as having an influence on human activity.
- making the user interaction implicit (*adapting* the information to the user's needs). For instance, QUALEG [19] proposes a unique combination of a global ontology with a dynamic context, for dynamically adapting eGovernment IT tools to a multi-lingual and multi-cultural setting.

– **Managing knowledge chunks:**
- determining the set of application/situation relevant *information* (the *information management* perspective). In [20, 21] information users specify their own current context when requesting data, in order to denote the part that is relevant to their specific situation. The work extends the relational model to deal with context: e.g. an attribute may not exist under some contexts or have different *facets* under different contexts. The approach provides a set of basic operations which extend relational algebra. In [8, 22] context is used as a viewpoint mechanism that takes into account implicit background knowledge to semi-automatically tailor *context-aware views* over a database.
- determining the set of application/situation relevant *services*. [23] proposes efficient context-aware service discovery in pervasive environments. In [24], perceptual processes provide a means to detect and track compositions of entities and to verify relations between them. The design problem is then to determine the appropriate entities (resp. relations) that must be determined (resp. verified) with respect to a task or service to be provided, in a potentially infinite set.

---

[2] http://www.mais-project.it/

- determining the set of application/situation relevant *behaviours*. In [25, 26] an information base is decomposed into (possibly overlapping) subsets, referred to as contexts, which could be recursively contained in other contexts. Each context is assigned one or more owners, authorised to perform *any operation or transaction* on their context. The framework supports context-specific naming and representation of conceptual entities, relativised transaction execution, operations for context construction and manipulation, authorisation mechanisms and change propagation.

As a matter of fact, the lack of a uniform approach for modelling context-related information makes it difficult to clearly understand the requirements that have to be considered when proposing or adopting a context model on the basis of its focus. While [10] presents a survey of literature on the context modelling problem, and introduces a framework useful for analysing context models and to select the most suitable one for a given application, the central issue of this paper is to propose a disciplined framework for the life-cycle of a context-aware system, in which context is explicitly considered and studied as an independent component. Although, with respect to the classification above, our approach is mostly oriented to the *management of knowledge chunks*, we believe that the general view on context-aware system design proposed in the next section can be adopted in each of the broad classes we have described.

## 3    A General Framework for the Design of Context-Aware Systems

The short review above emphasizes, from one viewpoint, the use of the concept of context in a considerably varied set of applications; on the other hand, and just because the applications are so different, it prompts the need for focusing on context modelling independently of the specific application. How context is represented and how the information derived from the context is exploited is fundamental to understand the design issues that must be solved during a specific design task.

Context is, thus, the key meta-knowledge which must be formally defined and whose role becomes essential within the process of application design, which must target two different realms: the reality of interest, captured by the application domain model e.g., by an Entity-Relationship (E/R), and the context meta-knowledge, which is used to reshape the available information (or behaviours) on the particular needs that the destination user is experiencing in each situation.

Note that the above two tracks of context-aware design may be totally independent since no feedback is needed between them until the final phase of the design process, when the contexts are associated with the domain aspects relevant to them.

Our proposal of a very general framework for context-aware system design envisages the intervention of context in the two traditional software life-cycle loops: the design-time loop and the run-time loop. The former is developed over three stages:

1. *Context modelling*, when the dimensions of context that are relevant to the specific scenario are understood and modelled, giving birth to the modelling of the possible situations the system may incur in.

2. *Application domain modelling*, where the traditional modelling of the system data and functions takes place.
3. *Design of the relationship between the context model and the application domain*: here, the designer establishes the relationships between the contexts envisaged in the first step and the data and behaviours that have to be raised when each context becomes active.

In Step 1, any appropriate context model may be adopted; throughout this work we will adopt the *Context Dimension Tree* (*CDT*), a general context model that we already used for context-aware view definition [8]. Step 2 can be performed adopting any software design methodology, while Step 3 is a very delicate phase, in which the relationships between the context meta-knowledge and the domain knowledge are established. In this paper we concentrate on the description of Steps 1 and 3, using Datalog and its extensions.

Consider now a context-aware system at run-time, when the elements of context must be involved in the system's behaviour to modify it. We envisage four main stages:

1. *Context sensing*, when sensors gather physical measurements from the environment. For instance, the system clock gives us time, the GPS gives us the location, or a thermometer measures a room's temperature.
2. *Context recognition*, when the numerical values gathered in the previous phase are transformed into contextual (symbolic) information. Just to give an example, the GPS reading can be transformed into "Magdalene College", which is the symbolic value associated to the area the GPS has sensed. Also take into account the fact that not necessarily the symbolic contextual information comes from sensors; for instance, the recognition, on the part of the system, of a user, might be performed autonomously by the system by means of an RFID tag, but also be input by the user him/herself.
3. *Context validation and binding*, when the discovered context (in terms of symbolic values attached to parameters) is first of all validated, to recognise whether this combination of values makes sense in the current state, and then adopted as the next valid context.
4. *Context exploitation*, when the system enacts a context-aware behaviour.

In the next subsection we illustrate the context model we propose for Step 1 of the design-time loop.

### 3.1   A Conceptual Context Model

In a common-sense interpretation, the context is perceived as a set of variables (*context dimensions*) whose values may be of interest for an agent (human or artificial). For instance, with reference to the running example of Section 1, the following attribute-value pairs:

$$\langle \ \text{role='professor', term='hilary', topic='seminar'} \ \rangle$$

may be used to characterise the context of a professor interested in seminars during the Hilary term. Note also that, given an application, not all the combinations of value assignments are necessarily meaningful, e.g., the following pairs:

⟨ role='student', term='trinity', topic='meeting' ⟩

characterise the situation of a student accessing the information about meetings that is typically a task done by professors.

Generally speaking, the precise definition of the *valid* combinations is usually obtained by means of a *context model* [10], also allowing the application designer to specify the constraints that determine all the possible (meaningful) contexts related to the application situation. Moreover, a context model should also be able to model the association between each context and the subset of the data which is relevant for that context.

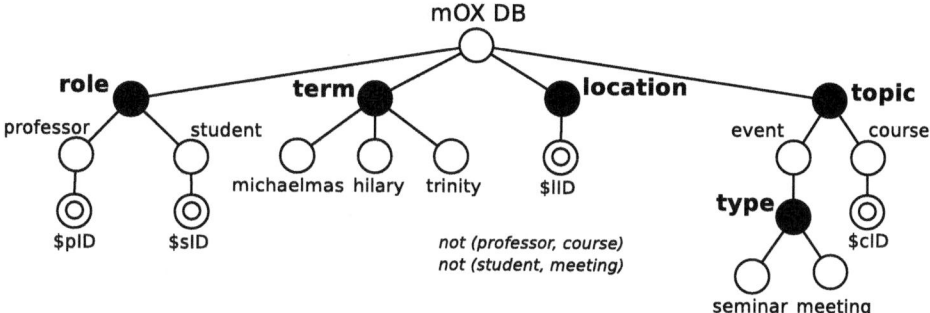

**Fig. 2.** A *CDT* for the mOX Application

A *CDT* is a tree-based context model able to represent multi-dimensional and hierarchical contexts. Figure 2 shows a *CDT* compatible with the domain and the contexts envisaged by our running example. In a *CDT*, black nodes represent dimensions (and possibly sub-dimensions) while white nodes represent values. An edge $(b, w)$, where $b$ is a black node and $w$ is a white node, represents an association between a value and its dimension (i.e., the context-model allows the association of the value $w$ to the dimension $b$), while an edge $(w, b)$ represents the specification of a sub-dimension, i.e., whenever a dimension assumes the value $w$, it is possible to further specify the context by assigning values to the sub-dimension $b$. Moreover, every time we want to explicitly parametrise the values that a dimension might assume (e.g., the identifier of an agent), we resort to *parameters*, represented in Figure 2 as nodes with a double border. Parameters may also be associated to dimensions (i.e., black nodes) especially in those situations where we have a large (or infinite) number of values for a given dimension (e.g., all the locations in Oxford or all the integer numbers) and we do not want (or it is impossible) to elicit all of them.

In a *CDT*, whenever we specify a set of values for the dimensions, we implicitly identify a point in the multidimensional space (see Figure 3) representing the possible contexts i.e., we *instantiate* a context. As already said, not all the combinations of dimension-value assignments are necessarily meaningful or even coherent. In order to prevent certain combinations of values from being present at the same time in a context, the *CDT* provides constraints of the form $not(w_1, \ldots, w_n)$, whose semantics is to forbid the contemporary presence of the values $w_1, \ldots w_n$ in a context.

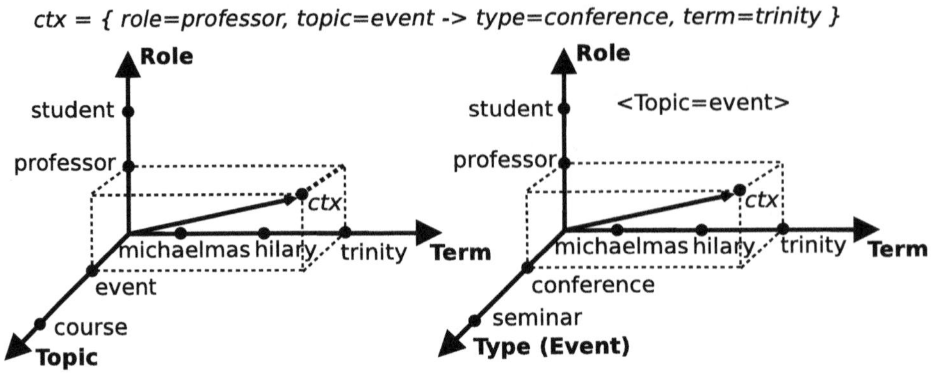
ctx = { role=professor, topic=event -> type=conference, term=trinity }
Role
student
professor
ctx
michaelmas
hilary
trinity
Term
event
course
Topic
Role
student
<Topic=event>
professor
ctx
michaelmas
hilary
trinity
Term
conference
seminar
Type (Event)

**Fig. 3.** A multi-dimensional representation for contexts

In the *CDT* model a valid context (i.e., compatible with the context-model) is a combination $C$ of the dimension-values such that:

1. for each black node at most one of its white (direct) children belongs to $C$,
2. $C$ does not contain two values $w,w'$ such that $not(w,w')$ is in the *CDT*,
3. if a white node belongs to $C$, then also all its white ancestors in the *CDT* do.

Condition (1) ensures that all the assignments dimension-value are unambiguous. Condition (2) ensures that all the forbidden combinations of values do not appear in the same context while the last condition (3) states that whenever we assign a value to a sub-dimension, the values for the corresponding super-dimensions are deterministically assigned according to the structure of the context model.

## 4 Datalog for Context Modelling and Reasoning

Datalog is a database query language based on the logic programming paradigm. A Datalog *program* consists of *facts* and *rules*. Both facts and rules are *Horn clauses* of the form $L_0 \leftarrow L_1,\ldots,L_n$ where each $L_i$ is a *literal* of the form $p_i(t_1,\ldots,t_m)$ such that each $p_i$ is a first-order predicate and each $t_j$ is a *term* i.e., either a *constant*, a *null* or a *variable*. The left-hand-side of a clause is called the *head* while the right-hand-side is called the *body*. Facts are clauses with an empty body and only constants and nulls as terms (i.e., *ground* facts), while Datalog rules are clauses with at least one atom in the body. A Datalog rule is *safe* if all the variables appearing in the head appear also in the body, it is called *unsafe* otherwise.

Linear Datalog$^{\pm}$ is a variant of Datalog introduced in [27] whose rules are: (i) linear (i.e., single literal in the body) and possibly unsafe Datalog rules (better known as *tuple-generating dependencies* (TGDs)), (ii) *equality-generating dependencies* (EGDs) and *negative constraints* (NCs).

An *equality-generating dependency* (EGD) is a clause of the form $X_i = X_j \leftarrow L_1, \ldots, L_n$ where $X_i, X_j$ are variables of some $L_i$. A *negative constraint* (NC) is a clause of the form $\perp \leftarrow L_1, \ldots, L_n$, where $\perp$ denotes the truth constant *false*. In other words, a negative constraint specifies that certain formulae must be false in every model of a given theory. NCs have been proven useful for modelling various forms of ontological structures [27] as well as conceptual schemas such as Entity-Relationship (E/R) diagrams [28]. When a set of EGDs is considered together with a set of TGDs, the problem of query answering is undecidable in the general case since EGDs generalise the well-known class of functional dependencies in databases. For this reason Linear Datalog$^\pm$ adopts restrictions to ensure a controlled interaction between EGDs and TGDs that retains decidability [27].

We adopt Datalog$^\pm$ for its capability to model ontological constraints that allow tractable query answering. It is also known that Datalog$^\pm$ captures well-known ontology languages such as DL-*Lite* (through linear Datalog$^\pm$) and F-Logic$_{Lite}$ (through weakly-guarded Datalog$^\pm$) [27].

We now show that *CDT*s can be represented by means of Linear Datalog$^\pm$ programs enabling context reasoning tasks, while it is possible to exploit safe Datalog to represent the associations between a context and the corresponding subset of the available information.

In order to represent the *CDT* in terms of Linear Datalog$^\pm$ programs we introduce the following structures:

- the *context-vocabulary* program defines the application-independent vocabulary (i.e., the meta-model) used to build a context model. The context-vocabulary is constituted by a set of Linear Datalog$^\pm$ rules expressing the high-level constraints common to all the *CDT*s; we call this program $\mathcal{P}_{Voc}$.
- the *context-model* program uses the predicates of the context-vocabulary to define the specific context model for a given application. In particular, this program specifies the (possibly hierarchical) context dimensions for the specific application, along with their possible values. The context-model is represented as a set of Linear Datalog$^\pm$ rules $\mathcal{P}_{Mod}$ but, differently from $\mathcal{P}_{Voc}$, we associate to it also a set of EDB predicates to ensure the existence of certain objects such as the dimensions and the values of the specific context model we are representing. This is the output of the (Context Modelling) Step 1 in the design-time loop of Section 3.
- the *context instances* correspond to all possible (logical) models for the context-vocabulary and the context-model and represent valid (i.e., consistent with the context model) contexts for a particular application. In Datalog terms, the context instances are the Herbrand models $\mathcal{H}$ such that $\mathcal{H} \models \mathcal{P}_{Voc} \cup \mathcal{P}_{Mod}$. These instances are the only ones that are legally acceptable during Step 3 of the run-time loop of Section 3, i.e. at context validation and binding time.

In the following we discuss in deeper detail the structures introduced above and provide also the Linear Datalog$^\pm$ implementation of the *CDT* of Figure 2 compatible with our running example.

## 4.1 Context Vocabulary

The context-vocabulary provides the building-block predicates for modelling *contexts*, their *dimensions* and their *values* (e.g., role='student', term='trinity'). It also provides the vocabulary for defining *parameters* and their values (e.g., $cID='C004', $pID='P006') while the dimension and value *hierarchies* and the *constraints* are modelled by means of Linear Datalog$^{\pm}$ formulae. In other words, the vocabulary provides the means for representing the structure and the semantics of the context-model. The full specification of the context-vocabulary is given in Table 1.

**Table 1.** The context-vocabulary

| *TGDs* | |
|---|---|
| context(X) | $\rightarrow$ $\exists$Y hasDimension(X,Y), d-ass(Y). |
| d-ass(X) | $\rightarrow$ $\exists$Y$\exists$Z d-dimension(X,Y), dimension(Y), d-value(X,Z), value(Z). |
| p-ass(X) | $\rightarrow$ $\exists$Y$\exists$Z$\exists$W p-parameter(X,Y), parameter(Y), p-value(X,Z), *XSDAny*(Z), hasParameter(W,X), value(W). |
| *EGDs* | |
| Y=Z | $\leftarrow$ hasDimension(Y,X), hasDimension(Z,X). |
| Y=Z | $\leftarrow$ hasParameter(Y,X), hasParameter(Z,X). |
| Y=Z | $\leftarrow$ d-value(X,Y), d-value(X,Z). |
| Y=Z | $\leftarrow$ p-value(X,Y), p-value(X,Z). |
| Y=Z | $\leftarrow$ p-parameter(X,Y), p-parameter(X,Z). |
| Y=Z | $\leftarrow$ d-dimension(X,Y), d-dimension(X,Z). |

The context vocabulary contains three concepts that act as *types* for the first-class entities of the context model namely dimension, parameter along with value and XSDAny representing the dimension and parameter values respectively. As a consequence, each dimension, value and parameter will be represented as a constant in the corresponding predicate. Moreover, since the parameter values usually belong to concrete data-types (e.g., strings, integers, etc.), the vocabulary provides a special predicate XSDAny representing the XSD (XML Schema Definition [3]) type xsd:AnyType that encompasses all the simple and derived data-types definable in an XML document. The assignments of values to parameters and dimensions are represented as first-class citizens in the context-model; to this aim, the vocabulary provides the predicates named d-ass and p-ass respectively; the predicate d-dimension (p-parameter) associates the dimensions (parameters) assignments to the corresponding formal entities while the predicate d-value (p-value) associates the assignments to the corresponding values. In addition, since a parameter must be assigned to a (single) dimension value, the vocabulary forces every p-ass to be associated with a value of a dimension through the predicate hasParameter. A context is then associated to a set of assignments for the dimensions, modelled through the hasDimension predicate. The EGDs in Table 1 force

---

[3] http://www.w3.org/TR/xmlschema-0/

functional constraints for the parameter and dimension values and inverse-functional constraints for hasParameter and hasDimension since a parameter can be associated to at most one dimension value and each dimension value can be associated to at most one dimension.

## 4.2   The Context Model

The context-model program uses the resources defined in the context-vocabulary to build an application-dependent context model.

Table 2 shows the Linear Datalog$^\pm$ program $\mathcal{T}_{Mod}$ representing the *CDT* of Figure 2, built using the entities of the context-vocabulary of Table 1 where the numbers $(1, 2, \ldots)$ denote groups of rules having the same modelling aim. Dimensions, values and parameters (corresponding to black, white and double-circled nodes in the *CDT*) are modelled as constants. With reference to group (1), EDB predicates of the form dimension($\cdot$) enumerate the dimensions of the context model of our running example, namely: the role, the term, the location and the topic; in the same way, we model the parameters by EDB predicates of the form parameter($\cdot$) (see group (2)). The predicates in group (3) define the values of each dimension (e.g., professor is a value for the role dimension); all the concepts defining a set of values for a dimension must specialise the concept value of the context-vocabulary as established by the rules in group (4). In the same way, the rules in group (5) state that the assignments of a value to a particular dimension are specialisations of the vocabulary predicate d-value.

Statements of the groups (6) and (7) show how assignments of values to dimensions and parameters are defined. Each $d_d$-ass($\cdot$) represents an assignment of a formal dimension $d$ to a (unique) value $v$; dually, a $p_v$-ass($\cdot$) represents the association between a formal parameter $p$ and a (unique) concrete value of a given XSD type. In addition, each hasParameter($\cdot$) specifies which value $v$ it is associated with. As an example, the axiom (7b) states that sID is a parameter of the value student of the dimension role and that it can assume values in the domain of strings. With Linear Datalog$^\pm$ it is also possible to enforce a hierarchical structure among the dimensions. As an example, axiom (6e) states that type is actually a sub-dimension of topic, since every assignment for type implies also an assignment for role.

Given such a set of rules, for a given application domain, a context is defined as a set of dimension and parameter assignments, possibly specifying which dimensions are mandatory as in assertion (8).

Finally, Datalog$^\pm$ provides constraint-rules that can further constrain the structure of the valid contexts. This is useful when we want to prevent certain combinations of dimension-value pairs to appear in the same context (9a) and (9b). Such constraints are defined using Datalog$^\pm$ negative constraints preventing, for example, the role student to appear in a context where the topic meeting is also present (see the corresponding constraint in Figure 2). The EGDs of the form of (9c) enforce uniqueness constraints for the assignments since in a valid context only one assignment for each dimension is allowed.

The valid contexts will be then represented as an EDB that is a model for the program constituted by $\mathcal{T}_{Voc}$ and $\mathcal{T}_{Mod}$.

**Table 2.** A Linear Datalog$^\pm$ context model $\mathcal{T}_{Mod}$

| | |
|---|---|
| (1a) dimension(role). | (3a) role(professor). |
| (1b) dimension(term). | (3b) role(student). |
| (1c) dimension(location). | (3c) term(michaelmas). |
| (1d) dimension(topic). | (3d) term(hilary). |
| (1e) dimension(type). | (3e) term(trinity). |
| | (3f) location(X) $\rightarrow$ *XSDString*(X). |
| (2a) parameter(pID). | (3g) topic(event). |
| (2b) parameter(sID). | (3h) topic(course). |
| (2c) parameter(cID). | (3i) type(seminar). |
| | (3j) type(meeting). |
| (4a) role(X)$\rightarrow$value(X). | (5a) $d_{role}$-value(X,Y)$\rightarrow$d-value(X,Y). |
| (4b) term(X)$\rightarrow$value(X). | (5b) $d_{term}$-value(X,Y)$\rightarrow$d-value(X,Y). |
| (4c) location(X)$\rightarrow$value(X). | (5c) $d_{location}$-value(X,Y)$\rightarrow$d-value(X,Y). |
| (4d) topic(X)$\rightarrow$value(X). | (5d) $d_{topic}$-value(X,Y)$\rightarrow$d-value(X,Y). |
| (4e) type(X)$\rightarrow$value(X). | (5e) $d_{type}$-value(X,Y)$\rightarrow$d-value(X,Y). |

(6a) $d_{role}$-ass(X)$\rightarrow$     $\exists$Y d-ass(X), $d_{role}$-value(X,Y),role(Y),d-dimension(X,role).

(6b) $d_{term}$-ass(X)$\rightarrow$     $\exists$Y d-ass(X), $d_{term}$-value(X,Y),term(Y),d-dimension(X,term).

(6c) $d_{location}$-ass(X)$\rightarrow$     $\exists$Y d-ass(X), $d_{location}$-value(X,Y),location(Y),d-dimension(X,Y).

(6d) $d_{topic}$-ass(X)$\rightarrow$     $\exists$Y d-ass(X), $d_{topic}$-value(X,Y),topic(Y),d-dimension(X,topic).

(6e) $d_{type}$-ass(X)$\rightarrow$     $\exists$Y$\exists$Z d-ass(X), $d_{type}$-value(X,Y),type(Y),d-dimension(X,type), hasDimension(Z,X),$d_{topic}$-ass(Z),$d_{topic}$-value(Z,event).

(7a) $p_{professor}$-ass(X)$\rightarrow$     $\exists$Y$\exists$Z p-ass(X),p-value(X,Y),*XSDString*(Y), p-parameter(X,pID),hasParameter(professor,X).

(7b) $p_{student}$-ass(X)$\rightarrow$     $\exists$Y$\exists$Z p-ass(X),p-value(X,Y),*XSDString*(Y), p-parameter(X,sID),hasParameter(student,X).

(7c) $p_{course}$-ass(X)$\rightarrow$     $\exists$Y$\exists$Z p-ass(X),p-value(X,Y),*XSDString*(Y), p-parameter(X,cID),hasParameter(course,X).

(8) context$_{mOX}$(X)$\rightarrow$     $\exists$Y$\exists$Z context(X), hasDimension(X,Y), $d_{role}$-ass(Y), hasDimension(X,Z),$d_{topic}$-ass(Z).

(9a) hasDimension(X,Y),d-value(Y,professor),hasDimension(X,Z),d-value(Z,course)$\rightarrow \perp$.
(9b) hasDimension(X,Y),d-value(Y,student),hasDimension(X,Z),d-value(Z,meeting)$\rightarrow \perp$.
(9c) hasDimension(X,Y),d-dimension(Y,role),hasDimension(X,Z),d-dimension(Z,role)$\rightarrow$Y=Z.
...

## 4.3   The Contexts

It is now clear that the context-model supports the representation of a (potentially infinite, due to parameters on dimension nodes) number of valid contexts which correspond to different EDBs *context instances* consistent with the context-model and the context-vocabulary. Examples of contexts consistent with the context model of Table 2 and the running example are shown in Table 3. We define the two contexts $c1$ and $c2$ such that $c1$ models the situation of a professor interested in seminars held at Oxford University during the Hilary term, while $c2$ models the situation of a student interested in the courses offered by the Computing Laboratory during Michaelmas term.

**Table 3.** $c1$ and $c2$ context instances

| | |
|---|---|
| hasDimension(c1, c1_role) | $d_{role}$-ass(c1_role) |
| hasDimension(c1, c1_term) | $d_{term}$-ass(c1_term) |
| hasDimension(c1, c1_type) | $d_{type}$-ass(c1_type) |
| | |
| d-value(c1_role, professor) | d-dimension(c1_role, role) |
| d-value(c1_term, hilary) | d-dimension(c1_term, term) |
| d-value(c1_term, seminar) | d-dimension(c1_situation, type) |
| | |
| $context_{mOX}(c1)$ | |
| hasDimension(c2, c2_role) | $d_{role}$-ass(c2_role) |
| hasDimension(c2, c2_term) | $d_{term}$-ass(c2_term) |
| hasDimension(c2, c2_location) | $d_{location}$-ass(c2_location) |
| hasDimension(c2, c2_topic) | $d_{topic}$-ass(c2_topic) |
| | |
| d-value(c2_role, student) | d-dimension(c2_position, role) |
| d-value(c2_term, michaelmas) | d-dimension(c2_term, term) |
| d-value(c2_location, COMLAB) | d-dimension(c2_location, location) |
| d-value(c2_topic, course) | d-dimension(c2_topic, topic) |
| | |
| $context_{mOX}(c2)$ | |

Notice that in $c1$ it is not necessary to specify a value for the `topic` dimension, since the instance of Table 3 and the context model together imply `topic='event'`. In addition, we do not specify any value for the `location` dimension; in our model, the missing specification of a value for a dimension acts as a *don't-care* assignment i.e., all the regions are taken into consideration.

A good modelling practice is to keep the contexts separated from the context-model since, once the configurations have been computed, the application could (in principle) disregard the context model from which they have been generated.

### 4.4  Context Reasoning

An important aspect in a context model is the possibility to reason over the context data in order to (i) make implicit information explicit or (ii) detect meaningless or forbidden combinations of values. The need for reasoning in context-aware systems originates from the intrinsic uncertainty that comes with context data [29], especially when context-data are produced by sensors or acquired from external sources that can be intermittently connected to the network. Also the data coming directly from the user can be equally noisy since users can input erroneous values. In these situations, reasoning over the context instances using the constraints imposed by the context model can detect possible inconsistent contexts or infer missing context data during the phase of run-time context validation and binding (see Section 3).

Another important aspect regards the efficiency of context-reasoning. Context-aware systems often require fast, on-the-fly reasoning procedures that can be implemented and executed using limited computational resources. This is extremely useful in mobile applications especially in wireless-sensor networks. Luckily, reasoning in Linear Datalog$^{\pm}$ is FO-reducible and this allows to efficiently perform reasoning over a large number of context-instances through query reformulation.

Consider, as an example, the context model of Table 2 and the context instances of Table 3. In context c1 we do not specify the value for the topic dimension but we specify that the value for the type dimension is seminar. Using this information it is possible to infer that the value for topic is event using rules (5a) and (6d) of Table 2 i.e., by using the knowledge coming from the context-model that type is a sub-dimension of topic related to the value event.

## 5  Data Tailoring with Datalog

As seen in Section 3 – Step 3 of the design-time loop – once the context model has been defined, it is necessary to link it to the representation of the domain of interest (in our case the database schema) in order for the system to provide, at run-time, the relevant fragment of the database that must be used to answer the queries. We now propose a procedure for generating this association, and show how it is possible to enable context-aware query-answering based on contextual views.

The procedure consists of three phases; the first two implement the Step 3 of design-time and the last one implements the context-exploitation step (Step 4) at run-time. In the first phase, each value of each dimension of the context model is manually associated with a set of views over the relations of the database schema $\mathcal{R}$. Each view associated with a value of a dimension is called *value-based relevant area*, since each view represents the part of each entity in the schema which is "relevant" for that dimension's value. In a second phase, these areas are combined in order to obtain the *context-based relevant areas*, which are composed starting from the value-based relevant areas and represent, for each context, the part of each relation that is relevant in a given context. At run-time, each query over $\mathcal{R}$ is handed over to a substitution process that, given an active context, replaces the atoms mentioned in the query with the corresponding *context-based relevant areas*. A rewriting process will then express the queries in terms of the value-based relevant areas and, from here, in terms of the relations in $\mathcal{R}$. We now go into the details of each step.

**Definition 1 ((Value-Based Relevant Area)).**
*Let v be a value for a dimension in the context model and r be a relation of $\mathcal{R}$. A value-based relevant area for v and r is an expression of the form $r_v(\mathbf{X}) \leftarrow r(\mathbf{X}), \phi(\mathbf{X}, \mathbf{Y})$ where $\phi$ is an conjunction of atoms over $\mathcal{R}$.*

The value-based relevant areas can be seen as conjunctive queries over $\mathcal{R}$ that "restricts" a given relation and are defined for each combination of dimension's values $v_i$ and relations $r_j$, producing a set of view definitions. Consider the value-based relevant areas of Table 4.

Note that the parameters used in the context model are mentioned in the area definitions, to be actually instantiated at run-time with the corresponding value.

**Table 4.** Value-based relevant areas (excerpt)

| | |
|---|---|
| $\text{COURSE}_{student}(\text{cID},X_1,X_2,X_3,X_4)$ | $\leftarrow \text{COURSE}(\text{cID},X_1,X_2,X_3,X_4), \text{ENROLMENT}(\text{sID},X_1).$ |
| $\text{COURSE}_{course}(\text{cID},X_1,X_2,X_3,X_4)$ | $\leftarrow \text{COURSE}(\text{cID},X_1,X_2,X_3,X_4).$ |
| $\text{COURSE}_{michaelmas}(\text{cID},X_1,X_2,X_3,X_4)$ | $\leftarrow \text{COURSE}(\text{cID},X_1,X_2,X_3,X_4), X_3=\text{'Michaelmas'}.$ |
| $\text{COURSE}_{lID}(\text{cID},X_1,X_2,X_3,X_4)$ | $\leftarrow \text{COURSE}(\text{cID},X_1,\text{lID},X_3,X_4).$ |
| | |
| $\text{PROFESSOR}_{professor}(\text{pID},X_1,X_2,X_3,X_4,X_5)$ | $\leftarrow \text{PROFESSOR}(\text{pID},X_1,X_2,X_3,X_4,X_5).$ |
| $\text{PROFESSOR}_{student}(\text{pID},X_1,X_2,X_3,X_4,X_5)$ | $\leftarrow \text{PROFESSOR}(\text{pID},X_1,X_2,X_3,X_4,X_5), \text{COURSE}(\text{cID},X_6,X_7,X_8,\text{pID}),$ |
| | $\text{ENROLMENT}(\text{sID},\text{cID}).$ |
| $\text{PROFESSOR}_{course}(\text{pID},X_1,X_2,X_3,X_4,X_5)$ | $\leftarrow \text{PROFESSOR}(\text{pID},X_1,X_2,X_3,X_4,X_5), \text{COURSE}(\text{cID},X_6,X_7,X_8,\text{pID}).$ |
| $\text{PROFESSOR}_{seminar}(\text{pID},X_1,X_2,X_3,X_4,X_5)$ | $\leftarrow \text{PROFESSOR}(\text{pID},X_1,X_2,X_3,X_4,X_5), \text{EVENT}(X_6,X_7,X_8,X_9,X_{10},\text{pID}),$ |
| | $X_9=\text{'seminar'}.$ |
| $\text{PROFESSOR}_{michaelmas}(\text{pID},X_1,X_2,X_3,X_4,X_5)$ | $\leftarrow \text{PROFESSOR}(\text{pID},X_1,X_2,X_3,X_4,X_5), \text{EVENT}(X_6,X_7,X_8,X_9,X_{10},\text{pID}),$ |
| | $dateToTerm(X_7)=\text{'Michaelmas'}.$ |
| $\text{PROFESSOR}_{michaelmas}(\text{pID},X_1,X_2,X_3,X_4,X_5)$ | $\leftarrow \text{PROFESSOR}(\text{pID},X_1,X_2,X_3,X_4,X_5), \text{COURSE}(\text{cID},X_6,X_7,X_8,\text{pID}),$ |
| | $X_8=\text{'Michaelmas'}.$ |
| $\text{PROFESSOR}_{hilary}(\text{pID},X_1,X_2,X_3,X_4,X_5)$ | $\leftarrow \text{PROFESSOR}(\text{pID},X_1,X_2,X_3,X_4,X_5), \text{EVENT}(X_6,X_7,X_8,X_9,X_{10},\text{pID}),$ |
| | $dateToTerm(X_7)=\text{'Hilary'}.$ |
| $\text{PROFESSOR}_{hilary}(\text{pID},X_1,X_2,X_3,X_4,X_5)$ | $\leftarrow \text{PROFESSOR}(\text{pID},X_1,X_2,X_3,X_4,X_5), \text{COURSE}(\text{cID},X_6,X_7,X_8,\text{pID}),$ |
| | $X_8=\text{'Hilary'}.$ |
| $\text{PROFESSOR}_{lID}(\text{pID},X_1,X_2,X_3,X_4,X_5)$ | $\leftarrow \text{PROFESSOR}(\text{pID},X_1,X_2,X_3,\text{lID},X_5).$ |
| $\text{PROFESSOR}_{lID}(\text{pID},X_1,X_2,X_3,X_4,X_5)$ | $\leftarrow \text{PROFESSOR}(\text{pID},X_1,X_2,X_3,X_4,X_5), \text{EVENT}(X_6,X_7,X_8,X_9,\text{lID},\text{pID}).$ |
| $\text{PROFESSOR}_{lID}(\text{pID},X_1,X_2,X_3,X_4,X_5)$ | $\leftarrow \text{PROFESSOR}(\text{pID},X_1,X_2,X_3,X_4,X_5), \text{COURSE}(\text{cID},X_6,\text{lID},X_8,\text{pID}).$ |
| | |
| $\text{EVENT}_{professor}(X_1,X_2,X_3,X_4,X_5,X_6)$ | $\leftarrow \text{EVENT}(X_1,X_2,X_3,X_4,X_5,X_6).$ |
| $\text{EVENT}_{seminar}(X_1,X_2,X_3,X_4,X_5,X_6)$ | $\leftarrow \text{EVENT}(X_1,X_2,X_3,X_4,X_5,X_6), X_4=\text{'seminar'}.$ |
| $\text{EVENT}_{hilary}(X_1,X_2,X_3,X_4,X_5,X_6)$ | $\leftarrow \text{EVENT}(X_1,X_2,X_3,X_4,X_5,X_6), dateToTerm(X_2)=\text{'Hilary'}.$ |

The value-based relevant areas can be combined in order to produce a relevant area for each given context. We recall that a context can be seen as a set of assignments of values to dimensions, thus a context-based relevant area can be constructed by combining the value-based relevant areas corresponding to the values of a context.

For modelling reasons we restrict the form of the combinations to *unions* and *intersections* of value-based relevant areas:

**Definition 2 ((Context-Based Relevant Area)).**
*Let c be a context and $\mathcal{V}_c = \{v_1, \ldots, v_n\}$ be the set of values for the dimensions of c. Given a table $r \in \mathcal{R}$, a context-based relevant area for r under c is either a formula $r_c^{\wedge}(\mathbf{X}) \leftarrow \bigwedge_{i=1}^n r_{v_i}(\mathbf{X})$ (conjunctive relevant area) or a formula $r_c^{\vee}(\mathbf{X}) \leftarrow \bigvee_{i=1}^n r_{v_i}(\mathbf{X})$ (disjunctive relevant area) for each $v_i$ in $\mathcal{V}_c$.*

Both ways of producing the context-based relevant areas are important from a modelling point of view. A conjunctive relevant area of the form $r_c^{\wedge}$ is strictly adherent to the considered context and includes only the data that are *strictly relevant* to a context. This form of combination should be used when the main target of the contextualisation is *data-reduction* e.g., for storing the data on a mobile device. On the contrary, a disjunctive relevant area of the form $r_c^{\vee}$ produces a larger area that consists of all the data that can be related to a given context. This second way of combining the value-based relevant areas excludes only the data that are *certainly unrelated* to a given context and should be used when the designer's target is *data-focusing* i.e., increasing the focus on certain information without excluding potentially interesting data. Note that the combination of value-based relevant areas producing a conjunctive relevant-area is still a conjunctive query while their combination in a disjunctive relevant-area is a union of conjunctive queries. Four possible context-based relevant areas compliant with our running example are shown in Table 5. These context-based areas are constructed by means of conjunctive views over the value-based areas that will tailor the data to support queries in the context c1.

**Table 5.** Context-based relevant areas

$\text{PROFESSOR}_{c1}^{\wedge}(\text{pID},X_1,X_2,X_3,X_4,X_5) \leftarrow \text{PROFESSOR}_{professor}(\text{pID},X_1,X_2,X_3,X_4,X_5),$
$\text{PROFESSOR}_{seminar}(\text{pID},X_1,X_2,X_3,X_4,X_5),$
$\text{PROFESSOR}_{hilary}(\text{pID},X_1,X_2,X_3,X_4,X_5).$

$\text{EVENT}_{c1}^{\wedge}(X_1,X_2,X_3,X_4,X_5,X_6) \leftarrow \text{EVENT}_{professor}(X_1,X_2,X_3,X_4,X_5,X_6),$
$\text{EVENT}_{seminar}(X_1,X_2,X_3,X_4,X_5,X_6),$
$\text{EVENT}_{hilary}(X_1,X_2,X_3,X_4,X_5,X_6).$

$\text{PROFESSOR}_{c2}^{\wedge}(\text{pID},X_1,X_2,X_3,X_4,X_5) \leftarrow \text{PROFESSOR}_{student}(\text{pID},X_1,X_2,X_3,X_4,X_5),$
$\text{PROFESSOR}_{course}(\text{pID},X_1,X_2,X_3,X_4,X_5),$
$\text{PROFESSOR}_{michaelmas}(\text{pID},X_1,X_2,X_3,X_4,X_5).$
$\text{PROFESSOR}_{IID}(\text{pID},X_1,X_2,X_3,X_4,X_5).$

$\text{COURSE}_{c2}^{\wedge}(\text{cID},X_1,X_2,X_3,X_4) \leftarrow \text{COURSE}_{student}(\text{cID},X_1,X_2,X_3,X_4),$
$\text{COURSE}_{course}(\text{cID},X_1,X_2,X_3,X_4),$
$\text{COURSE}_{michaelmas}(\text{cID},X_1,X_2,X_3,X_4),$
$\text{COURSE}_{IID}(\text{cID},X_1,X_2,X_3,X_4).$

Once the context-based relevant areas have been produced, it is possible to use them at run-time to contextualise the queries. The run-time phase of context exploitation (see Section 3, Step 4) is thus reduced to reformulating the query using the context-aware views defined by the context-based relevant areas. Given a query $q$ over a schema $\mathcal{R}$, a contextualised query $q_c$ is obtained by replacing the predicates mentioned in the body of the query with the corresponding context-based relevant areas. Since each context-based relevant area is created on a table-base i.e., by properly restricting each table depending on the context, each contextualised table is actually a subset of the corresponding relation in $\mathcal{R}$. As an example consider the following query asking for title and date of all the events in which "Letizia Tanca" is a speaker:

$$q(X_1,X_2) \leftarrow EVENT(X_1,X_2,X_3,X_4,X_5,X_6),$$
$$PROFESSOR(X_5,'Letizia','Tanca',X_7,X_8,X_9).$$

Since it holds that any relevant area is actually a sub-relation of the the corresponding relation in the original database, we can produce the contextualised query for c1 as:

$$q_{c1}(X_1,X_2) \leftarrow EVENT_{c1}(X_1,X_2,X_3,X_4,X_5,X_6),$$
$$PROFESSOR_{c1}(X_5,'Letizia','Tanca',X_7,X_8,X_9).$$

By applying the context-based relevant area definitions we will consequently obtain the following query:

$$q_{c1}(X_1,X_2) \leftarrow EVENT_{professor}(X_1,X_2,X_3,X_4,X_5,X_6),$$
$$EVENT_{seminar}(X_1,X_2,X_3,X_4,X_5,X_6),$$
$$EVENT_{hilary}(X_1,X_2,X_3,X_4,X_5,X_6),$$
$$PROFESSOR_{professor}(X_6,'Letizia','Tanca',X_7,X_8,X_9),$$
$$PROFESSOR_{seminar}(X_6,'Letizia','Tanca',X_7,X_8,X_9),$$
$$PROFESSOR_{hilary}(X_6,'Letizia','Tanca',X_7,X_8,X_9).$$

that corresponds to the following UCQ over $\mathcal{R}$:

$$q_{c1}^1(X_1,X_2) \leftarrow EVENT(X_1,X_2,X_3,X_4,X_5,X_6),$$
$$EVENT(X_1,X_2,X_3,'seminar',X_5,X_6),$$
$$EVENT(X_1,X_2,X_3,X_4,X_5,X_6),$$
$$dateToTerm(X_2)='Hilary',$$
$$PROFESSOR(X_6,'Letizia','Tanca',X_7,X_8,X_9),$$
$$PROFESSOR(X_6,'Letizia','Tanca',X_7,X_8,X_9),$$
$$EVENT(X_{10},X_{11},X_{12},'seminar',X_{13},X_6),$$
$$PROFESSOR(X_6,'Letizia','Tanca',X_7,X_8,X_9).$$
$$q_{c1}^2(X_1,X_2) \leftarrow EVENT(X_1,X_2,X_3,X_4,X_5,X_6),$$
$$EVENT(X_1,X_2,X_3,'seminar',X_5,X_6),$$
$$EVENT(X_1,X_2,X_3,X_4,X_5,X_6),$$
$$dateToTerm(X_2)='Hilary',$$
$$PROFESSOR(X_6,'Letizia','Tanca',X_7,X_8,X_9),$$
$$PROFESSOR(X_6,'Letizia','Tanca',X_7,X_8,X_9),$$
$$COURSE(X_{10},X_{11},X_{12},'Hilary',X_6),$$
$$PROFESSOR(X_6,'Letizia','Tanca',X_7,X_8,X_9).$$

After optimisation, the above UCQ is equivalent to the following conjunctive query since $q_{c1}^2 \subseteq q_{c1}^1$.

$$q_{c1}^3(X_1,X_2) \leftarrow EVENT(X_1,X_2,X_3,'seminar',X_5,X_6),$$
$$PROFESSOR(X_6,'Letizia','Tanca',X_7,X_8,X_9),$$
$$dateToTerm(X_2)='Hilary'.$$

In order to see how disjunctive context-based relevant areas differ from the previous ones, assume that the designer had specified disjunctive areas of Table 6 for c1 instead of conjunctive ones.

**Table 6.** Disjunctive, context-based relevant areas for c1

| |
|---|
| $PROFESSOR_{c1}^\vee(pID,X_1,X_2,X_3,X_4,X_5) \leftarrow PROFESSOR_{professor}(pID,X_1,X_2,X_3,X_4,X_5).$ |
| $PROFESSOR_{c1}^\vee(pID,X_1,X_2,X_3,X_4,X_5) \leftarrow PROFESSOR_{seminar}(pID,X_1,X_2,X_3,X_4,X_5).$ |
| $PROFESSOR_{c1}^\vee(pID,X_1,X_2,X_3,X_4,X_5) \leftarrow PROFESSOR_{hilary}(pID,X_1,X_2,X_3,X_4,X_5).$ |
| |
| $EVENT_{c1}^\vee(X_1,X_2,X_3,X_4,X_5,X_6) \qquad \leftarrow EVENT_{professor}(X_1,X_2,X_3,X_4,X_5,X_6),$ |
| $EVENT_{c1}^\vee(X_1,X_2,X_3,X_4,X_5,X_6) \qquad \leftarrow EVENT_{seminar}(X_1,X_2,X_3,X_4,X_5,X_6),$ |
| $EVENT_{c1}^\vee(X_1,X_2,X_3,X_4,X_5,X_6) \qquad \leftarrow EVENT_{hilary}(X_1,X_2,X_3,X_4,X_5,X_6).$ |

In this case the contextualisation of the query $q$ w.r.t. c1 would have been resulted in the following UCQ, where all the combinations of the value-based relevant areas have been produced:

$$q_{c1}^1(X_1,X_2) \leftarrow EVENT(X_1,X_2,X_3,X_4,X_5,X_6),$$
$$PROFESSOR(X_6,'Letizia','Tanca',X_7,X_8,X_9).$$
$$q_{c1}^2(X_1,X_2) \leftarrow EVENT(X_1,X_2,X_3,X_4,'Seminar',X_6),$$
$$PROFESSOR(X_6,'Letizia','Tanca',X_7,X_8,X_9).$$
$$q_{c1}^3(X_1,X_2) \leftarrow EVENT(X_1,X_2,X_3,X_4,X_5,X_6),$$
$$PROFESSOR(X_6,'Letizia','Tanca',X_7,X_8,X_9),$$
$$dateToTerm(X_2)='Hilary'.$$
$$q_{c1}^3(X_1,X_2) \leftarrow EVENT(X_1,X_2,X_3,X_4,X_5,X_6),$$
$$PROFESSOR(X_6,'Letizia','Tanca',X_7,X_8,X_9),$$
$$COURSE(X_{10},X_{11},X_{12},'Hilary',X_6).$$
$$q_{c1}^4(X_1,X_2) \leftarrow EVENT(X_1,X_2,X_3,X_4,'Seminar',X_6),$$
$$PROFESSOR(X_6,'Letizia','Tanca',X_7,X_8,X_9),$$
$$COURSE(X_{10},X_{11},X_{12},'Hilary',X_6).$$
$$q_{c1}^5(X_1,X_2) \leftarrow EVENT(X_1,X_2,X_3,X_4,'Seminar',X_6),$$
$$PROFESSOR(X_6,'Letizia','Tanca',X_7,X_8,X_9),$$
$$dateToTerm(X_2)='Hilary'.$$
$$q_{c1}^6(X_1,X_2) \leftarrow EVENT(X_1,X_2,X_3,X_4,'Seminar',X_6),$$
$$PROFESSOR(X_6,'Letizia','Tanca',X_7,X_8,X_9),$$
$$COURSE(X_{10},X_{11},X_{12},'Hilary',X_6),$$
$$dateToTerm(X_2)='Hilary'.$$

Note that, in this case, after checking containment for all the queries, the above UCQ is equivalent to the query $q_{c1}^1$ that, in turn, is equivalent to the original query $q$. The effect of disjunctive relevant areas w.r.t. the conjunctive ones is thus that of broadening the subset of the available information that is used to answer the queries under the constraints imposed by the current context.

# 6   Conclusions

This paper has made a case for the explicit representation of context as an autonomous component during context-aware system design. It is our firm opinion that the same general design framework can be adopted for any context-aware system, provided that the software modelling phase, and the run-time behaviours of the system, be appropriately adapted to the specific application. In particular, we have shown the use of the framework for the design and exploitation of context in the formulation and usage of context-aware database views, using the Datalog language.

# References

1. Chui, M., Löffler, M., Roberts, R.: The internet of things. McKinsey Quarterly (2), 1–9 (2010)
2. Brézillon, P., Abu-Hakima, S.: Using knowledge in its context. AI Magazine 16(1), 87–91 (1995)
3. Wang, X., Zhang, D., Gu, T., Pung, H.: Ontology based context modeling and reasoning using OWL. In: Proc. of 1st Intl. Workshop on Context Modelling and Reasoning, pp. 18–22 (2004)
4. Abowd, G., Dey, A., Brown, P., Davies, N., Smith, M., Steggles, P.: Towards a better understanding of context and context-awareness. In: Proc. of 1st Intl. Symp. on Handheld and Ubiquitous Computing, pp. 304–307 (1999)
5. Ghidini, C., Giunchiglia, F.: Local Models Semantics, or contextual reasoning=locality+compatibility. Artificial Intellicence 127(2), 221–259 (2001)
6. Benerecetti, M., Bouquet, P., Ghidini, C.: On the dimensions of context dependence: Partiality, approximation, and perspective. In: Proc. of 3rd Intl. and Interdisciplinary Conf. on Modeling and Using Context, pp. 59–72 (2001)
7. Bazier, M., Brézillon, P.: Understanding context before using it. In: Proc. of 5th Intl. and Interdisciplinary Conf. on Modeling and Using Context, pp. 29–40 (2005)
8. Bolchini, C., Curino, C., Quintarelli, E., Schreiber, F., Tanca, L.: Context information for knowledge reshaping. Intl. Journal of Web Engineering and Technology 5(1), 88–103 (2009)
9. Strang, T., Linnhoff-Popien, C.: A context modeling survey. In: Proc. of 1st Intl. Workshop on Advanced Context Modelling, Reasoning and Management (2004)
10. Bolchini, C., Curino, C.A., Quintarelli, E., Schreiber, F., Tanca, L.: A data-oriented survey of context models. SIGMOD Record 36(4), 19–26 (2007)
11. Baldauf, M., Dustdar, S., Rosenberg, F.: A survey on context-aware systems. Intl. Journal of Ad Hoc and Ubiquitous Computing 2(4), 263–277 (2007)
12. Raptis, D., Tselios, N., Avouris, N.: Context-based design of mobile applications for museums: a survey of existing practices. In: Proc. of the 7th Intl. Conf. on human-computer Interaction with Mobile Devices & Services, pp. 153–160 (2005)
13. Petrelli, D., Not, E., Strapparava, C., Stock, O., Zancanaro, M.: Modeling context is like taking pictures. In: Proc. of the What, Who, Where, When, Why and How of Context-Awareness Workshop (2000)
14. Buchholz, S., Hamann, T., Hübsch, G.: Comprehensive structured context profiles (CSCP): Design and experiences. In: Proc. of 1st Intl. Work. on Context Modelling and Reasoning, pp. 43–47 (2004)
15. Chen, H., Finin, T., Joshi, A.: An intelligent broker for context-aware systems. In: Proc. of Intl. Conf. on Ubiquitous Computing - Poster Session, pp. 183–184 (2003)

16. Ouksel, A.M.: In-context peer-to-peer information filtering on the web. SIGMOD Record 32(3), 65–70 (2003)
17. Preuveneers, D., van den Bergh, J., Wagelaar, D., Georges, A., Rigole, P., Clerckx, T., Berbers, E., Coninx, K., de Bosschere, K.: Towards an extensible context ontology for ambient intelligence. In: Proc. of the 2nd European Symp. on Ambient Intelligence, pp. 148–159 (2004)
18. Kaenampornpan, M., O'Neill, E.: An intergrated context model: Bringing activity to context. In: Proc. of Work. on Advanced Context Modelling, Reasoning and Management (2004)
19. Segev, A., Gal, A.: Putting things in context: a topological approach to mapping contexts to ontologies. Journal on Data Semantics IX, 113–140 (2007)
20. Roussos, Y., Stavrakas, Y., Pavlaki, V.: Towards a context-aware relational model. In: Proc. of 1st Intl. Context Representation and Reasoning Work, pp. 7.1–7.12 (2005)
21. Roussos, Y., Sellis, T.: A model for context aware relational databases. Technical Report TR-2008-6, National Technical University of Athens (2008)
22. Tanca, L.: Context-based data tailoring for mobile users. In: Proc. of Datenbanksysteme in Business, Technologie und Web Work, pp. 282–295 (2007)
23. Raverdy, P.G., Riva, O., de La Chapelle, A., Chibout, R., Issarny, V.: Efficient context-aware service discovery in multi-protocol pervasive environments. In: Proc of 7th Intl. Conf. on Mobile Data Management, pp. 3–11 (2006)
24. Gu, T., Pung, H.K., Zhang, D.Q.: A service-oriented middleware for building context-aware services. Journal of Network and Computer Applications 28(1), 1–18 (2005)
25. Motschnig-Pitrik, R., Mylopoulos, J.: Semantics, features, and applications of the viewpoint abstraction. In: Proc. Intl. Conf. Advances Information System Engineering, pp. 514–539 (1996)
26. Theodorakis, M., Analyti, A., Constantopoulos, P., Spyratos, N.: A theory of contexts in information bases. Information Systems 27(3), 151–191 (2002)
27. Calì, A., Gottlob, G., Lukasiewicz, T.: A general datalog-based framework for tractable query answering over ontologies. In: Proc. of the 28th Symp. on Principles of Database Systems, pp. 77–86 (2009)
28. Calì, A., Gottlob, G., Pieris, A.: Tractable query answering over conceptual schemata. In: Proc. of the 28th Intl. Conf. on Conceptual Modeling, pp. 175–190 (2009)
29. Henricksen, K., Indulska, J.: Modelling and using imperfect context information. In: Proc. of Intl. Conf. on Pervasive Computing, pp. 33–37 (2004)

# Using Datalog for Fast and Easy Program Analysis

Yannis Smaragdakis[1,2] and Martin Bravenboer[3]

[1] University of Massachusetts, Amherst, MA 01003, USA
yannis@cs.umass.edu
[2] University of Athens, Athens 15784, Greece
smaragd@di.uoa.gr
[3] LogicBlox Inc., Two Midtown Plaza, Atlanta, GA 30309, USA
martin.bravenboer@acm.org

**Abstract.** Our recent work introduced the Doop framework for points-to analysis of Java programs. Although Datalog has been used for points-to analyses before, Doop is the first implementation to express full end-to-end context-sensitive analyses in Datalog. This includes key elements such as call-graph construction as well as the logic dealing with various semantic complexities of the Java language (native methods, reflection, threading, etc.).

The findings from the Doop research effort have been surprising. We set out to create a framework that would be highly complete and elegant without sacrificing performance "too much". By the time Doop reached maturity, it was a full order-of-magnitude faster than Lhoták and Hendren's Paddle—the state-of-the-art framework for context-sensitive points-to analyses. For the exact same logical points-to definitions (and, consequently, identical precision) Doop is more than 15x faster than Paddle for a 1-call-site sensitive analysis, with lower but still substantial speedups for other important analyses. Additionally, Doop scales to very precise analyses that are impossible with prior frameworks, directly addressing open problems in past literature. Finally, our implementation is modular and can be easily configured to analyses with a wide range of characteristics, largely due to its declarativeness.

Although this performance difference is largely attributable to architectural choices (e.g., the use of an explicit representation vs. BDDs), we believe that our ability to efficiently optimize our implementation was largely due to the declarative specifications of analyses. Working at the Datalog level eliminated much of the artificial complexity of a points-to analysis implementation, allowing us to concentrate on indexing optimizations and on the algorithmic essence of each analysis.

## 1 Introduction

*Points-to analysis* is one of the most fundamental static program analyses. It consists of computing a static approximation of all the data that a pointer variable or expression can reference during program run-time. The analysis forms the basis for practically every other program analysis and is closely inter-related with mechanisms such as call-graph construction, since the values of a pointer determine the target of dynamically resolved calls, such as object-oriented dynamically dispatched method calls or functional lambda applications.

O. de Moor et al. (Eds.): Datalog 2010, LNCS 6702, pp. 245–251, 2011.

In recent work [2, 1], we presented DOOP: a versatile points-to analysis framework for Java programs. DOOP is crucially based on the use of Datalog for specifying the program analyses, and on the aggressive optimization at the Datalog level, by programmer-assisted indexing of relations so that highly recursive Datalog programs evaluate near-optimally. The optimization approach accounts for several orders of magnitude of performance improvement: unoptimized analyses typically run over 1000 times more slowly. The result is quite surprising: compared to the prior best-comparable system DOOP often achieves speedups of an order-of-magnitude (10x or more) for several important analyses, while yielding identical results. This performance improvement is not caused by any major algorithmic innovation: we discuss in Section 3 how performance is largely a consequence of the optimization opportunities afforded by using a higher-level programming language (Datalog). Declarative specifications admit automatic optimizations and at the same time enable the user to identify and apply straightforward manual optimizations.

An important aspect of DOOP is that it is full-featured and "all Datalog". That is, DOOP is a rich framework, containing context insensitive, call-site sensitive, and object-sensitive analyses for different context depths, all specified modularly as variations on a common code base. Additionally, DOOP achieves high levels of completeness, as it handles complex Java language features (e.g., native code, finalization, and privileged actions). As a result, DOOP emulates and often exceeds the rich feature set of the PADDLE framework [7], which is the state-of-the-art in terms of completeness for complex, context-sensitive analyses. All these features are implemented entirely in Datalog, i.e., declaratively. Past points-to analysis frameworks (including those using Datalog) typically combined imperative computation and some declarative handling of the core analysis logic. For instance, the bddbddb system [11, 10] expresses the core of a points-to analysis in Datalog, while important parts (such as normalization and call-graph computation—except for simple, context-insensitive, analyses) are done in Java code. It was a surprise to researchers even that a system of such complexity can be usefully implemented declaratively. Lhoták [6] writes: *"[E]ncoding all the details of a complicated program analysis problem (such as the interrelated analyses [on-the-fly call graph construction, handling of Java features]) purely in terms of subset constraints [i.e., Datalog] may be difficult or impossible."*

The more technical aspects of DOOP (including the analysis algorithms and features, as well as our optimization methodology) are well-documented in prior publications [2, 1, 9]. Here we only intend to give a brief introduction to the framework and to extrapolate on our lessons learned from the DOOP work.

## 2   Background: Points-To Analysis in Datalog

DOOP's primary defining feature is the use of Datalog for its analyses. Architecturally, however, an important factor in DOOP's performance discussion is that it employs an *explicit* representation of relations (i.e., all tuples of a relation are represented as an explicit table, as in a database), instead of using Binary Decision Diagrams (BDDs), which have often been considered necessary for scalable points-to analysis [11, 10, 7, 6].

We use a commercial Datalog engine, developed by LogicBlox Inc. This version of Datalog allows "stratified negation", i.e., negated clauses, as long as the negation is not part of a recursive cycle. It also allows specifying that some relations are functions, i.e., the variable space is partitioned into domain and range variables, and there is only one range value for each unique combination of values in domain variables.

Datalog is a great fit for the domain of program analysis and, as a consequence, has been extensively used both for low-level [8, 5, 11] and for high-level [3, 4] analyses. The essence of Datalog is its ability to define recursive relations. Mutual recursion is the source of all complexity in program analysis. For a standard example, the logic for computing a callgraph depends on having points-to information for pointer expressions, which, in turn, requires a callgraph. We can easily see such recursive definitions in points-to analysis alone. Consider, for instance, two relations, AssignHeapAllocation(?heap, ?var) and Assign(?to, ?from). (We follow the Doop convention of capitalizing the first letter of relation names, while writing variable names in lower case and prefixing them with a question-mark.) The former relation represents all occurrences in the Java program of an instruction "a = new A();" where a heap object is allocated and assigned to a variable. That is, a pre-processing step takes a Java program (in Doop this is in intermediate, bytecode, form) as input and produces the relation contents. A static abstraction of the heap object is captured in variable ?heap—it can be concretely represented as, e.g., a fully qualified class name and the allocation's bytecode instruction index. Similarly, relation Assign contains an entry for each assignment between two Java program (reference) variables.

The mapping between the input Java program and the input relations is straightforward and purely syntactic. After this step, a simple pointer analysis can be expressed entirely in Datalog as a transitive closure computation:

```
1 VarPointsTo(?heap, ?var) <- AssignHeapAllocation(?heap, ?var).
2 VarPointsTo(?heap, ?to) <- Assign(?to, ?from), VarPointsTo(?heap, ?from).
```

The Datalog program consists of a series of *rules* that are used to establish facts about derived relations (such as VarPointsTo, which is the points-to relation, i.e., it links every program variable, ?var, with every heap object abstraction, ?heap, it can point to) from a conjunction of previously established facts. In our syntax, the left arrow symbol (<-) separates the inferred fact (the *head*) from the previously established facts (the *body*).

The key for a precise points-to analysis is context-sensitivity, which consists of qualifying program variables (and possibly object abstractions—in which case the context-sensitive analysis is said to also have a *context-sensitive heap*), with context information: the analysis collapses information (e.g., "what objects this method argument can point to") over all possible executions that result in the same context, while separating all information for different contexts. Object-sensitivity and call-site-sensitivity are the main flavors of context sensitivity in modern points-to analyses. They differ in the contexts of a context, as well as in when contexts are created and updated. Here we will not concern ourselves with such differences—it suffices to know that a context-sensitive analysis qualifies its computed facts with extra information.

Context-sensitive analysis in Doop is, to a large extent, similar to the above context-insensitive logic. The main changes are due to the introduction of Datalog variables representing contexts for variables (and, in the case of a context-sensitive heap, also objects) in the analyzed program. For an illustrative example, the following two rules handle method calls as implicit assignments from the actual parameters of a method to the formal parameters, in a 1-context-sensitive analysis with a context-*insensitive* heap. (This code is the same for both object-sensitivity and call-site-sensitivity.)

```
1  Assign(?calleeCtx, ?formal, ?callerCtx, ?actual) <-
2    CallGraphEdge(?callerCtx, ?invocation, ?calleeCtx, ?method),
3    FormalParam[?index, ?method] = ?formal,
4    ActualParam[?index, ?invocation] = ?actual.
5
6  VarPointsTo(?heap, ?toCtx, ?to) <-
7    Assign(?toCtx, ?to, ?fromCtx, ?from),
8    VarPointsTo(?heap, ?fromCtx, ?from).
```

(Note that some of the above relations are functions, and the functional notation "Relation[?domainvar] = ?val" is used instead of the relational notation, "Relation(?domainvar, ?val)". Semantically the two are equivalent, only the execution engine enforces the functional constraint and produces an error if a computation causes a function to have multiple range values for the same domain value.)

The example shows how a derived Assign relation (unlike the input relation Assign in the earlier basic example) is computed, based on the call-graph information, and then used in deriving a context-sensitive VarPointsTo relation.

For deeper contexts, one needs to add extra variables, since pure Datalog does not allow constructors and therefore cannot support value combination. We have introduced in DOOP a macro system to hide the number of context elements so that such variations do not pollute the analysis logic.

Generally, the declarative nature of DOOP often allows for very concise specifications of analyses. We show in an earlier publication [2] the striking example of the logic for the Java cast checking—i.e., the answer to the question "can type A be cast to type B?" The Datalog rules are almost an exact transcription of the Java Language Specification. A small excerpt, with the Java Language Specification text included in comments, can be seen in Figure 1.

## 3    Discussion: DOOP and Large-Scale Development in Datalog

Perhaps the main lesson learned from our experience with DOOP and its definition in Datalog is quite simple: *Datalog is not an abstract logic and does not magically yield automatic programming capabilities, but it is still much higher-level than current mainstream programming languages.*

Recent Datalog research has often concentrated on generalizing the language (to full first-order logic and higher-order logics), and on applying automated reasoning techniques. Although this is certainly a valuable direction, we believe that one should not lose sight of the fact that Datalog is already a very high-level language when compared to mainstream general purpose languages, such as Java, C++, or C#. It is, therefore, perhaps more interesting to examine Datalog not as a proxy for a logic but as an application programming language. Many of the benefits that we obtained with DOOP are

```
//  If S is an ordinary (nonarray) class, then:
//     o If T is a class type, then S must be the
//        same class as T, or a subclass of T.
CheckCast(?s, ?s) <- ClassType(?s).
CheckCast(?s, ?t) <- Subclass(?t, ?s).
...
//     o If T is an array type TC[], that is, an array of components
//        of type TC, then one of the following must be true:
//           + TC and SC are the same primitive type
CheckCast(?s, ?t) <-
  ArrayType(?s), ArrayType(?t),
  ComponentType(?s, ?sc), ComponentType(?t, ?sc), PrimitiveType(?sc).

//           + TC and SC are reference types (2.4.6), and type SC can be
//             cast to TC by recursive application of these rules.
CheckCast(?s, ?t) <-
  ComponentType(?s, ?sc), ComponentType(?t, ?tc),
  ReferenceType(?sc), ReferenceType(?tc), CheckCast(?sc, ?tc).
```

**Fig. 1.** Excerpt of Datalog code for Java cast checking, together with Java Language Specification text in comments. The rules are quite faithful to the specification.

directly due to such an approach. Of course, this raises the question of whether plain Datalog is expressive enough for general application programming. As we saw, even for the domain of points-to analysis, researchers were highly skeptical of the feasibility of expressing all elements (including those consisting mostly of tedious engineering) of a complex analysis in Datalog. We believe that this is precisely what is missing at this point in the evolution of Datalog. The language needs to be developed as a real programming language, with appropriate library support (for, e.g., graphics, communication, etc., APIs), tool support, a mature engine (for advanced automatic optimization of rule evaluation and efficient representation of relations), and possibly expressiveness enhancements (e.g., macros, exponential-search, or other high-order capabilities). A final element, which we are still debating whether it is essential or an intermediate state, is the ability to manually optimize a Datalog program, by exposition of an easy-to-understand cost model and appropriate interfacing with the engine.

Such arguments are easy to see in the context of Doop. The use of Datalog in Doop is certainly not as a logic. Doop is not written as an abstract specification that a clever runtime system automatically optimizes and executes efficiently. We needed to develop an optimization methodology for highly recursive programs and to introduce indexes manually, in order to attain optimal performance. The difference in performance between optimized and unoptimized Doop rules is enormous. At the same time, Doop is expressed at a much higher level than a similar implementation of a points-to analysis in Java or C++. The declarativeness of Datalog and the suitability of the LogicBlox Datalog platform for application development were crucial for Doop in more than one way:

- We relied on query optimization (i.e., intra-rule, as opposed to inter-rule, optimization) being performed automatically. This was crucial for performance and, although a straightforward optimization in the context of database relations, results in far more automation than programming in a mainstream high-level language.
- The declarativeness and modularity of Doop specifications contributed directly to performance. The surprisingly high performance of Doop compared to past frameworks is due to combining two factors: simple algorithmic enhancements, and an explicit representation instead of BDDs. Eliminating either of these factors results in complete lack of scalability in Doop. For instance, an explicit representation alone makes many standard analyses infeasible in Doop: even a 1H-object-sensitive analysis (i.e., 1-object-sensitive with a context-sensitive heap) would be completely infeasible for realistic programs. Nevertheless, we observed that this lack of scalability was due to very high redundancy (i.e., large sizes of some relations without an increase in analysis precision) in the data that the analysis was computing. The redundancy was easy to eliminate with two simple algorithmic enhancements: *1)* we perform exception analysis on-the-fly [1], computing contexts that are reachable because of exceptional control flow while performing the points-to analysis itself. The on-the-fly exception analysis significantly improves both precision and performance; *2)* we treat static class initializers context-insensitively (since points-to results are equivalent for all contexts of static class initializers), thus improving performance while keeping identical precision. These enhancements (especially the former, which results in highly recursive definitions of core relations) would be quite hard to consider in a non-declarative context. In Doop, such enhancements could be added with minor changes to the rules or with just the addition of extra rules. Once redundancy is eliminated via our algorithmic enhancements, an explicit representation (with the help of our index optimizations) becomes much faster than using BDDs.

Based on our experience, we believe that Datalog can have a bright future for application development. In a programming setting that has a dire need for higher-level programming abstractions, Datalog holds a great promise. The elements missing in order to fulfill this promise are not in the direction of greater declarativeness and automated reasoning abilities. Pursuing more complete-logic-like variants of Datalog may turn out to be an unreachable goal and is certainly not what is missing in practice: Datalog is already much more declarative than the mainstream languages currently used for application programming. Instead, it is practical elements that are missing and that can propel actual Datalog implementations to the mainstream. An interesting question is whether it is necessary for a programmer to treat a Datalog program as a program and not as a specification, i.e., whether the programmer should have the ability to understand and manually influence the program's execution cost.

In summary, the Doop framework has raised the bar in the domain of points-to analysis by introducing fast, modular, and scalable implementations of precise points-to analysis algorithms, while yielding important lessons about the architecture of such implementations. At the same time, however, we hope that Doop will be representative of future successes for Datalog application development as a whole.

**Acknowledgments.** This work was funded by the NSF (CCF-0917774, CCF-0934631) and by LogicBlox Inc.

# References

1. Bravenboer, M., Smaragdakis, Y.: Exception analysis and points-to analysis: Better together. In: Dillon, L. (ed.) ISSTA 2009: Proceedings of the 2009 International Symposium on Software Testing and Analysis, New York, NY, USA (July 2009)
2. Bravenboer, M., Smaragdakis, Y.: Strictly declarative specification of sophisticated points-to analyses. In: OOPSLA 2009: 24th Annual ACM SIGPLAN Conference on Object Oriented Programming, Systems, Languages, and Applications, ACM, New York (2009)
3. Eichberg, M., Kloppenburg, S., Klose, K., Mezini, M.: Defining and continuous checking of structural program dependencies. In: ICSE 2008: Proc. of the 30th Int. Conf. on Software Engineering, pp. 391–400. ACM, New York (2008)
4. Hajiyev, E., Verbaere, M., de Moor, O.: Codequest: Scalable source code queries with Datalog. In: Hu, Q. (ed.) ECOOP 2006. LNCS, vol. 4067, pp. 2–27. Springer, Heidelberg (2006)
5. Lam, M.S., Whaley, J., Livshits, V.B., Martin, M.C., Avots, D., Carbin, M., Unkel, C.: Context-sensitive program analysis as database queries. In: PODS 2005: Proc. of the Twenty-fourth ACM SIGMOD-SIGACT-SIGART Symposium on Principles of Database Systems, pp. 1–12. ACM, New York (2005)
6. Lhoták, O.: Program Analysis using Binary Decision Diagrams. PhD thesis, McGill University (January 2006)
7. Lhoták, O., Hendren, L.: Evaluating the benefits of context-sensitive points-to analysis using a BDD-based implementation. ACM Trans. Softw. Eng. Methodol. 18(1), 1–53 (2008)
8. Reps, T.: Demand interprocedural program analysis using logic databases. In: Ramakrishnan, R. (ed.) Applications of Logic Databases, pp. 163–196. Kluwer Academic Publishers, Dordrecht (1994)
9. Smaragdakis, Y., Bravenboer, M., Lhoták, O.: Pick your contexts well: Understanding object-sensitivity (the making of a precise and scalable pointer analysis). In: POPL 2011: Proceedings of the 38th Annual ACM SIGPLAN-SIGACT Symposium on Principles of Programming Languages. ACM, New York (2011)
10. Whaley, J., Avots, D., Carbin, M., Lam, M.S.: Using Datalog with binary decision diagrams for program analysis. In: Yi, K. (ed.) APLAS 2005. LNCS, vol. 3780, pp. 97–118. Springer, Heidelberg (2005)
11. Whaley, J., Lam, M.S.: Cloning-based context-sensitive pointer alias analysis using binary decision diagrams. In: PLDI 2004: Proc. of the ACM SIGPLAN 2004 Conf. on Programming Language Design and Implementation, pp. 131–144. ACM, New York (2004)

# Distributed Datalog Revisited*

Serge Aboiteboul[1], Meghyn Bienvenu[2],
Alban Galland[1], and Marie-Christine Rousset[3]

[1] INRIA Saclay & ENS Cachan, France
`firstname.lastname@inria.fr`
[2] CNRS & Univ. Paris-Sud, France
`meghyn@lri.fr`
[3] Univ. Grenoble, France
`Marie-Christine.Rousset@imag.fr`

## 1 Introduction

The emergence of Web 2.0 and social network applications has enabled more and more users to share sensitive information over the Web. The information they manipulate has many facets: personal data (e.g., pictures, movies, music, contacts, emails), social data (e.g., annotations, recommendations, contacts), localization information (e.g., bookmarks), access information (e.g., login, keys), web services (e.g., legacy data, search engines), access rights, ontologies, beliefs, time and provenance information, etc. The tasks they perform are very diverse: search, query, update, authentication, data extraction, etc. We believe that all this should be viewed in the holistic context of the management of a distributed knowledge base. Furthermore, we believe that datalog (and its extensions) forms the sound formal basis for representing such information and supporting these tasks. In this paper, we revisit datalog with this goal in mind. The focus of the presentation is on the formal extension of the model of distributed datalog and does not consider the implementation or the evaluation of the corresponding system [8].

We use logical (datalog) statements to capture these different facets of information that are typically considered in isolation. Knowledge can be communicated, replicated, queried, updated, and monitored. The use of a formal model allows information to be obtained by performing complex reasoning. Our model encompasses a rich variety of scenarios ranging from information in centralized servers to massively distributed, from fully trusted to untrusted, and possibly encrypted information, thereby capturing the reality of today's Web. It also provides the possibility of formally proving or disproving desirable properties such as soundness (data is only acquired legally) and completeness (one can acquire all data that one can legally claim).

After some preliminaries in Section 2, we introduce the model in Section 3. We briefly mention extensions in Section 4. The last section is a conclusion.

* This work has been partially funded by the European Research Council under the European Community's Seventh Framework Programme (FP7/2007-2013) / ERC grant Webdam, agreement 226513. http://webdam.inria.fr/

O. de Moor et al. (Eds.): Datalog 2010, LNCS 6702, pp. 252–261, 2011.

## 2    Preliminaries

In this section, we first consider the alphabets we use, then the kind of knowledge we manipulate. Finally, we briefly recall distributed datalog.

*Alphabets.* A central notion is that of a *principal* that corresponds to a participant in the system. Our terminology is motivated by the notion of "principal" in the domain of security, i.e., an entity that can be identified and verified via authentication. In the same spirit, a principal is determined in our context by a URI (and possibly authentication keys). Some principals, the *peers*, have a physical address with storage and processing capabilities, e.g., Facebook or Alice's iPhone. Others may represent a user, e.g., Alice, or a community such as Alice's friends or the rock climbing group.

The information of a principal $p$ is organized in relations. The identification of a relation is of the form $r@p$ where $r$ is the relation name and $p$ the principal. For instance, one might have the relation *pictures@alice-iPhone* (the pictures album stored on Alice's iPhone) or the relation *expert@rockClimbing* (the experts known in this group).

One can query a peer since it has a URI that corresponds to a real system. For instance, one can obtain the relation *pictures@alice-iPhone* by accessing the iPhone (assuming one has access to it). On the contrary, one cannot query a non-peer principal. For instance, one cannot ask *rockClimbing* (a virtual entity) for the list of experts. To obtain such information, one needs rules that tell us how to get information, e.g. for the *rockClimbing* experts, typically by querying "real" relations (extensional or intentional) at some peers.

More formally, the model uses the following alphabets:

- A set $\mathcal{P}'$ of *principal* IDs, that includes a set $\mathcal{P}$ of *peer* IDs. The system provides a unique IDs for each different principal, in the spirit of the standard notion of URIs.
- A set $\mathcal{R}$ of *relation* IDs. An actual relation name is a pair $r@p$ where $r$ is a relation ID and $p$ is a principal ID.
- A set $\mathcal{D}$ of *constants*. It is the disjoint union of the set of principal IDs, relation IDs and a set of data constants. A data constant is some sequence of bits: e.g., a string, a file (picture, music), an XML document. Principal and relation IDs are also constants so that we can reason about them. Constants are typed, e.g., principal, relation, string, integer, dates, etc.
- A set of *variables*. Similarly to constants, variables are typed. We use words starting with small letters for constants and with capitals for variables.

*Knowledge.* The architecture is illustrated in Figure 1. Consider for instance Peer 2. It has data and rules defining personal relations $r1, r2, r3$. It also has data and rules about relation $s$ of principal $q_2$ (shared with Peer 1) and about $r@q_1$ (shared with Peer 3). Observe the distinction for each peer, between its local schema (e.g., $r_i$ for Peer 2) and its participation in the global schema (e.g., $r@q_1, s@q_2$ for Peer 2).

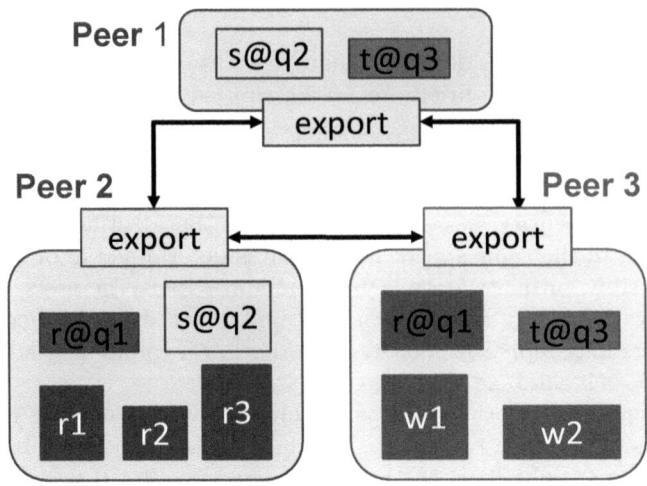

**Fig. 1.** Distributed datalog framework

Basic knowledge is expressed using facts of the form $r@p(a_1, ..., a_n)$. Note that peers and relations are reified[1]. It is therefore possible to have a fact $r@p(r', p')$ that speaks of a relation $r'$ and a peer $p'$. Furthermore, we can use peer and relation variables, e.g., $r@p(R, P)$ with $R$ a relation variable and $P$ a peer variable. From a formal viewpoint, we can see each fact $r@p(a, b)$ in a binary relation $r@p$ as a fact $univ_4(r, p, a, b)$ in a 4-ary relation. Indeed, we can even logically see it as a fact $univ(r, p, a, b, -, ..., -)$ in a unique relation, wide enough to accommodate all the tuples that are considered. Even if we introduced a more readable notation for our model, the reader should keep in mind that our model can then be fully described in terms of standard datalog.

In a distributed context, a peer $p$ is naturally led to possess data about other participants, for instance a principal who uses $p$ as server for his data, or another peer that replicates its data on $p$ to offer better performance or availability. For instance, consider the fact $album@alice(a)$. This fact may be known, e.g., by two peers, Picasa and Alice's iPhone. The knowledge of this fact by these peers, respectively, can be stated as:

$$picasa \; exports \; album@alice(a)$$
$$alice\text{-}iPhone \; exports \; album@alice(a)$$

The use of the *exports* word is motivated by the fact that one can now query Picasa or Alice's iPhone, to obtain such data, i.e., this data is *exported* by these two peers. Indeed, the primary goal of such a modality is to capture the essence of communications between peers. For instance, we can ask such data from Picasa using (informally) the query: *picasa exports album@alice(X)*.

---

[1] Reification is a process through which a computable/addressable object acts as a proxy for a non computable/addressable object.

More formally, we model such knowledge using a particular relation called *export*. The fact that some peer $p$ *exports* $r@q(a_1, ..., a_n)$ is stated as:

$$export@p(r, q, a_1, ..., a_n).$$

Note that the use of special relations such as *export* (or *univ* above) complicates typing. Suppose for instance that we store in relation *export@p* tuples in $r@q_1$ and $r@q_2$ and that the first contains pairs of peers and the second data elements. Then the "type" of a tuple in *export@p* is: $\langle r, q_1, peer, peer \rangle$ or $\langle r, q_2, data \rangle$. The use of these untyped relations may be seen as syntactic sugaring for some relations of distinct types.

As already mentioned, the relation *export* captures communications (interactions) between the peers. It therefore plays an essential role in the model. Particular applications may use other specific relations with particular associated semantics. For instance, one could consider:

- Localization: e.g., *where@q*$(r, p)$. Such a fact in the $q$ principal indicates that relation $r@q$ can be obtained from peer $p$.
- Access rights: *access@p*$(read, q)$. This fact states that $q$ has read access to principal $p$.

*Classical distributed datalog.* We briefly present distributed datalog which is a rather straightforward variation of standard datalog. We refer to, e.g., [4], for technical details on datalog. To our knowledge, the first attempts to distribute datalog on different peers are [16] and [19]. Since then, many works have followed. For instance, one of the authors of this article adapted query-sub-query optimization to a distributed setting in [1]. Distributed versions of datalog have also recently been used to implement Web routers [18], DHT [17] and Map-Reduce [7] very efficiently. These works only consider peer principals, since the focus is on the exchange of data between machines.

We present here a standard version of Distributed Datalog inspired by [1]. To illustrate, the following program defines the album of Alice's iPhone to include all the photos stored in her iPhone (a local relation) and on Picasa (a relation on another peer):

$$album@alice\text{-}iPhone(X) \leftarrow photos@alice\text{-}iPhone(X)$$
$$album@alice\text{-}iPhone(X) \leftarrow aliceAlbum@picasa(X)$$

Precisely, a *DDL* (for distributed datalog) *schema* is a triple $(\Pi, Rel, \sigma)$ where $\Pi$ is a finite set of peer IDs, for each $p \in \Pi$, $Rel(p)$ is a finite set of relation IDs, and for each $p, r$, $\sigma(r@p)$ specifies the type of relation $r@p$, i.e., its arity and the types of its columns.

A *DDL instance* $I$ of $(\Pi, \rho, \sigma)$ maps each $p$ to a finite set $I(p)$ of "safe" datalog *rules* defining relations in $p$.

We will formalize the notion of safety when we describe *distributed datalog revisited*. Rules with an empty body, e.g., $r@p(5) \leftarrow$, are called *facts*. Observe that, by definition, a rule of $p$ cannot have in its head a relation at peer $p'$. We will relax this restriction in Remark 3.

Let $I$ be an instance. The semantics $close(I)$ is defined as the smallest set of facts over $\cup_p Rel(p)$ that satisfies $\cup_p I(p)$.

*Remark 1.* Observe that a rule at peer $p$ may use in its body a relation at peer $p'$. This may be realized in practice by posing a query to $p'$. The query is continuous in the sense that $p'$ keeps sending matching tuples to $p$ as long as it derives them. We will ignore here the issue of detecting termination, which may be performed using some classical techniques.

We assume here to simplify that each peer knows how to query other peers and that it has access to all the data in other peers. This assumption may be relaxed in some contexts and in particular, when considering access rights.

Note that such specifications are very static, in particular with respect to localization. Also there is the assumption that each principal corresponds to a physical machine and is available all the time. The work presented here removes such limitations.

## 3   Distributed Datalog Revisited

In this section, we extend datalog, in order to capture the kind of knowledge one needs to handle in distributed information systems. We introduce two extensions, one based on the reification of relations and peers, and the second on the notion of principal.

*Reifying relations and peers.* The first extension we consider is based on reifying relations and peers. (We still ignore for now non-peer principals.) To illustrate, suppose that Alice is storing her album on some machine and Bob does not know where. Suppose also that their group of friends decided upon a global localization service, say *directory@server*. Then Bob may use the following rule:

$$alice\text{-}album@bob\text{-}iPhone(X) \leftarrow directory@server(album, alice, P),$$
$$export@P(album, alice, X)$$

Here $P, R$ are respectively peer and relation variables. The service *directory@server* provides bindings for $P$ (the name of the system) and $R$ (the name of the relation on this system) where Alice's album can be found. Observe that similar use of localization services are standard in distributed contexts, e.g., DHT or Ldap.

*Non-peer Principals.* We extend the notion of schema, instance, and their semantics to now include non-peer principals. To illustrate, assume that Alice, Bob and others created a principal *rockClimbing*. They may want to use a relation *album* in this shared principal. Bob may for instance use the rules:

$$album@rockClimbing(X) \leftarrow album@bob\text{-}iPhone(X)$$
$$album@rockClimbing(X) \leftarrow friends@bob\text{-}iPhone(Q),$$
$$directory@server(album, Q, P),$$
$$export@P(album, Q, X)$$

Now observe that *album@rockClimbing* is a "global" relation and that many peers may "publish" data in it and many peers may know how to retrieve data from it. The second rule highlights three main ways of obtaining information:

- *friends@bob-iPhone*($Q$) matches some facts in a (local) relation of this particular peer;
- *directory@server*(*album*, $Q$, $P$) matches some facts in a relation of another peer;
- *export@P*($Q$, *album*, $X$) matches some facts exported by another peer.

The difference between the second and third kind of atoms is that the second one is a form of syntactic sugaring which hides the explicit communication step. Indeed, from a communication point of view, the evaluation of *directory@server*(*album*, $Q$, $P$) results in a query to *server*, namely:

$$export@server(directory, server, album, Q, P)$$

There is yet a fourth kind of atom of the form $t@q(\bar{V})$ that matches the peer's knowledge of some non-peer principal relation $t@q$.

The example illustrates a key usage of our model for maintaining "external knowledge". Suppose that Alice is a friend of Bob ($Q$ is bound to Alice). Intuitively, we would like to get the album of Alice. What we query instead is a machine say Picasa ($P$ is bound to Picasa) where Alice stores her pictures.

*Formal model* A *term* is a constant or a variable. In particular, a relation term, a peer term and a principal term are terms of type relation, peer and principal respectively.

A *DDLR* (for distributed datalog revisited) *rule* is an expression of the form:

$$\alpha_0@\beta_0(V_0) \leftarrow \alpha_1@\beta_1(V_1), ..., \alpha_n@\beta_n(V_n)$$

where

- $\alpha_i, \beta_i$ are relation and principal terms respectively.
- $V_i$ are tuples of terms.
- The rule is *safe* in that (i) in the body, a principal or relation variable must be bound before appearing as $\alpha_i$ or $\beta_i$, and (ii) a variable occurring in the head must be bound in the body.

Note the ordering of atoms in the previous definition. This can be relaxed by imposing that for *some* ordering of the atoms, (i) and (ii) hold.

A *DDLR schema* is a quadruple $(\Pi', \Pi, Rel, \sigma)$ where $\Pi$ is a set of peer IDs, $\Pi' \supseteq \Pi$ a set of principals, $Rel$ assigns relation IDs to principals, and $\sigma$ gives their arities.

A *DDLR instance* $I$ of $(\Pi', \Pi, Rel, \sigma)$ maps each $p \in \Pi$ (each peer) to a finite set $I(p)$ of safe DDLR rules such that:

**(head)** The relation in the head is (+) either $R@p(\bar{V})$ for some relation term $R$; or (++) $R@Q(\bar{V})$ for some relation term $R$ and *non-peer* principal term $Q$.

**(body)** Each relation in the body is either of the form $R@Q(\bar{V})$ for some relation term $R$ and $Q=p$ or $Q$ is some non-peer principal term or of the form $export@P(\bar{V})$ for some peer term $P$.

**(typing)** Each rule respects the typing specified by the schema.

The constraint (body) can be relaxed to any kind of relation $R@Q(\bar{V})$. In this case, if $Q \neq p$ is a peer, it is interpreted as $export@Q(R,Q,\bar{V})$. Henceforth, unless otherwise specified, datalog means DDLR.

*Semantics.* There are subtleties in the inference of facts. First, note that the classical least-model semantics, i.e. $close(\cup_p I(p))$ is in general not attainable. For instance, suppose peer $p$ has no rule defining non-peer principal $q$ and has a rule $r@p(x) \leftarrow s@q(x)$. Then $p$ cannot call $q$ so this rule is useless, even if $q$ is defined on another peer.

   Observe another subtlety: (+) uses typing to prevent the derivation of information in other peer relations. We will show how to relax (+) in Remark 3.

   For a set $K$ of facts, a relation $r$ and a principal $q$, $K(r@q)$ is the sets of facts in $K$ about $r@q$.

**Definition 1.** *(Distributed least-model semantics) Let $I$ be an instance. The dclosure is a function (i) that maps each peer $p$, to a set $dclose(I,p)$ of facts over $\cup_q Rel(q)$ (facts over peers and non-peer principals) and (ii) that satisfies:*

1. *for each pair of peers $p,p'$, $dclose(I,p)(export@p) = dclose(I,p')(export@p)$.*
2. *for each peer $p$, $dclose(I,p)$ satisfies $I(p)$.*
3. *$\cup_p dclose(I,p)$ is minimum.*

Observe that all peers have the same view of the peer relations. Suppose peer $p$ does not even know of peer $p'$, i.e., $p'$ does not occur in its local knowledge. By the previous definition, $dclose(I,p)(export@p') = dclose(I,p')(export@p')$. This may seem unnatural. However, suppose someone asks the query $\leftarrow export@p'(x_1, ..., x_n)$ to $p$. Then $p$ discovers the existence of $p'$, can get data from $p'$ and can answer the query. This motivates (1) in the previous definition.

   Note that, in general, the different views the peers have of the principal relations may be incomplete. It is easy to see that in general, for a peer $p_0$:

$$dclose(I,p_0) \subseteq \cup_p dclose(I,p) \subseteq close(\cup_p I(p))$$

and that the inclusions are possibly strict. Note that this leads to complex reasoning about knowledge in the style of [13]. One may want to check whether a given set of rules guarantees completeness. Unfortunately, verifying such properties comes down to comparing datalog programs, which is undecidable [11].

   We conclude this section with two remarks: one on open vs. closed world assumptions, and one on relaxing (+) by allowing rules with other peer relations in the head.

*Remark 2 (Open vs. closed world).* It should be observed that such definitions of "global principal relations" typically rely on an open-world assumption since anyone (with proper access right) can participate in the definition of that relation and perhaps no one has the complete picture. This is in the spirit of Local-as-View mediator systems [14]. On the other hand, consider a peer relation. The value of that relation at the peer can be seen as its complete instance, so it is more in the spirit of the closed world assumption and Global-as-View. Clearly, both kinds of relations may be combined freely. For instance, a definition of a peer relation may use a non-peer principal relation.

*Remark 3 (Relaxing (+)).* Consider a peer $p_1$ with the rule $r@p_2(x) \leftarrow s@p_1(x)$. An issue is that when asked the query $\leftarrow r@p_2(X)$, peer $p_2$ may not be aware of the rule at $p_1$. We could allow such a rule if (intuitively), $p_1$ notifies $p_2$ that he wishes to participate in the definition of $r@p_2$ and $p_2$ reacts by installing locally the rule:

$$r@p_2(X) \leftarrow export@p1(r, p2, X)$$

that may be interpreted by "$p_1$ also has facts for $r@p_2$".

# 4    Extensions in Brief

A holistic knowledge-base model would also need to rely on a number of extensions of datalog that have so far been studied in isolation. We mention them next. Datalog has to be extended in the following ways:

**Nonmonotonicity.** One can first consider negation in rules with different semantics, e.g., stratified negation or well-founded negation, see [4]. Problems of nonmonotonicity also arise when one considers updates (which are necessary to capture real applications). One could also consider negation in heads of rules. So for instance, someone may state that Bill is not an expert in rock climbing. This may contradict the statement of someone else who states that he is. Clearly, such inconsistencies are frequent on the Web and a comprehensive model for Web data management should take this into account.

**Ontologies and incomplete information.** Ontologies can be used to structure a participant's vocabulary and to translate knowledge between the vocabularies of different participants in a distributed environment, cf. e.g., [6]. Some simply ontology statements, like predicate inclusions (e.g. *Photo* $\sqsubseteq$ *Document*), can be straightforwardly handled by our proposed framework. However, other important ontological constructs, like existential restrictions (*Parent* $\sqsubseteq$ $\exists hasChild$) which may introduce incomplete information, are not supported. Extensions of datalog in this direction have been considered, see [10].

**Intentional data.** We assumed in this paper that we answer queries with facts. It may be appropriate to answer with "rules". For instance, if one asks a machine for a relation, say $R$, in the *rockClimbing* principal, it may be preferable to obtain as answer, some rule for computing $R$, e.g., stating that one should first obtain some data from Bob and combine it with data from Alice. This presents the advantage of allowing learning about new relations, a feature typically needed on the Web. Extensions of datalog in this direction have been considered under the generic term of Active XML [2,5].

**Trees.** The data exchange format of the Web is XML, i.e. trees instead of relations. Active XML also extends datalog to trees.

**Time.** When we consider evolving data, time becomes an issue since a relation at time $t$ may be different than at time $t'$. Extensions of datalog with time have been studied, e.g. in [15]. The idea is to distinguish between relations $r@t$ and $r@t'$, just as we distinguished between knowledge of *rockClimbing* at two sites $s1$ and $s2$.

**Access rights.** Access rights have been considered in this setting in the WebdamExchange system [3]. For instance, we can augment the *export* relation with an extra column for the identity of the caller. Then to query a peer $p$, we use this extra column, e.g.,

$$exports@picasa(album,lulu,X,alice).$$

Alice uses this query (properly authenticated with her signature) for requesting pictures in Lulu's album from Picasa. Based on the access rights of Alice, Picasa chooses which data to return. Due to space limitations, this will not be detailed here.

**Beliefs.** Peers or principals may want to state information they believe in but are not sure. This may be captured, for instance, by extending the *export* relation with yet one more column. The fact

$$export@server(where,\ album,\ alice,\ bobIPhone,\ 72\%)$$

states that the server believes that the album of Alice can be found on Bob's iPhone with a strong probability (72%).

## 5   Conclusion

There has recently been renewed interest in datalog; see [12]. We presented a knowledge model for the management of distributed (Web) information based on datalog. We already discussed a number of extensions in Section 4, so possible directions for future works. Some of the authors are currently developing a system based on distributed datalog revisited, namely WebdamExchange, with a strong emphasis on access control [3].

The work presented here raises a number of issues. In particular, we need to investigate the reasoning needed to find information of interest or disseminate such information. A main issue is the efficient support of queries in systems based on distributed datalog. Optimization techniques such as QSQ [20] and Magic Set [9] have been adapted to similar setting, e.g., [19,16,1]. Also, it would be interesting to study properties of the resulting systems such as completeness, i.e., any available data can be obtained. In the context of access rights, completeness takes a new flavor: "any data one is entitled to see can be obtained". Also, this raises the issue of *soundness*: "only data one is entitled to see can be obtained".

# References

1. Abiteboul, S., Abrams, Z., Haar, S., Milo, T.: Diagnosis of asynchronous discrete event systems: datalog to the rescue! In: PODS, pp. 358–367 (2005)
2. Abiteboul, S., Benjelloun, O., Milo, T.: The Active XML project: an overview. The VLDB Journal 17, 1019–1040 (2008)
3. Abiteboul, S., Galland, A., Marian, A., Polyzotis, A.: A model for web information management with access control (2010) (in preparation)
4. Abiteboul, S., Hull, R., Vianu, V.: Foundations of Databases. Addison-Wesley, Reading (1995)
5. Abiteboul, S., Segoufin, L., Vianu, V.: Static analysis of Active XML systems. In: PODS, pp. 221–230 (2008)
6. Adjiman, P., Chatalic, P., Goasdoué, F., Rousset, M.-C., Simon, L.: Distributed reasoning in a peer-to-peer setting: Application to the semantic web. J. Artif. Intell. Res. (JAIR) 25, 269–314 (2006)
7. Alvaro, P., Condie, T., Conway, N., Elmeleegy, K., Hellerstein, J.M., Sears, R.: Boom analytics: exploring data-centric, declarative programming for the cloud. In: EuroSys, pp. 223–236 (2010)
8. Antoine, E., Galland, A., Lyngbaek, K., Marian, A., Polyzotis, N.: Social networking on top of the WebdamExchange system. In: ICDE (to appear, 2011)
9. Bancilhon, F., Maier, D., Sagiv, Y., Ullman, J.D.: Magic sets and other strange ways to implement logic programs. In: PODS, pp. 1–15 (1986)
10. Calì, A., Gottlob, G., Lukasiewicz, T.: Datalog$^{\pm}$: a unified approach to ontologies and integrity constraints. In: ICDT, pp. 14–30 (2009)
11. Cosmadakis, S.S., Gaifman, H., Kanellakis, P.C., Vardi, M.Y.: Decidable optimization problems for database logic programs (preliminary report). In: STOC, pp. 477–490 (1988)
12. Datalog 2.0. Oxford Univ. (2010), http://www.datalog20.org/
13. Fagin, R., Halpern, J.Y., Moses, Y., Vardi, M.Y.: Reasoning about knowledge. The MIT Press, Cambridge (2003)
14. Halevy, A.Y.: Answering queries using views: A survey. The VLDB Journal 10, 270–294 (2001)
15. Hellerstein, J.: The declarative imperative: Experiences and conjectures in distributed logic. SIGMOD Rec. 39, 5–19 (2010)
16. Hulin, G.: Parallel processing of recursive queries in distributed architectures. In: VLDB, pp. 87–96 (1989)
17. Loo, B.T., Condie, T., Hellerstein, J.M., Maniatis, P., Roscoe, T., Stoica, I.: Implementing declarative overlays. In: SOSP, pp. 75–90 (2005)
18. Loo, B.T., Hellerstein, J.M., Stoica, I., Ramakrishnan, R.: Declarative routing: extensible routing with declarative queries. In: SIGCOMM, pp. 289–300 (2005)
19. Nejdl, W., Ceri, S., Wiederhold, G.: Evaluating recursive queries in distributed databases. IEEE Trans. Knowl. Data Eng. 5, 104–121 (1993)
20. Vieille, L.: Recursive axioms in deductive databases: The query/subquery approach. In: Expert Database Conf., pp. 253–267 (1986)

# DEDALUS: Datalog in Time and Space

Peter Alvaro[1], William R. Marczak[1], Neil Conway[1],
Joseph M. Hellerstein[1], David Maier[2], and Russell Sears[3]

[1] University of California, Berkeley
{palvaro,wrm,nrc,hellerstein}@cs.berkeley.edu
[2] Portland State University
maier@cs.pdx.edu
[3] Yahoo! Research
sears@yahoo-inc.com

**Abstract.** Recent research has explored using Datalog-based languages to express a distributed system as a set of logical invariants. Two properties of distributed systems proved difficult to model in Datalog. First, the state of any such system evolves with its execution. Second, deductions in these systems may be arbitrarily delayed, dropped, or reordered by the unreliable network links they must traverse. Previous efforts addressed the former by extending Datalog to include updates, key constraints, persistence and events, and the latter by assuming ordered and reliable delivery while ignoring delay. These details have a semantics outside Datalog, which increases the complexity of the language and its interpretation, and forces programmers to think operationally. We argue that the missing component from these previous languages is a notion of *time*.

In this paper we present **DEDALUS**, a foundation language for programming and reasoning about distributed systems. DEDALUS reduces to a subset of Datalog with negation, aggregate functions, successor and choice, and adds an explicit notion of logical time to the language. We show that DEDALUS provides a declarative foundation for the two signature features of distributed systems: mutable state, and asynchronous processing and communication. Given these two features, we address two important properties of programs in a domain-specific manner: a notion of *safety* appropriate to non-terminating computations, and *stratified* monotonic reasoning with negation over time. We also provide conservative syntactic checks for our temporal notions of safety and stratification. Our experience implementing full-featured systems in variants of Datalog suggests that DEDALUS is well-suited to the specification of rich distributed services and protocols, and provides both cleaner semantics and richer tests of correctness.

**Keywords:** Datalog, distributed systems, logic programming, temporal logic.

## 1 Introduction

In recent years, there has been a resurgence of interest in Datalog as the foundation for applied, domain-specific languages in a wide variety of areas, including networking [20], distributed systems [2,5,8], natural language processing [11], robotics [4], compiler analysis [15], security [14,18,32] and computer games [31]. The resulting

O. de Moor et al. (Eds.): Datalog 2010, LNCS 6702, pp. 262–281, 2011.

languages have been promoted for their compact and natural representations of tasks in their respective domains, in many cases leading to code that is orders of magnitude shorter than equivalent imperative programs. Another stated advantage of these languages is their ability to directly capture intuitive specifications of protocols and programs as executable code.

While most of these efforts were intended to be "declarative" languages, many chose to extend Datalog with operational features natural to their application domain. These operational aspects limit the ability of the language designers to leverage the rich literature on Datalog: program checks such as safety and stratifiability, and optimizations such as magic sets and incremental maintenance of materialized views. In addition, in many of these languages the blend of operational and declarative constructs leads to semantic ambiguities. These aspects are of particular interest to us in the context of networking and other distributed systems, both because we have considerable practical experience with these languages [2,20], and because others have examined the semantic ambiguities of these languages in some depth [23,26].

In this paper we reconsider declarative programming for distributed systems from a model-theoretic perspective. We introduce a declarative language called DEDALUS[1] that enables the specification of rich distributed systems concepts without recourse to operational constructs. DEDALUS is a subset of a language with well-studied features: Datalog enhanced with negation, aggregate functions, choice, and a successor relation. DEDALUS provides a model-theoretic foundation for the two key features of distributed systems: mutable state, and asynchronous processing and communication. We show how these features are captured in DEDALUS via the incorporation of *time* as an attribute of Datalog predicates.

Given the ability to express programs with these two features, we address two important properties of DEDALUS programs: a temporal notion of *safety* appropriate to long-running services and protocols, and *stratified* monotonic reasoning with negation over time. We also provide conservative syntactic checks for our temporal notions of safety and stratification.

We begin by defining $\text{DEDALUS}_0$, a restricted sublanguage of Datalog (Section 2). We show how $\text{DEDALUS}_0$ supports state update in Section 3, and prove temporal safety and stratifiability properties of $\text{DEDALUS}_0$ in Section 4. Finally, we introduce DEDALUS by adding support for asynchrony to $\text{DEDALUS}_0$ in Section 5. Throughout, we demonstrate the expressivity and practical utility of our work with specific examples, including a number of building-block routines from classical distributed computing, such as sequences, queues, distributed clocks, and reliable broadcast. We also discuss the correspondence between DEDALUS and our prior work implementing full-featured distributed services in more operational Datalog variants [2,20].

---

[1] DEDALUS is intended as a precursor language for **Bloom**, a high-level language for programming distributed systems that will replace Overlog in the **BOOM** project [2]. As such, it is derived from the character Stephen Dedalus in James Joyce's *Ulysses*, whose dense and precise chapters precede those of the novel's hero, Leopold Bloom. The character Dedalus, in turn, was partly derived from Daedalus, the greatest of the Greek engineers and father of Icarus. Unlike Overlog, which flew too close to the sun, Dedalus remains firmly grounded.

## 2    DEDALUS$_0$

We take as our foundation the language Datalog¬ [30]: Datalog enhanced with negated subgoals. We will be interested in the classes of syntactically stratifiable and locally stratifiable programs [27], which we revisit below. For conciseness, when we refer to "Datalog" below our intent is to admit negation—i.e., Datalog¬.

As a matter of notation, we refer to a countably infinite universe of constants $C$—in which $C_1, C_2, \ldots$ are representations of individual constants—and a countably infinite universe of variable symbols $\mathcal{A} = A_1, A_2, \ldots$. We will capture time in DEDALUS$_0$ via an infinite relation successor isomorphic to the successor relation on the integers; for convenience we will in fact refer to the domain $\mathbb{Z}$ when discussing time, though no specific interpretation of the symbols in $\mathbb{Z}$ is intended beyond the fact that successor(x,y) is true exactly when $y = x + 1$.

### 2.1   Syntactic Restrictions

DEDALUS$_0$ is a restricted sublanguage of Datalog. Specifically, we restrict the admissible schemata and the form of rules with the four constraints that follow.

**Schema:** We require that the final attribute of every DEDALUS$_0$ predicate range over the domain $\mathbb{Z}$. In a typical interpretation, DEDALUS$_0$ programs will use this final attribute to connote a "timestamp," so we refer to this attribute as the *time suffix* of the corresponding predicate.

**Time Suffix:** In a well-formed DEDALUS$_0$ rule, every subgoal must use the same existential variable $\mathcal{T}$ as its time suffix. A well-formed DEDALUS$_0$ rule must also have a time suffix $S$ as its rightmost head attribute, which must be constrained in exactly one of the following two ways:

1. The rule is *deductive* if $S$ is bound to the value $\mathcal{T}$; that is, the body contains the subgoal $S = \mathcal{T}$.
2. The rule is *inductive* if $S$ is the successor of $\mathcal{T}$; that is, the body contains the subgoal successor($\mathcal{T}$, $S$).

In Section 5, we will define DEDALUS as a superset of DEDALUS$_0$ and introduce a third kind of rule to capture asynchrony.

*Example 1.* The following are examples of well-formed deductive and inductive rules, respectively.

deductive: p(A, B, S) ← e(A, B, $\mathcal{T}$), S = $\mathcal{T}$;

inductive: q(A, B, S) ← e(A, B, $\mathcal{T}$), successor($\mathcal{T}$, S);

**Positive and Negative Predicates:** For every extensional predicate r in a DEDALUS$_0$ program $P$, we add to $P$ two distinguished predicates r_pos and r_neg with the same schema as r. We define r_pos using the following rule:

r_pos($A_1, A_2, [\ldots], A_n, S$) ←
    r($A_1, A_2, [\ldots], A_n, \mathcal{T}$), $S = \mathcal{T}$;

That is, for every extensional predicate r there is an intensional predicate r_pos that contains at least the contents of r. Intuitively, this rule allows extensional facts to serve as ground for r_pos, while enabling other rules to derive additional r_pos facts.

The predicate r_pos may be referenced in the body or head of any DEDALUS$_0$ rule. We will make use of the predicate r_neg later to capture the notion of mutable state; we return to it in Section 3.2. Like r_pos, the use of r_neg in the heads and bodies of rules is unrestricted.

**Guarded EDB:** No well-formed DEDALUS$_0$ rule may involve any extensional predicate, except for a rule of the form above.

## 2.2  Abbreviated Syntax and Temporal Interpretation

We have been careful to define DEDALUS$_0$ as a subset of Datalog; this inclusion allows us to take advantage of Datalog's well-known semantics and the rich literature on the language.

DEDALUS$_0$ programs are intended to capture temporal semantics. For example, a fact, $p(C_1 \ldots C_n, C_{n+1})$, with some constant $C_{n+1}$ in its time suffix can be thought of as a fact that is true "at time $C_{n+1}$." Deductive rules can be seen as *instantaneous* statements: their deductions hold for predicates agreeing in the time suffix and describe what is true "for an instant" given what is known at that instant. Inductive rules are *temporal*—their consequents are defined to be true "at a different time" than their antecedents.

To simplify DEDALUS$_0$ notation for this typical interpretation, we introduce some syntactic "sugar" as follows:

- *Implicit time-suffixes in body predicates:* Since each body predicate of a well-formed rule has an existential variable $\mathcal{T}$ in its time suffix, we optionally omit the time suffix from each body predicate and treat it as implicit.
- *Temporal head annotation:* Since the time suffix in a head predicate may be either equal to $\mathcal{T}$ or equal to $\mathcal{T}$'s successor, we omit the time suffix from the head—and its relevant constraints from the body—and instead attach an identifier to the head predicate of each temporal rule, to indicate the change in time suffix. A temporal head predicate is of the form:
  $r(A_1, A_2, [\ldots], A_n)$@next
  The identifier @next stands in for successor$(\mathcal{T}, S)$ in the body.
- *Timestamped facts:* For notational consistency, we write the time suffix of facts (which must be given as a constant) outside the predicate. For example:
  $r(A_1, A_2, [\ldots], A_n)$@$C$

*Example 2.* The following are "sugared" versions of deductive and inductive rules from Example 1, and a temporal fact:

deductive: p(A, B) ← e(A, B);

inductive: q(A, B)@next ← e(A, B);

fact: e(1, 2)@10;

# 3   State in Logic

*Time is a device that was invented to keep everything from happening at once.*[2]

Given our definition of DEDALUS$_0$, we now address the persistence and mutability of data across time—one of the two signature features of distributed systems for which we provide a model-theoretic foundation.

The intuition behind DEDALUS$_0$'s successor relation is that it models the passage of (logical) time. In our discussion, we will say that ground atoms with lower time suffixes occur "before" atoms with higher ones. The constraints we imposed on DEDALUS$_0$ rules restrict how deductions may be made with respect to time. First, rules may only refer to a single time suffix variable in their body, and hence subgoals *cannot join across different "timesteps."* Second, rules may specify deductions that occur concurrently with their ground facts or in the next timestep—in DEDALUS$_0$, we rule out induction "backwards" in time or "skipping" into the future.

This notion of time allows us to consider the contents of the EDB—and hence a perfect model of the IDB—with respect to an "instant in time": we simply bind the time suffixes ($\mathcal{T}$) of all body predicates to a constant. Because this produces a sequence of models (one per timestep), it gives us an intuitive and unambiguous way to declaratively express persistence and state changes across time. In this section, we give examples of language constructs that capture state-oriented motifs such as persistent relations, deletion and update, sequences, and queues.

## 3.1   Simple Persistence

A fact in predicate $p$ at time $\mathcal{T}$ may provide ground for deductive rules at time $\mathcal{T}$, as well as ground for deductive rules in timesteps greater than $\mathcal{T}$, provided there exists a *simple persistence rule* of the form:

   p_pos($A_1$,$A_2$,[...],$A_n$)@next ← p_pos($A_1$,$A_2$,[...],$A_n$);

A simple persistence rule of this form ensures that a $p$ fact true at time $i$ will be true $\forall j \in \mathbb{Z} : j \geq i$.

## 3.2   Mutable State

To model deletions and updates of a fact, it is necessary to break the induction in a simple persistence rule. Adding a p_neg subgoal to the body of a simple persistence rule accomplishes this:

   p_pos($A_1, A_2, [...], A_n$)@next ←
       p_pos($A_1, A_2, [...], A_n$),
       ¬ p_neg($A_1, A_2, [...], A_n$);

If, at any time $k$, we have a fact p_neg($C_1, C_2, [...], C_n$)@k, then we do not deduce a p_pos($C_1, C_2, [...], C_n$)@k+1 fact. Furthermore, we do not deduce a p_pos($C_1, C_2, [...], C_n$)@j fact for any $j > k$, unless this p_pos fact is re-derived at some timestep $j > k$ by another rule. This behavior corresponds to the intuition that a persistent fact, once stated, remains true until it is retracted.

---

[2] Graffiti on a wall at Cambridge University [1].

*Example 3.* Consider the following DEDALUS$_0$ program and ground facts:

```
p_pos(A, B) ← p(A, B);
p_pos(A, B)@next ← p_pos(A, B), ¬p_neg(A, B);

p(1,2)@101;
p(1,3)@102;
p_neg(1,2)@300;
```

The following facts are true: p(1,2)@200, p(1,3)@200, p(1,3)@300. However, p(1,2) @301 is false because p(1,2) was "deleted" at timestep 300.

Since mutable persistence occurs frequently in practice, we provide the *persist* macro, which takes three arguments: a predicate name, the name of another predicate to hold "deleted" facts, and the (matching) arity of the two predicates. The macro expands to the corresponding mutable persistence rule. For example, the above p_pos persistence rule may be equivalently specified as persist[p_pos, p_neg, 2].

Mutable persistence rules enable *updates*. For some time $\mathcal{T}$, an update is any pair of facts:

```
p_neg(C₁, C₂, [...], Cₙ)@𝒯;
p_pos(D₁, D₂, [...], Dₙ)@𝒯 + 1;
```

Intuitively, an update represents deleting an old value of a tuple and inserting a new value. Every update is *atomic across timesteps*, meaning that the old value ceases to exist at the same timestep in which the new value is derived—timestep $\mathcal{T} + 1$ in the above definition.

## 3.3 Sequences

One may represent a database sequence—an object that retains and monotonically increases a counter value—with a pair of inductive rules. One rule increments the current counter value when some condition is true, while the other persists the value of the sequence when the condition is false. We can capture the increase of the sequence value without using arithmetic, because the infinite series of successor has the monotonicity property we require:

```
seq(B)@next ← seq(A), successor(A,B), event(_);
seq(A)@next ← seq(A), ¬event(_);
seq(0);
```

Note that these three rules produce only a single value of seq at each timestep, but they do so in a manner slightly different than our standard persistence template.

## 3.4 Queues

While sequences are useful for imposing an ordering on tuples, programs will in some cases require that tuples are processed in a particular (partial) order associated with specific timesteps. To this end, we introduce a queue template, which employs inductive persistence and aggregate functions in rule heads to process tuples according to a data-dependent order, rather than as a set.

Aggregate functions simplify our discussion of queues. Mumick and Shmueli observe correspondences in the expressivity of Datalog with stratified negation and stratified aggregation functions [25]. Adding aggregation to our language does not affect its expressive power, but is useful for writing natural constructs for distributed computing including queues and ordering.

In DEDALUS$_0$ we allow aggregate functions to appear in the heads of deductive rules in the form:

$$p(A_1, \ldots, A_n, \rho_1(A_{n+1}), \ldots, \rho_m(A_{n+m}))$$

In such a rule (whose body must bind $A_1, \ldots, A_{n+m}$), the predicate $p$ contains one row for each satisfying assignment of $A_1, \ldots, A_n$—akin to the distinct "groups" of SQL's "GROUP BY" notation.

Consider a predicate `priority_queue` that represents a series of tasks to be performed in some predefined order. Its attributes are a string representing a user, a job, and an integer indicating the priority of the job in the queue:

```
priority_queue('bob', 'bash', 200)@123;
priority_queue('eve', 'ls', 1)@123;
priority_queue('alice', 'ssh', 204)@123;
priority_queue('bob', 'ssh', 205)@123;
```

Observe that all the time suffixes are the same. Given this schema, we note that a program would likely want to process `priority_queue` events individually in a data-dependent order, in spite of their coincidence in logical time.

In the program below, we define a table `m_priority_queue` that serves as a queue to feed `priority_queue`. The queue must persist across timesteps because it may take multiple timesteps to drain it. At each timestep, for each value of **A**, a single tuple is projected into `priority_queue` and deleted (atomic with the projection) from `m_priority_queue`, changing the value of the aggregate calculated at the subsequent step:

```
persist[m_priority_queue_pos, m_priority_queue_neg, 3]

omin(A, min<C>) ←
  m_priority_queue(A, _, C);

priority_queue(A, B, C)@next ←
  m_priority_queue(A, B, C),
  omin(A, C);

m_priority_queue_neg(A, B, C) ←
  m_priority_queue(A, B, C),
  omin(A, C);
```

Under such a queueing discipline, deductive rules that depend on `priority_queue` are constrained to consider only min-priority tuples at each timestep per value of the variable **A**, thus implementing a per-user FIFO discipline. To enforce a global FIFO ordering over `priority_queue`, we may redefine `omin` and any dependent rules to exclude the **A** attribute.

A queue establishes a mapping between DEDALUS$_0$'s timesteps and the priority-ordering attribute of the input relation. By doing so, we take advantage of the monotonic property of timestamps to enforce an ordering property over our input that is otherwise difficult to express in a logic language. We return to this idea in our discussion of temporal "entanglement" in Section 5.5.

# 4    Stratification and Safety

In the previous section we demonstrated that DEDALUS$_0$ can capture intuitive notions of persistence and mutability of state via a stylized use of Datalog. However, the alert reader will note that even simple DEDALUS$_0$ programs make for unusual Datalog: among other concerns, persistence rules produce derivations for an infinite number of values of the time suffix. Traditional Datalog interpreters, which work against static databases, would attempt to enumerate these values, making this approach impractical.

However, in the context of distributed systems and networks, the need for non-terminating "services" or "protocols" is very common. In this section we show that expressing distributed systems properties such as persistence and mutable state in logic does not require dispensing with familiar notions of safety and stratification: we take traditional notions of acceptable Datalog programs, and extend them in a way that admits sensible non-terminating programs.

## 4.1    Stratification in DEDALUS$_0$

We first turn our attention to the semantics of programs with negation. As we will see, the inclusion of time enables a syntactic stratification condition for programs, and the existence of a unique model that corresponds to intuition [27].

**Lemma 1.** *A* DEDALUS$_0$ *program without negation has a unique minimal model.*

*Proof.* A DEDALUS$_0$ program without negation is a pure Datalog program. Every pure Datalog program has a unique minimal model.

We define syntactic stratification of a DEDALUS$_0$ program the same way it is defined for a Datalog program:

**Definition 1.** *A* DEDALUS$_0$ *program is* syntactically stratifiable *if there exists no cycle with a negative edge in the program's predicate dependency graph.*

We may evaluate such a program in *stratum order* as described in the Datalog literature [30]. It is easy to see that any syntactically stratified DEDALUS$_0$ instance has a unique perfect model [27] because it is a syntactically stratified Datalog program.

However, many programs we are interested in expressing are not syntactically stratifiable. Fortunately, we are able to define a syntactically checkable notion of *temporal stratifiability* of DEDALUS$_0$ programs that maps to a subset of locally stratifiable Datalog programs.

**Definition 2.** *The* deductive reduction *of a* DEDALUS$_0$ *program P is the subset of P consisting of exactly the deductive rules in P.*

**Definition 3.** *A* DEDALUS$_0$ *program is* temporally stratifiable *if its deductive reduction is syntactically stratifiable.*

**Lemma 2.** *Any temporally stratifiable* DEDALUS$_0$ *instance P has a unique perfect model.*

*Proof.* Every temporally stratifiable DEDALUS$_0$ instance is locally stratifiable [27], and thus has a unique perfect model.

*Example 4.* A simple temporally stratifiable DEDALUS$_0$ program that is not syntactically stratifiable.

```
persist[p_pos, p_neg, 3]

p_pos(A, B, T) ←
    insert_p(A, B, T);

p_neg(A, B, T) ←
    p_pos(A, B, T),
    delete_p(T);
```

In the DEDALUS$_0$ program above, *insert_p* and *delete_p* are captured in EDB relations. This reasonable program is unstratifiable because $p\_pos > p\_neg \wedge p\_neg > p\_pos$. But because the successor relation is constrained such that $\forall A, B, successor(A, B) \rightarrow B > A$, any such program is locally stratified on time suffixes. Therefore, we have $p\_pos_n \not>^+$ $p\_neg_n \not>^+ p\_pos_{n+1}$; informally, earlier values do not depend on later values.

## 4.2   Temporal Safety

Next we consider the issue of infinite results raised in the introduction to this section. In traditional Datalog, this concern is well studied. A Datalog program is considered *safe* if it has a finite minimal model, and hence has a finite execution. Safety in Datalog is traditionally ensured through the following syntactic constraints:

1. No functions are allowed.
2. Variables are *range restricted*: all attributes of the head goal appear in a non-negated body subgoal.
3. The EDB is finite.

These constraints ensure that the Herbrand Universe is finite: any atom that may be deduced by a safe program may only take its attributes from the set of all constant symbols appearing in the program and EDB. In fact, the set of all possible assignments of these constants to predicate attributes, representing every possible interpretation, is itself finite.

Since our definition of successor violates these rules, and indeed leads to an infinite set of facts, DEDALUS$_0$ programs violate this definition of safety. However, successor models time, not computation; later sections explain how DEDALUS implementations avoid enumerating the contents of successor at runtime. This section introduces a notion of termination that allows us to reason about the safety of DEDALUS$_0$ programs.

A DEDALUS$_0$ program containing only deductive rules is informally equivalent to a Datalog program in which all predicates have no time suffix. If all the rules in such a program meet the conditions above, then clearly we would like them to meet DEDALUS$_0$'s definition of safety.

**Definition 4.** *A rule is* instantaneously safe *if it is deductive, function-free and range-restricted. A DEDALUS$_0$ program is* instantaneously safe *if its deductive reduction is instantaneously safe.*

The successor relation complicates the discussion of safety, as it introduces the countably infinite set $\mathbb{Z}$ to our universe of constants.

Consider the following DEDALUS$_0$ program, which derives a single, persistent fact:

*Example 5.* An unsafe DEDALUS$_0$ instance?
```
persist[p_pos, p_neg, 2]
p(1, 2)@123;
```

The single ground fact will cause one deduction for each tuple in successor. Since successor is infinite, the corresponding Datalog program is unsafe.

However, observe that each of these deductions produces a tuple that changes only in its time suffix. We find it useful to distinguish between unsafe programs and programs that, given a finite EDB, eventually derive only tuples that are equivalent except in their time suffixes.

**Definition 5.** *Two sets of ground atoms $\Gamma$ and $\Gamma'$ are* equivalent modulo time *if each atom $\gamma \in \Gamma$ has a corresponding atom $\gamma' \in \Gamma'$ such that $\gamma$ and $\gamma'$ have the same predicate symbol, and the same assignment of constants to attributes for all attributes except the time suffix.*

**Definition 6.** *We say a DEDALUS$_0$ instance is* quiescent at time $T$ *if the set of all atoms with time suffix $T$ is equivalent modulo time to the set of all atoms with time suffix $T - 1$.*

**Lemma 3.** *A DEDALUS$_0$ instance that is quiescent at time $T$ will be quiescent until timestamp of the next EDB fact $V$, i.e. for all $U \in \mathbb{Z} : V > U \geq T$. If no EDB fact has a timestamp greater than $T$, then the instance will be henceforth quiescent.*

*Proof.* A DEDALUS$_0$ program admits only deductive and inductive rules, which derive new tuples at the same time as their ground tuples or in the immediate next timestep. Thus, the set of tuples true at time $T$ is completely determined by any tuples true at time $T - 1$, and any EDB facts true at time $T$. Observe that the integer value of the timestep does not influence the derivation.

If the instance is quiescent at $T$, then given $\mathbf{A}$, the set of atoms with timestamp $T - 1$, and the EDB at $T$, the program entails $\mathbf{A}$ at timestamp $T$. Thus in the absence of EDB facts at $T + 1$, it entails $\mathbf{A}$ at $T + 1$.

**Definition 7.** *A DEDALUS$_0$ instance with finite EDB is* temporally safe *if it is henceforth quiescent after some time $T$.*

**Definition 8.** *Given the depends-on relation $>$ and its transitive closure $>^*$, an intensional predicate $e$ in a program $P$ is called an* instantaneous predicate *if for every predicate $p$ for which $e >^* p$ (ie, $e$ depends transitively on $p$), either $p$ appears in the head of no inductive rules, or the body of each inductive rule with head $p$ contains at least one positive instantaneous predicate.*

We propose the following conservative test for temporal safety. A program is guaranteed to be temporally safe if every rule is either:

1. An instantaneously safe rule, or
2. An inductive rule in which the head predicate occurs also in the body with the same variable bindings for all attributes save the time suffix, or
3. An inductive rule that has at least one instantaneous predicate as a positive subgoal in the body.

While a temporally safe program is henceforth quiescent after some time $T$, a temporally unsafe program changes infinitely. Note that the DEDALUS$_0$ program in Example 5 is temporally safe because the basic persistence macro creates a rule that satisfies the second condition above.

**Lemma 4.** *A temporally stratifiable* DEDALUS$_0$ *instance is temporally safe if it has a finite EDB and every rule is one of the kinds 1-3 above.*

*Proof.* Assume the program is temporally unsafe. That is, there exists no time $T$ such that $\forall U \geq T$, the set of all atoms with timestamp $U$ is equivalent modulo time to the set of all atoms with timestamp $T - 1$. Let $E$ be the maximum timestamp of any fact in the EDB.

Observe that every rule $r$ of kind 3 may only entail a finite number of facts—as the EDB is finite—and thus may entail no facts at a timestamp greater than some maximum timestamp $V_r \leq E + 1 \in \mathbb{Z}$. Since a DEDALUS$_0$ program has a finite set of rules we know $\exists V \in \mathbb{Z} : \forall r : V \geq V_r$, and thus $V \leq E + 1$.

We now consider times $T$ such that $T > E + 1$. By the argument above, no rules of kind 3 entail any facts with a timestamp greater than $E + 1$. Recall that no EDB atoms are true at any timestamp greater than $E$. Thus, any facts with timestamp greater than $E + 1$ must be entailed by rules of kind 1 or 2.

Consider the set of equivalence classes modulo time of all possible atoms, **A**, given the Herbrand Universe. We know **A** is finite, as the Herbrand Universe is finite. Therefore, if the program is temporally unsafe, then **B**, the set of atoms entailed by the program, both contains and excludes infinitely many members of at least one equivalence class in **A** (i.e., something "infinitely oscillates in time" between being true and false). Since the program has finitely many rules, at least one rule must entail infinitely many atoms (from at least one of the equivalence classes from **A**). Thus, it is easy to see that there must be a cycle that contains some predicate $P$ and $\neg P$.

We show there exists such a cycle containing only rules of kind 1, which implies that the program is temporally unstratifiable. In order for such a cycle to exist, $P$ must transitively depend on $\neg P$, and $\neg P$ must transitively depend on $P$. Thus, the program contains a rule $J_1$ with $\neg P$ in its body, and some predicate $R$ in its head, as well as a rule $J_2$ that is transitively dependent on $R$, with $P$ in its head.

**Case 1:** $P \neq R$. In this case, $J_1$ must be of kind 1, as for any $Q \neq P$, a rule of kind 2 with $P$ in the head may not directly entail $Q$ given $P$. $J_2$ must also be of kind 1—if it is of kind 2, then it necessarily contains $P$ in its body, so it cannot entail $P$ unless $P$ is entailed by some other rule. If $J_2$ contains $R$ in its body, then the program is syntactically unstratifiable. But if $J_2$ does not contain $R$ in its body, then it contains some predicate $S$ transitively entailed by $R$; without loss of generality, the body contains $R$. Thus, the program is syntactically unstratifiable.

**Case 2:** $P = R$. In this case, $J_1$ and $J_2$ are the same rule: $P \leftarrow \neg P$. Thus, the program is syntactically unstratifiable.

Thus, the program is temporally unstratifiable, which contradicts our assumption.

*Example 6.* A DEDALUS$_0$ instance with a temporally unsafe deductive rule.

```
p(A, B) ← q(A);
```

The program above has a temporally unsafe deductive rule that corresponds to an unsafe rule in Datalog: it is not range-restricted. The head variable $B$ could range over an infinite set of constants.

*Example 7.* A DEDALUS$_0$ instance that is temporally unsafe due to infinite oscillation.

```
flip_flop(B, A)@next ← flip_flop(A, B);
flip_flop(0, 1)@1;
```

The above program exemplifies temporally unsafe induction. Even though it contains no function symbols and all variables are range-restricted, it entails infinite oscillation of the *flip_flop* predicate.

We can imagine interesting examples of temporally unsafe programs, and do not forbid them in DEDALUS$_0$.

## 5  Asynchrony

In this section we introduce DEDALUS, a superset of DEDALUS$_0$ that also admits the *choice* construct [13] to bind time suffixes. Choice allows us to model the inherent nondeterminism in communication over unreliable networks that may delay, lose or reorder the results of logical deductions. We then describe a syntactic convention for rules that model communication between agents, and show how DEDALUS can be used to implement common distributed computing idioms like Lamport clocks and reliable broadcast.

### 5.1  Choice

An important property of distributed systems is that individual computers cannot control or observe the temporal interleaving of their computations with other computers. One aspect of this uncertainty is captured in network delays: the arrival "time" of messages cannot be directly controlled by either sender or receiver. In this section, we enhance our language with a traditional model of nondeterminism from the literature to capture these issues: the *choice* construct as defined by Greco and Zaniolo [13].

The subgoal choose(($X_1$), ($X_2$)) may appear in the body of a rule, where $X_1$ and $X_2$ are vectors whose constituent variables occur elsewhere in the body. Such a subgoal enforces the functional dependency $X_1 \rightarrow X_2$, "choosing" a single assignment of values to the variables in $X_2$ for each variable in $X_1$.

The choice construct is nondeterministic. In a model-theoretic interpretation of logic programming, a nondeterministic program must have a multiplicity of *stable models*— that is, it must be unstratifiable. Greco and Zaniolo define choice in precisely this fashion: the choice construct is expanded into an unstratifiable strongly-connected component of rules, and each possible choice is associated with a different model. Each such model has a unique, non-deterministic assignment that respects the given functional dependencies. In our discussion, it may be helpful to think of one such model chosen non-deterministically—a non-deterministic "assignment of timestamps to tuples."

## 5.2  Distribution Model

The choice construct captures the non-determinism of communicating agents in a distributed system, but we want to use it in a stylized way to model typical notions of distribution. To this end, DEDALUS adopts the "horizontal partitioning" convention introduced by Loo et al. [21]. To represent a distributed system, we consider some number of agents, each running a copy of the same program against a disjoint subset (*horizontal partition*) of each predicate's contents. We require one attribute in each predicate to be used to identify the partitioning for tuples in that predicate. We call such an attribute a *location specifier*, and prefix it with a # symbol in Dedalus.

Finally, we constrain DEDALUS rules in such a way that the location specifier variable in each body predicate is the same—i.e., the body contains tuples from exactly one partition of the database, logically colocated (on a single "machine"). If the head of the rule has the same location specifier variable as the body, we call the rule "local," since its results can remain on the machine where they are computed. If the head has a different variable in its location specifier, we call the rule a *communication rule*. We now proceed to our model of the asynchrony of this communication, which is captured in a syntactic constraint on the heads of communication rules.

## 5.3  Asynchronous Rules

In order to represent the nondeterminism introduced by distribution, we admit a third type of rule, called an *asynchronous* rule. A rule is asynchronous if the relationship between the head time suffix $S$ and the body time suffix $\mathcal{T}$ is unknown. Furthermore, $S$ (but not $\mathcal{T}$) may take on the special value $\top$ which means "never." Derivation at $\top$ indicates that the deduction is "lost," as time suffixes in rule bodies do not range over $\top$.

We model network nondeterminism using the choice construct to choose from a value in the special time predicate, which is defined using the following Datalog rules:

```
time(⊤);
time(S) ← successor(S, _);
```

Each asynchronous rule with head predicate $p(A_1,\ldots,A_n)$ has the following additional subgoals in its body:

```
time(S), choose((A₁,...,Aₙ,T), (S)),
```

where $S$ is the timestamp of the rule head. Note that our use of choose incorporates all variables of each head predicate tuple, which allows a unique choice of $S$ for each head tuple. We further require that communication rules include the location specifier appearing in the rule body among the functionally-determining attributes of the choose predicate, even if it does not occur in the head.

*Example 8.* A well-formed asynchronous DEDALUS rule:

```
r(A, B, S) ←
  e(A, B, T),
  time(S),
  choose((A, B, T), (S));
```

We admit a new temporal head annotation to sugar the rule above. The identifier `async` implies that the rule is asynchronous, and stands in for the additional body predicates. The example above expressed using `async` is:

*Example 9.* A sugared asynchronous DEDALUS rule:

```
r(A, B)@async ← e(A, B);
```

## 5.4    Asynchrony and Distribution in DEDALUS

As noted above, communication rules must be asynchronous. This restricts our model of communication between agents in two important ways. First, by restricting bodies to a single agent, the only communication modeled in DEDALUS occurs via communication rules. Second, because all communication rules are asynchronous, agents may only learn about time values at another agent by receiving messages (with unbounded delay) from that agent. Note that this model says nothing about the relationship between the agents' clocks; they could be non-monotonically increasing, or they could respect a global order.

## 5.5    Temporal Monotonicity

Nothing in our definition of asynchronous rules prevents tuples in the head of a rule from having a timestamp that precedes the timestamp in the rule's body. This is a significant departure from DEDALUS$_0$, since it violates the monotonicity assumptions upon which we based our proof of temporal stratification. On an intuitive level, it may also trouble us that rules can derive head tuples that exist "before" the body tuples on which they are grounded; this situation violates intuitive notions of causality and admits the possibility of temporal paradoxes.

We have avoided restricting DEDALUS to rule out such issues, as doing so would reduce its expressiveness. Recall that simple monotonic Datalog (without negation) is insensitive to the values in any particular attribute. Hence DEDALUS programs without negation are also well-defined regardless of any "temporal ordering" of deductions: in monotonic programs, even if tuples with timestamps "in the future" are used to derive tuples "from the past," there is an unambiguous least minimal model. In Section 4.1 we showed that the monotonicity of time suffixes achieved by inductive rules ensures a unique perfect model even for non-monotonic DEDALUS$_0$ programs.

**Practical Implications.**  Given this discussion, in practice we are interested in three asynchronous scenarios: (a) monotonic programs (even with non-monotonicity in time), (b) non-monotonic programs whose semantics guarantee monotonicity of time suffixes and (c) non-monotonic programs where we have domain knowledge guaranteeing monotonicity of time suffixes. Each represents practical scenarios of interest.

P. Alvaro et al.

The first category captures the spirit of many simple distributed implementations that are built atop unreliable asynchronous substrates. For example, in some Internet publishing applications (weblogs, online fora), it is possible due to caching or failure that a "thread" of discussion arrives out of order, with responses appearing before the comments they reference. In many cases a monotonic "bag semantics" for the comment program is considered a reasonable interface for readers, and the ability to tolerate temporal anomalies simplifies the challenge of scaling a system through distribution.

The second scenario is achieved in DEDALUS$_0$ via the use of successor for the time suffix. The asynchronous rules of DEDALUS require additional program logic to guarantee monotonic increases in time for predicates with dependencies. In the literature of distributed computing, this constraint is known as a *causal ordering* and is enforced by distributed clock protocols. We review one classic protocol in the DEDALUS context in Section 5.6; including this protocol into DEDALUS programs ensures temporal monotonicity.

Finally, certain computational substrates guarantee monotonicity in both timestamps and message ordering—for example, some multiprocessor cache coherency protocols provide this property. When temporal monotonicity is given, the proof of temporal stratification applies.

**Entanglement.** Consider the asynchronous rule below:

```
p(A, B, N)@async ← q(A, B)@N;
```

Due to the async keyword in the rule head, each *p* tuple will take some unspecified time suffix value. Note however that the time suffix *N* of the rule body appears also in an attribute of *p* other than the time suffix, recording a binding of both the time value of the deduction and the time value of its consequence. We call such a binding an *entanglement*. Note that in order to write the rule it was necessary to not sugar away the time suffix in the rule body.

Entanglement is a powerful construct. It allows a rule to reference the logical clock time of the deduction that produced one (or more) of its subgoals; this capability supports protocols that reason about partial ordering of time across machines. More generally, it exposes the infinite successor relation to attributes other than the time suffix, allowing us to express concepts such as infinite sequences.

### 5.6 Lamport Clocks

Recall that DEDALUS allows program executions to order message timestamps arbitrarily, violating intuitive notions of causality by allowing deductions to "affect the past." This section explains how to implement Lamport clocks [16] atop DEDALUS, which allows programs to ensure temporal monotonicity by reestablishing a causal order despite derivations that flow backwards through time.

Consider a rule p(A,B)@async ← q(A,B). By rewriting it to:

```
persist[p_pos, p_neg, 2]
p_wait(A, B, N)@async ← q(A, B)@N;
p_wait(A, B, N)@next ← p_wait(A, B, N)@M, N ≥ M;
p(A, B)@next ← p_wait(A, B, N)@M, N < M;
```

we place the derived tuple in a new relation p_wait that stores any tuples that were "sent from the future" with their sending time "entangled"; these tuples stay in the p_wait predicate until the point in time at which they were derived. Conceptually, this causes the system to evaluate a potentially large number of timesteps (if N is significantly less than the timestamp of the system when the tuple arrives). However, if the runtime is able to efficiently evaluate timesteps when the database is quiescent, then instead of "waiting" by evaluating timesteps, it will simply increase its logical clock to match that of the sender. In contrast, if the tuple is "sent into the future," then it is processed using the timestep that receives it.

This manipulation of timesteps and clock values is equivalent to conventional descriptions of Lamport clocks, except that our Lamport clock implementation effectively "advances the clock" by preventing derivations until the clock is sufficiently advanced, by temporarily storing incoming tuples in the p_wait relation.

## 5.7 Reliable Broadcast

Distributed systems cope with unreliable networks by using mechanisms such as broadcast and consensus protocols, timeouts and retries, and often hide the nondeterminism behind these abstractions. DEDALUS supports these notions, achieving encapsulation of nondeterminism while dealing explicitly with the uncertainty in the model. Consider the simple broadcast protocol below:

```
sbcast(#Member, Sender, Message)@async ←
  smessage(#Agent, Sender, Message),
  members(#Agent, Member);

sdeliver(#Member, Sender, Message) ←
  sbcast(#Member, Sender, Message);
```

Assume that members is a persistent relation that contains the broadcast membership list. The protocol is straightforward: if a tuple appears in smessage (an EDB predicate), then it will be sent to all members (a multicast). The interpretation of the non-deterministic choice implied by the @async rule indicates that messaging order and delivery (i.e., finite delay) are not guaranteed.

The program shown below makes use of the multicast primitive provided by the previous program and uses it to implement a basic reliable broadcast using a textbook mechanism [24] that assumes any node that fails to receive a message sent to it has failed. When the broadcast completes, all nodes that have not failed have received the message.

Our simple two-rule broadcast program is augmented with the following rules, so that if a node receives a message, it also multicasts it to every member *before* delivering the message locally:

```
smessage(Agent, Sender, Message) ←
  rmessage(Agent, Sender, Message);

buf_bcast(Sender, Me, Message) ←
  sdeliver(Me, Sender, Message);
```

```
smessage(Me, Sender, Message)  ←
  buf_bcast(Sender, Me, Message);

rdeliver(Me, Sender, Message)@next  ←
  buf_bcast(Sender, Me, Message);
```

Note that all network communication is initiated by the @async rule from the original simple broadcast. The @next is required in the rdeliver definition in order to prevent nodes from taking actions based upon the broadcast before it is guaranteed to meet the reliability guarantee.

Implementing other disciplines like FIFO and atomic broadcast and consensus are similar exercises, requiring the use of ordered queueing and sequences.

## 6  Related Work

### 6.1  Deductive Databases and Updateable State

Many deductive database systems, including LDL [7] and Glue-Nail [10], admit procedural semantics to deal with updates using an assignment primitive. In contrast, languages proposed by Cleary and Liu [9,19,22] retain a purely logical interpretation by admitting temporal extensions into their syntax and interpreting assignment or update as a composite operation across timesteps [19] rather than as a primitive. We follow the approach of Datalog/UT [19] in that we use explicit time suffixes to enforce a stratification condition, but differ in several significant ways. First, we model persistence explicitly in our language, so that like updates, it is specified as a composite operation across timesteps. Partly as a result of this, we are able to enforce stricter constraints on the allowable time suffixes in rules: a program may only specify what deductions are visible in the current timestep, the immediate next timestep, and *some* future timestep, as opposed to the free use of intervals allowed in rules in Liu et al.

U-Datalog [6] addresses updates using syntax annotations that establish different interpretations for the set of updated relations and the IDB, interpreting update atoms as constraints and using constraint logic programming techniques to test for inconsistent derivations. Similarly, Timed Concurrent Constraint Programming (TCCP) [28,29] handles nonmonotonic constructs in a CLP framework by outputting a new (possibly diminished) store and constraint program at each timestep.

Our temporal approach to representing state change most closely resembles the Statelog language [12]. By contrast, our motivation is the logical specification and implementation of distributed systems, and our principal contribution is the use of time to model both local state change and communication over unreliable networks.

Lamport's TLA+ [17] is a language for specifying concurrent systems in terms of constraints over valuations of state and temporal logic that describes admissible transitions. Two distinguishing features of DEDALUS with respect to TLA+ are our minimalist use of temporal constructs (next and async), and our unified treatment of temporal and other attributes of facts; this enables the full literature of Datalog to be applied to both temporal and instantaneous properties of programs.

## 6.2   Distributed Systems

Significant recent work ([2,5,8,20], etc.) has focused on applying deductive database languages to the problem of specifying and implementing network protocols and distributed systems. Implementing distributed systems entails a data store that changes over time, so any useful implementation of such a language addresses the updateable state issue in some manner. Existing distributed deductive languages such as NDlog and Overlog adopt a *chain of fixpoints* interpretation. Evaluation proceeds in three phases:

1. Input from the external world, including network messages, clock interrupts and host language calls, is collected.
2. Time is frozen, the union of the local store and the batch of events is taken as EDB, and the program is run to fixpoint.
3. The deductions that cause side effects (e.g., deletions, updates, network messages and host language callbacks) are dealt with.

Unfortunately, the language descriptions give no careful specification of how and when deletions and updates should be made visible, so the third step is a "black box." Loo et al. [20] proved that classes of programs with certain monotonicity properties (i.e., programs without negation or fact deletion) are equivalent (specifically, eventually consistent) when evaluated globally (via a single fixpoint computation) or in a distributed setting in which the *chain of fixpoints* interpretation is applied at each participating node, and no messages are lost. Navarro et al. [26] proposed an alternate syntax that addressed key ambiguities in Overlog, including the *event creation vs. effect* ambiguity. Their solution solves the problem by introducing procedural semantics to the interpretation of the augmented Overlog programs. A similar analysis was offered by Mao [23].

# 7   Conclusion

Datalog has inspired a variety of recent applied work, which touts the benefits of declarative specifications for practical implementations. We have developed substantial experience building distributed systems [2,3,8,20] using hybrid declarative/imperative languages such as Overlog [20]. While our experience with those languages was largely positive, the combination of Datalog and imperative constructs often clouded our understanding of the "correct" execution of single-node programs that performed state updates. This work developed in large part as a reaction to the semantic difficulties presented by these distributed logic languages.

Through its reification of time as data, DEDALUS allowed us to achieve the goal of a purely declarative language, without sacrificing the ability to express two critical features of practical distributed systems: mutable state and asynchronous communication. We believe that DEDALUS is as expressive as Overlog, but formalizing this intuition is difficult because the semantics of Overlog are not well specified. Instead, we are currently validating the practicality of our work by "porting" many of our Overlog programs to DEDALUS.

In DEDALUS, state update and communication differ from logical deduction only in terms of timing. In the local case, this allows us to express state update without giving up the clean semantics of Datalog; unlike Datalog extensions that use imperative constructs to provide such functionality, each DEDALUS rule expresses a logical invariant that will hold over all program executions. However, interactions with external processes and asynchronous communication introduce nondeterminism which DEDALUS models with choose. Our hope is that modeling external processes and events with a single primitive will simplify efforts to formally verify the correctness of distributed systems implemented using DEDALUS. Two natural directions in this vein are to determine for a given DEDALUS program whether Church-Rosser confluence holds for all models produced by choice, or to capture finer-grained notions like serializability of such models with respect to transaction identifiers embedded in EDB facts.

**Acknowledgments.** Ras Bodík and Tyson Condie were intimately involved in discussions surrounding the development of DEDALUS. We are also indebted to Mark Utting and Erik Meijer for conversation and inspiration from their Starlog and LINQ experiences respectively, and to Phil Bernstein for suggestions on future work. Thanks to Kuang Chen and Jesse Trutna for comments on the paper. This work was supported by NSF grants 0917349, 0803690, 0722077, 0713661 and 0435496, Air Force Office of Scientific Research award 22178970-41070-F, the Natural Sciences and Engineering Research Council of Canada, and gifts from Yahoo Research, IBM Research and Microsoft Research.

# References

1. Abelson, H., Sussman, G.J. (eds.): Structure and Interpretation of Computer Programs, 2nd edn. McGraw Hill, New York (1996)
2. Alvaro, P., Condie, T., Conway, N., Elmeleegy, K., Hellerstein, J.M., Sears, R.C.: BOOM Analytics: Exploring Data-centric, Declarative Programming for the Cloud. In: EuroSys (2010)
3. Alvaro, P., Condie, T., Conway, N., Hellerstein, J.M., Sears, R.: I Do Declare: Consensus in a logic language. In: NetDB (2009)
4. Ashley-Rollman, M.P., et al.: Declarative programming for modular robots. In: Workshop on Self-Reconfigurable Robots/Systems and Applications (2007)
5. Belaramani, N., Zheng, J., Nayate, A., Soulé, R., Dahlin, M., Grimm, R.: PADS: A policy architecture for distributed storage systems. In: NSDI (2009)
6. Bertino, E., Catania, B., Gori, R.: Enhancing the Expressive Power of the U-Datalog Language. Theory and Practice of Logic Programming 1(1), 105–122 (2001)
7. Chimenti, D., Gamboa, R., Krishnamurthy, R., Naqvi, S., Tsur, S., Zaniolo, C.: The LDL System Prototype. IEEE Trans. on Knowl. and Data Eng. 2(1), 76–90 (1990)
8. Chu, D.C., Popa, L., Tavakoli, A., Hellerstein, J.M., Levis, P., Shenker, S., Stoica, I.: The design and implementation of a declarative sensor network system. In: 5th ACM Conference on Embedded Networked Sensor Systems, SenSys (2007)
9. Cleary, J.G., Utting, M., Clayton, R.: Data Structures Considered Harmful. In: Australasian Workshop on Computational Logic (2000)
10. Derr, M.A., Morishita, S., Phipps, G.: The Glue-Nail Deductive Database System: Design, Implementation, and Evaluation. The VLDB Journal 3, 123–160 (1994)
11. Eisner, J., Goldlust, E., Smith, N.A.: Dyna: a declarative language for implementing dynamic programs. In: Proc. ACL (2004)

12. Georg Lausen, W.M., Ludäscher, B.: On active deductive databases: The statelog approach. In: Kifer, M., Voronkov, A., Freitag, B., Decker, H. (eds.) Dagstuhl Seminar 1997, DYNAMICS 1997, and ILPS-WS 1997. LNCS, vol. 1472, pp. 69–106. Springer, Heidelberg (1998)

13. Greco, S., Zaniolo, C.: Greedy Algorithms in Datalog with Choice and Negation. In: Proceedings of the Joint International Conference and Symposium on Logic Programming, pp. 294–309 (1998)

14. Jim, T.: Sd3: A trust management system with certified evaluation. In: IEEE Symposium on Security and Privacy, pp. 106–115 (2001)

15. Lam, M.S., Whaley, J., Livshits, V.B., Martin, M.C., Avots, D., Carbin, M., Unkel, C.: Context-sensitive program analysis as database queries. In: PODS (2005)

16. Lamport, L.: Time, Clocks, and the Ordering of Events in a Distributed System. Communications of the ACM 21(7), 558–565 (1978)

17. Lamport, L.: The temporal logic of actions. ACM Toplas 16(3), 872–923 (1994)

18. Li, N., Mitchell, J.: Datalog with constraints: A foundation for trust-management languages. In: Dahl, V. (ed.) PADL 2003. LNCS, vol. 2562, pp. 58–73. Springer, Heidelberg (2002)

19. Liu, M., Cleary, J.: Declarative Updates in Deductive Databases. Journal of Computing and Information 1, 1435–1446 (1994)

20. Loo, B.T., Condie, T., Garofalakis, M., Gay, D.E., Hellerstein, J.M., Maniatis, P., Ramakrishnan, R., Roscoe, T., Stoica, I.: Declarative Networking. Communications of the ACM 52(11), 87–95 (2009)

21. Loo, B.T., Hellerstein, J.M., Stoica, I., Ramakrishnan, R.: Declarative routing: Extensible routing with declarative queries. In: SIGCOMM (2005)

22. Lu, L., Cleary, J.G.: An Operational Semantics of Starlog. In: Nadathur, G. (ed.) PPDP 1999. LNCS, vol. 1702, pp. 131–162. Springer, Heidelberg (1999)

23. Mao, Y.: On the declarativity of declarative networking. In: NetDB (2009)

24. Mullender, S. (ed.): Distributed Systems, 2nd edn. Addison-Wesley, Reading (1993)

25. Mumick, I.S., Shmueli, O.: How expressive is stratified aggregation? Annals of Mathematics and Artificial Intelligence 15(3-4), 407–435 (1995)

26. Navarro, J.A., Rybalchenko, A.: Operational Semantics for Declarative Networking. In: Gill, A., Swift, T. (eds.) PADL 2009. LNCS, vol. 5418, pp. 76–90. Springer, Heidelberg (2008)

27. Przymusinski, T.C.: On the Declarative Semantics of Deductive Databases and Logic Programs. In: Minker, J. (ed.) Foundations of Deductive Databases and Logic Programming, pp. 193–216. Morgan Kaufmann, Los Altos (1988)

28. Saraswat, V., Jagadeesan, R., Gupta, V.: Timed Default Concurrent Constraint Programming. Journal of Symbolic Computation 22(5-6), 475–520 (1996)

29. Saraswat, V.A., Jagadeesan, R., Gupta, V.: Foundations of Timed Concurrent Constraint Programming. In: LICS, pp. 71–80 (1994)

30. Ullman, J.D.: Principles of Database and Knowledge-Base Systems. The New Technologies, vol. II. W. H. Freeman & Co., New York (1990)

31. White, W., et al.: Scaling games to epic proportions. In: SIGMOD (2007)

32. Zhou, W., Mao, Y., Loo, B.T., Abadi, M.: Unified declarative platform for secure netwoked information systems. In: ICDE, pp. 150–161 (2009)

# The Disjunctive Datalog System DLV*

Mario Alviano, Wolfgang Faber, Nicola Leone, Simona Perri,
Gerald Pfeifer, and Giorgio Terracina

Department of Mathematics, University of Calabria, 87030 Rende (CS), Italy
{alviano,faber,leone,perri,terracina}@mat.unical.it, gerald@pfeifer.com

**Abstract.** DLV is one of the most successful and widely used answer set programming (ASP) systems. It supports a powerful language extending Disjunctive Datalog with many expressive constructs, including aggregates, strong and weak constraints, functions, lists, and sets. The system provides database connectivity offering a simple way for powerful reasoning on top of relational databases. In this paper, we provide an ample overview of the DLV system. We illustrate its input language and give indications on how to use it for representing knowledge. We also provide a panorama on the system architecture and the main optimizations it incorporates. We then focus on $\mathrm{DLV}^{DB}$, an extension of the basic system which allows for tight coupling with traditional database systems. Finally, we report on a number industrial applications which rely on DLV.

## 1 Introduction

In this paper, we provide an overview of the disjunctive datalog system DLV [26]. The DLV project has been active for more than fourteen years, and has led to the development and continuous enhancement of the DLV system. DLV is widely used by researchers all over the world, and has stimulated quite some interest also in industry (see Section 6).

The key reasons for the success of DLV can be summarized as follows:
**Advanced knowledge modeling capabilities.** DLV provides support for declarative problem solving in several respects:

- High expressiveness of its knowledge representation language, extending disjunctive datalog with many expressive constructs, including aggregates [17], weak constraints [4], functions, lists, and sets [7]. These constructs not only increase the expressiveness of the language; they also improve its knowledge modeling power, enhancing DLV's usability in real-world contexts.
- Full declarativeness: ordering of rules and subgoals is immaterial, the computation is sound and complete, and its termination is guaranteed.
- Front-ends for dealing with specific applications.

* This research has been partly supported by Regione Calabria and EU under POR Calabria FESR 2007-2013 within the PIA project of DLVSYSTEM s.r.l., and by MIUR under the PRIN project LoDeN.

O. de Moor et al. (Eds.): Datalog 2010, LNCS 6702, pp. 282–301, 2011.

**Solid Implementation.** Much effort has been spent on sophisticated algorithms and techniques for improving the performance (see Sections 4.1 and 5), including

- Database optimization techniques: magic sets [10,1], indexing and join ordering methods [25].
- Search optimization techniques: heuristics [18,28], backjumping techniques [34,31], pruning operators [8,16].
- Parallel evaluation [9,30].
- Evaluation in mass-memory [40].

**Interoperability.** A number of mechanisms have been implemented to allow DLV to interact with external systems:

- Interoperability with relational DBMSs: ODBC interface and $DLV^{DB}$ [40].
- Interoperability with Semantic Web reasoners: DLVHEX [14].
- Calling external (C++) functions from DLV programs: DLVEX [6].
- Calling DLV from Java programs: Java Wrapper [33].

In the following, we introduce the language constructs of DLV by examples, provide some use-cases of how knowledge can be represented in the DLV language. Subsequently, we provide an overview of the architecture and techniques of DLV, and we then focus on DLV $^{DB}$ – DLV version working (mostly) in mass-memory. Finally, we provide information on industrial products that rely on DLV.

## 2    The Language of DLV

In this section, we describe the language of the DLV system by examples, providing the intuitive meaning of the main constructs. For further details and the formal definition, we refer to [26,7,17]. We first introduce the basic language, which is based on the founding work by Gelfond and Lifschitz [20] and then we illustrate a number of extensions including aggregates [17], weak constraints [4], complex terms [7], queries and database interoperability constructs [40].

*Basic Language.* The main construct in the DLV language is a rule, an expression of the form $Head : - Body.$, where $Body$ is a conjunction of literals and $Head$ is a disjunction of atoms. Informally, a rule can be read as follows: "if $Body$ is true then $Head$ is true". A rule without a body is called a *fact*, since it models an unconditional truth (for simplicity :- is omitted); whereas a rule with an empty head, called *strong constraint*, is used to model a condition that must be false in any possible solution. A set of rules is called *program*. The semantics of a program is given by its *answer sets* [20]. A program can be used to model a problem to be solved: the problem's solutions correspond to the answer sets of the program (which are computed by DLV). Therefore, a program may have no answer set (if the problem has no solution), one (if the problem has a unique solution) or several (if the problem has more than one possible solutions).

As an example consider the problem of automatically creating an assessment test from a given database of questions where each question is identified by a unique string, covers a particular topic, and requires an estimated time to be answered. The input data about questions can be represented by means of a set of facts of type $question(q, topic, time)$; in addition, facts of the form $relatedTopic(topic)$ specify the topics related to the subject of the test.

For instance, consider the case in which only four questions are given, represented by facts: $question(q1, computerscience, 8)$, $question(q2, computerscience, 15)$, $question(q3, mathematics, 15)$, and $question(q4, mathematics, 25)$. Moreover, suppose that computer science is the only topic to be covered by the test, therefore $relatedTopic(computerscience)$ is also part of the input facts. The program consisting only of these facts has one answer set $A_1$ containing exactly the five facts.

Assessment creation amounts to selecting a set of questions from the database, according to a given specification. To single out questions related to the subject of the test, one can write the rule:

$$relatedQuestion(Q) :\text{-} question(Q, Topic, Time), relatedTopic(Topic).$$

that can be read: "$Q$ is a question related to the test if $Q$ has a topic related to some of the subjects that have to be assessed". Adding this rule to the input facts reported earlier yields one answer set $A_2 = A_1 \cup \{relatedQuestion(q1), relatedQuestion(q2)\}$.

For determining all the possible subsets of related questions the following disjunctive rule can be used:

$$inTest(Q) \text{ v } discard(Q) :\text{-} relatedQuestion(Q).$$

Intuitively, this rule can be read as: "if $Q$ identifies a related question, then either $Q$ is taken in the test or $Q$ is discarded." This rule has the effect of associating each possible choice of related questions with an answer set of the program. Indeed, the answer sets of the program $\mathcal{P}$ consisting of the above two rules and the input facts are:

$$A_3 = A_2 \cup \{discard(q1), discard(q2)\}, \quad A_4 = A_2 \cup \{inTest(q1), discard(q2)\},$$
$$A_5 = A_2 \cup \{discard(q1), inTest(q2)\}, \quad A_5 = A_2 \cup \{inTest(q1), inTest(q2)\}$$

corresponding to the four possible choices of questions $\{\}, \{q1\}, \{q2\}, \{q1, q2\}$. Note that the answer sets are minimal with respect to subset inclusion. Indeed, for each question $Q$ there is no answer set in which both $inTest(Q)$ and $discard(Q)$ appear.

At this point, some strong constraints can be used to single out some solutions respecting a number of specification requirements. For instance, suppose we are interested in tests containing only questions requiring less than 10 minutes to be answered. The following constraint models this requirement:

$$:\text{-} inTest(Q), question(Q, Topic, Time), Time >= 10.$$

The program obtained by adding this constraint to $\mathcal{P}$ has only two answer sets $A_3$ and $A_4$.

*Aggregate Functions.* More involved properties requiring operations on sets of values can be expressed by aggregates, a DLV construct similar to aggregation in the SQL language. DLV supports five aggregate functions, namely *#sum*, *#count*, *#times*, *#max*, *#min*.

In our running example we might want to restrict the included questions to be solvable in an estimated time of less than 60 minutes. This can be achieved by the following strong constraint:

$$:\text{-}\,not\#sum\{Time, Q : inTest(Q), question(Q, Topic, Time)\} < 60.$$

The aggregate sums up the estimated solution times of all questions in the test, and the constraint will eliminate all scenarios in which this sum is not less than 60.

*Optimization Constructs.* The DLV language also allows for specifying optimization problems (i.e. problems where some goal function must be minimized or maximized). This can be achieved by using *weak constraints*. From a syntactic point of view, a weak constraint is like a strong one where the implication symbol :- is replaced by :∼. Contrary to strong constraints, weak constraints allow for expressing conditions that *should* be satisfied, but not necessarily have to be.

The informal meaning of a weak constraint :∼ $B$ is "try to falsify $B$", or "$B$ should preferably be false". Additionally, a weight and a priority level for the weak constraint may be specified enclosed in square brackets (by means of positive integers or variables). The answer sets minimize the sum of weights of the violated (unsatisfied) weak constraints in the highest priority level and, among them, those which minimize the sum of weights of the violated weak constraints in the next lower level, and so on.

As an example, if we want to prefer quick-to-answer questions in tests, the following weak constraint represent this desideratum.

$$:\sim inTest(Q), question(Q, Topic, Time). \; [Time : 1]$$

Intuitively, each question in the test increases the total weight of the solution by its estimated solution time. Thus solutions where the total weight is minimal are preferred.

*Complex Terms.* The DLV language allows for the use of complex terms. In particular, it supports function symbols, lists, and sets. Prolog-like syntax is allowed for both function symbols and lists, while sets are explicitly represented by listing the elements in brackets.

As an example, we enrich the question database for allowing two types of questions, open and multiple choice. Input questions are now represented by facts like the following

$$question(q1, math, open(text), 10).$$
$$question(q2, physics, multiplechoice(text, \{c1, c2, c3\}, \{w1, w2, w3\}), 3).$$

where function symbols *open* and *multiplechoice* are used for representing the two different types of questions. In particular, *open* is a unary function whose only parameter represents the text of the question, while *multiplechoice* has three parameters, the text of the question, a set containing correct answers and another set of wrong answers.

The use of sets allows for modeling multi-valued attributes, while function symbols can be used for modeling "semi-structured" information.

Handling complex terms is facilitated by a number of built-in predicates. For instance, the following rule uses the *#member* built-in for selecting correct answers given by a student in the test.

$$correctAnswer(Student, QID, Ans) :- inTest(QID), answer(Student, QID, Ans),$$
$$question(QID, To, multiplechoice(Tx, Cs, Ws), Ti), \#member(Ans, Cs).$$

*Queries.* The DLV language offers the possibility to express conjunctive queries. From a syntactic point of view, a query in DLV is a conjunction of literals followed by a question mark. Since a DLV program may have more than one answer set, there are two different reasoning modes, brave and cautious, to compute a query answer. In the brave (resp. cautious) mode, a query answer is true if the corresponding conjunction is true in some (resp. all) answer sets.

For instance, the answers to the following simple query are the questions having as topic *computerscience* that are contained in some (resp. all) answer sets of the program when brave (resp.cautious) reasoning is used.

$$inTest(Q), question(Q, computerscience, T)?$$

*Database Interoperability.* The DLV system supports interoperability with databases by means of *#import/#export* commands for importing and exporting relations from/to a DBMS. The *#import* command reads tuples from a specified table of a relational database and stores them as facts with a predicate name provided by the user.

In our example, questions can be retrieved from a database by specifying in the program the following directive.

$$\#import(questionDB, \text{``user''}, \text{``passwd''}, \text{``}SELECT * FROM\ question\text{''}, question).$$

where *questionDB* is the name of the database, *"user"* and *"passwd"* are the data for the user authentication, *"SELECT * FROM question"* is an *SQL* query that constructs the table that will be imported and *question* is the predicate name which will be used for constructing the new facts.

In a similar way the *#export* command allows for exporting the extension of a predicate in an answer set to a database.

## 3   Knowledge Representation

In this section, we illustrate the usage of DLV as a tool for knowledge representation and reasoning. We consider a number of problems, from classical deductive database applications to search and optimization problems, and show how the language of DLV can be used to encode them in a highly declarative fashion.

## 3.1   Deductive Databases

We next present two problems motivated by classical deductive database applications, namely *Same Generation* and *Simple Paths*. For the first one, we provide an encoding consisting of positive datalog rules, while we encode the second one by using complex terms (lists).

*Same Generation.* Given a parent-child relationship (an acyclic directed graph), we want to find all pairs of persons belonging to the same generation. Two persons are of the same generation, if either (i) they are siblings, or (ii) they are children of two persons of the same generation.

Suppose that the input is provided by facts like *parent(thomas, joseph)* stating that *thomas* is a parent of *joseph*. Then, this problem can be encoded by the following program, which computes a relation *samegeneration(X, Y)* containing all facts such that $X$ is of the same generation as $Y$:

$$samegeneration(X, Y) \text{:-} parent(P, X), parent(P, Y).$$
$$samegeneration(X, Y) \text{:-} parent(P1, X), parent(P2, Y),$$
$$samegeneration(P1, P2).$$

*Simple Paths.* Given a directed graph, a *simple path* is a sequence of nodes, each one appearing exactly once, such that from each one (but the last) there is an edge to the next in the sequence.

The following program exploits complex terms for deriving all simple paths for a directed graph, starting from a given *edge* relation:

$$path([X, Y]) \text{ :- } edge(X, Y).$$
$$path([X|[Y|W]]) \text{ :- } edge(X, Y), path([Y|W]), \text{ not } \#member(X, [Y|W]).$$

The first rule builds a simple path as a list of two nodes directly connected by an edge. The second rule constructs a new path adding an element to the list representing an existing path. The new element will be added only if there is an edge connecting it to the head of an already existing path. The built-in predicate *#member* allows to avoid the insertion of an element that is already included in the list; without this check, the construction would never terminate in the presence of circular paths (note that, by default, DLV disallow programs which might not terminate [7]).

## 3.2   Search Problems

Here we illustrate two different usages of the DLV language for solving search problems. On the one hand we consider the *Seating problem* for showing how a search problem can be encoded in a DLV program whose answer sets correspond to the problem solutions. On the other hand, we consider a problem of number and graph theory, namely *Ramsey Numbers*, for showing how to build a DLV program whose answer sets witness that a property does not hold, i.e., the property at hand holds if and only if the DLV program has no answer set.

288    M. Alviano et al.

*Seating.* Consider the problem of generating a seating arrangement for $k$ guests, with $m$ tables and $n$ chairs per table. Guests who like each other should sit at the same table; guests who dislike each other should sit at different tables.

Suppose that the number of chairs per table is specified by $nChairs(X)$ and that $person(P)$ and $table(T)$ represent the guests and the available tables, respectively. Then, we can generate a seating arrangement by the following program:

$$at(P,T) \text{ v } not\_at(P,T) :\text{-} person(P), table(T).$$
$$:\text{-} table(T), nChairs(C), \text{not } \#count\{P : at(P,T)\} \leq C.$$
$$:\text{-} person(P), \text{not } \#count\{T : at(P,T)\} = 1.$$
$$:\text{-} like(P1,P2), at(P1,T), \text{not } at(P2,T).$$
$$:\text{-} dislike(P1,P2), at(P1,T), at(P2,T).$$

The disjunctive rule guesses whether person $P$ sits at table $T$ or not, thus generating all possible assignments of persons to tables (even those where a person is not assigned to any table or it is assigned to more than one). The strong constraints discard assignments that do not respect the problem specification. In particular the first constraint, for each table $T$, counts the number of persons assigned to $T$ and ensures that it does not exceed the number of chairs per table, whereas the second one, imposes that each person is seated at precisely one table. Finally, the last two constraints ensure that persons who like each other are seated at the same table and persons who dislike each other are not.

*Ramsey Numbers.* The Ramsey number $R(k,m)$ is the least integer $n$ such that, no matter how we color the arcs of the complete undirected graph (clique) with $n$ nodes using two colors, say red and blue, there is a red clique with $k$ nodes (a red $k$-clique) or a blue clique with $m$ nodes (a blue $m$-clique).

Ramsey numbers exist for all pairs of positive integers $k$ and $m$ [32]. We next show a program $\mathcal{P}$ that allows for deciding whether a given integer $n$ is <u>not</u> the Ramsey Number $R(3,4)$. By varying the input number $n$, we can determine $R(3,4)$, as described below. Let $\mathcal{F}$ be the collection of facts for input predicate *arc* encoding a complete graph with $n$ nodes. $\mathcal{P}$ is the following program:

$$blue(X,Y) \text{ v } red(X,Y) :\text{-} arc(X,Y).$$
$$:\text{-} red(X,Y), red(X,Z), red(Y,Z).$$
$$:\text{-} blue(X,Y), blue(X,Z), blue(Y,Z),$$
$$blue(X,W), blue(Y,W), blue(Z,W).$$

Intuitively, the disjunctive rule guesses a color for each edge. The first constraint eliminates the colorings containing a red clique (i.e., a complete graph) with 3 nodes, and the second constraint eliminates the colorings containing a blue clique with 4 nodes. The program $\mathcal{P} \cup \mathcal{F}$ has an answer set if and only if there is a coloring of the edges of the complete graph on $n$ nodes containing no red clique of size 3 and no blue clique of size 4. Thus, if there is an answer set for a particular $n$, then $n$ is <u>not</u> $R(3,4)$, that is, $n < R(3,4)$. On the other hand, if $\mathcal{P} \cup \mathcal{F}$ has no answer set, then $n \geq R(3,4)$. Thus, the smallest $n$ such that no answer set is found is the Ramsey number $R(3,4)$.

## 3.3  Optimization Problems

In this section, we present two optimization problems, the first one is a classical graph theory problem, while the second one concerns exam scheduling.

*Maximal Cut.* Given a graph $G = (V, E)$ we want to compute the maximal cuts of the graph, i.e. a partition of $V$ in two sets $V_1$ and $V_2$ such that the number of edges of $G$ having one endpoint in $V_1$ and one endpoint in $V_2$ is maximal.

Suppose that the graph $G$ is specified by facts over predicates *node* and *edge*. Then, the following program compute the maximal cuts of $G$:

$$v1(X) \, \mathsf{v} \, v2(X) :\text{-} \, node(X).$$
$$:\sim v1(X), v2(Y), not edge(X, Y). \, [1 : 1]$$
$$:\sim v2(X), v1(Y), not edge(X, Y). \, [1 : 1]$$

Here the disjunctive rule guesses whether $node(X)$ is in the subset $V_1$ or $V_2$, thus generating all the possible partitions of nodes into subsets. Then, the two weak constraints allow for preferring partitions where the number of edges with both nodes assigned to the same subset is minimum.

*Exam Scheduling.* Here we have to schedule the exams for several university courses in three time slots $t_1$, $t_2$, and $t_3$ at the end of the semester. In other words, each course should be assigned exactly to one of these three time slots. Specific instances $I$ of this problem are provided by sets $\mathcal{F}_I$ of facts specifying the exams to be scheduled. An example fact is $exam(cs1, lee, cs, 1)$ specifying the exam identified as $cs1$, taken by $lee$, of the first year of the curriculum $cs$.

Several exams can be assigned to the same time slot (the number of available rooms is sufficiently high), but the scheduling has to respect the following specifications:

S1 Two exams given by the same professor cannot run in parallel, i.e., in the same time slot.
S2 Exams of the same curriculum should be assigned to different time slots, if possible. If $S2$ is unsatisfiable for a curriculum $C$, one should:
($S2_1$) first of all, minimize the overlap between exams of the same year of $C$,
($S2_2$) then, minimize the overlap between exams of different years of $C$.

This problem can be encoded in the DLV language by the following program $\mathcal{P}$:

$$at(Id, t_1) \, \mathsf{v} \, at(Id, t_2) \, \mathsf{v} \, at(Id, t_3) :\text{-} \, exam(Id, P, C, Y).$$
$$:\text{-} \, at(Id, T), at(Id', T), Id <> Id', exam(Id, P, C, Y), exam(Id', P, C', Y').$$
$$:\sim at(Id, T), at(Id', T), exam(Id, P, C, Y), exam(Id', P', C, Y), Id <> Id'. \, [1 : 2]$$
$$:\sim at(Id, T), at(Id', T), exam(Id, P, C, Y), exam(Id', P', C, Y'), Y <> Y'. \, [1 : 1]$$

The disjunctive rule generates the possible assignments of exams to time slots and the strong constraint discards the assignments of the same time slot to two exams of the same professor, as required by the specification $S1$. Finally, the two weak constraints state that exams of the same curriculum should *possibly not* be assigned to the same time slot. However, the first one, which has higher priority (level 2), states this desire for the exams of the curriculum of the same year, while the second one, which has lower priority (level 1) states it for the exams of the curriculum of different years.

# 4    DLV Implementation

A main strength of DLV is its implementation which is based on solid theoretical foundations, and relies on sophisticated data structures and advanced optimization techniques. In this section we first outline the main aspects of the DLV computation, then we give an overview of the main techniques which were employed in the implementation. Finally, we describe the general architecture of the system.

The computation of the answer sets in DLV is characterized by two phases, namely *program instantiation (grounding)* and *answer set search*. The former transforms the input program into a semantically equivalent one with no variables (ground) and the latter applies propositional algorithms on the instantiated program to generate answer sets.

Grounding in DLV is more than a simple replacement of variables by all possible ground terms: It partially evaluates relevant program fragments, and efficiently produces a ground program which has precisely the same answer sets. The size of the instantiation is a critical aspect for the efficiency of the system: On the one hand, instantiated programs can require exponential space, on the other hand, the answer set search can take exponential time in the size of the grounded program. Therefore even a small reduction in the size of the generated instantiation can yield significant performance gains.

Answer set search is then performed by the *Model Generator (MG)* and the *Model Checker (MC)* on the program produced by the grounding. Roughly, the MG produces "candidate" answer sets, the stability of which is subsequently verified by the MC. MG is the non-deterministic core of the system, and it is implemented as a backtracking search similar to the Davis-Putnam-Logemann-Loveland (DPLL) procedure [13] for SAT solving. Basically, starting from the empty (partial) interpretation, the Model Generator repeatedly assumes truth-values for atoms (branching step), subsequently computing their deterministic consequences (propagation step). This is done until either an answer set candidate is found or an inconsistency is detected. Candidate answer sets are then checked by the *Model Checker* module; whereas, if an inconsistency is detected, chosen literals have to be undone. For disjunctive programs, model checking is as hard as the problem solved by the Model Generator, while it is trivial for non-disjunctive programs.

## 4.1    Main Optimization Techniques

Many optimization techniques have been incorporated into the DLV engine, including database techniques for efficient instantiation, advanced pruning operators, look-ahead and look-back techniques for model generation, and innovative techniques for answer-set checking. In the following, we recall the most relevant ones which have been adopted in the main phases of the evaluation.

*Instantiation Phase.* DLV implements several relevant optimization techniques for the instantiation, mainly descending from the databases field, aimed at reducing both the size of the instantiation and the time needed for generating it. For instance, the DLV instantiator implements a *Program Rewriting* [15] strategy descending from query optimization techniques in relational algebra which allows for reducing in many cases the size of the program instantiation. According to this technique, program rules are automatically rewritten by pushing projections and selections down the execution tree as much as possible. Another rewriting-based optimization technique used in DLV are *Dynamic Magic Sets* [10,1], an extension of the Magic Sets technique originally defined for standard Datalog for optimizing query answering over logic programs. The Magic Sets technique rewrites the input program for identifying a subset of the program instantiation which is sufficient for answering the query. The restriction of the instantiation is obtained by means of additional "magic" predicates, whose extensions represent relevant atoms w.r.t. the query. Dynamic Magic Sets, specifically conceived for disjunctive programs, inherit the benefits provided by standard magic sets and additionally allow for exploiting the information provided by the magic predicates also during the non-deterministic answer set search.

Another group of techniques concerns the instantiation process of each rule of the program. In particular, since computing all the possible instantiations of a rule is, basically, analogous to computing all the answers of a conjunctive query joining the extensions of literals of the rule body, DLV uses a *Join Ordering* [25] strategy for determining an efficient evaluation order of the literals in the rule and a main-memory *On-demand Indexing* technique, where a generic argument can be indexed (established according to a heuristic), indices are computed on demand during the evaluation. In addition, the rule instantiation procedure of DLV implements a *BackJumping* algorithm [31] which exploits both semantic and structural information about the rule for computing efficiently only a relevant subset of its ground instances, avoiding the generation of "useless" instances, while fully preserving the semantics of the program.

In the last few years, in order to make use of modern multi-core/multi-processor computers, a parallel version of the DLV instantiator has been realized based on a number of strategies [9,30] which allow for three levels of parallelism during the instantiation process, namely, components, rules and single rule level.

**Model Generation Phase.** One of the main optimizations used in the model generation phase concerns the propagation step, where an advanced pruning operator [8,16] is applied that allows to prune the search space by combining an extension of the well-founded operator for disjunctive programs.

The efficiency of the whole model generation process depends also on two crucial features: a good heuristic (branching rule) to choose the branching literal (i.e., the criterion determining the literal to be assumed true at a given stage of the computation); and a smart recovery procedure for undoing the choices causing inconsistencies. To this end, both *look-ahead* [18] and *look-back* [34,28] techniques and heuristics have been implemented in DLV. In a lookahead heuristic [18] each possible choice literal is tentatively assumed, its consequences are computed, and some characteristic values on the result are recorded. The look-ahead heuristics of [18] "layers" several criteria based on peculiar properties of DLV programs, and basically drives the search towards "supported" interpretations (since answer sets are supported interpretations – cf. [27,29,3]). In look-back heuristics choices are usually made in such a way that the atoms most involved in conflicts are chosen first. Look-back heuristics are mainly employed in conjunction with *backjumping*, where the set of chosen literals that are relevant for an inconsistency are detected, and the system goes back in the search until at least one choice that caused the inconsistency is undone. The *backjumping* technique of DLV makes use of a *reason calculus* [34] that allows for determining the relevance for an inconsistency; in particular, the information about the choices ("reasons") whose truth-values have caused truth-values of other deterministically derived atoms is collected and used for backjumping.

**Model Checking Phase.** A crucial step in the computation of the answer sets is model checking. There are two main reason for the importance of the model checking step: the exponential number of possible models (model candidates), and the hardness of stable model checking. Note that, when disjunction is allowed in the head, deciding whether a given model is a stable model of a propositional ASP program is co-NP complete in general [12]. For this phase DLV adopts a technique based on a transformation $\mathcal{T}$, which reduces stable model checking to UNSAT, i.e., to deciding whether a given CNF formula is unsatisfiable. Thus, the stability of a candidate answer set $M$ for a program $P$ is verified by calling a SAT solver on the CNF formula obtained by applying $\mathcal{T}$ to $P$. The transformation consumes logarithmic space and no new symbols are added.

## 4.2    DLV Architecture

The system architecture of DLV is shown in Figure 1. Upon startup, the input specified by the user is parsed and transformed into the internal data structures of the system. The input can be read from text files, but, as already mentioned, DLV also provides an interface to relational databases via ODBC. The *Intelligent Grounder* (IG) module efficiently generates a ground instantiation $Ground(\mathcal{P})$ of the input, using techniques described in Section 4.1. Note that for stratified programs the IG module already computes the single answer set and does not produce any instantiation. The subsequent computations, which constitute the non-deterministic part of the DLV system, are then performed on $Ground(\mathcal{P})$ by the *Model Generator* and the *Model Checker* as outlined in Section 4.1.

Once an answer set has been found, the Model Generator may resume in order to look for further answer sets. This process is continued until either no more answer sets exist or an explicitly specified number of answer sets has been computed.

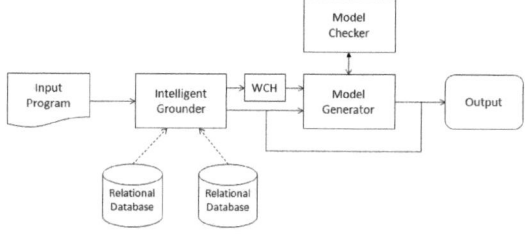

**Fig. 1.** General architecture of the DLV system

Note that, in presence of weak constraints, after the instantiation of the program, the computation is governed by the WCH module and consists of two phases: (i) the first phase determines the cost of an optimal answer set together with one "witnessing" optimal answer set and, (ii) the second phase computes all answer sets having that optimal cost. It is worthwhile noting that both the IG and the MG also have built-in support for weak constraints, which is activated (and therefore incurs higher computational cost) only if weak constraints are present in the input. The MC, instead, does not need to provide any support for weak constraints, since these do not affect answer-set checking at all.

# 5    Reasoning on Top of Databases: DLV$^{DB}$

In real world applications, reasoning is often done on existing data sources; in these contexts, current deductive database systems show some limitations, namely: *(i)* the amount of data that can be handled is limited since most of them work in main memory; *(ii)* the interaction with external (and autonomous) sources of data, like databases, is not trivial and, in several cases, not allowed at all; *(iii)* the efficiency of existing solutions is still not sufficient for their utilization in complex reasoning tasks involving massive amount of data.

DLV$^{DB}$ comes as a database oriented extension of DLV aiming to overcome these drawbacks. As it will be clear in the following, this extension is significantly more complex than the simple *#import/#export* commands introduced previously. In this section we provide a brief description of its main characteristics, inspiring ideas, and possible applications.

## 5.1    Main Features

The language supported by DLV$^{DB}$ consists of disjunctive and unstratified programs, with aggregates and strong constraints; moreover, it provides the possibility to introduce DBMS-stored function calls directly in the programs as external built-ins. Weak constraints and complex terms are not supported yet.

The basic idea underlying DLV$^{DB}$ is the translation of the input DLV program into a query plan composed of standard SQL queries. The evaluation strategy adopted by the system puts its basis on the sharp distinction existing between the grounding and the model generation phases. Two distinct strategies are adopted in case the input program is non-disjunctive and stratified or not.

If a program is non-disjunctive and stratified, it has a unique stable model corresponding exactly to its ground instantiation. The evaluation of these programs can be done by translating each rule into a corresponding SQL statement, and in the composition of a suitable query plan on the DBMS; the evaluation of recursive rules is carried out with an improved semi-naïve approach.

In presence of disjunctive rules or unstratified negation in a program, its ground instantiation is no more sufficient to compute its stable models. Then, grounding and model generation phases must both take place. The evaluation strategy, in this case, moves most of the grounding into the database, by the execution of suitable SQL queries. This phase generates two kinds of data: ground atoms (facts) valid in every stable model (and thus not requiring further elaboration in the model generation phase) and ground rules, summarizing possible values for a predicate and the conditions under which these can be inferred.

Facts compose the so called *solved* part of the program, whereas ground rules form the *residual program*. One of the main challenges in DLV$^{DB}$ is to keep the smallest amount of information as possible in main memory; consequently, the residual program generated by the system is as small as possible.

The minimal residual program is then loaded into the main memory, and the model generation is carried out with the standard DLV techniques, described previously.

DLV$^{DB}$ also ports DLV built-in predicates to databases, and extends this functionality to any stored function defined in the database (in the following, we call them external built-ins). The evaluation of such external built-ins is completely carried out during the grounding (this is true even for disjunctive or unstratified programs). As a consequence, their handling can be carried out completely within the SQL statements generated for the query plan. By convention, given an external built-in $\#f(X_1, \ldots, X_n, O)$ only the last variable $O$ can be considered as an output parameter, whereas all the other variables must be intended as input for $f$ and, thus, they must be safely bound to some other variables in the rule body. This corresponds to the database function call $f(X_1, \ldots, X_n) = O$. For example, consider the rule:

$$mergedNames(ID, Name) :\text{-} person(ID, FirstName, LastName),$$
$$\#concat(FirstName, LastName, Name).$$

This rule is translated into:

    INSERT INTO mergedNames (SELECT  person.ID,
    concat(person.FirstName,person.LastName) FROM  person);

In order to allow for a strict coupling between DLV and DBMSs, a set of auxiliary directives has been designed so as to instruct DLV$^{DB}$ on how to map intended input/output data onto DLV predicates; details on this aspect are given in the next section.

As for current and future work, we plan to add the following features to the system: *(i)* support for complex terms, *(ii)* introduction of techniques for the

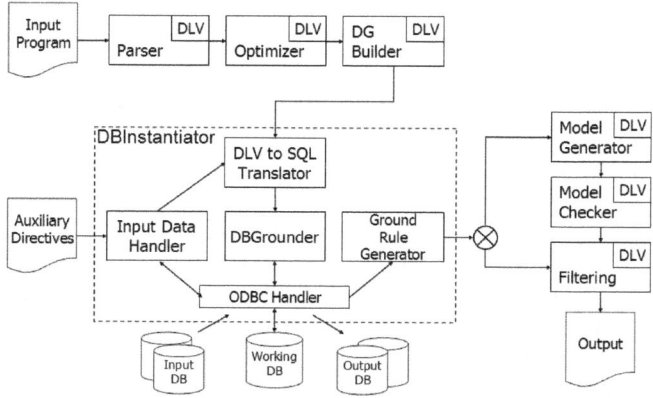

**Fig. 2.** Architecture of $\mathrm{DLV}^{DB}$

distribution of the evaluation on multiple databases, and *(iii)* introduction of techniques for improving query answering like unfolding and static filtering.

## 5.2   DLV DB Architecture

Figure 2 illustrates the architecture of $\mathrm{DLV}^{DB}$. In the figure, the boxes marked with DLV have already been developed in the DLV system. An input program $\mathcal{P}$ is first analyzed by the Parser which encodes the rules in the intensional database (IDB) and stores in the working database facts specified directly in the input program (if any). Then the Optimizer applies basic syntactic rewritings and the Dependency Graph Builder computes the dependency graph of the program, its connected components and a topological ordering of these components. Finally, the DB Instantiator module, the core of the system, is activated.

The DB Instantiator module receives the Dependency Graph (DG) generated by the Dependency Graph Builder and some auxiliary directives. Communication with databases is performed via ODBC. This allows $\mathrm{DLV}^{DB}$ both to be independent from a particular DBMS and to handle databases distributed over the Internet. Only strictly necessary information is transferred from the databases to the system in order to limit the inherent inefficiency of these operations.

If the input program is non-disjunctive and stratified, the result of the instantiation step is directly fetched to the filtering module; otherwise the Ground Rule Generator module produces the residual program. This is transferred in main memory to the standard DLV Model Generator for the identification of the stable models. Note that all the data derived to be true in every stable model by the DB Instantiator are kept inside the database.

As previously pointed out, $\mathrm{DLV}^{DB}$ can be coupled with external databases through some auxiliary directives. Intuitively, the user must specify the working database and can specify a set of table definitions; each specified table must be mapped onto one of the program predicates. Facts can reside on separate databases or they can be obtained as views on different tables. A USE or CREATE directive can be used to specify input or output data, respectively. Finally, the user can choose to copy the entire output of the evaluation or parts thereof in a database different from the working one.

## 5.3   Using DLV $^{DB}$ for Data Integration

Data integration systems provide a transparent access to different and possibly distributed sources. The user is provided with a uniform view of available information by the so-called *global schema*, which queries can be posed upon. The integration system is then in charge of accessing the single sources separately and merging data relevant for the query, guided by mapping rules that specify relationships holding between the sources and the global schema [2,23].

The global schema may contain integrity constraints (such as key dependencies, inclusion dependencies, etc.). The main issues in data integration arise when original sources independently satisfy the integrity constraints but, when they are merged through the mappings, they become inconsistent. As an example, consider students of two universities; each student has an unique ID in his university, but two different students in different universities may share the same ID. Clearly, when they are combined in a global database, the key constraint on student IDs of the global schema will be violated.

Most of the solutions to these problems are based on database repair approaches. Basically, a repair is a new database satisfying constraints of the global schema with minimal differences from the source data. Note that multiple repairs can exist for the same database. Then, answering queries over globally inconsistent sources consists in computing those answers that are true in every possible repair; these are called *consistent* answers in the literature.

Answer Set Programming is a powerful tool in this context, as demonstrated for example by the approaches formalized in [2,5,24]. In fact, if mappings and constraints on the global schema are expressed as disjunctive datalog programs, and the query $Q$ as a union of conjunctions on the global schema, the database repairs correspond to the stable models of the program, and the consistent answers to $Q$ correspond to the answers of $Q$ under cautious reasoning.

In this context, DLV$^{DB}$ provides: *(i)* the needed expressiveness to build multiple repairs and to perform cautious reasoning on them (not provided by standard SQL), *(ii)* the capability to deal with the massive amounts of data typical of real world data integration scenarios (not provided by available deductive systems), and *(iii)* an easy way to interact with autonomous and distributed databases, a frequent setting in data integration processes.

*Example 1.* To have an intuition on the simplicity to use DLV$^{DB}$ as a data integration engine, consider two student relations $s1(SID, Name)$ and $s2(SID, Name)$ of two different universities, and assume that the global schema is designed so as to merge these lists, but keeping SID as a key for the global database.

A program defining the mappings for the global relation $sG$ and handling the possible repairs for key constraint violations over student IDs is:

$$sR(ID, N) := s1(ID, N). \quad sR(ID, N) := s2(ID, N).$$
$$sC(ID, N1) \lor sC(ID, N2) := sR(ID, N1), sR(ID, N2), N1 \neq N2.$$
$$sG(ID, N) := sR(ID, N), \text{not } sC(ID, N).$$

Here the first two rules load all possible data from the sources, whereas the third one avoids to put conflicting tuples in the global relation sG. Note that the disjunctive rule allows the generation of the minimal repairs by singling out conflicting tuples only.

Now, assume that $s1$ contains $\{s1(1234, John), s1(2345, Andrew)\}$ and $s2$ contains $\{s2(1234, David)\}$. There is globally a conflict between John and David because they have the same ID. Then, there are two repairs for $sG$, namely $\{sG(1234, John), sG(2345, Andrew)\}$ and $\{sG(1234, David), sG(2345, Andrew)\}$.

If the user poses the query $q1(N) := sG(ID, N)$, the only consistent answer is: *Andrew*, but if the user asks for $q2(ID) := sG(ID, N)$, the consistent answers are: $\{1234, 2345\}$.

Finally, if the actual content of s1 and s2 is stored in two database tables s1r on database DB1 and s2r on database DB2, in order to perform the query evaluation on a database named workdb, the following auxiliary directives are sufficient:

USEDB workdb:myname:mypasswd.
USE s1r MAPTO s1 FROM DB1:u1:pw1.    USE s2r MAPTO s2 FROM DB2:u2:pw2.

# 6    Spin-Off and Applications

DLV is widely used by researchers all over the world, and, importantly, it has stimulated quite some interest also in industry. Indeed, even if the industrial exploitation of DLV has started fairly recently, it already has a history of applications on the industrial level.

The industrial application of DLV is mostly managed by two spin-off companies of the University of Calabria, EXEURA s.r.l. and DLVSYSTEM s.r.l. . EXEURA develops products and applications in the area of knowledge management based on DLV; while DLVSYSTEM maintains the DLV system and provides consulting on its use.

In this section we present some of the industrial applications of DLV. In particular, we first mention some industrial products of EXEURA incorporating DLV as computational core. Then, we recall a number of industrial applications based on DLV or on DLV-based products.

*DLV-based Industrial Products.* OntoDLV [35,36], OLEX [11,39], HιLεX [38,37], are three Knowledge Management products of EXEURA based on DLV.

OntoDLV [35,36] is a system for ontology specification and reasoning. The language of OntoDLV, called OntoDLP, is an extension of (disjunctive) ASP with all the main ontology constructs including classes, inheritance, relations, and axioms. Importantly, OntoDLV supports a powerful interoperability mechanism with OWL, allowing the user to retrieve information from external OWL Ontologies and to exploit this data in OntoDLP ontologies and queries. OntoDLV facilitates the development of complex applications in a user-friendly visual environment; it features a rich Application Programming Interface (API) [19], and it is endowed with a robust persistency-layer for saving information transparently on a DBMS, and it seamlessly integrates DLV [26].

OLEX [11,39] (OntoLog Enterprise Categorizer System) is a corporate classification system supporting the entire content classification life-cycle, including document storage and organization, ontology construction, pre-processing and classification. OLEX employs a reasoning-based approach to text classification which combines: ($i$) ontologies for the formal representation of the domain knowledge; ($ii$) pre-processing technologies for a symbolic representation of texts and ($iii$) ASP as categorization rule language and DLV as ASP engine. Logic rules, indeed, provides a natural and powerful way to encode how document contents may relate to ontology concepts.

HιLεX [38,37] is an advanced system for ontology-based information extraction from semi-structured and unstructured documents. HιLεX implements a semantic approach to the information extraction problem able to deal with different document formats (html, pdf, doc, ...). HιLεX is based on OntoDLP for describing ontologies, and supports a language that is founded on the concept of *ontology descriptor*. A "descriptor" looks like a production rule in a formal attribute grammar, where syntactic items are replaced by ontology elements. The obtained specification is rewritten in ASP and evaluated by means of the DLV system.

*Industrial Applications.* Commercial applications based on DLV include:

*Team Building in the Gioia-Tauro Seaport.* A system based on DLV has been developed to automatically produce an optimal allocation of the available personnel of the international seaport of Gioia Tauro [21]. The system currently employed by the transshipment company ICO BLG can build new teams satisfying a number of constraints or complete the allocation automatically when the roles of some key employees are fixed manually.

*E-Tourism.* IDUM [22] is an intelligent e-tourism system. IDUM system helps both employees and customers of a travel agency in finding the best possible travel solution in a short time. In IDUM an ontology modeling the tourism scenario was developed by using OntoDLV, and is automatically filled by processing the offers received by a travel agent with HιLεX. IDUM mimics the behavior of the typical employee of a travel agency by running a set of specifically devised logic programs that reason on the information contained in the tourism ontology.

*Automatic Itinerary Search.* In this application, a Web portal has been conceived for making the public transportation system of the Italian region Calabria more accessible, including both public and private companies. The system specifies locations and time tabling of start/transfers/arrival, as well as other information on the trip, like walking directions, duration, etc. A set of specifically devised ASP programs are used to build the required itineraries.

*e-Government.* An application of the OLEX system has been developed which classifies legal acts and decrees issued by public authorities. The system was validated with the help of the employees of the Calabrian Region administration, and it performed very well by obtaining a mean precision of 96% on real-world documents.

*e-Medicine.* OLEX has been used to develop a system capable of automatically classifying case histories and documents containing clinical diagnoses. The system was commissioned with the goal of conducting epidemiological analyses, by the ULSS n.8 (which is, a local authority for health services) of the area of Asolo, in the Italian region Veneto. The system has been deployed and is currently used by the personnel of the ULSS of Asolo.

# References

1. Alviano, M., Faber, W., Greco, G., Leone, N.: Magic sets for disjunctive datalog programs. Tech. Rep. 09/2009, Dipartimento di Matematica, Università della Calabria, Italy (2009), http://www.wfaber.com/research/papers/TRMAT092009.pdf
2. Arenas, M., Bertossi, L.E., Chomicki, J.: Specifying and Querying Database Repairs using Logic Programs with Exceptions. In: Larsen, H.L., Kacprzyk, J., Zadrozny, S., Andreasen, T., Christiansen, H. (eds.) Proceedings of the Fourth International Conference on Flexible Query Answering Systems, FQAS 2000 (2000)
3. Baral, C., Gelfond, M.: Logic Programming and Knowledge Representation. Journal of Logic Programming 19/20, 73–148 (1994)
4. Buccafurri, F., Leone, N., Rullo, P.: Enhancing Disjunctive Datalog by Constraints. IEEE Transactions on Knowledge and Data Engineering 12(5), 845–860 (2000)
5. Calì, A., Lembo, D., Rosati, R.: Query rewriting and answering under constraints in data integration systems. In: Int. Joint Conference on Artificial Intelligence (IJCAI 2003), pp. 16–21 (2003)
6. Calimeri, F., Cozza, S., Ianni, G.: External sources of knowledge and value invention in logic programming. Annals of Mathematics and Artificial Intelligence 50(3-4), 333–361 (2007)
7. Calimeri, F., Cozza, S., Ianni, G., Leone, N.: Computable Functions in ASP: Theory and Implementation. In: Garcia de la Banda, M., Pontelli, E. (eds.) ICLP 2008. LNCS, vol. 5366, pp. 407–424. Springer, Heidelberg (2008)
8. Calimeri, F., Faber, W., Leone, N., Pfeifer, G.: Pruning Operators for Disjunctive Logic Programming Systems. Fundamenta Informaticae 71(2-3), 183–214 (2006)
9. Calimeri, F., Perri, S., Ricca, F.: Experimenting with Parallelism for the Instantiation of ASP Programs. Journal of Algorithms in Cognition, Informatics and Logics 63(1-3), 34–54 (2008)
10. Cumbo, C., Faber, W., Greco, G., Leone, N.: Enhancing the magic-set method for disjunctive datalog programs. In: Demoen, B., Lifschitz, V. (eds.) ICLP 2004. LNCS, vol. 3132, pp. 371–385. Springer, Heidelberg (2004)
11. Cumbo, C., Iiritano, S., Rullo, P.: OLEX – A Reasoning-Based Text Classifier. In: Alferes, J.J., Leite, J. (eds.) JELIA 2004. LNCS (LNAI), vol. 3229, pp. 722–725. Springer, Heidelberg (2004)
12. Dantsin, E., Eiter, T., Gottlob, G., Voronkov, A.: Complexity and Expressive Power of Logic Programming. ACM Computing Surveys 33(3), 374–425 (2001)

13. Davis, M., Logemann, G., Loveland, D.: A Machine Program for Theorem Proving. Commun. ACM 5, 394–397 (1962)
14. Eiter, T., Ianni, G., Schindlauer, R., Tompits, H.: A Uniform Integration of Higher-Order Reasoning and External Evaluations in Answer Set Programming. In: International Joint Conference on Artificial Intelligence (IJCAI) 2005, Edinburgh, UK, pp. 90–96 (August 2005)
15. Faber, W., Leone, N., Mateis, C., Pfeifer, G.: Using Database Optimization Techniques for Nonmonotonic Reasoning. In: INAP Organizing Committee (ed.) Proceedings of the 7th International Workshop on Deductive Databases and Logic Programming (DDLP 1999), pp. 135–139. Prolog Association, Japan (1999)
16. Faber, W., Leone, N., Pfeifer, G.: Pushing Goal Derivation in DLP Computations. In: Gelfond, M., Leone, N., Pfeifer, G. (eds.) LPNMR 1999. LNCS (LNAI), vol. 1730, pp. 177–191. Springer, Heidelberg (1999)
17. Faber, W., Leone, N., Pfeifer, G.: Semantics and complexity of recursive aggregates in answer set programming. Artificial Intelligence (2010) (accepted for publication)
18. Faber, W., Leone, N., Pfeifer, G., Ricca, F.: On look-ahead heuristics in disjunctive logic programming. Annals of Mathematics and Artificial Intelligence 51(2-4), 229–266 (2007)
19. Gallucci, L., Ricca, F.: Visual Querying and Application Programming Interface for an ASP-based Ontology Language. In: Vos, M.D., Schaub, T. (eds.) Proceedings of the Workshop on Software Engineering for Answer Set Programming (SEA 2007), pp. 56–70 (2007)
20. Gelfond, M., Lifschitz, V.: Classical Negation in Logic Programs and Disjunctive Databases. New Generation Computing 9, 365–385 (1991)
21. Grasso, G., Iiritano, S., Leone, N., Lio, V., Ricca, F., Scalise, F.: An asp-based system for team-building in the gioia-tauro seaport. In: Carro, M., Peña, R. (eds.) PADL 2010. LNCS, vol. 5937, pp. 40–42. Springer, Heidelberg (2010)
22. Ielpa, S.M., Iiritano, S., Leone, N., Ricca, F.: An ASP-Based System for e-Tourism. In: Erdem, E., Lin, F., Schaub, T. (eds.) LPNMR 2009. LNCS, vol. 5753, pp. 368–381. Springer, Heidelberg (2009)
23. Lenzerini, M.: Data integration: A theoretical perspective. In: Proc. PODS 2002, pp. 233–246 (2002)
24. Leone, N., Gottlob, G., Rosati, R., Eiter, T., Faber, W., Fink, M., Greco, G., Ianni, G., Kałka, E., Lembo, D., Lenzerini, M., Lio, V., Nowicki, B., Ruzzi, M., Staniszkis, W., Terracina, G.: The INFOMIX System for Advanced Integration of Incomplete and Inconsistent Data. In: Proceedings of the 24th ACM SIGMOD International Conference on Management of Data (SIGMOD 2005), pp. 915–917. ACM Press, Baltimore (2005)
25. Leone, N., Perri, S., Scarcello, F.: Improving ASP Instantiators by Join-Ordering Methods. In: Eiter, T., Faber, W., Truszczyński, M. (eds.) LPNMR 2001. LNCS (LNAI), vol. 2173, pp. 280–294. Springer, Heidelberg (2001)
26. Leone, N., Pfeifer, G., Faber, W., Eiter, T., Gottlob, G., Perri, S., Scarcello, F.: The DLV System for Knowledge Representation and Reasoning. ACM Transactions on Computational Logic 7(3), 499–562 (2006)
27. Leone, N., Rullo, P., Scarcello, F.: Disjunctive Stable Models: Unfounded Sets, Fixpoint Semantics and Computation. Information and Computation 135(2), 69–112 (1997)
28. Maratea, M., Ricca, F., Faber, W., Leone, N.: Look-back techniques and heuristics in dlv: Implementation, evaluation and comparison to qbf solvers. Journal of Algorithms in Cognition, Informatics and Logics 63(1-3), 70–89 (2008)

29. Marek, V.W., Subrahmanian, V.: The Relationship between Logic Program Semantics and Non-Monotonic Reasoning. In: Proceedings of the 6th International Conference on Logic Programming – ICLP 1989, pp. 600–617. MIT Press, Cambridge (1989)
30. Perri, S., Ricca, F., Sirianni, M.: A parallel asp instantiator based on dlv. In: Proceedings of the POPL 2010 Workshop on Declarative Aspects of Multicore Programming, DAMP 2010, Madrid, Spain, January 19, pp. 73–82. ACM, New York (2010)
31. Perri, S., Scarcello, F., Catalano, G., Leone, N.: Enhancing DLV instantiator by backjumping techniques. Annals of Mathematics and Artificial Intelligence 51(2-4), 195–228 (2007)
32. Radziszowski, S.P.: Small Ramsey Numbers. The Electronic Journal of Combinatorics 1 (1994) (revision 9: July 15, 2002)
33. Ricca, F.: The DLV Java Wrapper. In: de Vos, M., Provetti, A. (eds.) Proceedings ASP 2003 - Answer Set Programming: Advances in Theory and Implementation, Messina, Italy, pp. 305–316 (September 2003), http://CEUR-WS.org/Vol-78/
34. Ricca, F., Faber, W., Leone, N.: A Backjumping Technique for Disjunctive Logic Programming. AI Communications – The European Journal on Artificial Intelligence 19(2), 155–172 (2006)
35. Ricca, F., Gallucci, L., Schindlauer, R., Dell'Armi, T., Grasso, G., Leone, N.: OntoDLV: an ASP-based system for enterprise ontologies. Journal of Logic and Computation (2009)
36. Ricca, F., Leone, N.: Disjunctive Logic Programming with types and objects: The DLV$^+$ System. Journal of Applied Logics 5(3), 545–573 (2007)
37. Ruffolo, M., Leone, N., Manna, M., Saccà, D., Zavatto, A.: Exploiting ASP for Semantic Information Extraction. In: de Vos, M., Provetti, A. (eds.) Proceedings ASP 2005 - Answer Set Programming: Advances in Theory and Implementation, Bath, UK, pp. 248–262 (July 2005)
38. Ruffolo, M., Manna, M.: HiLeX: A System for Semantic Information Extraction from Web Documents. In: Manolopoulos, Y., Filipe, J., Constantopoulos, P., Cordeiro, J. (eds.) ICEIS (Selected Papers). LNBIP, vol. 3, pp. 194–209 (2008)
39. Rullo, P., Cumbo, C., Policicchio, V.L.: Learning rules with negation for text categorization. In: Cho, Y., Wainwright, R.L., Haddad, H., Shin, S.Y., Koo, Y.W. (eds.) Proceedings of the 2007 ACM Symposium on Applied Computing (SAC), Seoul, Korea, March 11-15, pp. 409–416. ACM, New York (2007)
40. Terracina, G., Leone, N., Lio, V., Panetta, C.: Experimenting with recursive queries in database and logic programming systems. Theory and Practice of Logic Programming 8, 129–165 (2008)

# Datalog as a Query Language for
# Data Exchange Systems

Marcelo Arenas[1], Pablo Barceló[2], and Juan L. Reutter[3]

[1] Dept. of Computer Science, Pontificia Universidad Católica de Chile
[2] Dept. of Computer Science, University of Chile
[3] School of Informatics, University of Edinburgh

**Abstract.** The class of unions of conjunctive queries (UCQ) has been shown to be particularly well-behaved for data exchange; its certain answers can be computed in polynomial time (in terms of data complexity). However, this is not the only class with this property; the certain answers to any DATALOG program can also can be computed in polynomial time. The problem is that both UCQ and DATALOG do not allow for negated atoms, while most database query languages are equipped with negation. Unfortunately, adding an unrestricted form of negation to these languages yields to intractability of the problem of computing certain answers.

In order to face this challenge, we have recently proposed a language, called DATALOG$^{C(\neq)}$ [5], that extends DATALOG with a restricted form of negation while keeping the good properties of DATALOG, and UCQ, for data exchange. In this article, we provide evidence in favor of the use of DATALOG$^{C(\neq)}$ as a query language for data exchange systems. More precisely, we introduce the syntax and semantics of DATALOG$^{C(\neq)}$, we present some of the fundamental results about this language shown in [5], and we extend those results to the case of data exchange settings that allow for constraints in the target schema. All of these results provide justification for the use of DATALOG$^{C(\neq)}$ in practice.

## 1   Introduction

Data exchange is the problem of computing an instance of a *target* schema, given an instance of a *source* schema and a specification of the relationship between source and target data. Although data exchange is considered to be an old database problem, its theoretical foundations have only been laid out very recently by the seminal work of Fagin, Kolaitis, Miller and Popa [10]. Both the study of data exchange and schema mappings have become an active area of research during the last few years in the database community (see e.g. [10,11,4,9,17,13,18,12]).

In its simplest form, a data exchange setting is a triple $\mathcal{M} = (\mathbf{S}, \mathbf{T}, \Sigma_{st})$, where $\mathbf{S}$ is a *source* schema, $\mathbf{T}$ is a *target* schema, and $\Sigma_{st}$ is a mapping defined as a set of *source-to-target* dependencies of the form $\forall \bar{x} \forall \bar{y} \, (\phi_{\mathbf{S}}(\bar{x}, \bar{y}) \rightarrow \exists \bar{z} \, \psi_{\mathbf{T}}(\bar{x}, \bar{z}))$, where $\phi_{\mathbf{S}}$ and $\psi_{\mathbf{T}}$ are conjunctions of relational atoms over $\mathbf{S}$ and $\mathbf{T}$, respectively. Given a source instance $I$, the goal in data exchange is to materialize a target instance $J$ that is a *solution* for $I$, that is, $J$ together with $I$ satisfies each dependency in $\Sigma_{st}$.

An important issue in data exchange is that the existing specification languages usually do not completely determine the relationship between source and target data and, thus, each source instance has an infinite number of solutions. This immediately raises the question of which solution should be materialized. Initial work on data exchange [10] has identified a class of "good" solutions, called *universal* solutions. In formal terms, a solution is universal if it can be homomorphically embedded into every other solution. It was proved in [10] that for the class of data exchange settings defined above, a particular universal solution – called the *canonical* universal solution – can be computed in polynomial time.

A second important issue in data exchange is query answering. Queries in the data exchange context are posed over the target schema, and –given that there may be many solutions for a source instance– there is a general agreement in the literature that their semantics should be defined in terms of *certain* answers [14,1,15,10]. More formally, given a data exchange setting $\mathcal{M} = (\mathbf{S}, \mathbf{T}, \Sigma_{st})$ and a query $Q$ over $\mathbf{T}$, a tuple $\bar{t}$ is said to be a certain answer to $Q$ over $I$ under $\mathcal{M}$, if $\bar{t}$ belongs to the evaluation of $Q$ over every possible solution $J$ for $I$ under $\mathcal{M}$.

The definition of certain answers is highly non-effective, as it involves computing the intersection of infinitely many sets. Thus, it becomes particularly important to understand for which classes of relevant queries, the certain answers can be computed efficiently. In particular, it becomes relevant to understand whether it is possible to compute the certain answers to any of these classes by using some materialized solution. Fagin, Kolaitis, Miller, and Popa [10] have shown that this is the case for the class of union of conjunctive queries (UCQ); the certain answers to each union of conjunctive queries $Q$ over a source instance $I$ can be computed in polynomial time by directly posing $Q$ over the canonical universal solution for $I$. It is important to notice that in this result the complexity is measured only in terms of the size of the source instances (in particular, the data exchange setting and the query are assumed to be fixed). Thus, the previous result is stated in terms of *data* complexity [20].

The good properties of UCQ for data exchange can be completely explained by the fact that unions of conjunctive queries are preserved under homomorphisms. But this is not the only language that satisfies this condition, as queries definable in DATALOG, the recursive extension of UCQ, are also preserved under homomorphisms. Thus, DATALOG retains several of the good properties of UCQ for data exchange. In particular, the certain answers to a DATALOG program $\Pi$ over a source instance $I$ can be computed efficiently by first materializing the canonical universal solution $J$ for $I$, and then evaluating $\Pi$ over $J$ (since DATALOG programs can be evaluated in polynomial time in the size of the data).

Unfortunately, both UCQ and DATALOG keeps us in the realm of the positive, while most database query languages are equipped with negation. However, adding an unrestricted form of negation to DATALOG (and even to the class of conjunctive queries) leads to intractability of the problem of computing certain answers. Thus, extending DATALOG with some form of negation that, on the one hand, allows to express interesting data exchange queries, and, on the other hand, retains the good properties of DATALOG for data exchange, is a nontrivial task that must be handled carefully.

In order to face this challenge, we have recently proposed a language, called DATALOG$^{C(\neq)}$ [5], that extends DATALOG with a restricted form of negation while keeping the good properties of DATALOG, and UCQ, for data exchange. In this article, we provide evidence in favor of the use of $\text{DATALOG}^{C(\neq)}$ as a query language for data exchange systems. More precisely, we start by introducing the syntax and semantics of $\text{DATALOG}^{C(\neq)}$. Then we continue by presenting some of the fundamental results about this language shown in [5], which provide justification for the use of $\text{DATALOG}^{C(\neq)}$ in practice. In particular, we show that the certain answers to a $\text{DATALOG}^{C(\neq)}$ program can be computed in polynomial time, and that the language $\text{DATALOG}^{C(\neq)}$ can be used to express interesting queries in the data exchange context, as every union of conjunctive queries with at most one inequality or negated relational atom per disjunct can be efficiently expressed as a $\text{DATALOG}^{C(\neq)}$ program in the context of data exchange. We finish the paper by extending these results to the case of data exchange settings with constraints in the target, as explained below.

In addition to the data exchange scenario we have seen so far, it is common in the literature to assume that target schemas come with its own set of dependencies; i.e. each data exchange setting $\mathcal{M} = (\mathbf{S}, \mathbf{T}, \Sigma_{st})$ is extended with a set $\Sigma_t$ of dependencies over the schema $\mathbf{T}$, which are called target constraints. In that case, a target instance $J$ is said to be a solution for the source instance $I$ under the setting $\mathcal{M} = (\mathbf{S}, \mathbf{T}, \Sigma_{st}, \Sigma_t)$, if not only the pair $(I, J)$ satisfies each dependency in $\Sigma_{st}$, but also $J$ satisfies each dependency in $\Sigma_t$.

As it is to be expected, the addition of target dependencies makes the fundamental data exchange tasks more difficult, starting from the fact that it is no longer true that solutions exist for each source instance. Even worst, it follows from [13] that even for simple data exchange settings with target dependencies, the problem of checking for the existence of solutions may be undecidable. In order to solve this problem, the data exchange literature has identified a relevant class of target dependencies – those that consist of a set of equality-generating dependencies (that subsume keys) and a *weakly-acyclic* set of tuple-generating dependencies – that have the following good properties for data exchange [10]: Checking the existence of solutions is a tractable problem; and for every source instance that has a solution, a canonical universal solution can be computed in polynomial time. The latter implies that, for the class of data exchange settings extended with a set of target dependencies that consists of a set of equality-generating dependencies and a weakly-acyclic set of tuple-generating dependencies, the certain answers to each union of conjunctive queries $Q$ can still be computed in polynomial time (by simply posing $Q$ over the canonical universal solution $J$ for a given source instance $I$, in case such $J$ exists).

In this paper, we investigate the feasibility of using $\text{DATALOG}^{C(\neq)}$ as a query language for data exchange settings extended with equality-generating target dependencies and weakly-acyclic sets of tuple-generating target dependencies. In particular, we prove that for this class of data exchange settings, the certain answers to each $\text{DATALOG}^{C(\neq)}$ program can be computed in polynomial time. Also, we study the expressiveness of $\text{DATALOG}^{C(\neq)}$ in this context, and show that every union of conjunctive queries with at most one inequality or negated relational atom per disjunct can be efficiently expressed as a $\text{DATALOG}^{C(\neq)}$ program if only equality-generating target dependencies are considered. We also show that this result fails if, in addition, target constraints are allowed to contain weakly-acyclic sets of tuple-generating target dependencies; indeed, we prove in the paper that there exist a data exchange setting $\mathcal{M} = (\mathbf{S}, \mathbf{T}, \Sigma_{st}, \Sigma_t)$, where $\Sigma_t$

is the union of a set of equality-generating dependencies and a weakly-acyclic set of tuple-generating dependencies, and a conjunctive query $Q$ over $\mathbf{T}$ with one negated relational atom such that the problem of computing certain answers to $Q$ under $\mathcal{M}$ is undecidable.

**Organization of the paper.** In Section 2, we introduce the terminology used in the paper. Then, in Section 3, we define the syntax and semantics of $\text{DATALOG}^{C(\neq)}$ programs, and show their good properties for data exchange. In Section 4 we study the expressive power of $\text{DATALOG}^{C(\neq)}$ programs. Concluding remarks are given in Section 5.

## 2    Background

A *schema* $\mathbf{R}$ is a finite set $\{R_1, \ldots, R_k\}$ of relation symbols, with each $R_i$ having a fixed arity $n_i > 0$. Let $\mathbf{D}$ be a countably infinite domain. An *instance* $I$ of $\mathbf{R}$ assigns to each relation symbol $R_i$ of $\mathbf{R}$ a finite $n_i$-ary relation $R_i^I \subseteq \mathbf{D}^{n_i}$. The *domain* $\text{dom}(I)$ of instance $I$ is the set of all elements that occur in any of the relations $R_i^I$. We often define instances by simply listing the tuples attached to the corresponding relation symbols.

We assume familiarity with first-order logic (FO) and DATALOG. In this paper, CQ is the class of conjunctive queries and UCQ is the class of unions of conjunctive queries. If we extend these classes by allowing inequalities or negation (of relational atoms), then we use superscripts $\neq$ and $\neg$, respectively. Thus, for example, $\text{CQ}^{\neq}$ is the class of conjunctive queries with inequalities, and $\text{UCQ}^{\neg}$ is the class of unions of conjunctive queries with negation. As usual in the database literature, we assume that every query $Q$ in $\text{UCQ}^{\neq,\neg}$ is *safe*: (1) if $Q_1$ and $Q_2$ are disjuncts of $Q$, then $Q_1$ and $Q_2$ have the same free variables, (2) if $Q_1$ is a disjunct of $Q$ and $x \neq y$ is a conjunct of $Q_1$, then $x$ and $y$ appear in some non-negated relational atoms of $Q_1$, (3) if $Q_1$ is a disjunct of $Q$ and $\neg R(\bar{x})$ is a conjunct of $Q_1$, then every variable in $\bar{x}$ appears in a non-negated relational atom of $Q_1$.

### 2.1    Data Exchange Settings and Solutions

As is customary in the data exchange literature, we consider instances with two types of values: constants and nulls [10,11]. More precisely, let $\mathbf{C}$ and $\mathbf{N}$ be infinite and disjoint sets of constants and nulls, respectively, and assume that $\mathbf{D} = \mathbf{C} \cup \mathbf{N}$. If we refer to a schema $\mathbf{S}$ as a *source* schema, then we will assume that for every instance $I$ of $\mathbf{S}$, it holds that $\text{dom}(I) \subseteq \mathbf{C}$. On the other hand, if we refer to a schema $\mathbf{T}$ as a *target* schema, then for every instance $J$ of $\mathbf{T}$, it holds that $\text{dom}(J) \subseteq \mathbf{C} \cup \mathbf{N}$. Slightly abusing notation, we also use $\mathbf{C}$ to denote a built-in unary predicate such that $\mathbf{C}(a)$ holds if and only if $a$ is a constant, that is $a \in \mathbf{C}$.

A *data exchange setting* is a tuple $\mathcal{M} = (\mathbf{S}, \mathbf{T}, \Sigma_{st})$, where $\mathbf{S}$ is a source schema, $\mathbf{T}$ is a target schema, $\mathbf{S}$ and $\mathbf{T}$ do not have predicate symbols in common and $\Sigma_{st}$ is a set of FO-dependencies over $\mathbf{S} \cup \mathbf{T}$ (in [10] and [11] a more general class of data exchange settings is presented, that also includes *target* dependencies; we consider these settings in Section 4.1). As usual in the data exchange literature (e.g., [10,11]), we restrict the study to data exchange settings in which $\Sigma_{st}$ consists of a set of *source-to-target tuple-generating* dependencies. A source-to-target tuple-generating dependency (st-tgd) is an

FO-sentence of the form $\forall \bar{x} \forall \bar{y} \, (\phi(\bar{x}, \bar{y}) \rightarrow \exists \bar{z} \, \psi(\bar{x}, \bar{z}))$, where $\phi(\bar{x}, \bar{y})$ is a conjunction of relational atoms over $\mathbf{S}$ and $\psi(\bar{x}, \bar{z})$ is a conjunction of relational atoms over $\mathbf{T}$.[1] A *source* (resp. *target*) instance $K$ for $\mathcal{M}$ is an instance of $\mathbf{S}$ (resp. $\mathbf{T}$). We usually denote source instances by $I, I', I_1, \ldots$, and target instances by $J, J', J_1, \ldots$.

The class of data exchange settings considered in this paper is usually called GLAV (global-&-local-as-view) in the database literature [15]. One of the restricted forms of this class that has been extensively studied for data integration and exchange is the class of LAV settings. Formally, a LAV setting (local-as-view) [15] is a data exchange setting $\mathcal{M} = (\mathbf{S}, \mathbf{T}, \Sigma_{st})$, in which every st-tgd in $\Sigma_{st}$ is of the form $\forall \bar{x} \, (S(\bar{x}) \rightarrow \exists \bar{z} \, \psi(\bar{x}, \bar{z}))$, for some $S \in \mathbf{S}$.

An instance $J$ of $\mathbf{T}$ is said to be a *solution* for an instance $I$ under $\mathcal{M} = (\mathbf{S}, \mathbf{T}, \Sigma_{st})$, if the instance $K = (I, J)$ of $\mathbf{S} \cup \mathbf{T}$ satisfies $\Sigma_{st}$, where $S^K = S^I$ for every $S \in \mathbf{S}$ and $T^K = T^J$ for every $T \in \mathbf{T}$. If $\mathcal{M}$ is clear from the context, we shall say that $J$ is a solution for $I$.

*Example 1.* Let $\mathcal{M} = (\mathbf{S}, \mathbf{T}, \Sigma_{st})$ be a data exchange setting. Assume that $\mathbf{S}$ consists of one binary relation symbol $P$, and $\mathbf{T}$ consists of two binary relation symbols $Q$ and $R$. Further, assume that $\Sigma_{st}$ consists of st-tgds $P(x, y) \rightarrow Q(x, y)$ and $P(x, y) \rightarrow \exists z R(x, z)$. Then $\mathcal{M}$ is also a LAV setting.

Let $I = \{P(a, b), P(a, c)\}$ be a source instance. Then $J_1 = \{Q(a, b), Q(a, c), R(a, b)\}$ and $J_2 = \{Q(a, b), Q(a, c), R(a, n)\}$, where $n \in \mathbf{N}$, are solutions for $I$. In fact, $I$ has infinitely many solutions. □

## 2.2 Universal Solutions and Canonical Universal Solution

It has been argued in [10] that the preferred solutions in data exchange are the *universal* solutions. In order to define this notion, we first have to revise the concept of *homomorphism* in data exchange. Let $K_1$ and $K_2$ be instances of the same schema $\mathbf{R}$. A homomorphism $h$ from $K_1$ to $K_2$ is a function $h : \mathrm{dom}(K_1) \rightarrow \mathrm{dom}(K_2)$ such that: (1) $h(c) = c$ for every $c \in \mathbf{C} \cap \mathrm{dom}(K_1)$, and (2) for every $R \in \mathbf{R}$ and every tuple $\bar{a} = (a_1, \ldots, a_k) \in R^{K_1}$, it holds that $h(\bar{a}) = (h(a_1), \ldots, h(a_k)) \in R^{K_2}$. Notice that this definition of homomorphism slightly differs from the usual one, as the additional constraint that homomorphisms are the identity on the constants is imposed.

Let $\mathcal{M}$ be a data exchange setting, $I$ a source instance and $J$ a solution for $I$ under $\mathcal{M}$. Then $J$ is a *universal solution* for $I$ under $\mathcal{M}$, if for every solution $J'$ for $I$ under $\mathcal{M}$, there exists a homomorphism from $J$ to $J'$.

*Example 2 (Example 1 continued).* Solution $J_2$ is a universal solution for $I$, while $J_1$ is not since there is no homomorphism from $J_1$ to $J_2$. □

It follows from [10] that for the class of data exchange settings studied in this paper, every source instance has universal solutions. In particular, one of these solutions - called the *canonical universal solution* - can be constructed in polynomial time from the given source instance (assuming the setting to be fixed), using the *chase* procedure [6] (see e.g. [10]).

---

[1] We usually omit universal quantification in front of st-tgds and express them simply as $\phi(\bar{x}, \bar{y}) \rightarrow \exists \bar{z} \, \psi(\bar{x}, \bar{z})$.

*Remark:* Notice that each target instance $J'$ that contains the canonical universal solution $J$ of a source instance $I$, is also a solution for $I$. Thus, each source instance has infinitely many solutions.

### 2.3  Certain Answers

Queries in a data exchange setting $\mathcal{M} = (\mathbf{S}, \mathbf{T}, \Sigma_{st})$ are posed over the target schema $\mathbf{T}$. Given that there are infinitely many solutions for a given source instance $I$ with respect to $\mathcal{M}$, the standard approach in the data exchange literature is to define the semantics of the query based on the notion of certain answers [14,1,15,10].

Let $I$ be a source instance. For a query $Q$ of arity $n \geq 0$, in any of our logical formalisms, we denote by certain$_{\mathcal{M}}(Q, I)$ the set of *certain answers* of $Q$ over $I$ under $\mathcal{M}$, that is, the set of $n$-tuples $\bar{t}$ such that $\bar{t} \in Q(J)$, for every $J$ that is a solution for $I$ under $\mathcal{M}$. If $n = 0$, then we say that $Q$ is *Boolean*, and certain$_{\mathcal{M}}(Q, I) =$ true if and only if $Q$ holds for every $J$ that is a solution for $I$ under $\mathcal{M}$. We write certain$_{\mathcal{M}}(Q, I) =$ false if it is not the case that certain$_{\mathcal{M}}(Q, I) =$ true.

Let $\mathcal{M} = (\mathbf{S}, \mathbf{T}, \Sigma_{st})$ be a data exchange setting and $Q$ a query over $\mathbf{T}$. The main problem studied in this paper is:

> PROBLEM    : CERTAIN-ANSWERS($\mathcal{M}, Q$).
> INPUT         : A source instance $I$ and a tuple $\bar{t}$ of constants from $I$.
> QUESTION : Does $\bar{t} \in$ certain$_{\mathcal{M}}(Q, I)$?

## 3  Extending Query Languages for Data Exchange: DATALOG$^{C(\neq)}$ Programs

The class of unions of conjunctive queries is particularly well-behaved for data exchange; the certain answers of each union of conjunctive queries $Q$ can be computed by directly posing $Q$ over an arbitrary universal solution [10]. More formally, given a data exchange setting $\mathcal{M}$, a source instance $I$, a universal solution $J$ for $I$ under $\mathcal{M}$, and a tuple $\bar{t}$ of constants, $\bar{t} \in$ certain$_{\mathcal{M}}(Q, I)$ if and only if $\bar{t} \in Q(J)$. This implies that for each data exchange setting $\mathcal{M}$, the problem CERTAIN-ANSWERS($\mathcal{M}, Q$) can be solved in polynomial time if $Q$ is a union of conjunctive queries (because the canonical universal solution for $I$ can be computed in polynomial time and $Q$ can be evaluated in polynomial time in the size of the data).

The fact that the certain answers of a union of conjunctive queries $Q$ can be computed by posing $Q$ over a universal solution, can be fully explained by the fact that $Q$ is *preserved* under homomorphisms, that is, for every pair of instances $J, J'$, homomorphism $h$ from $J$ to $J'$, and tuple $\bar{a}$ of elements in $J$, if $\bar{a} \in Q(J)$, then $h(\bar{a}) \in Q(J')$. But UCQ is not the only class of queries that is preserved under homomorphisms; also DATALOG, the *recursive* extension of the class UCQ, has this property. Since each DATALOG program can be evaluated in polynomial time in the size of the data, we have that the certain answers to each DATALOG query $Q$ can be obtained efficiently by first computing a universal solution $J$, and then evaluating $Q$ over $J$. Thus, DATALOG preserves the good properties of UCQ for data exchange.

Unfortunately, both UCQ and DATALOG keep us in the realm of the positive (i.e. negated atoms are not allowed in queries), while most database query languages are equipped with negation. It seems then natural to extend UCQ (or DATALOG) in the context of data exchange with some form of negation. Indeed, query languages with different forms of negation have been considered in the data exchange context [3,8], as they can be used to express interesting queries. Next, we show an example of this fact.

*Example 3.* Consider a data exchange setting with $\mathbf{S} = \{E(\cdot, \cdot), A(\cdot), B(\cdot)\}$, $\mathbf{T} = \{G(\cdot, \cdot), P(\cdot), R(\cdot)\}$ and

$$\Sigma_{st} = \{E(x, y) \rightarrow G(x, y),\ A(x) \rightarrow P(x),\ B(x) \rightarrow R(x)\}.$$

Notice that if $I$ is a source instance, then the canonical universal solution $\text{CAN}(I)$ for $I$ is such that $E^I = G^{\text{CAN}(I)}$, $A^I = P^{\text{CAN}(I)}$ and $B^I = R^{\text{CAN}(I)}$.

Let $Q(x)$ be the following UCQ$^\neg$ query over $\mathbf{T}$:

$$\exists x \exists y\, (P(x) \wedge R(y) \wedge G(x, y)) \vee \exists x \exists y \exists z\, (G(x, z) \wedge G(z, y) \wedge \neg G(x, y)).$$

It is not hard to prove that for every source instance $I$, $\text{certain}_{\mathcal{M}}(Q, I) = \texttt{true}$ if and only if there exist elements $a, b \in \text{dom}(\text{CAN}(I))$ such that $a$ belongs to $P^{\text{CAN}(I)}$, $b$ belongs to $R^{\text{CAN}(I)}$ and $(a, b)$ belongs to the transitive closure of the relation $G^{\text{CAN}(I)}$. That is, $\text{certain}_{\mathcal{M}}(Q, I) = \texttt{true}$ if and only if there exist elements $a, b \in \text{dom}(I)$ such that $a$ belongs to $A^I$, $b$ belongs to $B^I$ and $(a, b)$ belongs to the transitive closure of the relation $E^I$.     □

It is well-known (see e.g. [16]) that there is no union of conjunctive queries (indeed, not even an FO-query) that defines the transitive closure of a graph. Thus, if $Q$ and $\mathcal{M}$ are as in the previous example, then there is no union of conjunctive queries $Q'$ such that $Q'(\text{CAN}(I)) = \text{certain}_{\mathcal{M}}(Q', I) = \text{certain}_{\mathcal{M}}(Q, I)$, for every source instance $I$. It immediately follows that negated relational atoms add expressive power to the class UCQ in the context of data exchange (see also [4]). And not only that, it follows from [10] that inequalities also add expressive power to UCQ in the context of data exchange.

Unfortunately, adding an unrestricted form of negation to DATALOG (or even to CQ) not only destroys preservation under homomorphisms, but also easily leads to intractability of the problem of computing certain answers [1,10]. More precisely, there is a setting $\mathcal{M}$ and a query $Q$ in CQ$^{\neq}$ such that the problem CERTAIN-ANSWERS$(\mathcal{M}, Q)$ cannot be solved in polynomial time (unless PTIME $=$ NP). In particular, the set of certain answers of $Q$ cannot be computed by evaluating $Q$ over a polynomial-time computable universal solution.

## 3.1 DATALOG$^{C(\neq)}$ Programs

We have recently proposed a language DATALOG$^{C(\neq)}$ [5] that adds negation in a natural way to DATALOG, while keeping the good properties of this language for data exchange. We define this language below.

**Definition 1 (DATALOG$^{C(\neq)}$ programs).** *A constant-inequality Datalog rule is a rule of the form:*

$$S(\bar{x}) \leftarrow S_1(\bar{x}_1), \ldots, S_\ell(\bar{x}_\ell), \mathbf{C}(y_1), \ldots, \mathbf{C}(y_m), u_1 \neq v_1, \ldots, u_n \neq v_n, \quad (1)$$

*where*

*(a) $S, S_1, \ldots, S_\ell$ are (non necessarily distinct) predicate symbols,*
*(b) every variable in $\bar{x}$ is mentioned in some tuple $\bar{x}_i$ ($i \in [1, \ell]$),*
*(c) every variable $y_j$ ($j \in [1, m]$) is mentioned in some tuple $\bar{x}_i$ ($i \in [1, \ell]$), and*
*(d) every variable $u_j$ ($j \in [1, n]$), and every variable $v_j$, is equal to some variable $y_i$*
*($i \in [1, m]$).*

*Further, a* constant-inequality Datalog program (DATALOG$^{C(\neq)}$ *program) $\Pi$ is a finite set of constant-inequality Datalog rules.*

For example, the following is a constant-inequality Datalog program:

$$R(x, y) \leftarrow T(x, z), S(z, y), \mathbf{C}(x), \mathbf{C}(z), x \neq z$$
$$S(x) \leftarrow U(x, u, v, w), \mathbf{C}(x), \mathbf{C}(u), \mathbf{C}(v), \mathbf{C}(w), u \neq v, u \neq w$$

For a rule of the form (1), we say that $S(\bar{x})$ is its head. The set of predicates of a DATALOG$^{C(\neq)}$ program $\Pi$, denoted by $Pred(\Pi)$, is the set of predicate symbols mentioned in $\Pi$, while the set of intensional predicates of $\Pi$, denoted by $IPred(\Pi)$, is the set of predicates symbols $R \in Pred(\Pi)$ such that $R(\bar{x})$ appears as the head of some rule of $\Pi$.

Assume that $\Pi$ is a DATALOG$^{C(\neq)}$ program and $I$ is a database instance of the relational schema $Pred(\Pi)$. Then $\mathcal{T}(I)$ is an instance of $Pred(\Pi)$ such that for every $R \in Pred(\Pi)$ and every tuple $\bar{t}$, it holds that $\bar{t} \in R^{\mathcal{T}(I)}$ if and only if there exists a rule $R(\bar{x}) \leftarrow R_1(\bar{x}_1), \ldots, R_\ell(\bar{x}_\ell), \mathbf{C}(y_1), \ldots, \mathbf{C}(y_m), u_1 \neq v_1, \ldots, u_n \neq v_n$ in $\Pi$ and a variable assignment $\sigma$ such that (a) $\sigma(\bar{x}) = \bar{t}$, (b) $\sigma(\bar{x}_i) \in R_i^I$, for every $i \in [1, \ell]$, (c) $\sigma(y_i)$ is a constant, for every $i \in [1, m]$, and (d) $\sigma(u_i) \neq \sigma(v_i)$, for every $i \in [1, n]$. Operator $\mathcal{T}$ is used to define the semantics of constant-inequality Datalog programs. More precisely, define $\mathcal{T}_\Pi^0(I)$ to be $I$ and $\mathcal{T}_\Pi^{n+1}(I)$ to be $\mathcal{T}(\mathcal{T}_\Pi^n(I)) \cup \mathcal{T}_\Pi^n(I)$, for every $n \geq 0$. Then the evaluation of $\Pi$ over $I$ is defined as $\mathcal{T}_\Pi^\infty(I) = \bigcup_{n \geq 0} \mathcal{T}_\Pi^n(I)$.

A constant-inequality Datalog program $\Pi$ is said to be defined over a relational schema $\mathbf{R}$ if $\mathbf{R} = Pred(\Pi) \smallsetminus IPred(\Pi)$ and ANSWER $\in IPred(\Pi)$. Given an instance $I$ of $\mathbf{R}$ and a tuple $\bar{t}$ in dom$(I)^n$, where $n$ is the arity of ANSWER, we say that $\bar{t} \in \Pi(I)$ if $\bar{t} \in$ ANSWER$^{\mathcal{T}_\Pi^\infty(I_0)}$, where $I_0$ is an extension of $I$ defined as: $R^{I_0} = R^I$ for $R \in \mathbf{R}$ and $R^{I_0} = \emptyset$ for $R \in IPred(\Pi)$.

## 3.2 Certain Answers for DATALOG$^{C(\neq)}$ Programs

As we mentioned before, the homomorphisms in data exchange are not arbitrary; they are the identity on the constants. Thus, given that inequalities are witnessed by constants in DATALOG$^{C(\neq)}$ programs, we have that these programs are preserved under homomorphisms. From this we conclude that the certain answers to a DATALOG$^{C(\neq)}$ program $\Pi$ can be computed by directly evaluating $\Pi$ over a universal solution. Thus, DATALOG$^{C(\neq)}$ programs preserve the good properties of DATALOG, and UCQ, for data exchange.

**Proposition 1 ([5]).** *Let $\mathcal{M} = (\mathbf{S}, \mathbf{T}, \Sigma_{st})$ be a data exchange setting, $I$ a source instance, $J$ a universal solution for $I$ under $\mathcal{M}$, and $\Pi$ a* DATALOG$^{C(\neq)}$ *program over* $\mathbf{T}$. *Then for every tuple $\bar{t}$ of constants, $\bar{t} \in$ certain$_\mathcal{M}(\Pi, I)$ iff $\bar{t} \in \Pi(J)$.*

Thus, the certain answers of a DATALOG$^{C(\neq)}$ program $\Pi$ over $I$ can be computed by directly posing $\Pi$ over CAN$(I)$ and discarding tuples that contain nulls. This implies that for each data exchange setting $\mathcal{M}$, the problem CERTAIN-ANSWERS$(\mathcal{M}, \Pi)$ can be solved in polynomial time if $\Pi$ is a DATALOG$^{C(\neq)}$ program (since CAN$(I)$ can be computed in polynomial time and $\Pi$ can be evaluated in polynomial time in the size of the data).

**Corollary 1.** *The problem* CERTAIN-ANSWERS$(\mathcal{M}, \Pi)$ *can be solved in polynomial time, for every data exchange setting* $\mathcal{M}$ *and* DATALOG$^{C(\neq)}$ *program* $\Pi$.

## 4   On the Expressive Power of DATALOG$^{C(\neq)}$ Programs

We have shown in [5] that DATALOG$^{C(\neq)}$ programs are capable of expressing relevant data exchange properties. In particular, these programs are expressive enough to capture the class of unions of conjunctive queries with at most one negated atom per disjunct. This class has proved to be relevant for data exchange, as its restriction with inequalities (that is, the class of queries in UCQ$^{\neq}$ with at most one inequality per disjunct) not only can express relevant queries but also is one of the few known extensions of the class UCQ for which the problem of computing certain answers is tractable [10].

**Theorem 1 ([5]).** *Let $Q$ be a* UCQ$^{\neq, \neg}$ *query over a schema* **T**, *with at most one inequality or negated relational atom per disjunct. Then there exists a* DATALOG$^{C(\neq)}$ *program $\Pi_Q$ over* **T** *such that for every data exchange setting* $\mathcal{M} = (\mathbf{S}, \mathbf{T}, \Sigma_{st})$ *and instance $I$ of* **S**, certain$_\mathcal{M}(Q, I)$ = certain$_\mathcal{M}(\Pi_Q, I)$. *Moreover, $\Pi_Q$ can be effectively constructed from $Q$ in polynomial time.*

We sketch the proof of this theorem by means of an example, since we prove a stronger result later (Theorem 4).

*Example 4.* Let $\mathcal{M}$ be a data exchange setting such that $\mathbf{S} = \{E(\cdot, \cdot), A(\cdot)\}$, $\mathbf{T} = \{G(\cdot, \cdot), P(\cdot)\}$ and

$$\Sigma_{st} = \{E(x, y) \rightarrow \exists z (G(x, z) \wedge G(z, y)), \; A(x) \rightarrow P(x)\}.$$

Also, let $Q(x)$ be the following query in UCQ$^{\neq, \neg}$:

$$(P(x) \wedge G(x, x)) \vee \exists y \, (G(x, y) \wedge x \neq y) \vee \exists y \exists z \, (G(x, z) \wedge G(z, y) \wedge \neg G(x, y)).$$

We construct a DATALOG$^{C(\neq)}$ program $\Pi_Q$ such that certain$_\mathcal{M}(Q, I)$ = certain$_\mathcal{M}(\Pi_Q, I)$. The set of intensional predicates of the DATALOG$^{C(\neq)}$ program $\Pi_Q$ is $\{U_1(\cdot, \cdot, \cdot), U_2(\cdot, \cdot), \text{DOM}(\cdot), \text{EQUAL}(\cdot, \cdot, \cdot), \text{ANSWER}(\cdot)\}$. The program $\Pi_Q$ over **T** is defined as follows.

First, the program collects in DOM$(x)$ all the elements that belong to the active domain of the instance of **T** where $\Pi_Q$ is evaluated:

$$\text{DOM}(x) \leftarrow G(x, z) \tag{2}$$
$$\text{DOM}(x) \leftarrow G(z, x) \tag{3}$$
$$\text{DOM}(x) \leftarrow P(x) \tag{4}$$

Second, the program $\Pi_Q$ includes the following rules that formalize the idea that $\text{EQUAL}(x, y, z)$ holds if $x$ and $y$ are the same elements:

$$\text{EQUAL}(x, x, z) \leftarrow \text{DOM}(x), \text{DOM}(z) \tag{5}$$

$$\text{EQUAL}(x, y, z) \leftarrow \text{EQUAL}(y, x, z) \tag{6}$$

$$\text{EQUAL}(x, y, z) \leftarrow \text{EQUAL}(x, w, z), \text{EQUAL}(w, y, z) \tag{7}$$

Predicate $\text{EQUAL}$ includes an extra argument that keeps track of the element $z$ where the query is being evaluated. Notice that we cannot simply use the rule $\text{EQUAL}(x, x, z) \leftarrow$ to say that $\text{EQUAL}$ is reflexive, as $\text{DATALOG}^{C(\neq)}$ programs are *safe*, i.e. every variable that appears in the head of a rule also has to appear in its body.
     Third, $\Pi_Q$ includes the rules:

$$U_1(x, y, z) \leftarrow G(x, y), \text{DOM}(z) \tag{8}$$

$$U_2(x, z) \leftarrow P(x), \text{DOM}(z) \tag{9}$$

$$U_1(x, y, z) \leftarrow U_1(u, v, z), \text{EQUAL}(u, x, z), \text{EQUAL}(v, y, z) \tag{10}$$

$$U_2(x, z) \leftarrow U_2(u, z), \text{EQUAL}(u, x, z) \tag{11}$$

Intuitively, the first two rules create in $U_1$ and $U_2$ a copy of $G$ and $P$, respectively, but again with an extra argument for keeping track of the element where $\Pi_Q$ is being evaluated. The last two rules allow to replace equal elements in the interpretation of $U_1$ and $U_2$.
     Fourth, $\Pi_Q$ includes the following rule for the third disjunct of $Q(x)$:

$$U_1(x, y, x) \leftarrow U_1(x, z, x), U_1(z, y, x) \tag{12}$$

Intuitively, this rule expresses that if $a$ is an element that does not belong to the set of certain answers to $Q(x)$, then for every pair of elements $b$ and $c$ such that $(a, b)$ and $(b, c)$ belong to the interpretation of $G$, it must be the case that $(a, c)$ also belongs to it.
     Fifth, $\Pi_Q$ includes the following rule for the second disjunct of $Q(x)$:

$$\text{EQUAL}(x, y, x) \leftarrow U_1(x, y, x) \tag{13}$$

Intuitively, this rule expresses that if $a$ is an element that does not belong to the set of certain answers to $Q(x)$, then for every element $b$ such that the pair $(a, b)$ belongs to the interpretation of $G$, it must be the case that $a = b$.
     Finally, $\Pi_Q$ includes two rules for collecting the certain answers to $Q(x)$:

$$\text{ANSWER}(x) \leftarrow U_2(x, x), U_1(x, x, x), \mathbf{C}(x) \tag{14}$$

$$\text{ANSWER}(x) \leftarrow \text{EQUAL}(y, z, x), \mathbf{C}(x), \mathbf{C}(y), \mathbf{C}(z), y \neq z \tag{15}$$

Intuitively, rule (14) says that if a constant $a$ belongs to the interpretation of $P$ and $(a, a)$ belongs to the interpretation of $G$, then $a$ belongs to the set of certain answers to $Q(x)$. Indeed, this means that if $J$ is an arbitrary solution where the program is being evaluated, then $a$ belongs to the evaluation of the first disjunct of $Q(x)$ over $J$.
     Rule (15) says that if in the process of evaluating $\Pi_Q$ with parameter $a$, two distinct constants $b$ and $c$ are declared to be equal ($\text{EQUAL}(b, c, a)$ holds), then $a$ belongs to

the set of certain answers to $Q(x)$. We show the application of this rule with an example. Let $I$ be a source instance, and assume that $(a, n)$ and $(n, b)$ belong to $G$ in the canonical universal solution for $I$, where $n$ is a null value. By applying rule (2), we have that $\text{DOM}(a)$ holds in $\text{CAN}(I)$. Thus, we conclude by applying rule (8) that $U_1(a, n, a)$ and $U_1(n, b, a)$ hold in $\text{CAN}(I)$ and, therefore, we obtain by using rule (13) that $\text{EQUAL}(a, n, a)$ holds in $\text{CAN}(I)$. Notice that this rule is trying to prove that $a$ is not in the certain answers to $Q(x)$ and, hence, it forces $n$ to be equal to $a$. Now by using rule (6), we obtain that $\text{EQUAL}(n, a, a)$ holds in $\text{CAN}(I)$. But we also have that $\text{EQUAL}(b, b, a)$ holds in $\text{CAN}(I)$ (by applying rules (3) and (5)). Thus, by applying rule (10), we obtain that $U_1(a, b, a)$ holds in $\text{CAN}(I)$. Therefore, by applying rule (13) again, we obtain that $\text{EQUAL}(a, b, a)$ holds in $\text{CAN}(I)$. This time, rule (13) tries to prove that $a$ is not in the certain answers to $Q(x)$ by forcing constants $a$ and $b$ to be the same value. But this cannot be the case since $a$ and $b$ are distinct constants and, thus, rule (15) is used to conclude that $a$ is in the certain answers to $Q(x)$. It is important to notice that this conclusion is correct. If $J$ is an arbitrary solution for $I$, then we have that there exists a homomorphism $h : \text{CAN}(I) \to J$. Given that $a$ and $b$ are distinct constants, we have that $a \neq h(n)$ or $b \neq h(n)$. It follows that there is an element $c$ in $J$ such that $a \neq c$ and the pair $(a, c)$ belongs to the interpretation of $G$. Thus, we conclude that $a$ belongs to the evaluation of the second disjunct of $Q(x)$ over $J$.

It is now an easy exercise to show that the set of certain answers to $Q(x)$ coincide with the set of certain answers to $\Pi_Q$, for every source instance $I$.                    □

As an immediate corollary to Theorem 1 and Corollary 1 we obtain the following:

**Corollary 2.** *The problem* CERTAIN-ANSWERS$(\mathcal{M}, Q)$ *can be solved in polynomial time, for every data exchange setting $\mathcal{M}$ and every union of conjunctive queries $Q$ with at most one inequality or negated relational atom per disjunct.*

We note that this slightly generalizes one of the polynomial time results in [10], which is stated for the class of unions of conjunctive queries with at most one inequality per disjunct. The proof of the result in [10] uses different techniques, based on the chase procedure.

It is important to notice that Corollary 2 is, in a sense, optimal, as there is a LAV data exchange setting $\mathcal{M}$ and a conjunctive query with two inequalities, such that CERTAIN-ANSWERS$(\mathcal{M}, Q)$ is coNP-complete [19]. This shows that Theorem 1 cannot be further extended to deal with arbitrary conjunctive queries with negated atoms.

A natural question at this point is whether the problem CERTAIN-ANSWERS$(\mathcal{M}, Q)$ is PTIME-complete for some data exchange setting $\mathcal{M}$ and union of conjunctive queries $Q$ with at most one negated atom per disjunct. The following proposition shows that this is indeed the case.

**Proposition 2 ([5]).** *There exist a* LAV *data exchange setting $\mathcal{M}$ and a Boolean conjunctive query $Q$ with one inequality such that* CERTAIN-ANSWERS$(\mathcal{M}, Q)$ *is* PTIME-*complete, under* LOGSPACE *reductions.*

The previous result establishes a difference with the class of unions of conjunctive queries (UCQ), for which the problem of computing certain answers under a setting $\mathcal{M}$ can be solved in LOGSPACE.

## 4.1  Adding Target Dependencies

In addition to the simple data exchange scenario we have seen so far, it is common in the literature to assume that target schemas come with its own set of dependencies $\Sigma_t$. Formally, data exchange settings with target dependencies (as presented, for instance, in [10,11]) are tuples of the form $\mathcal{M} = (\mathbf{S}, \mathbf{T}, \Sigma_{st}, \Sigma_t)$, where $\mathbf{S}$, $\mathbf{T}$ and $\Sigma_{st}$ are as before, and $\Sigma_t$ is the union of (1) a set of *tuple-generating* dependencies (tgds), i.e. dependencies of the form $\forall \bar{x} \forall \bar{y} \, (\phi(\bar{x}, \bar{y}) \rightarrow \exists \bar{z} \, \psi(\bar{x}, \bar{z}))$, where $\phi(\bar{x}, \bar{y})$ and $\psi(\bar{x}, \bar{z})$ are conjunctions of atomic formulas in $\mathbf{T}$, and (2) a set of *equality-generating* dependencies (egds), i.e. dependencies of the form $\forall \bar{x} \, (\phi(\bar{x}) \rightarrow x_i = x_j)$, where $\phi(\bar{x})$ is a conjunction of atomic formulas in $\mathbf{T}$, and $x_i, x_j$ are variables among those in $\bar{x}$.[2]

For settings with target dependencies, the solutions also have to satisfy the dependencies in $\Sigma_t$. That is, if $\mathcal{M} = (\mathbf{S}, \mathbf{T}, \Sigma_{st}, \Sigma_t)$ is a data exchange setting and $I$ is an instance of $\mathbf{S}$, then an instance $J$ of $\mathbf{T}$ is a solution for $I$ if not only the pair $(I, J)$ satisfies each dependency in $\Sigma_{st}$, but also $J$ satisfies each dependency in $\Sigma_t$.

As it is to be expected, the addition of target dependencies makes the fundamental data exchange tasks more difficult, starting from the fact that it is no longer true that solutions exist for each source instance. Even worst, it follows from [13] that there exists a data exchange setting $\mathcal{M} = (\mathbf{S}, \mathbf{T}, \Sigma_{st}, \Sigma_t)$ with target dependencies such that the problem of checking for the existence of solutions under $\mathcal{M}$ is undecidable.

In order to overcome the aforementioned limitations, the data exchange community has identified a relevant class of target dependencies that has good properties for data exchange. To define this class, we need to introduce some terminology. Assume that $\Sigma$ is a set of tgds over a schema $\mathbf{T}$. Then the *dependency* graph $G_\Sigma$ of $\Sigma$ is defined as follows:

(1)  add a node $(R, i)$ to $G_\Sigma$ for every relation $R \in \mathbf{T}$ and $i \in \{1, \dots, n\}$, where $n$ is the arity of $R$;
(2)  add an edge $(R, i) \rightarrow (T, j)$ to $G_\Sigma$ if there exist a tgd $\phi(\bar{x}, \bar{y}) \rightarrow \exists \bar{z} \, \psi(\bar{x}, \bar{z})$ in $\Sigma$ and a variable $x$ such that $x$ is mentioned in $\bar{x}$, $x$ occurs in the $i$-th attribute of $R$ in $\phi$ and $x$ occurs in the $j$-th attribute of $T$ in $\psi$;
(3)  add a special edge $(R, i) \rightarrow^* (T, j)$ to $G_\Sigma$ if there exists a tgd $\phi(\bar{x}, \bar{y}) \rightarrow \exists \bar{z} \, \psi(\bar{x}, \bar{z})$ in $\Sigma$ such that a variable $x$ occurs in the $i$-th attribute of $R$ in $\phi$ and an existentially quantified variable $z$ occurs in the $j$-th attribute of $T$ in $\psi$.

Moreover, $\Sigma$ is said to be *weakly acyclic* if the dependency graph $G_\Sigma$ of $\Sigma$ does not have a cycle going through an edge labeled $*$ [10]. Next theorem shows that the class of settings with weakly acyclic sets of tgds has good properties for data exchange.

**Theorem 2 ([10]).** *Let $\mathcal{M} = (\mathbf{S}, \mathbf{T}, \Sigma_{st}, \Sigma_t)$ be a data exchange setting, where $\Sigma_t$ is the union of a set of egds and a weakly-acyclic set of tgds. Then there is a polynomial time algorithm such that for every source instance $I$, it first decides whether a solution for $I$ exists, and if that is the case, it computes a canonical universal solution for $I$ in polynomial time.*

---

[2] As usual, we omit universal quantifiers in front of tgds and egds.

The latter implies that for the class of data exchange settings whose target dependencies consist of a set of equality-generating dependencies and a weakly-acyclic set of tuple-generating dependencies, the certain answers to each union of conjunctive queries $Q$ for a source instance $I$, can be computed in polynomial time by simply posing $Q$ over the canonical universal solution $J$ for $I$ and then discarding the tuples that contain nulls (in case such a solution $J$ exists). Notice, however, that using exactly the same argument one can prove the stronger result that certain answers to $\text{DATALOG}^{C(\neq)}$ programs can be computed in polynomial time under the class of settings specified in Theorem 2. This is because $\text{DATALOG}^{C(\neq)}$ programs are preserved under data exchange homomorphisms and can be evaluated in polynomial time in the size of the data. Indeed,

**Corollary 3.** *Let* $\mathcal{M} = (\mathbf{S}, \mathbf{T}, \Sigma_{st}, \Sigma_t)$ *be a data exchange setting, where* $\Sigma_t$ *is the union of a set of egds and a weakly acyclic set of tgds, and let* $\Pi$ *be a* $\text{DATALOG}^{C(\neq)}$ *program over* $\mathbf{T}$. *Then the problem* CERTAIN-ANSWERS$(\mathcal{M}, \Pi)$ *can be solved in polynomial time.*

Let us recall Corollary 2. It says that the certain answers to a union of conjunctive queries with at most one negated atom per disjunct, can be computed in polynomial time for settings without target dependencies. A natural question at this point is whether this positive result continues to hold if target schemas are allowed to contain dependencies of the form specified in Theorem 2. The following result shows that not only this is not the case, but also that the problem of computing certain answers to unions of conjunctive queries with at most one negated atom per disjunct is undecidable for this class of settings

**Theorem 3.** *There exists a data exchange setting* $\mathcal{M} = (\mathbf{S}, \mathbf{T}, \Sigma_{st}, \Sigma_t)$, *where* $\Sigma_t$ *is the union of a set of egds and a weakly-acyclic set of tgds, and a Boolean* $\text{CQ}^{\neg}$ *query* $Q$ *over* $\mathbf{T}$ *with a single negated relational atom such that* CERTAIN-ANSWERS$(\mathcal{M}, Q)$ *is undecidable.*

*Proof.* Let $\mathbf{S}^{\star}$ be a source schema consisting of a ternary relation $P$, $T^{\star}$ a target schema consisting of a ternary relation $R$ and $\mathcal{M}^{\star} = (\mathbf{S}^{\star}, T^{\star}, \Sigma_{st}^{\star}, \Sigma_t^{\star})$ a data exchange setting, where $\Sigma_{st}^{\star}$ consists of the following dependency:

$$P(x, y, x) \rightarrow R(x, y, z),$$

and $\Sigma_t^{\star}$ consists of the egd:

$$R(x, y, z) \wedge R(x, y, w) \rightarrow z = w,$$

and the following tgds:

$$R(x, y, u) \wedge R(y, z, v) \wedge R(u, z, w) \rightarrow R(x, v, w),$$
$$R(x, y, z) \wedge R(x', y', z') \rightarrow \exists w_1 \exists w_2 \exists w_3 \exists w_4 \exists w_5 \exists w_6 \exists w_7 \exists w_8 \exists w_9 \, (R(x, x', w_1) \wedge$$
$$R(x, y', w_2) \wedge R(x, z', w_3) \wedge R(y, x', w_4) \wedge R(y, y', w_5) \wedge$$
$$R(y, z', w_6) \wedge R(z, x', w_7) \wedge R(z, y', w_8) \wedge R(z, z', w_9)).$$

In [13], it was proved that the problem of verifying, given an instance $I$ of $\mathbf{S}^\star$, whether there exists at least one solution for $I$ under $\mathcal{M}^\star$ is undecidable. Next we show how to reduce this problem to the complement of our problem. More precisely, we define a data exchange setting $\mathcal{M} = (\mathbf{S}, \mathbf{T}, \Sigma_{st}, \Sigma_t)$, where $\mathbf{S} = \mathbf{S}^\star$ and $\Sigma_t$ is the union of a set of egds and a weakly-acyclic set of tgds, and a Boolean $\mathrm{CQ}^\neg$ query $Q$ over $\mathbf{T}$ with a single negated relational atom such that for every instance $I$ of $\mathbf{S}^\star$: There exists at least one solution for $I$ under $\mathcal{M}^\star$ if and only if $\mathrm{certain}_\mathcal{M}(Q, I) = \mathtt{false}$. From this, we conclude that CERTAIN-ANSWERS$(\mathcal{M}, Q)$ is undecidable.

Let $\mathbf{S} = \mathbf{S}^\star$, $\mathbf{T} = \mathbf{T}^\star \cup \{S\}$, where $S$ is a ternary predicate, $\Sigma_{st} = \Sigma_{st}^\star$ and $\Sigma_t$ be a set of target dependencies consisting of the egd:

$$R(x, y, z) \wedge R(x, y, w) \rightarrow z = w,$$

and the following tgds:

$$R(x, y, u) \wedge R(y, z, v) \wedge R(u, z, w) \rightarrow R(x, v, w),$$
$$R(x, y, z) \wedge R(x', y', z') \rightarrow \exists w_1 \exists w_2 \exists w_3 \exists w_4 \exists w_5 \exists w_6 \exists w_7 \exists w_8 \exists w_9 \, (S(x, x', w_1) \wedge$$
$$S(x, y', w_2) \wedge S(x, z', w_3) \wedge S(y, x', w_4) \wedge S(y, y', w_5) \wedge$$
$$S(y, z', w_6) \wedge S(z, x', w_7) \wedge S(z, y', w_8) \wedge S(z, z', w_9)).$$

Moreover, let $Q$ be the following Boolean query:

$$\exists x \exists y \exists z \, (S(x, y, z) \wedge \neg R(x, y, z)).$$

It is important to notice that the set of tgds in $\Sigma_t^\star$ is not weakly acyclic, while the set of tgds in $\Sigma_t$ is weakly acyclic. Next we show that for every instance $I$ of $\mathbf{S}^\star$, it holds that there exists at least one solution for $I$ under $\mathcal{M}^\star$ if and only if $\mathrm{certain}_\mathcal{M}(Q, I) = \mathtt{false}$.

($\Rightarrow$) Let $I$ be an instance of $\mathbf{S}^\star$ and $J^\star$ a solution for $I$ under $\mathcal{M}^\star$. Define $J$ as the following instance of $\mathbf{T}$: $R^T = R^{T^\star}$ and $S^T = R^{T^\star}$. Given that $(I, J^\star)$ satisfies $\Sigma_{st}^\star$ and $J^\star$ satisfies $\Sigma_t^\star$, we have that $(I, J)$ satisfies $\Sigma_{st}$ and $J$ satisfies $\Sigma_t$ and, therefore, $J$ is a solution for $I$ under $\mathcal{M}$. Thus, given that $Q$ does not hold in $J$ (since $R^T = S^T$), we conclude that $\mathrm{certain}_\mathcal{M}(Q, I) = \mathtt{false}$.

($\Leftarrow$) Assume that $I$ is an instance of $\mathbf{S}^\star$ such that $\mathrm{certain}_\mathcal{M}(Q, I) = \mathtt{false}$. Then let $J$ be a solution of $I$ under $\mathcal{M}$ such that $Q$ does not hold in $J$, and $J^\star$ an instance of $\mathbf{T}^\star$ defined as $R^{T^\star} = R^T$. Given that $(I, J)$ satisfies $\Sigma_{st}$, we have that $(I, J^\star)$ satisfies $\Sigma_{st}^\star$. Furthermore, given that $Q$ does not hold in $J$, we have that $J$ satisfies dependency:

$$\forall x \forall y \forall z \, (S(x, y, z) \rightarrow R(x, y, z)).$$

Thus, given that $J$ satisfies $\Sigma_t$, we conclude that $J^\star$ satisfies $\Sigma_t^\star$. Hence, we have that $J^\star$ is a solution for $I$ under $\mathcal{M}^\star$, from which we deduce that there exists at least one solution for $I$ under $\mathcal{M}^\star$. This concludes the proof of the theorem. $\qquad\square$

A natural way to ensure that the problem of computing certain answers to unions of conjunctive queries with at most one negated atom per disjunct remains tractable, in the presence of target dependencies, is by restricting the class of target dependencies allowed. Indeed, we prove below that this is the case for the class of data exchange settings that only allow egds in the target. The interesting part of this is not the result itself – which is a slight extension of a result in [10] – but the fact that our proof relies again on the translation of the problem of computing certain answers for this class of queries, under the settings described above, into the problem of computing certain answers to $\text{DATALOG}^{C(\neq)}$ programs.

A naïve approach to prove this result would be the following. Let $\mathcal{M} = (\mathbf{S}, \mathbf{T}, \Sigma_{st}, \Sigma_t)$ be a data exchange setting, where $\Sigma_t$ consists of a set of equality-generating dependencies, and let $\mathcal{M}'$ be the setting obtained from $\mathcal{M}$ by removing $\Sigma_t$. As we have mentioned above, for each union of conjunctive queries $Q$, with at most one inequality or negated relational atom per disjunct, one can construct a $\text{DATALOG}^{C(\neq)}$ program $\Pi_Q$ such that the certain answers to $Q$ under $\mathcal{M}'$ coincide with the certain answers to $\Pi_Q$ under $\mathcal{M}'$. Then one could implement the following algorithm for computing certain answers to $Q$ under $\mathcal{M}$: Given a source instance $I$, compute the canonical universal solution $J$ for $I$ under $\mathcal{M}$ (in case such a solution exists); evaluate $\Pi_Q$ over $J$; discard tuples that contain nulls.

Unfortunately, this simple algorithm is not correct for the following reason. Evaluating the program $\Pi_Q$ over $J$ may force some elements in $J$ to be equal, which, in turn, may imply some of the dependencies in $\Sigma_t$ to be triggered in the process. This suggests that if one wants to compute the certain answers to $Q$ (under $\mathcal{M}$) with a $\text{DATALOG}^{C(\neq)}$ program $\Pi_Q$, then $\Pi_Q$ must take into consideration not only $Q$ but also $\Sigma_t$. Indeed, we show next that for each union of conjunctive queries, with at most one negated atom per disjunct, it is possible to construct a $\text{DATALOG}^{C(\neq)}$ program $\Pi_{Q,\Sigma_t}$ such that the certain answers to $Q$ and to $\Pi_{Q,\Sigma_t}$ (under $\mathcal{M}$) coincide. Formally,

**Theorem 4.** *Let $Q$ be a $\text{UCQ}^{\neq,\neg}$ $k$-ary query over a schema $\mathbf{T}$ ($k \geq 0$), with at most one inequality or negated relational atom per disjunct. Further, let $\Sigma_t$ be a set of egds over $\mathbf{T}$. Then there exists a $\text{DATALOG}^{C(\neq)}$ program $\Pi_{Q,\Sigma_t}$ over $\mathbf{T}$ such that for every data exchange setting $\mathcal{M} = (\mathbf{S}, \mathbf{T}, \Sigma_{st}, \Sigma_t)$, instance $I$ of $\mathbf{S}$ and tuple $\bar{a} \in dom(I)^k$:*

$$\bar{a} \in \text{certain}_\mathcal{M}(Q, I) \quad \text{if and only if} \quad \bar{a} \in \text{certain}_\mathcal{M}(\Pi_{Q,\Sigma_t}, I).$$

*Moreover, $\Pi_{Q,\Sigma_t}$ can be effectively constructed from $Q$ and $\Sigma_t$ in polynomial time.*

*Proof.* Assume that $\mathbf{T} = \{T_1, \ldots, T_k\}$, where each $T_i$ has arity $n_i > 0$, that $Q(\bar{x}) = Q_1(\bar{x}) \vee \cdots \vee Q_\ell(\bar{x})$, where $\bar{x} = (x_1, \ldots, x_m)$ and each $Q_i(\bar{x})$ is a conjunctive query with at most one inequality or negated relational atom, and that $\Sigma_t = \{\alpha_1, \ldots, \alpha_q\}$ is a set of egds.

Then the set of intensional predicates of $\text{DATALOG}^{C(\neq)}$ program $\Pi_{Q,\Sigma_t}$ is

$$\{U_1, \ldots, U_k, \text{DOM}, \text{EQUAL}, \text{ANSWER}\},$$

where each $U_i$ ($i \in [1, k]$) has arity $n_i + m$, $\text{DOM}$ has arity 1, $\text{EQUAL}$ has arity $2 + m$ and $\text{ANSWER}$ has arity $m$. Moreover, the set of rules of $\Pi_{Q,\Sigma_t}$ is defined as follows.

- For every predicate $T_i \in \mathbf{T}$, $\Pi_{Q,\Sigma_t}$ includes the following $k$ rules:

$$\text{DOM}(x) \leftarrow T_i(x, y_2, y_3, \ldots, y_{n_i-1}, y_{n_i})$$
$$\text{DOM}(x) \leftarrow T_i(y_1, x, y_3, \ldots, y_{n_i-1}, y_{n_i})$$
$$\cdots$$
$$\text{DOM}(x) \leftarrow T_i(y_1, y_2, y_3, \ldots, y_{n_i-1}, x)$$

- $\Pi_{Q,\Sigma_t}$ includes the following rules for predicate $\text{EQUAL}$:

$$\text{EQUAL}(x, x, z_1, \ldots, z_m) \leftarrow \text{DOM}(x), \text{DOM}(z_1), \ldots, \text{DOM}(z_m)$$
$$\text{EQUAL}(x, y, z_1, \ldots, z_m) \leftarrow \text{EQUAL}(y, x, z_1, \ldots, z_m)$$
$$\text{EQUAL}(x, y, z_1, \ldots, z_m) \leftarrow \text{EQUAL}(x, w, z_1, \ldots, z_m), \text{EQUAL}(w, y, z_1, \ldots, z_m)$$

- For every predicate $U_i$, $\Pi_{Q,\Sigma_t}$ includes the following rules:

$$U_i(y_1, \ldots, y_{n_i}, z_1, \ldots, z_m) \leftarrow T_i(y_1, \ldots, y_{n_i}), \text{DOM}(z_1), \ldots, \text{DOM}(z_m)$$
$$U_i(y_1, \ldots, y_{n_i}, z_1, \ldots, z_m) \leftarrow U_i(w_1, \ldots, w_{n_i}, z_1, \ldots, z_m),$$
$$\text{EQUAL}(w_1, y_1, z_1, \ldots, z_m), \ldots,$$
$$\text{EQUAL}(w_{n_i}, y_{n_i}, z_1, \ldots, z_m)$$

- Let $i \in [1, \ell]$. First, assume that $Q_i(\bar{x})$ does not contain any negated atom. Then $Q_i(\bar{x})$ is equal to $\exists \bar{u}\, (T_{p_1}(\bar{u}_1) \wedge \cdots \wedge T_{p_n}(\bar{u}_n))$, where $p_j \in [1, k]$ and every variable in $\bar{u}_j$ is mentioned in either $\bar{u}$ or $\bar{x}$, for every $j \in [1, n]$. In this case, program $\Pi_{Q,\Sigma_t}$ includes the following rule:

$$\text{ANSWER}(\bar{x}) \leftarrow U_{p_1}(\bar{u}_1, \bar{x}), \ldots, U_{p_n}(\bar{u}_n, \bar{x}), \mathbf{C}(x_1), \ldots, \mathbf{C}(x_m) \qquad (16)$$

Notice that this rule is well defined since the set $\bar{x}$ is the set of free variables of $\exists \bar{u}\, (T_{p_1}(\bar{u}_1) \wedge \cdots \wedge T_{p_n}(\bar{u}_n))$. Second, assume that $Q_i(\bar{x})$ contains a negated relational atom. Then $Q_i(\bar{x})$ is equal to $\exists \bar{u}\, (T_{p_1}(\bar{u}_1) \wedge \cdots \wedge T_{p_n}(\bar{u}_n) \wedge \neg T_{p_{n+1}}(\bar{u}_{n+1}))$, where $p_j \in [1, k]$ and every variable in $\bar{u}_j$ is mentioned in either $\bar{u}$ or $\bar{x}$, for every $j \in [1, n+1]$. In this case, program $\Pi_{Q,\Sigma_t}$ includes the following rule:

$$U_{p_{n+1}}(\bar{u}_{n+1}, \bar{x}) \leftarrow U_{p_1}(\bar{u}_1, \bar{x}), \ldots, U_{p_n}(\bar{u}_n, \bar{x}). \qquad (17)$$

This rule is well defined since $\exists \bar{u}\, (T_{p_1}(\bar{u}_1) \wedge \cdots \wedge T_{p_n}(\bar{u}_n) \wedge \neg T_{p_{n+1}}(\bar{u}_{n+1}))$ is a safe query. Finally, assume that $Q_i(\bar{x})$ contains an inequality. Then $Q_i(\bar{x})$ is equal to $\exists \bar{u}\, (T_{p_1}(\bar{u}_1) \wedge \cdots \wedge T_{p_n}(\bar{u}_n) \wedge v_1 \neq v_2)$, where $p_j \in [1, k]$ and every variable in $\bar{u}_j$ is mentioned in either $\bar{u}$ or $\bar{x}$, for every $j \in [1, n]$, and $v_1$, $v_2$ are mentioned in $\bar{u}$ or $\bar{x}$. In this case, program $\Pi_{Q,\Sigma_t}$ includes the following rule:

$$\text{EQUAL}(v_1, v_2, \bar{x}) \leftarrow U_{p_1}(\bar{u}_1, \bar{x}), \ldots, U_{p_n}(\bar{u}_n, \bar{x}) \qquad (18)$$

We note that the rule above is well defined since $\exists \bar{u}\, (T_{p_1}(\bar{u}_1) \wedge \cdots \wedge T_{p_n}(\bar{u}_n) \wedge v_1 \neq v_2)$ is a safe query.

- For each $i \in [1, q]$, assume that dependency $\alpha_i$ is of form $(T_{p_1}(\bar{x}_1) \wedge \cdots \wedge T_{p_n}(\bar{x}_n) \to u = v)$, where each $p_j \in [1, k]$ and variables $u$ and $v$ are mentioned in $\bar{x}_1, \ldots, \bar{x}_n$. Then the program $\Pi_{Q, \Sigma_t}$ includes the following rule:

$$\text{EQUAL}(u, v, \bar{x}) \leftarrow U_{p_1}(\bar{x}_1, \bar{x}), \ldots, U_{p_n}(\bar{x}_n, \bar{x}) \qquad (19)$$

- Finally, if $Q$ has at least one inequality, or if $\Sigma_t$ is nonempty, program $\Pi_{Q, \Sigma_t}$ includes the rule:

$$\text{ANSWER}(\bar{x}) \leftarrow \text{EQUAL}(u, v, \bar{x}), \mathbf{C}(u), \mathbf{C}(v), u \neq v, \mathbf{C}(x_1), \ldots, \mathbf{C}(x_m) \qquad (20)$$

Let $\bar{a}$ be a tuple of elements from the domain of a source instance $I$. Each predicate $U_i$ in $\Pi_{Q, \Sigma_t}$ is used as a copy of $T_i$ but with $m$ extra arguments that store tuple $\bar{a}$. These predicates are used when testing whether $\bar{a}$ is a certain answer for $Q$ over $I$. More specifically, the rules of $\Pi_{Q, \Sigma_t}$ try to construct from the canonical universal solution $\text{CAN}(I)$ a solution $J$ for $I$ such that $\bar{a} \notin Q(J)$. Thus, if in a solution $J$ for $I$, it holds that $\bar{a} \in Q(J)$ because $\bar{a} \in Q_i(J)$, where $Q_i(\bar{x})$ is equal to $\exists \bar{u} \, (T_{p_1}(\bar{u}_1) \wedge \cdots \wedge T_{p_n}(\bar{u}_n) \wedge \neg T_{p_{n+1}}(\bar{u}_{n+1}))$, then $\Pi_{Q, \Sigma_t}$ uses rule (17) to create a new solution where the negative atom of $Q_i$ does not hold. In the same way, if in a solution $J$ for $I$, it holds that $\bar{a} \in Q(J)$ because $\bar{a} \in Q_i(J)$, where $Q_i(\bar{x})$ is equal to $\exists \bar{u} \, (T_{p_1}(\bar{u}_1) \wedge \cdots \wedge T_{p_n}(\bar{u}_n) \wedge v_1 \neq v_2)$, then $\Pi_{Q, \Sigma_t}$ uses rule (18) to create a new solution where the values assigned to $v_1$ and $v_2$ are equal (predicate EQUAL is used to store this fact). If $v_1$ or $v_2$ is assigned a null value, then it is possible to create a solution where the values assigned to these variables are the same. But this is not possible if both $v_1$ and $v_2$ are assigned different constant values. In fact, it follows from [10] that this implies that it is not possible to find a solution $J'$ for $I$ where $\bar{a} \notin Q(J')$, and in this case rule (20) is used to indicate that $\bar{a}$ is a certain answer for $Q$ over $I$. Notice, however, that every solution for $I$ must satisfy the dependencies in $\Sigma_t$. Thus, if for some $Q_i$ the program uses rules (17) or (18) to create an instance $J$ such that $\bar{a} \notin Q_i(J)$, but $J$ does not satisfies a dependency $\phi(\bar{x}) \to x_i = x_j$ in $\Sigma_t$, then rule (19) must be used to *repair* that instance, obtaining a solution $J'$ for $I$ in which the values assigned to $x_i$ and $x_j$ are the same, but still holds that $\bar{a} \notin Q_i(J)$. This will not be possible if both $x_i$ and $x_j$ are assigned different constant values; in this case, it can be proved using results in [10] that it is not possible to create a solution such that $\bar{a} \notin Q_i(J)$, and thus rule (20) is used to indicate that $\bar{a}$ is a certain answer for $Q$ over $I$.

By using the above observations, it is not difficult to prove that the statement of the theorem holds, which was to be shown.    □

As a corollary of Theorem 4 and Corollary 1, we immediately obtain the following desired result:

**Corollary 4.** *Let $Q$ be a $\text{UCQ}^{\neq, \neg}$ query over a schema* **T**, *with at most one inequality or negated relational atom per disjunct, and let $\mathcal{M} = (\mathbf{S}, \mathbf{T}, \Sigma_{st}, \Sigma_t)$ be a data exchange setting such that $\Sigma_t$ consists of a set of egds. Then the problem* $\text{CERTAIN-ANSWERS}(\mathcal{M}, Q)$ *can be solved in polynomial time.*

Another possible way to retain tractability of the problem CERTAIN-ANSWERS$(\mathcal{M}, Q)$, where $Q$ is a union of conjunctive queries with at most one negated atom per disjunct and $\mathcal{M}$ is a setting with target dependencies, is by restricting the class of queries allowed. Indeed, it has been proved in [10] that for the class of settings whose sets of target dependencies consist of egds and weakly-acyclic sets of tgds, the certain answers to a union of conjunctive queries with at most one inequality per disjunct can be computed in polynomial time by using an algorithm based on the *chase* procedure. It is an interesting open problem whether this result can also be proved with the help of DATALOG$^{C(\neq)}$ programs, in the style of Theorem 4 and Corollary 4.

## 5    Concluding Remarks

In this paper, we presented the language DATALOG$^{C(\neq)}$ that extends DATALOG with a restricted form of negation, and studied some of its fundamental properties. In particular, we showed that the certain answers to a DATALOG$^{C(\neq)}$ program can be computed in polynomial time, and we used this property to find tractable fragments of the class of unions of conjunctive queries with inequalities (even in the presence of target dependencies).

Both the problem of the existence of solutions and the computation of certain answers are defined in the paper assuming settings to be fixed. That is, in terms of Vardi's taxonomy [20], we study the *data* complexity of these problems. This makes sense in the database context, as usually specifications and queries are much smaller than source instances. However, a more refined complexity analysis of these problems should not consider any of their parameters to be fixed. This corresponds to the *combined* complexity of the problems mentioned above. The combined complexity of the problem of existence of solutions was studied in [13,7], while the combined complexity of the problem of computing certain answers was studied in [5].

Many problems related to DATALOG$^{C(\neq)}$ programs remain open. In particular, it would be interesting to know if it is decidable whether the certain answers to a query $Q$ in UCQ$^{\neq}$ can be computed as the certain answers to a DATALOG$^{C(\neq)}$ program $\Pi_Q$, and whether there exist a setting $\mathcal{M}$ and a query $Q$ in UCQ$^{\neq}$ such that the problem CERTAIN-ANSWERS$(\mathcal{M}, Q)$ is in PTIME, but the certain answers to $Q$ cannot be computed as the certain answers to a DATALOG$^{C(\neq)}$ program $\Pi_Q$.

**Acknowledgments.** We are very grateful to Jorge Pérez for many helpful discussions. The authors were supported by: Arenas - FONDECYT grant 1090565; Barceló - FONDECYT grant 11080011; Reutter - EPSRC grant G049165.

## References

1. Abiteboul, S., Duschka, O.: Answering queries using materialized views. Gemo report 383
2. Abiteboul, S., Hull, R., Vianu, V.: Foundations of databases. Addison-Wesley, Reading (1995)
3. Afrati, F.N., Li, C., Pavlaki, V.: Data exchange in the presence of arithmetic comparisons. In: EDBT, pp. 487–498 (2008)

4. Arenas, M., Barceló, P., Fagin, R., Libkin, L.: Locally consistent transformations and query answering in data exchange. In: PODS, pp. 229–240 (2004)
5. Arenas, M., Barceló, P., Reutter, J.: Query languages for data exchange: Beyond unions of conjunctive queries. Accepted for publication in Theory of Computing Systems, ToCS (2010); Preliminary version in Proceedings 12th International Conference on Database Theory (ICDT 2009), pp. 73–83 (2009)
6. Beeri, C., Vardi, M.Y.: A proof procedure for data dependencies. Journal of the ACM 31(4), 718–741 (1984)
7. Calì, A., Gottlob, G., Pieris, A.: Query answering under non-guarded rules in datalog+/-. In: Hitzler, P., Lukasiewicz, T. (eds.) RR 2010. LNCS, vol. 6333, pp. 1–17. Springer, Heidelberg (2010)
8. Deutsch, A., Nash, A., Remmel, J.B.: The chase revisited. In: PODS, pp. 149–158 (2008)
9. Fagin, R., Kolaitis, P., Popa, L., Tan, W.C.: Composing schema mappings: Second-order dependencies to the rescue. In: PODS, pp. 83–94 (2004)
10. Fagin, R., Kolaitis, P.G., Miller, R.J., Popa, L.: Data exchange: semantics and query answering. Theoretical Computer Science 336(1), 89–124 (2005)
11. Fagin, R., Kolaitis, P.G., Popa, L.: Data exchange: getting to the core. ACM Transactions on Database Systems 30(1), 174–210 (2005)
12. Kolaitis, P.: Schema mappings, data exchange, and metadata management. In: PODS, pp. 61–75 (2005)
13. Kolaitis, P., Panttaja, J., Tan, W.-C.: The complexity of data exchange. In: PODS, pp. 30–39 (2006)
14. Imielinski, T., Lipski, W.: Incomplete information in relational databases. Journal of the ACM 31, 761–791 (1984)
15. Lenzerini, M.: Data integration: A theoretical perspective. In: PODS, pp. 233–246 (2002)
16. Libkin, L.: Elements of Finite Model Theory. Springer, Heidelberg (2004)
17. Libkin, L.: Data exchange and incomplete information. In: PODS, pp. 60–69 (2006)
18. Libkin, L., Sirangelo, C.: Data exchange and schema mappings in open and closed worlds. In: PODS, pp. 139–148 (2008)
19. Mądry, A.: Data exchange: On the complexity of answering queries with inequalities. Information Processing Letters 94(6), 253–257 (2005)
20. Vardi, M.Y.: The complexity of relational query languages. In: STOC, pp. 137–146 (1982)

# Datalog Relaunched: Simulation Unification and Value Invention

François Bry[1], Tim Furche[2], Clemens Ley[2],
Bruno Marnette[2], Benedikt Linse[3], and Sebastian Schaffert[4]

[1] Institute for Informatics, Ludwig-Maximilians-Universität München,
Oettingenstr. 67, 80538 München, Germany
[2] Computing Laboratory, University of Oxford
Wolfson Building, Parks Road, Oxford OX1 3QD, UK
[3] Thomson Reuters, Landsberger Straße 191a, 80687 München, Germany
[4] Knowledge and Media Technologies, Salzburg Research,
Jakob Haringer Str. 5/III, 5020 Salzburg, Austria

**Abstract.** For reasoning on the Web, Datalog is lacking data extraction and value invention. This article proposes to overcome these limitations with "simulation unification" and "RDFLog".

Simulation unification is a non-standard unification inspired from regular path queries. Like standard unification, it yields bindings for variables in both terms to unify. Unlike standard unification, it does not try to make the two terms identical but instead to embed the query into the data. Simulation unification is decidable. Without variables, it has polynomial complexity. With variables it is, like standard unification, NP-complete. We identify a number of interesting special cases of unification, e.g., in presence or absence of term injectivity. In particular, we show that simulation unification without term injectivity on tree data is linear and in presence of injectivity it is still polynomial even on unordered trees in contrast to the NP-complete unordered tree inclusion problem.

RDFLog is Datalog with arbitrary quantifier alternation: Blank nodes, i.e., existentially quantified variables, in rule heads may be governed by universally quantified variables, universally quantified variables by blank nodes. RDFLog's declarative semantics is defined in terms of RDF entailment; its sound and complete operational semantics, in terms of Skolemization, standard Datalog evaluation, and un-Skolemization. We show that RDFLog limited to $\forall^*\exists^*$ prefixes is (up to unique helper predicates) equivalent to RDFLog with full quantifier alternation. A light-weight implementation points to the efficiency of the approach.

**Keywords:** Datalog, Unification, Value Invention, Un-Skolemization, Query Language, Regular Path Queries, Semi-Structured Data, HTML, XML, XPath, RDF.

## 1 Introduction

Datalog is a fragment of the logic programming language Prolog [87] aiming at combining rule-based reasoning with relational databases. Datalog is declarative,

O. de Moor et al. (Eds.): Datalog 2010, LNCS 6702, pp. 321–350, 2011.

or "pure", in the sense that it includes none of the procedural features of Prolog such as a pre-defined evaluation order and language constructs such as the cut for modifying this order. The integration of Prolog-style rule-based reasoning and databases has been first advertised at the end of the 70es, beginning of the 80es of the 20th century in three workshops on "Logic and Databases" [62] and on "Advances in Database Theories" [64,65] – cf. also [63]. The name Datalog, a contraction of the then widespread expression "Database Prolog", has been coined by David Maier and David S. Warren for lecture notes [91]. Datalog provides first-order queries that, up to the syntax, correspond to SQL queries without negation. Datalog also provides definite rules that correspond to SQL views. Methods have been developed for a set-oriented evaluation of Datalog queries [40], i.e., an evaluation building upon relational algebra and therefore efficiently accessing large amounts of data on secondary storage. Sophisticated methods have been developed for implementing backward chaining relying on forward chaining [112,8,14,117,110,31] (cf. [127,41,42,111] for overviews) thus ensuring a terminating and set-oriented evaluation of recursive Datalog programs. Datalog and the aforementioned evaluation methods have two salient traits:

1. They are restricted to "flat terms",[1] i.e., terms containing no function symbols other than constants.
2. They are restricted to universal facts and rules, i.e., facts and rules where all the variables of which are universally quantified.

Datalog's restriction to flat terms is no stringent limitation if relational data are accessed. Indeed, even though non-first-normal-form relational databases have been considered in research, the focus of relational database technology is on first-normal-form databases that correspond to "flat" logic terms, i.e., logic terms containing no function symbols other than constants. If, however, instead of flat relational data, data on the Web are accessed, then the two aforementioned traits of Datalog must be overcome. Indeed, HTML and XML documents are semi-structured [1], i.e., can be formalized as labelled unranked trees or nested relations. Datalog's restriction to universally quantified variables must be overcome if Datalog is to be used for RDF querying and reasoning. Indeed, RDF graphs might contain so-called blank node, i.e., existentially quantified variables.

This article describes two approaches to adapt Datalog to semi-structured data (such as HTML and XML documents) and to RDF graphs respectively.

The first approach, called "simulation unification", is a non-standard form of unification tuned to data extraction from semi-structured data. Simulation unification is inspired from regular path queries [2,3]. Like standard unification, simulation unification determines bindings for variables in both terms to unify. Unlike standard unification, simulation unification does not make the two terms identical but instead searches for an embedding of the query into the data. Simulation unification is decidable, sound and complete, and has polynomial data complexity. Without variables and some incompleteness query constructs,

---

[1] The article [117] is an exception: It describes an extension of the magic set method [8,14] to a restricted type of rules with nested terms.

it has polynomial, on tree data even linear time complexity; with variables it is, like standard unification, NP-hard. Simulation unification is closely related to the fragment of XPath [46] with only forward axes, a restriction that does not affect the expressiveness of XPath [103].

The second approach, called RDFLog, is an extension of Datalog with arbitrary quantifier alternation. In RDFLog programs, blank nodes, i.e., existentially quantified variables in rule heads, may occur in the scope of all, some, or none of the universal variables of a rule. In other words, in RDFLog rules, existentially quantified variables may be governed by universally quantified variables, universally quantified variables by existentially quantified variables.

This articles is organized as follows. Section 2 discusses related work. Section 3 describes simulation unification. Section 4 is devoted to RDFLog. Section 5 suggest a notion of "rich unification" as a framework for adapting Datalog to various data types and a direction for further research.

## 2    Related Work

### 2.1    Wrapping

Since the end of the 90es of the 20th century, the extraction of data from the Web and from large Thesauri, i.e., from semi-structured documents such as HTML documents, has been investigated from several angles. One commonly distinguishes between text extraction, or text wrapping, and structure extraction, or structure wrapping. Text wrapping is the retrieval of portions of text regardless of the documents' structures. Text wrapping techniques returning so-called "bag of words" is one of the core functions of current search engines and is therefore well-mastered [88]. A more sophisticated form of text wrapping is targeted at so-called "factoids", or entities and relationships between entities, related to a query and extracted from unstructured text [4,70,68,128,129]. Structure wrapping, i.e., the retrieval of structured portions of text such as a section with its sub-sections from a (structured) document is another from of wrapping. Currently, structure wrapping is deployed on the limited scale of Web query and transformation languages such as XPath [46,17], XQuery [19] and XSLT [45]. XPath, which is part of both XQuery and XSLT, can be seen as the most used structure wrapping language.

The approaches to structure wrapping considered so far can be understood by formalizing semi-structured documents as node-labelled unranked trees, i.e., trees such that two nodes similarly labelled do not necessarily have the same number of children.[2] A structure-aware wrapper can be seen as a language for selecting nodes, or equivalently the sub-trees rooted at these nodes, from labelled unranked trees while possibly performing simple changes such as renaming labels and removing some-subtrees. More sophisticated structure reorganizations – such as transposing a table, adding sums to table rows or columns, or constructing

---

[2] "Semi-structured" is used instead of "structured" for stressing this characteristic of Web documents as well as the lack of schema [35,1].

from a bibliography by years a bibliography by authors, and more generally most forms of data aggregation – are not considered part of data extraction: They are out of the range of structure-aware wrappers.

XPath [46,17], which appeared in 1999 and follows the regular path approach introduced with [2], is the best-known and most used structure wrapper language. It is, however, far from being the only one. Others approach to structure wrapping are as follows: Regular path queries (with constraints) have been proposed in [3]; regular tree languages and (regular tree automata for their evaluation) have been proposed in [30] and further investigated amongst other in [102]; a Datalog-style language called WebOQL has been proposed in [5]; regular path queries with nesting (or RPN) have been proposed in [66,67]; exploiting the fact that regular tree languages coincide with tree languages expressible in monadic second order logic or MSO,[3] MSO is proposed in [66,67] as a reference language for investigations of the expressive power of structure-aware wrapper languages; monadic Datalog, the inspiration of Elog [12], the language of the commercial wrapper Lixto [68], has been proposed in [13,66,67]. More on Web wrapping and Web query languages can be found in the survey [7].

Common to the afore-mentioned proposals is that

1. they are designed for tree-shaped data,
2. the majority, in particular XPath, is designed for querying only for sets of nodes,
3. their query paradigm is navigational.

Being designed for tree-shaped data, they can neither exploit the hypertext links and references within an HTML or XML document, nor fully access structure of RDF graphs. This restriction might not be that significant if standard documents and Web pages are queried. If instead Semantic Web documents such as RDF graphs are queried, the restriction is more significant. Indeed, RDF graphs are almost never tree-shaped. The majority is designed for querying for sets of nodes, but not for sets of tuples of nodes. In logic terms, they are tuned to monadic, i.e., single answer-variable, queries. A navigational query paradigm is quite natural for monadic queries. [69,18,20] stress the drawbacks of navigational queries. Arguably, navigational queries in languages like XPath [46,17] that offer so called "reverse axes" compromise declarativity. Note that reverse axes do not increase XPath's expressive power [103], though it has been recently shown [89] that this does not hold for more expressive path languages containing a Kleene-star type construct (such as conditional XPath [92]).

The language UnQL [36] has introduced simulation as a means for query answering. This has been further investigated with the language XMAS [10]. UnQL and simulation unification differ from each other as follows. First, a query in UnQL can be processed by matching, or "half unification", of a query pattern containing variables with a data item containing no variables. In contrast, simulation unification gives rise to unifying two query patterns both containing variables. Furthermore, variables in UnQL can only occur as leaves of query

---

[3] This is a classical result mentioned amongst other in [102].

patterns while simulation unification gives rise to (constrained) variables at any depth of a query term.

Simulation unification is not limited to querying tree-shaped data but can instead accommodate graph-shaped queries against graph-shaped data, is not limited to monadic queries but instead can accommodate querying for tuples of nodes, and its paradigm is not navigational but instead, like logic queries, pattern-oriented.

## 2.2 Rules Languages for the Semantic Web

The considerable literature on Web and Semantic Web rule languages falls generally into four groups:

1. markup for rule languages,
2. implementation of description logics or of RDF-based reasoning in Datalog, in Logic Programming, or in Answer Set Programming,
3. Datalog or Logic Programming style rule languages for RDF,
4. "hybrid reasoning", i.e., integrations of description logic primitives, or built-ins, into Datalog or (Disjunctive) Logic Programming.

The prominent markup languages for rules are the Rule Markup Language RuleML [28,21,22] and the languages, called "dialects", of the Rule Interchange Format RIF [26,24,23,106,25,49,47]. The focus here is on the interchange on the Web relying on XML of rule programs of various kinds. Both have been developed to express various forms of reasoning, especially forward and backward chaining, and, as far as RIF is concerned, production rules. SWRL [77,78,79,76], a rule language integrating sublanguages of OWL [93,123,50,104,39,74,75,97] in RuleML is both, a markup language, and an integration of a description logic in Logic Programming.

The large number of implementations of description logics in Datalog or, more generally, in Logic Programming or Disjunctive Logic Programming, amongst others [15,99,71,11,80,81,82,97], reflects the diversity of description logics. An implementations of RDF/S rule-based reasoning in Answer Set Programming is described in [107].

RDF's syntax makes it rather natural a candidate for Datalog or Logic Programming rules. [85,27,33] are mostly devoted to syntax, markup and interoperability issues of RDF rule languages, [121,130,96,72,124,105,120,34] investigate various forms of rule-based reasoning with RDF/S data. See [61] for a survey on RDF query and rule languages.

Various forms of hybrid reasoning, i.e., integration of description logics into Datalog, Logic Programming, Disjunctive Logic Programming or Answer Set Programming are described amongst others in [78,76,114,113,125,48,79,98,115,55] [54,38,116,53,95,94,52,109,33].

Most of the rule languages considered in the afore-mentioned articles support neither existential variables nor blank nodes in rule heads [121,122,96,58,105].

Some support blank nodes in rule heads but only with limited quantifier alternations [130,72,120]. To the best of the authors' knowledge, existential variable in rule heads with unrestricted quantifier alternation has been first proposed in [34]. The second part of the present paper describes this approach.

# 3    Simulation Unification: Unification for Web Wrapping

Simulation unification has been developed as a technique for evaluating "query patterns", called in the following "query terms", that are both, in the style of logic queries and better adapted to Web querying. Like logic queries, the query terms might include several variables. Variables in a query term are logic variables, that is, all their occurrences must be consistently bound. In contrast to logic queries, query terms are incomplete specification of the data to retrieve. Query terms may contain constructs for expressing incompleteness in *breadth,* in *depth,* with respect to *order,* and with respect to *optional subterms:*

- Incompleteness in breath: While the query term $a[X, b]$ corresponds to a logic query $a(X, b)$, the query term $a[[X]]$ retrieves a-labelled nodes with *at least one* child (bound to the variable $X$).
- Incompleteness in depth: The query term $a[\text{desc } b]$ retrieves a-labelled nodes with a b-labelled descendant node.
- Incompleteness with respect to order: The order of the matches for b and desc $c$ is irrelevant in the queries $a\{b, \text{desc } c\}$ and $a\{\{b, \text{desc } c\}\}$.
- Incompleteness with respect to optional subterms: The query $a[b, \text{optional} c[X]]$ binds the variable $X$ to some value only if in the data retrieved the a-labeled node has a c-labelled child having itself a child node (bound to $X$).

Furthermore, references in query terms and in data are resolved during simulation unification allowing *graph-shaped queries graph-shaped data.* Additional constructs ease the expression of queries frequently needed on the Web. The comparison [29] with the XQuery programs from the XQuery Use Cases [43] demonstrates that these features, as well as a few others described in [119], considerably ease the expression of practical queries.

**Definition 1 (Data Terms).** Data terms *are expressions inductively defined as follows that satisfy Conditions 1 and 2 below:*

1. *If $l$ is a label, then $l$ is a (atomic) data term.*
2. *If $id$ is an identifier and $t$ is a data term neither of the form $id_0: t_0$ nor of the form $\uparrow id_0$, then $id: t$ is a data term.*
3. *If $id$ is an identifier, then $\uparrow id$ is a data term.*
4. *If $l$ is a label and $t_1, \ldots, t_n$ are $n \geq 1$ data terms, then $l[t_1, \ldots, t_n]$ and $l\{t_1, \ldots, t_n\}$ are data terms.*

**Condition 1:** *For a given identifier $id$ an identifier definition $id: t_0$ occurs at most once in a term.*
**Condition 2:** *For every identifier reference $\uparrow id$ occurring in a term $t$ an identifier definition $id: t_0$ occurs in $t$.*

**Definition 2 (Query Terms).** Query terms *are expressions inductively defined as follows and satisfying Conditions 1 and 2 of Definition 1:*

1. *If $l$ is a label and $L$ is a label variable, then $l$, $L$, $l\{\{\}\}$, and $L\{\{\}\}$ are (atomic) query terms.*
2. *A term variable is a query term.*
3. *If id is an identifier and $t$ is a query term neither of the form $id_0 : t_0$ nor of the form $\uparrow id_0$, then $id : t$ is a query term.*
4. *If id is an identifier, then $\uparrow id$ is a query term.*
5. *If $X$ is a variable and $t$ a query term, then $X \rightsquigarrow t$ is a query term.*
6. *If $X$ is a variable and $t$ is a query term, then $X \rightsquigarrow \mathsf{desc}\ t$ is a query term.*
7. *If $l$ is a label, $L$ a label variable and $t_1, \ldots, t_n$ are $n \geq 1$ query terms, then $l[t_1, \ldots, t_n]$, $L[t_1, \ldots, t_n]$, $l\{t_1, \ldots, t_n\}$, $L\{t_1, \ldots, t_n\}$, $l[[t_1, \ldots, t_n]]$, $L[[t_1, \ldots, t_n]]$, $l\{\{t_1, \ldots, t_n\}\}$, and $L\{\{t_1, \ldots, t_n\}\}$ are query terms.*

*Query terms in which no variables occur are* ground. *Query terms that are not of the form $\uparrow id$, are* strict. *The* leftmost label *of strict and ground query terms of the form $l$, $l\{\{\}\}$, $l\{t_1, \ldots, t_n\}$, and $l[t_1, \ldots, t_n]$ is $l$; the* leftmost label *of a strict and ground query term of the form $id : t$ is the leftmost label of $t$.*

Note that *desc* never occurs in a ground query term (for it is always coupled with a variable), data terms are (simple) query terms, in a query term, multiple occurrences of a same variable are possible. *Child subterms* and *subterms* of query terms are defined such that if $t = f[a, g\{Y \rightsquigarrow \mathsf{desc}\ b\{X\}, h\{a, X \rightsquigarrow k\{c\}\}]$, then $a$ and $g\{Y \rightsquigarrow \mathsf{desc}\ b\{X\}, h\{a, X \rightsquigarrow k\{c\}\}$ are the only child subterms of $t$ and e.g. $a$ and $X$ and $Y \rightsquigarrow \mathsf{desc}\ b\{X\}$ and $h\{a, X \rightsquigarrow k\{c\}\}$ and $X \rightsquigarrow k\{c\}$ and $t$ itself are subterms of $t$. Note that $f$ is not a subterm of $t$.

We allow in the following a query term $\mathsf{desc}\ t$ without leading $\rightsquigarrow$ as an abbreviation for $X \rightsquigarrow \mathsf{desc}$ where $X$ is a fresh variable.

**Definition 3 (Variable Well-Formed Query Terms).** *A term variable $X$* depends *on a term variable $Y$ in a query term $t$ if $X \rightsquigarrow t_1$ is a subterm of $t$ and $Y$ is a subterm of $t_1$. A query term $t$ is* variable well-formed *if $t$ contains no term variables $X_0, \ldots, X_n$ $(n \geq 1)$ such that 1. $X_0 = X_n$ and 2. for all $i = 1, \ldots, n$, $X_i$ depends on $X_{i-1}$ in $t$.*

Thus, $f\{X \rightsquigarrow g\{X\}\}$ and $f\{X \rightsquigarrow g\{Y\}, Y \rightsquigarrow h\{X\}\}$ are not variable well-formed. Variable well-formedness precludes queries specifying infinite answers. In the following, query terms are assumed to be variable well-formed.

The declarative semantics of simulation unification is based on graph simulation. A simulation of a graph $G_1$ in a graph $G_2$ is a mapping of the nodes of $G_1$ in the nodes of $G_2$ preserving the edges. The graphs considered are directed, ordered and rooted and their nodes are labelled.

**Definition 4 (Simulation).** *Let $G_1 = (V_1, E_1)$ and $G_2 = (V_2, E_2)$ be two graphs. Let $\sim$ be an equivalence relation on $V_1 \cup V_2$. A relation $\mathcal{S} \subseteq V_1 V_2$ is a* simulation *with respect to $\sim$ of $G_1$ in $G_2$ if:*

1. If $(v_1, v_2) \in \mathcal{S}$, then $v_1 \sim v_2$.
2. If $(v_1, v_2) \in \mathcal{S}$ and $(v_1, v_1') \in E_1$, then there exists $v_2' \in V_2$ such that $(v_1', v_2') \in \mathcal{S}$ and $(v_2, v_2') \in E_2$.

Let $\mathcal{S}$ be simulation $\mathcal{S}$ of $G_1 = (V_1, E_1)$ in $G_2 = (V_2, E_2)$. $\mathcal{S}$ is total, if for each $v_1 \in V_1$ there exists at least one $v_2 \in V_2$ such that $(v_1, v_2) \in \mathcal{S}$. If $G_1$ has a root $r_1$, $G_2$ has a root $r_2$ and $(r_1, r_2) \in \mathcal{S}$, then $\mathcal{S}$ is a rooted simulation. $\mathcal{S}$ is minimal, if there are no simulations $\mathcal{S}' \subseteq \mathcal{S}$ of $G_1$ in $G_2$ such that $\mathcal{S}' \neq \mathcal{S}$.

Note that every rooted simulation is total.

**Definition 5 (Strict and Ground Query Term Simulation).** $\preceq$ is the relation on strict and ground query terms defined by $t^1 \preceq t^2$ if there exists a (minimal) rooted simulation with respect to label identity $\mathcal{S}$ of $t^1$ in $t^2$ such that:

1. if $v_1 = l\{\}$ occurs in $t^1$ and $(v_1, v_2) \in \mathcal{S}$, then $v_2$ has no children in $t^2$.
2. if $v_1 = l[[t_1^1, \ldots, t_n^1]]$ $(n \geq 1)$ occurs in $t^1$, $(v_1, v_2) \in \mathcal{S}$ and $(t_i^1, t_j^2) \in \mathcal{S}$ $(1 \leq j \leq m \leq n)$, then $t_1^2, \ldots, t_m^2$ occur in this indexing order as children of $v_2$ in the graph induced by $t^2$.
3. if $v_1 = l[t_1^1, \ldots, t_n^1]$ $(n \geq 1)$ occurs in $t^1$, $(v_1, v_2) \in \mathcal{S}$ and if $(t_i^1, t_j^2) \in \mathcal{S}$ $(1 \leq j \leq m \leq n)$, then $t_1^2, \ldots, t_m^2$ are pairwise distinct (i.e. $m = n$), they occur in this indexing order as children of $v_2$ in the graph induced by $t^2$ and $v_2$ has no other children than the $t_j^2$ in $t^2$.
4. if $v_1 = l\{t_1^1, \ldots, t_n^1\}$ occurs in $t^1$, $(v_1, v_2) \in \mathcal{S}$ and $(t_i^1, t_j^2) \in \mathcal{S}$ $(1 \leq j \leq m \leq n)$, then $t_1^2, \ldots, t_m^2$ are pairwise distinct (i.e. $m = n$) and $v_2$ has no other children than the $t_j^2$ in $t^2$.
5. if $v_1 = l\{\{t_1^1, \ldots, t_n^1\}\}$ occurs in $t^1$, $(v_1, v_2) \in \mathcal{S}$ and $(t_i^1, t_j^2) \in \mathcal{S}$ $(1 \leq j \leq m \leq n)$, then $t_1^2, \ldots, t_m^2$ are pairwise distinct (i.e. $m = n$).

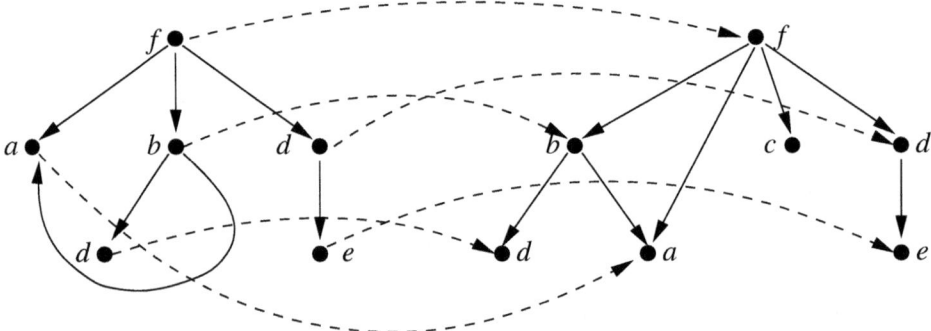

**Fig. 1.** A minimal simulation of the (graph induced by the) ground query term $t^q = f\{id_1 : a, b[d\{\{\}\}, \uparrow id_1], desc\}$ in the (graph induced by the) data term $t^{db} = f[b[d, id_2 : a], \uparrow id_2, c, d\{e\}]$

By Definition 4, $\preceq$ is reflexive and transitive, i.e. it is a preorder on the set of data terms. $\preceq$ is not a partial order, for although $t_1 = f\{\{a\}\} \preceq t_2 = f\{\{a, a\}\}$ and $t_2 = f\{\{a, a\}\} \preceq t_1 = f\{\{a\}\}$ (both $a$ of $t_2$ can be simulated by the same $a$ of $t_1$), $t_1 = f\{\{a\}\} \neq t_2 = f\{\{a, a\}\}$.

Rooted simulation with respect to label equality is a first step towards a formalisation of answers to query terms: If there exists a rooted simulation of (the graph induced by) a data term $t_1$, considered as a query term, in (the graph induced by) a data term $t_2$, then $t_2$ is an answer to $t_1$. Ground instances of a query term (cf. Definition 6) gives rise to extend this notion of answers to query terms. An answer in a database $D$ to a query term $t^q$ is characterized by bindings for the variables in $t^q$ such that the database term $t$ resulting from applying these bindings to $t^q$ is an element of $D$. Consider e.g. the query $t^q = f\{\{ X \rightsquigarrow g\{\{b\}\}, X \rightsquigarrow g\{\{c\}\} \}\}$ against the database $D = \{f\{g\{a, b, c\}, g\{a, b, c\}, h\}, f\{g\{b\}, g\{c\}\}\}$. The $\rightsquigarrow$ constructs in $t^q$ yield the constraint $g\{\{b\}\} \preceq X \wedge g\{\{c\}\} \preceq X$. Matching $t^q$ with the first data term in $D$ yields the constraint $X \preceq g\{a, b, c\}$. Matching $t^q$ with the second data term in $D$ yields the constraint $X \preceq g\{b\} \wedge X \preceq g\{c\}$. $g\{b\} \preceq X \wedge g\{c\} \preceq X$ is not compatible with $X \preceq g\{b\} \wedge X \preceq g\{c\}$. Thus, the only possible value for $X$ is $g\{a, b, c\}$, i.e. the only possible answer to $t^q$ in $D$ is $f\{g\{a, b, c\}, g\{a, b, c\}, h\}$.

**Definition 6 (Ground Instances of Query Terms).** *A grounding substitution is a function which assigns a label to each label variable and a database term to each term variable of a finite set of (label or term) variables. Let $t^q$ be a query term, $V_1, \ldots, V_n$ be the (label or term) variables occurring in $t^q$ and $\sigma$ be a grounding substitution assigning $v_i$ to $V_i$. The ground instance $t^q\sigma$ of $t^q$ with respect to $\sigma$ is the ground query term that can be constructed from $t^q$ as follows:*

1. *Replace each subterm $X \rightsquigarrow t$ by $X$.*
2. *Replace each occurrence of $V_i$ by $v_i$ $(1 \leq i \leq n)$.*

Requiring in Definition 2 *desc* to occur to the right of $\rightsquigarrow$ makes it possible to characterize a ground instance of a query term by a grounding substitution. This is helpful for formalizing answers but not necessary for language implementations.

Not all ground instances of a query term are acceptable answers, for some instances might violate the conditions expressed by the $\rightsquigarrow$ and *desc* constructs.

**Definition 7 (Allowed Instances).** *The constraint induced by a query term $t^q$ and a substitution $\sigma$ is the conjunction of all inequalities $t\sigma \preceq X\sigma$ such that $X \rightsquigarrow t$ is a subterm of $t^q$ not of the form desc $t_0$, and of all expressions $X\sigma \lhd t\sigma$ (read "$t\sigma$ subterm of $X\sigma$") such that $X \rightsquigarrow desc\ t$ is a subterm of $t^q$, if $t^q$ has such subterms. If $t^q$ has no such subterms, the constraint induced $t^q$ and $\sigma$ is the formula true. Let $\sigma$ be a grounding substitution and $t^q\sigma$ a ground instance of $t^q$. $t^q\sigma$ is allowed if:*

1. *Each inequality $t_1 \preceq t_2$ in the constraint induced by $t^q$ and $\sigma$ is satisfied.*
2. *For each $t_1 \lhd t_2$ in the constraint induced by $t^q$ and $\sigma$, $t_2$ is a subterm of $t_1$.*

**Table 1.** Query terms and matching data (; separates different data terms)

| | Query term | | Data terms |
|---|---|---|---|
| T1 | a{ } | $\preceq$  <br> $\npreceq$ | a{ }; a[ ]  <br> b{ } |
| T2 | a[ ] | $\preceq$  <br> $\npreceq$ | a[ ]  <br> b{ }; a{ } |
| T3 | a{ b } | $\preceq$  <br> $\npreceq$ | a{ b }  <br> a{ b, b } |
| T4 | a{ b, b } | $\preceq$  <br> $\npreceq$ | a{ b, b }  <br> a{ b }; a{ b, b, b } |
| P1 | a{{ b }} | $\preceq$  <br> $\npreceq$ | a{ b }; a{ c, b, d }; a{ b, b }  <br> a{ }; |
| P2 | a[[ b, c ]] | $\preceq$  <br> $\npreceq$ | a[ b, c ]; a[ d, b, e, c ]  <br> a[ c, b ]; a{ b, c } |
| D1 | a{ <u>desc</u> b } | $\preceq$  <br> $\npreceq$ | a[ b ]; a[ c{ b, e } ];  <br> a{ d, c{ b } }; |
| D2 | a{ <u>desc</u> b, <u>desc</u> c } | $\preceq$  <br> $\npreceq$ | a[ b, e[ c ] ];  <br> a{ b, c, d }; a{ e[b, c] }; |
| D3 | a{{ <u>desc</u> b, <u>desc</u> c }} | $\preceq$  <br> $\npreceq$ | a[ b, e[ c ] ]; a{ b, c, d };  <br> a{ e[b, c] }; |

**Definition 8 (Answers).** *Let $t^q$ be a query term and $D$ a database. An answer to $t^q$ in $D$ is a database term $t^{db} \in D$ such that there exists an allowed ground instance $t$ of $t^q$ satisfying $t \preceq t^{db}$.*

### 3.1 Examples of Simulation

Table 1 illustrates the simulation between (variable-free) query terms and data terms. For space reasons, we omit in query terms empty double braces and in data terms empty single braces, i.e., c reads c{{ }} in a query term and c{ } in a data term.

The first examples T1–T4 illustrate matching of ordered and unordered total query terms. Note, that unordered query terms match against ordered data terms (since the use of the curly braces indicates only that we do not care about the order). In total query terms both terms have exactly the same number of children in all cases. This is what sets partial query terms (P1–P2, I1–I2) apart from total query terms. Here, we may have additional query terms in the data that are ignored. The remaining examples of Table 1 illustrate the effect of desc. It allows matching at any depth (cf. D1–D3). Totality and injectivity are still enforced between the children of a matching data term (observe the difference between D2 and D3).

The effect of variables on term matching is illustrated in Table 2: Essentially, a variable matches any single term (or label, or position, or node, if so placed), but

**Table 2.** Query terms containing variables and their bindings

| Query term | Data terms | Bindings |
|---|---|---|
| V1 a{ <u>var</u> X } | $\preceq$ a[ b ];<br>$\npreceq$ a{ }; a[ b, c ] | $\{X/b\}$ |
| V2 a{{ <u>var</u> X }} | $\preceq$ a[ b, c ];<br>$\npreceq$ a{ }; | $\{X/b, X/c\}$ |
| V3 a{{ <u>var</u> X, <u>var</u> X }} | $\preceq$ a[ b, b ]; a{ c, b, b, d } <br> $\npreceq$ a[ b, c ]; a{ b } | $\{X/b_1, X/b_2\}$ |
| V5 a{ <u>var</u> X{ <u>var</u> X } } | $\preceq$ a[ b{ "b"} ];<br>$\npreceq$ a{ b, c }; | $\{X/\text{"b"}\}$ |
| V6 a{ <u>var</u> X ⤳c, <u>var</u> X } | $\preceq$ a[ c, c ];<br>$\npreceq$ a{ b, b }; | $\{X/b\}$ |
| V7 a{ <u>desc</u> <u>var</u> X } | $\preceq$ a[ c{ b, e[ f ] } ];<br><br>$\npreceq$ a{ d, c{ b } }; | $\{X/c\{...\}, X/b,$<br>$X/e[...], X/f\}$ |

matches are recorded in the bindings of the query. If a variable occurs multiple
times (V3), the matched query terms must be structurally equivalent. A variable
may occur as a label (V5), in which case it is bound to the value of the label
and can only match with other labels or character data (as the ''b'' in V5).
A variable may occur in a term restriction before ⤳ (V6), in which case the
right hand query term restricts the matching bindings for $X$. Finally, it can be
combined with <u>desc</u> yielding the expected result (V7).

## 3.2   Simulation Unification

Simulation unification is a non-deterministic algorithm for solving in the data
term lattice $(\mathcal{T}_{db}/ \equiv, \preceq)$ induced by the relation $\preceq$. Inequations of the form
$t^q \preceq t^c$, where $t^q$ is a query term, $t^c$ is a so-called "construct term", i.e., a query
term without ⤳ and *desc* constructs.[4] (possibly a data term), and $t^q$ and $t^c$ are
variable disjoint.[5] Thus, simulation unification computes substitutions $\sigma$ such
that $t^q\sigma$ and $t^c\sigma$ have instances $t^q\sigma\tau$ and $t^c\sigma\tau$ with $t^q\sigma\tau$ and $t^c\sigma\tau$ data terms
and $t^q\sigma\tau \preceq t^c\sigma\tau$.

Simulation unification consists in repeated applications of Term Decomposition phases followed by a Consistency Verification phase to a formula $C$ (for
constraint store) consisting in disjunctions of conjunctions of inequations of the
form $t^q \preceq t^c$ (with $t^q$ query term and $t^c$ construct term) and/or equations of
the form $t_1^c = t_2^c$ (with $t_1^c$ and $t_2^c$ construct terms). At the beginning $C$ consists

---

[4] Simulation unification is in fact defined for more general construct terms in which
grouping and aggregation constructs à la $\mathcal{LDL}$ [101,44] might occur.

[5] Variable disjointness is achieved in deduction systems by the so-called "standardiza-
tion apart."

in a single inequation $t^q \preceq t^c$. Both phases Term Decomposition and Consistency Verification consist in stepwise changes of the constraint store $C$. These changes are expressed in the following formalism inspired from [59]: A "simplification" $L \Leftrightarrow R$ replaces $L$ by $R$. Trivially satisfied inequations or equations are replaced by the atomic formula *true*. Inconsistent conjunctions of inequations or equations are replaced by the atomic formula *false*. Memoing ensures that the recursive traversal cyclic query terms terminates. For space reasons, memoing is not discussed in the following, i.e., references in query terms are disregarded, and only the decomposition rules for terms of the form a{} or {{}} are given. See [118] for a full treatment.

**Definition 9 (Term Decomposition Rules).** *Let $l$ (with or without indices) denote a label. Let $t^1$ and $t^2$ (with or without indices) denote query terms.*

- **Root Elimination:**

  (1)  $l \preceq l\{t_1^2, \ldots, t_m^2\} \Leftrightarrow true$          *if $m \geq 1$*
         $l \preceq l\{\{\}\} \Leftrightarrow true$

  (2)  $l\{t_1^1, \ldots, t_n^1\} \preceq l \Leftrightarrow false$          *if $n \geq 1$*
         $l\{t_1^1, \ldots, t_n^1\} \preceq l\{\{\}\} \Leftrightarrow false$          *if $n \geq 1$*

  (3)  Let $\Pi$ be the set of (total) functions $\{t_1^1, \ldots, t_n^1\} \to \{t_1^2, \ldots, t_m^2\}$:
         $l\{t_1^1, \ldots, t_n^1\} \preceq l\{t_1^2, \ldots, t_m^2\} \Leftrightarrow \bigvee_{\pi \in \Pi} \bigwedge_{1 \leq i \leq n} t_i^1 \preceq \pi(t_i^1)$
                                              *if $n \geq 1$ and $m \geq 1$*

  (4)  $l_1\{t_1^1, \ldots, t_n^1\} \preceq l_2\{t_1^2, \ldots, t_m^2\} \Leftrightarrow false$ *if $l_1 \neq l_2$ and $n \geq 0$ and $m \geq 0$*

- $\rightsquigarrow$ **Elimination:**

  $$X \rightsquigarrow t^1 \preceq t^2 \quad \Leftrightarrow \quad t^1 \preceq t^2 \wedge t^1 \preceq X \wedge X \preceq t^2$$

- **Descendant Elimination:**

  $$desc \; t^1 \preceq l_2\{t_1^2, \ldots, t_m^2\} \Leftrightarrow t^1 \preceq l_2\{t_1^2, \ldots, t_m^2\} \vee \bigvee_{1 \leq i \leq m} desc \; t^1 \preceq t_i^2$$
  $$if \; m \geq 0$$

Applying the $\rightsquigarrow$ and descendant elimination rules to a constraint store $C$ in disjunctive normal form may yield a constraint store not in disjunctive normal form. Thus, the method has to repeatedly restore the disjunctive normal form of $C$.

In the following, $mgcu(t_1, \ldots, t_n)$ (with $t_1, \ldots, t_n$ query terms) returns a most general commutative-unifier of $t_1, \ldots, t_n$ (in the sense of [6]) expressed as either *false*, if $t_1$ and $t_2$ are not commutative-unifiable, or as *true* if $t_1$ and $t_2$ are commutative-unifiable and do not contain variables, or else as a conjunction of equations of the form $X = t$. Note that most general commutative-unifiers are only computed for construct terms (i.e., query terms without $\rightsquigarrow$ and *desc* constructs). Recall that commutative unification is decidable.

In the definition below, simulation unification is initialized with $X_0 \rightsquigarrow t^q \preceq t^c$, where $X_0$ is a variable occurring neither in $t^q$ nor in $t^c$, instead of simply $t^q \preceq t^c$. The additional variable $X_0$ serves a complete specification of the answers returned. This is useful in proving the correctness of simulation unification but can sometimes be dispensed of in practice.

**Definition 10 (Simulation Unification).**

1. **Initialization:**
   $C := X_0 \rightsquigarrow t^q \preceq t^c$
   *(with $t^q$ query term, $t^c$ construct term and $t^q$, $t^c$ and $X_0$ variable disjoint).*
2. **Term Decomposition:**
   *Until $C$ can no longer be modified, repeat performing one of:*
   *– Apply a (applicable) Term Decomposition rule to $C$*
   *– Put $C$ in disjunctive normal form*
   *end-until*
3. **Variable Binding:**
   *Replace each $X \preceq t$ in $C$ with $X = t$.*
4. **Consistency Verification:**
   *For each disjunct $D$ of $C$ and for each variable $X$ occurring in $D$ do:*
   *Replace in $D$ the equations $X = t_1, \ldots, X = t_n$ by $mgcu(t_1, \ldots, t_n)$.*
   *end-for*

Note that the constraint store $C$ returned at the end of the Term Decomposition step is necessarily in disjunctive normal form. Indeed, if $C$ is not in disjunctive normal form, then the halting condition of the until loop (Step 2 of Definition 10) is not satisfied.

For efficiency reasons it is preferable to intertwine the Term Decomposition and Consistency Verification phases instead of performing them one after another. The sequential processing of both phases in Definition 10 simplifies the proofs.

**Proposition 1 (Correctness and Completeness).** *Let $t^q$ be a query term, $t^c$ a construct term, i.e., a query term without $\rightsquigarrow$ and desc constructs, and $X_0$ a variable such that $t^q$, $t^c$ and $X_0$ are variable disjoint. There exists a substitution $\tau$ such that $t^q\tau$ and $t^c\tau$ are database terms and $t^q\tau = t^c\tau$ if and only if a simulation unification initialized with $X_0 \rightsquigarrow t^q \preceq t^c$ returns a substitution $\sigma$ such that*

– *For each variable $X$ in $t^q$, $X\sigma$ is a subterm of $t^q\sigma$.*
– *$t^q\tau$ is an instance of $t^q\sigma$.*
– *$t^c\tau$ is an instance of $t^c\sigma$.*

The proof is given in [118].

## 3.3 Complexity of Simulation Unification

The complexity of standard unification is famously linear. The complexity picture for simulation unification is considerably more "complex": It is easy to see that full simulation unification is NP-complete. It is in NP, e.g., by translation to first-order logic [60]. It is NP-hard, e.g., by reduction from subgraph isomorphism [90] or 3SAT. In presence of incomplete term specifications and variables this is not surprising and in line with similarly expressive XML query languages such as XPath 2 (see [16]).

In this section, we thus introduce a family of restrictions to the query terms defined in Definition 2 and briefly summarize the complexity of simulation unification for these languages.

We denote with $\mathrm{SU}^{\mathrm{tree};-\mathrm{bi},-\mathrm{di}}_{-\mathrm{var},-\mathrm{inj},-\mathrm{u}}$ the simulation unification problem over query terms without variables ($-\mathrm{var}$), term injectivity ($-\mathrm{inj}$), and unordered terms ($-\mathrm{u}$), where query terms may only be tree-shaped (i.e., no references) and may be neither incomplete in depth ($-\mathrm{di}$) nor breadth ($-\mathrm{bi}$). Note, that all these restrictions only apply to query terms, not to data terms. For $-\mathrm{var}$, we can also use $-\mathrm{tvar}$ to only disallow term variables, such that label variables can still be used. For $-\mathrm{u}$ we can also use $-\mathrm{o}$ to disallow ordered terms. We can drop any of these restrictions, e.g., $\mathrm{SU}^{-\mathrm{bi}}_{-\mathrm{var}}$ denotes the simulation unification problem over the sub-language of query terms without variables and with no breadth-incomplete terms.

Table 3 summarizes the complexity results for simulation unification over the most interesting classes of restricted query terms.

The first three lines recall NP-complete fragments: (1) simulation unification over unrestricted query terms is NP-complete. (2) It remains so even if we allow no variables, but query terms may be graph-shaped. (3) It also remains NP-complete if we allow only tree shaped query terms, but any form of variables (including only label variables).

**Table 3.** Complexity of simulation unification. $q$ size of query term; $d$ size of data term (number of nodes, see [60])

|   | Fragment | Complexity |
|---|----------|------------|
| 1 | SU | NP-complete |
| 2 | $\mathrm{SU}_{-\mathrm{var}}$ | NP-complete |
| 3 | $\mathrm{SU}^{\mathrm{tree}}_{-\mathrm{tvar}}$ | NP-complete |
| 4 | $\mathrm{SU}^{\mathrm{tree}}_{-\mathrm{var},-\mathrm{inj}}$ | $q \cdot d^2$, $q \cdot d$ if *data terms* are trees or CIGs [60] |
| 5 | $\mathrm{SU}^{\mathrm{tree}}_{-\mathrm{var}}$ | $q \cdot d \cdot \frac{(q+d)^{1.5} \cdot q \cdot d}{log(q+d)}$ |
| 6 | $\mathrm{SU}^{\mathrm{tree}}_{-\mathrm{var},-\mathrm{o}}$ | $q \cdot d \cdot \frac{(q+d)^{1.5} \cdot q \cdot d}{log(q+d)}$ |
| 7 | $\mathrm{SU}^{\mathrm{tree}}_{-\mathrm{var},-\mathrm{u}}$ | $q \cdot d^2$ |
| 8 | $\mathrm{SU}^{\mathrm{tree};-\mathrm{di}}_{-\mathrm{var}}$ | $q^{1.5} \cdot d$ |
| 9 | $\mathrm{SU}^{\mathrm{tree};-\mathrm{di}}_{-\mathrm{var},-\mathrm{o}}$ | $q^{1.5} \cdot d$ |
| 10 | $\mathrm{SU}^{\mathrm{tree};-\mathrm{di}}_{-\mathrm{var},-\mathrm{u}}$ | $q \cdot d$ |
| 11 | $\mathrm{SU}^{\mathrm{tree};-\mathrm{di},-\mathrm{bi}}_{-\mathrm{var}}$ | $q + d$ |
| 12 | $\mathrm{SU}^{\mathrm{tree};-\mathrm{di},-\mathrm{bi}}_{-\mathrm{var},-\mathrm{o}}$ | $q + d$ |
| 13 | $\mathrm{SU}^{\mathrm{tree};-\mathrm{di},-\mathrm{bi}}_{-\mathrm{var},-\mathrm{u}}$ | $q + d$ |

*Proof (Sketch).* It is easy to see that (1) (and thus (2) and (3)) is in NP, cf. [60] for a reduction to first-order logic.

NP-hardness for (1) and (2) can be shown by reduction from subgraph isomorphism: Let $P, G$ be arbitrary graphs. Then we can test if $P$ is isomorphic to a subgraph in $G$ by the following construction (let $\lambda \neq mu$ be arbitrary labels): For each node of $P$, we construct a *breadth-incomplete* query term $q_i$ with label $\lambda$ containing a reference to the query term of each adjacent node. Let $q = \mu\{\{q_1, q_2, \ldots\}\}$. For each node of $G$, we construct a breadth-complete data term $d_i$ with label $\lambda$ and references to each query term of adjacent nodes. Let $d = \mu\{d_1, d_2, \ldots\}$. Then, $q$ simulates in $d$, if and only if $P$ is a subgraph of $G$. For instance, for the graph $P_1$ with edges $(1, 2), (2, 3), (1, 4)$ and the graph $G_1$ with edges $(1, 2), (2, 3), (2, 4), (1, 4), (1, 5), (4, 5)$ the terms are $\mu\{\{\lambda\{\{\lambda\{\{\lambda\{\{\}\}\}\}\}\}, \lambda\{\{\}\}\}\}$ and $\mu\{\lambda\{\lambda\{\}, \uparrow 4\}, 4@\lambda\{\uparrow 5\}, 5@\lambda\{\}\}$.

NP-hardness for (3) is shown in [90] by reduction from Clique.

Fragment 4 of Table 3 highlights a major result of [60]: If we relax the injectivity requirement, i.e., that the $t_1^2, \ldots t_m^2$ must be pairwise distinct in Definition 5, simulation unification becomes polynomial for query terms without of references and variables. In fact, there is a large class of graph-shaped data terms, called CIGs in [60], that includes all trees and forests on which simulation unification has linear data complexity in this case.

Fragments 5-7 consider the effect of injectivity in case of tree shaped query terms without variables. Fragment 5 is the general case, fragment 6 if we allow no ordered query terms (no []), fragment 7 if we allow no unordered query terms (no {}). The complexity of fragments 5 and 6 has been an open issue as stated in [90] and is first shown here. It turns out that all three fragments have polynomial complexity.

*Proof.* The polynomial complexity for Fragment 7 follows from equivalence of this fragment to a fragment of navigational XPath, see [60], for whose complexity see [16]. For instance, $a[[\text{desc } b, c[\text{desc } e]]]$ is equivalent to

```
/a[./*[descendant-or-self::b]/following-sibling::c[./*[1]
[descendant-or-self::e][not(following-sibling::*)]]
```

The complexity for fragment 6 can be shown by reduction to maximum matching for bipartite graphs (or a non-linear assignment problem): We consider bottom-up each sub-term $c$ in the given query $q$. For each $c$, $M_c$ denotes the set of nodes in the data term that match with $c$. We start with the leaf terms and set $M_c$ to the set of nodes with the appropriate label and arity ($|M_c| \leq d$). For inner query terms, if $c$ is incomplete, let $c = \lambda\{\{s_1, \ldots, s_n\}\}$. If $c$ is complete let $c = \lambda\{s_1, \ldots, s_n\}$. For each node $n$ in the data term $d$, that has the appropriate label and arity for $c$, for consider all $s_i$ and let $M_{s_i}^n$ be the restriction of $M_c$ to children of $n$. Thus the $M_{s_i}^n$ are the possible matches for each $s_i$ under the assumption that $c$ matches with $n$. From the $M_{s_i}^n$ we construct a bipartite graph in the following way: $G = (P, C; E)$ where $P$ is all the $s_i$, $C = \cup_i M_{s_i}^n$, and $E = \{(s_i, c) : c \in M_{s_i}^n\}$, i.e., there is an edge from $s_i$ to a node in $C$, if that node is a possible match for $s_i$.

For this bipartite graph, we compute the *maximum matching* $S$. A subset $M$ of $E$ is called a *matching* if every vertex of $G$ coincides with at most one edge from $M$. A matching is called maximal if it cannot be enlarged by any edge of the graph. A matching is called maximum, if it has maximal cardinality among all matchings for that graph.

If $S$ has cardinality $n$, $n$ is a match for $c$ and is added to $M_c$. If $M_q \neq$ after all query terms have been processed, then $q$ simulates in $d$.

Computing the maximum matching can be done in $O(\frac{(q+d)^{1.5} \cdot q \cdot d}{log(q+d)})$, cf.[37]. Thus, the whole algorithm takes $q \cdot d \cdot \frac{(q+d)^{1.5} \cdot q \cdot d}{log(q+d)}$.

For fragment 5 finally, we can use the same algorithm as for 6, but if $c$ is ordered we walk over the $s_i$ and the children of $n$ at the same time and compare matches in order, which can be done in $q + n$ time. Thus, it has the same complexity as fragment 6.

This result is indeed surprising, as unordered tree inclusion is NP-complete [84]. The difference between our case and unordered tree inclusion is that simulation unification does not consider a query term such as $a\{\{\textsf{desc } b, \textsf{desc } c\}\}$ to simulate with $a\{d\{b, c\} \}$ due to the injectivity requirement in Definition 5. For unordered tree inclusion the graph with edges $(a, b), (a, c)$ is included in the graph $(a, d), (d, b), (d, c)$, as unordered tree inclusion only preserves the ancestor relationships.

Fragments 8-10 are the cases, where we also restrict the use of desc. All three cases following immediately from the complexity of ordered, resp. unordered *path* inclusion problems shown in [83].

Finally, fragments 11-13 are the cases, where we consider only complete terms (without either desc, [[]] or {{ }}). In this case, simulation unification is the same problem as tree isomorphism for node-labeled trees, for which well-known linear algorithms exist.

To summarize, there are two surprising results when considering simulation unification over restricted fragments of the full query terms defined in Definition 2:

- Even in presence of incomplete terms and for terms mixing unordered and ordered specifications, simulation unification has linear data complexity on tree and CIG data and quadratic data complexity on arbitrary graphs, if we *ignore the injectivity requirement.*
- In presence of the injectivity requirement, simulation unification still remains polynomial in contrast to closely related problems such as unordered tree inclusion.

Though most of the results above have been proven in [60] and [90], the latter case has been stated as an open issue even in [90]. In this paper, we close this remaining gap in the complexity picture for simulation unification with a positive result: Simulation unification remains polynomial as long as we do not use (multiple occurrences of) variables or graph-shaped query terms, even in presence of unordered terms. It is especially, interesting that thanks to the particular variant of injectivity chosen for query terms, simulation unification remains polynomial, as this requirement has been made for practical reasons: An intuition—so far often confirmed, admittedly on unsystematic observations— is that injectivity eases in practice the programming of queries.

## 4  RDFLog: Datalog with Value Invention

RDFLog extends Datalog to support two distinguishing features of RDF: blank nodes and the logical core [100] of the RDFS vocabulary. In RDFLog, Blank nodes can be specified by existentially quantified variables in rule heads. RDFLog allows *unrestricted quantifier alternation* between existential and universal quantifiers in a rule. The following examples illustrate the benefit of unrestricted quantifier alternation.

**(1)** "Someone knows each professor" can be represented in RDFLog as

$$\exists stu \forall prof \left( (prof, \mathsf{rdf{:}type}, \mathsf{uni{:}professor}) \rightarrow (stu, \mathsf{uni{:}knows}, prof) \right) \tag{1}$$

We call such rules $\exists\forall$ rules. Some approaches such as [130] are limited to rules of this form.

**(2)** "Each lecture must be "practiced" by another course (such as a tutorial or practice lab) without knowing more about that course". This statement can not be expressed by $\exists\forall$ rules. In RDFLog it can be represented as

$$\forall lec \exists crs \left( (lec, \mathsf{rdf{:}type}, \mathsf{uni{:}lecture}) \rightarrow (crs, \mathsf{uni{:}practices}, lec) \right) \tag{2}$$

Such rules are referred to as $\forall\exists$ rules. Recent proposals for rule extensions to SPARQL are limited to this form, if they consider blank nodes in rule heads at all. Indeed, with SPARQL's `CONSTRUCT` patterns a fresh blank node is constructed for each binding of the universal variables (cf. Section 10.2.1 in [108]).

**(3)** "For each lecture there is a course that "practices" that lecture and is attended by all students attending the lecture". This is represented in RDFLog as

$$\forall lec \exists crs \forall stu \left( (lec, \mathsf{rdf{:}type}, \mathsf{uni{:}lecture}) \wedge (stu, \mathsf{uni{:}attends}, lec) \rightarrow \right.$$
$$\left. (crs, \mathsf{uni{:}practices}, lec) \wedge (stu, \mathsf{uni{:}attends}, crs) \right) \tag{3}$$

To the authors' knowledge, RDFLog is the first RDF query language that supports rules of this third kind. RDFLog furthermore is a closed RDF query language, i.e., the answer to an RDFLog program is again an RDF graph, and RDFLog can express the logical core $\rho$df of the RDFS semantics [100].

In [86] it is suggested to extend Logic Programming—called Computational Logic—with existential quantifications in rule's heads, that is, with the very extension RDFLog provides. However, in this book, no method is described for the processing such rules.

The proofs of all results of this section on RDFLog and value invention can be found in [32].

## 4.1  Preliminaries

**Definition 11 (RDF Graph [73]).** *An* RDF *vocabulary* V *consists of two disjoint sets called* URIs U *and literals* L. *The* blank nodes B *is a set disjoint from* U *and* L. *An* RDF *graph is a set of RDF triples where an* RDF *triple is an element of* $(U \cup B) \times U \times (U \cup L \cup B)$. *If* $t = (s, p, o)$ *is an RDF triple then* s *is the* subject, p *is the* predicate, *and* o *is the* object *of* $t$.

The set L of literals consists of three subsets, *plain literals*, *typed literals* and *literals with language tags*. In this work we consider only plain literals (and thus drop IL, the interpretation function for typed literals, see Section 1.3 in [73], in the following definitions).

**Definition 12 (RDF Interpretation [73]).** *An* interpretation I *of an RDF vocabulary* V = (U, L) *is a tuple* (IR, LV, IP, IEXT, IS) *where* IR *is a non-empty set of resources such that* $L \subseteq LV \subseteq IR$, IP *is a set of* properties *and* IEXT : IP → $2^{IR \times IR}$, *and* IS : U → IR ∪ IP *are mappings*.

IR and IP are not necessarily disjoint since a same URI can be used both as a resource and as a property. RDF interpretations are used to assign a truth value to an RDF graph. RDF assigns a special meaning to a predefined vocabulary, called RDFS vocabulary. It is, e.g., required that IEXT(IP(rdfs : subPropertyOf)) is transitive and reflexive. The formulation of theses constraints on RDF interpretation makes use of a notion of a *class* which is omitted in the definition above for simplicity. The logical core of RDFS, denoted as $\rho df$, has been identified in [100]. An RDF interpretation I is a $\rho df$ *interpretation* if I satisfied the constraints specified in Definition 3 of [100].

The semantics of RDF is completed by the notion of entailment: An RDF graph g *RDF-entails* ($\rho df$-*entails*) an RDF graph h if for all RDF ($\rho df$) interpretations I, I(h) = true if I(g) = true [73].

The following uses formulas, terms, structures, Herbrand structures, satisfaction $\models$, models, entailment $\models$, logic and Datalog programs, and the *immediate consequence operator* $T_P$ of a logic program $P$. Infinite formulas [6] are also used: if $\Phi$ is a recursively enumerable set of formulas, then $\bigwedge(\Phi)$ is a formula; if $\bar{x} = x_1, x_2, \ldots$ is a recursively enumerable sequence of variables and if $\varphi$ is a formula, then $\exists \bar{x}(\varphi)$ is a formula. We write $\varphi(\bar{x})$ to indicate that the free variables of a formula $\varphi$ are amongst $\bar{x} = x_1, \ldots, x_n$.

We show that the semantics of RDF can be defined in terms of standard logic. In particular, RDF graphs can be translated to formulas so that logical entailment coincides with RDF entailment. For any RDF vocabulary V = (U, L) we define the alphabet $\Sigma_V = U \cup L \cup \{T\}$ where U and L are constant symbols and $T$ is an arbitrary ternary relation symbol.

---

[6] Of a limited form: infinite conjunctions all variables of which are existentially quantified.

**Definition 13 (Canonical Formula of an RDF Graph).** *Let* $g = \{t_1, \ldots, t_n\}$ *be an RDF graph over* $V$. *The canonical formula of* $g$ *is the formula* $\varphi_g :=$ $\exists \bar{x} (\psi_1(\bar{x}) \wedge \ldots \wedge \psi_n(\bar{x}))$ *over* $\Sigma_V$ *and variables from* $B$ *where* $\psi_i = T(s, p, o)$ *if* $t_i = (s, p, o)$ *and* $\bar{x}$ *is the set of blank nodes occurring in* $g$.

It is easy to see that $\rho df$ [100] corresponds to a finite set of Datalog rules $\Phi^{\rho df}$.

**Proposition 2.** *Let* $g$, $h$ *be RDF graphs and* $\varphi_g$, $\varphi_h$ *their canonical formulas. Then* $g$ *RDF-entails* $h$ *iff* $\varphi_g \models \varphi_h$ *and* $g$ *$\rho df$-entails* $h$ *iff* $\varphi_g \wedge \Phi^{\rho df} \models \varphi_h$.

## 4.2   RDFLog Syntax

**Definition 14 (Syntax of RDFLog Programs).** *Let* $V = (U, L)$ *be an RDF vocabulary and* $Var$ *a set of variables. An* RDFLog *atom over* $V$ *is an atom* $T(t_1, t_2, t_3)$ *where* $t_1, t_2 \in (U \cup Var)$ *and* $t_3 \in (U \cup L \cup Var)$. *An* RDFLog *rule over* $V$ *is a formula*

$$\forall \bar{x}_1 \exists \bar{y}_1 \ldots \forall \bar{x}_n \exists \bar{y}_n \, (body(\bar{x}) \rightarrow head(\bar{x}, \bar{y}))$$

*over* $\Sigma_V$ *and* $Var$ *where* $\bar{x} = \bar{x}_1, \ldots, \bar{x}_n$ *and* $\bar{y} = \bar{y}_1, \ldots, \bar{y}_n$ *are finite sequences from* $Var$ *and* $body(\bar{x})$ *and* $head(\bar{x}, \bar{y})$ *are finite conjunctions of RDFLog atoms. In addition we require that RDFLog rules are* range restricted*: if* $x \in Var(head)$ *is universal or there is an existential* $y \in Var(head)$ *such that* $y$ *is in the scope of* $x$, *then* $x \in Var(body)$. *An* RDFLog *program over* $V$ *is a finite set of RDFLog rules over* $V$.

Any finite RDF graph $g = \{t_1, \ldots, t_n\}$ with blank nodes $\bar{x}$ can be encoded into the RDFLog rule $\exists \bar{x} \, (true \rightarrow t_1 \wedge \ldots \wedge t_n)$ where $true$ denotes the empty conjunction. As it makes the notation simpler, we always assume that the input RDF graph is encoded into such a rule in the RDFLog program. As there is only one predicate symbol ($T$) in an RDFLog program, it can be omitted.

## 4.3   Declarative Semantics

The following RDFLog program shows that it is problematic to define the semantics of an RDF query language in terms of models. Let the *canonical structure* $A_g$ of an RDF graph $g$ be the structure over the domain of URIs, literals and blank nodes where $(t_1, t_2, t_3)$ is true in $A_g$ iff $(t_1, t_2, t_3)$ is an RDF triple in $g$. As (2) is a fact in $P$ and (1) is a rule in $P$, any canonical structure of an RDF graph that is a model of $P$ must contain the triple ('Logic', uni:located_in, _:b) for some blank node _:b. Since this triple contains a literal in the subject position, it is not an RDF triple. Thus, that $P$ has no model which is the canonical structures of an RDF graph. Even if, as with SPARQL, literals in subject position are allowed, one can similarly argue with blank nodes in predicate position.

$$P = \{\forall sem \exists rm \forall stu\big((stu, \text{uni:attends}, sem)$$
$$\rightarrow (sem, \text{uni:located\_in}, rm) \wedge (stu, \text{uni:knows}, rm)\big), \qquad (1)$$
$$true \rightarrow (\text{uni:julie}, \text{uni:attends}, \text{'Logic'}) \wedge (\text{uni:john}, \text{uni:attends}, \text{uni:RDF})\} \quad (2)$$

$$[\![P]\!] \ni \{(\_\text{:b3}, \text{uni:located\_in}, \_\text{:b1}), (\text{uni:julie}, \text{uni:knows}, \_\text{:b1}),$$
$$(\text{uni:RDF}, \text{uni:located\_in}, \_\text{:b2}), (\text{uni:john}, \text{uni:knows}, \_\text{:b2}),$$
$$(\text{uni:julie}, \text{uni:attends}, \text{'Logic'}), (\text{uni:julie}, \text{uni:attends}, \_\text{:b3}),$$
$$(\text{uni:john}, \text{uni:attends}, \text{uni:RDF})\}$$

The difficulty is overcome by defining the semantics of RDFLog in terms of RDF entailment. More precisely, the semantics of an RDFLog program $P$ is defined as the set of all RDF graphs $g$ that entail exactly the same RDF graphs as $P$ (and satisfying in particular $P \models g$).

**Definition 15 (Denotational Semantics of RDFLog).** *Let $P$ be an RD-FLog program and* RDF *the set of RDF graphs. The denotational semantics $[\![P]\!]$ of $P$ is the set $[\![P]\!] := \{g \in \text{RDF} \mid \forall h \in \text{RDF} (P \models \varphi_h \text{ iff } \varphi_g \models \varphi_h)\}$ where $\varphi_g$ and $\varphi_h$ are the canonical formulas of $g$ and $h$ respectively.*

Observe that the semantics of an RDFLog program is an infinite set of possibly infinite RDF graphs. As we formalized RDF graphs as formulas, we have to consider the special kind of infinite formulas defined above. Nonetheless it is immediate from the definition that the RDF graphs in $[\![P]\!]$ form an equivalence class under RDF entailment. Therefore any element of $[\![P]\!]$ characterizes the infinite set $[\![P]\!]$. In the next section we show how such a representative can be computed.

Observe that $\Phi^{\rho df}$ encoded in RDFLog. Therefore it is up to the programmer to enclose $\Phi^{\rho df}$ into $P$ if the semantics of $P$ is supposed to be aware of the $\rho df$ vocabulary.

subsectionOperational Semantics

RDFLog operational semantics consists in (1) Skolemization, (2) standard Datalog evaluation, (3) un-Skolemization, and (4) normalization. Normalisation discards intermediary triples that may contain blank nodes in predicate position (see [126] for cases where this is useful), the final answer of an RDFLog program never contains such triples.

**Definition 16 (Skolemisation).** *Let $\Sigma$ and $\Gamma$ be disjoint alphabets, $\varphi = \forall \bar{x} \exists y$ $(\psi)$ a formula over $\Sigma \cup \Gamma$ and $f \in \Gamma$. A $\Gamma$-Skolemisation step $s_f$ maps $\varphi$ to $s_f(\varphi) := \forall \bar{x} \psi \{y \leftarrow f(\bar{x})\}$. A $\Gamma$-Skolemisation $s$ is a composition $s_{f_1} \circ \ldots \circ s_{f_n}$ of $\Gamma$-Skolemisation steps such that $f_i$ does not occur in $s_{f_{i+1}} \circ \ldots \circ s_{f_n}(\varphi)$ and $s(\varphi)$ contains no existential variables. The definition of a Skolemisation is extended to sets in the usual way.*

The Skolemised of an RDFLog program $P$ is equivalent to a range restricted logic program $s(P)$. Any logic programming engine can compute the minimal Herbrand model $M_{s(P)}$ of $s(P)$.

We define $\varphi_{M_{s(P)}}$ to be the conjunction of all ground atoms that are true in $M_{s(P)}$. However, $\varphi_{M_{s(P)}}$ might not be the canonical formula of an element of $[\![P]\!]$ for two reasons. First, the example shows that $\varphi_{M_{s(P)}}$ might contain atoms with skolem terms, such as (uni:RDF, uni:located_in, $s_{rm}$(uni:RDF)), which are not entailed by $P$. Second, $\varphi_{M_{s(P)}}$ can contain atoms that contain literals in subject or predicate position and blank nodes in predicate position. In the example the atom ('Logic', uni:located_in, $s_{rm}$('Logic')) contains the literal 'Logic' in subject position.

The first problem is solved by "undoing" the Skolemisaton, i.e., replacing each Skolem term in $\varphi_{M_{s(P)}}$ by a fresh, distinct blank node. We call this operation *UnSkolemisaton*.

**Definition 17 (Unskolemisation).** *Let $\Sigma$ and $\Gamma$ be disjoint alphabets and $\varphi$ a ground, possibly infinite, and quantifier free formula over $\Sigma \cup \Gamma$. Let $\bar{t}$ be the sequence of all ground terms $f(\bar{u})$ where $f$ is in $\Gamma$ and $\bar{u}$ is a sequence of terms over $\Sigma \cup \Gamma$. Then the $\Gamma$-Unskolemisation $u$ maps $\varphi$ to $u(\varphi) := \exists \bar{x} \, (\varphi\{\bar{t} \leftarrow \bar{x}\})$. where $\bar{x}$ is a sequence of fresh variables.*

To solve the second problem, we remove all triples with literals or blank nodes in predicate position (no RDF graph may contain such a triple or any triple entailed by it). In addition we remove each triple $t$ that contains a literal $l$ in object position and add two triples $t_1$ and $t_2$ where $t_1$ is obtained from $t$ by replacing an occurrence of a literal $l$ in subject position by a fresh blank node $b_l$ and $t_2$ is obtained from $t$ by replacing all occurrences of $l$ by $b_l$.

This is necessary to preserve information about the identity of domain elements that are denoted by blank nodes. For example observe that the RDF graph {(uni:julie, uni:attends, _:b), (_:b, uni:located_in, $s_{rm}$('Logic'))} follows from the RDFLog program $P$ above. To maintain this information we need to insert the triple (uni:julie, uni:attends, _:b3) into $[\![P]\!]$. We formalise this step by defining the normalisation operator.

**Definition 18 (Normalisation Operator).** *Let $\varphi$ be a formula of the form $\exists \bar{x} \, (a_1(\bar{x}) \wedge \ldots \wedge a_n(\bar{x}))$ where each $a_i(\bar{x}) = T(t_1, t_2, t_3)$ for some $t_1, t_2, t_3 \in (U \cup B \cup L)$. Let $L' \subseteq L$ be the set of literals that occur in the first argument of an atom in $\varphi$. We define $\mu : U \cup B \cup L \to U \cup B \cup L$ to be the injection such that $\mu(t) = b$ for some fresh blank node $b$ (not in $\varphi$) if $t \in L'$ and $\mu(t) = t$ otherwise. Then $\Pi(\varphi) = \{\Pi(a_1(\bar{x})), \ldots \Pi(a_n(\bar{x}))\}$ and*

$$\Pi(T(t_1, t_2, t_3)) = \begin{cases} \top & \text{if } t_2 \in B \cup L \\ (\mu(t_1), t_2, t_3) \wedge (\mu(t_1), t_2, \mu(t_3)) & \text{otherwise} \end{cases}$$

The normalisation operator ensures that, though intermediary triples may contain blank nodes in predicate position (see [126] for examples where this is useful), the final answer of an RDFLog program never contains such triples.

**Definition 19 (Operational Semantics of RDFLog).** *Let $P$ be an RDFLog program over $\Sigma$, $s$ a $\Gamma$-Skolemisation for $P$, and $u$ an $\Gamma$-Unskolemisation. Then the operational semantics of $P$ is $[P] := \Pi\left(u(\varphi_{M_{s(P)}})\right)$ where $\varphi_{M_{s(P)}}$ is as defined above: the conjunction of all ground atoms that are true in the minimal Herbrand model of $s(P)$.*

## 4.4 Properties and Experimental Evaluation

Even though we do not require that elements of the denotational semantics $[\![P]\!]$ of an RDFLog program $P$ are models of $P$ it holds that $u(\varphi_{M_{s(P)}})$ has a canonical structure that is not only a model of $P$ but even a universal model [56,57]. Thus if we allow literals in subject position and blank nodes in subject or predicate position, we can omit $\Pi$ from the operational semantics and compute a model of $P$.

To formulate this more precisely, we define an *extended Herbrand structure $A$* over alphabet $\Sigma$ and variables *Var* as a structure $(D, Rel, Fun)$ where $D$ is the set of (possibly non-ground) terms over $\Sigma$ and *Var*, and every function $f^A$ is defined by $f^A(t_1, \ldots, t_n) = f(t_1, \ldots, t_n)$. We extend the definition of Unskolemisation from formulas to extended Herbrand structures: if $u$ is an Unskolemisation that replaces $\bar{t}$ by $\bar{x}$ then $u(M)$ is the extended Herbrand structure obtained from $M$ by renaming the domain elements $\bar{t}$ by $\bar{x}$.

**Lemma 1.** *Let $P$ be an RDFLog program, $A_P = u(M_{s(P)})$ and $\varphi_P = u\left(\varphi_{M_{s(P)}}\right)$. Then $A_P \models P$ and $P \models \varphi_P$.*

Intuitively, $A_P \models P$ means that $\varphi_P$ captures all the information in $P$ and $P \models \varphi_P$ means that it does not assert anything that is not asserted by $P$. From these two key observations, we can prove that the operational semantics of RDFLog is both sound and complete with respect to the denotational semantics.

**Theorem 1.** *Let $P$ be an RDFLog program. Then $[P] \in [\![P]\!]$.*

The reduction of RDFLog to standard logic programs allows for a direct implementation of RDFLog on top of any logic programming or database engine that supports value invention and recursion. In the following, we we compare experimentally the performance of a very simple prototype based on that principle with two of the more common SPARQL implementations. Our implementation of RDFLog uses a combination of Perl pre- and post-filters for Skolemisation, Unskolemisation, and normalisation of RDFLog programs and XSB Prolog to evaluate the Skolemised programs.

We compare our implementation with the ARQ SPARQL processor of Jena (Version 2.1) and the SPARQL engine provided by the Sesame RDF Framework. For Sesame, we choose the main-memory store as it is "by far the fastest type of repository that can be used" according to Sesame's authors. With this store, Sesame becomes a main-memory, ad-hoc query engine just like RDFLog and ARQ. As common for ad-hoc queries we measure overall execution time including both loading of the RDF data and execution of the SPARQL or RDFLog query.

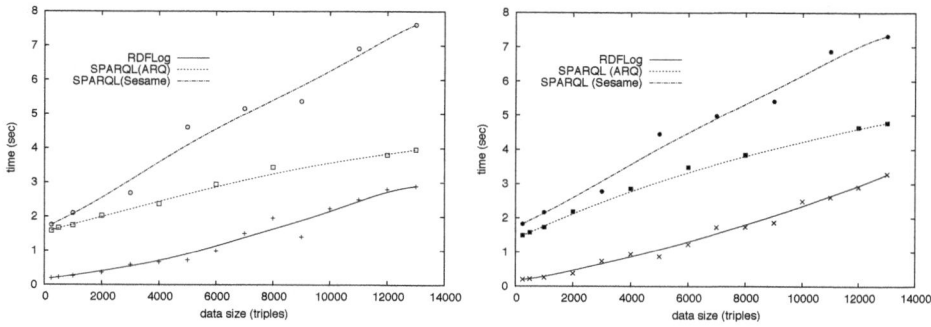

**Fig. 2.** Performance comparison on rule 1 (left) and on rule 2 (right)

In the experiments we evaluate three different queries against an RDF graph consisting of Wikipedia data. The experiments have been carried out on a Intel Pentium M Dual-Core with 1.86 GHz, 1 MB cache and 2 GB main memory. For each setting, the running time is averaged over 25 runs. We compare the following rules:

- *Rule 1:* $\forall x \forall y \left( (x, \mathsf{wiki:internalLink}, y) \rightarrow (x, \mathsf{test:connected}, y) \right)$
- *Rule 2:* $\forall x \forall y \exists z \left( (x, \mathsf{wiki:internalLink}, y) \rightarrow (x, \mathsf{test:connected}, z) \right)$

Figure 2 compares the performance of RDFLog with that of ARQ and Sesame for rule 1 and rule 2 (we omit rule 3 as it is not expressible in SPARQL). Despite its light-weight, ad-hoc implementation, RDFLog outperforms ARQ and Sesame in this setting. The figures show moreover that also for ARQ and Sesame, blank node construction does not bear any significant additional computational effort.

## 5   Conclusion

Datalog has proven a useful vehicle for research and advanced database systems. However, to remain such it must adapt to the ever more dominant Web. To that end, we describe two approaches for addressing two of the most glaring deficiencies of Datalog: simulation unification, for an easy access to semi-structured Web data, and RDFLog, for arbitrary quantifier alternation in rule heads needed for constructing RDF graphs. Both approaches pose new challenges to Datalog evaluation and analysis, but we show that in both cases polynomial core languages—at the cost of mild restrictions—can be identified.

**Acknowledgements.** The research leading to these results has received funding from the European Commission and the Swiss Federal Office for Education and Science within the 6th Framework Programme project REWERSE no. 506779 and the European Research Council under the European Communitys Seventh Framework Programme (FP7/2007-2013)/ERC grant agreement no. 246858—DIADEM.

# References

1. Abiteboul, S., Buneman, P., Suciu, D.: Data on the Web: From Relations to Semistructured Data and XML. Morgan Kaufmann, San Francisco (1999)
2. Abiteboul, S., Quass, D., McHugh, J., Widom, J., Wiener, J.L.: The Lorel Query Language for Semistructured Data. Int. J. on Digital Libraries 1(1), 68–88 (1997)
3. Abiteboul, S., Vianu, V.: Regular Path Queries with Constraints. In: PODS, pp. 122–133 (1997)
4. Appelt, D.E.: Introduction to Information Extraction. AI Commun. 12(3), 161–172 (1999)
5. Arocena, G.O., Mendelzon, A.O.: WebOQL: Restructuring Documents, Databases, and Webs. In: ICDE, pp. 24–33. IEEE Computer Society, Los Alamitos (1998)
6. Baader, F.: Unification in Commutative Theories. In: Unification, pp. 417–435. Academic Press, London (1989)
7. Bailey, J., Bry, F., Furche, T., Schaffert, S.: Web and Semantic Web Query Languages: A Survey. In: Eisinger, N., Małuszyński, J. (eds.) Reasoning Web. LNCS, vol. 3564, pp. 35–133. Springer, Heidelberg (2005)
8. Bancilhon, F., Maier, D., Sagiv, Y., Ullman, J.D.: Magic Sets and Other Strange Ways to Implement Logic Programs. In: PODS, pp. 1–15. ACM, New York (1986)
9. Barahona, P., Bry, F., Franconi, E., Henze, N., Sattler, U. (eds.): Reasoning Web 2006. LNCS, vol. 4126. Springer, Heidelberg (2006)
10. Baru, C., Ludäscher, B., Papakonstantinou, Y., Velikhov, P., Vianu, V.: Features and Requirements for an XML View Definition Language: Lessons from XML Information Mediation. In: QL 1998, W3C (1998)
11. Bassiliades, N., Vlahavas, I.P.: R-DEVICE: A Deductive RDF Rule Language. In: Antoniou, G., Boley, H. (eds.) RuleML 2004. LNCS, vol. 3323, pp. 65–80. Springer, Heidelberg (2004)
12. Baumgartner, R., Flesca, S., Gottlob, G.: The Elog Web Extraction Language. In: Nieuwenhuis, R., Voronkov, A. (eds.) LPAR 2001. LNCS (LNAI), vol. 2250, pp. 548–560. Springer, Heidelberg (2001)
13. Baumgartner, R., Flesca, S., Gottlob, G.: Visual Web Information Extraction with Lixto. In: Apers, P.M.G., Atzeni, P., Ceri, S., Paraboschi, S., Ramamohanarao, K., Snodgrass, R.T. (eds.) VLDB, pp. 119–128. Morgan Kaufmann, San Francisco (2001)
14. Beeri, C., Ramakrishnan, R.: On the Power of Magic. In: PODS, pp. 269–284. ACM, New York (1987)
15. Belleghem, K.V., Denecker, M., Schreye, D.D.: A Strong Correspondence between Description Logics and Open Logic Programming. In: ICLP, pp. 346–360 (1997)
16. Benedikt, M., Koch, C.: Xpath leashed (2007)
17. Berglund, A., Boag, S., Chamberlin, D., Fernàndez, M.F., Kay, M., Robie, J., Siméon, J. (eds.): XML Path Language (XPath) Version 2.0. Recommendation. W3C (2007)
18. Berlea, A., Seidl, H.: fxt – A Transformation Language for XML Documents. J. of Computing and Information Technology (CIT), Special Issue on Domain-Specific Languages (2001)
19. Boag, S., Chamberlin, D., Fernaàndez, M.F., Robie, J., Siméon, J. (eds.): XQuery 1.0: An XML Query Language. Recommendation. W3C (2007)
20. Boley, H.: Relationships Between Logic Programming and XML. In: Proc. 14th Workshop Logische Programmierung, Würzburg (January 2000)

21. Boley, H.: The RuleML Family of Web Rule Languages. In: Alferes, J.J., Bailey, J., May, W., Schwertel, U. (eds.) PPSWR 2006. LNCS, vol. 4187, pp. 1–17. Springer, Heidelberg (2006)
22. Boley, H.: Are Your Rules Online? Four Web Rule Essentials. In: Paschke, A., Biletskiy, Y. (eds.) RuleML 2007. LNCS, vol. 4824, pp. 7–24. Springer, Heidelberg (2007)
23. Boley, H., Halmark, G., Kifer, M., Paschke, A., Polleres, A., Reynolds, D. (eds.): RIF Core Dialect. W3C Recommendation. World Wide Web Consortium, W3C (2010)
24. Boley, H., Kifer, M. (eds.): RIF Basic Logic Dialect. W3C Recommendation. World Wide Web Consortium, W3C (2010)
25. Boley, H., Kifer, M. (eds.): RIF Framework for Logic Dialects. W3C Recommendation. World Wide Web Consortium, W3C (2010)
26. Boley, H., Kifer, M., Patranjan, P.-L., Polleres, A.: Rule Interchange on the Web. In: Antoniou, G., Aßmann, U., Baroglio, C., Decker, S., Henze, N., Patranjan, P.-L., Tolksdorf, R. (eds.) Reasoning Web. LNCS, vol. 4636, pp. 269–309. Springer, Heidelberg (2007)
27. Boley, H., Mei, J., Sintek, M., Wagner, G.: RDF/RuleML Interoperability. In: Rule Languages for Interoperability (2005)
28. Boley, H., Tabet, S., Wagner, G.: Design Rationale for RuleML: A Markup Language for Semantic Web Rules. In: Cruz, I.F., Decker, S., Euzenat, J., McGuinness, D.L. (eds.) SWWS, pp. 381–401 (2001)
29. Bolzer, O., Bry, F., Furche, T., Kraus, S., Schaffert, S.: Development of Use Cases, Part I. Technical Report PMS-FB-2005-23, Institute for Informatics, University of Munich (2005)
30. Brügemann-Klein, A., Wood, D.: Regular Tree Languages over Non-ranked Alphabets (1998) (unpublished manuscript)
31. Bry, F.: Query Evaluation in Deductive Databases: Bottom-Up and Top-Down Reconciled. Data Knowledge Engineering 5, 289–312 (1990)
32. Bry, F., Furche, T., Ley, C., Linse, B., Marnette, B.: RDFLog: It's like Datalog for RDF. Technical Report PMS-FB-2008-1, Institute for Informatics, University of Munich (2005)
33. Bry, F., Furche, T., Ley, C., Linse, B., Marnette, B.: RDFLog: It's like Datalog for RDF. In: Workshop on (Constraint) Logic Programming, WLP 2008 (2008)
34. Bry, F., Furche, T., Linse, B.: The perfect match: Rpl and rdf rule languages. In: Polleres, A., Swift, T. (eds.) RR 2009. LNCS, vol. 5837, pp. 227–241. Springer, Heidelberg (2009)
35. Buneman, P.: Tutorial Semistructured Data. In: PODS, pp. 117–121 (1997)
36. Buneman, P., Fernandez, M.F., Suciu, D.: Unql: A query language and algebra for semistructured data based on structural recursion. VLDB J. 9(1), 76–110 (2000)
37. Burkard, R., Dell'Amico, M., Martello, S.: Assignment Problems. SIAM, Philadelphia (2009)
38. Calvanese, D., Giacomo, G.D., Lenzerini, M., Rosati, R.: View-Based Query Answering over Description Logic Ontologies. In: Brewka, G., Lang, J. (eds.) KR, pp. 242–251. AAAI Press, Menlo Park (2008)
39. Carroll, J.J., Roo, J.D. (eds.): OWL Web Ontology Language Test Cases. W3C Recommendation. World Wide Web Consortium, W3C (2004)
40. Ceri, S., Gottlob, G., Lavazza, L.: Translation and Optimization of Logic Queries: The Algebraic Approach. In: Chu, W.W., Gardarin, G., Ohsuga, S., Kambayashi, Y. (eds.) VLDB, pp. 395–402. Morgan Kaufmann, San Francisco (1986)

41. Ceri, S., Gottlob, G., Tanca, L.: What you Always Wanted to Know About Datalog (And Never Dared to Ask). IEEE Trans. Knowl. Data Eng. 1(1), 146–166 (1989)
42. Ceri, S., Gottlob, G., Tanca, L.: Logic Programming and Databases. Springer, Heidelberg (1990)
43. Chamberlin, D., Fankhauser, P., Marchiori, M., Robie, J. (eds.): XML Query Use Cases. W3C Working Group Note. World Wide Web Consortium, W3C (2007)
44. Chimenti, D., Gamboa, R., Krishnamurthy, R., Naqvi, S.A., Tsur, S., Zaniolo, C.: The ldl system prototype. IEEE Trans. Knowl. Data Eng. 2(1), 76–90 (1990)
45. Clark, J. (ed.): XSL Transformations (XSLT) Version 1.0. Recommendation. W3C (1999)
46. Clark, J., DeRose, S. (eds.): XML Path Language (XPath) Version 1.0. Recommendation. W3C (1999)
47. de Bruijn, J. (ed.): RIF RDF and OWL Compatibility. W3C Recommendation. World Wide Web Consortium, W3C (2010)
48. de Bruijn, J., Eiter, T., Polleres, A., Tompits, H.: On Representational Issues About Combinations of Classical Theories with Nonmonotonic Rules. In: Lang, J., Lin, F., Wang, J. (eds.) KSEM 2006. LNCS (LNAI), vol. 4092, pp. 1–22. Springer, Heidelberg (2006)
49. de Sainte Marie, C., Halmark, G., Paschke, A. (eds.): RIF Production Rule Dialect. W3C Recommendation. World Wide Web Consortium, W3C (2010)
50. Dean, M., Schreiber, G. (eds.): OWL Web Ontology Language Reference. W3C Recommendation. World Wide Web Consortium, W3C (2004)
51. Deutsch, A. (ed.): Proceedings of the Twenty-third ACM SIGACT-SIGMOD-SIGART Symposium on Principles of Database Systems. ACM, New York (2004)
52. Drabent, W., Eiter, T., Ianni, G., Krennwallner, T., Lukasiewicz, T., Maluszynski, J.: Hybrid Reasoning with Rules and Ontologies. In: Bry, F., Małuszyński, J. (eds.) Semantic Techniques for the Web. LNCS, vol. 5500, pp. 1–49. Springer, Heidelberg (2009)
53. Eiter, T., Ianni, G., Krennwallner, T., Polleres, A.: Rules and Ontologies for the Semantic Web. In: Baroglio, C., Bonatti, P.A., Małuszyński, J., Marchiori, M., Polleres, A., Schaffert, S. (eds.) Reasoning Web. LNCS, vol. 5224, pp. 1–53. Springer, Heidelberg (2008)
54. Eiter, T., Ianni, G., Polleres, A., Schindlauer, R., Tompits, H.: Reasoning with Rules and Ontologies. In: Barahona, et al. (eds.) [9], pp. 93–127
55. Eiter, T., Ianni, G., Schindlauer, R., Tompits, H., Wang, K.: Forgetting in Managing Rules and Ontologies. In: Web Intelligence, pp. 411–419. IEEE Computer Society, Los Alamitos (2006)
56. Fagin, R., Kolaitis, P.G., Miller, R.J., Popa, L.: Data Exchange: Semantics and Query Answering. In: Calvanese, D., Lenzerini, M., Motwani, R. (eds.) ICDT 2003. LNCS, vol. 2572, pp. 207–224. Springer, Heidelberg (2002)
57. Fagin, R., Kolaitis, P.G., Miller, R.J., Popa, L.: Data Exchange: Semantics and Query Answering. Theor. Comput. Sci. 336(1), 89–124 (2005)
58. Fensel, D., Sycara, K., Mylopoulos, J. (eds.): ISWC 2003. LNCS, vol. 2870. Springer, Heidelberg (2003)
59. Frühwirth, T.: Theory and practice of constraint handling rules. Journal of Logic Programming, Special Issue on Constraint Logic Programming 37(1-3), 95–138 (1998)
60. Furche, T.: Implementation of Web Query Language Reconsidered: Beyond Tree and Single-Language Algebras at (Almost) No Cost. Dissertation/doctoral thesis, Ludwig-Maxmilians University Munich (2008)

61. Furche, T., Linse, B., Bry, F., Plexousakis, D., Gottlob, G.: Rdf querying: Language constructs and evaluation methods compared. In: Barahona, et al. (eds.) [9], pp. 1–52
62. Gallaire, H., Minker, J. (eds.): Logic and Data Bases, Symposium on Logic and Data Bases. Advances in Data Base Theory. Plenum Press, New York (1978)
63. Gallaire, H., Minker, J., Nicolas, J.-M.: Logic and Databases: A Deductive Approach. ACM Comput. Surv. 16(2), 153–185 (1984)
64. Gallaire, H., Nicolas, J.-M., Minker, J. (eds.): Advances in Data Base Theory, Centre d'Études et de Recherches de l'École Nationale Supérieure de l'Aéronautique et de l'Espace de Toulouse (CERT), France, December 12-14, 1979. Based on the Proceedings of the Workshop on Formal Bases for Data Bases, vol. 1. Plenum Press, New York (1981)
65. Gallaire, H., Nicolas, J.-M., Minker, J. (eds.): Advances in Data Base Theory, Centre d'études et de recherches de Toulouse, France, December 14-17, 1982. Based on the Proceedings of the Workshop on Logical Data Bases, vol. 2. Plenum Press, New York (1984)
66. Gottlob, G., Koch, C.: Monadic Datalog and the Expressive Power of Languages for Web Information Extraction. In: Popa, L. (ed.) PODS, pp. 17–28. ACM, New York (2002)
67. Gottlob, G., Koch, C.: Monadic datalog and the expressive power of languages for Web information extraction. J. ACM 51(1), 74–113 (2004)
68. Gottlob, G., Koch, C., Baumgartner, R., Herzog, M., Flesca, S.: The Lixto Data Extraction Project - Back and Forth between Theory and Practice. In: Deutsch (ed.) [51], pp. 1–12
69. Grahne, G., Lakshmanan, L.V.S.: On the Difference between Navigating Semistructured Data and Querying It. In: Workshop on Database Programming Languages, pp. 271–296 (1999)
70. Grishman, R.: Information Extraction. In: The Oxford Handbook of Computational Linguistics, pp. 545–559. Oxford University Press, Oxford (2003)
71. Grosof, B.N., Horrocks, I., Volz, R., Decker, S.: Description logic programs: combining logic programs with description logic. In: WWW, pp. 48–57 (2003)
72. Gutiérrez, C., Hurtado, C.A., Mendelzon, A.O.: Foundations of semantic web databases. In: Deutsch (ed.) [51], pp. 95–106
73. Hayes, P. (ed.): RDF Semantics. W3C Recommendation. World Wide Web Consortium, W3C (2004)
74. Heflin, J. (ed.): OWL Web Ontology Language Use Cases and Requirements. W3C Recommendation. World Wide Web Consortium, W3C (2004)
75. Hori, M., Euzenat, J., Patel-Schneider, P.F. (eds.): OWL Web Ontology Language XML Presentation Syntax. W3C Recommendation. World Wide Web Consortium, W3C (2004)
76. Horrocks, I.: OWL Rules, OK?. In: Rule Languages for Interoperability (2005)
77. Horrocks, I., Angele, J., Decker, S., Kifer, M., Grosof, B.N., Wagner, G.: Where Are the Rules? IEEE Intelligent Systems 18(5), 76–83 (2003)
78. Horrocks, I., Patel-Schneider, P.F.: A proposal for an Owl rules language. In: Feldman, S.I., Uretsky, M., Najork, M., Wills, C.E. (eds.) WWW, pp. 723–731. ACM, New York (2004)
79. Horrocks, I., Patel-Schneider, P.F., Bechhofer, S., Tsarkov, D.: OWL rules: A proposal and prototype implementation. J. Web Sem. 3(1), 23–40 (2005)
80. Hustadt, U., Motik, B., Sattler, U.: Reducing SHIQ-Description Logic to Disjunctive Datalog Programs. In: Dubois, D., Welty, C.A., Williams, M.-A. (eds.) KR, pp. 152–162. AAAI Press, Menlo Park (2004)

81. Hustadt, U., Motik, B., Sattler, U.: Reasoning in Description Logics by a Reduction to Disjunctive Datalog. J. Autom. Reasoning 39(3), 351–384 (2007)
82. Ianni, G., Krennwallner, T., Martello, A., Polleres, A.: A Rule System for Querying Persistent RDFS Data. In: Aroyo, L., Traverso, P., Ciravegna, F., Cimiano, P., Heath, T., Hyvönen, E., Mizoguchi, R., Oren, E., Sabou, M., Simperl, E. (eds.) ESWC 2009. LNCS, vol. 5554, pp. 857–862. Springer, Heidelberg (2009)
83. Kilpeläinen, P.: Tree Matching Problems with Applications to Structured Text Databases. PhD thesis, University of Helsinki, Faculty of Science, Department of Computer Science (1992)
84. Kilpelainen, P., Mannila, H.: Ordered and Unordered Tree Inclusion. SIAM J. Comput. 24(2), 340–356 (1995)
85. Klyne, G.: Representring Facts and Rules in RDF – Bridging Cconventional predicate representation and RDF (2001),
    http://www.ninebynine.org/RDFNotes/RDFFactsAndRules.html
86. Kowalski, R.: Computational logic and human life: How to be artificially intelligent. Preprint, Department of Computing, Imperial College London (2010),
    http://www.doc.ic.ac.uk/~rak/papers/newbook.pdf to be published by Cambridge University Press
87. Kowalski, R.A.: The Early Years of Logic Programming. Commun. ACM 31(1), 38–43 (1988)
88. Langville, A.N., Meyer, C.D.: Google's PageRank and Beyond – The Science of Search Engine Ranking. Princetoon University Press (2006)
89. Ley, C., Benedikt, M.: How big must complete xml query languages be? In: ICDT 2009: Proceedings of the 12th International Conference on Database Theory, pp. 183–200. ACM, New York (2009)
90. Linse, B.: Data Integration on the (Semantic) Web with Rules and Rich Unification. PhD thesis, Ludwig-Maximilians-Universität München (2010)
91. Maier, D.: Communication during the Workshop Datalog 2.0 (2010)
92. Marx, M.: Conditional xpath. ACM Trans. Database Syst. 30(4), 929–959 (2005)
93. McGuinness, D.L., van Harmelen, F. (eds.): OWL Web Ontology Language Overview. W3C Recommendation. World Wide Web Consortium, W3C (2004)
94. Meditskos, G., Bassiliades, N.: A Rule-Based Object-Oriented OWL Reasoner. IEEE Trans. Knowl. Data Eng. 20(3), 397–410 (2008)
95. Meditskos, G., Bassiliades, N.: Combining a DL Reasoner and a Rule Engine for Improving Entailment-Based OWL Reasoning. In: Sheth, A.P., Staab, S., Dean, M., Paolucci, M., Maynard, D., Finin, T., Thirunarayan, K. (eds.) ISWC 2008. LNCS, vol. 5318, pp. 277–292. Springer, Heidelberg (2008)
96. Miklós, Z., Neumann, G., Zdun, U., Sintek, M.: Querying semantic web resources using triple views. In: Fensel, et al. (eds.) [58], pp. 517–532
97. Motik, B., Grau, B.C., Horrocks, I., Wu, Z., Fokoue, A., Lutz, C. (eds.): OWL 2 Web Ontology Language Profiles. W3C Recommendation. World Wide Web Consortium, W3C (2009)
98. Motik, B., Horrocks, I., Rosati, R., Sattler, U.: Can OWL and Logic Programming Live Together Happily Ever After? In: Cruz, I., Decker, S., Allemang, D., Preist, C., Schwabe, D., Mika, P., Uschold, M., Aroyo, L.M. (eds.) ISWC 2006. LNCS, vol. 4273, pp. 501–514. Springer, Heidelberg (2006)
99. Motik, B., Volz, R.: Optimizing Query Answering in Description Logics using Disjunctive Deductive Databases. In: Bry, F., Lutz, C., Sattler, U., Schoop, M. (eds.) KRDB. CEUR Workshop Proceedings, vol. 79. CEUR-WS.org (2003)

100. Muñoz, S., Pérez, J., Gutierrez, C.: Minimal Deductive Systems for RDF. In: Franconi, E., Kifer, M., May, W. (eds.) ESWC 2007. LNCS, vol. 4519, pp. 53–67. Springer, Heidelberg (2007)
101. Naqvi, S.A., Tsur, S.: A Logical Language for Data and Knowledge Bases. Computer Science Press, Rockville (1989)
102. Neven, F., Schwentick, T.: Query automata over finite trees. Theoretical Computer Science 275(1-2), 633–674 (2002)
103. Olteanu, D., Meuss, H., Furche, T., Bry, F.: XPath: Looking Forward. In: Chaudhri, A.B., Unland, R., Djeraba, C., Lindner, W. (eds.) EDBT 2002. LNCS, vol. 2490, pp. 109–127. Springer, Heidelberg (2002)
104. Patel-Schneider, P.F., Hayes, P., Horrocks, I. (eds.): OWL Web Ontology Language Semantics and Abstract Syntax. W3C Recommendation. World Wide Web Consortium, W3C (2004)
105. Polleres, A.: From SPARQL to rules (and back). In: Williamson, C.L., Zurko, M.E., Patel-Schneider, P.F., Shenoy, P.J. (eds.) WWW, pp. 787–796. ACM, New York (2007)
106. Polleres, A., Boley, H., Kifer, M. (eds.): RIF Datatypes and Built-Ins 1.0. W3C Recommendation. World Wide Web Consortium, W3C (2010)
107. Polleres, A., Schindlauer, R.: DLVHEX-SPARQL: A SPARQL Compliant Query Engine Based on DLVHEX. In: Polleres, A., Pearce, D., Heymans, S., Ruckhaus, E. (eds.) ALPSWS. CEUR Workshop Proceedings, vol. 287. CEUR-WS.org (2007)
108. Prud'hommeaux, E., Seaborne, A. (eds.): SPARQL Query Language for RDF. W3C Recommendation. World Wide Web Consortium, W3C (2008)
109. Pührer, J., Heymans, S., Eiter, T.: Dealing with Inconsistency When Combining Ontologies and Rules Using DL-Programs. In: Aroyo, L., Antoniou, G., Hyvönen, E., ten Teije, A., Stuckenschmidt, H., Cabral, L., Tudorache, T. (eds.) ESWC 2010. LNCS, vol. 6088, pp. 183–197. Springer, Heidelberg (2010)
110. Ramakrishnan, R.: Magic Templates: A Spellbinding Approach to Logic Programs. In: ICLP/SLP, pp. 140–159 (1988)
111. Ramakrishnan, R., Ullman, J.D.: A survey of deductive database systems. J. Log. Program. 23(2), 125–149 (1995)
112. Rohmer, J., Lescoeur, R., Kerisit, J.-M.: The Alexander Method - A Technique for The Processing of Recursive Axioms in Deductive Databases. New Generation Comput. 4(3), 273–285 (1986)
113. Rosati, R.: On the decidability and complexity of integrating ontologies and rules. J. Web Sem. 3(1), 61–73 (2005)
114. Rosati, R.: Semantic and Computational Advantages of the Safe Integration of Ontologies and Rules. In: Fages, F., Soliman, S. (eds.) PPSWR 2005. LNCS, vol. 3703, pp. 50–64. Springer, Heidelberg (2005)
115. Rosati, R.: Integrating Ontologies and Rules: Semantic and Computational Issues. In: Barahona, et al. (eds.) [9], pp. 128–151
116. Rosati, R.: On Combining Description Logic Ontologies and Nonrecursive Datalog Rules. In: Calvanese, D., Lausen, G. (eds.) RR 2008. LNCS, vol. 5341, pp. 13–27. Springer, Heidelberg (2008)
117. Saccà, D., Zaniolo, C.: Implementation of recursive queries for a data language based on pure horn logic. In: ICLP, pp. 104–135 (1987)
118. Schaffert, S.: Xcerpt: A Rule-Based Query and Transformation Language for the Web. Dissertation. PhD Thesis, Institute for Informatics, University of Munich (2004)
119. Schaffert, S., Bry, F.: Querying the Web Reconsidered: A Practical Introduction to Xcerpt. Extreme Markup Languages (2004)

120. Schenk, S., Staab, S.: Networked graphs: a declarative mechanism for SPARQL rules, SPARQL views and RDF data integration on the web. In: Huai, J., Chen, R., Hon, H.-W., Liu, Y., Ma, W.-Y., Tomkins, A., Zhang, X. (eds.) WWW, pp. 585–594. ACM, New York (2008)
121. Sintek, M., Decker, S.: Triple - an rdf query, inference, and transformation language. In: INAP, pp. 47–56 (2001)
122. Sintek, M., Decker, S.: Triple - a query, inference, and transformation language for the semantic web. In: Horrocks, I., Hendler, J. (eds.) ISWC 2002. LNCS, vol. 2342, pp. 364–378. Springer, Heidelberg (2002)
123. Smith, M.K., Welty, C., McGuinness, D.L. (eds.): OWL Web Ontology Language Guide. W3C Recommendation. World Wide Web Consortium, W3C (2004)
124. Swift, T.: Deduction in ontologies via asp. In: Lifschitz, V., Niemelä, I. (eds.) LPNMR 2004. LNCS (LNAI), vol. 2923, pp. 275–288. Springer, Heidelberg (2003)
125. ter Horst, H.J.: Combining RDF and Part of OWL with Rules: Semantics, Decidability, Complexity. In: Gil, Y., Motta, E., Benjamins, V.R., Musen, M.A. (eds.) ISWC 2005. LNCS, vol. 3729, pp. 668–684. Springer, Heidelberg (2005)
126. ter Horst, H.J.: Completeness, decidability and complexity of entailment for rdf schema and a semantic extension involving the owl vocabulary. J. Web Sem. 3(2-3), 79–115 (2005)
127. Ullman, J.D.: Principles of Database and Knowledge-Base Systems, vol. I. Computer Science Press, Rockville (1988)
128. Wilks, Y., Brewster, C.: Natural Language Processing as a Foundation of the Semantic Web. Foundations and Trends in Web Science 1(3-4), 199–327 (2009)
129. Wilks, Y., Brewster, C.: Natural Language Processing as a Foundation of the Semantic Web. Now Publishers Inc. (2009)
130. Yang, G., Kifer, M.: Reasoning about anonymous resources and meta statements on the semantic web. J. Data Semantics 1, 69–97 (2003)

# Datalog+/-: A Family of Languages for Ontology Querying

Andrea Calì[3,2], Georg Gottlob[1,2], Thomas Lukasiewicz[1], and Andreas Pieris[1]

[1] Computing Laboratory, University of Oxford, UK
[2] Oxford-Man Institute of Quantitative Finance, University of Oxford, UK
[3] Department of Computer Science, University of London, Birkbeck College, UK
`andrea@dcs.bbk.ac.uk`,
`{georg.gottlob,thomas.lukasiewicz,andreas.pieris}@comlab.ox.ac.uk`

**Abstract.** In ontology-based data access, an extensional database is enhanced by an ontology that generates new intensional knowledge which has to be considered when answering queries. In this setting, tractable data complexity (i.e., complexity w.r.t. the data only) of query answering is crucial, given the need to deal with large data sets. This paper summarizes results on a recently introduced family of Datalog-based languages, called Datalog+/-, which is a new framework for tractable ontology querying. Plain Datalog is extended by allowing existential quantifiers, the equality predicate, and the truth constant false to appear in rule heads. At the same time, the resulting language is syntactically restricted, so as to achieve decidability and even tractability.

## 1 Introduction

This paper is a survey of recently introduced variants of Datalog. On the one hand, Datalog is extended by allowing features such as existential quantifiers, the equality predicate, and the truth constant *false* to appear in rule heads. On the other hand, the resulting language is syntactically restricted, so as to achieve decidability, and in some relevant cases even tractability. The family of all such (existing and future) variants was dubbed *Datalog*$^{\pm}$ (also written Datalog+/- whenever appropriate). Before delving into this new language family, let us very briefly review the well-known Datalog language.

Datalog (see, e.g., [1]) has been used as a paradigmatic database programming and query language for over three decades. While Datalog is rarely used directly as a query language in corporate application contexts, the language has influenced the development of popular query languages such as SQL, whose newer versions allow one to express recursive queries. Moreover, Datalog has been used as an inference engine for knowledge processing within several software tools, and has recently gained popularity in the context of various applications, such as web data extraction [7,29,8], source code querying and program analysis [31], and modeling distributed systems [2].

A basic Datalog program consists of a set of universally quantified function-free Horn clauses. When writing a Datalog program, as usual in logic programming, we consider sets of rules to be conjunctions, use the comma for conjoining

O. de Moor et al. (Eds.): Datalog 2010, LNCS 6702, pp. 351–368, 2011.

atoms, and assume all variables of a rule to be universally quantified, while omitting the universal quantifiers. The predicate symbols appearing in such a program either refer to *extensional database (EDB) predicates*, whose values are given via an input database, or to *intensional database (IDB) predicates*, whose values are computed by the program. In standard Datalog, EDB predicate symbols may appear in rule bodies only.

*Example 1.* Consider a program that takes as input EDB a directed graph, given by a binary edge relation $e$, plus a set of special vertices of this graph given by a unary relation $s$. The recursive Datalog program

$$s(X) \rightarrow r(X),$$
$$r(X), e(X, Y) \rightarrow r(Y)$$

computes the set $r$ of all vertices in the graph reachable via a directed path of nonnegative length from special vertices, while the recursive program

$$e(X, Y) \rightarrow c(X, Y),$$
$$e(X, Y), c(Y, Z) \rightarrow c(X, Z)$$

computes the transitive closure $c$ of the binary relation $e$.     ∎

A *Boolean conjunctive query (BCQ)* is an existentially quantified conjunction of atoms. For example, the BCQ $q$ of whether a directed triangle is reachable in the graph $e$ of Example 1 from the set $s$ of special vertices can be written as $\exists X \exists Y \exists Z \, r(X), r(Y), r(Z), e(X, Y), e(Y, Z), e(Z, X)$. Alternatively, $q$ can be represented as a Datalog rule with a head predicate of arity 0, i.e., a Boolean head predicate: $r(X), r(Y), r(Z), e(X, Y), e(Y, Z), e(Z, X) \rightarrow triangle$. A *conjunctive query (CQ)* is defined similarly to a BCQ but has free variables defining the output tuples (see Section 2).

Given an EDB $D$ and a Datalog program $\Sigma$, let us denote by $D \cup \Sigma$ the logical theory containing both the facts (i.e., ground atoms) of $D$ and the rules of $\Sigma$. It is well-known that $D \cup \Sigma$ has a unique *least Herbrand model* $LHM(D \cup \Sigma)$ which consists of all ground atoms $\underline{a}$ such that $D \cup \Sigma \models \underline{a}$. This model can be computed by a least fixpoint iteration starting from the EDB $D$ and adding at each iteration step all new facts generated by a single rule application. We say that a BCQ $q$ evaluates to true over $D$ and $\Sigma$ iff $D \cup \Sigma \models q$. This is equivalent to the existence of a homomorphism from (the atoms of) $q$ to $LHM(D \cup \Sigma)$.

Note that the unique least Herbrand model of a Datalog program and a database is always finite, and all values appearing in it are from the *active domain* of the given EDB, i.e., all values that appear as arguments of EDB facts or that are explicitly mentioned in the Datalog program. For ontology querying, however, it would be desirable that a Datalog extension could be able to express the existence of certain values that are not necessarily from the active domain of the EDB. This can be achieved by allowing existentially quantified variables in rule heads [36]. Let us give a brief example, and refer to Section 6, and to the references therein, for more detailed treatment.

*Description logics (DLs)* [4] are used to formalize so-called ontological knowledge about relationships between objects, entities, and classes in a certain application domain. For example, we could express that every person has exactly one father who, moreover, is himself a person, by the following DL clauses, where *person* is a set of objects whose initial value is specified in the form of an EDB relation, called *concept*, and *father* is a binary relation, a so-called *role* in DL terminology: *(i) person* $\sqsubseteq \exists father$, *(ii)* $\exists father^- \sqsubseteq person$, *(iii)* (funct *father*). In an appropriate version of Datalog$^\pm$, the same can be expressed as:

$$
\begin{aligned}
person(X) &\rightarrow \exists Y\, father(X, Y), \\
father(X, Y) &\rightarrow person(Y), \\
father(X, Y), father(X, Y') &\rightarrow Y = Y'.
\end{aligned}
$$

Note that here the relation *person*, which is supplied in the input with an initial value, is actually modified. Therefore, we no longer require (as in standard Datalog) that EDB relation symbols cannot occur in rule heads.

DLs usually rely on classical first-order semantics, and so arbitrary (finite or infinite) models are considered. In the above example, models with infinite chains of ancestors are perfectly legal. Rather than "materializing" such models, i.e., computing and storing them, we are interested in reasoning and query answering. For example, whenever the initial value of *person* is nonempty, then the BCQ $\exists X \exists Y \exists Z\, father(X, Y), father(Y, Z)$ will evaluate to *true*, while the query $\exists X \exists Y\, father(X, Y), father(Y, X)$ to *false* since it is false in some models.

In summary, as we have briefly tried to sketch, ontology querying (and possibly a number of other applications such as Data Exchange and Web Data Extraction—for more details we refer the reader to [15]) could possibly profit from appropriate forms of Datalog extended by the possibility of using rules with existential quantifiers in their heads (such rules are known as *tuple-generating dependencies (TGDs)*, and they capture the well-known *inclusion dependencies*—see, e.g., [1]), and by several additional features such as, for example, equality in rule heads (such rules are known as *equality-generating dependencies (EGDs)*, and they capture the well-known *functional dependencies*—see, e.g., [1]).

Unfortunately, already for sets of TGDs alone, most basic reasoning and query answering problems are undecidable. In particular, given a database $D$ and a set $\Sigma$ of TGDs, checking whether $D \cup \Sigma \models q$ for a ground fact $q$ is undecidable [9]. Worse than that, undecidability holds even in case both $q$ and $\Sigma$ are *fixed*, and only $D$ is given as input [11]. It is thus important to identify large classes of formalisms for rule sets $\Sigma$ that *(i)* are based on Datalog, and thus enable a modular rule-based style of knowledge representation, *(ii)* are syntactical fragments of first-order logic so that answering a BCQ $q$ under a database $D$ and $\Sigma$ is equivalent to the classical entailment check $D \cup \Sigma \models q$, *(iii)* are expressive enough for being useful in real applications, *(iv)* have decidable query answering, and finally *(v)* query answering is tractable in *data complexity*, that is, the complexity calculated by considering only the data as part of the input, whereas $q$ and $\Sigma$ are fixed; this type of complexity is an important measure, because we can realistically assume that the EDB $D$ is the only really large object in the input. This paper reports on some recent languages that fulfill these criteria. We dubbed the family of such languages Datalog$^\pm$, because, as already explained, they add features to Datalog, and on the other hand make some syntactical restrictions.

One of the main tools used for proving favorable results about a number of Datalog$^\pm$ languages is the *chase procedure* [34,32]. The chase is an algorithm that, roughly speaking, executes the rules of a Datalog$^\pm$ program $\Sigma$ on input $D$ in a forward chaining manner by inferring new atoms, creating null values (Skolem constants) whenever an existential quantifier needs to be satisfied, and unifying such nulls with other nulls or with non-null values whenever required by an equality atom in the head of a rule whose body has become satisfied. The key property of the chase procedure is that, independently of the order in which rules are processed, the result $chase(D, \Sigma)$ is a universal model of $D \cup \Sigma$, i.e., an "initial" model which can be homomorphically embedded into every other model (see, e.g., [28]). As a consequence, for each BCQ $q$, $D \cup \Sigma \models q$ iff $chase(D, \Sigma) \models q$ iff there is a homomorphism from (the atoms of) $q$ to $chase(D, \Sigma)$.

The chase procedure may terminate or not. The most notable syntactic restriction guaranteeing chase termination is *weak acyclicity* of TGDs, for which we refer the reader to the landmark paper [26]. More general syntactic restrictions were studied in [25,35]. However, this is not appropriate for ontology querying. Fortunately, even in case the chase does not terminate and has an infinite result, it is a useful tool for studying query answering, since in relevant cases, it is sufficient to execute the chase up to a certain finite level (or derivation depth) for being able to answer a BCQ.

Section 3 reports on the class of *guarded* TGDs, where each rule body is required to have an atom that covers all body variables of the rule. For instance, the first Datalog program in Example 1 is guarded, while the second one is not. Guarded TGDs ensure polynomial time data complexity of query answering, even though the chase may be infinite. We then consider the even more restricted class of *linear* TGDs, for which query answering is *first-order rewritable* which means that $q$ and $\Sigma$ can be transformed into a first-order query $q_\Sigma$ such that $D \models q_\Sigma$ iff $D \cup \Sigma \models q$. This property, introduced in [20] in the context of DLs, is essential if $D$ is a very large database. It means that query answering can be deferred to a standard query language such as (basic, non-recursive) SQL.

Stickiness, a completely different paradigm for decidable and tractable query answering is discussed in Section 4. Let us give a very informal explanation. First, stickiness requires that every TGD $\sigma$ that has a double occurrence of a variable $X$ in the rule body, has at least one occurrence of $X$ in the rule head. Further, whenever such a TGD fires and produces a new atom $\underline{a}$ that has a value $v$ in place of the variable $X$, then the value $v$ is never lost by any derivation sequence that uses chase steps (i.e., forward chaining) for producing new atoms, and that involves $\underline{a}$. In other words, every value that arises in a new atom $\underline{a}$ through a *join* in a rule body must be present in all further atoms derived from $\underline{a}$. We will introduce stickiness by a syntactic criterion that is easily testable.

In Section 5, we first deal with *negative constraints*, i.e., rules whose head is the truth constant *false* denoted by $\bot$. It turns out that negative constraints come for free, and can be used without any increase of complexity. The reason is that checking whether a rule of the form $\phi(\mathbf{X}) \to \bot$ is satisfied by a database $D$ given a Datalog$^\pm$ program $\Sigma$ is tantamount to showing that $D \cup \Sigma \not\models \phi(\mathbf{X})$, i.e., to the evaluation of a BCQ. We then proceed by drawing our attention to equality-generating dependencies (EGDs) that we would like to use together with TGDs. Unfortunately, as well-known in database theory, query answering becomes undecidable even when putting together some extremely week forms of TGDs and EGDs such as inclusion dependencies and functional dependencies [23]. In this paper, we therefore concentrate on a very simple, nevertheless extremely useful class of EGDs, namely *key dependencies* (or simply *keys*). We discuss semantic and syntactic conditions ensuring that keys are usable without destroying decidability and tractability.

Section 6 briefly describes how highly relevant DLs such as *DL-Lite$_\mathcal{F}$* and *DL-Lite$_\mathcal{R}$* can be modeled in the Datalog$^\pm$ framework. We conclude with a brief outlook on further research.

## 2   Preliminaries

In this section we recall some basics on databases, (Boolean) conjunctive queries, tuple-generating dependencies, and the TGD chase procedure.

**General.** We define the following pairwise disjoint (infinite) sets of symbols: a set $\Gamma$ of *constants* (constitute the "normal" domain of a database), and a set $\Gamma_N$ of *labeled nulls* (used as placeholders for unknown values, and thus can be also seen as variables). Different constants represent different values (*unique name assumption*), while different nulls may represent the same value. A lexicographic order is defined on $\Gamma \cup \Gamma_N$, such that every value in $\Gamma_N$ follows all those in $\Gamma$. We denote by $\mathbf{X}$ sequences of variables $X_1, \ldots, X_k$, with $k \geqslant 0$.

A *relational schema* $\mathcal{R}$ (or simply *schema*) is a set of *relational symbols* (or *predicates*), each with its associated arity. We write $r/n$ to denote that the predicate $r$ has arity $n$. A *position* $r[i]$ (in a schema $\mathcal{R}$) is identified by a predicate $r \in \mathcal{R}$ and its $i$-th argument (or attribute). A *term* $t$ is a constant, null, or variable. An *atomic formula* (or simply *atom*) has the form $r(t_1, \ldots, t_n)$, where $r/n$ is a relation, and $t_1, \ldots, t_n$ are terms. For an atom $\underline{a}$, we denote by $dom(\underline{a})$ the set of its terms. This notation naturally extends to sets and conjunctions of atoms. Conjunctions of atoms are often identified with the sets of their atoms.

A *substitution* from one set of symbols $S_1$ to another set of symbols $S_2$ is a function $h : S_1 \to S_2$ defined as follows: *(i)* $\varnothing$ is a substitution (empty substitution), *(ii)* if $h$ is a substitution, then $h \cup \{X \to Y\}$ is a substitution, where $X \in S_1$ and $Y \in S_2$, and $h$ does not already contain some $X \to Z$ with $Y \neq Z$. If $X \to Y \in h$, then we write $h(X) = Y$. A *homomorphism* from a set of atoms $A_1$ to a set of atoms $A_2$, both over the same schema $\mathcal{R}$, is a substitution $h : dom(A_1) \to dom(A_2)$ such that: *(i)* if $t \in \Gamma$, then $h(t) = t$, and *(ii)* if $r(t_1, \ldots, t_n)$ is in $A_1$, then $h(r(t_1, \ldots, t_n)) = r(h(t_1), \ldots, h(t_n))$ is in $A_2$. The notion of homomorphism naturally extends to conjunctions of atoms.

**Databases and Queries.** A *database (instance)* $D$ for a schema $\mathcal{R}$ is a (possibly infinite) set of atoms of the form $r(\mathbf{t})$ (a.k.a. *facts*), where $r/n \in \mathcal{R}$ and $\mathbf{t} \in (\Gamma \cup \Gamma_N)^n$. We denote as $r(D)$ the set $\{\mathbf{t} \mid r(\mathbf{t}) \in D\}$. A *conjunctive query (CQ)* $q$ of arity $n$ over a schema $\mathcal{R}$, written as $q/n$, has the form $q(\mathbf{X}) = \exists \mathbf{Y} \varphi(\mathbf{X}, \mathbf{Y})$, where $\varphi(\mathbf{X}, \mathbf{Y})$ is a conjunction of atoms over $\mathcal{R}$, $\mathbf{X}$ and $\mathbf{Y}$ are sequences of variables or constants in $\Gamma$, and the arity of $q$ is $n$. $\varphi(\mathbf{X}, \mathbf{Y})$ is called the *body* of $q$, denoted as $body(q)$. A *Boolean CQ (BCQ)* is a CQ of zero arity. The *answer* to a CQ $q/n$ over an instance $I$, denoted as $q(I)$, is the set of all $n$-tuples $\mathbf{t} \in \Gamma^n$ for which there exists a homomorphism $h : \mathbf{X} \cup \mathbf{Y} \to \Gamma \cup \Gamma_N$ such that $h(\varphi(\mathbf{X}, \mathbf{Y})) \subseteq I$ and $h(\mathbf{X}) = \mathbf{t}$. A BCQ has only the empty tuple $\langle \rangle$ as possible answer, in which case it is said that has positive answer. Formally, a BCQ has *positive* answer over $I$, denoted as $I \models q$, iff $\langle \rangle \in q(I)$.

**Tuple-Generating Dependencies.** A *tuple-generating dependency (TGD)* $\sigma$ over a schema $\mathcal{R}$ is a first-order formula $\forall \mathbf{X} \forall \mathbf{Y} \, \varphi(\mathbf{X}, \mathbf{Y}) \to \exists \mathbf{Z} \, \psi(\mathbf{X}, \mathbf{Z})$, where $\varphi(\mathbf{X}, \mathbf{Y})$ and $\psi(\mathbf{X}, \mathbf{Z})$ are conjunctions of atoms over $\mathcal{R}$, called the *body* and the *head* of $\sigma$, denoted as $body(\sigma)$ and $head(\sigma)$, respectively. Henceforth, to avoid notational clutter, we will omit the universal quantifiers in TGDs. Such $\sigma$ is satisfied by an instance $I$ for $\mathcal{R}$ iff, whenever there exists a homomorphism $h$ such that $h(\varphi(\mathbf{X}, \mathbf{Y})) \subseteq I$, there exists an extension $h'$ of $h$ (i.e., $h' \supseteq h$) such that $h'(\psi(\mathbf{X}, \mathbf{Z})) \subseteq I$.

We now define the notion of *query answering* under TGDs. Given a database $D$ for $\mathcal{R}$, and a set $\Sigma$ of TGDs over $\mathcal{R}$, the *models* of $D$ w.r.t. $\Sigma$, denoted as $mods(D, \Sigma)$, is the set of all instances $I$ such that $I \models D \cup \Sigma$, which means that $I \supseteq D$ and $I$ satisfies $\Sigma$. The *answer* to a CQ $q$ w.r.t. $D$ and $\Sigma$, denoted as $ans(q, D, \Sigma)$, is the set $\{\mathbf{t} \mid \mathbf{t} \in q(I) \text{ for each } I \in mods(D, \Sigma)\}$. The *answer* to a BCQ $q$ w.r.t. $D$ and $\Sigma$ is *positive*, denoted as $D \cup \Sigma \models q$, iff $ans(q, D, \Sigma) \neq \varnothing$. Note that query answering under general TGDs is undecidable [9], even when the schema and the set of TGDs are fixed [11].

The *combined complexity* of query answering is the complexity of determining whether a given tuple is among the answers to a query $q$ w.r.t a database $D$ and a set $\Sigma$ of TGDs, where $q$, $D$ and $\Sigma$ are part of the input. The *data complexity* is the complexity of the same problem, where $q$ and $\Sigma$ are considered fixed, and only $D$ is part of the input. The latter complexity is the most important in the context of data-oriented settings, where the data size is usually much larger than the size of the constraints and of the query.

The two problems of CQ and BCQ evaluation under TGDs are LOGSPACE-equivalent [22,32,27,25]. Henceforth, we thus focus only on the BCQ evaluation problem. All complexity results carry over to the other problems. We also recall that query answering under TGDs is equivalent to query answering under TGDs with singleton atoms in the head [11]. This is shown by means of a transformation from general TGDs to TGDs with single-atom heads [11]. Moreover, the transformation preserves the properties of the classes of TGDs that we consider in this survey. Therefore, all results for TGDs with singleton atoms in the head carry over to TGDs with multiple head-atoms. We thus always assume w.l.o.g. (unless stated otherwise) that every TGD has a singleton atom in its head.

**The TGD Chase.** The *chase procedure* (or simply *chase*) is a fundamental algorithmic tool introduced for checking implication of dependencies [34], and later for checking query containment [32]. Informally, the chase is a process of repairing a database w.r.t. a set of dependencies so that the resulted database satisfies the dependencies. We shall use the term chase interchangeably for both the procedure and its result. The chase works on an instance through the so-called TGD *chase rule*. The TGD chase rule comes in two equivalent fashions: *oblivious* and *restricted* [11], where the restricted one repairs TGDs only when they are not satisfied. In the sequel, we focus on the oblivious one for technical clarity. The TGD chase rule defined below is the building block of the chase.

TGD CHASE RULE: Consider a database $D$ for a schema $\mathcal{R}$, and a TGD $\sigma = \varphi(\mathbf{X}, \mathbf{Y}) \to \exists \mathbf{Z}\, \psi(\mathbf{X}, \mathbf{Z})$ over $\mathcal{R}$. If $\sigma$ is *applicable* to $D$, i.e., there exists a homomorphism $h$ such that $h(\varphi(\mathbf{X}, \mathbf{Y})) \subseteq D$ then: *(i)* define $h' \supseteq h$ such that $h'(Z_i) = z_i$, for each $Z_i \in \mathbf{Z}$, where $z_i \in \Gamma_N$ is a "fresh" labeled null not introduced before, and following lexicographically all those introduced so far, and *(ii)* add to $D$ the set of atoms in $h'(\psi(\mathbf{X}, \mathbf{Z}))$ if not already in $D$.

Given a database $D$ and a set of TGDs $\Sigma$, the chase algorithm for $D$ and $\Sigma$ consists of an exhaustive application of the TGD chase rule in a breadth-first fashion, which leads as result to a (possibly infinite) chase for $D$ and $\Sigma$, denoted as $chase(D, \Sigma)$. For the formal definition of the chase algorithm we refer the reader to [12]. The (possibly infinite) chase for $D$ and $\Sigma$ is a *universal model* of $D$ w.r.t. $\Sigma$, i.e., for each instance $I \in mods(D, \Sigma)$, there exists a homomorphism from $chase(D, \Sigma)$ to $I$ [26,25]. Using this fact it can be shown that for a BCQ $q$, $D \cup \Sigma \models q$ iff $chase(D, \Sigma) \models q$.

# 3 Guarded and Linear Datalog$^{\pm}$

Clearly, for ontology querying purposes, we do not want to limit our attention to cases where the chase terminates, but consider cases where the chase produces an infinite universal solution, and where, in general, no finite universal solution exists. Unfortunately, as already mentioned, query answering is undecidable in such cases, and we are looking for decidable subclasses. In this section we present the languages *guarded* and *linear Datalog$^{\pm}$*.

## 3.1 Guarded Datalog$^{\pm}$

We first discuss the class of *guarded* TGDs, which forms the language *guarded Datalog$^{\pm}$*, as a special class of TGDs relative to which query answering is decidable, and even tractable in data complexity. Queries relative to such TGDs can be evaluated on a finite part of the chase, which is of constant size when the query and the TGDs are fixed.

A TGD $\sigma$ is *guarded* iff it contains an atom in its body that contains all the universally quantified variables of $\sigma$. The leftmost such atom is the *guard atom* (or *guard*) of $\sigma$. The non-guard atoms in the body of $\sigma$ are the *side atoms* of $\sigma$. For example, the TGD $r(X, Y), s(Y, X, Z) \to \exists W\, s(Z, X, W)$ is guarded (via the

guard $s(Y, X, Z)$), while the TGD $r(X, Y), r(Y, Z) \rightarrow r(X, Z)$ is not guarded.
Note that sets of guarded TGDs (with single-atom heads) are theories in the
*guarded fragment* of first-order logic [3].

**Combined Complexity.** The next theorem establishes combined complexity
results for conjunctive query evaluation under guarded Datalog$^\pm$. The EXPTIME
and 2EXPTIME-completeness results hold even if the input database is fixed.

**Theorem 1 ([11]).** *Let $D$ be a database for a schema $\mathcal{R}$, and $\Sigma$ be a set of
guarded TGDs over $\mathcal{R}$. Moreover, let $w$ be the maximum arity over all predicates
of $\mathcal{R}$, and let $|\mathcal{R}|$ denote the total number of predicate symbols. Then:*

a) *If $q$ is an atomic query, then deciding whether $D \cup \Sigma \models q$ is PTIME-complete
   in case both $w$ and $|\mathcal{R}|$ are bounded, and remains PTIME-complete even
   when $\Sigma$ is fixed. This problem is EXPTIME-complete if $w$ is bounded; and
   2EXPTIME-complete in general, even when $|\mathcal{R}|$ is bounded.*
b) *If $q$ is a general BCQ, deciding whether $D \cup \Sigma \models q$ is NP-complete in case
   both $w$ and $|\mathcal{R}|$ are bounded, and thus also in case of a fixed $\Sigma$. Checking
   whether $D \cup \Sigma \models q$ is EXPTIME-complete if $w$ is bounded; and 2EXPTIME-
   complete in general, even when $|\mathcal{R}|$ is bounded.*

**Data Complexity.** The data complexity of evaluating BCQs relative to guarded
TGDs turns out to be polynomial in general, and linear in the case of atomic
queries. In the sequel, let $\mathcal{R}$ be a relational schema, $D$ be a database for $\mathcal{R}$,
and $\Sigma$ be a set of guarded TGDs over $\mathcal{R}$. The *chase graph* for $D$ and $\Sigma$ is the
directed graph with $chase(D, \Sigma)$ be the set of nodes, and having an edge from $\underline{a}$
to $\underline{b}$ iff $\underline{b}$ is obtained from $\underline{a}$, and possibly other atoms, by a one-step application
of a TGD $\sigma \in \Sigma$. Here, we mark $\underline{a}$ as *guard* iff $\underline{a}$ is the guard of $\sigma$. The *guarded
chase forest* for $D$ and $\Sigma$ is the restriction of the chase graph for $D$ and $\Sigma$ to
all atoms marked as guards and their children. The *guarded chase* of level up to
$k \geqslant 0$ for $D$ and $\Sigma$, denoted as $g\text{-}chase^k(D, \Sigma)$, is the set of all atoms in the
forest of depth at most $k$.

It can be shown that (homomorphic images of) the query atoms are contained
in a finite, initial part of the guarded chase forest, whose size is determined only
by the query and $\mathcal{R}$. However, this does not yet assure that also the whole derivation of the query atoms are contained in such a portion of the guarded chase
forest. This slightly stronger property is captured by the following definition.

**Definition 1.** *We say that $\Sigma$ has the* bounded guard-depth property (BGDP)
*iff, for each database $D$ for $\mathcal{R}$ and for each BCQ $q$, whenever there is a homo-
morphism $\mu$ that maps $q$ into $chase(D, \Sigma)$, then there is a homomorphism $\lambda$ of
this kind such that all ancestors of $\lambda(q)$ in the chase graph for $D$ and $\Sigma$ are
contained in $g\text{-}chase^{\gamma_g}(D, \Sigma)$, where $\gamma_g$ depends only on $q$ and $\mathcal{R}$.*

It is possible to show that guarded TGDs have also this stronger bounded guard-
depth property. The proof is based on the observation that all side atoms that
are necessary in the derivation of the query atoms are contained in a finite, initial
portion of the guarded chase forest, whose size is determined only by the query

and $\mathcal{R}$ (which is slightly larger than the one for the query atoms only). By this result, deciding BCQs in the guarded case is in PTIME in the data complexity [11]. It is also hard for PTIME, as can be proved by reduction from propositional logic programming [13].

**Theorem 2 ([11,13]).** *Let $D$ be a database for a schema $\mathcal{R}$, $\Sigma$ be a set of guarded TGDs over $\mathcal{R}$, and $q$ be a BCQ over $\mathcal{R}$. Then, deciding whether $D \cup \Sigma \models q$ is PTIME-complete in data complexity. If $q$ is atomic, then the same problem is feasible in linear time in data complexity.*

**Extensions.** It is important to say that guarded TGDs can be enriched by *stratified negation*, where non-monotonic negations may be used in TGD bodies and queries. A natural stratified negation for query answering over ontologies, which is in general based on several strata of infinite models, is proposed in [13]. An expressive language, which forms a generalization of guarded Datalog$^{\pm}$, is *weakly-guarded Datalog$^{\pm}$* introduced in [11]. Roughly speaking, a set $\Sigma$ of TGDs is weakly-guarded iff, for each $\sigma \in \Sigma$, there exists an atom in $body(\sigma)$, called a *weak-guard*, that contains only the universally quantified variables of $\sigma$ that occur at positions where a "fresh" null of $\Gamma_N$ can appear during the construction of the chase (and not all the universally quantified variables).

## 3.2   Linear Datalog$^{\pm}$

*Linear Datalog$^{\pm}$* is a variant of guarded Datalog$^{\pm}$, where query answering is even first-order rewritable in data complexity. A TGD is *linear* iff it contains only a singleton body-atom. Linear Datalog$^{\pm}$ is strictly more expressive than inclusion dependencies; for example, the linear TGD $supervises(X, X) \rightarrow manager(X)$, which asserts that everyone supervising her/himself is a manager, is not expressible with inclusion dependencies.

**Combined Complexity.** Query answering under linear Datalog$^{\pm}$ is PSPACE-complete in combined complexity. This result can be seen by results in [32,39,21,30].

**Theorem 3 ([32,39,21,30]).** *Let $D$ be a database for a schema $\mathcal{R}$, $\Sigma$ be a set of linear TGDs over $\mathcal{R}$, and $q$ be a BCQ over $\mathcal{R}$. Then, deciding whether $D \cup \Sigma \models q$ is PSPACE-complete, even when $q$ is fixed.*

**Data Complexity.** Towards the data complexity, we start from some preliminaries. A class $\mathcal{C}$ of TGDs is *first-order rewritable* (or *FO-rewritable*) iff for every set of TGDs $\Sigma$ in $\mathcal{C}$, and for every BCQ $q$, there exists a first-order query $q_\Sigma$ such that, for every database $D$, it holds $D \cup \Sigma \models q$ iff $D \models q_\Sigma$. Since answering first-order queries is in the class AC$_0$ in data complexity [40], it immediately follows that for FO-rewritable TGDs, BCQ answering is in AC$_0$ in data complexity. The *chase of level up to* $k \geqslant 0$ for $D$ and $\Sigma$, denoted as $chase^k(D, \Sigma)$, is the set of all atoms of $chase(D, \Sigma)$ of derivation level at most $k$.

We next define the bounded derivation-depth property, which is strictly stronger than the bounded guard-depth property. Informally, this property says that (homomorphic images of) the query atoms along with their derivations are contained in a finite, initial portion of the chase graph (rather than the guarded chase forest), whose size is determined only by the query and $\mathcal{R}$.

**Definition 2.** *A set of TGDs $\Sigma$ over a schema $\mathcal{R}$ has the* bounded derivation-depth property (BDDP) *iff, for every database $D$ for $\mathcal{R}$, and for every BCQ $q$ over $\mathcal{R}$, whenever $D \cup \Sigma \models q$, then $chase^{\gamma_d}(D, \Sigma) \models q$, where $\gamma_d$ depends only on $q$ and $\mathcal{R}$.*

Clearly, in the case of linear TGDs, for every $\underline{a} \in chase(D, \Sigma)$, the subtree of $\underline{a}$ in the guarded chase forest is now determined only by $\underline{a}$ itself. Therefore, for a single atom, its depth coincides with the number of applications of the TGD chase rule that are necessary to generate it. That is, the guarded chase forest coincides with the chase graph. By this observation, we obtain that linear TGDs have the bounded derivation-depth property.

It is known that, given a class of TGDs $\mathcal{C}$, if $\mathcal{C}$ has the BDDP, then it is also FO-rewritable [13]. The main ideas behind the proof of this result are informally as follows. Since the derivation depth and the number of body atoms in TGDs is bounded, the number of all database ancestors of query atoms is also bounded. Thus, the number of all non-isomorphic sets of potential database ancestors with variables as arguments is also bounded. Take the existentially quantified conjunction of every such ancestor set where the query $q$ is answered positively. Then, the FO-rewriting of $q$ is the disjunction of all these formulas. As an immediate consequence we get the following result.

**Theorem 4 ([13]).** *BCQ answering under linear TGDs is in* AC$_0$ *in data complexity.*

## 4   Sticky Datalog$^\pm$

In this section, we present another language in the Datalog$^\pm$ family, which hinges on a paradigm that is very different from guardedness, and that we call *stickiness*. Stickiness, formally defined below by an efficiently testable condition involving variable-marking, is a sufficient condition that ensures the so-called *sticky property* of the chase, which is as follows. For every database $D$, assume that during the chase of $D$ under a set $\Sigma$ of TGDs, we apply a TGD $\sigma \in \Sigma$ that has a variable $V$ appearing more than once in its body; assume also that $V$ maps (via homomorphism) on the symbol $z$, and that by virtue of this application the atom $\underline{a}$ is introduced. In this case, for each atom $\underline{b} \in body(\sigma)$, we say that $\underline{a}$ is *derived* from $\underline{b}$. Then, we have that $z$ appears in $\underline{a}$, and in all atoms resulting from some chase derivation sequence starting from $\underline{a}$, "sticking" to them (hence the name "sticky TGDs") [16]. We now come to the formal definition.

**Definition 3.** *Consider a set $\Sigma$ of TGDs. We mark the variables that occur in the body of the TGDs of $\Sigma$ according to the following procedure. First, for each TGD $\sigma \in \Sigma$, and for each variable $V$ in body$(\sigma)$, if there exists an atom $\underline{a} \in head(\sigma)$ such that $V$ does not appear in $\underline{a}$, then we mark each occurrence* *of $V$ in body*($\sigma$). *Now, we apply exhaustively (i.e., until a fixpoint is reached) the following: for each pair* $\langle \sigma, \sigma' \rangle \in \Sigma \times \Sigma$ *(including the case* $\sigma = \sigma'$ *), if a universally quantified variable $V$ occurs in head*($\sigma$) *at positions* $\pi_1, \dots, \pi_m$, *for* $m \geqslant 1$, *and there exists an atom* $\underline{a} \in body(\sigma')$ *such that at each position* $\pi_1, \dots, \pi_m$ *a marked variable occurs, then we mark each occurrence of $V$ in body*($\sigma$). *We say that $\Sigma$ is* sticky *iff there is no TGD $\sigma \in \Sigma$ such that a marked variable occurs in body*($\sigma$) *mote than once.*

**Example 2.** Consider the following set $\Sigma$ of TGDs:

$$p(X, Y) \rightarrow \exists Z \, p(Y, Z)$$
$$p(X, Y) \rightarrow q(X)$$
$$q(X), q(Y) \rightarrow r(X, Y)$$
$$p(X, Y), p(Z, X) \rightarrow q(X).$$

Clearly, on an input database as simple as $\{p(a, a)\}$, the chase does not terminate. Moreover, $\Sigma$ is non-guarded. In fact, the third rule is a prime example of non-guardedness. Also, $\Sigma$ is not weakly-guarded, since at the positions $q[1]$ and $q[2]$ it is possible to have a "fresh" null of $\Gamma_N$ during the construction of the chase, and thus the third rule is not weakly-guarded w.r.t. $\Sigma$. However, $\Sigma$ is sticky since the only variable that occurs more than once in the body of a TGD, i.e., the variable $X$ in the body of the last TGD, is non-marked. ∎

Observe that in the chase for the database $D = \{p(a, a)\}$, and the sticky set $\Sigma$ of TGDs given in the above example, the extension of the relation $r$ is an infinite clique, and thus $chase(D, \Sigma)$ has infinite treewidth. Interestingly, stickiness is a sufficient property that ensures that the TGDs are a so-called *finite unification set*, an abstract decidability paradigm defined in [5]. The next theorem establishes combined complexity results for BCQ answering under sticky sets of TGDs.

**Theorem 5 ([16]).** *Let $D$ be a database for a schema $\mathcal{R}$, $\Sigma$ be a sticky set of TGDs over $\mathcal{R}$, and $q$ be a BCQ over $\mathcal{R}$. Then, deciding whether $D \cup \Sigma \models q$ is* NP-*complete if $\Sigma$ is fixed, and* EXPTIME-*complete in general.*

As shown in [16], the class of sticky sets of TGDs enjoys the BDDP (see Definition 2), and thus sticky sets of TGDs are FO-rewritable. The next result follows immediately.

**Theorem 6 ([16]).** *BCQ answering under sticky sets of TGDs is in* AC$_0$ *in data complexity.*

**Extensions.** Several convincing arguments for the usefulness of sticky sets of TGDs are given in [16]. However, they are not expressive enough for being able to model simple cases such as the TGD $r(X, Y, X) \rightarrow \exists Z \, s(Y, Z)$; clearly, the variable $X$ is marked, and thus the stickiness condition is violated. Note that the above rule falls in the FO-rewritable class of linear TGDs (see Subsection 3.2). A language that captures both linear and sticky Datalog$^{\pm}$, without losing the desirable property of FO-rewritability, is *sticky-join Datalog*$^\pm$ introduced in [17]. A more general class of TGDs, which is called *weakly-sticky* sets of TGDs, and which constitute *weakly-sticky Datalog*$^\pm$, is studied in [17]. Roughly, in a weakly-sticky set of TGDs, the variables that occur more than once in the body of a TGD are non-marked or occur at positions where a finite number of symbols can appear during the construction of the chase.

## 5  Additional Features

In this section we discuss how Datalog$^\pm$ can be extended with negative constraints and key dependencies.

**Negative Constraints.** A *negative constraint* (or simply *constraint*) is a first-order sentence of the form $\forall \mathbf{X} \, \phi(\mathbf{X}) \to \bot$, where $\phi(\mathbf{X})$ is a conjunction of atoms (with no restrictions) and $\bot$ is the constant *false*; the universal quantifier is omitted for brevity. As we shall see in Section 6, constraints are vital when representing ontologies.

*Example 3.* Suppose that the unary predicates $c$ and $c'$ represent two classes. The fact that these two classes have no common instances can be expressed by the constraint $c(X), c'(X) \to \bot$. Moreover, if the binary predicate $r$ represents a relationship, the fact that no instance of the class $c$ participates to the relationship $r$ (as the first component) can be stated by the constraint $c(X), r(X, Y) \to \bot$. ∎

Checking whether a set of constraints is satisfied by a database given a set of TGDs is tantamount to query answering [13]. In particular, given a set of TGDs $\Sigma_T$, a set of constraints $\Sigma_\bot$, and a database $D$, for each constraint $\nu = \phi(\mathbf{X}) \to \bot$ we evaluate the BCQ $q_\nu = \exists \mathbf{X} \, \phi(\mathbf{X})$ over $D \cup \Sigma_T$. If at least one of such queries answers positively, then $D \cup \Sigma_T \cup \Sigma_\bot \models \bot$ (i.e., the theory is inconsistent), and thus for every BCQ $q$ it holds that $D \cup \Sigma_T \cup \Sigma_\bot \models q$; otherwise, given a BCQ $q$, we have that $D \cup \Sigma_T \cup \Sigma_\bot \models q$ iff $D \cup \Sigma_T \models q$, i.e., we can answer $q$ by ignoring the constraints.

**Theorem 7 ([13]).** *Consider a database $D$ for a schema $\mathcal{R}$, a set $\Sigma_T$ of TGDs over $\mathcal{R}$, a set $\Sigma_\bot$ of constraints over $\mathcal{R}$, and a BCQ $q$ over $\mathcal{R}$. Then, $D \cup \Sigma_T \cup \Sigma_\bot \models q$ iff (i) $D \cup \Sigma_T \models q$ or (ii) $D \cup \Sigma_T \models q_\nu$, for some constraint $\nu \in \Sigma_\bot$.*

As an immediate consequence, constraints do not increase the complexity of BCQ answering under TGDs alone [13].

**Key Dependencies.** The addition of keys is more problematic than that of constraints, since the former easily makes query answering undecidable (see, e.g., [18]). For this reason, we consider a restricted class of keys, namely, *non-conflicting KDs*, which have a controlled interaction with TGDs, and thus decidability of query answering is guaranteed. Nonetheless, as we shall see in Section 6, this class is expressive enough for modeling ontologies.

A *key dependency (KD)* $\kappa$ is an assertion of the form $key(r) = \mathbf{A}$, where $r$ is a predicate symbol and $\mathbf{A}$ is a set of attributes of $r$. It is equivalent to the set of EGDs $\{r(\mathbf{X}, Y_1, \ldots, Y_m), r(\mathbf{X}, Y_1', \ldots, Y_m') \rightarrow Y_i = Y_i'\}_{1 \leqslant i \leqslant m}$, where the variables $\mathbf{X} = X_1, \ldots, X_n$ appear exactly at the attributes of $\mathbf{A}$ (w.l.o.g., the first $n$ of $r$). Such a KD $\kappa$ is *applicable* to a set of atoms $B$ iff there exist two (distinct) tuples $\mathbf{t_1}, \mathbf{t_2} \in \{\mathbf{t} \mid r(\mathbf{t}) \in B\}$ such that $\mathbf{t_1}[\mathbf{A}] = \mathbf{t_2}[\mathbf{A}]$, where $\mathbf{t}[\mathbf{A}]$ is the projection of tuple $\mathbf{t}$ over $\mathbf{A}$. If there exists an attribute $i \notin \mathbf{A}$ of $r$ such that $\mathbf{t_1}[i]$ and $\mathbf{t_2}[i]$ are two (distinct) constants of $\Gamma$, then there is a *hard violation* of $\kappa$, and the chase *fails*. Otherwise, the result of the application of $\kappa$ to $B$ is the set of tuples obtained by either replacing each occurrence of $\mathbf{t_1}[i]$ in $B$ with $\mathbf{t_2}[i]$, if $\mathbf{t_1}[i]$ follows lexicographically $\mathbf{t_2}[i]$, or vice-versa otherwise.

The chase of a database $D$, in the presence of two sets $\Sigma_T$ and $\Sigma_K$ of TGDs and KDs, respectively, is computed by iteratively applying: *(i)* a single TGD once, and *(ii)* the KDs as long as they are applicable.

We continue by introducing the semantic notion of separability, which formulates a controlled interaction of TGDs and KDs, so that the KDs do not increase the complexity of BCQ answering.

**Definition 4 ([18,13]).** *Let $\mathcal{R}$ be a relational schema. Consider a set $\Sigma = \Sigma_T \cup \Sigma_K$ over $\mathcal{R}$, where $\Sigma_T$ and $\Sigma_K$ are sets of TGDs and KDs, respectively. Then, $\Sigma$ is* separable *iff for every database $D$ for $\mathcal{R}$ the following conditions are satisfied: (i) if $chase(D, \Sigma)$ fails, then there is a hard violation of some KD $\kappa \in \Sigma_K$, when $\kappa$ is applied directly on $D$, and (ii) if there is no chase failure, then for every BCQ $q$ over $\mathcal{R}$, $chase(D, \Sigma) \models q$ iff $chase(D, \Sigma_T) \models q$.*

In the presence of separable sets of TGDs and KDs, the complexity of query answering is the same as in the presence of the TGDs alone. This is proved in [13], generalizing [18], by showing that in such a case we can first perform a chase failure check, which has the same complexity as BCQ answering, and then, if is negative, proceed with query answering under the TGDs alone.

We now give a sufficient syntactic condition for separability. The next definition generalizes the notion of *non-key-conflicting IDs* introduced in [18]. This condition is crucial for using TGDs to capture ontology languages, as we will show in Section 6. Notice that, in the following definition, TGDs are assumed to have single-atom heads; this is, as stated in Section 2, without loss of generality.

**Definition 5 ([13]).** *Let $\mathcal{R}$ be a relational schema. Consider a TGD $\sigma = \varphi(\mathbf{X}, \mathbf{Y}) \rightarrow \exists \mathbf{Z}\, r(\mathbf{X}, \mathbf{Z})$ over $\mathcal{R}$, and a set $\Sigma_K$ of KDs over $\mathcal{R}$. We say that $\Sigma_K$ is* non-conflicting (NC) *relative to $\sigma$ if for each $\kappa \in \Sigma_K$ of the form $key(r) = \mathbf{A}$, the following conditions are satisfied: (i) the set of the attributes of $r$ in $head(\sigma)$ where a universally quantified variable occurs is not a strict superset of $\mathbf{A}$, and (ii) each existentially quantified variable in $\sigma$ occurs just once. We say that $\Sigma_K$ is* NC relative to a set $\Sigma_T$ of TGDs iff $\Sigma_K$ is NC relative to every $\sigma \in \Sigma_T$.*

*Example 4.* Consider the TGD $\sigma$ of the form $p(X, Y) \rightarrow \exists Z\, r(X, Y, Z)$, and the KDs $\kappa_1 : key(r) = \{1, 2\}$ and $\kappa_2 : key(r) = \{1\}$. Clearly, the set of the $\forall$-attributes of $r$ in $head(\sigma)$ is $\mathbf{U} = \{1, 2\}$. Observe that $\{\kappa_1\}$ is NC relative to $\sigma$; roughly, every atom generated during the chase by applying $\sigma$ will have a "fresh" null of $\Gamma_N$ in some key attribute of $\kappa_1$, thus never firing this KD. On the contrary, $\{\kappa_2\}$ is not NC relative to $\sigma$ since $\mathbf{U} \supset \{1\}$. ∎

## 6    Ontology Querying

We now briefly describe how the description logics (DLs) $DL\text{-}Lite_{\mathcal{F}}$ and $DL\text{-}Lite_{\mathcal{R}}$ [20] can both be reduced to linear Datalog$^\pm$ with (negative) constraints and NC keys, called Datalog$^\pm_0$, and that the former are strictly less expressive than the latter. Note that $DL\text{-}Lite_{\mathcal{R}}$ is able to fully capture the (DL fragment of) RDF Schema [10], the vocabulary description language for RDF; see [24] for a translation. Note also that other DLs of the $DL\text{-}Lite$ family can be similarly translated to Datalog$^\pm_0$; for more details we refer the reader to [14].

Intuitively, DLs model a domain of interest in terms of concepts and roles, which represent classes of individuals and binary relations on classes of individuals, respectively. A DL knowledge base (or ontology) in $DL\text{-}Lite_{\mathcal{F}}$ encodes in particular subset relationships between concepts and between roles, the membership of individuals to concepts and of pairs of individuals to roles, and functional dependencies on roles. The following example illustrates some DL axioms in $DL\text{-}Lite_{\mathcal{F}}$ and their translation to Datalog$^\pm_0$.

*Example 5.* The following are some concept inclusion axioms, which informally express that *(i)* conference and journal papers are articles, *(ii)* conference papers are not journal papers, *(iii)* every scientist has a publication, *(iv)* isAuthorOf relates scientists and articles:

$$CPaper \sqsubseteq Article,\ JPaper \sqsubseteq Article,$$
$$CPaper \sqsubseteq \neg JPaper,\ Scientist \sqsubseteq \exists isAuthorOf,$$
$$\exists isAuthorOf \sqsubseteq Scientist,\ \exists isAuthorOf^- \sqsubseteq Article.$$

They are translated to the following TGDs and constraints (we identify atomic concepts and roles with their predicates):

$$CPaper(X) \rightarrow Article(X),$$
$$JPaper(X) \rightarrow Article(X),$$
$$CPaper(X), JPaper(X) \rightarrow \bot,$$
$$Scientist(X) \rightarrow \exists Z\ isAuthorOf(X, Z),$$
$$isAuthorOf(X, Y) \rightarrow Scientist(X),$$
$$isAuthorOf(Y, X) \rightarrow Article(X).$$

The following role inclusion and functionality axioms express that *(v)* isAuthorOf is the inverse of *hasAuthor*, and *(vi)* *hasFirstAuthor* is a functional binary relationship:

$$isAuthorOf^- \sqsubseteq hasAuthor,$$
$$hasAuthor^- \sqsubseteq isAuthorOf,$$
$$(\text{funct } hasFirstAuthor).$$

They are translated to the following TGDs and KDs:

$$isAuthorOf(Y, X) \rightarrow hasAuthor(X, Y),$$
$$hasAuthor(Y, X) \rightarrow isAuthorOf(X, Y),$$
$$hasFirstAuthor(X, Y), hasFirstAuthor(X, Y') \rightarrow Y = Y'.$$

The following concept and role memberships express that the individual $i_1$ is a scientist who authors the article $i_2$:

$$Scientist(i_1), \ isAuthorOf(i_1, i_2), \ Article(i_2).$$

They are translated to identical database atoms (where we also identify individuals with their constants). ∎

Formally, every knowledge base $\mathcal{K}$ in *DL-Lite$_\mathcal{F}$* or *DL-Lite$_\mathcal{R}$* is translated into a database $D_\mathcal{K}$, a set of TGDs $\Sigma_\mathcal{K}$, and a set of queries $Q_\mathcal{K}$ representing a set of KDs, which are in fact linear TGDs and NC keys, respectively. The next result shows that BCQs from knowledge bases in *DL-Lite$_\mathcal{F}$* and *DL-Lite$_\mathcal{R}$* can be reduced to BCQs in Datalog$_0^\pm$.

**Theorem 8 ([13]).** *Let $\mathcal{K}$ be a knowledge base in DL-Lite$_\mathcal{F}$ or DL-Lite$_\mathcal{R}$, and $q$ be a BCQ for $\mathcal{K}$. Then, $q$ holds in $\mathcal{K}$ iff either (i) $D_\mathcal{K} \cup \Sigma_\mathcal{K} \models q_c$, for some $q_c \in Q_\mathcal{K}$, or (ii) $D_\mathcal{K} \cup \Sigma_\mathcal{K} \models q$.*

Consequently, the satisfiability of knowledge bases in *DL-Lite$_\mathcal{F}$* and *DL-Lite$_\mathcal{R}$* can be reduced to BCQs in Datalog$_0^\pm$.

**Corollary 1 ([13]).** *Let $\mathcal{K}$ be a knowledge base in DL-Lite$_\mathcal{F}$ or DL-Lite$_\mathcal{R}$. Then, $\mathcal{K}$ is unsatisfiable iff $D_\mathcal{K} \cup \Sigma_\mathcal{K} \models q_c$, for some $q_c \in Q_\mathcal{K}$.*

The next result follows immediately from the fact that the simple linear TGD $r(X) \to s(X, X)$ is not expressible neither in *DL-Lite$_\mathcal{F}$* nor in *DL-Lite$_\mathcal{R}$* [13].

**Theorem 9 ([13]).** *Datalog$_0^\pm$ is strictly more expressive than both DL-Lite$_\mathcal{F}$ and DL-Lite$_\mathcal{R}$.*

Note that the TGDs used in our translation are in fact inclusion dependencies. Since a set of inclusion dependencies is trivially sticky, we have that also sticky Datalog$^\pm$ (plus negative constraints and non-conflicting keys) is strictly more general than both *DL-Lite$_\mathcal{F}$* and *DL-Lite$_\mathcal{R}$*.

# 7    Conclusion and Future Research

In this paper we reviewed a number of languages in the Datalog$^\pm$ family. These languages can be considered specifically-engineered (syntactic) fragments of first-order logic (possibly with non-monotonic negation) that are suited for ontological query answering. We find these languages rather attractive: they are simple, easy to understand, easy to analyze, decidable, and they have good complexity properties. Moreover, they are extremely versatile and expressive. In fact, we have shown that languages as simple as linear Datalog$^\pm$ with negative constraints and non-conflicting keys (both simple first-order features) can express very popular DLs. But unlike these DLs, the Datalog$^\pm$ languages are not restricted to a binary signature, and can be augmented, without problems and without additional complexity, by non-monotonic stratified negation, a desirable expressive feature not present in DLs.

Datalog$^{\pm}$ is still a young research topic, and there are many challenging research problems to be tackled. Some of the issues that we want to address in the near future follow.

- In general, we would like to extend our decidable fragments as much as possible. As a first step, we plan to combine the two tractability paradigms guardedness and stickiness in a smart way, so to obtain a formalism that generalizes both in the best possible way.
- More expressive DLs allow for restricted forms of *transitive closure* or of transitivity constraints. Transitive closure is easily expressible in Datalog (see Example 1), but only through non-guarded rules, whose addition to decidable sets of rules may easily lead to undecidability. We would like to study under which conditions closure can be safely added to various versions of Datalog$^{\pm}$.
- Finite controllability was shown recently for the guarded fragment of first-order logic [6], and thus holds for guarded TGDs (and it easily extends to the class of weakly-guarded TGDs). We plan to study this property in the context of sticky sets of TGDs.
- For non-finitely-controllable Datalog$^{\pm}$ languages, we would like to study the complexity of *query answering under finite models*. Pioneering work on finite model reasoning in the DL area was done in [37,38,33,19].
- For those logics where query answering is FO-rewritable, the resulting FO-query is usually very large. We plan to study the optimization of such FO-rewritings from both a theoretical and a practical point of view.

**Acknowledgments.** This work was supported by the European Research Council under the European Community's 7-th Framework Programme (FP7/2007-2013)/ERC grant no. 246858 – DIADEM. The authors also acknowledge support by the EPSRC project "Schema Mappings and Automated Services for Data Integration and Exchange" (EP/E010865/1), and by the German Research Foundation (DFG) under the Heisenberg Programme. Georg Gottlob's work was also supported by a Royal Society Wolfson Research Merit Award.

# References

1. Abiteboul, S., Hull, R., Vianu, V.: Foundations of Databases. Addison-Wesley, Reading (1995)
2. Alvaro, P., Marczak, W., Conway, N., Hellerstein, J.M., Maier, D., Sears, R.C.: Towards scalable architectures for clickstream data warehousing. Technical report, EECS Department, University of California, Berkeley (2009)
3. Andréka, H., van Benthem, J., Németi, I.: Modal languages and bounded fragments of predicate logic. J. Philosophical Logic 27, 217–274 (1998)
4. Baader, F., Calvanese, D., McGuinness, D.L., Nardi, D., Patel-Schneider, P.F. (eds.): The Description Logic Handbook: Theory, Implementation, and Applications. Cambridge University Press, Cambridge (2003)

5. Baget, J.-F., Leclère, M., Mugnier, M.-L., Salvat, E.: Extending decidable cases for rules with existential variables. In: Proc. of IJCAI, pp. 677–682 (2009)
6. Bárány, V., Gottlob, G., Otto, M.: Querying the guarded fragment. In: Proc. of LICS, pp. 1–10 (2010)
7. Baumgartner, R., Flesca, S., Gottlob, G.: Visual web information extraction with Lixto. In: Proc. of VLDB, pp. 119–128 (2001)
8. Baumgartner, R., Gatterbauer, W., Gottlob, G.: Monadic Datalog and the expressive power of web information extraction languages. In: Liu, L., Özsu, M.T. (eds.) Encyclopedia of Database Systems, pp. 3465–3471. Springer-Verlag New York, Inc., New York (2009)
9. Beeri, C., Vardi, M.Y.: The implication problem for data dependencies. In: Proc. of ICALP, pp. 73–85 (1981)
10. Brickley, D., Guha, R.V.: RDF vocabulary description language 1.0: RDF Schema. W3C Recommendation (2004), http://www.w3.org/TR/2004/REC-rdf-schema-20040210/
11. Calì, A., Gottlob, G., Kifer, M.: Taming the infinite chase: Query answering under expressive relational constraints. In: Proc. of KR, pp. 70–80 (2008)
12. Calì, A., Gottlob, G., Lukasiewicz, T.: Datalog$^\pm$: A unified approach to ontologies and integrity constraints. In: Proc. of ICDT, pp. 14–30 (2009)
13. Calì, A., Gottlob, G., Lukasiewicz, T.: A general Datalog-based framework for tractable query answering over ontologies. In: Proc. of PODS, pp. 77–86 (2009)
14. Calì, A., Gottlob, G., Lukasiewicz, T.: A general Datalog-based framework for tractable query answering over ontologies. Technical Report RR-10-21, Computing Laboratory, University of Oxford (2010)
15. Calì, A., Gottlob, G., Lukasiewicz, T., Marnette, B., Pieris, A.: Datalog+/-: A family of logical knowledge representation and query languages for new applications. In: Proc. of LICS, pp. 228–242 (2010)
16. Calì, A., Gottlob, G., Pieris, A.: Advanced processing for ontological queries. Proc. of VLDB 3(1), 554–565 (2010)
17. Calì, A., Gottlob, G., Pieris, A.: Query answering under non-guarded rules in Datalog+/-. In: Hitzler, P., Lukasiewicz, T. (eds.) RR 2010. LNCS, vol. 6333, pp. 1–17. Springer, Heidelberg (2010)
18. Calì, A., Lembo, D., Rosati, R.: On the decidability and complexity of query answering over inconsistent and incomplete databases. In: Proc. of PODS, pp. 260–271 (2003)
19. Calvanese, D.: Finite model reasoning in description logics. In: Proc. of KR, pp. 292–303 (1996)
20. Calvanese, D., De Giacomo, G., Lembo, D., Lenzerini, M., Rosati, R.: Tractable reasoning and efficient query answering in description logics: The DL-Lite family. J. Autom. Reasoning 39(3), 385–429 (2007)
21. Casanova, M.A., Fagin, R., Papadimitriou, C.H.: Inclusion dependencies and their interaction with functional dependencies. J. Comput. Syst. Sci. 28, 29–59 (1984)
22. Chandra, A.K., Merlin, P.M.: Optimal implementation of conjunctive queries in relational data bases. In: Proc. of STOC, pp. 77–90 (1977)
23. Chandra, A.K., Vardi, M.Y.: The implication problem for functional and inclusion dependencies. SIAM J. Comput. 14, 671–677 (1985)
24. de Bruijn, J., Heymans, S.: Logical foundations of (e)RDF(S): Complexity and reasoning. In: Aberer, K., Choi, K.-S., Noy, N., Allemang, D., Lee, K.-I., Nixon, L.J.B., Golbeck, J., Mika, P., Maynard, D., Mizoguchi, R., Schreiber, G., Cudré-Mauroux, P. (eds.) ASWC 2007 and ISWC 2007. LNCS, vol. 4825, pp. 86–99. Springer, Heidelberg (2007)

25. Deutsch, A., Nash, A., Remmel, J.B.: The chase revisisted. In: Proc. of PODS, pp. 149–158 (2008)
26. Fagin, R., Kolaitis, P.G., Miller, R.J., Popa, L.: Data exchange: Semantics and query answering. Theor. Comput. Sci. 336(1), 89–124 (2005)
27. Fagin, R., Kolaitis, P.G., Miller, R.J., Popa, L.: Data exchange: semantics and query answering. Theor. Comput. Sci. 336(1), 89–124 (2005)
28. Fagin, R., Kolaitis, P.G., Popa, L.: Data exchange: getting to the core. ACM Trans. Database Syst. 30(1), 174–210 (2005)
29. Gottlob, G., Koch, C.: Monadic Datalog and the expressive power of web information extraction languages. J. ACM 51(1), 71–113 (2004)
30. Gottlob, G., Papadimitriou, C.H.: On the complexity of single-rule Datalog queries. Inf. and Comput. 183(1), 104–122 (2003)
31. Hajiyev, E., Verbaere, M., de Moor, O.: *codeQuest:* scalable source code queries with datalog. In: Hu, Q. (ed.) ECOOP 2006. LNCS, vol. 4067, pp. 2–27. Springer, Heidelberg (2006)
32. Johnson, D.S., Klug, A.C.: Testing containment of conjunctive queries under functional and inclusion dependencies. J. Comput. Syst. Sci. 28(1), 167–189 (1984)
33. Lutz, C., Sattler, U., Tendera, L.: The complexity of finite model reasoning in description logics. Inf. and Comput. 199(1-2), 132–171 (2005)
34. Maier, D., Mendelzon, A.O., Sagiv, Y.: Testing implications of data dependencies. ACM Trans. Database Syst. 4(4), 455–469 (1979)
35. Marnette, B.: Generalized schema-mappings: From termination to tractability. In: Proc. of PODS, pp. 13–22 (2009)
36. Patel-Schneider, P.F., Horrocks, I.: A comparison of two modelling paradigms in the semantic web. J. Web Semantics 5(4), 240–250 (2007)
37. Rosati, R.: Finite model reasoning in *dl-lite*. In: Bechhofer, S., Hauswirth, M., Hoffmann, J., Koubarakis, M. (eds.) ESWC 2008. LNCS, vol. 5021, pp. 215–229. Springer, Heidelberg (2008)
38. Rosati, R.: On the finite controllability of conjunctive query answering in databases under open-world assumption. Journal of Computer and System Sciences (2010) (to appear)
39. Vardi, M.Y.: Personal communication reported in [32] (1984)
40. Vardi, M.Y.: On the complexity of bounded-variable queries. In: Proc. of PODS, pp. 266–276 (1995)

# Knowledge Representation Language P-Log – A Short Introduction

Michael Gelfond

Texas Tech University, USA
michael.gelfond@ttu.edu

**Abstract.** The paper gives a short informal introduction to the knowledge representation language P-Log. The language allows natural and elaboration tolerant representation of commonsense knowledge involving logic and probabilities. The logical framework of P-Log is *Answer Set Prolog* which can be viewed as a significant extension of Datalog. On the probabilistic side, the authors adopt the view which understands probabilistic reasoning as *commonsense reasoning about degrees of belief of a rational agent*, and use causal Bayes nets as P-log probabilistic foundation. Several examples are aimed at explaining the syntax and semantics of the language and the methodology of its use.

## 1 Introduction

The purpose of this paper is to give a short introduction to the knowledge representation (KR) language P-Log [4]. The goal of the P-Log designers was to create a KR-language allowing natural and elaboration tolerant representation of commonsense knowledge involving logic and probabilities. The logical framework of P-Log is *Answer Set Prolog* (ASP) — a language for knowledge representation and reasoning based on the answer set semantics (*aka* stable model semantics) of logic programs [8,9]. ASP has roots in declarative programing, the syntax and semantics of standard Prolog and Datalog, and non-monotonic logic. The semantics of ASP captures the notion of possible beliefs of a reasoner who adheres to the *rationality principle* which says that "*One shall not believe anything one is not forced to believe*". The entailment relation of ASP is non-monotonic[1], which facilitates a high degree of elaboration tolerance in ASP theories. ASP allows natural representation of defaults and their exceptions, causal relations (including effects of actions), agents' intentions and obligations, and other constructs of natural language. ASP has a number of efficient reasoning systems including those in [10,6,11], a well developed mathematical theory, and a well tested methodology of representing and using knowledge for computational tasks (see, for instance, [2]). This, together with the fact that two of the designers of P-Log came from the ASP community, made the choice of a logical foundation

---

[1] Roughly speaking, a language $L$ is *monotonic* if whenever $\Pi_1$ and $\Pi_2$ are collections of statements of $L$ with $\Pi_1 \subset \Pi_2$, and $W$ is a model of $\Pi_2$, then $W$ is a model of $\Pi_1$. A language which is not monotonic is said to be *non-monotonic*.

O. de Moor et al. (Eds.): Datalog 2010, LNCS 6702, pp. 369–383, 2011.

for P-Log comparatively easy. On the probabilistic side, the authors adopt the view which understands probabilistic reasoning as *commonsense reasoning about degrees of belief of a rational agent*. This matches well with the ASP-based logic side of the language. The ASP part of a P-Log program can be used for describing possible beliefs, while the probabilistic part would allow knowledge engineers to quantify the degrees of these beliefs. Another important influence on the design of P-Log is the separation between *doing* and *observing* and the notion of *Causal Bayesian Net* (see [12]).

## 2  Syntax and Semantics

In this section we give an informal introduction to the syntax and semantics of P-Log using a very simple example.

*Example 1.* [The jungle story]
*Imagine yourself lost in a dense jungle. A group of natives has found you and offered to help you survive, provided you can pass their test. They tell you they have an Urn of Decision from which you must choose a stone at random. (The urn is sufficiently wide for you to easily get access to every stone, but you are blindfolded so you cannot cheat.) You are told that the urn contains nine white stones and one black stone. Now you must choose a color. If the stone you draw matches the color you chose, the tribe will help you; otherwise, you can take your chances alone in the jungle. (The reasoning of the tribe is that they do not wish to help the exceptionally stupid, or the exceptionally unlucky.)*

It does not take knowledge of probability theory to realize that you will have a much better chance of obtaining their help if you choose *white* for the color of the stone. Our task is to *automate the simple commonsense argument which led to this conclusion*. To do that we need a language which will allow us to represent all the information relevant to the story, including the available choices. We will show how this can be done in P-Log.

The syntax of P-Log is rather similar to that of ASP. But, unlike ASP, the signature of a P-Log program is sorted, each function symbol comes with sorts for its parameters and its range, and atoms are properly-typed expressions of the form $a(\bar{t}) = y$, where $y$ is a constant from the range of a function symbol $a$. In addition to the usual ASP rules formed from such atoms (and equalities[2] and inequalities of elements of a sort), the P-Log programmer may declare some of the terms of the language (called *attributes*) to be random. These declarations and rules are called the *logical part* of a P-Log program, $\Pi$. This part defines sets of beliefs of a rational reasoner associated with $\Pi$, called *possible worlds* of $\Pi$. In addition program $\Pi$ may contain some information about the likelihood of different random events. This information together with the *principle of indifference which says that possible values of random attributes are assumed to be equally probable if we have no reason to prefer one of them to any other*, may be

---

[2] Equality in P-Log is understood as identity.

used to define a *probability function* $P_\Pi$ on the sets of possible worlds of $\Pi$. We will often refer to $P_\Pi$ as the probability function *induced* by $\Pi$.

We will illustrate the language by using it to formalize the rules of the jungle test from Example 1. Our formalization will not be the simplest possible. Instead we aim for modeling enough features for a reasonably complete description of P-Log syntax and semantics.

*Example 2.* [The jungle test rules in P-Log]
We start with defining *sorts* and *functions* of the program. For simplicity, we number the stones by integers from one to ten and introduce a sort

$stones = \{1, 2, 3, 4, 5, 6, 7, 8, 9, 10\}$.

The sort *colors* and a function *color* from *stones* to *colors* will be declared in P-Log as follows:

$colors = \{black, white\}$.

$color : stones \to colors$.

Without loss of generality we assume that the first stone is black — and hence the others are white. This will be specified by the rules:

$color(1) = black$.
$color(X) = white \leftarrow X \neq 1$.

The test requires the traveler to do two selections: selection of the color (*select_color*) and selection of the stone (*select_stone*). (Note that these selections can refer to a mental experiment conducted by a reasoner or to an actual physical selection. No distinction is necessary.) The traveler, whose reasoning we are trying to model will, hopefully, deliberate before making the first selection. The outcome of the second selection can not, of course, be determined by deliberation. But, independently of the strategy decided upon by the agent, both selections can be performed randomly, so we will declare them as random. The corresponding declarations in P-Log will look like this:

$select\_color : colors$.
$random(select\_color)$.

$select\_stone : stones$.
$random(select\_stone)$.

We will also need to declare

$help : boolean$.

The tribal laws will then be represented by the rules:

$help \ \leftarrow select\_stone = X,$
$\qquad\qquad color(X) = C,$
$\qquad\qquad select\_color = C.$
$\neg help \leftarrow select\_stone = X,$
$\qquad\qquad color(X) = C_1,$
$\qquad\qquad select\_color = C_2,$
$\qquad\qquad C_1 \neq C_2.$

(Here *help* and ¬*help* are used as shorthands for $help = true$ and $help = false$, respectively.) Let us denote the resulting program by $\Pi_{test}$.

We will use this program to explain the P-Log definition of possible worlds and probability function induced by a P-Log program. Due to space restrictions, we will omit some technical details which can be found in [4] and aim instead at conveying the general idea. The possible worlds of program $\Pi_{test}$ will be defined by simply translating it into the program $\tau(\Pi_{test})$ of Answer Set Prolog as follows.

For every attribute $a(\bar{t})$ with $range(a) = \{y_1, \ldots, y_n\}$, the mapping $\tau$

1. Represents the sort information by the corresponding set of atoms; e.g.

   $s = \{1, 2\}$ is turned into facts $s(1)$ and $s(2)$.
2. Replaces every rule of the form

   $$random(a(\bar{t})) \leftarrow body$$

   by

   $$a(\bar{t}) = y_1 \ or \ \ldots \ or \ a(\bar{t}) = y_n \leftarrow body, not \ ab(a(\bar{t})).$$

   where $ab$ is a new predicate symbol.
3. Replaces every occurrence of an atom $a(\bar{t}) = y$ by $a(\bar{t}, y)$, and expands the program by rules of the form

   $$\neg a(\bar{t}, Y_2) \leftarrow a(\bar{t}, Y_1), Y_1 \neq Y_2.$$

4. Grounds the resulting program by replacing variables with elements of the corresponding sorts.

The second item in the definition gives us an intuitive reading of randomness in P-Log; $random(a(\bar{t}))$ *says that, under normal circumstances, during a construction of a possible set of beliefs, the reasoner associated with the program must randomly select exactly one value of $a(\bar{t})$ from $a$'s range.*
Actually, P-Log allows more-general random selection rules which have the form:

$$random(a(\bar{t}) : \{X : p(X)\}) \leftarrow body.$$

This limits the selection of the value of $a(\bar{t})$ to elements of $a$'s range which satisfy property $p$. For each such rule, $\tau$ creates an additional ASP rule:

$$\leftarrow body, a(\bar{t}, Y), not \ p(Y), not \ ab(a(\bar{t})).$$

Answer sets of $\tau(\Pi)$ are called *possible worlds* of $\Pi$. (The new term is used to simply stay close to the traditional terminology of probability theory.)

It is easy to see that possible worlds of program $\Pi_{test}$ from Example 3 are

$W_1 = \{select\_color = white, select\_stone = 1, \neg help\}$
$W_i = \{select\_color = white, select\_stone = i, help\}$ for $1 < i \leq 10$.

$W_{11} = \{select\_color = black, select\_stone = 1, help\}$
$W_{10+i} = \{select\_color = black, select\_stone = i, \neg help\}$ for $1 < i \leq 10$.

We do not show $random(select\_color)$ and $random(select\_stone)$ which belong to every possible world. (We are also omitting sorts, negative information, and some inessential atoms.) Each possible world represents a possible set of beliefs of the reasoner associated with $\Pi_{test}$.

Now we explain how to define a (normalized) probabilistic *measure* on possible worlds of a P-Log program. This measure, a real number from the interval $[0, 1]$, represents the degree of a reasoner's belief that a possible world $W$ matches the true state of the world. As usual *the probability of a set of possible worlds is the sum of measures of its elements*, (and the probability of a proposition $F$ is the probability of the set of its models – possible worlds satisfying $F$).

We start with defining probability measure, say $\mu$, for the possible worlds of program $\Pi_{test}$ from Example 3. First notice that every possible world $W$ of $\Pi_{test}$ is determined by the reasoner's choice of the values of its random attributes $select\_color$ and $select\_stone$. This means that to compute the measure $\mu(W)$ assigned to a possible world $W$, we need to compute the probability of the reasoner making the corresponding selections of values. The *probability of the reasoner selecting value y of a random attribute a in the process of construction of W* will be denoted by $P(W, a = y)$. The computation of $P$ for our program $\Pi_{test}$ will be based on the *Principle of Indifference* — a commonsense rule which says that *possible values of random attribute are assumed to be equally probable if we have no reason to prefer one of them to any other*. Consider a possible world $W_1$ and random attribute $select\_color$. The reasoner constructing $W_1$ has two possible choices for his selection, and has no reason to prefer one to another. Hence, by the Principle of Indifference, $P(W_1, select\_color = white) = 1/2$. Similarly, the reasoner has ten different choices for the value of $select\_color$ and hence $P(W_1, select\_stone = 1) = 1/10$. To compute the probability measure $\mu(W_1)$, we need to compute the probability of the agent making both of these selections. Since the selections are independent from each other, we simply multiply their probabilities: $\mu(W_1) = 1/2 \times 1/10 = 1/20$. (In the general case, the sum of measures of possible worlds may not sum up to 1; in that case it should be normalized in the usual manner.) Clearly a similar argument works for other possible worlds and hence, for every $W$, $\mu(W) = 1/20$. Since the proposition $select\_color = white$ is true in 18 of these worlds we, as expected, have that

$P_{\Pi_{test}}(select\_color = white \wedge help) = 0.05 \times 9 = 0.45$ and
$P_{\Pi_{test}}(select\_color = black \wedge help) = 0.05 \times 1 = 0.05$.

The above construction is rather general. It forms the basis of the definition of probabilistic measure for P-Log programs not containing any specific information about probabilities of outcomes of the program selections. In such cases the probabilistic measure is assigned according to the Indifference Principle. In some cases, however, the reasoner has some additional information about plausibility of various values of the random selection process. To show how the semantics of a P-Log program can be expanded to this case, we consider a slight modification of our program $\Pi_{test}$. Let us assume that *the traveler from Example 1 came from a culture in which the white color is associated with death. A statistical study demonstrated that, given a choice between white and black, the people from this culture select black 8 out of 10 times.*

To incorporate this information into our program, we need a new syntactic construct — *causal probability atom*, or *pr-atom*. A *pr*-atom takes the form[3]

$$pr(a(\bar{t}) = y|_c B) = v$$

where $a(\bar{t})$ is a random attribute, $B$ a conjunction of literals, $v \in [0,1]$, and $y$ is a possible value of $a(\bar{t})$. The "causal stroke" '$|_c$' and the "rule body" $B$ may be omitted in case $B$ is empty. The statement says that *if the value of $a(\bar{t})$ is selected at random, and $B$ holds, then the probability that the process of selection causes $a(\bar{t}) = y$ is $v$.*

We can use the new construct to add the knowledge of the statistics about the color preference to $\Pi_{test}$. We simply add the statement

$pr(select\_color = black) = 0.8$

Clearly, the new program, $\Pi'_{test}$, has the same possible worlds as $\Pi_{test}$. However, the probabilistic measure $\mu'$ of the new program will be different. As before, each possible world is determined by the corresponding random selections. Now the probability, $P(W, select\_color = white)$, of the reasoner selecting value *white* in the process of construction of possible world $W$ will be equal to 0.2; $P(W, select\_color = black)$ will be equal to 0.8. This means that for every $1 \le i \le 10$, $\mu'(W_i) = 0.2 \times 0.1 = 0.02$. Similarly, for every $10 \le i \le 20$, $\mu'(W_i) = 0.8 \times 0.1 = 0.08$. Thus

$P_{\Pi_{test'}}(select\_color = white \wedge help) = 0.02 \times 9 = 0.18$, while
$P_{\Pi_{test'}}(select\_color = black \wedge help) = 0.08 \times 1 = 0.08$.

Even though the advantages of not doing a random selection are less obvious, some deliberation may still substantially improve the traveler's chances of survival.

To complete our description of syntax and semantics of P-Log, let us discuss how the traveler could use his knowledge base to decide on the right choice of color. The task, of course, is to find out what choice of color maximizes his chances of getting help. We adopt a solution of this type of problem suggested in [12]. The book introduces the notion of *deliberate action*, $do(a(\bar{t}) = y)$, which stops normally random attribute $a(\bar{t})$ from being random and sets its value to $y$. It also uses specification of probability via graphical models to define probability, $P(G \mid do(a(\bar{t}) = y))$ of a goal $G$ conditioned on the deliberate assignment of $y$ to $a(\bar{t})$. (The definition involves *surgery* of the graph consisting of cutting some of its causal links. ) It is important to notice that $P(G \mid do(a(\bar{t}) = y))$ may differ

---

[3] The actual construct of P-Log is slightly more general. The definition given here works for P-Log programs containing exactly one rule defining an attribute $a$ as random.

substantially from a more traditional $P(G \mid a(\bar{t}) = y)$. The later conditions $G$ on the *observation* of the outcome of a random experiments. (In fact the difference between doing and observing was one of the most important lessons learned by the authors of P-Log from reading [12].)

To solve the problem of our traveler, the method from [12] suggests representing the tribal test as a causal Bayesian net or a set of structural equations defining a probability function $P$ and computing $P(help \mid do(select\_color = white)$ and $P(help \mid do(select\_color = black)$. Using $do$ allows us to ask the question "What will the probability of obtaining help be if the reasoner chooses white (or black)?" Clearly the former will be a larger number and, hence, the traveler will know that selecting *white* will increase his chances of getting help.

To model this type of reasoning in P-Log, we first need to expand its syntax by allowing statements

$$do((a(\bar{t}) = y))$$

and

$$obs(a(\bar{t}) = y))$$

$$obs(a(\bar{t}) \neq y))$$

The mapping $\tau$ defined above will also be expanded as follows: for every P-Log program $\Pi$, ASP program $\tau(\Pi)$ will contain rules:

$$\leftarrow obs(a(\bar{t}) = y)), not\ a(\bar{t}, y)$$

$$\leftarrow obs(a(\bar{t}) \neq y)), not\ \neg a(\bar{t}, y)$$

$$a(\bar{t}, y) \leftarrow do(a(\bar{t}) = y)$$

$$ab(a(\bar{t})) \leftarrow do(a(\bar{t}) = y)$$

The first two rules guarantee that no possible world of the program fails to satisfy observations. The third specifies that $do(a(\bar{t}) = y)$ indeed assigns the value $y$ to $a(\bar{t})$. The fourth is used to stop $a(\bar{t})$ from being random. The definition of possible world does not change. We slightly refine the definition of measure; $\mu(W)$ is defined as the product $P(W, a(\bar{t}) = y)$ for all $a(\bar{t}) = y$ such that $random(a(\bar{t}) = y) \in W$. (The last condition was not explicitly mentioned before).

Now we can define the P-Log analogue of Pearl's conditioning on actions. Given a probability function $P_\Pi$ induced by P-Log program $\Pi$:

$$P_\Pi(G \mid do(a(\bar{t}) = y)) =_{def} P_{\Pi \cup do(a(\bar{t})=y}(G)$$

The usual conditional probability of $G$ given literal $l$ is expressed in P-Log terms as

$$P_\Pi(G \mid obs(l)) =_{def} P_{\Pi \cup obs(l)}(G).$$

Here $l$ is understood as an observation. (The definition can be easily expanded to arbitrary formula $F$.)

Of course the definition of probability outlined in this section is only applicable to programs which satisfy a number of natural conditions. There should be possible worlds; i.e., the program $\tau(\Pi)$ should be consistent. In the process of construction of a possible world a random attribute $a(\bar{t})$ should be defined by a unique random selection rule. There are a few others. It is not difficult to show that if these conditions are satisfied, then the function $P_\Pi$ defined on sets of possible worlds satisfies the so called Kolmogorov axioms of probability.

This completes our introduction of syntax and semantics of P-Log. In the next section we use several examples to demonstrate the use of P-Log for some short but sophisticated problems whose solutions employ natural combination of logical and probabilistic reasoning.

## 3    Reasoning in P-Log

We start with completing our jungle example.

*Example 3.* [Traveler is making a decision]
To make the decision, the traveler must compare $P_{\Pi_{test}}(help \mid do(select\_color = white))$ and $P_{\Pi_{test}}(help \mid do(select\_color = black))$. In accordance with the above definition, to compute the former one considers program $\Pi_{test}^{white} = \Pi_{test} \cup do(select\_color = white)$ and computes its possible worlds. They are

$W_1 = \{random(select\_stone), select\_color = white, select\_stone = 1, \neg help\}$
$W_i = \{random(select\_stone), select\_color = white, select\_stone = i, help\}$ for every $1 < i \le 10$.

Note that, unlike the possible worlds of $\Pi_{test}$, the possible worlds of the new program do not contain $random(select\_color)$. This reflects the deliberate character of the traveler's color selection. Consequently, for every $1 \le i \le 10$, $\mu(W_i) = P(W_i, select\_stone = i) = 0.1$, and $P_{\Pi_{test}^{white}}(help) = 0.9$. A similar argument will show that $P_{\Pi_{test}^{black}}(help) = 0.1$. Clearly the traveler is better off selecting *white*.

The jungle example addresses a rather simple probabilistic problem, which could be easily solved without building a knowledge base of the corresponding domain. In what follows we consider several examples where the use of P-Log allows to substantially clarify the modeling process. The first example, Monty Hall Problem, is a difficult puzzle which is frequently incorrectly solved even by people with some knowledge of probability theory.

*Example 4.* [Monty Hall problem]
The Monty Hall Problem gets its name from the TV game show hosted by Monty Hall. *A player is given the opportunity to select one of three closed doors, behind one of which there is a prize. Behind the other two doors are empty rooms. Once the player has made a selection, Monty is obligated to open one of the remaining closed doors which does not contain the prize, showing that the room behind it is empty. He then asks the player if he would like to switch his selection to the other unopened door, or stay with his original choice. Does it matter if he switches?*

The answer is YES. In fact switching doubles the player's chance to win. This problem is quite interesting, because the answer is felt by many people — even some mathematicians — to be counter-intuitive. Often a person immediately comes up with a (wrong) negative answer and is not easily persuaded that he made a mistake. We believe that part of the reason for the difficulty is some disconnect between modeling probabilistic and non-probabilistic knowledge about the problem. In P-Log this disconnect disappears which leads to a natural correct solution. In other words, the standard probability formalisms lack the ability to explicitly represent certain non-probabilistic knowledge that is needed in solving this problem. In the absence of this knowledge, wrong conclusions are made. The P-Log solution, adopted from [4], is meant to show how P-Log can be used to avoid this problem by allowing us to specify relevant knowledge explicitly.

*The game's rules*:

The domain contains the set of three doors and three 0-arity random attributes, *selected*, *open* and *prize*. This will be represented by the following P-Log declarations (the numbers are not part of the declaration; we number statements so that we can refer back to them):

1. $doors = \{1, 2, 3\}$.
2. $open, selected, prize : doors$.

The regular part contains rules that state that Monty can open any door to a room which is not selected and which does not contain the prize.

3. $\neg can\_open(D) \leftarrow selected = D$.
4. $\neg can\_open(D) \leftarrow prize = D$.
5. $can\_open(D) \leftarrow not\ \neg can\_open(D)$.

The first two rules are self-explanatory. The last rule, which uses both classical and default negations, is a typical ASP representation of the closed world assumption — Monty can open any door except those which are explicitly prohibited.

Assuming that both, Monty and the player, select a door at random, the probabilistic information about the three attributes of doors can now be expressed as follows:

6. $random(prize)$.
7. $random(selected)$.
8. $random(open : \{X : can\_open(X)\})$.

Notice that rule (8) guarantees that Monty selects only those doors which can be opened according to rules (3)–(5). The knowledge expressed by these rules (which can be extracted from the specification of the problem) is often not explicitly represented in probabilistic formalisms leading reasoners (who usually do not realize this) to insist that their wrong answer is actually correct.

The P-Log program $\Pi_{monty0}$ consisting of the logical rules (1)-(8) represents our knowledge of the problem domain. It has the following 12 possible worlds:

$W_1 = \{selected = 1, prize = 1, open = 2, ...\}$.
$W_2 = \{selected = 1, prize = 1, open = 3, ...\}$.
$W_3 = \{selected = 1, prize = 2, open = 3, ...\}$.
$W_4 = \{selected = 1, prize = 3, open = 2, ...\}$.
$W_5 = \{selected = 2, prize = 1, open = 3, ...\}$.
$W_6 = \{selected = 2, prize = 2, open = 1, ...\}$.
$W_7 = \{selected = 2, prize = 2, open = 3, ...\}$.
$W_8 = \{selected = 2, prize = 3, open = 1, ...\}$.
$W_9 = \{selected = 3, prize = 1, open = 2, ...\}$.
$W_{10} = \{selected = 3, prize = 2, open = 1, ...\}$.
$W_{11} = \{selected = 3, prize = 3, open = 1, ...\}$.
$W_{12} = \{selected = 3, prize = 3, open = 2, ...\}$.

According to our definitions they will be assigned various probability measures. For instance, *selected* has three, equally plausible, possible values in each $W_i$. Hence

$$P(W_i, selected = j) = 1/3$$

for each $i$ and $j$. Similarly for *prize*

$$P(W_i, prize = j) = 1/3$$

Consider $W_1$. Since $can\_open(1) \notin W_1$ the atom $open = 1$ is not possible in $W_1$ and the corresponding probability $P(W_1, open = 1)$ is undefined. The only possible values of *open* in $W_1$ are 2 and 3. Hence

$$P(W_1, open = 2) = 1/2$$

$$P(W_1, open = 3) = 1/2$$

Now consider $W_4$. $W_4$ contains $can\_open(2)$ and no other $can\_open$ atoms. Hence the only possible value of *open* in $W_4$ is 2, and therefore

$$P(W_4, open = 2) = 1$$

The computations of other values of $P(W_i, open = j)$ are similar.

To proceed with the story, first let us eliminate an orthogonal problem of modeling time by assuming that we observed that the player has already (randomly) selected door 1, and Monty (randomly) opened door 2 revealing that it did not contain the prize. This is expressed as:

$$obs(selected = 1). \quad obs(open = 2). \quad obs(prize \neq 2).$$

Let us refer to the above P-Log program as $\Pi_{monty1}$. Because of the observations $\Pi_{monty1}$ has two possible worlds $W_1$ and $W_4$, the first containing $prize = 1$ and the second containing $prize = 3$. It follows that the unnormalized measure of $W_1$ is equal to $P(W_1, selected = 1) \times P(W_1, prize = 1) \times P(W_1, open = 2) = 1/18$; the unnormalized measure of $W_4$ is 1/9. After normalization we have

$$\mu(W_1) = 1/3$$

$$\mu(W_4) = 2/3$$

and hence

$$P_{\Pi_{monty1}}(prize = 1) = \mu(W_1) = 1/3$$

$$P_{\Pi_{monty1}}(prize = 3) = \mu(W_4) = 2/3$$

*Changing the door doubles the player's chance to win.*

Now consider a situation when the player assumes (either consciously or without consciously realizing it) that *Monty could have opened any one of the unopened doors (including one which contains the prize).* Then the corresponding program will have a new definition of *can_open*. The rules (3–5) will be replaced by

$\neg can\_open(D) \leftarrow selected = D.$
$can\_open(D) \leftarrow not \ \neg can\_open(D).$

The resulting program $\Pi_{monty2}$ will also have two possible worlds containing $prize = 1$ and $prize = 3$ respectively, each with unnormalized probability of $1/18$, and therefore $P_{\Pi_{monty2}}(prize = 1) = 1/2$ and $P_{\Pi_{monty2}}(prize = 3) = 1/2$. In that case changing the door will not increase the probability of getting the prize.

*Example 5.* [Bayesian squirrel]
In this example we illustrate the use of P-Log for Bayesian learning. One common type of learning problem consists of selecting from a set of models for a random phenomenon by observing repeated occurrences of that phenomenon. The Bayesian approach to this problem is to begin with a "prior density" on the set of candidate models and update it in light of our observations. As an example, Hilborn and Mangel [14] describe the Bayesian squirrel. *The squirrel has hidden its acorns in one of two patches, say Patch 1 and Patch 2, but can't remember which. The squirrel is 80% certain the food is hidden in Patch 1. Also, it knows there is a 20% chance of finding food per day when it is looking in the right patch (and, of course, a 0% probability if it is looking in the wrong patch).*

To represent this knowledge in P-Log program $\Pi$, we introduce sorts

$patch = \{p1, p2\}.$

$day = \{1 \ldots n\}.$

(where $n$ is some constant, say, 5)

and attributes

$hidden\_in : patch.$

$found : patch * day \rightarrow boolean.$

$look : day \rightarrow patch.$

Attribute *hidden_in* is always random. Hence we include

random ($hidden\_in$).

*found* is random only if the squirrel is looking for food in the right patch; i.e. we have

random $(found(P, D)) \leftarrow hidden\_in = P,\ look(D) = P.$

The regular part of the program consists of the closed world assumption for *found*:

$\neg found(P, D) \leftarrow not\ found(P, D).$

Probabilistic information of the story is given by statements:

$pr(hidden\_in = p1) = 0.8$

$pr(found(P, D)) = 0.2$

This knowledge, in conjunction with a description of the squirrel's activity, can be used to compute probabilities of possible outcomes of the next search for food.

Consider for instance program $\Pi_1 = \Pi \cup \{do(look(1) = p_1)\}$. The program has three possible worlds

$W_1^1 = \{look(1) = p_1, hidden\_in = p_1, found(p_1, 1), \ldots\},$

$W_2^1 = \{look(1) = p_1, hidden\_in = p_1, \neg found(p_1, 1), \ldots\},$

$W_3^1 = \{look(1) = p_1, hidden\_in = p_2, \neg found(p_1, 1), \ldots\},$

with probability measures $\mu(W_1) = 0.16$, $\mu(W_2) = 0.64$, $\mu(W_3) = 0.2$.

As expected

$P_{\Pi_1}(hidden\_in = p_1) = 0.8$, and

$P_{\Pi_1}(found(p_1, 1)) = 0.16.$

Suppose now that the squirrel failed to find its food during the first day, and decided to continue its search in the first patch next morning.

The failure to find food on the first day should decrease the squirrel's degree of belief that the food is hidden in patch one, and consequently decreases its degree of belief that it will find food by looking in the first patch again. This is reflected in the following computation:

Let $\Pi_2 = \Pi_1 \cup \{obs(\neg found(p_1, 1)), do(look(2) = p_1)\}.$

The possible worlds of $\Pi_2$ are

$W_1^2 = W \cup \{hidden\_in = p_1, look(2) = p_1, found(p_1, 2) \ldots\},$

$W_2^2 = W \cup \{hidden\_in = p_1, look(2) = p_1, \neg found(p_1, 2) \ldots\},$

$W_3^2 = W \cup \{hidden\_in = p_2, look(2) = p_1, \neg found(p_1, 2) \ldots\}.$

where $W = \{look(1) = p_1, \neg found(p_1, 1)\}.$

Their (normalized) probability measures are

$\mu(W_1^2) = .128/.84 = .152$, $\mu(W_2^2) = .512/.84 = .61$, $\mu(W_3^2) = .2/.84 = .238$.

Consequently,

$P_{\Pi_2}(hidden\_in = p_1) = 0.762$, and $P_{\Pi_2}(found(p_1, 2)) = 0.152$. ...

After a number of unsuccessful attempts to find food in the first patch the squirrel can come to the conclusion that food is probably hidden in the second patch and change her search strategy accordingly.

Notice that each new experiment changes the squirrel's probabilistic model in a non-monotonic way, i.e. the set of possible worlds resulting from each successive experiment is not merely a subset of the possible worlds of the previous model. The program, however, is changed only by the addition of new actions and observations. Distinctive features of P-Log such as the ability to represent observations and actions, as well as conditional randomness, play an important role in allowing the squirrel to learn new probabilistic models from experience.

## 4 Conclusion

When P-Log designers started their work they had (at least) three common goals. They wanted to have the language which would

- allow elegant and elaboration tolerant formalizations of non-trivial combinations of logical and probabilistic reasoning,
- help the language designers (and hopefully others) to better understand the meaning of probability and probabilistic reasoning,
- better understand how to design and implement knowledge-based software systems.

P-Log is a comparatively new language[4] so it may be too early to judge if the authors achieved their goal. From the standpoint of the author of this paper, however, substantial steps have already being made in achieving the first two goals. This is mainly due to several distinctive features of P-Log. Even though it can be argued that some of them exist in other languages aimed at combining logic and probability, we are not aware of any work combining all of these features. First, *P-Log probabilities are defined with respect to an explicitly stated knowledge base*, written in the language of ASP. This allows to explicitly specify the background knowledge which is normally "hidden" in classical approaches. Making the agent's knowledge a part of the probabilistic model makes the "degree of belief" interpretation of probability more concrete. As we attempted to demonstrate with the Monty Hall example, this feature of P-Log proves to be very useful for modeling probabilistic domains. In addition to logical non-monotonicity

---

[4] The first publication on P-Log appeared in 2004 [3] but the reasonably comprehensive journal paper [4] was published much later.

guaranteed by ASP, P-Log is *probabilistically non-monotonic* – addition of new information can add new possible worlds and substantially change the original probabilistic model. This feature was illustrated in the Bayesian squirrel example. The reliance on an explicitly stated knowledge base also greatly facilitates modeling various types of probabilistic update. In classical probability theory, changes in probability caused by obtaining new knowledge are normally handled by *conditional probability*. This limits the possible updates by knowledge expressible by propositional formulas. This can be modeled in P-Log by simply expanding the agent's knowledge by observations. But the *P-Log approach allows other types of updates including defaults, rules introducing new terms, and deliberate actions in the sense of Pearl*. Interested readers can look for other examples of P-Log modeling in [4,7,5]. The use of P-Log for the design and implementation of knowledge intensive systems is still in its infancy. There are some initial implementations and applications of P-log (see for instance [1] and [13]) which show promise, but much work is needed to develop really efficient algorithms and interesting applications.

# References

1. Anh, H.T., Kencana Ramli, C.D.P., Damásio, C.V.: An implementation of extended p-log using xasp. In: Garcia de la Banda, M., Pontelli, E. (eds.) ICLP 2008. LNCS, vol. 5366, pp. 739–743. Springer, Heidelberg (2008)
2. Baral, C.: Knowledge Representation, Reasoning, and Declarative Problem Solving. Cambridge University Press, Cambridge (2003)
3. Baral, C., Gelfond, M., Rushton, N.: Probabilistic Reasoning with Answer Sets. In: Lifschitz, V., Niemelä, I. (eds.) LPNMR 2004. LNCS (LNAI), vol. 2923, pp. 21–33. Springer, Heidelberg (2003)
4. Baral, C., Gelfond, M., Rushton, N.: Probabilistic reasoning with answer sets. Journal of Theory and Practice of Logic Programming (TPLP) 9(1), 57–144 (2009)
5. Baral, C., Hunsaker, M.: Using the probabilistic logic programming language p-log for causal and counterfactual reasoning and non-naive conditioning. In: Proceedings of IJCAI 2007, pp. 243–249 (2007)
6. Gebser, M., Kaufman, B., Neumann, A., Schaub, T.: Conflict-deriven answer set enumeration. In: Baral, C., Brewka, G., Schlipf, J. (eds.) LPNMR 2007. LNCS (LNAI), vol. 4483, pp. 136–148. Springer, Heidelberg (2007)
7. Gelfond, M., Rushton, N.: Causal and Probabilistic Reasoning in p-log. In: Dechter, R., Geffner, H., Halpern, J. (eds.) Heuristics, Probabilities and Causality. A tribute to Judea Pearl, pp. 337–359. College Publications (2010)
8. Gelfond, M., Lifschitz, V.: The stable model semantics for logic programming. In: Proceedings of ICLP 1988, pp. 1070–1080 (1988)
9. Gelfond, M., Lifschitz, V.: Classical negation in logic programs and disjunctive databases. New Generation Computing 9(3/4), 365–386 (1991)
10. Leone, N., Pfeifer, G., Faber, W., Eiter, T., Gottlob, G., Perri, S., Scarcello, F.: The dlv system for knowledge representation and reasoning. ACM Transactions on Computational Logic 7, 499–562 (2006)

11. Niemela, I., Simons, P., Soininen, T.: Extending and implementing the stable model semantics. Artificial Intelligence 138(1-2), 181–234 (2002)
12. Pearl, J.: Causality. Cambridge University Press, Cambridge (2000)
13. Pereira, L.M., Anh, H.T.: Evolution prospection in decision making. Intelligent Decision Technologies 3(3), 157–171 (2009)
14. Hilborn, R., Mangel, L.: The Ecological Detective. Princeton University Press, Princeton (1997)

# Living with Inconsistency and Taming Nonmonotonicity*

Jan Małuszyński[1] and Andrzej Szałas[1,2]

[1] Department of Computer and Information Science, Linköping University,
S-581 83 Linköping, Sweden
[2] Institute of Informatics, Warsaw University, 02-097 Warsaw, Poland
{jan.maluszynski,andrzej.szalas}@liu.se

**Abstract.** In this paper we consider rule-based query languages with negation in bodies and heads of rules, traditionally denoted by DATALOG$^{\neg\neg}$. Tractable and at the same time intuitive semantics for DATALOG$^{\neg\neg}$ has not been provided even though the area of deductive databases is over 30 years old. In this paper we identify sources of the problem and propose a query language, which we call 4QL.

The 4QL language supports a modular and layered architecture and provides a tractable framework for many forms of rule-based reasoning both monotonic and nonmonotonic. As the underpinning principle we assume openness of the world, which may lead to the lack of knowledge. Negation in rule heads may lead to inconsistencies. To reduce the unknown/inconsistent zones we introduce simple constructs which provide means for application-specific disambiguation of inconsistent information, the use of Local Closed World Assumption (thus also Closed World Assumption, if needed), as well as various forms of default and defeasible reasoning.

## 1  Introduction

This paper introduces a rule-based query language 4QL with negation in bodies and heads of rules, belonging to the family of DATALOG$^{\neg\neg}$ languages. Tractable and at the same time intuitive semantics for DATALOG$^{\neg\neg}$ has not been provided even if the area of deductive databases is over 30 years old. In this paper we identify sources of the problem and propose a solution based on a four-valued semantics with 'true', 'false', 'inconsistent' and 'unknown' as truth values (further denoted by $t$, $f$, $i$ and $u$, respectively). An important feature of 4QL is that it permits to directly address problems related to inconsistent information and the lack of knowledge. Such problems are crucial in many applications and have been addressed in extensions of query languages, based on non-monotonic logics initially derived from the Closed World Assumption (CWA), where unknown facts are, by default, assigned the value $f$. In many applications, including Semantic Web technologies and robotics systems, CWA is not necessarily applicable and developments in these fields usually follow the Open World Assumption (OWA), where facts not included in or inferred from the database are assigned the value $u$.

---

* Supported in part by grant N N206 399334 from Polish Ministry of Science and National Education.

O. de Moor et al. (Eds.): Datalog 2010, LNCS 6702, pp. 384–398, 2011.

Inconsistent and unknown information is often addressed taking DATALOG with negation as the starting point for paraconsistent extensions. Then inconsistency has to be dealt with together with nonmonotonicity, making the proposals unsuitable for many applications and technically quite complex. In this paper we present a novel, lightweight approach, separating the issues of incomplete/inconsistent knowledge and nonmonotonicity. Using the four-valued paraconsistent logic introduced in [32], we define a modular language 4QL with unrestricted negation and layered architecture. At the base layers OWA is accepted. This is crucial in the proposed approach for dealing with inconsistencies and the lack of knowledge in a monotonic way. Modules of higher layers may use additional simple yet powerful constructs allowing one to express various mechanisms of nonmonotonic reasoning. In particular, these constructs provide means for application-specific disambiguation of inconsistent information obtained at lower layers, the use of Local CWA (thus also CWA, if needed), and various forms of default reasoning. The resulting query language is still tractable as regards its data complexity. Moreover, it captures PTIME queries on ordered domains (see [31]).

The paper is organized as follows. Section 2 gives a brief survey of related work on paraconsistent logic programming and the four-valued logic of [32,42]. Sections 3 and 4 introduce 4QL and discuss its architecture. Section 5 discusses the constructs of 4QL, allowing one to express various kinds of nonmonotonicity and illustrates their use on examples. Conclusions are presented in Section 6.

# 2 Living with Inconsistency

## 2.1 Related Work

In the context of logic programming the problem of inconsistency was first addressed by Blair and Subrahmanian [8]. The logic programs considered in this paper (called *Generally Horn logic programs*) consist of clauses where each literal is annotated t or f. The annotation f plays the role of negation. Programs are interpreted using Belnap's four-valued logic [6]. A fixpoint semantics defines the least model of each program, and associates one of the four truth values with any element of the Herbrand base. In this approach the negation, modeled by the annotations, is a four-valued logical negation in contrast to the negation-as-failure used in logic programming. The work of Kifer and Lozinski [28] extends the approach to theories which may include also this kind of negation.

Several publications (see e.g. [2,4,13,40] and references therein) address reasoning with inconsistencies in extended logic programs and disjunctive extended logic programs introduced by Gelfond and Lifschitz [25]. Such programs admit so called *explicit negation* in addition to the negation-as-failure. Thus the issue of inconsistency has to be considered together with the issue of nonmonotonic reasoning. These proposals usually extend the semantics of normal logic programs such as stable model semantics or well-founded semantics.

It was observed by Fitting (see e.g. [23]) that bilattices [26] are convenient for treatment of inconsistency. In many of the papers mentioned above the definition of the paraconsistent semantics is based on bilattices. A commonly used four-valued logic is

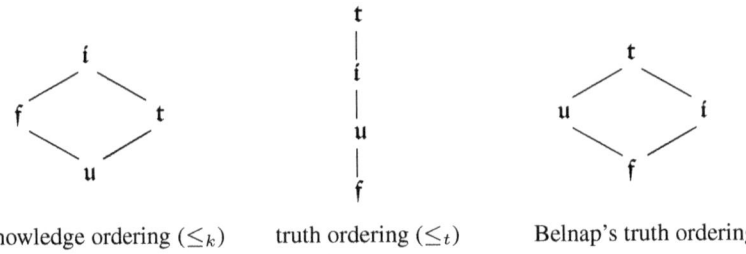

knowledge ordering ($\leq_k$)     truth ordering ($\leq_t$)     Belnap's truth ordering

**Fig. 1.** Truth and knowledge orderings

Belnap's logic [6] where two orderings on truth values are considered, known as *knowledge ordering* $\leq_k$ and *Belnap's truth ordering* (see Figure 1). As shown, e.g., in [19,42], Belnap's truth ordering is problematic in areas we focus on. A different truth ordering $\leq_t$ was used in [14] presenting a paraconsistent logic programming approach to querying inconsistent databases and in [42].

The starting point for this paper are some results reported in [32,42,41], providing a four-valued framework for reasoning with rough sets [37]. We adopt here the four-valued logic defined therein as a basis for the semantics of 4QL. However, 4QL is substantially different from the rule language discussed in [42] and in [41]. While the work in [42,41] concentrates on approximate reasoning and knowledge fusion, here we accept a different kind of disjunction and existential quantification which make 4QL "back compatible" with DATALOG when restricting truth values to the two classical ones and closing the world using CWA.

### 2.2  A Four-Valued Logic for Paraconsistent Reasoning

We adopt the four-valued logic introduced by Małuszyński, Szałas and Vitória in [32]. It results from a combination of truth ordering $\leq_t$ and knowledge ordering $\leq_k$ shown in Figure 1. The truth tables for the connectives are shown in Table 1.

Let us emphasize that known facts about connectives in the classical two-valued logic may not hold in the four-valued case. For instance, $p \to q$ in our logic is not equivalent to $\neg q \to \neg p$. Such deviations from the classical semantics are rather typical in many-valued logics (see [9]). In the context of databases, DATALOG¬ with the well-founded semantics uses a three-valued logic not preserving some classical laws (see [1]). However, when truth values are restricted to t and f, all considered connectives are classical and preserve all laws known from classical propositional calculus.

**Table 1.** Truth tables for $\wedge$, $\vee$, $\to$ and $\neg$

| $\wedge$ | f | u | i | t |   | $\vee$ | f | u | i | t |   | $\to$ | f | u | i | t |   | | $\neg$ |
|---|---|---|---|---|---|---|---|---|---|---|---|---|---|---|---|---|---|---|
| f | f | f | f | f |   | f | f | u | i | t |   | f | t | t | t | t |   | f | t |
| u | f | u | u | u |   | u | u | u | i | t |   | u | t | t | t | t |   | u | u |
| i | f | u | i | i |   | i | i | i | i | t |   | i | f | f | t | f |   | i | i |
| t | f | u | i | t |   | t | t | t | t | t |   | t | f | f | t | t |   | t | f |

The truth tables for conjunction $\wedge$ and disjunction $\vee$ are respectively defined as minimum and maximum w.r.t. truth ordering.

The implication $\rightarrow$ is a four-valued extension of the classical implication. It is used to interpret clauses of 4QL. Whenever the body of a clause has the value $f$ or $u$, we make the clause $t$. Intuitively, this reflects our intention not to draw conclusions from false or unknown information. Namely, a clause with unknown or false body is always satisfied, so one does not have to update its head.

From inconsistent body we want to conclude that the head is also inconsistent:

- we do not want to derive conclusions as to truth or falsity of a fact on the basis of inconsistent assumptions
- the unknown conclusion should not follow from inconsistency, namely having the implication $p \rightarrow q$ with $p$ inconsistent, we have a positive evidence both about $p$ and $\neg p$, so we also have a positive evidence indicating truth of $q$. Therefore $q$ is not totally unknown, as the assignment of $u$ to $q$ would indicate. As already argued, we cannot assign $t$ to $q$ on the basis of inconsistent $p$, so $q$ is to be assigned $i$.

The implication is $t$ if the predecessor takes value $t$ and the successor is $t$ or $i$. The latter case is needed to handle the situation when both head and its negation are to be derived on the basis of true assumptions.

**Definition 1.** By an *interpretation* we mean any set of literals. By the *truth value* of a literal $\ell$ in interpretation $\mathcal{I}$, denoted by $\mathcal{I}(\ell)$, we mean the value defined as follows:

$$\mathcal{I}(\ell) \stackrel{def}{=} \begin{cases} t \text{ if } \ell \in \mathcal{I} \text{ and } (\neg\ell) \notin \mathcal{I} \\ i \text{ if } \ell \in \mathcal{I} \text{ and } (\neg\ell) \in \mathcal{I} \\ u \text{ if } \ell \notin \mathcal{I} \text{ and } (\neg\ell) \notin \mathcal{I} \\ f \text{ if } \ell \notin \mathcal{I} \text{ and } (\neg\ell) \in \mathcal{I}. \end{cases}$$

The definition of interpretation is extended for formulas built from literals using $\vee, \wedge, \neg$ and $\rightarrow$ according to Table 1. $\triangleleft$

## 3  4QL: The Monotonic Layer

### 3.1  Syntax

The alphabet of 4QL consists of predicate symbols, constants and variables. Atomic formulas and literals are built in the usual way. For a negative literal $\ell = \neg\ell'$ the notation $\neg\ell$ stands for its positive counterpart $\ell'$. We treat propositions as zero-argument relation symbols.

**Definition 2.**

- By a *rule* we mean any expression of the form:

$$\ell :\!- (b_{11}, \ldots, b_{1i_1}) \vee (b_{21}, \ldots, b_{2i_2}) \vee \ldots \vee (b_{m1}, \ldots, b_{mi_m}). \tag{1}$$

where $\ell, b_{11}, \ldots, b_{1i_1}, b_{21}, \ldots, b_{2i_2}, \ldots, b_{m1}, \ldots, b_{mi_m}$ are ground literals.

- If $\varrho$ is a rule of the form (1) then:
  - $rule(\ell) \overset{\text{def}}{=} \varrho$
  - $head(\varrho) \overset{\text{def}}{=} \ell$
  - $body(\varrho) \overset{\text{def}}{=} (b_{11}, \ldots, b_{1i_1}) \vee (b_{21}, \ldots, b_{2i_2}) \vee \ldots \vee (b_{m1}, \ldots, b_{mi_m})$
  - for $1 \leq j \leq m$, $\beta_j(\rho) \overset{\text{def}}{=} b_{j1}, \ldots, b_{ji_j}$.
- By a 4QL *program* we understand any finite set $S$ of rules such that there are no two rules $\rho_1, \rho_2 \in S$ with $head(\rho_1) = head(\rho_2)$.  ◁

In the sequel, the empty body is denoted by the empty symbol or the symbol $\emptyset$.

*Remark 1.*

- We consider ground rules only in order to simplify the presentation. However, typical rules with variables are allowed, too. We assume that whenever there is a variable appearing in the body of a rule but not in its head then it is assumed to be existentially quantified in its body. The existential quantifier $\exists x q(x)$ is then understood as the disjunction $q(a_1) \vee \ldots \vee q(a_k)$, where $a_1, \ldots, a_k$ are all constants appearing in the database.
- The intention behind the disjunction in (1) is that it gathers all ground bodies with $\ell$ as their head. This cannot be achieved by the use of many rules, as in the case of DATALOG, since $(p \to q) \wedge (r \to q)$ is not equivalent to $(p \vee r) \to q$.  ◁

### 3.2 Declarative Semantics

The declarative semantics of 4QL is defined in terms of Herbrand models.

**Definition 3.** By a *Herbrand base* of a program we mean the set of all ground literals constructed with predicate symbols and constants which occur in the program.  ◁

**Definition 4.** A set of literals $\mathcal{I}$ is a *model of a set of rules* $S$ iff for each rule $\varrho \in S$ we have that $\mathcal{I}\big(body(\varrho) \to head(\varrho)\big) = \mathbf{t}$, where it is assumed that the empty body takes the value $\mathbf{t}$ in any interpretation.  ◁

It should be noticed that the Herbrand base is a model of any set of rules. However, our intuition is that the knowledge represented by a set of rules should be based on the explicit knowledge represented by facts. Minimal models, if exist, may not fulfill this requirement, as shown in the following example.

*Example 1.* Let $S$ be the following set of rules:

$wait :\!-\, overloaded \vee rest\_time\,.$
$rest\_time :\!-\, wait\,.$
$\neg\, overloaded :\!-\, rest\_time\,.$
$overloaded\,.$

A minimal model of $S$ is $\{overloaded, \neg overloaded, wait, rest\_time\}$ but the only fact of $S$ (i.e., $overloaded$) has in this model value $\mathfrak{i}$ so there are no facts supporting the truth of $wait$ and $rest\_time$ in this model. The intuitively correct model for $S$ is $\{overloaded, \neg overloaded, wait, \neg wait, rest\_time, \neg rest\_time\}$.  ◁

The following definitions reflect our intuitions. Note that intuitions closest to ours are those behind well-supportedness of Fages [22].

**Definition 5.** Let $\mathcal{I}$ be an interpretation and $\prec$ be a strict partial order on $\mathcal{I}$. Given a set of rules $S$, we say that a model $\mathcal{I}$ of $S$ *supports a rule* $\varrho \in S$ w.r.t. $\prec$ provided that:

$body(\varrho) = \emptyset$ or there is $\beta_j(\varrho)$ such that $\mathcal{I}(\beta_j(\varrho)) = \mathbf{t}$
and for all literals $\imath \in \beta_j(\varrho)$ we have that $\imath \prec head(\varrho)$.  ◁

**Definition 6.** A model $\mathcal{I}$ of a set of rules $S$ is *well-supported* provided that there exists a strict partial order $\prec$ on $\mathcal{I}$ such that for every literal $\ell \in \mathcal{I}$,

- if $\mathcal{I}(\ell) = \mathbf{t}$ then $\mathcal{I}$ supports $rule(\ell)$ w.r.t. $\prec$. (2)

- if $\mathcal{I}(\ell) = \mathbf{i}$ then (at least) one of the following conditions hold: (3)

  – $\mathcal{I}$ supports $rule(\ell)$ w.r.t. $\prec$

  – there is a rule $\varrho \in \{rule(\ell), rule(\neg \ell)\}$ with $\mathcal{I}(body(\varrho)) = \mathbf{i}$ for which there is $\beta_j(\varrho) = \mathbf{i}$ such that for all literals $\imath$ in $\beta_j(\varrho)$, $\imath \prec head(\varrho)$.  ◁

*Remark 2.* In condition (3) one could also expect a clause concerning $\mathcal{I}(\neg \ell) = \mathbf{i}$. On the other hand, $\mathcal{I}(\ell) = \mathbf{i}$ implies that also $\mathcal{I}(\neg \ell) = \mathbf{i}$ so the respective condition for $\mathcal{I}(\neg \ell) = \mathbf{i}$ is already included in Definition 6. For example, interpretation $\{rest, \neg rest, overloaded, \neg overloaded\}$ is a well-supported model for the set of rules:

$\neg rest :\!- overloaded.$ (4)
$rest.$ (5)
$overloaded.$ (6)
$\neg overloaded.$ (7)

as well as for the set of rules $\{[\neg rest.], (5), (6), (7)\}$.  ◁

The following theorem is proved in [31].

**Theorem 1.** For any set $S$ of rules there is the unique well-supported model for $S$.  ◁

### 3.3  Computing the Unique Well-Supported Model

Let us now present an algorithm for computing the unique well-supported model for a given set of rules. Its correctness is proved in [31]. We need the following notation.

**Definition 7.** Let $S$ be a set of rules.

- By $\mathcal{L}(S)$ we denote the set of relation symbols appearing in $S$.
- By a *duplicate* of a relation symbol $\ell \in \mathcal{L}(S)$ we understand a fresh relation symbol, for simplicity denoted by $\ell'$.
- By $\mathcal{L}'(S)$ we understand the set of *duplicates* of relation symbols of $\mathcal{L}(S)$, i.e., $\mathcal{L}'(S) = \{\ell' \mid \ell \in \mathcal{L}(S)\}$.
- By $Pos(S)$ we understand the DATALOG program obtained from $S$ by replacing each negative literal $\neg \ell$ of $S$ by its duplicate $\ell'$.  ◁

390 J. Małuszyński and A. Szałas

---

**Input:** a set of rules $S$
**Output:** the unique well-supported model $\mathcal{I}^S$ for $S$

Phase 1 (*finding basic inconsistencies*):
    (a) compute the least Herbrand model $\mathcal{I}_0^S$ of $Pos(S)$
    (b) let $\mathcal{I}_1^S \stackrel{\text{def}}{=} \{\ell, \neg\ell \mid \ell, \ell' \in \mathcal{I}_0^S\}$
Phase 2 (*finding potentially true literals*):
    (a) let $S' = \{\varrho \mid \varrho \in S$ and $\mathcal{I}_1^S(head(\varrho)) \neq \mathbf{i}\}$
    (b) set $\mathcal{I}_2^S$ to be the least Herbrand model for $Pos(S')$
        with literals $\ell'$ substituted by $\neg\ell$
Phase 3 (*reasoning with inconsistency*):
    (a) define the following transformation $\Phi^S$ on interpretations:

$$\Phi^S(\mathcal{I}) \stackrel{\text{def}}{=} \mathcal{I} \cup \{\ell, \neg\ell \mid \text{ there is a rule } [\ell :\!- \beta_1 \vee \ldots \vee \beta_m] \in S \quad (8)$$
$$\text{such that } \exists k \in \{1, \ldots, m\}[\mathcal{I}(\beta_k) = \mathbf{i}] \quad (9)$$
$$\text{and } \neg\exists n \in \{1, \ldots, m\}[\,(\mathcal{I}_2^S - \mathcal{I})(\beta_n) = \mathbf{t}]\}. \quad (10)$$

    The transformation $\Phi^S$ is monotonic (see [31]).
    Denote by $\mathcal{I}_3^S$ the fixpoint of $\Phi^S$ obtained by iterating $\Phi^S$ on $\mathcal{I}_1^S$, i.e.,

$$\mathcal{I}_3^S = \bigcup_{i \in \omega} (\Phi^S)^i(\mathcal{I}_1^S)$$

    (b) set $\mathcal{I}^S = \mathcal{I}_2^S \cup \mathcal{I}_3^S$.

---

**Fig. 2.** The method of computing the well-supported model for the set of rules $S$

The algorithm is presented in Figure 2.

*Example 2.* To illustrate the algorithm, consider set of rules discussed in Example 1 together with rules:

$good\_mood :\!- rested \vee success\,.$
$\neg rested :\!- \neg rest\_time\,.$
$rested\,.$
$success\,.$

Phase 1 gives $\mathcal{I}_1^S = \{overloaded, \neg overloaded\}$.
The set $S'$ of Phase 2 is:

$wait :\!- overloaded \vee rest\_time\,.$
$rest\_time :\!- wait\,.$
$good\_mood :\!- rested \vee success\,.$
$\neg rested :\!- \neg rest\_time\,.$
$rested\,.$
$success\,.$

Phase 2 returns $\mathcal{I}_2^S = \{success, rested, good\_mood\}$.

Phase 3 goes through the following iterations of $\Phi^S$:

> $\{overloaded, \neg overloaded\}$
> $\{overloaded, \neg overloaded, wait, \neg wait\}$
> $\{overloaded, \neg overloaded, wait, \neg wait, rest\_time, \neg rest\_time\}$
> $\{overloaded, \neg overloaded, wait, \neg wait, rest\_time, \neg rest\_time,$
> $\quad rested, \neg rested\}$ — fixpoint.

Hence $\mathcal{I}_3^S = \{overloaded, \neg overloaded, wait, \neg wait, rest\_time, \neg rest\_time,$
$\quad\quad rested, \neg rested\}$.
  Finally $\mathcal{I}^S = \{success, good\_mood, overloaded, \neg overloaded, wait, \neg wait,$
$\quad\quad rest\_time, \neg rest\_time, rested, \neg rested\}$.  ◁

The following theorem is proved in [31].

**Theorem 2**

- The interpretation $\mathcal{I}^S$ is the well-supported model of $S$.
- Algorithm given in Figure 2 computes $\mathcal{I}^S$ in time polynomial w.r.t. the size of the domain.  ◁

# 4    4QL: Modular Architecture

In this section we add constructs substantially extending expressiveness of the base 4QL language described so far. The intended modular and layered architecture is shown in Figure 3. Modules are allowed to read values of literals from modules of a lower layer. This way we do not allow recursion through nonmonotonic operators. The idea is somehow similar to that of stratified logic programs, where negation is the only nonmonotonic operator (for a more detailed discussion of this issue see [31]).

**Definition 8**

- An *external literal* is an expression of one of the forms:
  $$A.R, \neg A.R, A.R \text{ IN } T, \neg A.R \text{ IN } T,$$
  where:
  - $A$ is a module name and $R$ is a positive literal ($A$ is called the *reference module* of the external literal)[1]
  - $T \subseteq \{\mathsf{f}, \mathsf{u}, \mathsf{i}, \mathsf{t}\}$.[2]
- An external literal may only appear in rule bodies of a module $B$, provided that its reference module is in a strictly lower layer than $B$.
- We write $\ell = v$ to stand for $\ell \text{ IN } \{v\}$. The literal $\neg A.R \text{ IN } T$ is to be read as "$(\neg A.R) \text{ IN } T$" rather than "$\neg (A.R \text{ IN } T)$".  ◁

---

[1] If $R$ is not defined in the module $A$ then the value of $A.R$ is $\mathsf{u}$.
[2] The intended meaning of $A.R \text{ IN } T$ is that the truth value of $A.R$ is in the set $T$.

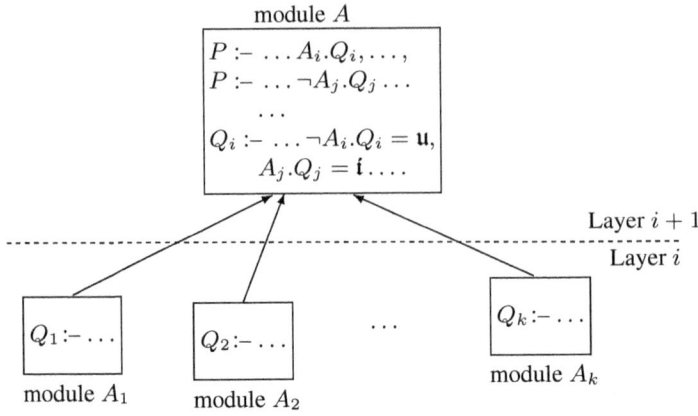

module $A$

$$P :- \ldots A_i.Q_i, \ldots,$$
$$P :- \ldots \neg A_j.Q_j \ldots$$
$$\ldots$$
$$Q_i :- \ldots \neg A_i.Q_i = \mathbf{u},$$
$$A_j.Q_j = \mathbf{i} \ldots.$$

Layer $i + 1$

Layer $i$

$$Q_1 :- \ldots$$

$$Q_2 :- \ldots$$

$$\ldots$$

$$Q_k :- \ldots$$

module $A_1$        module $A_2$

module $A_k$

**Fig. 3.** The intended architecture

Semantics of modules and external literals can easily be defined by assuming that:

- formally, positive literal $R$ (respectively, negative literal $\neg R$) occurring in module $A$ is an abbreviation for $A.R$ (respectively, for $\neg A.R$), so that $A.R$ is not the same as $B.R$ when $B \neq A$
- each module operates on its "local" literals, accessing "foreign" literals only via dotted notation
- external literals, when used in a given module, are fully defined in modules in lower layers
- truth values assigned to external literals, when used, cannot change.

Under these assumptions each external literal occurring in a module $A$ has a fixed truth value determined at lower levels. The semantics of $A$ is now defined as the unique well-supported model of the program $A'$ obtained from $A$ by replacing each external literal of $A$ by the respective constant $\mathbf{f}, \mathbf{u}, \mathbf{i}$ or $\mathbf{t}$ corresponding to the truth value of this literal.

## 5  Taming Nonmonotonicity

The goal of this section is to show that very simple concepts of modules and external literals allow one to express many useful nonmonotonic rules. We do not intend to provide a detailed analysis of the discussed techniques. Instead, we illustrate their usefulness by examples.

Typical sources of nonmonotonicity are generally caused by attempts to fill gaps in missing knowledge, e.g.,

- efficient representation of (negative) information (like CWA, LCWA)
- drawing rational conclusions from non-conclusive information (e.g., circumscription, default logics)
- drawing rational conclusions from the lack of knowledge (e.g., autoepistemic reasoning)
- resolving inconsistencies (e.g., defeasible reasoning).

Reasoning in traditional nonmonotonic logics is of heavyweight complexity [5,11,12,20,27]. In the following subsections we provide examples indicating how to represent lightweight forms of nonmonotonicity in 4QL. The term "lightweight" indicates that we do not exactly mirror the semantics of nonmonotonic formalisms, but still capture the underlying intuitions. Moreover, our shift in semantics results in tractable nonmonotonic reasoning over databases.

## 5.1  Local Closed-World Assumption

Local Closed World Assumption (LCWA) generalizes the Closed World Assumption introduced by Reiter [38]. It has been considered in many sources, including [21,18,15,16]. Intuitively, one often wants to contextually close part of the world, not necessarily all relations in the database.

*Example 3.* The following rules in a module other than $B$ locally close *loc*, where $loc(X, Y, T)$ means that object $X$ has location $Y$ at timepoint $T$:

$$
\begin{aligned}
loc(X,Y,T)\text{:-} \quad & nextTime(T,S), && - T \text{ is the timepoint next to } S \\
& house(X), && - X \text{ is a house} \\
& B.chLoc(X,S) \text{ IN } \{\mathsf{u},\mathsf{f}\}, && - B \text{ reports change of location being } \mathsf{u} \text{ or } \mathsf{f} \\
& C.loc(X,Y,S). && - C \text{ reports that location of } X \text{ at time } S \text{ is } Y \\
\neg loc(X,Y,T)\text{:-} \quad & nextTime(T,S), && - T \text{ is the timepoint next to } S \\
& movingCar(X), && - X \text{ is a moving car} \\
& B.chLoc(X,S) \text{ IN } \{\mathsf{u},\mathsf{t}\}, && - B \text{ reports change of location being } \mathsf{u} \text{ or } \mathsf{f} \\
& C.loc(X,Y,S). && - C \text{ reports that location of } X \text{ at time } S \text{ is } Y
\end{aligned}
$$

These rules state that houses do not change their location in contrast to moving cars, no matter whether the $B$'s database contains information as to the change of location or not.                                                                                          ◁

## 5.2  Lightweight Default Reasoning

Default reasoning has been introduced by Reiter [39] and intensively studied by numerous authors (see, e.g., [7,10,30,33] and references there).

Default rules have the form:

$$prerequisite : justification \vdash consequent, \tag{11}$$

with the intuitive meaning

> "deduce *consequent* whenever *prerequisite* is true
> and *justification* is consistent with current beliefs".

Assuming that *consequent*, *justification* are literals and *prerequisite* is a conjunction of literals, rules of the form (11) can be translated into:

$$consequent \text{:-} prerequisite, justification \in \{\mathsf{t},\mathsf{u}\}.$$

If *consequent*, *justification*, *prerequisite* are not in required form, one first has to transform them into rules using standard techniques known from logic programming.[3]

The following example shows how to represent such rules in 4QL.

*Example 4.* Consider the following default rule:

$$car(X) \wedge speed(X, high) : onRoad(X) \vdash onRoad(X)$$

stating that cars moving with high speed typically are on road. An 4QL rule capturing similar intuitions can be:

$$onRoad(X) :- car(X), \qquad\qquad - X \text{ is a car}$$
$$speed(X, high), \qquad - \text{ speed of } X \text{ is high}$$
$$B.onRoad(X) \text{ IN } \{\mathsf{t}, \mathsf{u}\}. - B \text{ reports that } onRoad(X) \text{ is } \mathsf{t} \text{ or } \mathsf{u}. \quad \lhd$$

In 4QL we can also consider defaults for resolving inconsistencies as shown in the following example.

*Example 5.* Let module $A$ contain, among others, the following rules:

$$stop \quad :- red\_light.$$
$$\neg stop :- policeman\_directs\_to\_go\_through.$$

A possible inconsistency may be resolved in a module in layer higher than $A$, using the rule:

$$\neg stop :- A.stop = \mathsf{i}.$$

That is, when there is both red light and a policeman directing to go through then one should not stop. $\qquad\qquad \lhd$

### 5.3 Lightweight Autoepistemic Reasoning

Autoepistemic reasoning, introduced by Moore [35], concentrates around the reasoning of the form:

"If you do not know $R$, conclude $\neg R$." $\qquad\qquad (12)$

Assuming that $R$ is a literal, formulas of the form (12) can be translated into 4QL rules of the form:

$$\neg R :- A.R = \mathsf{u}$$

placed in a module of layer higher than $A$.

*Example 6.* Consider the rule stating that "if you do not know that you have a sister, conclude that you do not have a sister". It can be represented by the rule

$$\neg have\_sister :- A.have\_sister = \mathsf{u}.$$

Such a rule should be placed in a module in layer higher than $A$. $\qquad\qquad \lhd$

---

[3] This may cause an exponential blow up of formulas.

## 5.4   Lightweight Circumscriptive Reasoning

Circumscription has been introduced by McCarthy [34] and then intensively studied (see, e.g., [11,17,20,27,29,24]).

In general, replacing circumscription by rules is not doable. However, in 4QL one can express typical abnormality theories, where formulas involving abnormalities have the pattern, where $ab$ is minimized and $conclusion$ is varied:

$$(condition \land \neg abnormal) \rightarrow conclusion. \tag{13}$$

In such cases one can:

- locally close abnormality
- make varied predicates heads of rules.[4]

In the case of formulas of the form (13), one can first provide the following rule necessary to locally close $ab$, say in module $A$:

$$abnormal(X) :- condition \land \neg conclusion.$$

Then the following rules both locally close $ab$ and provide (in a module of a higher layer than $A$) the following rules expressing the required circumscriptive policy:

$\neg abnormal(X) :- A.abnormal(X)$ IN $\{\mathsf{f}, \mathsf{u}\}$.  $-$ local closure of $abnormal$
$conclusion :- condition, \neg abnormal$.      $-$ representation of (13) .

*Example 7.* Consider the theory stating that ill persons normally consult their doctors:

$$\forall X [(ill(X) \land \neg ab(X)) \rightarrow consults\_doctor(X)]$$

and assume one minimizes the abnormality predicate $ab$ varying $consults\_doctor$.
    Let $A$ be a module with (among others) the following rule:

$$ab(X) :- ill(X), \neg consults\_doctor(X).$$

We define a module $B$ in a layer higher than $A$, consisting of rules:

$\neg ab(X) :- A.ab(X)$ IN $\{\mathsf{f}, \mathsf{u}\}$.
$consults\_doctor(X) :- ill(X), \neg ab(X)$.                    ◁

## 5.5   Lightweight Defeasible Reasoning

A rule-based form of defeasible reasoning has been introduced by Nute [36]. It is used, among others, in Semantic Web technologies [3]. Rules have the form similar to 4QL, but the underlying semantics is two-valued. Possible inconsistencies are resolved by placing priorities on rules. Such priorities can easily be modeled in 4QL, as the following example shows.

---

[4] This sometimes requires finding explicit definitions of varied predicates. Even if often can be done automatically, e.g., using second-order quantifier elimination, this is not a lightweight task [24].

*Example 8.* Consider the following defeasible rules reflecting buyer's requirements as to apartments:

$$r1 : size(X, large) \Rightarrow acceptable(X)$$
$$r2 : \neg pets\_allowed(X) \Rightarrow \neg acceptable(X)$$

with priorities $r2 > r1$.

Assume module $B$ contains rules:

$$acceptable(X) \quad :- \; size(X, large).$$
$$\neg acceptable(X) \; :- \; \neg pets\_allowed(X).$$

The following rules in a module in higher layer resolves possible inconsistencies according to required priority:

$$acceptable(X) \quad :- \; B.acceptable(X) = \mathbf{t}.$$
$$\neg acceptable(X) \; :- \; B.acceptable(X) = \mathbf{i}.$$

Note that in 4QL we can also address cases with **u**, not covered by defeasible rules. For example, one can additionally express rules like:

$$\neg acceptable(X) :- B.acceptable(X) = \mathbf{u}.$$

not expressible by means of defeasible rules.                                      ◁

## 6   Conclusions

The paper proposes a new DATALOG$^{\neg\neg}$-like query language 4QL, which is shown powerful but still lightweight and intuitive. It provides means for monotonic reasoning supported by facts together with a very simple mechanism for expressing nonmonotonic rules.

The intended methodology is based on the assumption that conclusions monotonically derived from facts are well supported. This idea is reflected by the intended architecture, where:

– the lowest layer provides solid knowledge, supported by facts, e.g., reflecting perception, expert knowledge, etc.
– higher layers allow one to derive conclusions still supported by facts or using various forms of nonmonotonic reasoning, usually reflecting expert knowledge.

We have provided an algorithm for computing well-supported models. The algorithm runs in deterministic polynomial time w.r.t. size of the databases.

As shown in [31], the layered 4QL language captures PTIME queries over ordered domains.

# References

1. Abiteboul, S., Hull, R., Vianu, V.: Foundations of Databases. Addison-Wesley Pub. Co., Reading (1996)
2. Alcântara, J., Damásio, C.V., Pereira, L.M.: An encompassing framework for paraconsistent logic programs. J. Applied Logic 3(1), 67–95 (2005)
3. Antoniou, G., van Harmelen, F.: A Semantic Web Primer. The MIT Press, Cambridge (2004)
4. Arieli, O.: Paraconsistent declarative semantics for extended logic programs. Ann. Math. Artif. Intell. 36(4), 381–417 (2002)
5. Baumgartner, R., Gottlob, G.: On the complexity of model checking for propositional default logics: New results and tractable cases. In: IJCAI, pp. 64–69 (1999)
6. Belnap, N.D.: A useful four-valued logic. In: Eptein, G., Dunn, J.M. (eds.) Modern Uses of Many Valued Logic, pp. 8–37. Reidel, Dordrechtz (1977)
7. Besnard, P.: An Introduction to Default Logic. Springer, Heidelberg (1989)
8. Blair, H.A., Subrahmanian, V.S.: Paraconsistent logic programming. Theor. Comput. Sci. 68(2), 135–154 (1989)
9. Bolc, L., Borowik, P.: Many-Valued Logics, 1. Theoretical Foundations. Springer, Berlin (1992)
10. Brewka, G.: Non-Monotonic Reasoning: Logical Foundations of Commonsense. Cambridge University Press, Cambridge (1991)
11. Cadoli, M., Eiter, T., Gottlob, G.: Complexity of propositional nested circumscription and nested abnormality theories. ACM Trans. Comput. Log. 6(2), 232–272 (2005)
12. Cadoli, M., Schaerf, M.: A survey on complexity results for non-monotonic logics. Journal Logic Programming 17, 127–160 (1993)
13. Damásio, C.V., Pereira, L.M.: A survey of paraconsistent semantics for logic programs. In: Handbook of Defeasible Reasoning and Uncertainty Management Systems, pp. 241–320 (1998)
14. de Amo, S., Pais, M.S.: A paraconsistent logic approach for querying inconsistent databases. International Journal of Approximate Reasoning 46, 366–386 (2007)
15. Doherty, P., Kachniarz, J., Szałas, A.: Using contextually closed queries for local closed-world reasoning in rough knowledge databases. In: Pal, S.K., Polkowski, L., Skowron, A. (eds.) Rough-Neural Computing: Techniques for Computing with Words, Cognitive Technologies, pp. 219–250. Springer, Heidelberg (2004)
16. Doherty, P., Łukaszewicz, W., Skowron, A., Szałas, A.: Knowledge representation techniques. A rough set approach. Studies in Fuzziness and Soft Computing, vol. 202. Springer, Heidelberg (2006)
17. Doherty, P., Łukaszewicz, W., Szałas, A.: Computing circumscription revisited. Journal of Automated Reasoning 18(3), 297–336 (1997); See also 14th International Joint Conference on AI (IJCAI 1995). Morgan Kaufmann Pub. Inc., San Francisco (1995)
18. Doherty, P., Łukaszewicz, W., Szałas, A.: Efficient reasoning using the local closed-world assumption. In: Cerri, S.A., Dochev, D. (eds.) AIMSA 2000. LNCS (LNAI), vol. 1904, pp. 49–58. Springer, Heidelberg (2000)
19. Dubois, D.: On ignorance and contradiction considered as truth-values. Logic Journal of the IGPL 16(2), 195–216 (2008)
20. Eiter, T., Gottlob, G.: Propositional circumscription and extended closed-world reasoning are $\Pi_2^P$-complete. Theoretical Computer Science 114(2), 231–245 (1993)
21. Etzioni, O., Golden, K., Weld, D.S.: Sound and efficient closed-world reasoning for planning. Artificial Intelligence 89, 113–148 (1997)
22. Fages, F.: Consistency of Clark's completion and existence of stable models. Methods of Logic in Computer Science 1, 51–60 (1994)

23. Fitting, M.C.: Fixpoint semantics for logic programming. A survey. Theoretical Computer Science 278(1-2), 25–51 (2002)
24. Gabbay, D.M., Schmidt, R., Szałas, A.: Second-Order Quantifier Elimination. Foundations, Computational Aspects and Applications. Studies in Logic, vol. 12. College Publications (2008)
25. Gelfond, M., Lifschitz, V.: Classical negation in logic programs and disjunctive databases. New Generation Comput. 9(3/4), 365–386 (1991)
26. Ginsberg, M.: Multi-valued logics. In: Proceedings of AAAI 1986, Fifth National Conference on Artificial Intelligence, pp. 243–247 (1986)
27. Gottlob, G.: Complexity results for nonmonotonic logics. Journal of Logic and Computation 2(3), 397–425 (1992)
28. Kifer, M., Lozinski, E.L.: A logic for reasoning with inconsistency. J. Autom. Reasoning 9(2), 179–215 (1992)
29. Lifschitz, V.: Circumscription. In: Gabbay, D.M., Hogger, C.J., Robinson, J.A. (eds.) Handbook of Artificial Intelligence and Logic Programming, vol. 3, pp. 297–352. Oxford University Press, Oxford (1991)
30. Łukaszewicz, W.: Non-Monotonic Reasoning - Formalization of Commonsense Reasoning. Ellis Horwood Series in Artificial Intelligence. Ellis Horwood, England (1990)
31. Małuszyński, J., Szałas, A.: Logical foundations and complexity of 4QL, a query language with unrestricted negation (2010) (to appear); Journal of Applied Non-Classical Logics, http://arxiv.org/abs/1011.5105
32. Małuszyński, J., Szałas, A., Vitória, A.: Paraconsistent logic programs with four-valued rough sets. In: Chan, C.-C., Grzymala-Busse, J.W., Ziarko, W.P. (eds.) RSCTC 2008. LNCS (LNAI), vol. 5306, pp. 41–51. Springer, Heidelberg (2008)
33. Marek, V.W., Truszczyński, M.: Nonmonotonic Logic. Springer, Heidelberg (1993)
34. McCarthy, J.: Circumscription: A form of non-monotonic reasoning. Artificial Intelligence Journal 13, 27–39 (1980)
35. Moore, R.C.: Possible-world semantics for autoepistemic logic. In: Proc. 1st Nonmonotonic Reasoning Workshop, New Paltz, NY, pp. 344–354 (1984)
36. Nute, D.: Defeasible logic. In: Handbook of Logic in Artificial Intelligence and Logic Programming, pp. 353–395 (1994)
37. Pawlak, Z.: Rough Sets. Theoretical Aspects of Reasoning about Data. Kluwer Academic Publishers, Dordrecht (1991)
38. Reiter, R.: On closed world data bases. In: Gallaire, H., Minker, J. (eds.) Logic and Data Bases, pp. 55–76. Plenum Press, New York (1978)
39. Reiter, R.: A logic for default reasoning. Artificial Intelligence Journal 13, 81–132 (1980)
40. Sakama, C., Inoue, K.: Paraconsistent stable semantics for extended disjunctive programs. J. Log. Comput. 5(3), 265–285 (1995)
41. Vitória, A.: Reasoning with Rough Sets and Paraconsistent Rough Sets. University of Linköping, Ph.D. Thesis (2010), http://urn.kb.se/resolve?urn=urn:nbn:se:liu:diva-60794
42. Vitória, A., Małuszyński, J., Szałas, A.: Modeling and reasoning with paraconsistent rough sets. Fundamenta Informaticae 97(4), 405–438 (2009)

# Author Index

GPSR Compliance

The European Union's (EU) General Product Safety Regulation (GPSR) is a set of rules that requires consumer products to be safe and our obligations to ensure this.

If you have any concerns about our products, you can contact us on ProductSafety@springernature.com

In case Publisher is established outside the EU, the EU authorized representative is:

Springer Nature Customer Service Center GmbH
Europaplatz 3
69115 Heidelberg, Germany

**Batch number: 09473985**

Printed by Printforce, the Netherlands